INTRODUCTORY GEOGRAPHIC INFORMATION SYSTEMS

Pearson Series in
Geographic Information Science
Keith C. Clarke, Series Editor

Berlin/Avery, *Fundamentals of Remote Sensing and Airphoto Interpretation,* 5th edition

Clarke, *Getting Started with Geographic Information Systems,* 5th edition

Greene/Pick, *Exploring the Urban Community: A GIS Approach,* 2nd edition

Jensen, *Introductory Digital Image Processing: A Remote Sensing Perspective,* 3rd edition

Jensen, *Remote Sensing of the Environment: An Earth Resource Perspective,* 2nd edition

Jensen/Jensen, *Introductory Geographic Information Systems*

Lo/Yeung, *Concepts and Techniques in Geographic Information Systems,* 2nd edition

Slocum, McMaster, Kessler, and Howard, *Thematic Cartography and Geovisualization,* 3rd edition

INTRODUCTORY GEOGRAPHIC INFORMATION SYSTEMS

John R. Jensen
University of South Carolina

Ryan R. Jensen
Brigham Young University

PEARSON

Boston Columbus Indianapolis New York San Francisco Upper Saddle River
Amsterdam Cape Town Dubai London Madrid Milan Munich Paris Montréal Toronto
Delhi Mexico City São Paulo Sydney Hong Kong Seoul Singapore Taipei Tokyo

Geography Editor: Christian Botting
Marketing Manager: Maureen McLaughlin
Project Editor: Anton Yakovlev
Editorial Assistant: Bethany Sexton
Marketing Assistant: Nicola Houston
Media Producer: Ziki Dekel
Managing Editor, Geosciences and Chemistry: Gina M. Cheselka
Project Manager, Production: Edward Thomas
Project Manager, Full Service: Erin Donahue, PreMediaGlobal
Full Service and Composition: PreMediaGlobal
Copyeditor: Kelly Birch
Proofreader: Martha Ghent
Senior Technical Art Specialist: Connie Long
Illustrator: Kevin Lear, Spatial Graphics
Cover Designer: Richard Whitaker, Seventeenth Street Studios
Photo Editor: Maya Melenchuk
Text Permissions Project Manager: Beth Wollar
Text Permissions: Jean Smith, Carlisle
Operations Specialist: Michael Penne
Front Cover Art Credit: NASA/Jet Propulsion Laboratory/National Geospatial-Intelligence Agency

Credits and acknowledgments for material borrowed or adapted from other sources and reproduced, with permission, in this textbook appear on the pages at the end of the figure captions.

Library of Congress Cataloging-in-Publication Data

Jensen, John R.
Introductory geographic information systems / John R. Jensen, Ryan R. Jensen.
p. cm. – (Pearson series in geographic information science)
ISBN 978-0-13-614776-3
1. Geographic information systems. I. Jensen, Ryan R. II. Title.
G70.2.J63 2012
910.285–dc23

2011040750

2 3 4 5 6 7 8 9 10—CRK—15 14 13 12

www.pearsonhighered.com

ISBN-10: 0-13-614776-3
ISBN-13: 978-0-13-614776-3

BRIEF CONTENTS

CONTENTS

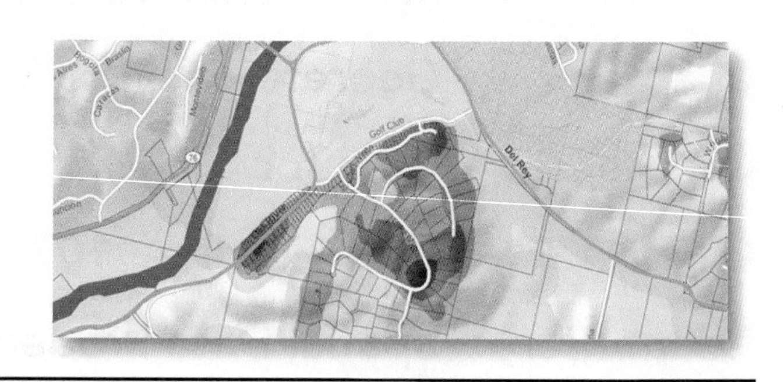

CHAPTER 1 INTRODUCTION TO GIS

CHAPTER 2 GEOREFERENCING

CHAPTER 3 DATA FOR GIS

CHAPTER 4 DATA QUALITY

CHAPTER 5
SPATIAL DATA MODELS AND DATABASES

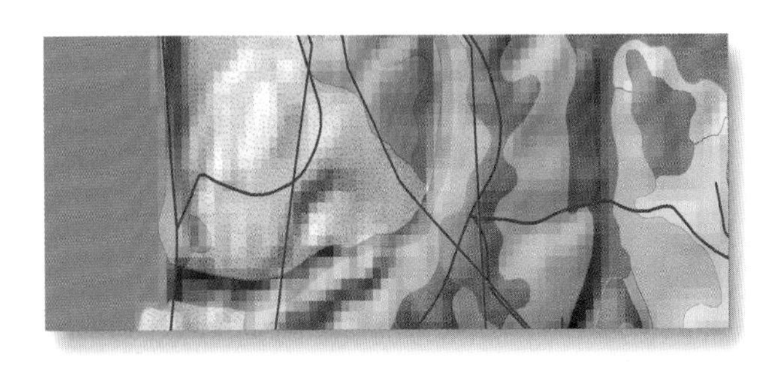

CHAPTER 6 SPATIAL ANALYSIS OF VECTOR AND RASTER DATA

CHAPTER 7 NETWORK ANALYSIS

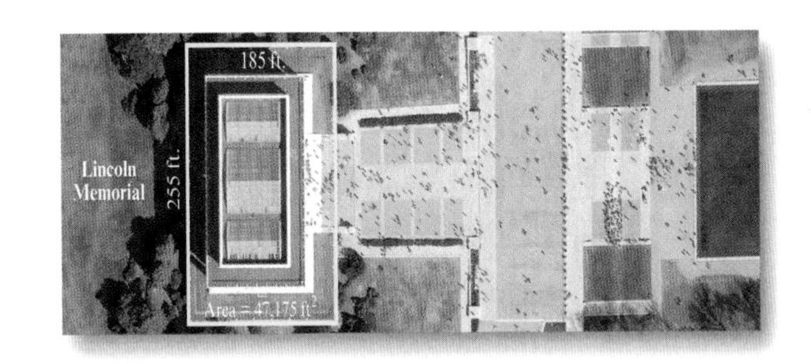

CHAPTER 8 STATISTICS AND SPATIAL DATA MEASUREMENTS

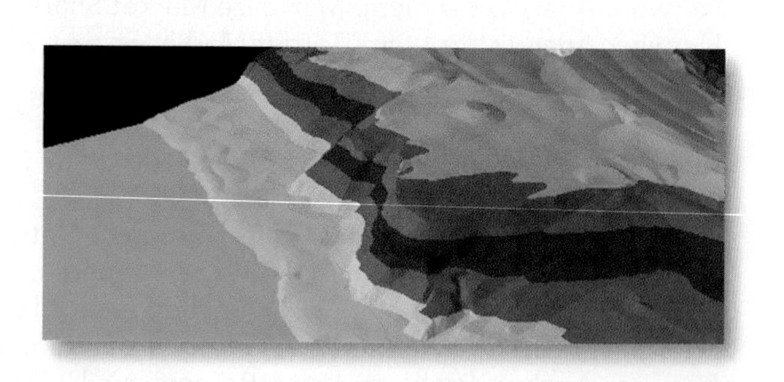

CHAPTER 9 SPATIAL ANALYSIS OF 3-DIMENSIONAL DATA

CHAPTER 10
CARTOGRAPHY USING A GIS

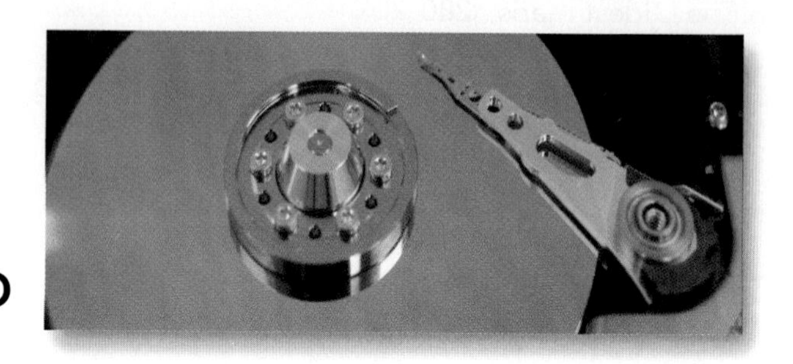

CHAPTER 11 GIS HARDWARE/SOFTWARE AND PROGRAMMING

CHAPTER 12 FUTURE CONSIDERATIONS

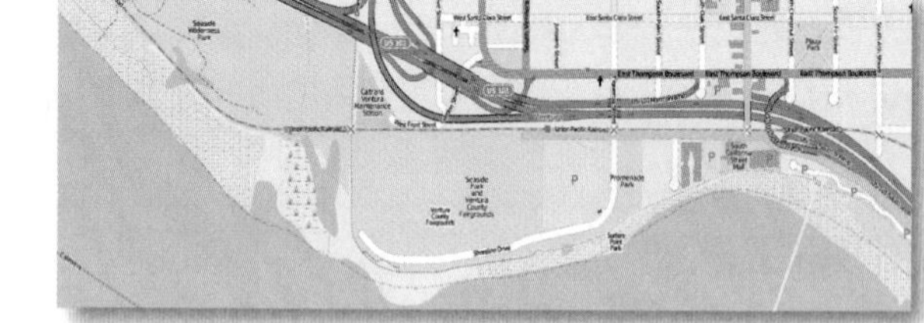

PREFACE

Geographic information systems (GIS) are designed to input, display, and analyze spatial data to solve spatial problems. Geographic information systems are one of the mapping sciences along with geodesy, surveying, cartography, and remote sensing. The ability to address important geospatial questions using a geographic information system is improving daily because of advances in the quality of geospatial data, spatial analysis algorithms, and computer hardware. Because of these improvements, geographic information systems are used in a great variety of applications such as network analysis, environmental studies, land use and transportation planning, terrain visualization, sea-level-rise prediction, socioeconomic and population analysis, business location/allocation modeling, and many others. The U.S. Department of Labor and other organizations have recognized the use of geographic information systems as a key emerging occupation with strong potential career opportunities.

Introductory Geographic Information Systems will be of value to GIScience students and educators for several reasons. The book covers the basic principles associated with GIS at an introductory, practical level. It was written for those who know very little about GIS and spatial analysis. Relatively complex GIScience principles are introduced as simply as possible, often using specially prepared color illustrations, rather than mathematical equations, to communicate principles. When equations are required, they are presented using simple algebra or trigonometry terms. Review questions and a glossary are provided at the end of each chapter. All the illustrations and tables in the book are available in digital format in a Microsoft PowerPoint™ file. Instructors may download the PowerPoint™ file from **www.pearsonhighered.com/irc**, and use the illustrations and tables in addition to their own teaching materials.

Each copy of the book includes access to a Premium Website at **www.mygeoscienceplace.com** with quizzes, web links, "In the News" RSS feeds, images and line drawings from the book, and other resources.

Chapter 1: Introduction to GIS

This chapter describes the characteristics of spatial data and the role and importance of a geographic information system in spatial-data analysis. The chapter briefly introduces the difference between vector and raster data structures and provides several formal and informal definitions of geographic information systems. Important misconceptions about GIS are clarified. The components of typical geographic information systems are introduced, including hardware, software, humanware, and data. Numerous trends in the use of geographic information systems are reviewed, including the business of GIS and careers in GIS.

Chapter 2: Georeferencing

Quality geographic information system analysis requires spatial data that are accurately referenced to a coordinate system. This chapter provides basic information about geodetic datums, ellipsoids, geoids, and common coordinate systems. The global (spherical) coordinate system based on latitude and longitude is presented first. Then, several projected coordinate systems are introduced such as the Universal Transverse Mercator, Albers Equal-area, Lambert Conformal Conic, and State Plane Coordinate Systems. The ability to create custom map projections and coordinate systems is discussed. Tissot's Indicatrix and its use for understanding the distortion associated with various map projections is introduced.

Chapter 3: Data for GIS

This chapter reviews the basic techniques used to obtain geospatial data for analysis in a GIS. In situ spatial-data collection methods are discussed, including the use of Global Navigation Satellite Systems (GNSS) such as the U.S. NAVSTAR Global Positioning System (GPS), land surveying, ground-based sampling or the taking of a census, and digitization of hard-copy maps and images. The chapter then presents how geospatial data are collected using remote-sensing instruments placed on board aircraft and spacecraft. The remote-sensing process, terminology, and resolution considerations (spatial, spectral, temporal, and radiometric) are discussed. Several remote-sensing data-collection systems are described, including aerial photography, multispectral, hyperspectral, thermal-infrared, LiDAR, and RADAR. A brief overview of analog- and digital-image processing is provided.

Chapter 4: Data Quality

Data-quality assessment is an important part of GIS analysis. This chapter describes the concept of metadata (data about data) and how it can be used to help determine the usefulness of a dataset for a particular project. The difference between accuracy and precision is introduced. Common types of attribute and positional (spatial) error are discussed as well as how the error can be measured and, in certain instances, corrected. Map-accuracy standards from several organizations are provided. The importance of error visualization and error propagation are described. The concepts of ecological fallacy and the modifiable area unit problem are reviewed.

Chapter 5: Spatial Data Models and Databases

This chapter reviews detailed characteristics of vector and raster data models. Vector-data topology and georelational and object-based vector models are discussed. Then, raster file format and georeferencing are described. Sometimes vector or raster data must be transformed into a different data structure. Vector-to-raster and raster-to-vector data conversions are described that perform this function. The chapter concludes with a discussion of how geographic information systems are used to store, relate, join, and query attribute data associated with the vector and raster data models using specially prepared databases.

Chapter 6: Spatial Analysis of Vector and Raster Data

This chapter provides basic information about geographic information system spatial analysis using vector and raster data. Methods of buffering point, line, and area vector data are introduced. Vector topological overlay is discussed, including point-in-polygon, line-in-polygon, and polygon-on-polygon. Raster data analysis is introduced, including physical-distance measurement, buffering, local operations applied to a single raster dataset, local operations applied to multiple raster datasets, neighborhood operations (e.g., spatial filtering), and regional (zonal) operations and statistics.

Chapter 7: Network Analysis

This chapter begins with a brief introduction to geocoding and address matching. Two general types of geodatabase networks are discussed (undirected and directed). The general process of creating a topologically correct network geodatabase using geographic information stored in a GIS is considered. Potential sources of network information are discussed. Network elements such as edges, junctions, and turns are described. The concepts of network cost (e.g., impedances such as time or distance), barriers (e.g., temporary road closures or accidents), and hierarchy are presented. Various types of location-allocation modeling used to locate facilities are introduced. The chapter concludes with a discussion of how to determine flow direction, trace edges and junctions upstream or downstream, and use barriers to solve problems in a directed hydrologic network.

Chapter 8: Statistics and Spatial Data Measurements

This chapter presents some of the fundamental descriptive and spatial statistics and how these can be used to enhance our understanding of spatial relationships. Simple Euclidean and Manhattan distance measurements are introduced. Common polygon measurements are considered, such as polygon perimeter and area measurements. Useful descriptive and spatial statistics are discussed, such as the mean center and standard distance of a spatial distribution. The concept of spatial autocorrelation and its measurement using Moran's I is introduced. Point pattern analysis techniques using quadrat and nearest-neighbor analysis are reviewed.

Chapter 9: Spatial Analysis of 3-Dimensional Data

This chapter describes how control-point observations (e.g., x, y, and z-elevation) can be transformed into vector and raster data structures for visualization and surface processing. The control point data can be transformed into a Triangular Irregular Network (TIN). The data can also be transformed into a raster (matrix) format using spatial interpolation techniques such as nearest-neighbor, inverse-distance-weighting, kriging, and splining. The chapter reviews how TIN and raster datasets can be processed to extract slope, aspect, and isolines. Various methods of analytical hill-shading and color rendition are discussed that are often used to improve the interpretability of 3-dimensional surfaces.

Chapter 10: Cartography Using a GIS

GIS analysis often involves the creation of high-quality cartographic (map) products. The chapter begins with a brief history of several major cartographic milestones. The cartographic process is then introduced to help the reader understand the practical and perceptual stages involved in map-making. Fundamental map-design elements are described that can lead to high-quality cartographic products (e.g., layout, balance, use of color and symbols, the figure-ground relationship, north arrows and compass roses, scale bars). Detailed information about mapping point (e.g., graduated circles), line (e.g., contours), and area (e.g., choropleth) features using a GIS are presented with examples. The characteristics of photomaps and orthophotomaps are discussed.

Chapter 11: GIS Hardware/ Software and Programming

This chapter begins with an overview of typical GIS computer hardware, including computer type, central processing unit (CPU), memory, mass storage, display, input and output devices, and archiving considerations. Important GIS software characteristics are introduced, including commonly used GIS software, operating systems, data capture and data formats, databases, cartographic capabilities, and cost. The importance of GIS software customer support is discussed. Sometimes standard GIS software may not have all of the capabilities required to complete a project. When this occurs, a GIS professional should be able to program new geospatial code that can function within the standard GIS software. The fundamental characteristics of performing GIS-related computer programming are reviewed. An example of object-oriented programming using the Python language is provided.

Chapter 12: Future Considerations

GIS career and education considerations are introduced, including wage and employment trends, information about public and private sector employment, certification, and continuing education. The importance of belonging to professional geospatial organizations is emphasized. Various GIS technical considerations are then discussed, including cloud computing and GIS, web-based GIS, mobile GIS, the collection of volunteered geographic information (VGI), improvement in data formats and standards, and 3-dimensional visualization. Public access to geospatial data and legal/privacy issues are introduced. The chapter concludes with observations about improvements in remote sensing–derived information and its increased importance in GIS analysis.

Appendix: Sources of Geospatial Information

The Appendix introduces four U.S. federal geospatial data repositories, one open-source repository, and a single representative commercial geospatial data repository. A list of selected geospatial datasets that can be downloaded via the Internet is provided, including digital elevation, hydrology, land use/land cover and biodiversity/habitat, network (road) and population demographic data, and several types of public remote-sensor data. Map or image examples of the datasets are presented where appropriate. The Appendix concludes with a summary of the GIS-data clearinghouses in each of the 50 states.

ACKNOWLEDGEMENTS

We would like to acknowledge the help of the following individuals:

Paul Beaty, ERDAS, Intergraph Inc., Atlanta, GA.

Keith Clarke, Department of Geography, University of California at Santa Barbara, CA.

John Copple, CEO at Sanborn Map Company, Colorado Springs, CO.

Dave Cowen, Department of Geography, University of South Carolina, Columbia, SC.

Jay Gatrell, Editor of *Applied Geography* and Dean of the School of Graduate Studies, Indiana State University, Terre Haute, IN.

Chris Gentry, Department of Geosciences, Austin Peay State University, Clarksville, TN.

Brian Hayman, Publisher, *GIScience & Remote Sensing*, Bellwether Publishing, Columbia, MD.

Mike Hodgson, Department of Geography, University of South Carolina, Columbia, SC.

Lisa Horn, Intellectual Property Coordinator, Esri, Inc., Redlands, CA.

Spencer Jenkins, Director, Utah Automated Geographic Reference Center, Salt Lake City, UT.

Marsha Jensen, copy-editing and proofing.

Dan Johnson, Department of Geography, Indiana University School of Liberal Arts, Indianapolis, IN.

Marguerite Madden, Department of Geography, University of Georgia, Athens, GA.

Charlie Mandello, Executive Vice-president, PICTOMETRY International, Inc., Rochester, NY.

Dan Morgan, Director of Information Technology and GIS Department, Beaufort County, SC.

Mike Morgan, Department of Geography, University of South Carolina, Columbia, SC.

Victor Mesev, Department of Geography, Florida State University, Tallahassee, FL.

Kevin Remington, Department of Geography, University of South Carolina, Columbia, SC.

Lynn Shirley, Department of Geography, University of South Carolina, Columbia, SC.

Xiaofang Wei, International Center for Water Resources Management, Central State University, Wilberforce, OH.

Chang Yi, Department of Geography, University of South Carolina, Columbia, SC.

We would like to thank the following individuals, agencies, and commercial firms who provided data used to create the illustrations:

©Alamy, Inc.: selected photographs.

Beaufort County, SC, GIS Department: digital aerial photography, LiDAR data, and parcel and transportation network data.

©Bellwether Publishing, Ltd: selected figures published in *GIScience & Remote Sensing*.

©Cindy Brewer and Mark Harrower and the Pennsylvania State University, *ColorBrewer*: Sequential and diverging color scheme specifications from *ColorBrewer*.org.

Dave Cowen and Mike Morgan: 3-dimensional GIS building examples.

©DeLorme®, Inc.: picture of the world's largest globe, *Eartha*.

©Esri, Inc: ArcGIS®, ArcMap™, and ArcCatalog™ graphical user interfaces are the intellectual property of Esri and are used herein by permission. Also for the use of *ArcWorld Supplement* and *ArcGIS® Online*. Copyright© Esri. All rights reserved.

©Google®, Inc.: photograph of *Google® Earth* interface.

©GeoEye®, Inc.: use of IKONOS and GeoEye-1 satellite imagery.

IndianaMap: aerial photography and other geospatial information of Indiana.

Lexington County, SC, GIS Internet Property, Mapping, and Data Services: aerial photography and parcel data.

Library of Congress, Geography and Map Division: photographs of historical maps.

National Aeronautics & Space Administration (NASA) and Jet Propulsion Laboratory (JPL): ASTER, AVIRIS, *G-Projector* software, GRACE, Landsat Thematic Mapper, MODIS, SRTM.

National Archives and Records Administration (NARA): gray-scale and color cards.

National Oceanic and Atmospheric Administration (NOAA): AVHRR, Coastal Change Analysis Program (C-CAP), NOAA Geophysical Data System (GEODAS).

National Geodetic Survey (NGS): photographs of CORS and surveying instruments.
©Oak Ridge National Laboratory (ORNL): LandScan description.
©OpenStreetMap: open-source geospatial data.
©PICTOMETRY International, Inc.; digital vertical and oblique aerial photography and pictures of people using PICTOMETRY data.
©Sanborn Map Company, Inc.: aerial photography, LiDAR data, and several thematic maps.
©Sensefly, Inc: unmanned aerial vehicle (UAV) photograph.
South Carolina Department of Natural Resources (SCDNR): thematic datasets of South Carolina.
State of Utah, Automated Geographic Reference Center (AGRC): aerial photography and thematic datasets of Utah.
U.S. Census Bureau: TIGER/Line® Shapefiles, population density and median age data.
U.S. Department of Agriculture (USDA): National Agricultural Imagery Program (NAIP) aerial photography.
U.S. Fish & Wildlife Service (USF&WS): National Wetlands Inventory (NWI) data.
U.S. Geological Survey (USGS): Declassified satellite imagery, Digital Orthophoto Quadrangles (DOQ), *Earth Explorer* website, Elevation Derivatives for National Applications (EDNA), GAP Analysis Program, *Geo.Data.gov* website, GTOPO30, historical terrestrial photographs, LiDAR, *The National Map*, National Elevation Dataset (NED), National Hydrography Dataset (NHD), National Land Cover Dataset (NLCD), Map Projections, US Topo data.
©The Nature Conservancy: permission to use sponsored research results.
©TeleAtlas, Inc., and Esri, Inc.: San Francisco, CA, network data used by permission.
©Zev Radovan, *Bible Land Pictures* / Alamy, Inc.: picture of clay table of a map of the world used by permission.

We appreciate the GIScience series editor, Keith Clarke, for his thoughtful reviews, guidance, and recommendations. Christian Botting provided timely management decisions and kept the project on track. Anton Yakovlev was very thorough in his role as Project Editor, constantly making wise decisions about presentation format and permissions. Members of the Pearson Education, Inc., editorial and production staff worked carefully to publish this book, especially Edward Thomas, Gina Cheselka, Kelly Birch, Martha Ghent, Maya Melenchuk, and Erin Donahue (PreMediaGlobal). Finally, we appreciate the encouragement and patience of our wives, Marsha and Tricia.

John R. Jensen
University of South Carolina

Ryan R. Jensen
Brigham Young University

ABOUT THE AUTHORS

John R. Jensen received a BA in geography from California State University at Fullerton, an MS from Brigham Young University (BYU), and a PhD from the University of California at Los Angeles (UCLA). He is a Carolina Distinguished Professor of Geography at the University of South Carolina and is co-director of the GIS & Remote Sensing Laboratory. He is a certified photogrammetrist and a past president of the American Society for Photo-grammetry & Remote Sensing: The Geospatial Information Society (6,500 members). He has published more than 130 GIScience-related articles. He received the SAIC John E. Estes Memorial Teaching Award for education, mentoring, and training in remote sensing and GIS. He received the USGS/NASA William T. Pecora Award for his GIScience research contributions. He has mentored 34 PhD and 62 master's students. He has conducted more than 50 GIScience-related projects sponsored by NASA, DOE, and NOAA. He is the editor of the journal *GIScience & Remote Sensing*. He received the Association of American Geographers Lifetime Achievement Award for research and education in GIScience. He is the author of *Introductory Digital Image Processing: A Remote Sensing Perspective,* 3rd edition, and *Remote Sensing of the Environment: An Earth Resource Perspective,* 2nd edition, also published by Pearson.

Ryan R. Jensen received a BS in cartography and GIS from Brigham Young University (BYU), an MS in geography from BYU, and a PhD in geography with a minor in botany and a concentration in interdisciplinary GIS from the University of Florida. He is an Associate Professor of Geography at BYU. He is a certified Geographic Information System Professional (GISP) who specializes in GIS and remote-sensing applications in human-environment interactions. He has mentored four PhD and six master's students. He has published more than 40 GIScience-related articles based on research funded by NASA, NSF, and USAID. He teaches GIS courses at BYU and has been involved in many GIScience-related practical projects. He serves on the editorial board of *Applied Geography* and as co-editor of the GIS and Earth Observation section of *Geography Compass.*

ABOUT OUR SUSTAINABILITY INITIATIVES

Pearson recognizes the environmental challenges facing this planet, as well as acknowledges our responsibility in making a difference. This book is carefully crafted to minimize environmental impact. The binding, cover, and paper come from facilities that minimize waste, energy consumption, and the use of harmful chemicals. Pearson closes the loop by recycling every out-of-date text returned to our warehouse.

Along with developing and exploring digital solutions to our market's needs, Pearson has a strong commitment to achieving carbon-neutrality. As of 2009, Pearson became the first carbon- and climate-neutral publishing company. Since then, Pearson remains strongly committed to measuring, reducing, and offsetting our carbon footprint.

The future holds great promise for reducing our impact on Earth's environment, and Pearson is proud to be leading the way. We strive to publish the best books with the most up-to-date and accurate content, and to do so in ways that minimize our impact on Earth. To learn more about our initiatives, please visit **www.pearson.com/responsibility.**

INTRODUCTORY GEOGRAPHIC INFORMATION SYSTEMS

1 Introduction to GIS

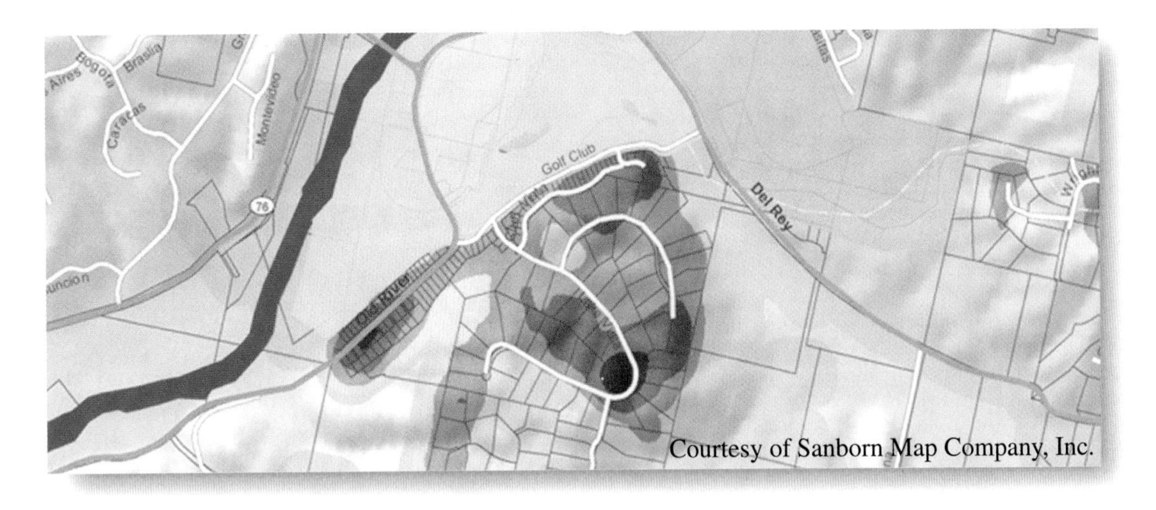

Courtesy of Sanborn Map Company, Inc.

Although you may not be aware of it, you have obtained quite a bit of geographic knowledge having lived on planet Earth for some time. During this time, you have probably heard about **geographic information systems (GIS)** but are not exactly sure what they are or how they might be used in scientific investigations or to improve decision making. Perhaps your employer knows about the usefulness of a GIS and wants you to learn the fundamentals of GIS so you can be a more valuable employee. Maybe you already use a GIS and simply want to learn more about it to make yourself more marketable. This book introduces you to the fundamental principles of GIS in a simple, straightforward manner.

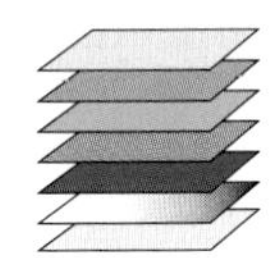

What Are Spatial Data?

Spatial data have unique geographic coordinates or other spatial identifiers that allow the data to be located in geographic space (Jensen et al., 2005). **Aspatial data** such as your age or height have no geographic information associated with them. There is a high probability that you have already been exposed to spatial information in the form of maps, aerial photographs, or satellite images especially if you have used Internet mapping services such as:

- *Bing Maps* (www.microsoft.com/maps/default.aspx),

- *Google Earth* (www.earth.google.com),

- *Google Maps* (www.maps.google.com),

- *MapQuest* (www.mapquest.com), or

- *Yahoo! Maps* (www.maps.yahoo.com).

Therefore, geographic information analysis will simply be an extension of many things that you have already experienced. For example, have you ever wondered:

- What happens when you call 911 in an emergency? The dispatcher immediately locates your address in a geospatial database. Ideally, the dispatcher can see your location on a map or aerial image and the location of all the potential emergency response vehicles (e.g., fire, police, paramedics) within the general vicinity (Figure 1-1). If properly configured, the GIS-enabled emergency response software will then identify the optimum route for an emergency response vehicle to travel to your residence or workplace. Thus, the quality of the geographic data and the effectiveness of the GIS software could save your life.
- What happens when you give your postal Zipcode to the cashier at your local department store? Typically, your Zipcode and its associated geographic coordinates are transferred to an electronic geospatial database along with information about the products you purchased and their cost. People trained in business and GIS accumulate such information from millions of customers each day and use the information to a) place new stores at an optimum location within a community to maximize profits, and/or b) stock stores with the specific products that the people in the nearby community are most likely to purchase.
- How do navigation devices, cell phones, and iPads help you identify the shortest distance or the fastest route from location A to location B? Devices such as these in the United States use Global Positioning

911 Dispatcher Using GIS and Remote Sensing Technology

©Pictometry International

FIGURE 1–1 A 911 dispatcher receives an incoming call. Geospatial information stored in the GIS database is analyzed automatically to identify the geographic location of the caller. The dispatcher is then able to see the location of the caller on a digital map or digital aerial image as shown. In addition, the GIS may contain information about the current location of each of the potential first responders (e.g., police, fire, paramedics). The dispatcher or the GIS system then selects the responder that can reach the caller's location most efficiently (image courtesy of Pictometry International, Inc.).

System (GPS) technology to identify where you are on the Earth at any moment. This spatial information is stored in a geospatial database along with the coordinates of the destination (location B). Special GIS functions are then used to locate the optimum route to location B and display it on the screen. A navigation device mounted in a car can provide the driver with detailed driving instructions as shown in Figure 1-2a. Similarly, hand-held GPS-enabled cell phones (Figure 1-2b) can be located in geographic space. In this example, the cell phone is located on George Rogers Blvd. in Columbia, SC (Figure 1-2c). The user can also search the database to identify the location of other features of interest in the area (e.g., Williams-Brice Stadium in Columbia, SC) and determine their proximity to the cell phone. The location information can be symbolized using traditional cartography (Figure 1-2c) or overlaid on high-resolution satellite imagery or digital aerial photography (Figure 1-2d).

- How are environmentally sensitive areas such as wetlands protected from environmental degradation in developing areas? These sensitive areas are usually studied and modeled using several types of geographic information placed in a GIS, such as the spatial distribution of existing wetlands, the surrounding land use/land cover, the proposed zoning ordinances, terrain slope and elevation, the hydrologic network, and the existing transportation network. The GIS is used to analyze all these spatial data at one time and predict the impact of the proposed land use on the existing wetland.

Each of these applications requires spatial data and spatial data analysis. Spatial data and spatial data analysis have been around for a long time, but only within the last 30 years have they begun to make a significant, almost daily, difference in the lives of the general public (Foresman, 1998). Interestingly, geographic information and analysis are becoming so commonplace that society often takes them for granted. For example, most people are not concerned about how the fastest route to a location is determined when they use one of the mapping sites on the Internet (e.g., *Bing Maps*, *Google Maps*, *Yahoo! Maps*, etc.) or their personal navigation device (e.g., an iPhone). They are only concerned that it works properly. Therefore, it is imperative that people such as yourself who perform GIS analysis do it as accurately and efficiently as possible. This book introduces many geospatial applications and ways in which geographic information systems can be used to make improved decisions that protect human life and allow sustainable development of the environment (Jensen et al., 2002). This book is devoted to educating you so that you can use geographic data and geographic information systems wisely.

Dashboard-mounted Navigation Devices Use Global Positioning System (GPS) Technology

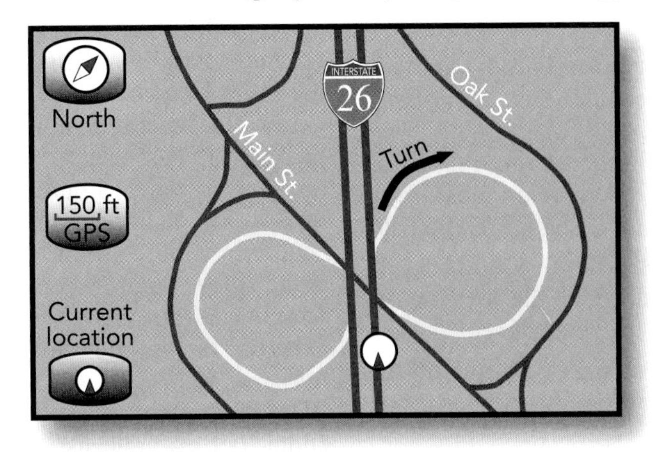

a. Typical information displayed on a navigation device.

Cell Phones Can Find their Location (*x*,*y*) Using a Combination of GPS, Wi-Fi, and Cellular Tower Triangulation

b. iPhone mapping application.

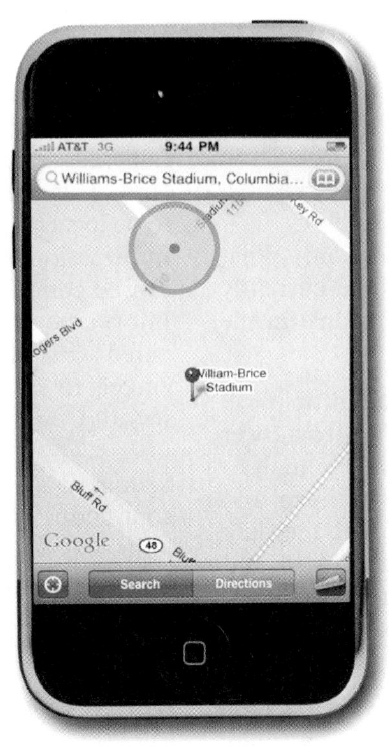

c. Planimetric map showing the location of the iPhone and Williams-Brice Stadium.

d. Satellite image overlaid with iPhone location and map information.

FIGURE 1–2 a) Navigation devices that use GPS technology are routinely mounted on car dashboards. Typical information displayed includes the navigation device's location, the direction it is traveling (N, S, E, W), road names, and directions to specific locations, if requested. b) A cell phone with mapping capabilities. The iPhone mapping application outlined in red utilizes GPS, Wi-Fi, and cellular towers to locate it on the surface of the Earth (iPhone photograph courtesy of D. Hurst / Alamy). c) The location of the iPhone on George Rogers Blvd. in Columbia, SC, is displayed as a blue dot using *Google* mapping technology. The user can also search the geospatial database to identify the location of other features of interest in the area, such as Williams-Brice Stadium, and determine their proximity to the cell phone. The location information can be symbolized using c) traditional cartography, or d) overlaid on satellite imagery or aerial photography.

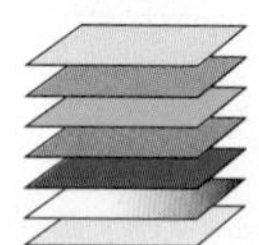

Spatial Questions

People in many disciplines ask a tremendous variety of spatial questions every day. Here are some examples:

- Law enforcement: "Where in the city are the majority of the drug arrests made? Where do most of the violent crimes occur? Is there a spatial relationship between these two variables?"
- Developer: "What is the slope of the land in this area? Is the slope too steep for development?"
- Realtor: "What is the average price of homes in this neighborhood relative to those in nearby neighborhoods?"
- University admissions administrator: "Where do most of the student applicants live? Where are the economically disadvantaged areas? How can we attract more applicants from these areas?"
- Aid worker: "Where is the area of greatest human suffering and greatest property damage? How can we maximize the impact of our relief efforts?"
- Delivery truck driver: "What is the most efficient route for my 25 deliveries today?"
- Legislator: "Where should we draw the Congressional district boundaries so that all of the people in a large city are represented in Congress equally?"
- Centers for Disease Control and Prevention: "What is the geographic distribution of people currently infected by a disease and how many people in the immediate vicinity could be infected?"

Whether or not they are aware of it, these people will have to use spatial data and spatial analysis to answer the questions. The results of their spatial data analysis will likely impact our lives (Koch, 2005; Green and Pick, 2006). Therefore, it is important that the data that each of these people uses are collected, stored, and analyzed in an accurate manner. Geographic information systems have been developed for this purpose.

How Are Spatial Data Organized in a GIS?

As previously mentioned, spatial data are data that have a spatial component associated with them (Morrison and Veregin, 2010). This means that we know where the feature is in *x*, *y*, and often *z* space. The location may be described in a common global or spherical coordinate system (e.g., latitude/longitude), in a projected coordinate system (e.g., a Universal Transverse Mercator map projection), in a local coordinate system (e.g., a spatial system unique to a building that maps the building's utility infrastructure), or with something as simple as a street address (e.g., 222 Springdale Road). This spatial component allows GIS users to map the location of features and subsequently perform spatial analysis. In the example described earlier, the shopper's Zipcode information allows the company to know the general area where the shopper lives. The *aspatial* data associated with the business transaction (i.e., the products purchased and amount of money spent) are of limited value to the company until they can be attributed to the shopper's address. Once attributed, these data, in conjunction with the information obtained from many other customers, can be used to identify the optimum location for a new store.

The same principle holds true for many other kinds of data. For example, assume you are the local tax assessor who must make sure that all properties are assessed—and therefore taxed—equitably. Now, assume you know many things about the Jones family lot (parcel) in your town. In particular, you know that the house has 3000 ft.^{2} of heated living space, it occupies 0.5 acres, and was assessed at $300,000 the previous tax year. This is important aspatial information. For this aspatial information to become of value, you must associate it with spatial information. All of the aspatial information becomes spatial when a geographic location (address) is associated with the Jones parcel of land. This spatial information allows the Jones parcel to be located on a property ownership (cadastral) map. Information associated with the Jones parcel this year can be compared to information from previous years. Information about the Jones parcel can also be compared with information about surrounding or nearby parcels to ensure that the Jones parcel is equitably assessed (Cowen et al., 2007).

Spatial data are typically categorized as being discrete, continuous, or summarized by a geographic area. The following sections describe each of these kinds of geographic data.

Discrete Geographic Features

Discrete geographic features may consist of:

- points,
- lines, and
- areas.

Discrete point features are typically displayed using point symbols. For example, the geographic location associated with individual houses in Beaufort, SC, is displayed as circular point symbols in Figure 1-3a. If desired, the point symbols could be graduated (sized) according to the value of each home, which is additional attribute information typically stored and associated with each street address.

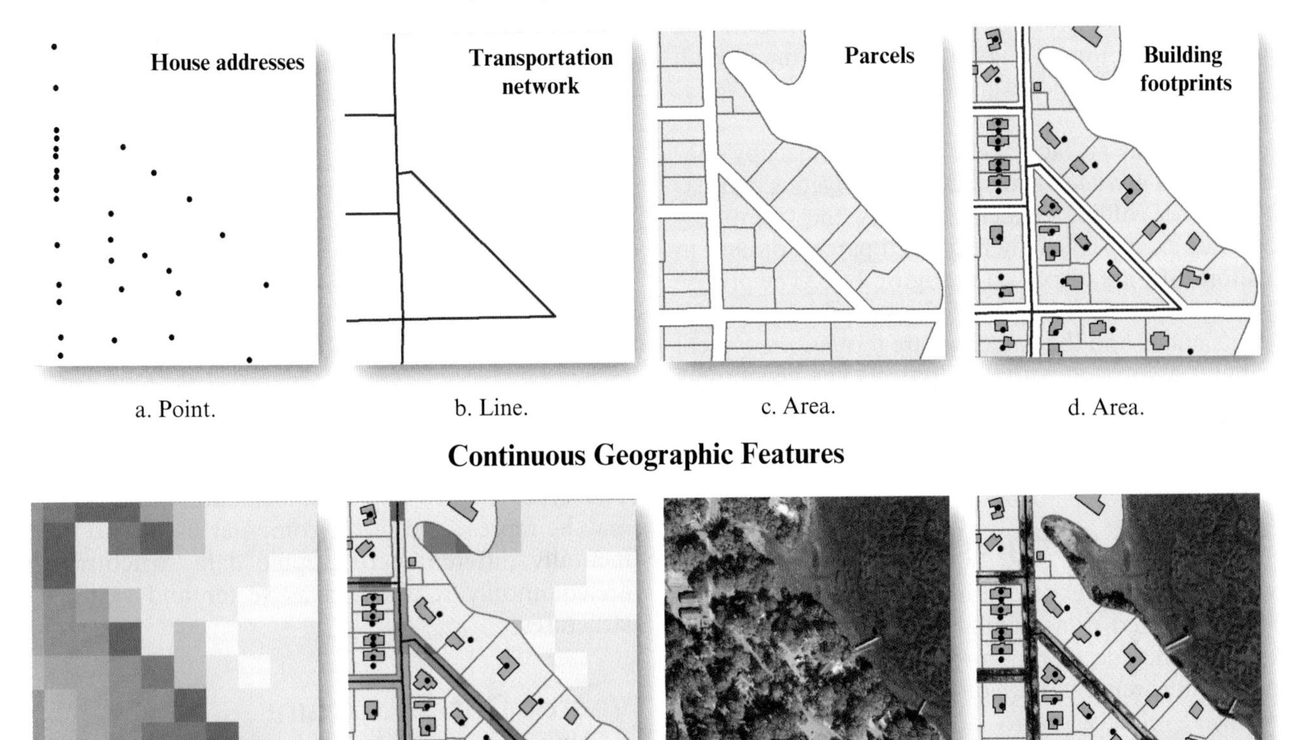

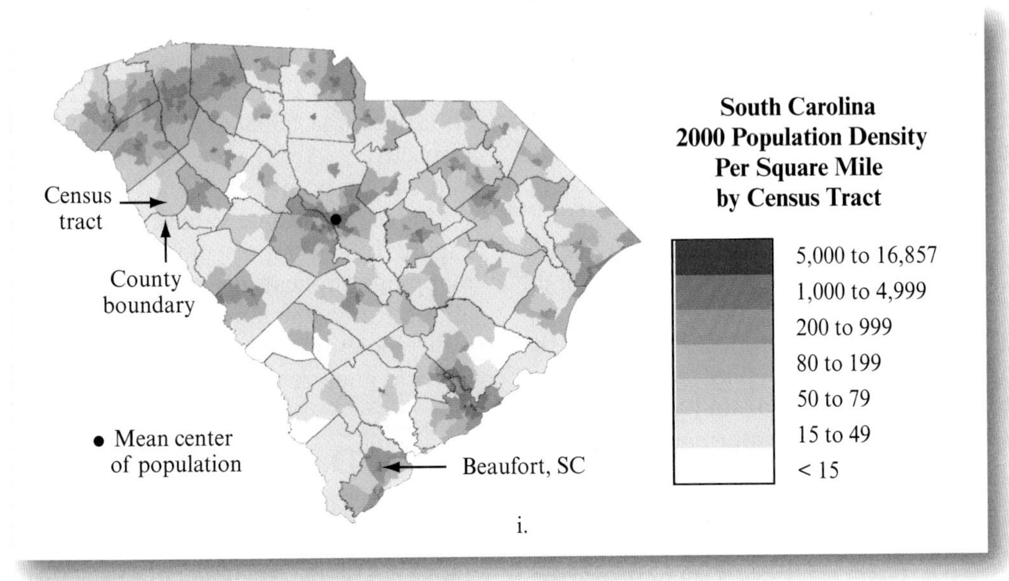

FIGURE 1–3 a-d) Point, line, and area discrete features present in a part of Beaufort, SC. e-h) Elevation and color-infrared orthophotography may be represented as continuous data. i) Features may be summarized by area such as the population density of South Carolina in 2000 by Census Tract (data courtesy of Beaufort County GIS Department [a-h] and the U.S. Census Bureau [i]).

Linear features are usually displayed as lines (vectors) with beginning, intermediate, and end points. A portion of the road network of Beaufort, SC, is shown as a collection of vectors in Figure 1-3b. The name of each road is typically stored as an attribute.

Features on the surface of the Earth that occupy geographic area are usually displayed as polygons consisting of a series of line segments (vectors) that eventually close. For example, legally registered parcels of land in Beaufort, SC, are displayed in Figure 1-3c. The precise *x,y* geographic coordinates of the parcel corners, the owner's name, and the parcel square footage are typical attributes associated with each parcel. The geographic area of each building footprint associated with each parcel shown in Figure 1-3d are also area features because they occupy geographic space.

Continuous Geographic Features

Some phenomena exist continuously in the landscape and are referred to as **continuous geographic features**. Examples include elevation (Maidment et al., 2007), temperature, relative humidity, reflected solar radiation, wind velocity, gravity, atmospheric pressure, and so on. Scientists, surveyors, and others often collect measurements of these variables at discrete point locations and then interpolate the data to fill a grid. For example, the elevation above sea level for the same geographic area in Beaufort, SC, is shown in grid (often called raster) format in Figure 1-3e. Each 30 x 30 m cell contains a single elevation value that has been color-coded. The darker the color, the higher the elevation. Note that the cells are continuous across the landscape, i.e., there are no gaps in the coverage. The area information shown in Figure 1-3d is overlaid on the elevation data in Figure 1-3e to create a composite in Figure 1-3f.

Most remote sensor data are continuous in nature (Warner et al., 2009). For example, during daylight hours, reflective near-infrared, red, green, and blue light are continuously reflected from the terrain. A color-infrared aerial photograph created from reflected near-infrared, red, and green light is shown in Figure 1-3g. The area information shown in Figure 1-3d is overlaid on the color-infrared orthophoto in Figure 1-3h.

Features Summarized by Geographic Area

Another very important type of geographic data involves taking a number of discrete measurements within a geographic area (i.e., a polygon) and then summarizing these data with a single value associated with the region. For example, population and other socio-economic data are often summarized by geographic area. The U. S. Census Bureau compiles population data by census tract, block, block group, county, and state. If the population data within a geographic area are divided by the amount of land associated with the area, then it is possible to report and map the population data in terms of population density, e.g., population per square mile or per square kilometer. There are 46 counties in South Carolina. A map depicting the population density of South Carolina per square mile per census tract is shown in Figure 1-3i. The Beaufort, SC, census tract is highlighted.

Vector and Raster Data Structures

The types of geographic information just described may be represented in the computer using two fundamentally different cartographic data structures that are commonly referred to as **vector** and **raster data structures**.

Vector Data Structure

Points are often stored in a vector data structure according to their unique *x* and *y* coordinates. For example, point #2 in Figure 1-4a is located at *x*-coordinate 530,971 m and *y*-coordinate 3,589,686 m in a Universal Transverse Mercator (UTM) map projection. A line in vector format is simply an assemblage of connected points (i.e., beginning point, *n* intermediate points, and an end point). Each of the points associated with a line has unique *x,y* coordinates. For example, line segment #11 shown in Figure 1-4b consists of two points with coordinates at 530886, 3589858 and 531017, 3589342, respectively. A polygon is created when the beginning and ending points of at least three line segments have the same coordinate values. For example, parcel #5 in Figure 1-4c is represented by four points. When the mapping application calls for detailed information about point, line, and area (polygon) features such as utility poles, roads, and parcels, it is often best to collect and analyze the data in vector format.

Raster Data Structure

Point, line, and area data can also be stored in a raster (matrix) format. The house at Point #2 located at 530971, 3589686 is shown in raster format in Figure 1-4d. It is in its proper planimetric location. However, the process of rasterization has caused the point symbol to be symbolized as a square picture element (i.e., pixel) instead of a point. Pixels are usually made the same size in *x* and *y* directions, e.g., 10 x 10 m. Unfortunately, unless the rasterization process is performed at a very high spatial resolution, it usually plays havoc

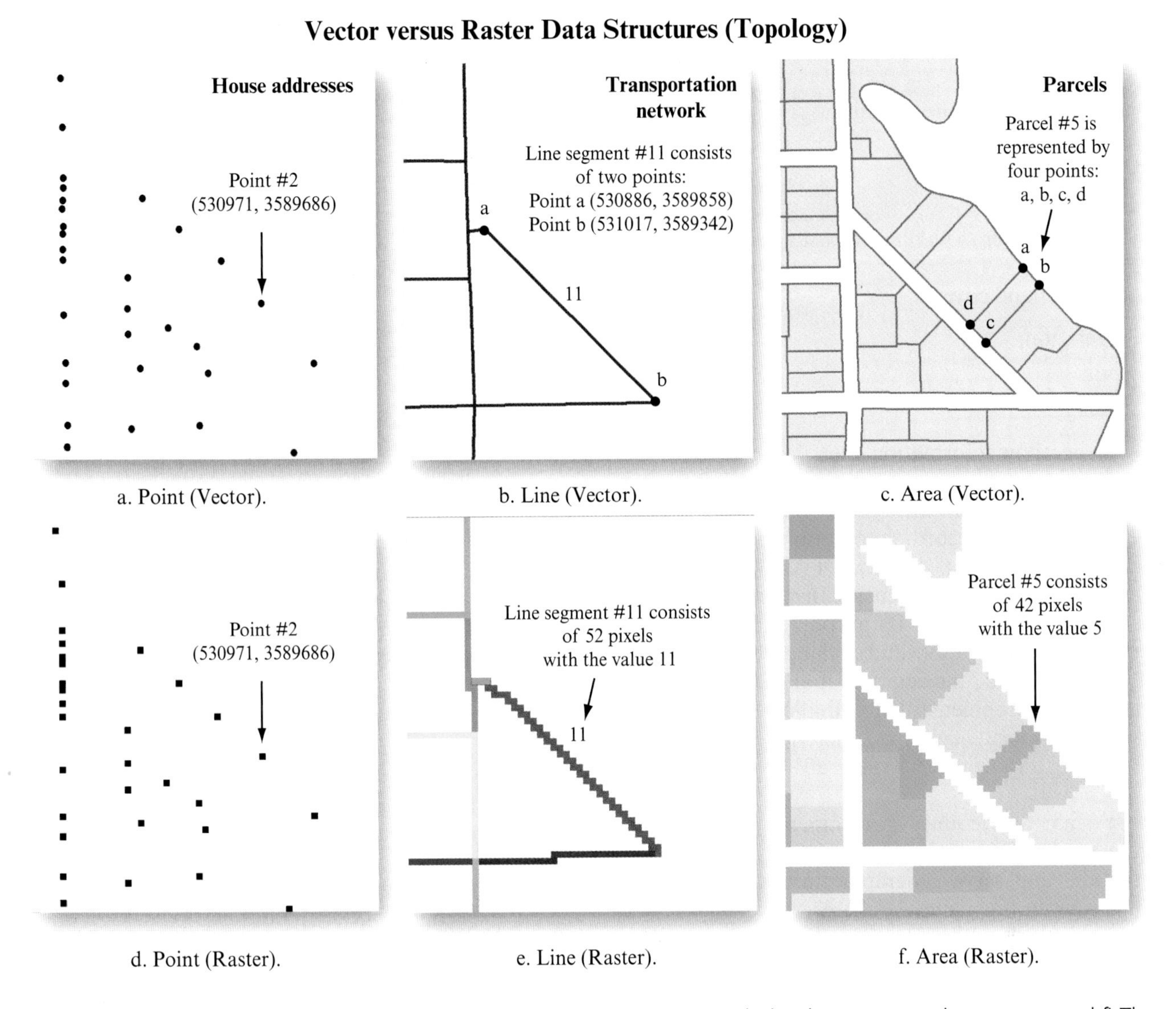

FIGURE 1–4 a-c) Point, line, and area information in a part of Beaufort, SC, symbolized using vector data structures. d-f) The same point, line, and area information symbolized using a raster data structure (data courtesy of Beaufort County GIS Department).

with linear features, often causing them to lose spatial precision and appear jagged as shown in Figure 1-4e. Polygons in raster format can experience the same fate (Figure 1-4f). Fortunately, it is still possible to maintain thematic information about the linear features and polygons. For example, Line segment #11 in Figure 1-4e consists of 51 pixels all with the value 11. Parcel #5 in Figure 1-4f consists of 42 pixels all with the value 5. The raster data structure is ideal for storing spatial information about continuous data such as temperature, humidity, elevation, reflectance, etc. (e.g., Figure 1-3e and g).

Spatial Data Infrastructures

In addition to knowing about the various types of geographic features in vector and raster format, it is important to be aware of national and international standards associated with how these data are stored and shared. In the United States, the **Federal Geographic Data Committee (FGDC)** promotes the coordinated development, use, sharing, and dissemination of the nation's digital geographic information (FGDC, 2011). This nationwide data publishing effort is known as the **National Spatial Data Infrastructure (NSDI).** The NSDI consists of three geometrically registered *framework foundation spatial databases* (Figure 1-5):

- geodetic control,
- digital terrain (elevation and bathymetry),
- digital orthorectified imagery,

four *framework thematic databases*:

- cadastral,
- boundaries or political units,
- hydrology,
- transportation,

and several other *thematic databases*, such as:

- land use/land cover,
- vegetation,
- soils,
- geology,
- demographic information, etc.

Many governments throughout the world organize their spatial data according to Global Spatial Data Infrastructures (GSDI). "The GSDI Association is an inclusive organization of agencies, firms, and individuals from around the world. Its purpose is to promote international cooperation and collaboration in support of local, national, and international spatial data infrastructure developments that will allow nations to better address social, economic, and environmental issues of pressing importance" (GSDI, 2011).

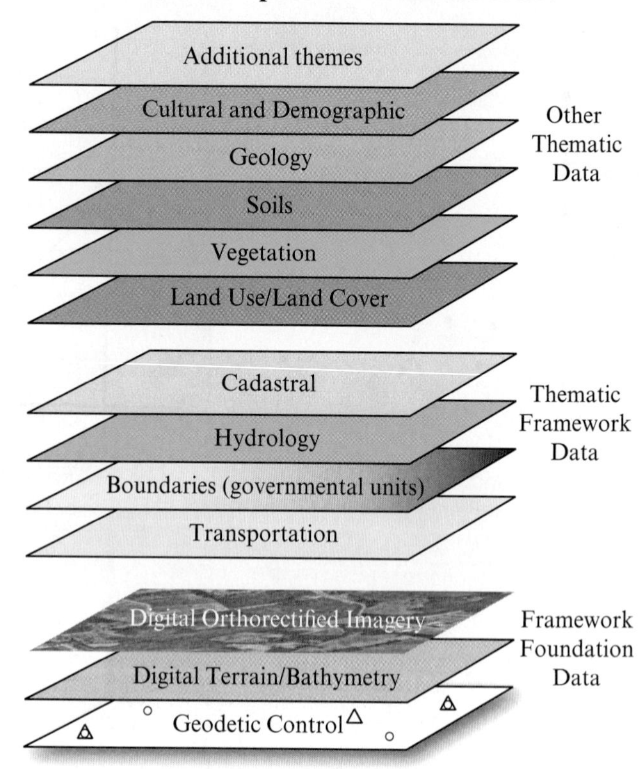

FIGURE 1–5 The United States' National Spatial Data Infrastructure (NSDI) consists of framework foundation data, thematic framework data, and other thematic data.

Most state and county governments in the United States use FGDC standards and NSDI logic to design, maintain, and serve geographic information. For example, seven thematic databases (coverages) of the Beaufort area in Beaufort County, SC, are shown in Figure 1-6. These datasets are stored in the Beaufort County Geographic Information System according to FGDC standards and NSDI specifications. Note that the database contains geodetic control, digital terrain, orthophotography, transportation, and cadastral information such as parcels and building footprints. The Beaufort County GIS contains hundreds of thematic coverages that are used to manage the affairs of the county by personnel in the various departments, including Fire, Police, Emergency Response (911), utility management, flood control, and so on. Much of the spatial data are available free to the public via the Internet.

Formal and Informal Definitions of GIS

Now that you have a preliminary appreciation for the nature of geographic features (e.g., discrete, continuous, area-based), how they are stored in vector or raster data structures, and how they are organized in spatial data infrastructures, it is useful to provide some formal GIS definitions. Because GIS are used by diverse multidisciplinary groups of people for a great variety of applications, it is not surprising that there are multiple definitions of what constitutes a GIS. For example, consider the following definitions of GIS.

A **GIS** is:

- a set of tools for collecting, storing, retrieving at will, transforming, and displaying spatial data from the real world for a particular set of purposes (Burroughs, 1986).
- an information system used to manipulate, summarize, query, edit, and visualize spatial and non-spatial information stored in a computer database (Goodchild, 1997).
- a digital system for the acquisition, management, analysis, and visualization of spatial data for the purposes of planning, administering, and monitoring the natural and socioeconomic environment (Konecny, 2003).
- an automated system for the capture, storage, retrieval, analysis, and display of spatial data (Slocum et al., 2005).

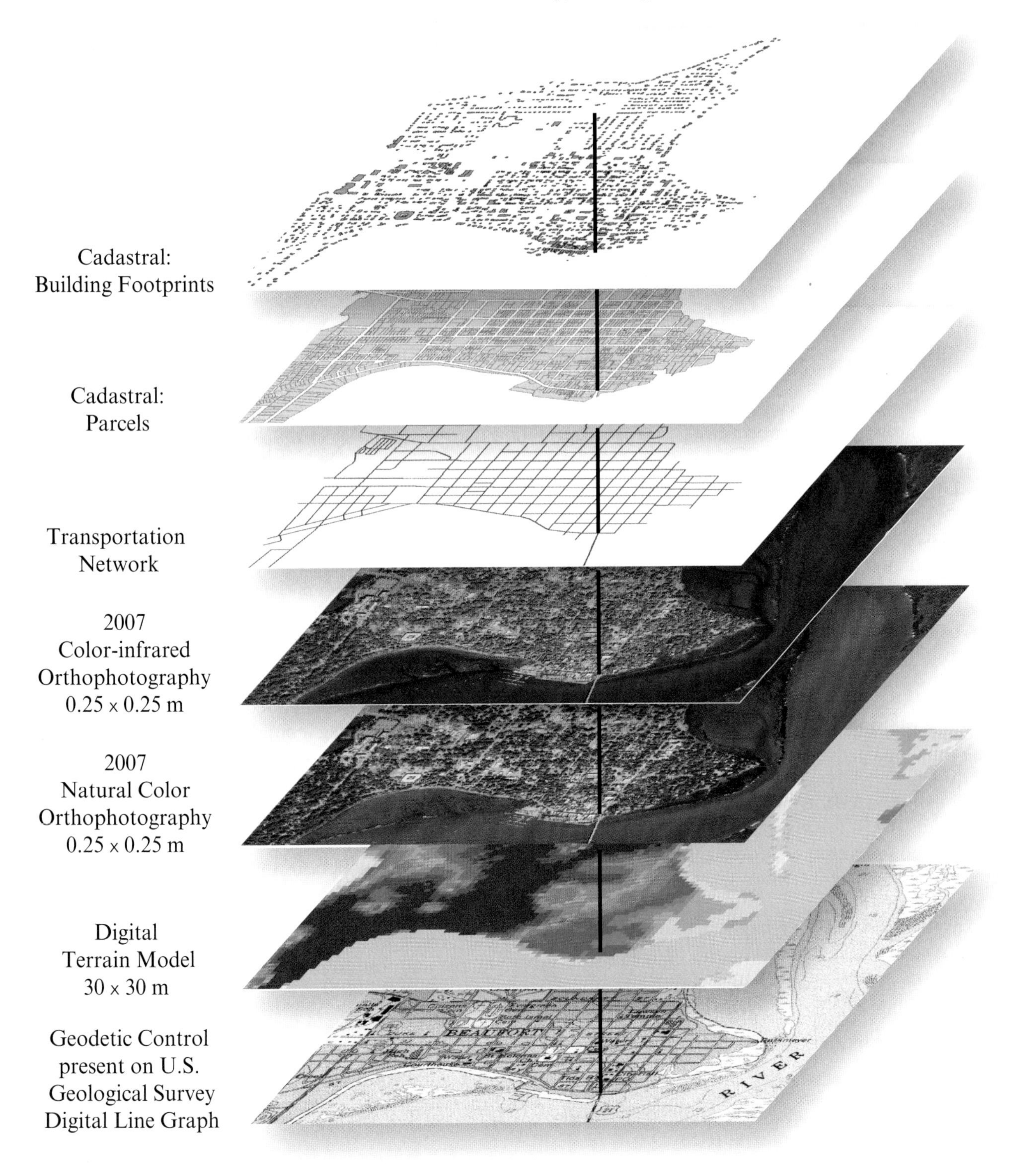

FIGURE 1–6 The Beaufort County GIS Department maintains hundreds of spatial data files. Many of these meet National Spatial Data Infrastructure (NSDI) specifications. Three framework foundation files (geodetic control, digital terrain model, and orthophotography) and three thematic framework files (transportation, cadastral parcels, and building footprints) are displayed (data courtesy of Beaufort County GIS Department).

Emergency Response

a. Firefighter evaluating a hard-copy image map of an alarm area.

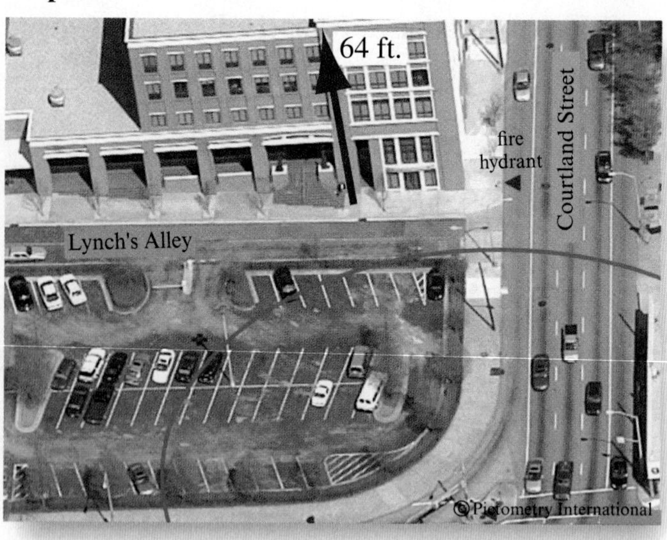

b. Unique oblique aerial photography displayed using a special GIS that contains detailed building elevation data and other attribute information such as street names and fire hydrant locations.

FIGURE 1–7 The amount of time it takes to dispatch and route emergency vehicles can have an impact on the survival of the people needing help. If you or a loved one need a fireman or ambulance you would want the professionals to have every tool available to get them to your location as quickly as possible. a) A firefighter is examining a hard-copy map of the alarm area. b) Detailed digital information in the GIS can be used to locate the building at the corner of Lynch's Alley and Courtland Street, determine its height (64 ft.), allocate the proper hook-and-ladder fire engine to the site, and identify the nearest fire hydrants (red triangles) before ever reaching the location (images courtesy of Pictometry International, Inc.).

- a computer-based system designed to manage and use geospatial data to solve spatial problems (Lo and Yeung, 2007).

How one defines a GIS is often dependent on how a person uses it. Below are several examples of how professionals who commonly perform spatial analysis might informally define a GIS:

- A transportation engineer might define a GIS as a spatial system designed to maintain, update, model, and map transportation networks.
- A biologist might define a GIS as a system for monitoring and mapping the spatial dynamics of species and ecosystems.
- A geographer might define a GIS as a system for storing, retrieving, and analyzing spatial data for the purpose of identifying spatial patterns.
- A zoologist might define a GIS as a system for mapping, modeling, and tracking flora and fauna movements and migration in selected ecosystems.
- A city planner might define a GIS as a tool for zoning.
- A tax assessor might define a GIS as a system to accurately map and monitor assessed property values to ensure assessment equity and tax compliance and to identify illegal building development.
- A phone company employee might define a GIS as a system to map existing telephone poles and underground lines for maintenance and infrastructure improvements.
- An emergency operator might define a GIS as a tool used for a) locating the scene of an accident, emergency, or crime; and b) determining the most efficient route so that the proper resources can arrive as quickly as possible (Figure 1-7).

While almost all of the definitions contain a clause about analyzing spatial data, there is no universally accepted GIS definition. One of the drawbacks of not having an absolute definition of GIS is that it allows for misconceptions to be perpetuated.

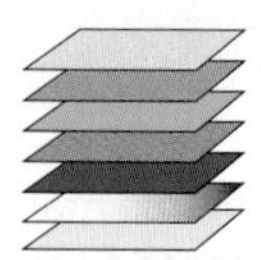

Misconceptions about GIS

Below are several misconceptions about the nature and use of geographic information systems.

Misconception: A GIS Is Simply a Modified Graphic Arts or Computer-Aided-Design (CAD) Program

Both computer-aided-design (CAD) and graphic arts programs are very useful. For example, CAD programs are often used by architects and engineers to create and edit architectural and engineering drawings. Similarly, graphic arts programs such as Adobe Photoshop and Adobe Illustrator enable artists and web designers to create and edit photographs and digital drawings. Unfortunately, some people mistakenly think a GIS is simply a graphic arts or CAD program. While some of the capabilities are the same, the analytical spatial analysis capabilities of a GIS are usually significantly greater than those of most graphic arts or CAD programs. One of the most important differences is that all *bona fide* geographic information systems contain a database management system (DBMS) whereas many CAD and graphic arts programs do not. In addition, many CAD and graphic arts programs do not allow thematic map overlay, geocoding, and network analysis, which are several of the most important GIS functions. Most high-quality GIS have the ability to process remotely sensed data to extract useful information for input to the GIS.

Misconception: A GIS Is Simply a Cartographic Mapping Program

The science of cartography (map making) has been with us for several thousand years. In fact, many of the fundamental principles associated with a high-quality GIS are based on long-standing cartographic theory (Slocum et al., 2005). Unfortunately, some people mistakenly think that a mapping program is equivalent to a GIS. A standard cartographic mapping program is concerned mainly with making an accurate cartographic map that effectively communicates spatial information. Such programs have little ability to apply spatial analytical operations to the content of the map (e.g., network analysis) or to compare one map with another (e.g., map overlay).

Conversely, a GIS can be used to edge-match, compare, and correlate two or more maps. For example, perhaps a user wants to examine the relationship between soil and vegetation in an ecosystem. Before GIS was developed, cartographers had to a) make sure that both the soil and vegetation maps were created at the same scale and map projection, and then b) create a Mylar (clear plastic) version of the maps so that they could be manually overlaid on top of one another to identify spatial relationships between the two variables (McHarg, 1967). This manual map overlay method was useful, but it was very difficult to calculate statistical relationships between the variables. Evaluation of more than two maps was especially problematic. A GIS is specifically designed to compare and contrast the information content associated with *n* thematic maps that are registered to one another. The GIS can be instructed to rapidly extract numerous types of geospatial information and statistics associated with the relationships between the various thematic maps.

Actually, when it comes to creating interim and final cartographic map products, a high-quality GIS is superior to many commercially available cartographic mapping programs. A high-quality GIS can create standard and expanded symbol sets, change line weights, manipulate font characteristics, and perform real-time color adjustment. GIS are also easily able to transform spatial data into various coordinate systems, map projections, datums, and ellipsoids (defined in Chapter 2). Scale is also easily manipulated in a GIS, allowing users to quickly and efficiently change from large-scale to small-scale and back again. Chapter 10 describes how high-quality maps can be produced using a GIS.

Misconception: A GIS Is Simply a Software Package without Theoretical Foundation

Abler (1987) suggested that "GIS technology is to geographical analysis what the microscope, telescope and computers have been to other sciences." A GIS is much more than a software package. The development of geographic information systems is based on geographic information science (often referred to as *GIScience*) (Goodchild, 1992; 1997). **GIScience** seeks to improve our knowledge about the nature of geographic data and how it may be collected, analyzed, and viewed using the theory and logic found in the mapping sciences (i.e., cartography, GIS, surveying, and remote sensing of the environment). GIS is also a professional culture where fellow practitioners discuss GIS applications, trends, and solutions to real-world problems. They model physical systems (e.g., to predict the geographic extent of hurricane storm surge) and human-environmental systems (e.g., to predict population dispersion in floodplains) (Clarke et al., 2002; Maidment et al., 2007).

As GIScience has developed over the years, so too has the community of GIS users and user groups. These people and local/regional user groups are very valuable when you encounter things you haven't seen before or that you need guidance with when using a GIS. For example, the ESRI-sponsored Southeast Regional User Group organizes a user conference every year and attempts to answer GIS questions on-line.

Misconception: Traditional Paper Maps Are Just as Useful as a GIS

One might ask, "Why is a GIS better than simply analyzing the information found on a paper map?" First, it is very difficult to compare two or more maps when they are in analog (hard-copy) paper format. In addition, it is generally more difficult to make quantitative measurements on hard-copy paper maps. Storing paper maps is a significant problem that can consume a large amount of office space. Archiving and accessing paper maps is also problematic. Conversely, a GIS database consisting of registered digital maps is a) relatively easy to store in a digital format, b) easy to access when the attributes of the various thematic layers are stored as metadata (data about data) in a database management system (DBMS) (Onsrud, 2007), c) able to compare or correlate the information content found in *n* maps, and d) able to extract quantitative information from individual or multiple maps.

If it is necessary to incorporate the information stored in a historical paper map in a GIS, then the information content of the paper map can be digitized and placed in a map projection. In this way the information content found in historical paper maps can be related to current digital spatial information in the GIS. For example, the 1:24,000 7.5-minute topographic map of Provo, UT, provided by the U.S. Geological Survey's National Map US Topo program is shown in Figure 1-8. This topographic map includes elevation (contour) information from the National Elevation Dataset (NED) collected in 2002, hydrology information from the National Hydrology Dataset (NHD) collected in 2009, and aerial photography from the National Agriculture Imagery Program (NAIP) collected in 2009. The data in the map can be viewed in GeoPDF format (www.nationalmap.gov/ustopo). In addition, all of the data found in the US Topo map can be downloaded from the USGS National Map database (www.nationalmap.gov/ustopo) for direct input to a GIS. Chapter 3 describes the digitization process.

Misconception: A GIS Is No Different than Any Other Information System

Information systems are computerized tools that assist users in the transformation of data into information. Information systems help people store, retrieve, and analyze data to solve problems. The goal of a GIS is the same as that of any information system. However, there is one notable difference between a GIS and other information systems—much of the information in a GIS is spatial and can be analyzed using special spatial analysis algorithms (Dale, 2005).

Components of a GIS

A typical geographic information system consists of four components (Maguire, 1991):

- Hardware,
- Software,
- Humanware (i.e., liveware), and
- Data.

GIS Hardware

Hardware refers to the computer platform and peripherals associated with the GIS (Figure 1-9 and Table 1-1). Geographic information systems can function using the hardware components found in relatively inexpensive laptop computers or more expensive desktop computers that may contain one or more central processing units (CPUs). The greater the speed of the CPUs, the more rapidly the GIS data input/output and analytical operations can be performed. It is good practice to have greater than 6 GB of random access memory (RAM) and more than 1 TB of mass storage so that large spatial datasets can be stored, analyzed, and output rapidly in near real-time (Table 1-1).

Peripheral input devices such as scanners and digitizing tablets allow hard-copy paper maps or images to be input to the GIS. Special graphics processors and large amounts of graphics RAM (e.g., >1 GB) are needed to rapidly display vector and raster data on the computer screen. It is wise to purchase computer monitors that can display a large number of pixels, (e.g., 1900 x 1200). The system should be able to display a minimum of 16.7 millions colors (referred to as 24-bit color) so that high-color-resolution images and maps can be displayed without color distortion. Peripheral output devices such as printers and plotters are used to create hard-copy cartographic maps and images for presentation (Table 1-1). Additional information about computer hardware commonly used in GIS analysis is found in Chapter 11.

GIS Software

The GIS analyst should select a GIS that uses a standard operating system such as the current version of Microsoft Windows, UNIX, LINEX, or Apple Macintosh OS (Figure 1-9 and Table 1-1). While most GIS offer many of the same fundamental spatial analysis capabilities, the user should carefully decide which GIS has the spatial data analysis capabilities that are optimum for his or her application(s). For example, if a GIS is going to be used primarily to analyze vector

The National Map US Topo Data: 7.5-minute Quadrangle of Provo, UT

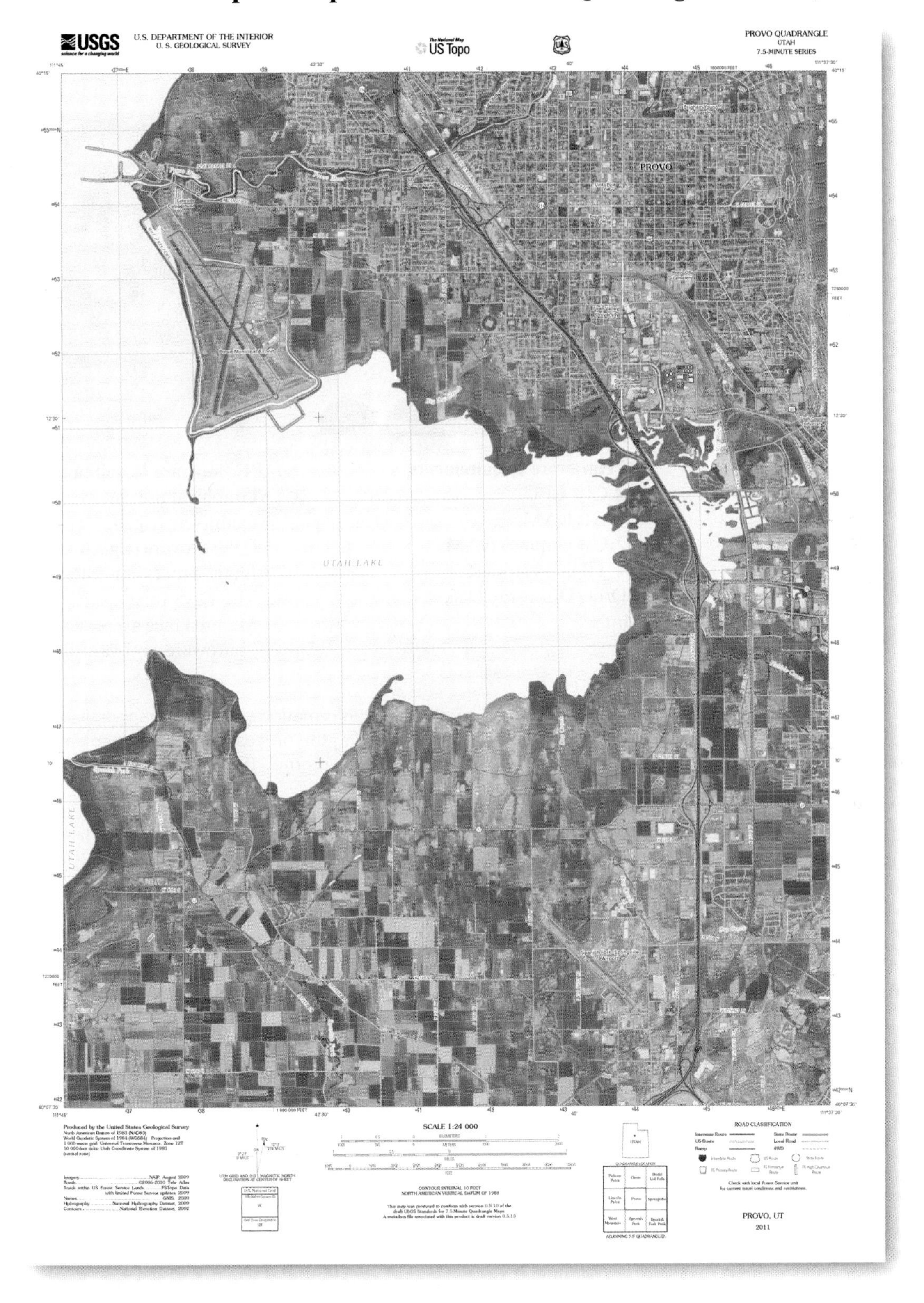

FIGURE 1–8 The U.S. Geological Survey's *National Map* program provides quantitative geospatial information for input to a GIS. This example is a US Topo GeoPDF of the Provo, UT, 7.5-minute quadrangle with elevation data from the National Elevation Dataset (NED), hydrology data from the National Hydrology Dataset (NHD), and aerial photography from the National Agriculture Imagery Program (NAIP). The US Topo information can be viewed using a PDF viewer. The spatial information can be downloaded directly from *The National Map* website (data courtesy of the U.S. Geological Survey).

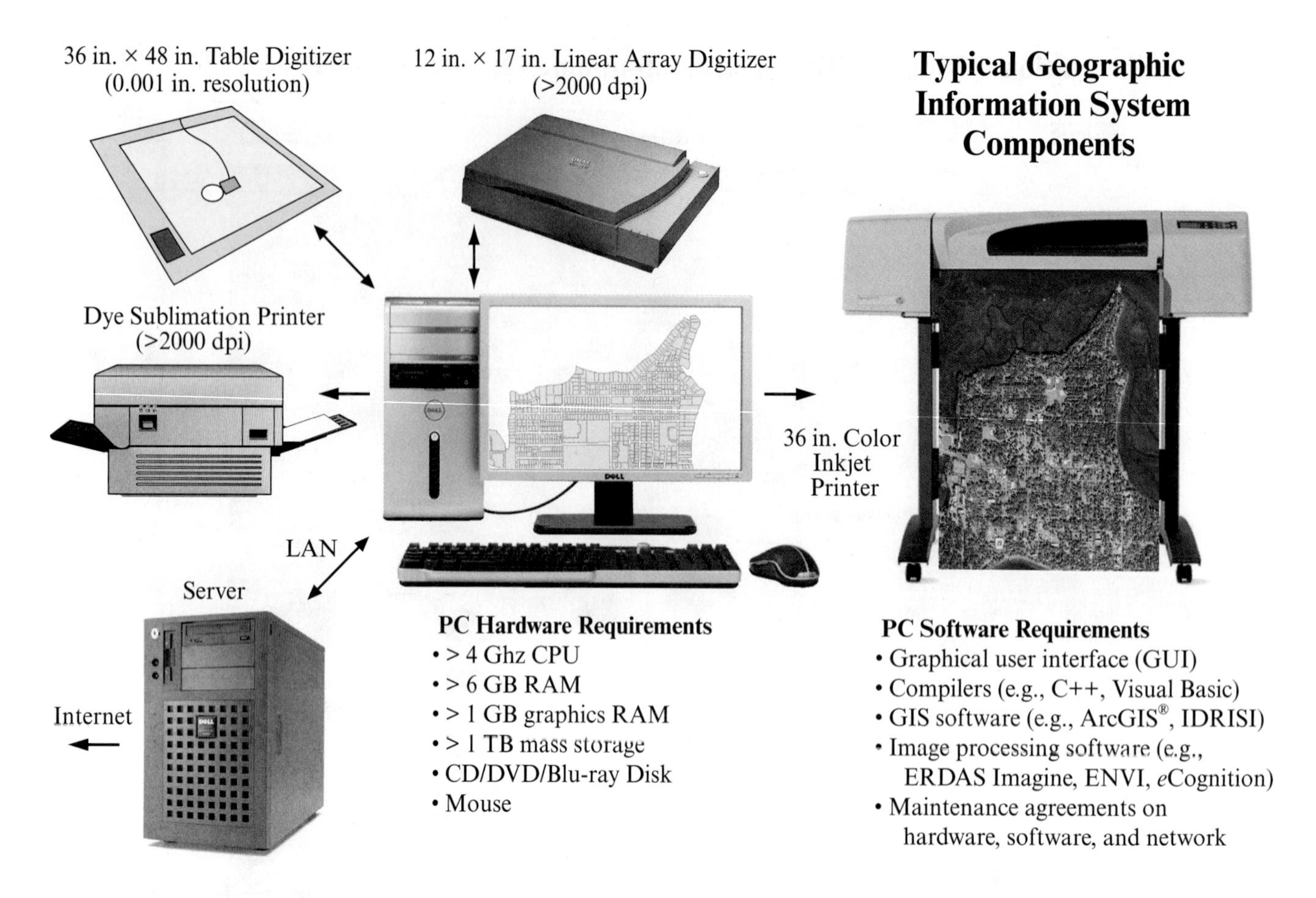

FIGURE 1–9 Typical hardware and software components of a geographic information system. The server is present to share GIS-related datasets and output products with other users without impacting the processing taking place on the PC. The individual units are connected via a local area network (LAN) and also with the Internet. (Source of map and airphoto Beaufort County GIS Department.)

utility data for a municipal government, he or she will want to purchase a GIS (e.g., ESRI ArcGIS®, Bentley MicroStation, Pitney Bowes Business Insight) that has excellent vector analysis functionality such as a robust ability to process linear networks (e.g., roads) and polygons (e.g., land parcels). Conversely, if most of the analysis involves various types of raster data, then a GIS that is especially adept at raster data analysis should be selected (e.g., Leica Geosystems ERDAS, IDRISI Taiga, GRASS, ArcGIS®).

The statistical capabilities of a GIS are another important consideration. Many of the spatial and database analyses conducted using a GIS rely on statistics, and different GIS have different statistical analysis capabilities—especially spatial statistics. Only a few of the major GIS are able to provide most of the functionality required for complex spatial analyses (Price, 2008). Table 1-1 summarizes many of the functions found in major GIS software.

One of the most important GIS software components is the database management system (DBMS). A high-quality GIS must have a powerful DBMS with adequate tools, rules, and procedures for effective data management, query, analysis, and output. Using these properties, the DBMS performs the input, storage, and retrieval of data that are linked to either vector or raster spatial data. You have probably used a spatial database before when searching for a store near your home by inputting your postal Zipcode. In this instance, the program searches for nearby stores based on the coordinates of your Zipcode, which is stored in a DBMS. One of the unique things about a GIS DBMS is that it allows tabular data (e.g., the square footage of your house) to be spatially linked to a location (Zipcode, address, latitude/longitude, UTM coordinates, etc.).

A high-quality GIS will also have excellent networking capabilities, including the ability to rapidly input, output, and process data via the Internet and/or cloud computing using specialized GIS functions. **Cloud computing** is a model of computer use in which data and/or services stored on the Internet are provided to users on a temporary basis (see Chapter 12). The GIS also includes Internet GIS functionality that allows not only data to be shared between different locations and computers but also specialized GIS algorithms

TABLE 1–1 Typical GIS computer hardware and software characteristics. Additional information about computer hardware/software, and GIS computer programming is provided in Chapter 11.

Computer Hardware	Characteristics	Importance
Central Processing Unit (CPU)	Single CPU Multiple CPUs	Multiple CPUs significantly increase the speed of operations associated with GIS data analysis and the processing of large datasets.
Arithmetic Co-processor	Reduced instruction set code	Increases the speed of calculations.
Memory	Read only memory (ROM) Random access memory (RAM) Graphics memory	Used to perform system operations. > 6 GB > 1 TB graphics RAM
Mass Storage	Hard Disk Compact Disk (CD) Digital Video Disk (DVD) Blu-ray Disk (BD)	> 1 TB is ideal Dual-layered if possible
Display	Minimum of 1900 x 1200 pixels 24 to 32-bit color look-up tables	Goal is to view the maximum geographic space possible at the highest color resolution.
Peripheral Input and Output Devices	Mouse Scanner (≥2000 dpi) Tablet digitizer (≥2000 dpi) Printers/plotters	Projects may require digitization of hard-copy maps or hard-copy remote sensor data. High quality printers and plotters are used to display GIS-related products.
Networking	Local area network (LAN) Internet backbone Cloud computing	Essential for sharing spatial data, GIS processing, and distributing GIS-related products.
Computer Software	**Characteristics**	**Importance**
Operating System	Microsoft, UNIX, LINUX, Apple	Use a widely adopted, reputable system.
Database Management System (DBMS)	Store and access attribute data	Critical to the usefulness of the GIS.
Functions	Cartography Data coordinate conversion Data interoperability Data management Digital image processing Geocoding/address matching Geostatistical analysis Linear referencing Network analysis Programming software Spatial analysis Spatial statistics 3-dimensional analysis	The GIS software must be able to perform the tasks required for specific geospatial applications.
Network	Local area network software Internet data access software Internet GIS software	Facilitates data sharing and processing between computers in a local area network (LAN) and on the Internet.

TABLE 1–2 Selected types of geospatial data and their sources in the United States. Additional sources of geospatial data are provided in Chapter 3 and in the Appendix.

Geospatial Data	Representative Public Source	Representative Commercial Source
Cadastral		
Parcels	Tax Assessor	Surveying and photogrammetric engineering companies
Building footprints	Tax Assessor	
Demography		
Population density	U.S. Census Bureau	Demographic consulting firms
Socio-economic characteristics	U.S. Census Bureau	Demographic consulting firms
Remote Sensor Data		
Very high spatial resolution <0.25 m	U.S. Dept. of Agriculture	Photogrammetric engineering firms
High spatial resolution 1 to 5 m	U.S. Dept. of Agriculture	GeoEye, DigitalGlobe, SPOT
Moderate spatial resolution 5 to 100 m	NASA Landsat TM, ETM, ETM+	SPOT, RADARSAT
Low spatial resolution >100 m	NASA MODIS, NOAA AVHRR	SPOT
High spectral resolution > 30 bands	NASA MODIS, NASA HYPERION	HiVista Hymap, CASI
Light Detecting and Ranging (LiDAR)	U.S. Geological Survey	EarthData, Sanborn, Optech
Soils and Geology		
Soils	U.S. Natural Resources Cons. Service	Soils consulting firms
Geology	U.S. Geological Survey	Oil and gas companies
Topography/Bathymetry		
Digital elevation models	U.S. Geological Survey	Photogrammetric and lidargrammetric engineering companies
Digital bathymetric models	U.S. Geological Survey	
Transportation Network		
Road centerlines	U.S. Department of Transportation	Transportation and photogrammetric engineering consulting firms
As-built engineering drawings	U.S. Department of Transportation	
Urban Infrastructure		
Land Use/Land Cover	U.S. National Map Local, regional, state planning agencies	Planning and photogrammetric engineering consulting firms
Utilities		
Power, sewer, water, communication	U.S. Census Bureau	Utility and photogrammetric firms
Vegetation		
Agriculture	U.S. Dept. of Agriculture	Agriculture consulting firms
Forestry	U.S. and State Forest Service	Forestry consulting firms
Rangeland	U.S. Bureau of Reclamation	Rangeland consulting firms
Wetland	U.S. Fish & Wildlife Service	Wetland consulting firms
Water		
Drainage network	U.S. Geological Survey	Hydrology consulting firms
Discharge	U.S. Geological Survey	Hydrology consulting firms
Weather		
Current	U.S. NOAA Weather Service	Weather consulting firms

and methods to be used (Peng and Tsou, 2006) (Table 1-1).

Humanware (Liveware)

One of the most important components of a GIS is **humanware** (sometimes referred to as **liveware**), defined as the characteristics and capabilities of the people responsible for designing, implementing, and using the GIS (Unwin, 1997; Schuurman, 2000). In fact, people are the most important component of a GIS because proper use of a GIS depends on people to structure the research questions, perform the analysis, and then judge whether the information extracted from the GIS is of value. The benefits of GIS technology may be minimal without users skilled at managing the GIS, applying GIS to real-world problems, and correctly interpreting the results (Satti, 2002). Generally, the cost of well-qualified GIS professionals is increasing dramatically whereas the cost of GIS hardware is decreasing.

GIS Data

Specially prepared geospatial data are a prerequisite for successful GIS analysis. Previous sections in this chapter described the nature of vector and raster data used in a GIS. Selected types of geospatial data and their sources in the United States are listed in Table 1-2 and discussed in Chapter 3. Additional information about geospatial data sources is provided in the Appendix.

Trends in GIS

GIS development has been closely associated with advances in the development of the computer. As a result, GIS-related hardware has become faster (more efficient), more affordable, and generally smaller in size. Geographic information systems now function using easy-to-use-and-understand graphical user interfaces (GUI) rather than simple text commands. Also, most early GIS were relative islands of technology that could not communicate with other machines. Advances in computer networking allow geographic information systems throughout the world to communicate with one another and rapidly share and disseminate spatial and non-spatial information. The majority of GIS data and algorithm sharing takes place via the Internet. To this end, the **Open Geospatial Consortium (OGC)** was initiated in 1994. OGC is a group of over 100 universities, corporations, and government agencies whose mission is to make GIS interoperable by building links that allow the accurate and efficient transfer of information derived using many of the most popular commercial and public GIS. In addition, a considerable amount of GIS analysis is conducted via web-based GIS analysis.

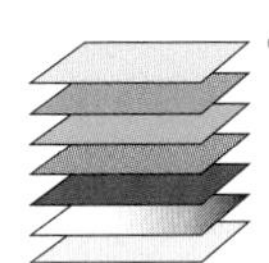

The Business of GIS

Recent studies suggest that GIS is a multi-billion dollar industry with many facets, including (Mondello et al., 2008; Bureau of Labor Statistics, 2011): the GIS software development industry, the GIS data acquisition industry, and GIS value-added service industry.

GIS Software Development Industry

As one might expect, not all GIS are created equally. Some research will be required to determine which GIS is best for you or your organization. Each GIS has various strengths and weaknesses. Some of the most common GIS software includes:

- *ArcGIS®* by Environmental Systems Research Institute, Inc. (www.esri.com; Price, 2008),
- *AutoCAD* with *MapGuide* by Autodesk, Inc. (www.autodesk.com),
- *ERDAS Imagine* by Leica-Geosystems, Inc. (www.ERDAS.com),
- *GRASS,* developed by the U.S. Army Construction Engineering Research Laboratories, a branch of the U.S. Army Corps of Engineers. GRASS is now maintained by an international development team. GRASS is important because it is free and publicly available via the Internet (http://grass.fbk.eu/),
- *IDRISI Taiga* by the Clark University Laboratory, (www.clarklabs.org),
- *MicroStation* by Bentley, Inc. (www.bentley.com/en-US/Products/MicroStation/), and
- *Pitney Bowes Business Insight* (formerly MapInfo) (www.pbinsight.com/welcome/mapinfo/).

Additional information about several of these GIS software programs is provided in Chapter 11.

The GIS software industry employs programmers, software designers, and applications specialists with backgrounds in geography, computer science, and many other disciplines. They develop software that GIS professionals want and will pay to use. The competition between the main software companies is intense as each seeks to obtain a greater share of the world-wide GIS software market.

GIS Data Acquisition Industry

A GIS is of little value if there is no valuable spatial information to analyze. Fortunately, there are many publicly available (free) spatial datasets. In fact, the U.S. government provides a significant amount of spatial data associated with a variety of disciplines. In addition, most state and municipal governments maintain, collect, and store relatively accurate spatial data. Many states and counties provide GIS data clearinghouses that can be accessed via the Internet. These clearinghouses allow the user to interactively view spatial data on their computer screen in real-time and download geospatial data.

International governments provide many GIS datasets as well. An advantage of using data published by a government agency is that the data usually adhere to a set of NSDI accuracy standards. The quality of the data is documented in attached metadata files that contain information about how the data were collected, processed, and stored. Selected types of geospatial data and representative public sources are listed in Table 1-2. Private commercial companies also provide a tremendous amount of geospatial data as shown in Table 1-2. The user must normally pay for the use of such data.

One might assume that given the tremendous amount of public and private geospatial data that have been collected through the years that the world has been mapped sufficiently. This assumption is inaccurate because geographic phenomena are continually changing (Estes and Mooneyhan, 1994; Warner et al., 2009). For example, Figure 1-10 demonstrates the rapid rate at which the geographic landscape is changing in Spanish

Landscape Change in Spanish Fork, UT

a. Aerial photograph in 2000.

b. Aerial photograph in 2006.

FIGURE 1–10 Black and white aerial photography of Spanish Fork, UT, obtained in 2000 and color aerial photography obtained in 2006 document the rapid conversion of prime agricultural land to residential development. Monitoring the geographic distribution and rate of change in land cover is critical for many applications (courtesy (a) U.S. Department of Agriculture and (b) state of Utah).

Fork, UT, during a six-year period. High-quality agricultural land is being converted to residential development very rapidly.

Similarly, transportation networks can change very rapidly. This can be a particularly vexing problem for those with personal navigation devices. It is frustrating to be directed by your personal navigation device along a route that no longer exists. Fortunately, most navigation devices access constantly updated geospatial information. Another example of the ever-changing nature of geographic phenomena are coastlines, which can change very rapidly. Also, just as geographic features (e.g., roads, buildings, etc.) are constantly changing, geographic attributes change rapidly, such as the assessed values of homes or the average daily traffic volume along a street.

When geospatial data are required that are not readily available from government sources, GIS users will need to make a decision about how to acquire the data they need. Fortunately, there are many different GIS-related businesses that continuously collect and analyze spatial data that can be incorporated into a GIS. One of the most important decisions that a GIS-user must make when acquiring new geospatial data is how detailed the spatial data should be. This necessitates that the user be concerned with scale. Different applications require different scales of data. For example, if you are mapping the hydrology of the United States, relatively small-scale (coarse) hydrologic vector information would probably be sufficient. However, if you were charged with mapping a very small portion of the Wabash River near Terre Haute, IN, you would most likely need to have very detailed, large-scale hydrologic vector data (Figure 1-11).

GIS Value-added Service Industry

Thousands of people are employed in the GIS value-added service industry. People in these companies use GIS technology and geospatial data on a daily basis to answer geographic questions for their clients. Examples include helping farmers maximize their crop yield using precision agriculture, scheduling the optimum route to deliver all of the packages for a fleet of delivery trucks, and identifying 10 homes that meet a potential real estate buyer's requirements, where the homes are located and the optimum route to visit them in the shortest possible time.

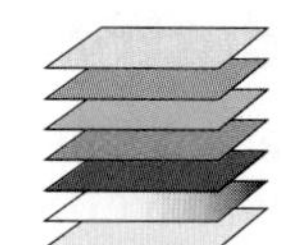

Careers in GIS

People in many different disciplines and vocations use GIS. A number of them have been discussed in this chapter. GIS jobs are available in public agencies (e.g., national, state, and local government; colleges and universities) and private commercial firms. The demand for GIS professionals continues to increase as spatial data and spatial analysis become more common (Bureau of Labor Statistics, 2011). For example, 20 years ago very few people foresaw that consumers would be able to purchase GPS-enabled navigation devices from a department store for less than $200 and that there would be no service fee to use them! Similarly, few envisioned that it would be possible to freely view high-spatial-resolution satellite imagery of much of the

TABLE 1–3 Selected GIS-related occupations defined by the U.S. Department of Labor Employment and Training Administration (Data from O*NET Online, http://online.onetcenter.org/find/quick?s=gis; accessed July 9, 2011. Also see DiBiase et al., 2010). Employment and growth estimates do not include geospatial software programmers and application developers. Wage information about several of these occupations is provided in Chapter 12.

Geospatial Occupation	Estimated Employment (2008)	Projected Growth (2008–2018)	Projected Growth Rate (2008–2018)
Geographic Information Scientists and Technologists Geographic Information Systems Technicians	209,000	72,600	Average (7% to 13%)
Mapping Technicians	77,000	29,400	Much faster than average (≥20%)
Cartographers and Photogrammetrists	12,000	6,400	Much faster than average (≥20%)
Geodetic Surveyors	58,000	23,300	Faster than average (14 to 19%)
Remote Sensing Scientists and Technologists	27,000	10,100	Average (7% to 13%)
Remote Sensing Technicians	65,000	36,400	Average (7% to 13%)
Surveyors	58,000	23,300	Faster than average (14 to 19%)
Surveying Technicians	77,000	29,400	Much faster than average (≥20%)

world via the Internet (e.g., via *Google Earth, Google Maps, MapQuest, Bing Maps*), stimulating increased interest by the general public in geospatial matters. Universities and colleges teach the principles of GIS in a great variety of disciplines such as geography, geology, civil engineering, natural resource management, forestry, agriculture, marine science, and so on. In fact, the educational system cannot currently keep up with the demand for educated GIScience professionals (Mondello et al., 2008).

The U.S. Department of Labor Employment and Training Administration provides online information about GIS-related occupations. Selected results are summarized in Table 1-3. A significant number of GIS-related jobs will need to be filled in the time period 2008 to 2018 to keep up with projected demand. Additional geospatial workforce considerations are discussed in DiBiase et al. (2010).

There are several Internet locations where you can learn about current GIS job openings and post your resume. Examples include: *GIS Jobs* (www.gisjobs.com), *GIS Jobs Clearinghouse* (www.gjc.org), and *GeoJobs* (www.geojobs.org). It is useful to visit these sites occasionally to see the type of GIS skills that are in demand in the marketplace, typical starting salaries, and common GIS job opportunities.

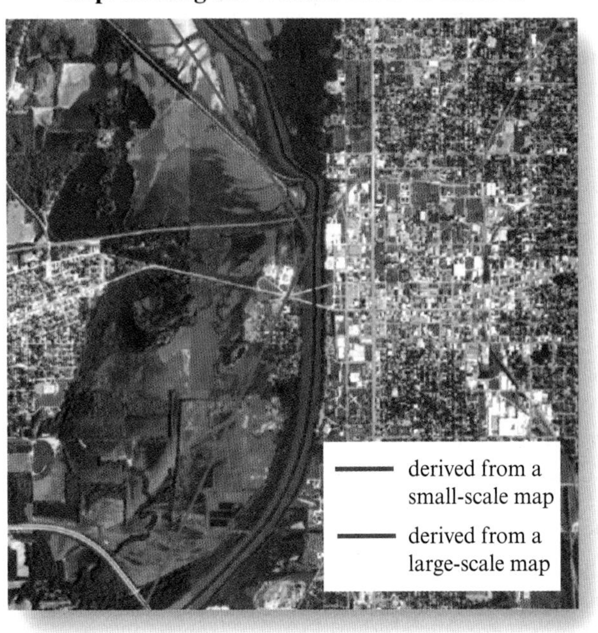

FIGURE 1–11 The blue line represents the *Wabash River* extracted from a small-scale (less-detailed) map. When used at the appropriate scale of analysis (e.g., continental studies), this line symbolization is adequate for most applications. However, when very large-scale (fine detail) studies are necessary, you will probably need to have the level of precision afforded by the red line, which was extracted from a 1:24,000 topographic map (data courtesy of IndianaMap).

Investing in GIS

Based on what has been presented so far, it probably sounds like every organization that studies anything in geographic space and maintains spatial information about it should implement a GIS. It is true that GIS is a powerful technology for storing, processing, and analyzing spatial data that allows for spatial relationships to be studied and modeled. However, GIS requires substantial initial and continuing investments in both personnel and financial resources. In fact, the history of GIS is replete with examples of GIS failures of government agencies, organizations, and private companies that did not understand the resource intensive task of creating and maintaining a comprehensive GIS. To this end, the design and implementation of a functional GIS can often take longer than a year—depending on the size of the organization and the amount and type of geographic data that will be used. This may not seem like much time, but if you are an elected official who is trying to justify a tax-payer expense or a county board member who is promoting the virtues of GIS to other board members not familiar with the technology, one or more years may seem like an eternity. Also, to successfully maintain a GIS, dedicated, full-time employees must be hired and/or trained.

Once a GIS has been created it can be an invaluable tool for making informed spatial decisions and mapping and monitoring human and natural systems. However, GIS is not a panacea that will address all of a given municipalities' problems with regard to issues of urban sprawl, inequitable property taxation, or any other number of spatial issues. One must always remember that a standard GIS does not actually make decisions. It is up to people to intelligently use GIS data and results to make good decisions. It should be noted, however, that a GIS can be specially configured to be a spatial decision support system that has the unique ability to make logical decisions based on the data and rules provided (Jensen et al., 2009). A **spatial decision support system (SDSS)** is a computer-based spatial information system that supports business or organizational decision-making activities.

GIS users must be competent in the use and analysis of spatial data. GIS has provided a way for geographic information to be accurately analyzed in a wide range of applications. However, users who are unfamiliar with GIS and geographic information may incorrectly use a GIS or may use spatial data in an inappropriate way. Therefore, a good understanding of GIS and spatial data is essential before beginning work on GIS projects. For example, users must understand how data in the GIS were acquired and verified for accuracy before performing any spatial data analysis. This information is usually found within a dataset's metadata.

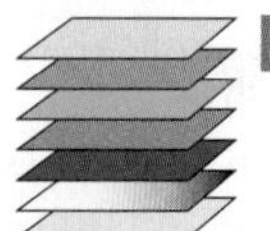

Book Organization

This book was written for people who want to learn the basic principles of GIS. It assumes no prior knowledge about GIS, spatial data, or spatial data analysis. It introduces the basics of GIS through chapters that build upon one another.

Chapter 2 introduces the user to the fundamental principles of georeferencing with information about datums, ellipsoids, geoids, and map projections, which are important to the successful use of GIS technology. Chapter 3 describes how data are collected for input to a GIS using in situ and remote-sensing data collection methods. It also reviews how hard-copy map data are digitized for input to a GIS. Chapter 4 summarizes data-quality issues, including metadata, accuracy and precision, error, data standards, and models of uncertainty. Chapter 5 provides more detailed information about vector and raster data structures plus an introduction to Database Management Systems and spatial databases. Chapter 6 describes how vector and raster data are analyzed using various algorithms, including buffering and overlay analysis. Chapter 7 describes how to use a GIS for geocoding/address matching, network analysis, and spatial location/allocation modeling. Chapter 8 reviews descriptive statistics, descriptive spatial statistics, and spatial data measurements using a GIS. Chapter 9 introduces the spatial analysis of 3-dimensional data using Triangular Irregular Network (TIN) surface processing, raster spatial interpolation, and surface processing. Chapter 10 describes how high-quality cartographic products may be created using a GIS. Chapter 11 provides detailed information about GIS computer hardware/software requirements and GIS computer programming basics. Chapter 12 peers into the future of GIS technology, applications, and demand for GIS professionals.

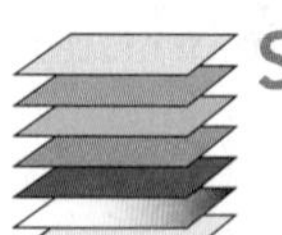

Summary

Over the past several decades the importance of geographic information in general and GIS in particular have become extremely important for improving the quality of life for humans, flora, and fauna (Jensen et al., 2004; 2009; Bureau of Labor Statistics, 2011). This importance may be the result of our increased recognition that spatial data and spatial data analysis play a critical role in understanding the complex spatial dynamics of our world (Madden, 2009). We hope that this book will be an excellent starting point—and continuing resource—as you journey along the GIScience path. Welcome to the world of GIS and spatial data.

Review Questions

1. What are the two primary types of data structures used to store information in a geographic information system?

2. Why are National Spatial Data Infrastructure (NSDI) standards important to the United States and other countries of the world?

3. Is the future of GIScience on a positive or negative trajectory? Provide reasons for your decision.

4. How is GIS information used when you request your cell phone to identify the route to the nearest fast-food restaurant?

5. Describe some of the major hardware and software components of a GIS and how the technology is changing.

6. Describe the difference between a typical computer-aided-design (CAD) program and a true geographic information system.

7. Describe the difference between a remote sensing data collection system (e.g., Landsat 7 Enhanced Thematic Mapper) and a GIS.

8. Based on your preliminary knowledge, where would you go to obtain the following types of geospatial information for your GIS: transportation network data, elevation data, population density data, per capita income data, property ownership information?

9. Identify seven major applications that are often performed using a GIS.

10. Why is it important that all of the geospatial information stored in a GIS be geometrically rectified (registered) to one another?

11. What is the difference between a GIS and a spatial decision support system?

12. Where can you go to learn about GIS-related jobs and projected trends in GIS employment?

Glossary

Cloud Computing: A model of computer use in which data and/or services stored on the Internet are provided to users on a temporary basis.

Continuous Geographic Features: The type of geospatial data that exists continuously in the landscape. Examples include elevation, temperature, atmospheric pressure, and slope.

Discrete Geographic Features: Discrete geospatial data generally consist of points (e.g., the centroid of a building), lines (e.g., a road network), or polygons (e.g., building footprints).

Features Summarized by Geographic Area: Geographic data summarized by an enumeration district such as a watershed, school district, county, state, or country.

Federal Geographic Data Committee (FGDC): Interagency committee that promotes the coordinated development, use, sharing, and dissemination of geospatial data on a national basis.

Geographic Information System (GIS): A spatial information system used to import, edit, visualize, analyze, and output spatial and non-spatial information stored in a computer database.

GIScience: The body of theory and knowledge that seeks to improve our understanding about the nature of geographic data and how it may be collected, analyzed, and viewed using the logic found within the mapping sciences (i.e., cartography, GIS, surveying, and remote sensing of the environment).

Humanware: The characteristics and capabilities of the people responsible for designing, implementing, and using a GIS (sometimes referred to as liveware).

Information System: Computerized tools that assist people to transform data into information.

National Spatial Data Infrastructure (NSDI): The NSDI includes geospatial framework foundation data (e.g., geodetic control, digital orthophotos), framework thematic data (e.g., cadastral, transportation), and other types of thematic spatial data (e.g., soils, land cover) used by the United States and other governments throughout the world to manage natural and cultural resources.

Open Geospatial Consortium (OGC): A group of more than 100 universities, corporations, and government agencies whose mission is to make GIS interoperable by building links that allow the accurate and efficient transfer of information derived using many of the most popular commercial and public geographic information systems.

Raster Data Structures: Geospatial data stored in a raster (matrix) format where each picture element (pixel) is associated with a row and column of the raster dataset.

Spatial Data: Any data or information that have spatial attributes (e.g., latitude/longitude).

Spatial Decision Support System (SDSS): A spatial information system that supports business or organizational decision-making activities.

Vector Data Structures: Point, line, and area (polygon) data stored according to their *x,y,* and/or *z*-coordinates.

References

Abler, R. F., 1987, "The National Science Foundation Center for Geographic Information and Analysis," *International Journal of Geographic Information Systems,* 1(4):303–326.

Bureau of Labor Statistics, 2011, *Occupational Outlook Handbook, 2010-2011 Edition*, Washington: U. S. Bureau of Labor Statistics (www.bls.gov./oco/ocos040.htm).

Burroughs, P. A., 1986, *Principles of Geographic Information Systems for Land Resources*, Oxford, UK: Clarendon Press.

Clarke, K. C., Parks, B. O. and M. P. Crane, 2002, *Geographic Information Systems and Environmental Modeling*, Upper Saddle River: Pearson Prentice-Hall, 306 p.

Cowen, D. J., Coleman, D. J., Craig, W. J., Domenico, C., Elhami, S., Johnson, S., Marlow, S., Roberts, F., Swartz, M. T. and N. Von Meyer, 2007, *National Land Parcel Data: A Vision for the Future*, Washington: National Academy Press, 158 p.

Dale, P., 2005, *Introduction to Mathematical Techniques Used in GIS*, Boca Raton: CRC Press, 202 p.

DiBiase, D., Corbin, T., Fox, T., Francica, J., Green, K., Jackson, J., Jeffress, G., Jones, B., Jones, B., Mennis, J., Schuckman, K., Smith, C. and J. Van Sickle, 2010, "The New Geospatial Technology Competency Model: Bringing Workforce Needs into Focus," *URISA Journal*, 22(2):55–72.

Estes, J. E. and D.W. Mooneyhan, 1994, "Of Maps and Myths," *Photogrammetric Engineering & Remote Sensing*, 60(5):515–524.

FGDC, 2011, *Federal Geographic Data Committee*, Washington: FGDC, (www.fgdc.gov/).

Foresman, T. W., 1998, *The History of Geographic Information Systems*, Upper Saddle River: Pearson Prentice-Hall, Inc., 397 p.

Goodchild, M. F., 1992, "Geographic Information Science," *International Journal of Geographical Information Systems*, 6(1):31–45.

Goodchild, M. F., 1997, "What is Geographic Information Science?" *NCGIA Core Curriculum in GIScience* (www.ncgia.ucsb.edu/giscc/units/u002/u002.html).

Green, R. P. and J. B. Pick, 2006, *Exploring the Urban Community: A GIS Approach*, Upper Saddle River: Pearson Prentice-Hall, 495 p.

GSDI, 2011, *Global Spatial Data Infrastructure Association* (www.GSDI.org).

Jensen, J. R., Botchwey, K., Brennan-Galvin, E., Johannsen, C. J., Juma, C., Mabogunje, A. L., Miller, R. B., Price, K. P., Reining, P. A. C., Skole, D. L., Stancioff, A. and D. R. F. Taylor, 2002, *Down To Earth: Geographic Information for Sustainable Development in Africa*, Washington: National Academy Press, 155 p.

Jensen, J. R., Hodgson, M. E., Garcia-Quijano, M., Im, J. and J. Tullis, 2009, "A Remote Sensing and GIS-assisted Spatial Decision Support System for Hazardous Waste Site Monitoring," *Photogrammetric Engineering & Remote Sensing*, 75(2):169–177.

Jensen, J. R. and J. Im., 2007, "Remote Sensing Change Detection in Urban Environments," in R. R. Jensen, J. D. Gatrell and D. D. McLean (Eds.), *Geo-Spatial Technologies in Urban Environments Policy, Practice, and Pixels*, 2nd Ed., Berlin: Springer-Verlag, 7–32.

Jensen, J. R., Im, J., Hardin, P. and R. R. Jensen, 2009, "Chapter 19: Image Classification," in Warner, T. A., Nellis, M. D. and G. M. Foody (Eds.), *The SAGE Handbook of Remote Sensing*, London: SAGE Publications, 269–296.

Jensen, J. R., Saalfeld, A., Broome, F., Cowen, D., Price, K., Ramsey, D., Lapine, L. and E. L. Usery, 2005, "Chapter 2: Spatial Data Acquisition and Integration," in *A Research Agenda for Geographic Information Science*, Boca Raton: CRC Press, 17–60.

Jensen, R. R., Gatrell, J. D., Boulton, J. and B. Harper, 2004, "Using Remote Sensing and Geographic Information Systems to Study Urban Quality of Life and Urban Forest Amenities," *Ecology & Society*, 9(5):5, (www.ecologyandsociety.org/vol9/iss5/art5/).

Koch, T., 2005, *Cartographies of Disease: Maps, Mapping, and Medicine*, Redlands: ESRI Press, 388 p.

Konecny, G., 2003, *Geoinformation: Remote Sensing, Photogrammetry and Geographic Information Systems*, New York: Taylor & Francis, 248 p.

Lo, C. P. and A. K. W. Yeung, 2007, *Concepts and Techniques in Geographic Information Systems*, Upper Saddle River: Pearson Prentice-Hall, Inc., 532 p.

Madden, M. (Ed.), 2009, *Manual of Geographic Information Systems*, Bethesda: American Society for Photogrammetry & Remote Sensing, 1352 p.

Maidment, D. R., Edelman, S., Heiberg, E. R., Jensen, J. R., Maune, D. F., Schuckman, K. and R. Shrestha, 2007, *Elevation Data for Floodplain Mapping*, Washington: National Academy Press, 151 p.

Maguire, D. J., 1991, "An Overview and Definition of GIS," in Maguire, D. J., Goodchild, M. F., and D. W. Rind, (Eds.), *Geographical Information Systems: Principles & Applications*, New York: John Wiley & Sons, 9–20.

McHarg, I. L., 1967 (1995: 25th Anniversary Ed.), *Design with Nature*, New Jersey: John Wiley & Sons, 208 p.

Mondello, C., Hepner, G. and R. M. Medina, 2008, "ASPRS 10 Year Remote Sensing Industry Forecast: Phase V," *Pho-*

togrammetric Engineering & Remote Sensing, 74(11): 1297–1305.

Morrison, J. and H. Veregin, 2010, "Spatial Data Quality," in *Manual of Geospatial Science & Technology*, J. D. Bossler, Ed., Boca Raton: CRC Press, 593–610.

Onsrud, H., 2007, *Research and Theory in Advancing Spatial Data Infrastructure Concepts*, Redlands: ESRI Press, 293 p.

Peng, X. and M. Tsou, 2003, *Internet GIS: Distributed Geographic Information Services for the Internet and Wireless Networks*, New York: John Wiley & Sons, 679 p.

Price, M., 2008, *Mastering ArcGIS®*, 3rd Ed., New York: McGraw Hill, Inc., 607 p.

Satti, S. R., 2002, *GWRAPPS: A GIS-based Decision Support System for Agricultural Water Resources Management*, Masters Thesis, Gainesville: University of Florida, 116 p.

Schuurman, N., 2000, "Trouble in the Heartland: GIS and its Critics in the 1990s," *Progress in Human Geography*, 24(4):569–590.

Slocum, T., McMaster, R. B., Kessler, F. C. and H. H. Howard, 2005, *Thematic Cartography and Geographic Visualization*, 2nd Ed., Upper Saddle River: Pearson Prentice-Hall, Inc., 475 p.

Unwin, D. J., 1997, "Unit 160 - Teaching and Learning GIS in Laboratories," in *NCGIA Core Curriculum in GIScience*, Santa Barbara: National Center for Geographic Information and Analysis (www.ncgia.ucsb.deu/giscc/units/u160/u160.html).

Warner, T. A., Nellis, M. D. and G. M. Foody, 2009, *Handbook of Remote Sensing*, London: SAGE Publications Ltd., 504 p.

2 GEOREFERENCING

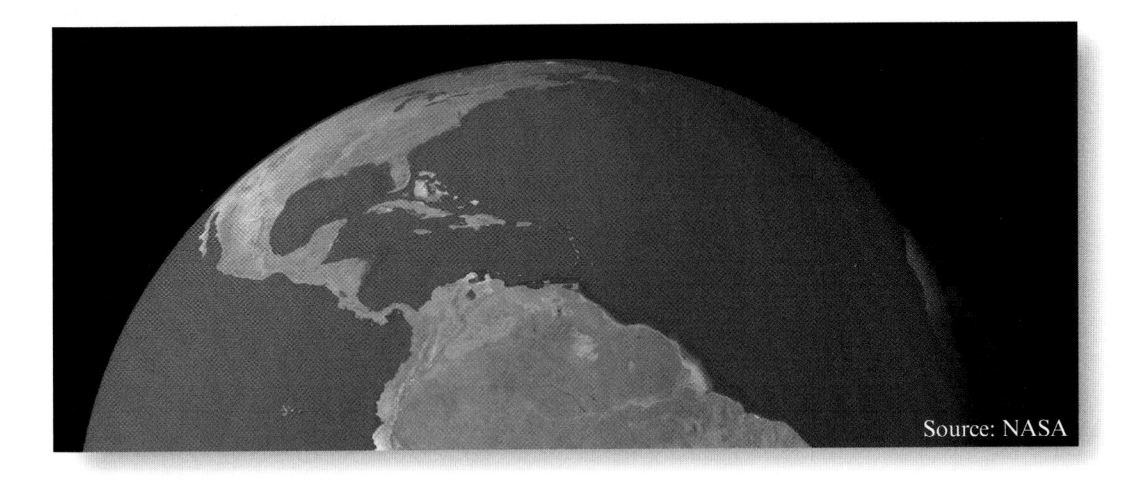

All the features in a GIS geodatabase, such as telephone poles, building footprints, or road segments, must have accurate geographic location and extent information associated with them. The ability to locate these features accurately in geographic space is commonly referred to as **georeferencing**. Perhaps you are asking yourself, "Why do I need to learn about georeferencing, which includes information about datums, ellipsoids, geoids, and coordinate systems, when all I want to do is use a GIS to inventory and analyze the spatial data of my study area?" The answer is that without a basic knowledge of these concepts, it is likely that the results produced using the GIS will not meet your expectations. In fact, the results could be inaccurate or misleading. Consequently, it is important that GIScientists understand basic georeferencing concepts.

Overview

This chapter provides introductory information about geodetic datums, ellipsoids, geoids, and common coordinate systems. The global (spherical) coordinate system based on latitude and longitude is presented along with several of the more important projected coordinate systems such as the Universal Transverse Mercator (UTM), Albers Equal-area, Lambert Conformal Conic, and State Plane Coordinate Systems. Tissot's indicatrix and its use for understanding the distortion associated with various map projections is introduced. The reader should be able to use the information in this chapter to help select an appropriate map projection for a particular GIS project.

Datums

The Earth is an irregularly shaped sphere that is difficult to model. Accurate *x*, *y*, and *z* position measurements are required for a great variety of applications including mapping (e.g., thematic, topographic), nautical charting, flood risk determination, transportation, land use, and ecosystem management. The term **datum** refers to a reference or foundation surface against which accurate position measurements are made. Basically, a datum identifies "zero" on a measurement scale (Maidment et al., 2007).

Two main datums are the foundation for navigation in the United States. These datums—called the horizontal and vertical datums—make up the **National Spatial Reference System (NSRS)**. Geodesists, surveyors, cartographers, and others interested in precise positioning use the NSRS as their foundation for georeferencing. To develop horizontal and vertical datums, it is first necessary to define the shape of the Earth. This requires familiarity with geodesy. The U.S. National Geodetic Survey (NGS) defines **geodesy** as the science concerned with determining the size and shape of the Earth and the location of points upon its surface (NGS, 2011c). Geodesists describe the shape of the Earth using ellipsoids, geoids, and gravitational measurements.

Ellipsoids

Human beings often think of the Earth as a perfect, 3-dimensional sphere (Figure 2-1a). However, geodesists have carefully measured the Earth and found that it is not a perfect sphere. In fact, there is a slight, but important difference between the distance around the Earth from North Pole to South Pole (39,939,593.9 m)

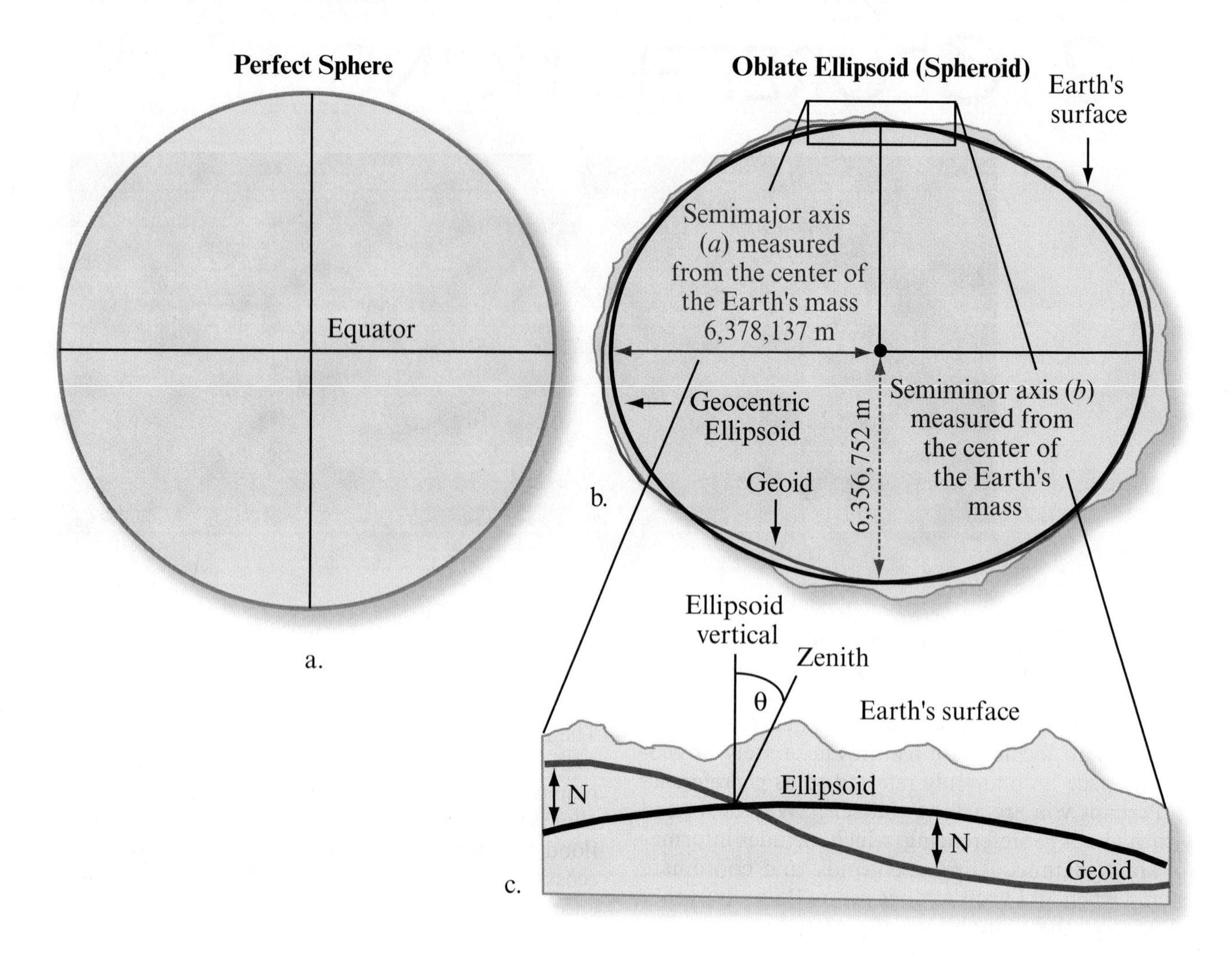

FIGURE 2–1 a) The Earth is not a perfect sphere. b) The Earth is an oblate ellipsoid (i.e., a spheroid) with the distance from the center of the Earth to the Equator (semimajor axis) being slightly greater than the distance from the center of the Earth to the poles (semiminor axis). c) Relationships associated with the Earth's surface, the geoid and the WGS84 geocentric ellipsoid. The height difference between the geoid and the geocentric ellipsoid (N) is the geoid separation. The angle between a perpendicular to the ellipsoid and a perpendicular to the geoid is called the vertical deflection angle (θ).

when compared to the distance around the Equator (40,075,452.7 m). The distance from the center of the Earth to the poles is 6,356,752.3142 m. The distance from the center of the Earth to the Equator is 6,378,137 m. The Earth's shape is an **oblate ellipsoid** (also called a **spheroid)**, that has been slightly flattened at the north and south poles (Maidment et al., 2007).

The Earth's oblateness is caused by the rotation of the Earth on its somewhat shorter axis (Figure 2-1b). The amount of polar flattening is computed using the equation (Esri, 2004):

$$f = \frac{(a-b)}{a} \tag{2.1}$$

where a and b are the lengths of the semimajor and semiminor axes of the ellipse which represent the Equatorial and polar radii of the Earth, respectively (Figure 2-1b). Therefore, the amount of flattening, f, is very close to 1/300:

$$f = \frac{(6378137 - 6356752)}{6378137} = 0.00335 = \frac{1}{300}$$

The ellipsoid is typically used as the reference surface for making horizontal (longitude and latitude) measurements in geodetic networks. The World Geodetic System of 1984 (WGS84) was developed by the U.S. Defense Mapping Agency (now the National Geospatial-Intelligence Agency). This is the global reference ellipsoid used by the U.S. Global Positioning System (GPS). There are about 25 different ellipsoids used throughout the world today for mapping purposes. Characteristics of six ellipsoids used for GIS applications and general mapping are summarized in Table 2-1.

TABLE 2–1 Selected common ellipsoids used for regional, national, and international mapping and GIS applications (adapted from Lo and Yeung, 2007; Leica Geosystems, 2008).

Ellipsoid	Semimajor axis, *a* (m)	Semiminor axis, *b* (m)	Use
Australian National 1966	6,378,160	6,356,774.719	Australia
Clarke 1866	6,378,206.4	6,356,584.467	North America
International 1924	6,378,388	6,356,911.946	Remaining parts of the world
GRS80: Geodetic Reference System 1980	6,378,137	6,356,752.3141	Adopted in North America for1983 Earth-centered coordinate system (satellite)
WGS84: World Geodetic System 1984	6,378,137	6,356,752.3142	Used with the Global Positioning System (GPS) and by NASA (satellite)
Nominal Radius of the Earth	6,370,997	6,370,997	A perfect sphere

Geoids

You are probably aware that the contours found on a topographic map normally refer to the elevation above mean sea level. What you may not know is that the most accurate representation of mean sea level is through the use of a geoid. The NGS (2007) defines a **geoid** as the equipotential surface of the Earth's gravity field that best fits global mean sea level. In simple terms, a geoid (Figure 2-1bc) is the shape of the Earth if the oceans were allowed to flow freely under the continents to create a single, undisturbed global sea level covering the entire planet (Lo and Yeung, 2007). Therefore, our vertical reference system is defined by gravity.

Gravity pulls all objects downward toward the center of the Earth.You might think that gravity is uniform all over the Earth and that mean sea level (i.e., the geoid) should be constant all over the Earth. Interestingly, it is not. The Earth's shape and gravity field are complex and vary over space and time. For example, the Earth's surface rises and falls about 30 cm (about 1 ft.) every day due to the gravitational influences of the moon and the sun (NGS, 2011c).

A map of the Earth's gravity field measured by the National Aeronautics & Space Administration (NASA) Gravity Recovery and Climate Experiment (GRACE) satellite is shown in Figure 2-2 (NASA, 2007). The gravity information in this illustration was summarized over 111 days. This illustration demonstrates how gravitational forces are generally greater over the continents and especially the mountain ranges, where the continental crust is thickest, and generally lower over the oceans where the Earth's crust is not as thick. For example, gravity averaged over these 111 days was greater over the Andes Mountains, Rocky Mountains, and the Himalayas than in the Amazon Basin in South America or much of the Pacific Ocean.

Sometimes a location on the Earth may have zero elevation with respect to the geoid and be several meters above or below zero with respect to the ellipsoid. (Maidment, et al., 2007). The difference is known as the geoid separation, *N*, as shown in Figure 2-1c.

Horizontal Datums

A **horizontal datum** is a collection of points on the Earth that have been identified according to their precise northerly or southerly location (latitude) and easterly or westerly location (longitude) (NGS, 2011a). To create a horizontal datum (which is really a network of horizontally distributed points) surveyors mark each of the positions they identify on the Earth with a brass, bronze, or aluminum disk monument. They locate each of the monuments in geographic space very accurately with GPS technology and use this information to create a "connected" unified network of measurements, i.e., a datum.

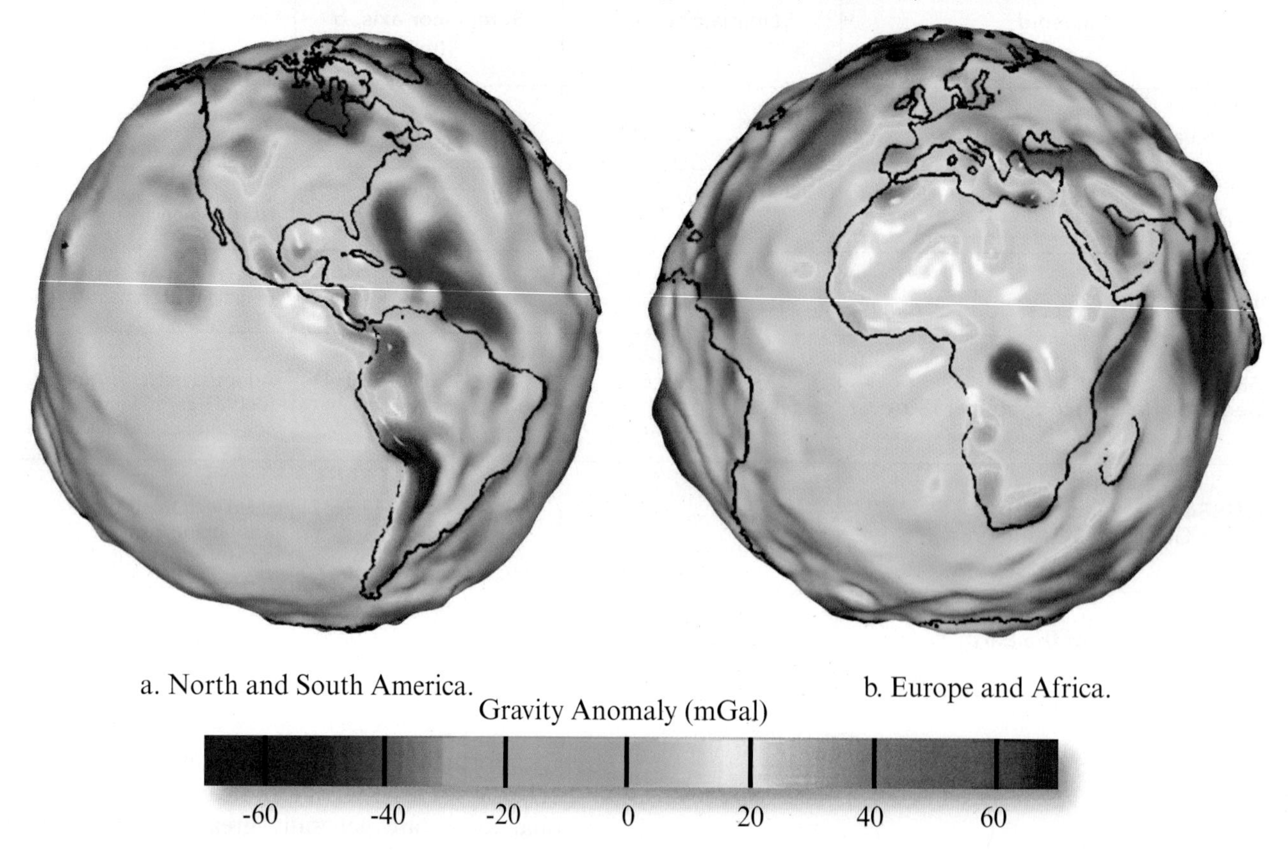

FIGURE 2–2 Earth Gravity Model 01 based on 111 days of measurement by the National Aeronautics & Space Administration (NASA) GRACE satellite. A milligal is used to describe variations in gravity over the surface of the Earth. One milligal (or mGal) = 0.00001 m/s^2 can be compared to the total gravity on the Earth's surface of approximately 9.8 m/s^2. One milligal is about 1 millionth of the standard acceleration on the Earth's surface (courtesy NASA/JPL/University of Texas Center for Space Research).

In 1927, the U.S. Coast and Geodetic Survey, connected all of the existing horizontal monuments together using terrestrial surveying triangulation procedures and created the North American Datum of 1927 (NAD27). The National Geodetic Survey subsequently created the North American Datum of 1983 (NAD83), which is the most commonly used horizontal control datum in the United States.

Vertical Datums

A **vertical datum** is a collection of spatially distributed points on the Earth with known heights either above or below mean sea level. Near coastal areas, mean sea level is determined with a tide gauge. In areas far away from the shore, mean sea level is determined by the shape of the geoid (NGS, 2011b). Similar to the survey markers used to identify known positions in the horizontal datum, round brass plates mark positions in the vertical datum.

In 1929, the NGS compiled all of the existing vertical benchmarks and created the National Geodetic Vertical Datum of 1929 (NGVD 29). Since then, movements of the Earth's crust have changed the elevations of many benchmarks. In 1988, NGVD 29 was adjusted to remove inaccuracies and to correct distortions. The new datum, called the North American Vertical Datum of 1988 (NAVD 88), is the most commonly used vertical datum in the United States today. For example, Federal Emergency Management Agency (FEMA) digital flood insurance rate maps (DFIRMS) are referenced to the NAVD 88.

The **elevation** of a geographic location is its height above a fixed reference point, most commonly a reference geoid, a mathematical model of the Earth's sea level. For example, right now you may be standing on the ground at an elevation of 500 m above sea level. The term digital elevation model (DEM) is a generic term used to describe a continuous digital elvation surface above sea level. A digital surface model

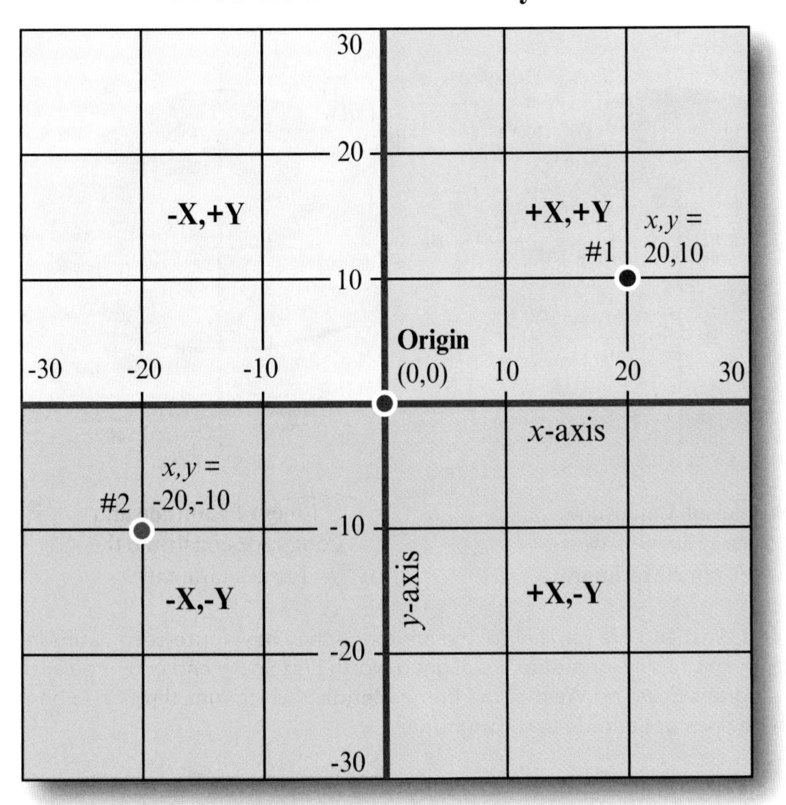

FIGURE 2–3 An example of a simple cartesian coordinate system. Note how x and y values change from positive to negative depending on where the point is located in relation to the origin. A false-easting and false-northing origin (0,0) could be introduced in the lower left corner of this grid to ensure that all coordinates are in the positive quadrant (+X, +Y) of the coordinate system.

(DSM) includes the elevation of all the features in the terrain above sea level such as bare ground, buildings, trees, powerlines, etc. A digital terrain model (DTM) contains only elevations of the bare ground above sea level without any buildings, trees, etc.

Bathymetry is the study of the underwater depth of lake, sea, or ocean floors. Bathymetric (or hydrographic) charts are typically produced to support the safety of surface or sub-surface navigation, and usually show seafloor relief or terrain as contour lines (called depth contours or isobaths) and selected depths (called soundings).

Coordinate Systems

There are two common types of coordinate systems typically used in geographic information systems: a) global or spherical coordinate systems based on latitude and longitude, and b) projected coordinate systems based on a map projection such as a conformal conic map projection (Esri, 2011). Map projections define how positions on the Earth's curved 3-dimensional surface are transformed onto a flat map surface. A coordinate system is then superimposed on the flat map surface to provide the referencing framework by which positions are measured and computed (Lo and Yeung, 2007).

Cartesian Coordinate Systems

A cartesian coordinate system is one that assigns two coordinates (x and y) to every point on a flat surface. The two coordinates are distances from an origin (e.g., 0,0) in the x- and y-direction. For example, point #1 in Figure 2-3 is located at coordinates $x,y = 20,10$. A cartesian coordinate system is relatively simple to envision and devise. However, it is important to remember that a cartesian coordinate system may have both positive and negative x- and y-coordinate values, as shown in Figure 2-3 (e.g., point #2 coordinates $x,y = -20,-10$). These positive and negative coordinate values can be confusing when used for mapping. Consequently, some map coordinate systems use *false-eastings* (x) or *false-northings* (y) so that the extent of the study area is forced to lie within the positive region of the coordinate system (+X,+Y). For example, the heavily used Universal Transverse Mercator (UTM) coordinate system (to be discussed) uses false-easting logic.

Latitude and Longitude

Latitude and longitude represent one of the most basic coordinate systems and form the base of the Earth's only "global" coordinate system. Lines of latitude begin at the Equator and run East-West parallel to the Equator (Figure 2-4a). Latitude measures degrees north and south of the Equator from the center of the

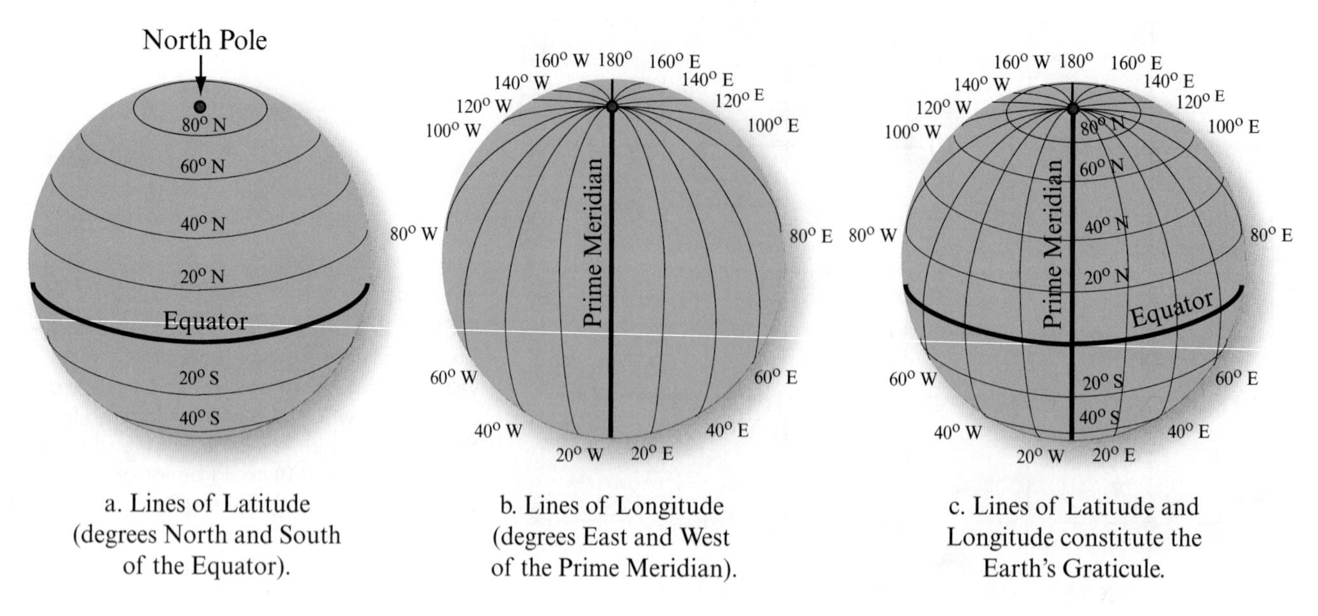

FIGURE 2–4 a) Lines of latitude are aligned East and West and are parallel to one another – they never intersect. Latitude is measured in degrees North and South of the Equator. b) Lines of longitude are aligned North and South and converge at the North and South Poles. Longitude is measured in degrees East and West of the Prime Meridian which runs through Greenwich, England. c) The Earth's Graticule consists of the lines of Latitude and Longitude.

Earth from 90° to -90°. Some prominent lines of latitude include the Equator (0°), the Tropic of Cancer (23.5° N), and Tropic of Capricorn (23.5° S).

Lines of longitude run North-South and measure degrees East and West of the Prime Meridian (0°) from 0° to 180° (Figure 2-4b). Some prominent lines of longitude include the Prime Meridian (0°) and 180° West longitude, which is generally associated with the International Date Line. The origin of the latitude, longitude coordinate system is where the Prime Meridian intersects the Equator. This is the point where both latitude and longitude = 0°. To the east of this point longitude is positive and to the west it is negative. To the north of this point latitude is positive and to the south latitude is negative.

Many datasets are provided in unprojected geographic (latitude, longitude) coordinates. Often, one of the first things that GIS analysts do with a dataset is to project the data into one of the map projections to be discussed.

Measuring Distance Using Latitude and Longitude

The latitude (ϕ) and longitude (λ) coordinates of a location on the surface of the Earth are measured from a theoretical point at the center of the Earth. The coordinates may be reported in degrees, minutes, and seconds or in decimal degrees (Figure 2-5). Latitude is the angular distance between the plane of the Equator and a line passing through the point under investigation and the center of the Earth. Longitude is the angular distance between the Prime Meridian and the meridian of the point under investigation.

The distance in curvature of a degree of latitude is always equal to about 111 km. However, the distance in curvature of a degree of longitude is not constant because longitude converges at the poles. Therefore, it is not possible to use distances in curvature in longitude consistently throughout the Earth. At the Equator, 1° of longitude is equal to about 111 km. As latitude increases to the north and south, longitude converges causing it to have less distance in curvature. You can calculate the distance in curvature of longitude if you know the latitude using the following equation:

$$1°longitude = 111 \times \cos(latitude) \tag{2.2}$$

At 60° north or south latitude, the distance of 1° of longitude equals 55.5 km because the cosine of 60° = 0.5 (i.e., $111 \times 0.5 = 55.5$). At 90° north or south latitude the distance of 1° of longitude is 0 km because the cosine of 90° = 0.0.

Latitude and longitude are measured using degrees, minutes, and seconds or decimal degrees. In addition, some researchers prefer degrees with decimal minutes. There are 60 minutes in each degree and 60 seconds in each minute. Knowing this, it is relatively easy to con-

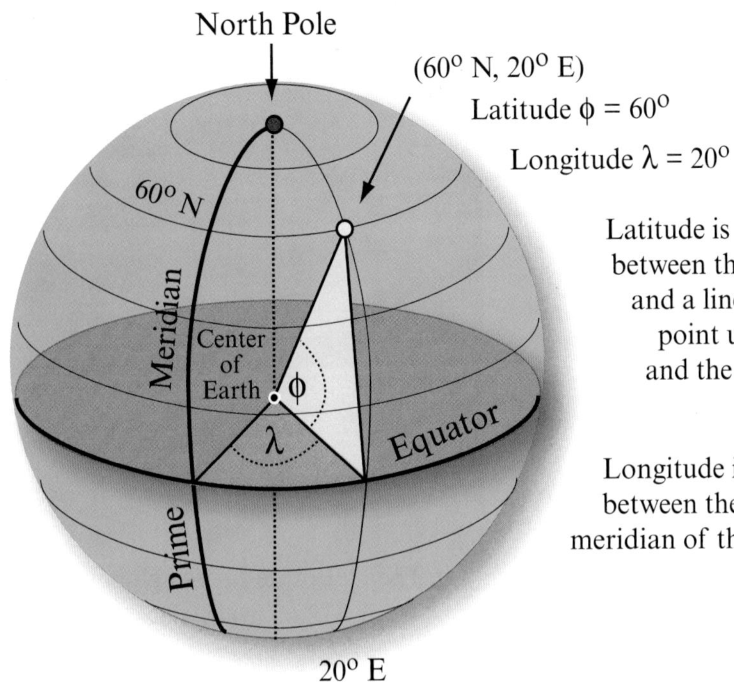

FIGURE 2–5 The latitude (ϕ) and longitude (λ) coordinates of a location on the surface of the Earth are measured from a theoretical point at the center of the Earth. The coordinates may be reported in degrees, minutes, and seconds or in decimal degrees.

vert from decimal degrees to degrees, minutes, and seconds and vice versa. For example, if you are provided a spatial dataset in decimal degrees, you first truncate the degrees and multiply the decimal portion by 60 to calculate decimal minutes. Then, do the same thing with your newly created decimal minutes to determine seconds.

Below is an example of the conversion of 111.2358° in decimal degrees to degrees, minutes, and seconds:

111° remains the same. Take 0.2358 and multiply by 60:

$$0.2358 \times 60 = 14.148$$

14 is the number of minutes. Take 0.148 and multiply it by 60:

$$0.148 \times 60 = 8.88$$

8.88 is the number of seconds. So, the conversion of 111.2358° to degrees, minutes, and seconds is 111° 14' 8.88".

You may also receive a spatial dataset that has latitude and longitude measured in degrees, minutes, and seconds and you need to convert these values into decimal degrees. This is also a relatively simple procedure. For example, assume a location is given as 35° 25' 45.2". To convert this value to decimal degrees you start by dividing the seconds by 60:

$$45.2/60 = 0.75333$$

Take this number (0.75333) and add it to the minutes:

$$0.75333 + 25 = 25.75333$$

Then, take this newly calculated decimal minute number and divide it by 60:

$$25.75333/60 = 0.429222$$

Finally, add this number to the number of degrees:

$$0.429222 + 35 = 35.429222°.$$

Unfortunately, because of the convergence of longitude at the poles, accurate distance and area measurements are very difficult to obtain using latitude and longitude when the area or distance between two points extend north to south. To remedy this, the geographic grid is used instead as the base to define custom map projections and coordinate systems. All of the custom map

a. A globe 1.5 ft. (45.7 cm) in diameter.

The World's Largest Globe

b. The DeLorme *Eartha* globe is 41.5 ft. (12.65 m) in diameter.

FIGURE 2–6 a) Globes are scale reductions of the Earth. Unfortunately, they are costly, difficult to create and transport, and the viewer can only see approximately one-half of the sphere (globe) at one time. Note that the Earth is inclined on its axis 23.5° (D. Hurst / Alamy). *Eartha*, the world's largest rotating and revolving globe, is located at DeLorme, Inc., in Yarmouth, ME. The globe weighs approximately 5,600 pounds (2,500 kg) and has a diameter of approximately 41.5 ft. (12.65 m). It has a scale of 1:1,000,000, where 1 in. = 16 miles (26 km) and 1 mm = 10 km. It is mounted at a 23.5° angle, causing the Equator to be diagonal to the floor. It uses a cantilever mount with two motors, and simulates one day's revolution and rotation every minute (*Eartha* Globe at DeLorme, Yarmouth, ME. Reprinted with permission).

projections that you create for GIS projects will be based on the geographic grid.

The Globe

No map can rival a globe in truly representing the surface of the entire Earth (Figure 2-6a). An accurate 3-dimensional globe depicts true shapes, directions, distances, and areas. The largest freely rotating globe in the world is inside the headquarters of DeLorme, Inc. located in Yarmouth, ME. It is 41.5 ft. (12.65 m) in diameter (Figure 2-6b) (DeLorme, 2011).

A **graticule** is usually superimposed on the globe and consists of the spherical coordinate system based on lines of latitude (parallels) and longitude (meridians). On a globe, lines of latitude are parallel and spaced equally on lines of longitude (meridians) (Figure 2-4a; 2-6a) A simulated *Google Earth* globe is shown in Figure 2-7b. The Equator, each meridian, and every other full circumference of the Earth form a great circle. A **great circle** is a circle formed on the surface of a sphere by a plane that passes through the center of the sphere. You can draw or measure along an infinite number of great circles using a globe. The arc of a great circle can be used to measure the shortest distance between any two points on the surface of the Earth (USGS, 2011). The Equator is the only parallel that is a great circle.

The lines of longitude converge to a point at the north and south poles and diverge uniformly as they approach the Equator (Figures 2-4b; 2-7b). The scale on a globe does not vary from region to region; a globe has only one scale. For example, a single 12-in. diameter globe has a scale of approximately 1:42,000,000 (1 in. = 660 statute miles). The geographic area on the surface of the Earth (or on a globe) bounded by any two lines of latitude and any two lines of longitude is the same anywhere between the same two lines of latitude. For example, the geographic area of the region between 30° and 40° N latitude and 60° and 70° E longitude has exactly the same area as the region bounded by 30° and 40° N latitude and 90° and 100° E longitude.

Unfortunately, physical globes (as opposed to virtual computer-generated globes) are not very useful for

Earth as Seen from Space

a. Photograph of the Earth taken by the crew of NASA Apollo 17.

Simulated Earth with Graticule

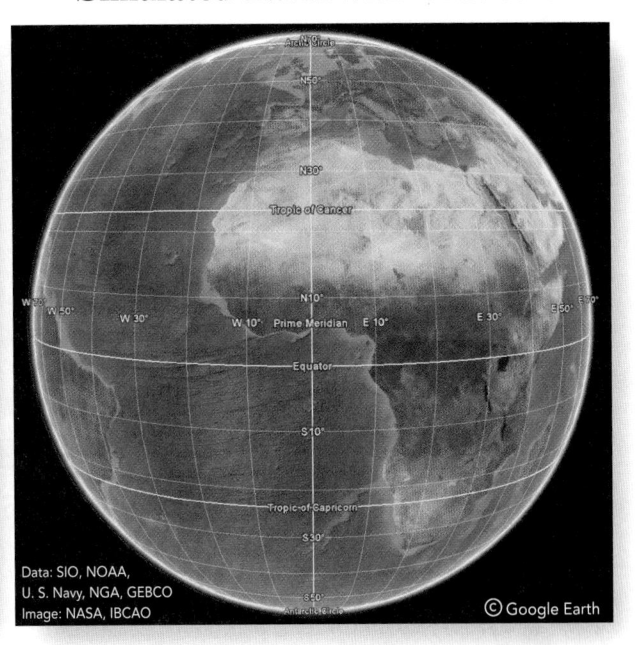

b. A graticule superimposed on a simulated globe.

FIGURE 2–7 a) The Earth is a 3-dimensional oblate ellipsoid (spheroid). The Apollo 17 crew took this photograph through a specially-prepared window of the Apollo 17 spacecraft while on their way to the moon (courtesy of National Aeronautics & Space Administration). b) The 3-dimensional Earth can be simulated and overlaid with a graticule consisting of latitude and longitude. The Equator, Prime Meridian, Tropic of Cancer, and Tropic of Capricorn are superimposed on this simulated globe (data provided by: SIO, NOAA, U.S. Navy, NGA, GEBCO; images provided by NASA, IBCAO; Copyright Google Earth).

most GIS-related projects because they have disadvantages, including:

- even large globes (e.g., 41.5 ft. in diameter) have very small scales (e.g., 1:1,000,000) and provide relatively little detail about the surface of the Earth,
- globes are very expensive to create, update, transport, and store, and
- a person can only look at approximately one-half of the globe at one time.

This is the reason that most GIS analyses use projected geospatial information.

Map Projections

A **map projection** is a systematic transformation of the 3-dimensional Earth into a 2-dimensional flat map (Iliffe, 2008; Garnett, 2009). There are many kinds of projections, but all involve transfer of the distinctive global patterns of parallels of latitude and meridians of longitude onto a developable surface (e.g., a plane, cylinder, or cone) (Bugayevskiy and Snyder, 1995) (Figure 2-8). Unfortunately, this transformation cannot be accomplished without some distortion, resulting in every map projection having unique advantages and disadvantages (Grafarend and Krumm, 2006; Kanters, 2007; Krygier, 2011) (Table 2-2). Consequently, there is no universal "best" map projection for each mapping project (USGS, 2011). Instead, the GIS professional must select the map projection best suited to his or her needs, which minimizes the distortion of the most important features to be portrayed on the map.

Cartographers and mathematicians have devised a great variety of map projections to project (flatten) the 3-dimensional characteristics of the globe onto a 2-dimensional flat map (Robinson and Snyder, 1991; Maher, 2010). Many of the most useful map projections are summarized in John Snyder's USGS Professional Paper *Map Projection: A Working Manual* (1987) and in *Flattening the Earth* (1995). The following material summarizes some of the key properties, characteristics, and preferred uses of several of the most important map projections frequently used by GIS professionals today.

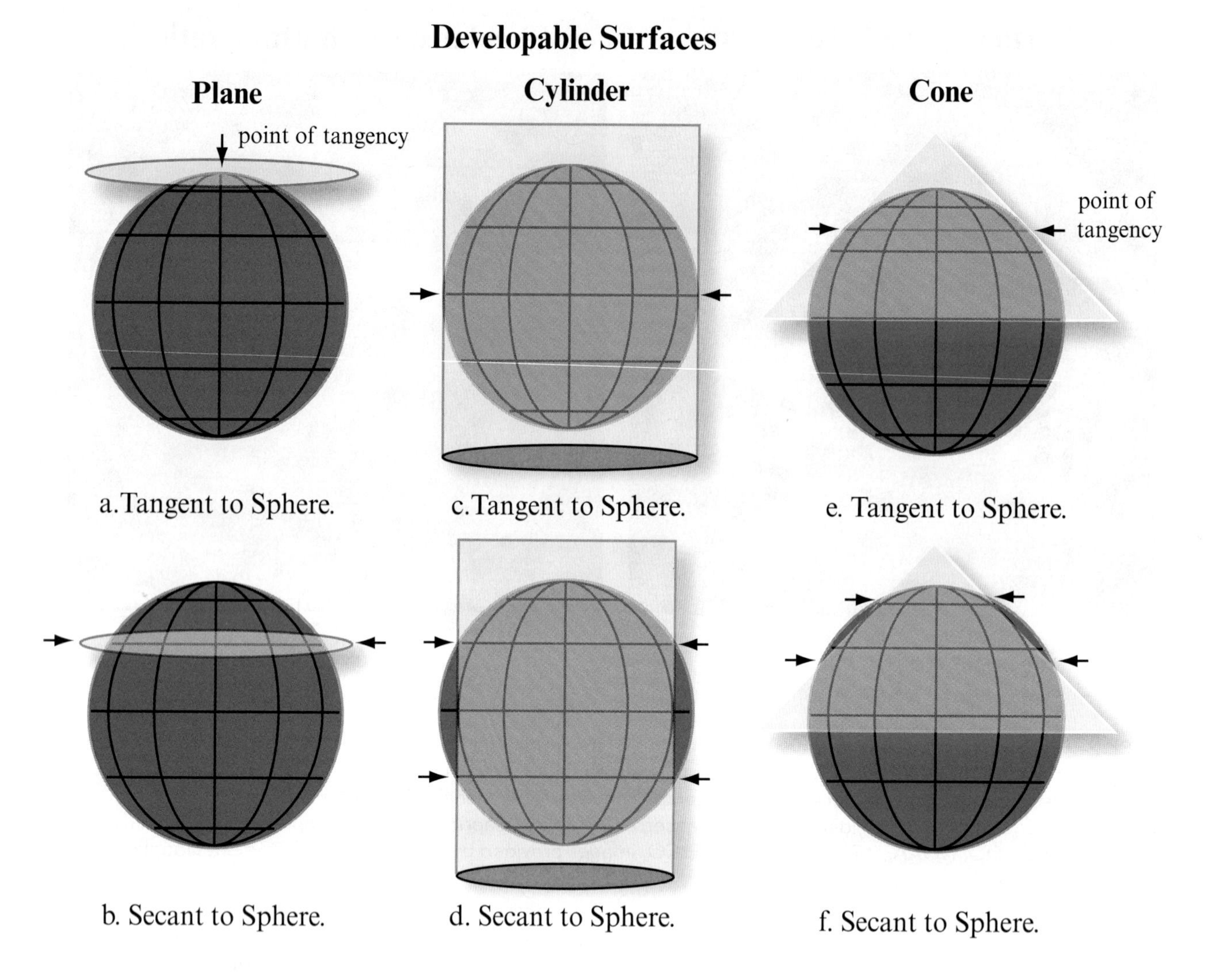

FIGURE 2–8 Three types of developable surfaces are often used to create map projections: plane, cylinder, and cone. a,b) A planar developable surface may just touch (i.e., be tangent with) or intersect (i.e., be secant with it) a sphere. c,d) A cylindrical developable surface may be tangent or secant to a sphere. e,f) A cone developable surface may be tangent or secant to a sphere (adapted from Slocum et al., 2005, and Krygier, 2011).

It is important to remember that every 2-dimensional flat map misrepresents (distorts) the surface of the 3-dimensional Earth in some way. A projected flat map or parts of a map can have some, but never all, of the following characteristics (Table 2-2):

- true directions,
- true distances (i.e., equidistant),
- true areas, and/or
- true shapes (i.e., conformality).

A map projection is said to be **conformal** when at any point on the map the scale is the same in every direction (USGS, 2011). Therefore, meridians and parallels in conformal map projections intersect at right angles and the shapes of very small areas and angles with very short sides are preserved. The size of most areas, however, is distorted.

A map projection is **equal-area** (also referred to as equivalent) if every part on the map, as well as the whole, has the same area as the corresponding part on the Earth, at the same reduced scale. No flat map can be both equal-area and conformal at the same time (USGS, 2011).

Equidistant maps show true distances only from the center of the projection or along a special set of lines (USGS, 2011). They correctly represent azimuths about the point of tangency (i.e., where a map touches the globe) but do not correctly represent areas. For example, an Azimuthal Equidistant map centered on Washington, DC, shows the correct distance between Washington, DC, and any other point in the projec-

TABLE 2–2 Summary of selected map projection properties associated with cylindrical, azimuthal, and conic developable surfaces. P = partly (data from USGS, 2011).

Developable Surface Type	Projection	Conformal	Equal-area	Equi-distant	True Direction	Perspective	Straight Rhumb Lines
Sphere	Globe						
Cylindrical	Mercator				P		
	Transverse Mercator						
	Space Oblique Mercator						
Azimuthal	Gnomonic				P		
	Stereographic				P		
	Orthographic				P		
	Azimuthal Equidistant			P	P		
	Lambert Azimuthal Equal-area				P		
Conic	Albers Equal-area						
	Lambert Conformal				P		
	Equidistant			P			
	Polyconic			P			

tion, i.e., it shows the correct distance between Washington, DC, and Philadelphia, PA, and between Washington, DC, and Richmond, VA. But it does not show the correct distance between Philadelphia, PA, and Richmond, VA, because the projection is not centered on Philadelphia, PA. No flat map can be both equidistant and equal-area at the same time.

Azimuthal map projections correctly represent selected angular relationships. **Azimuthal** projections are projections to a plane placed *tangent* to (just touching) the globe at a point. As with distances, not all angular relationships can be represented correctly on a single map, but it is possible to correctly represent all angular relationships about a single point.

A basic knowledge of the properties of commonly used map projections helps when selecting a map projection that comes closest to fulfilling a specific need.

Developable Surfaces Used in Map Projections

Cartographers have developed methods to project the information found on the surface of a globe onto simple geometric forms, called developable surfaces, including (Figure 2-8):

- planes,
- cylinders, and
- cones.

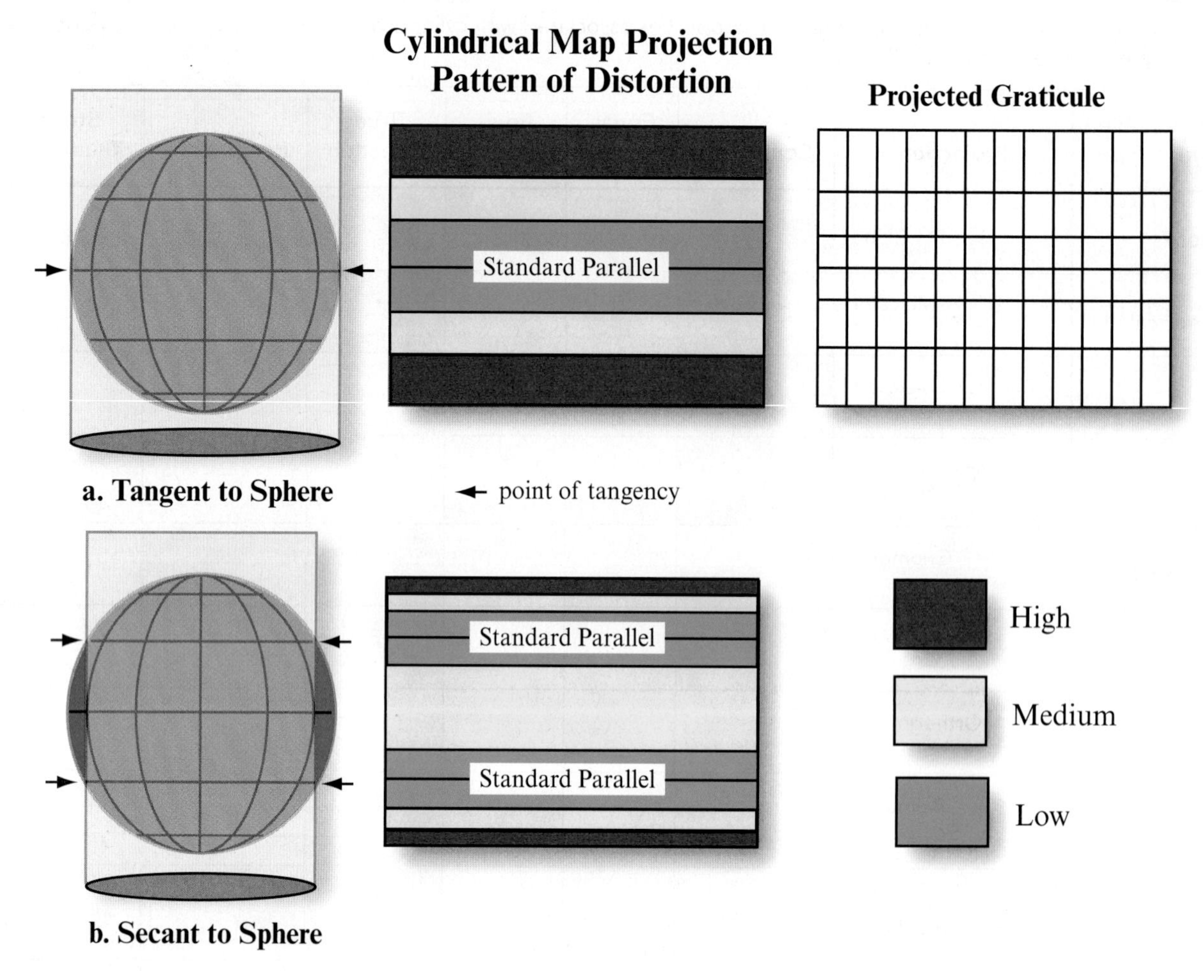

FIGURE 2–9 The pattern of distortion associated with cylindrical map projections. a) The pattern of distortion when the cylinder just touches the sphere, i.e., it is tangent. b) The pattern of distortion when the cylinder intersects the sphere, i.e., it is secant. The greater the distance from a standard parallel (i.e., where the cylinder touches or intersects the sphere), the greater the distortion (adapted from Slocum et al., 2005, and Krygier, 2011).

A **developable surface** is a simple geometric form capable of being flattened without compressing or stretching (Slocum et al., 2005). A plane is already flat, whereas a cylinder or cone may be cut and laid out flat, without stretching or compressing the content. Map projections are typically classified into three general families: cylindrical, conical, and azimuthal (planar).

One of the most important characteristics of map projections is where the developable surface just touches or intersects the sphere. For example, if the sphere (globe) just touches the developable surface at a single point, it is said to be *tangent* to the surface (Figure 2-8a,c,e). If the sphere intersects the developable surface it is said to be *secant* to the surface (Figure 2-8b,d,f). The place(s) where the sphere intersects the developable surface (i.e., it is either tangent or secant to the surface) is the most accurate area of a map projection.

It is not possible to describe or show examples of all the map projections available (Esri, 2004; Leica Geosystems, 2008; Furuti, 2011). Rather, the following sections briefly identify representative map projections that are widely used by GIS professionals and cartographers. Tissot's Indicatrix is then introduced, which can be used to model or understand the geometric distortion in map projections.

Cylindrical Map Projections

Standard cylindrical map projections are mathematically projected onto a cylinder that a) just touches the sphere (i.e., it is tangent to the sphere), or b) is made to intersect the sphere (i.e., it is secant to the sphere) (Figure 2-9).

Mercator

The Mercator map projection was developed by Flemish cartographer Gerardus Mercator (1512–1594) in 1569 for navigation purposes (Figure 2-10a). Meridians and parallels are straight lines and cross one another at 90°. Angular relationships are maintained in this map projection. However, to preserve conformali-

Cylindrical Map Projections

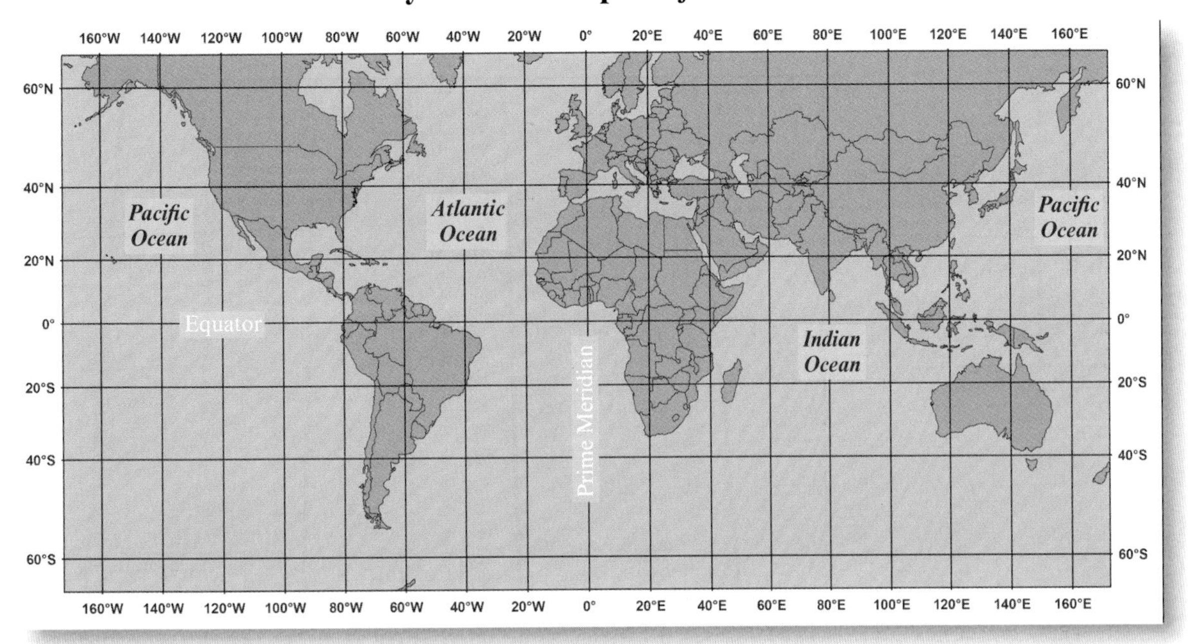

a. Mercator conformal map projection.

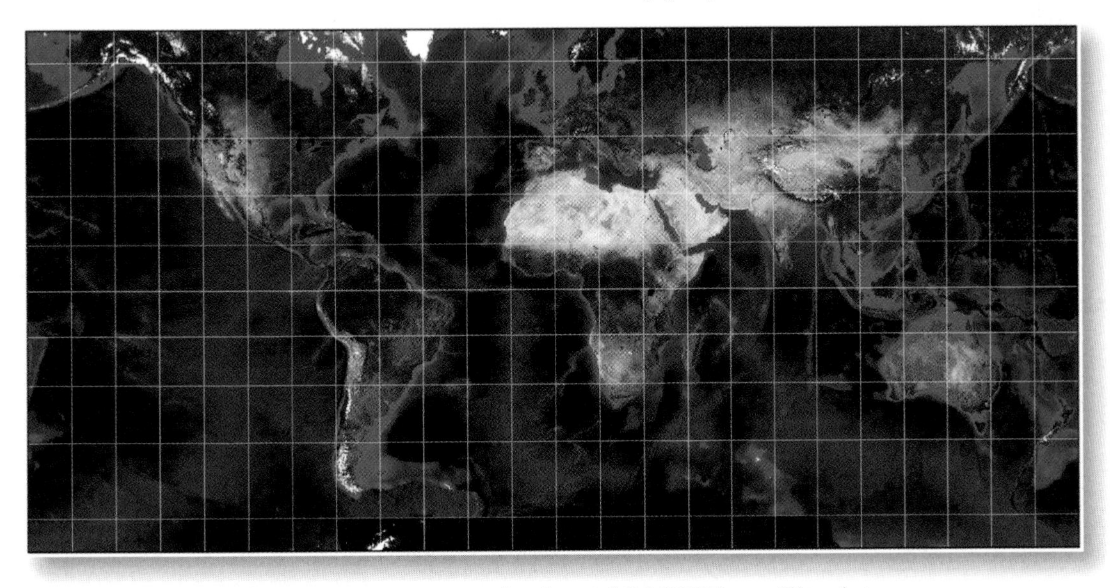

b. Mercator map projection of MODIS satellite data.

FIGURE 2–10 a) The Mercator conformal map projection is based on a cylindrical developable surface. The Equator is the standard parallel. Note the extreme distortion of land masses at higher latitudes. The projection was created using Esri ArcMap™ (data courtesy of ArcWorld Supplement and Esri, Inc.). b) Mercator map projection of NASA Moderate Resolution Imaging Spectrometer (MODIS) satellite data (MODIS imagery courtesy of NASA). The projection was created using NASA's *G.Projecter* software (NASA, 2011).

ty, parallels of latitude are placed increasingly farther apart with increasing distance from the Equator (Figure 2-10a). Any straight line on a Mercator map projection is a **rhumb line** (a line of constant angular direction), which is not necessarily the shortest distance between points. Distances are true only along the Equator (i.e., the standard parallel), but are reasonably correct within 12° to 15° north or south of the Equator (Figure 2-9a). If the developable surface is secant to the sphere, two standard parallels will have the correct scale instead of the Equator (Figure 2-9b) (Slocum et al., 2005; Krygier, 2011).

Areas and shapes of large areas like continents are usually distorted in Mercator map projections. The distortion increases away from the Equator and there is

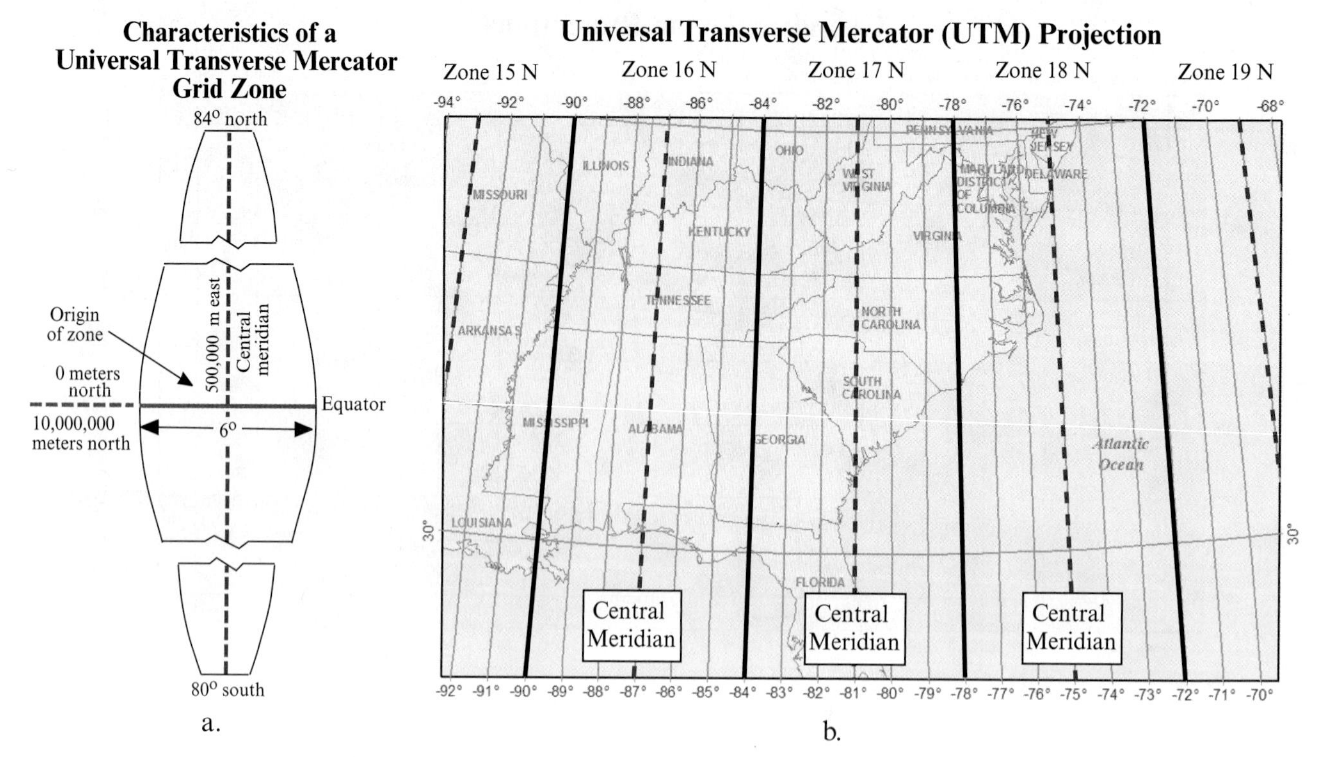

FIGURE 2–11 a) Characteristics of a Universal Transverse Mercator (UTM) Grid Zone. There are 60 zones, each 6° in size encompassing the Earth. b) UTM grid Zone 17 N with a Central Meridian at 81° W longitude is useful for GIS mapping projects in South Carolina. UTM Zone 16 N centered on 87° W longitude is useful for GIS mapping projects in Alabama (data courtesy of ArcWorld Supplement and Esri, Inc.).

extreme distortion in the polar regions. The poles are typically not shown in a Mercator map projection because of the extreme distortion in these areas. A Mercator map projection of MODIS satellite image data is shown in Figure 2-10b.

The Mercator map projection is excellent for mapping equatorial regions. Otherwise, the Mercator projection should be considered to be a special-purpose map projection best suited for navigation. Secant Mercator map projections are used for large-scale coastal charts. In fact, the use of the Mercator map projection for nautical charting is universal. Examples are the charts published by the National Ocean Survey, U.S. Dept. of Commerce (Leica Geosystems, 2008).

Mercator map projections are conformal in that angles and shapes within any small area (such as that found in a typical USGS 7.5-minute topographic map) are essentially true (USGS, 2011). The patterns of distortion associated with cylindrical map projections that just touch (tangent) or intersect (secant) the globe are shown in Figure 2-9 (Slocum et al., 2005; Krygier, 2011).

Universal Transverse Mercator

One of the most widely used map projections for rectifying remotely sensed data and for large-scale topographic mapping applications is the Transverse Mercator projection. It is made from a normal Mercator projection by rotating the cylinder (the developable surface) 90° so that it lies tangent along a *meridian* (line of longitude) instead of line of latitude.

The Universal Transverse Mercator (UTM) coordinate system is based on a cartesian coordinate system. It is composed of 60 zones, each 6° of longitude wide, with a Central Meridian placed every sixth meridian beginning with 177° west longitude. Zone 1 is located from 180° to 174° west longitude. Zone 2 extends from 174° west to 168° west longitude and so forth. Each UTM zone has both a north and a south zone (Figure 2-11a). The north zone extends from the Equator to 84° N latitude. The southern zone extends from 80° S latitude to the Equator. The UTM map projection is not used to map the poles.

The intersection of the Central Meridian of a UTM zone and the Equator is the origin of the zone (Figure 2-11a). It has a central scale factor of 0.9996. The Central Meridians, the Equator, and each line 90° from the Central Meridian are straight lines (Figure 2-11a). The Central Meridian normally has a constant scale. Any lines parallel to the Central Meridian are lines of constant scale. UTM maps can be edge-matched only if they are in the same zone with one Central Meridian.

Each UTM zone has a Central Meridian that remains perpendicular to the zone's southern boundary throughout the north-south extent of the zone. Each zone also has a false-easting of 500,000 m west of the zone's central meridian. This ensures that all easting and northing values remain positive throughout the zone. Otherwise, you would have negative values west of the Central Meridian.

The UTM projection is often used for mapping large areas that are mainly north-south in extent. For example, the UTM projection is often used by the U.S. Geological Survey in its topographic mapping program at scales from 1:24,000 to 1:250,000. UTM Zone 17 N is useful for mapping South Carolina with a Central Meridian of 81° W (Figure 2-11b). UTM Zone 16 N is useful for mapping Alabama and is centered on 87° W longitude (Figure 2-11b).

Distances are true only along the Central Meridian selected by the mapmaker or along two lines parallel to it, but all distances, directions, shapes, and areas are reasonably accurate within 15° of the Central Meridian. Distortion of distances, directions, and size of areas increases rapidly outside the 15° band. Because the map is conformal, however, shapes and angles within any small area (such as that found on a 1:24,000-scale USGS topographic map) are essentially true.

UTM coordinates are in meters and referenced according to the *x* (easting) and *y* (northing) values. Easting refers to the meters east of the artificial zone boundary. Northing refers to meters north of the artificial zone boundary. In the northern hemisphere, northing refers to meters north of the Equator. For example, suppose that you are given the following UTM coordinate information:

12N 444782 E 4455672 N

This means that the location is in Zone 12 north of the Equator, 444,782 meters east of the UTM origin and 4,455,672 meters north of the Equator. Of course, you can also convert this location to other units. For example, you can divide these values by 1,000 to convert the units to kilometers. In this case, you could determine that the location is 444.782 km east of the UTM origin and 4,455.672 km north of the Equator.

UTM coordinates are easy to use and virtually all GPS devices allow for locations to be mapped in UTM coordinates. In addition, the UTM coordinate system covers most of the world (except for the poles). Also, because the system uses meters as its base unit, it is easy to convert to other units and to calculate useful areal units such as meters^2, hectares, and kilometers^2. Internet mapping applications, such as *Google Earth*, allow for coordinates to be displayed and queried in UTM.

Some disadvantages to the UTM coordinate system must be noted. It is often difficult to use a UTM map projection when the study area crosses multiple UTM zones from east to west. Therefore, if your study area is located across two UTM zones, a UTM map projection may not be the best choice. This makes using UTM very difficult for large, continental-sized areas such as all of the conterminous United States or the entire area of the Amazon Basin.

Space Oblique Mercator

The Space Oblique Mercator (SOM) projection is a modified cylindrical projection with the map surface defined by a satellite orbit. It was developed by USGS scientists in the 1970s to reduce the amount of distortion caused when satellite images of the ellipsoidal Earth were printed on a flat page. It was originally developed to map the imagery obtained by the Landsat Multispectral Scanner (MSS). The projection is used to map the continuous swath of data collected by a satellite remote sensing system during each orbital pass. The scale is true along the ground track (Snyder, 1987; 1995).

The SOM projection is useful mainly for the relatively narrow swath along the groundtrack of the satellite. SOM maps are basically conformal with the extent of the map defined by the orbital characteristics of the remote sensing system. The SOM may be used for any satellite orbiting the Earth in a circular or elliptical orbit and at any inclination.

Mollweide

The Mollweide map projection was created in 1805 by Karl Mollweide. It is a pseudocylindrical map projection in which the Equator is represented as a straight horizontal line perpendicular to a Central Meridian that is one-half its length. All the other meridians are elliptical arcs that are equally spaced. All the other parallels are compressed in length as they progress toward the poles.

It is an equal-area projection designed to inscribe the entire world onto a 2:1 ellipse, that keeps parallels straight (but not standard) while still preserving areas (Figure 2-12). The proportion of the area of the ellipse between any given parallel (e.g., 20° N latitude) and the Equator is the same as the proportion of the area on a globe between that parallel and the Equator. However, this relationship is maintained at the expense of shape distortion, which is significant at the corners of the map projection. Therefore, the Mollweide map projection is equal-area but not conformal. The Mollweide map projection of MODIS satellite image data is

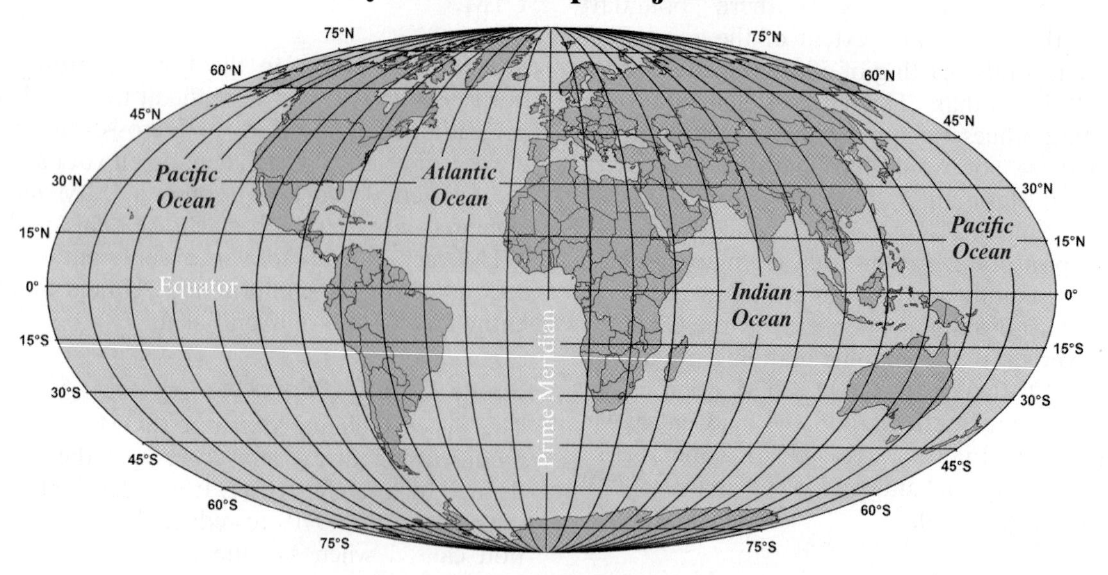

a. Mollweide pseudocylindrical equal-area.

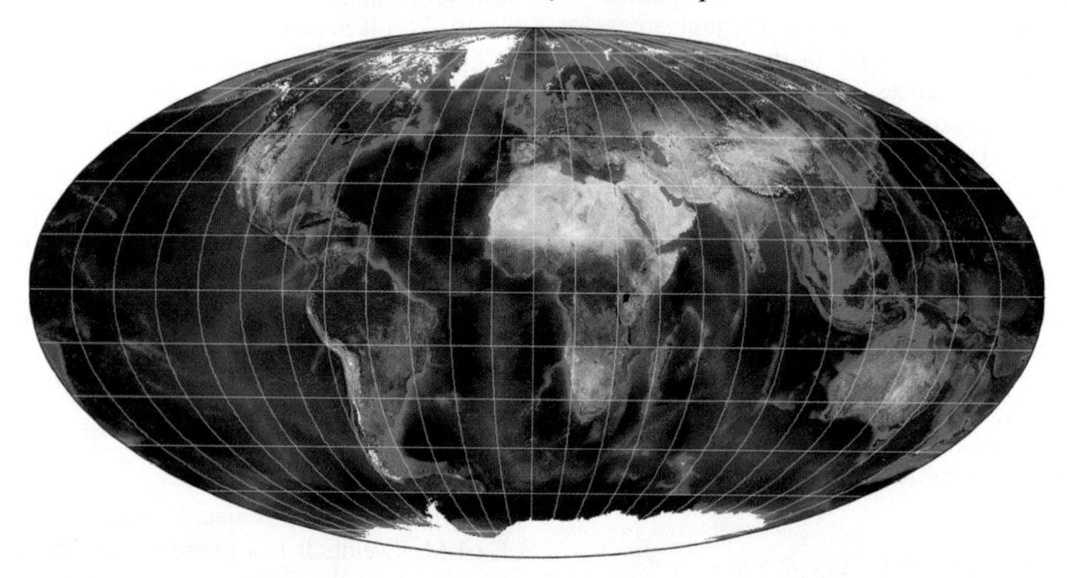

b. Mollweide projection of MODIS satellite data.

FIGURE 2–12 a) The Mollweide Pseudocylindrical Equal-area map projection is based on a cylindrical developable surface. The projection is centered on the Prime Meridian but the user can center the projection on any meridian desired (data courtesy of ArcWorld Supplement and Esri, Inc.). b) Mollweide map projection of MODIS satellite image data (MODIS imagery courtesy of NASA). Projection was created using NASA's G.Projector software (NASA, 2011).

shown in Figure 2-12b. The Mollweide projection is also called homolographic (Greek, *homo* = "same"), or elliptical (Furuti, 2011). The Mollweide projection is generally used to create world maps.

Azimuthal (Planar) Map Projections

Azimuthal map projections are mathematically projected onto a plane *tangent* to (touching) any point on the globe, such as at the North Pole (90° N, 0° W) (Figure 2-13a). They can also be created by intersecting the sphere with a plane, e.g., along 40° N (Figure 2-13b). The patterns of distortion associated with azimuthal map projections that just touch (tangent to) or intersect (secant to) the globe are shown in Figure 2-13ab (Slocum et al., 2005; Krygier, 2011). Azimuthal map projections may be centered on the poles (referred to as Polar-aspect), at a point on the Equator (referred to as Equatorial-aspect), or at any other orientation desired (referred to as Oblique-aspect).

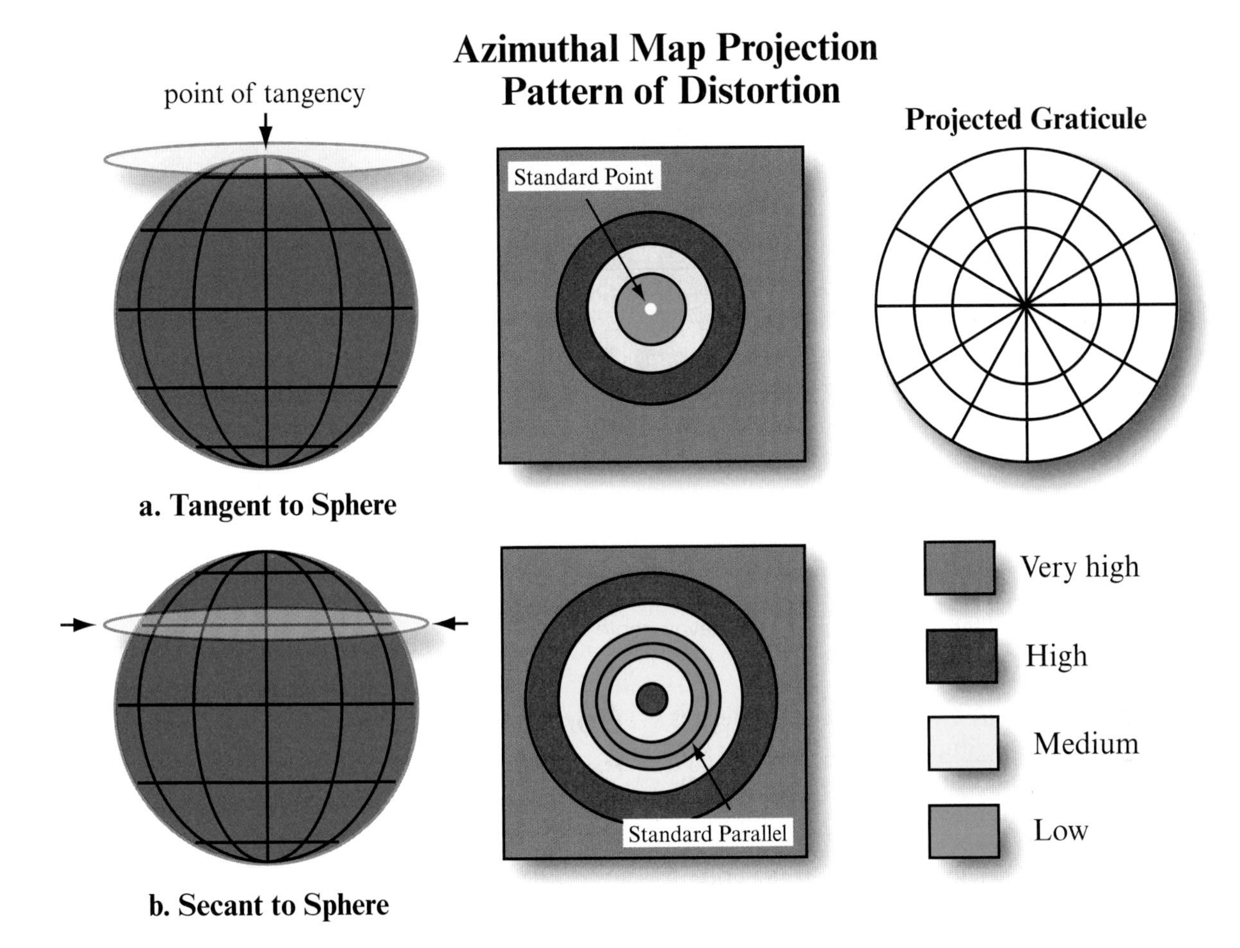

FIGURE 2–13 The pattern of distortion associated with azimuthal map projections. a) The distortion when the plane is tangent to the sphere. b) The distortion when the plane is secant to the sphere. The greater the distance from the point of tangency or the standard parallel, the greater the distortion (adapted from Slocum et al., 2005, and Krygier, 2011).

Perspective Azimuthal Map Projections

Perspective Azimuthal map projections may be constructed geometrically using a light source placed at a certain location within or outside of a transparent globe that contains parallels of latitude and meridians of longitude (Figure 2-14). Rays of light from the light source project shadows of the meridians and parallels onto the planar surface.

The location of the light source can be inside the sphere (referred to as *gnomonic*), on the opposite side of the sphere (the antipode) at the point of tangency (referred to as *stereographic*), or at an infinite distance from the point of tangency, yielding parallel light rays (referred to as *orthographic*) (Figure 2-14). In reality, the graticule (grid) of the globe is projected mathematically onto the plane rather than by using light projected through the sphere.

The Azimuthal Gnomonic projection is believed to be the oldest projection, developed around the sixth century B.C. Its most important property is that the Equator and all meridians are mapped as straight lines, making it possible to find the shortest route between any two points.

Azimuthal Stereographic maps are often used to display the hemisphere that is opposite the light source point. It is not possible to show both hemispheres in their entirety. It is the only azimuthal projection that preserves true angles and local shape. It is often used to map large continent-sized areas of similar extent in all directions (USGS, 2011).

The Azimuthal Orthographic projection is often used to display the Earth, moon, and other planets as if the viewer was infinitely far away in outer space. The display closely resembles a 3-dimensional view of the spheres. It is the most familiar of the azimuthal map projections (Leica Geosystems, 2008).

Lambert Azimuthal Equal-area

The Lambert Azimuthal Equal-area map projection (Figure 2-15) is best suited for regions extending equally in all directions from a standard point of tangency. It is possible to locate the point of tangency at the

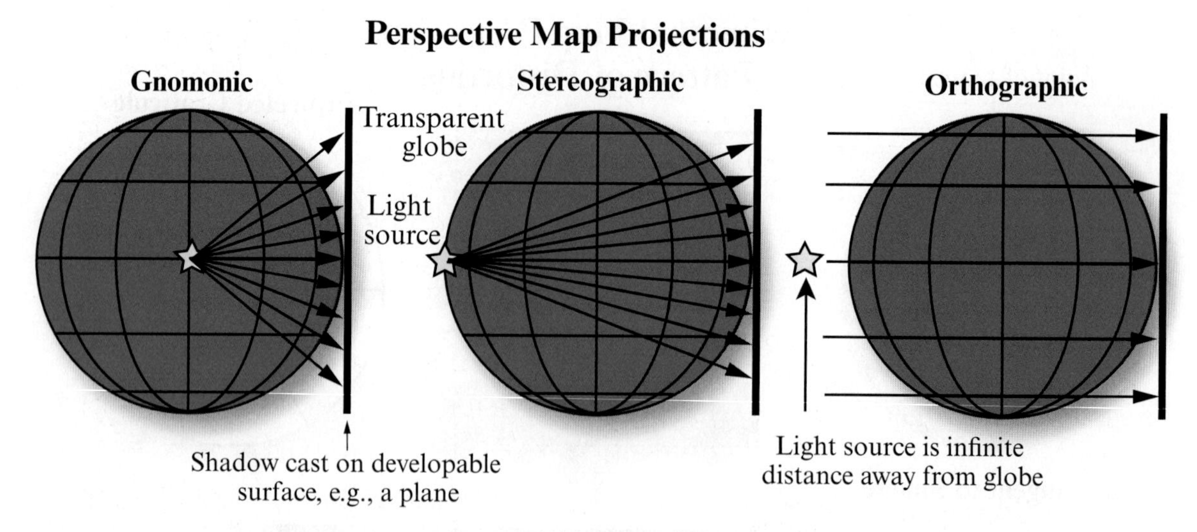

FIGURE 2–14 Perspective map projections: Gnomonic, Stereographic, and Orthographic. Note the location of the light source in relation to the location of the transparent globe and the developable surface, which in this particular example is a plane. Also note the angle of the shadows cast on the developable surface.

poles (Figure 2-15ab) or anywhere else the user desires such as at 40° N, 0° W longitude (Figure 2-15c) or 40° N, 80° W longitude as demonstrated using MODIS imagery of the Earth (Figure 2-15d).

Areas on the map are shown in their true proportion to the same areas on the Earth. Therefore, any two quadrangles that are bounded by two parallels and two meridians at the same latitude are equal in area. Directions are true only from the standard point of tangency. The scale decreases (becomes smaller) gradually away from the standard point of tangency. The distortion of shapes increases away from the standard point of tangency. Any straight line drawn through the standard point is on a great circle. The map is equal-area but not conformal, perspective, or equidistant (USGS, 2011).

Azimuthal Equidistant

In an Azimuthal Equidistant map projection, distances and directions to all places are true only from the standard point of tangency of the projection. Distances are correct between points along straight lines through the standard (center) point. All other distances are inaccurate. Any straight line drawn through the standard (center) point is on a great circle. The distortion of areas and shapes increases away from the standard point (USGS, 2011). Azimuthal Equidistant projections are useful for showing airline distances from the standard point of the projection. A polar aspect (Figure 2-16) is often used for world maps and maps of polar hemispheres. An oblique aspect is used for atlas maps of continents and world maps for aviation use.

Conical Map Projections

Conical map projections are mathematically projected onto a cone-developable surface. The cone can be tangent or secant to the sphere. If it is tangent, there is one standard parallel. If it is secant, there are two standard parallels (Figure 2-17). The greater the distance from the point of tangency or intersection of the sphere with the cone, the greater the distortion (Slocum et al., 2005; Krygier, 2011).

Albers Equal-area Conic

The Albers Equal-area Conic map projection is used by the U.S. Geological Survey for maps showing the conterminous United States (i.e., the 48 mainland states) or for mapping large areas of the United States (Figure 2-18a). The map projection is secant at two standard parallels. The projection is ideal when mapping large areas that are mainly east-west in geographic extent and when it is important to maintain equal-area relationships. The projection is not conformal, perspective, or equidistant. Directional measurement is reasonably accurate within limited geographic regions. Distance measurements are accurate along both of the standard parallels. The scale is true only along the two standard parallels. Maps created using the Albers Equal-area Conic projection can be edge-matched only if they have the same standard parallels and the same scale (USGS, 2011).

Lambert Conformal Conic

The Lambert Conformal Conic map projection (Figure 2-18b) is one of the most widely used map projections. It is secant at two standard parallels. It looks like the Albers Equal-area Conic (Figure 2-18a), but the

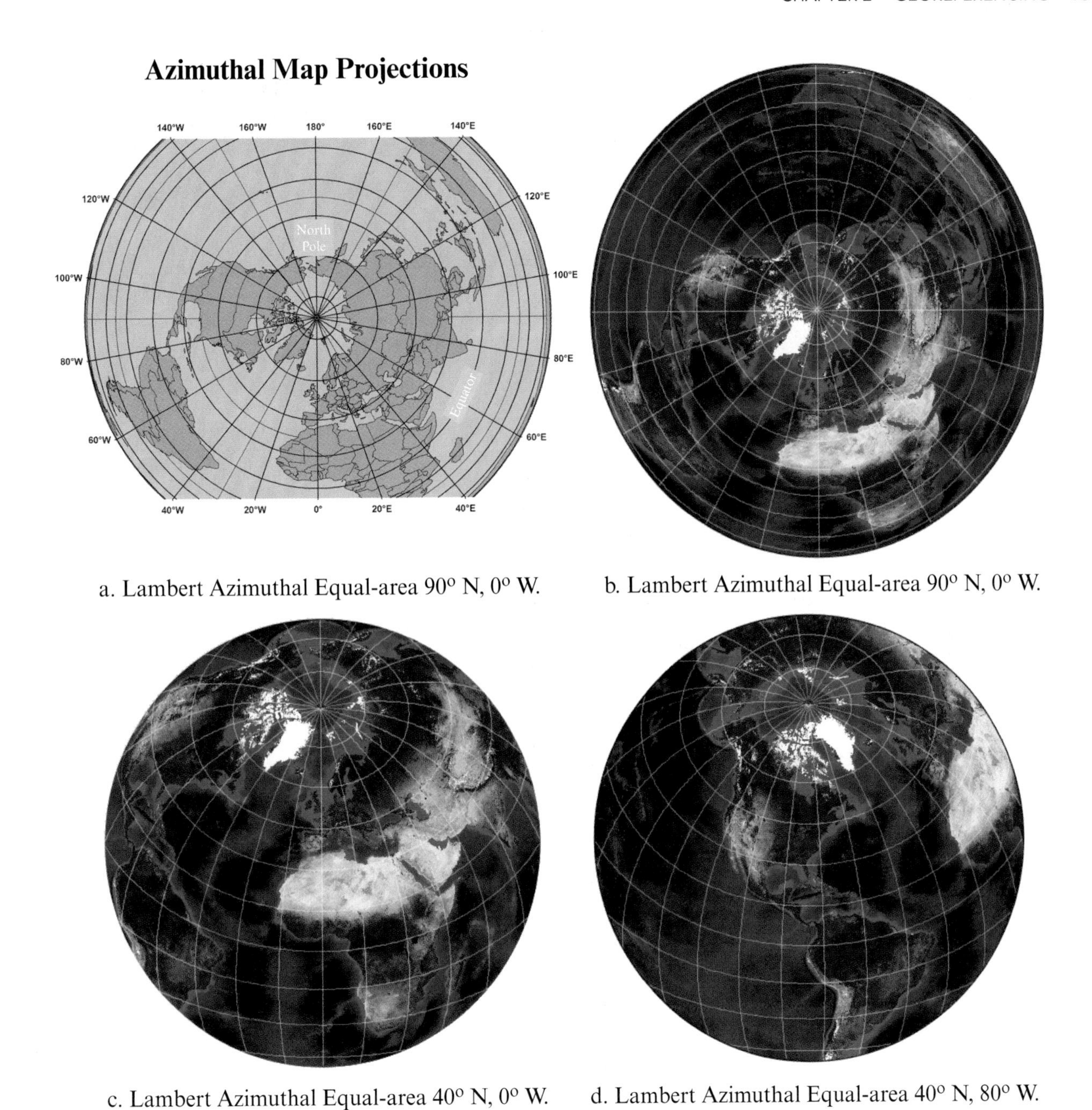

FIGURE 2–15 Lambert Azimuthal Equal-area map projections. a) Lambert Azimuthal Equal-area map projection with the standard point of tangency at 90° N, 0° W (data courtesy of ArcWorld Supplement and Esri, Inc.) b) Lambert Azimuthal Equal-area map projection of MODIS data. The point of tangency is 90° N, 0° W. c) The point of tangency is 40° N, 0° W. d) Point of tangency is 40° N, 80° W (MODIS imagery courtesy of NASA; projection created using G.Projector software).

graticule spacing is different. It is used by the USGS for many 7.5- and 15-minute topographic maps and for the State Base Map series. It is also used to map countries or regions that are mainly east-west in extent (USGS, 2011).

The Lambert Conformal Conic projection is not perspective, equal-area, or equidistant. Distance measurement is true only along the two standard parallels and reasonably accurate elsewhere in limited regions. Directional measurements are reasonably accurate, especially near the standard parallels. The distortion of shapes and areas is minimized along the two standard parallels selected by the mapmaker, but increases the greater the distance away from the standard parallels. The shapes of areas on large-scale maps of relatively small geographic areas are essentially true.

The two standard parallels are 33° N and 45° N for the USGS Base Map series for the 48 conterminous States. The standard parallels are varied for the very impor-

Equidistant Map Projection

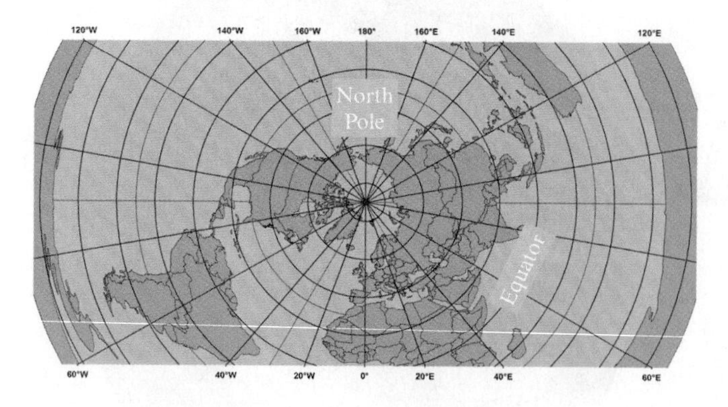

a. Azimuthal Equidistant 90° N, 0° W.

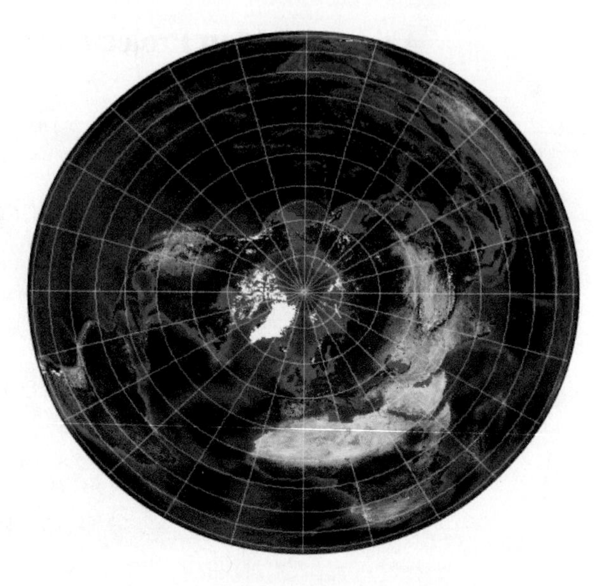

b. Azimuthal Equidistant 90° N, 0° W.

FIGURE 2–16 a) Azimuthal Equidistant map projection with the standard point of tangency at 90° N and 0° W (data courtesy of ArcWorld Supplement and Esri, Inc.) b) Azimuthal Equidistant projection of MODIS imagery with the standard point of tangency at 90° N and 0° W (MODIS imagery courtesy of NASA; projection created using NASA's G.Projector software).

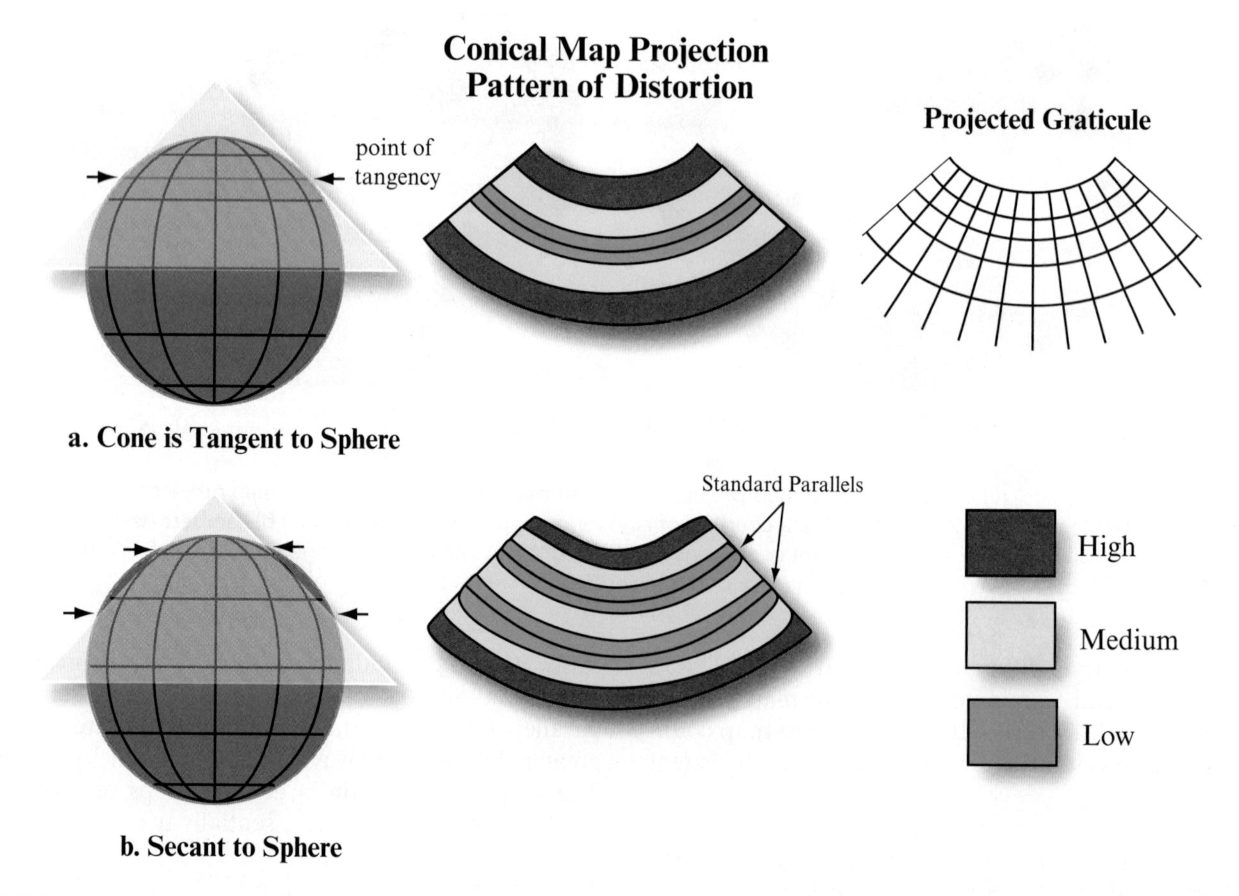

FIGURE 2–17 The pattern of distortion associated with Conical map projections. a) The pattern of distortion when the cone is tangent to the sphere. b) The pattern of distortion when the cone is secant to the sphere. The greater the distance from the standard parallel(s), the greater the distortion (adapted from Slocum et al., 2005, and Krygier, 2011).

Conical Map Projections

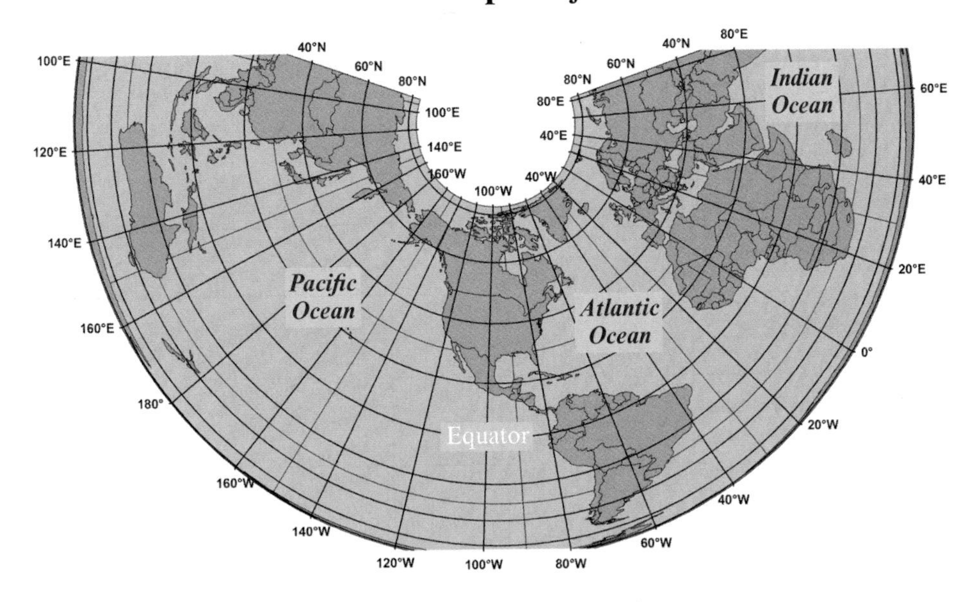

a. Albers Equal-area Conic.

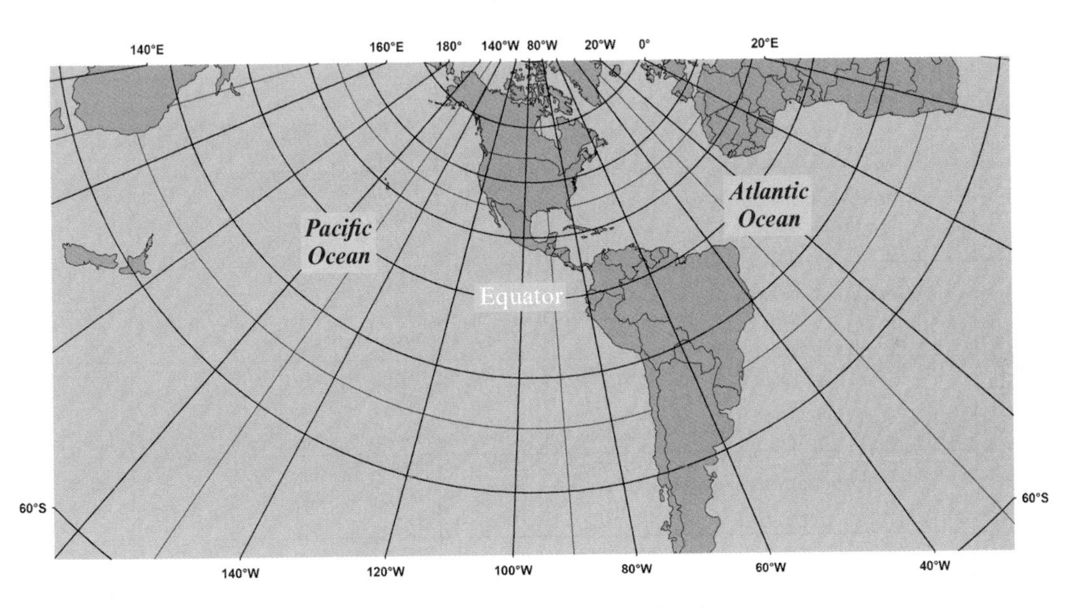

b. Lambert Conformal Conic.

FIGURE 2–18 Selected conical map projections (data courtesy of ArcWorld Supplement and Esri, Inc.). a) Albers Equal-area Conic map projection. b) Lambert Conformal Conic map projection.

tant USGS Topographic Map series (7.5- and 15-minute) (USGS, 2011).

Selected map projections ideally suited to mapping different geographic areas are summarized in Table 2-3. The globe is best at portraying the world. Azimuthal projections are especially useful for mapping entire hemispheres, continents, and regions. The cylindrical Transverse Mercator and several conic map projections are especially useful for medium- and large-scale mapping projects.

Other Projections and Coordinate Systems

Sometimes map projections or coordinate systems are specially prepared for political or other considerations. For example, in the 1930s each of the states agreed to develop their own map projection and coordinate system based on either the Transverse Mercator or the Lambert Conformal Conic map projections. These projections and coordinates systems came to be known as the State Plane Coordinate Systems (SPCS).

TABLE 2–3 Selected map projections associated with cylindrical, azimuthal, and conic developable surfaces that are ideally suited to mapping different geographic areas. P = partly (USGS, 2011).

Developable Surface Type	Projection	World	Hemisphere	Continent/ Ocean	Region/ Sea	Medium Scale	Large Scale
Sphere	Globe						
Cylindrical	Mercator	P					
	Transverse Mercator						
	Space Oblique Mercator						
Azimuthal	Gnomonic				P		
	Stereographic						
	Orthographic		P				
	Azimuthal Equidistant	P					P
	Lambert Azimuthal Equal Area						
Conic	Albers Equal Area						
	Lambert Conformal						
	Equidistant						
	Polyconic					P	P

State Plane Coordinate Systems

Individual state projections were chosen to decrease distortion and minimize error. These projections were chosen based on an individual state's shape and geographic location on the sphere. In addition, some states decided to break up their State Plane Coordinate System into different zones. For example, Utah's State Plane Coordinate System contains three different zones (North, Central, and South) based on the state's geographic shape and location (Figure 2-19). Utah's State Plane Coordinate System uses a Lambert Conformal Conic projection.

Most local government thematic data layers are based on the use of State Plane Coordinate Systems. Most legal descriptions used by governments include details in State Plane Coordinate System coordinates. So, if you plan on working for a local city or government agency, you should be prepared to use the State Plane Coordinate System.

As with UTM, there are disadvantages to working with the State Plane Coordinate System. Similar to UTM, the State Plane Coordinate System used in most states has multiple zones that are difficult to move across if your study area happens to straddle the zones. In addition, State Plane Coordinate Systems end at the state line. Therefore, any projects that wish to examine multiple states will need to select another coordinate system. The original unit of measurement for the State

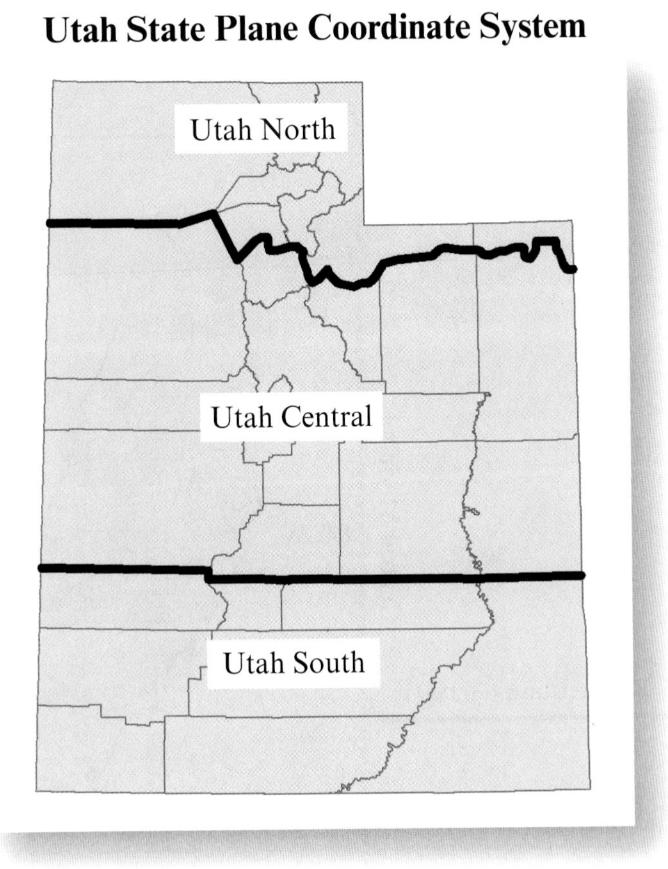

Utah State Plane Coordinate System

Utah North

Utah Central

Utah South

FIGURE 2–19 Each state has its own State Plane Coordinate System. The size and shape of each state determines the number of zones. Utah has three State Plane Coordinate zones (North, Central, and South) (data courtesy of ArcWorld Supplement and Esri, Inc.).

Plane Coordinate System was based on the NAD27 datum in feet. Recently, the U.S. Geological Survey began releasing metric topographic maps. These maps are based on a new State Plane Coordinate System that is based on the NAD83 datum, with meters as the measurement unit.

Custom Map Projections

Sometimes the map projections previously discussed are not adequate for a GIS-related mapping project. When this occurs, the analyst can use or create custom projections or coordinate systems to complete the project. For example, consider the Florida Geographic Data Library (FGDL) map projection (Figure 2-20). Its authors determined that they wanted a single projection and coordinate system for the entire state of Florida because Florida is intersected by UTM zones 16 and 17 and its State Plane Coordinate System has three zones—East, West, and North. They wanted a custom map projection and coordinate system that enabled the entire state to have positive (+) values for both easting and northing (x and y).

The Florida Geographic Data Library map projection is based on the Albers Conic Equal-area map projection using Standard Parallels at 24° N and 31.5° N. The Central Meridian of the projection is 84° W. A false-easting of 400,000 m is used so that all coordinates within the map projection area are positive. Figure 2-20 shows the projection with the two standard parallels (24° N and 31.5° N) and the Central Meridian (84° W). The units are in meters, and the zero values begin at the origin in the southwest part of the projection.

Implementation in a GIS

A robust GIS can effectively transform spatial data into various datums, coordinate systems, and map projections. These are features that make a GIS unique when compared to high-quality graphic arts programs such as Freehand, Adobe Illustrator, Adobe Photoshop, etc.

Therefore, regardless of what map projection or coordinate system your spatial data are in, you should be able to change the format to meet the needs of your particular project. For example, suppose you were

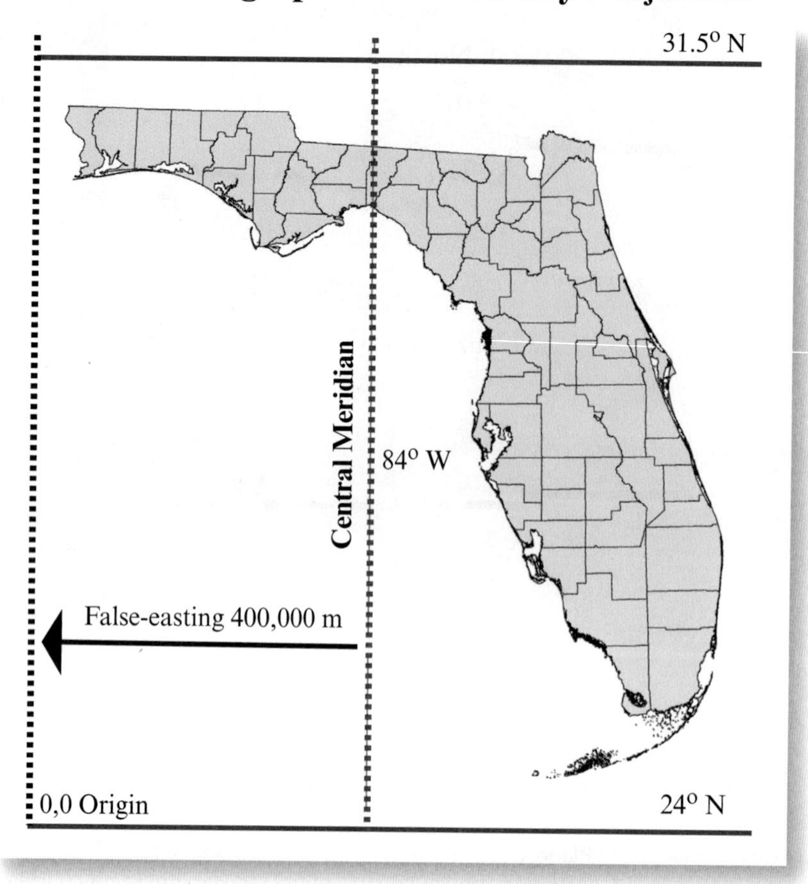

FIGURE 2–20 The characteristics of the custom Florida Geographic Data Library map projection and coordinate system (data courtesy of ArcWorld Supplement and Esri, Inc.). Two standard parallels (24° N and 31.5° N) and one standard meridian (84° W) are used to create the projection. Also note that a false-easting of 400,000 m is used to create an origin of 0,0 off the southwest coast of Florida in the Caribbean. This ensures that all easting and northing coordinate values are positive.

working on a project in Florida and for some reason you needed to convert the custom Florida Geographic Data Library map projection previously discussed into a UTM map projection. A GIS could be used to perform this function using the information about the input Florida Geographic Data Library map projection (Figure 2-21a) and the desired output UTM map projection parameters (Figure 2-21b). The ArcGIS® user interface shown in Figure 2-22 can be used to create an entirely new projected coordinate system if desired.

Tissot's Indicatrix

Nicholas Auguste Tissot, a French mathematician, developed the Indicatrix to measure and graphically illustrate the geometric distortion associated with various map projections. The **Indicatrix** is a geometric deformation indicator that is an infinitely small circle on the surface of the Earth projected as a small ellipse on a map projection plane. This ellipse describes characteristics locally at and near the infinitely small ellipse.

Tissot's Indicatrix is used to graphically illustrate linear, angular and area distortions on maps (Laskowski, 1989). Characteristics of a Tissot Indicatrix are shown in Figure 2-23. ABCD is a circle with unit area defined in a spherical or ellipsoidal model of the Earth, and the dashed A'B'C'D' is the Tissot's Indicatrix that results from its projection onto the map plane. Depending upon the map projection characteristics, segment OA is transformed to OA', and segment OB is transformed to OB'. Linear scale is not conserved along these two directions, since OA' is not equal to OA and OB' is not equal to OB. Angle MOA, in the unit circle, is transformed into angle M'OA' in the distorted ellipse. Because angle MOA>M'OA', angular distortion is present. The area of circle ABCD is, by definition,

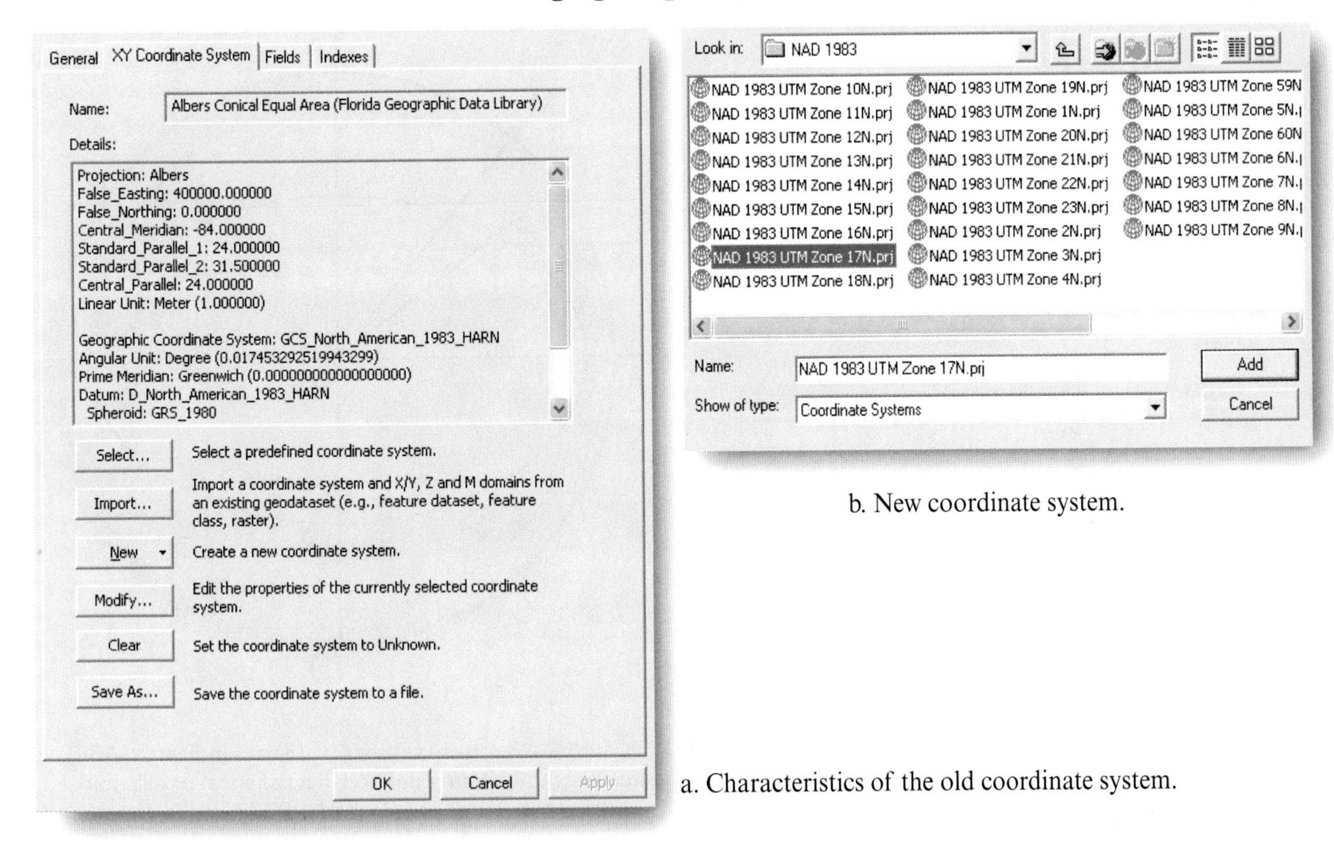

FIGURE 2–21 A robust GIS allows users to transform data between map projections, coordinate systems, and datums. This is an example of a) a spatial dataset in an Albers Conical Equal-area projection (from the Florida Geographic Data Library) that is being converted to b) a North American Datum 1983 UTM map projection for Zone 17N using Esri ArcGIS® software. Note in (a) that the Central Meridian is located at 84° W with a false-easting of 400,000 m and the two Standard Parallels at 24° N and 31.5° N, respectively. The input map projection is based on the 1983 North American Datum and the GRS 1980 spheroid (interfaces courtesy of Esri, Inc.).

equal to 1. Because the area of ellipse A'B' is < 1, area distortion is present.

In conformal map projections, where angles are preserved around every location, the Tissot's Indicatrices are all circles, with varying sizes. In equal-area map projections, where area proportions between objects are conserved, the indicatrices all have unit area, although their shapes and orientations vary with location.

As expected, indicatrices associated with a true sphere are all circular and the same size, as shown in Figure 2-24a, which is associated with an orthographic projection. Note in Figure 2-24 how the circles vary in size for the conformal projections (e.g., Mercator, Mollweide, Lambert Conformal Conic). Equal-area map projections such as the Albers Conic Equal-area projection exhibit ellipses that vary in shape and size, making it clear that angles have been distorted to maintain equal area relationships. One can learn much about various map projections by evaluating their characteristics using Tissot's Indicatrix.

Below are several useful Internet sites that provide additional information about map projections and Tissot's Indicatrix:

- *Flex Projector* (www.flexprojector.com).
- *Furuti Map Projections* (www.progonos.com/furuti).
- *Gallery of Map Projections* (http://www.csiss.org/map-projections/index.html).
- *Mapthematics GeoCart 3* (www.mapthematics.com).
- *Generic Mapping Tools* (http://gmt.soest.hawaii.edu).
- *MicroCAM* (http://www.csiss.org/map-projections/microcam/index.html).

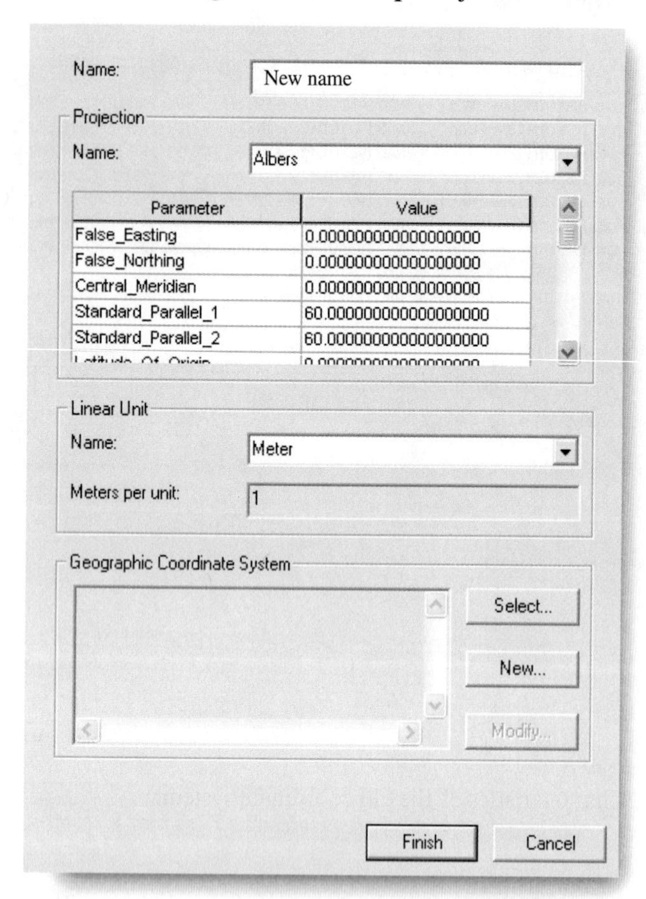

FIGURE 2–22 The ArcGIS® user interface can be used to create a new projected coordinate system (interface courtesy of Esri, Inc.). Note that the user must provide the Central Meridian, parallels, false-easting, and false-northing. You can create a projected coordinate system once and use it with multiple datasets.

- *NASA Global Map Projector* (www.giss.nasa.gov/tools/gprojector).
- USGS Decision Support System for Map Projections of Small Scale Data (http://mcmcweb.er.usgs.gov/DSS/).

Summary

It is wise for GIS users to have an understanding of the basic characteristics of datums, ellipsoids, and coordinate systems including map projections. Each datum, coordinate system, and/or map projection has unique advantages and disadvantages that should be weighed carefully when conducting a GIS project. Sometimes it is necessary to convert or transform the geospatial information from one datum or geographic coordinate system into another. Most high-quality GIS have robust transformation capabilities.

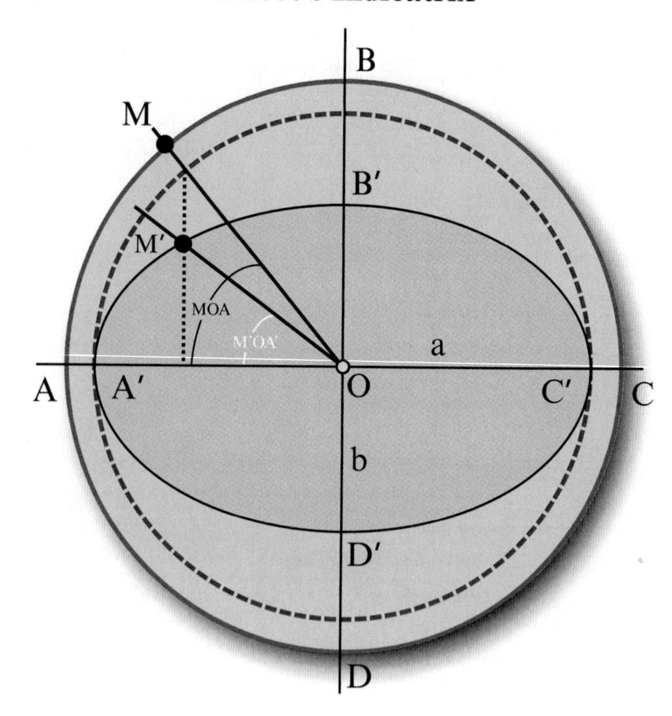

FIGURE 2–23 Characteristics of Tissot's Indicatrix. ABCD is a circle with unit area defined in a spherical or ellipsoidal model of the Earth. The dashed A′B′C′D′ is the Tissot's Indicatrix that results from its projection onto a map plane. In *conformal* map projections, where angles are preserved around every location, the indicatrices are circles of varying sizes. In *equal-area* map projections, where area proportions between objects are conserved, the indicatrices all have the same area, although their shapes and orientations will vary with location in the projection.

Review Questions

1. What are the primary developable surfaces used to create various map projections?

2. Which map projection would you use if you wanted to simulate a view of the Earth from outer space? What are the characteristics of this map projection?

3. What are some inherent advantages and disadvantages of using globes to display important cartographic information?

4. Describe what Tissot's Indicatrix measures and why it is important.

5. What is the difference between an oblate ellipsoid and a true sphere? Why is the difference important?

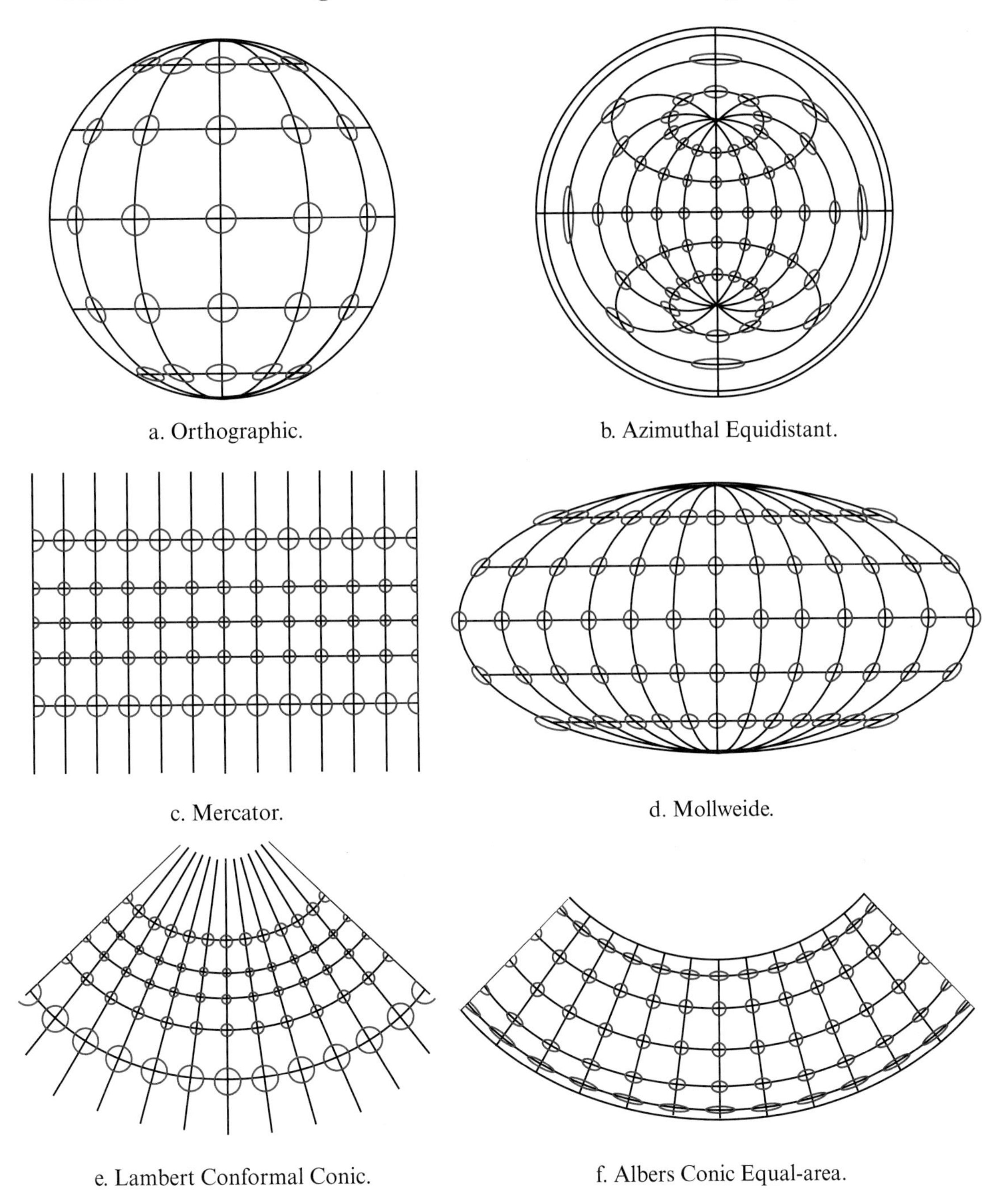

FIGURE 2–24 Tissot's Indicatrix diagrams associated with six selected map projections created using *MicroCAM*, 2011).

6. What is the difference between topographic elevation and bathymetric depth?

7. What coordinate system is heavily used by each of the United States? Why is this coordinate system important to each of the states?

8. You have been asked to conduct a GIS project that maps the land cover of western Europe. Which map projection would you choose for this project and why?

9. Why are many of the ellipses found in the Tissot's Indicatrix diagram of the Albers Conic Equal-area projection in Figure 2-24f so distorted?

10. Describe what it means when a developable surface is tangent or secant to a sphere. Why are standard parallels or standard meridians important in map projections?

Glossary

Azimuthal: Projection to a plane placed *tangent* to (just touching) the globe at a point.

Bathymetry: The study of the underwater depth of lake, sea, or ocean floors.

Conformal: A map projection is conformal when at any point the scale is the same in every direction. Unfortunately, the size of most areas is distorted. No flat map can be both equal-area and conformal at the same time.

Datum: A reference surface against which position measurements are made.

Developable Surface: A developable surface is a simple geometric form capable of being flattened without stretching. Many map projections can be organized according to the developable surface used such as a cylinder, cone, or plane.

Elevation: Refers to a specific type of height, an orthometric height, which is what most people think of as height above mean sea level.

Equal-area (also referred to as Equivalent): A map projection is equal-area if every part on the map, as well as the whole, has the same area as the corresponding part on the Earth, at the same reduced scale. No flat map can be both equal-area and conformal at the same time.

Equidistant: Maps that show true distances only from the center of the projection or along a special set of lines.

Geodesy: The scientific discipline concerned with determining the size and shape of the Earth and the location of points upon its surface.

Geoid: The equipotential surface of the Earth's gravity field that best fits global mean sea level.

Georeferencing: The ability to locate objects and/or areas accurately in geographic space.

Graticule: A graticule is often superimposed on a globe and consists of the spherical coordinate system based on lines of latitude (parallels) and longitude (meridians).

Great Circle: A circle is formed on the surface of a sphere by a plane that passes through the center of the sphere. The Equator, each meridian, and each other full circumference of the Earth forms a great circle. The arc of a great circle shows the shortest distance between points on the surface of the Earth.

Horizontal Datum: A collection of points on the Earth that have been identified according to their precise northerly or southerly location (latitude) and easterly or westerly location (longitude).

Indicatrix: A geometric deformation indicator that is an infinitely small circle on the surface of the Earth projected as a small ellipse on a map projection plane. It is used to measure and graphically illustrate the geometric distortion associated with various map projections.

Map Projection: A systematic transformation of the 3-dimensional Earth (or other body) onto a flat plane surface.

National Spatial Reference System (NSRS): Consists of the horizontal and vertical datums used by the U. S. National Geodetic Survey.

Oblate Ellipsoid or Oblate Spheroid: A sphere where the polar axis is shorter than the equatorial axis.

Rhumb Line: A line on the surface of the Earth crossing all meridians at the same angle. A rhumb line shows true direction.

Vertical Datums: A collection of spatially distributed points on the Earth with known heights either above or below mean sea level.

References

Bugayevskiy, L. M. and J. P. Snyder, 1995, *Map Projections: A Reference Manual*, London: Taylor & Francis, 352 p.

DeLorme, 2011, "DeLorme - Eartha, the World's Largest Revolving and Rotating Globe" (http://www.delorme.com/about/eartha.aspx).

Esri, 2011, *ARCGIS® 9.3: Map Projection Templates*, Redlands: Esri, Inc.

Esri, 2004, *Understanding Map Projections*, Redlands: Esri, Inc., 120 p.

Furuti, C. A., 2011, *Map Projections* (http://www.progonos.com/furuti).

Garnett, W., 2009, *A Little Book on Map Projection*, London: General Books, 62 p.

Grafarend, E. W. and Krumm, F. W., 2006, *Map Projections: Cartographic Information Systems*, London: Springer, Inc., 714 p.

Iliffe, J.C., 2008, *Datums and Map Projections for Remote Sensing, GIS, and Surveying*, 2nd Ed., New York: Whittles Publishing, 208 p.

Kanters, F., 2007, *Small-scale Map Projection Design*, London: Taylor & Francis, 352 p.

Krygier, J. B., 2011, Course on *Cartography and Visualization*, Delaware, OH: Department of Geology & Geography, Ohio Wesleyan University (http://krygier.owu.edu/krygier_html/geog_353/geog_353_lo/geog_353_lo05.html).

Laskowski, P. H., 1989, "The Traditional and Modern Look at Tissot's Indicatrix," Chapter 14 in *Accuracy of Spatial Databases*, M. Goodchild and S. Gopal (Eds.), Bristol, PA: Taylor and Francis, 155-174 p.

Leica Geosystems, 2008, *ERDAS Field Guide*, Volume 1, Atlanta: Leica Geosystems Geospatial Imaging, 444 p.

Lo, C. P. and A. K. W. Yeung, 2007, *Concepts and Techniques in Geographic Information Systems*, Upper Saddle River: Pearson Prentice-Hall, Inc., 532 p.

Maher, M. M., 2010, *Lining Up Data in ArcGIS®: A Guide to Map Projections*, Redlands: Esri Press, 200 p.

Maidment, D. R., Edelman, S., Heiberg, E. R., Jensen, J. R., Maune, D. F., Schuckman, K. and R. Shrestha, 2007, *Elevation Data for Floodplain Mapping*, Washington: National Academy Press, 151 p.

MicroCAM, 2011, *MicroCAM for Windows* (www.csiss.org/map-projections/microcam/index.html.).

NASA, 2007, *GRACE - Gravity Recovery and Climate Experiment*, (http://www.csr.utexas.edu/grace/).

NASA, 2011, *G.Projector*, New York: NASA Goddard Institute for Space Studies. *G.Projector* was written by R. B. Schmunk. Software can be downloaded from www.giss.nasa.gov/tools/gprojector.

NGS, 2007, *What is a Geoid?* (http://www.ngs.noaa.gov/GEOID/geoid_def.html).

NGS, 2011a, *The Horizontal Datum* (http://oceanservice.noaa.gov/education/tutorial_geodesy/geo05_horiz.html).

NGS, 2011b, *The Vertical Datum* (http://oceanservice.noaa.gov/education/tutorial_geodesy/geo06_vert.html).

NGS, 2011c, *What is Geodesy?* (http://www.ngs.noaa.gov/INFO/WhatWeDo.shtml).

Robinson, A. and J. P. Snyder, 1991, *Matching the Map Projection to the Need,* Bethseda: American Congress on Surveying and Mapping, 30 p.

Slocum, T. A., McMaster, R. B., Kessler, F. C. and H. H. Howard, 2005, "Chapter 8: Elements of Map Projections," *Thematic Cartography and Geographic Visualization*, Upper Saddle River: Pearson Prentice-Hall, Inc., 137-159 p.

Snyder, J. P., 1987, *Map Projections: A Working Manual*, U.S. Geological Survey Professional Paper #1395, Washington: U.S. Government Printing Office.

Snyder, J. P., 1995, *Flattening the Earth: Two Thousand Years of Map Projections*, Chicago: University of Chicago Press.

USGS, 2011, *Map Projections*, Washington: U.S. Geological Survey (http://egsc.usgs.gov/isb/pubs/MapProjections/projections.html).

3 DATA FOR GIS

Geographic information systems are used to analyze spatial data. But where do the spatial data come from? Most of the spatial data stored and analyzed in a GIS are collected using two primary data collection methods: in situ (in place) data collection and remote sensing of the environment.

Overview

This chapter reviews the fundamental techniques used to collect geospatial data for input to a GIS using in situ and/or remote sensing data collection methods. In situ spatial data collection methods are discussed first, including:

- the use of the NAVSTAR Global Positioning System (GPS),
- land surveying,
- ground-based sampling or the taking of a census, and
- digitization of historical hard-copy maps and other types of geospatial data.

The chapter then reviews how geospatial information can be obtained by different types of remote sensing instruments placed onboard aircraft and spacecraft. The remote sensing process and resolution considerations are presented. Several types of remote sensing data collection systems are introduced, including:

- aerial photography (vertical and oblique),
- multispectral,
- hyperspectral,
- thermal-infrared,
- LiDAR (light detection and ranging), and
- RADAR (radio detection and ranging).

Additional sources of geospatial information often analyzed using a GIS are found in the Appendix.

In Situ Data Collection

In situ data are collected on the ground by a human being or special data collection instruments. For example, it is common to use thermometers, anemometers, or a rain gauge to collect temperature, wind, and precipitation data, respectively. You might go door-to-door and interview people to obtain social, economic, and demographic (population) data. One of the most important characteristics of these in situ datasets is that you identify where each measurement was collected in geographic space. One of the most important instruments used to locate the data collected in the field is a global positioning system device.

Global Positioning System (GPS)

You have probably heard of the United States' **Global Positioning System (GPS)** (Figure 3-1). In fact, you may own a hand-held GPS unit or you may have one inside your car that is used for navigation purposes. As of 2011, the United States' GPS was the only globally operational, publicly available **Global Navigation Satellite System (GNSS)**. The GPS consists of up to 32 orbital satellites in six different orbital planes. The exact number of satellites varies as older satellites are retired and replaced with new satellites. The GPS became globally available in 1995. The United States' GPS is one of several Global Navigation Satellite Systems to be discussed.

GIS Applications of GPS

Some of the most important applications of GPS data collection technology include:

- determining your exact *x*, *y*, and *z* location anywhere on the surface of the Earth whether you are on land or at sea, as long as the GPS satellites are not obstructed from view.
- identifying your current location using the GPS and and then having the GIS network software identify the optimum route to a desired location.
- the use of GPS onboard an aircraft in support of the collection of digital aerial photography, LiDAR, or other types of remote sensor data. The GPS determines the *x*, *y*, and *z* position of the aircraft at the exact instant that an aerial photograph is taken or a LiDAR pulse of laser energy is emitted or received.
- information from airborne GPS receivers is used on commercial aircraft to constantly transmit the plane's position to air-traffic controllers and to help the pilot land the plane.
- collecting GPS points as you navigate in an area to document the exact location of the route you have taken or to compute the speed that you traveled the route.
- navigating to a previously collected GPS point to locate a favorite fishing spot, a benchmark, a property boundary, or buried treasure.
- determining the location of an important object (e.g., telephone pole, water or power meter) and then inputting attributes about the object such as the height of the pole or the number and type of transformers on the pole.
- the use of GPS-derived location information in precision agriculture to control special tractors and farm implements during land preparation, planting, fertilization, and harvesting.
- **geotagging,** which is the process of adding geographical identification metadata to various media such as terrestrial photographs, videos, etc. The geotagged information usually consists of latitude and longitude coordinates, though they can also include altitude, bearing, distance, accuracy data, and place names (Sorrell, 2008). Additional information on geotagging is provided in Chapter 12.
- **crowd sourcing,** which is the act of outsourcing tasks traditionally performed by an employee or contractor, to an undefined, large group of people or community (i.e., a crowd), through an open call usually via the Internet (Howe, 2006). This is especially useful when the call goes out for information about a particular geographic location (e.g., a landmark or a particular store) and many users respond, often with geotagged information.
- accurate terrestrial land surveying.

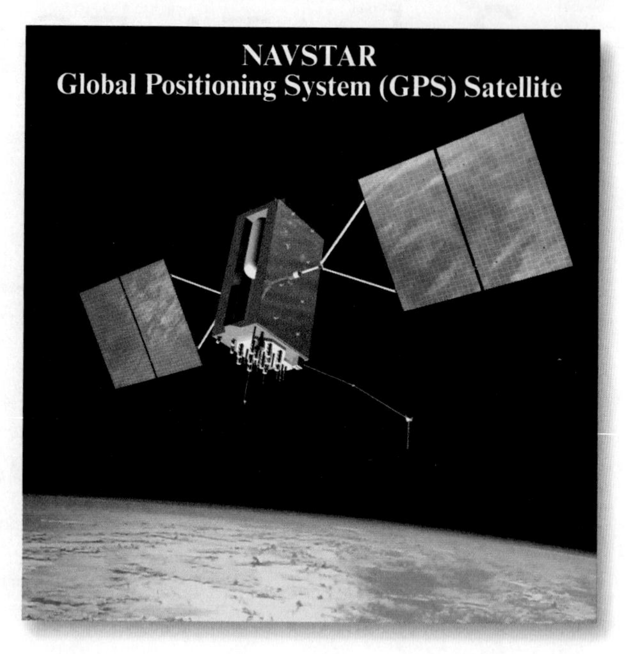

FIGURE 3–1 At least 24 NAVSTAR Global Positioning System (GPS) satellites orbit the Earth at 20,200 km (12,600 mi) each day. This is an artist's rendition of a new GPS III satellite. A GPS receiver on the ground communicates with at least four GPS satellites and computes the distance (range) to each of the satellites. This information is used to accurately identify the ground-based GPS receiver's latitude, longitude, and elevation. The accuracy of the GPS signal in space is the same for both the civilian GPS service (called SPS) and the military GPS service (called PPS). However, the civilian SPS broadcasts on only one frequency, while the military PPS uses two frequencies. This allows the military to perform ionospheric correction, which provides better accuracy than the civilian SPS (courtesy of www.gps.gov).

History of the GPS

It is not surprising that GNSS technology was initially developed by the military (the U.S. Department of Defense). The military always needs to know the exact location of all its personnel and equipment in a theatre of war, even in the dark. Real-time GPS-derived geographic information has also led to precision in the delivery of ordinance to targets, greatly increasing their lethality while hopefully reducing the number of casualties from misguided ordinance. Satellite navigation information allows the military to locate their forces more rapidly and accurately, greatly reducing the "fog of war" and the probability of troops being killed by friendly fire. The Gulf War from 1990 to 1991 was the first war in which GPS technology was widely used.

Inaccurate knowledge of one's geographic location can lead to unfortunate events. For example, Korean Air Lines Flight 007 was tragically shot down by a Soviet jet fighter in 1983, killing 269 people. Supposedly, the commercial airliner had drifted accidently into prohibited Soviet airspace. After this significant event, U.S. President Ronald Reagan issued a directive making the GPS system available free for civilian use once it was completed. The first GPS satellite was launched in 1989. The 24th satellite was launched in 1994.

Accurate positional information derived from the GPS has become a worldwide aid to improved public and personal navigation, accurate land surveying and thematic mapmaking, the creation of entirely new geospatial-related businesses, and an indispensable component for many scientific studies. GPS also provides a precise time reference used in many applications including the scientific study of earthquakes and the synchronization of various telecommunications networks.

GPS System Components

The **NAVigation System Using Timing And Ranging (NAVSTAR) Global Positioning System (GPS)** is a U.S.-owned utility that provides users with position, navigation, and timing (PNT) services (Figure 3-1). It consists of three segments: a space segment, a control segment, and a user segment (GPSgov, 2011).

Space Segment The basic GPS design consists of 24 satellites orbiting the Earth in 6 orbital planes, each 60° apart. A conceptual diagram of the constellation of 24 satellites is shown in Figure 3-2. Four satellites are placed in each orbit so that at any moment there are at least four satellites within the line-of-sight of almost anywhere on the Earth's surface. Typically, about nine satellites are visible from any point on the ground at any moment if they are not obstructed from view by trees, mountains, tall buildings, etc. The greater the number of GPS satellites observed by the ground-based receiver at any time, the higher the probability of obtaining accurate geographic coordinate information.

The GPS satellites orbit at an altitude of approximately 20,200 km (12,600 mi). Each satellite makes two complete orbits per day. In June, 2011, the U.S. Air Force expanded the GPS constellation to include a total of 27 satellites (GPSgov, 2011) (Table 3-1).

Control Segment The U.S. Air Force goes to great expense to launch, maintain, and constantly determine the exact location of the GPS satellites in space. There is a very precise atomic clock onboard each GPS satellite that continually transmits messages containing the current time at the start of the message, parameters to calculate the location of the satellite, and the general

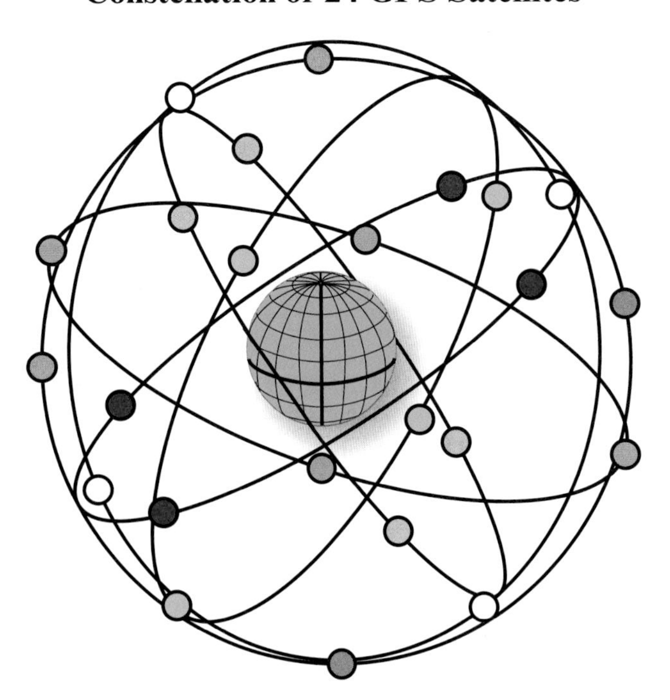

FIGURE 3–2 The basic constellation of 24 GPS satellites orbiting the Earth. There are six orbits each containing four satellites. The satellites are arranged in orbit so that at any moment at least four satellites are within line-of-sight from almost anywhere on the Earth's surface. Ideally, the signals from four or more satellites can be received by the GPS receiver without obstruction by trees, buildings, or mountains.

health of the system. The accuracy of the GPS signal in space is actually the same for both the civilian GPS service (called SPS) and the military GPS service (called PPS). However, the civilian SPS broadcasts on only one frequency, while the military PPS uses two frequencies. This allows the military to perform ionospheric correction, which provides better accuracy than the basic SPS.

The GPS receiver on the ground can be thought of as being located on the outside of a sphere that is centered on the GPS satellite with radius (R_1) equal to the distance measurement. A diagram of this relationship is shown in Figure 3-3a, where the GPS receiver on the ground is at location **A**. If only one GPS satellite is used, the location of **A** can be virtually anywhere on the 3-dimensional sphere as shown. If two GPS satellites are used, then two 3-dimensional spheres will be generated and location **A** can be anywhere within the area of intersection of the two spheres (Figure 3-3b). If three GPS satellites are used, the intersection of the three spheres yields much more accurate location **A** position information (Figure 3-3c). Theoretically, only three time measurements should be required to obtain accurate x,y position information using a ground-

TABLE 3–1 Characteristics of several international Global Navigational Satellite Systems (GNSS).

Global Navigational Satellite System (GNSS)	Country of Origin	Date Initiated	Status	Number of Satellites
Global Positioning System (GPS)	United States	1978	Operational since 1994	31–32
Global'naya Navigatsionnaya Sputnikovaya Sistema (GLONASS)	Russia (formerly the Soviet Union)	1976	Being restored	23 of 24 in 2011
***Galileo* Positioning System**	European Union and European Space Agency	2005	Being deployed	18 of 24 by 2015
Indian Regional Navigational Satellite System (IRNSS)	India	2006	Being deployed	1st satellite to be launched in 2011
Quasi-Zenith Satellite System (QZSS)	Japan	2002	Being deployed	1st satellite launched 2010
COMPASS (also called **BeiDou-2**)	China	2000	Being deployed	35 by 2020

based GPS receiver. Unfortunately, this is not the case because of clock (timing) problems associated with the GPS receiver on the ground.

The atomic clocks on all the GPS satellites are very accurate (to 10^{-9} seconds) and in phase with one another. The clocks on ground-based GPS receivers are relatively inexpensive and inaccurate. The use of an additional (fourth) satellite makes it possible to determine the timing error associated with the ground-based GPS receiver. In other words, the GPS receiver on the ground uses four measurements to solve for 4 variables: x, y, z, and t.

An important characteristic of a ground-based GPS receiver is the number of satellites that it can lock onto at any moment. Current GPS receivers can lock onto 10 to 20 satellites (i.e., channels). A GPS receiver may be tracking more than four satellites at any moment (e.g., eight), but it generally only uses the optimum four visible satellites to compute the x, y, and z measurements. These measurements are then turned into more useful forms of spatial information such as accurate latitude, longitude, and elevation.

User Segment People on the ground use GPS receivers to communicate with the GPS satellites to obtain continuous, accurate, worldwide, all-weather x, y, and z position (latitude, longitude, and elevation) information. GPS receivers are composed of an antenna (carefully tuned to the frequencies transmitted by the GPS satellites), a central processing unit, and a relatively inexpensive clock. They usually have a small color display so that the user can interact with the GPS unit and see location information. Many people input a digital map or a digital remotely sensed image of the study area into the GPS receiver so that the x,y location of the GPS receiver can be seen superimposed on the map or image. GPS receivers come in a variety of configurations. Examples of hand-held GPS receivers and a tractor-mounted GPS receiver used for precision agriculture are shown in Figure 3-4.

The accuracy of the x, y, and z location information obtained by the ground-based GPS receiver is based on several factors. One of the most important factors is the quality of the GPS receiver. Some GPS receivers have more accurate clocks, can track more satellites, can store more location information, and have superior software (firmware). Generally, the greater the capability desired, the more expensive the ground-based GPS receiver.

The mode of operation of the GPS receiver by the user can also significantly affect the accuracy of the measurements. A GPS receiver can be operated by itself or in conjunction with other GPS receivers on the ground. For example, a single *static* (non-moving) GPS receiver can communicate with ≥ 4 GPS satellites to locate its x, y position to within 5 to 10 m. Conversely, surveyors are usually interested in knowing the precise location of specific points on the surface of the Earth as well as the accurate distance between them (e.g., to identify property boundaries). This can be accom-

Locating the Position of an Object on the Ground Using the Global Positioning System (GPS) and Trilateration Principles

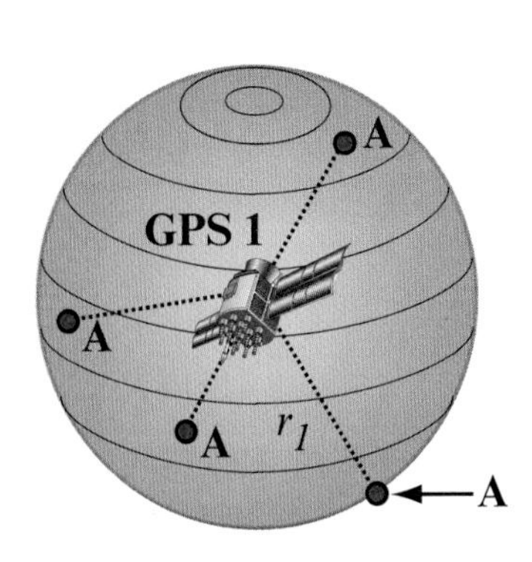

a. Location **A** can be anywhere on the circumference of the sphere if only one GPS satellite is used.

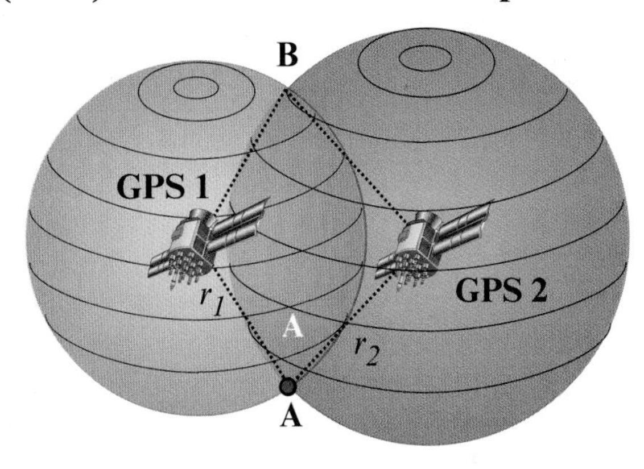

b. Using two GPS satellites narrows down the location of **A** to anywhere the two spheres intersect from **A** to **B**.

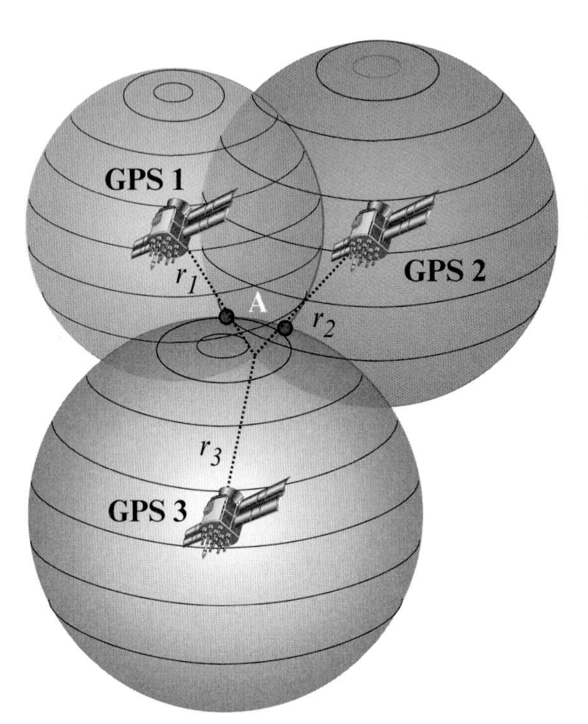

c. Using three GPS satellites narrows down the position of **A** to just two distinct points.

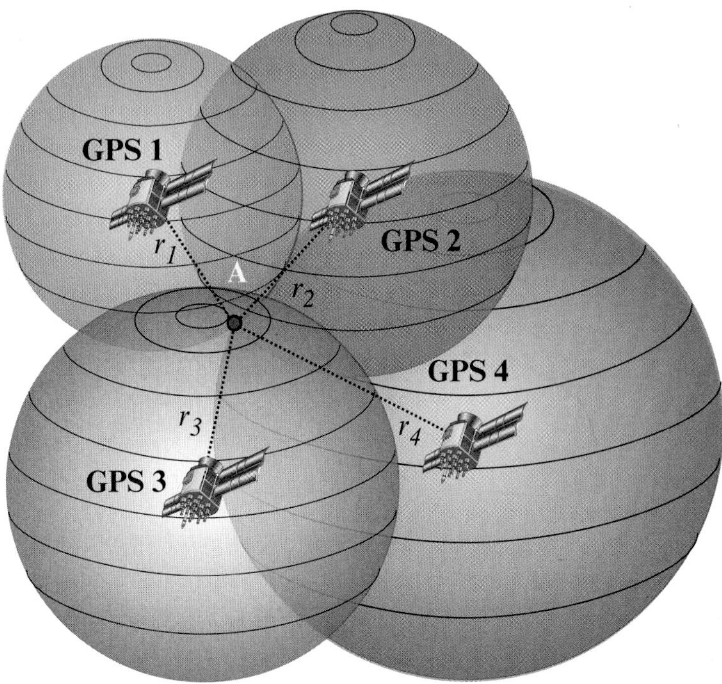

d. Using four GPS satellites provides accurate x,y, and z (elevation) measurements for location **A**.

FIGURE 3–3 Consider a single global positioning system (GPS) satellite as being located at the center of a hypothetical sphere. You want to locate the *x*, *y*, and *z* position of point **A** on the ground. a) If you use just one GPS satellite, you can determine that you are distance r_1 from the satellite. Unfortunately, this is not very precise location information since point **A** could be located anywhere on the perimeter of the 3-dimensional sphere with a radius of r_1. b) Measuring the distance to point **A** from two GPS satellites narrows down your location considerably. However, you could also be anywhere the two spheres intersect from **A** to **B**. c) Calculating the distance to point **A** from three GPS satellites causes three hypothetical spheres to intersect and narrows down the position of **A** to just two distinct points. d) Observing four GPS satellites helps remove the time bias associated with the relatively inexpensive clocks in the ground-based GPS receivers and allows more accurate *x*, *y*, and *z* (elevation) measurements to be obtained for point **A**.

Global Positioning System (GPS) Data Collection

a. Data collection using a hand-held receiver.

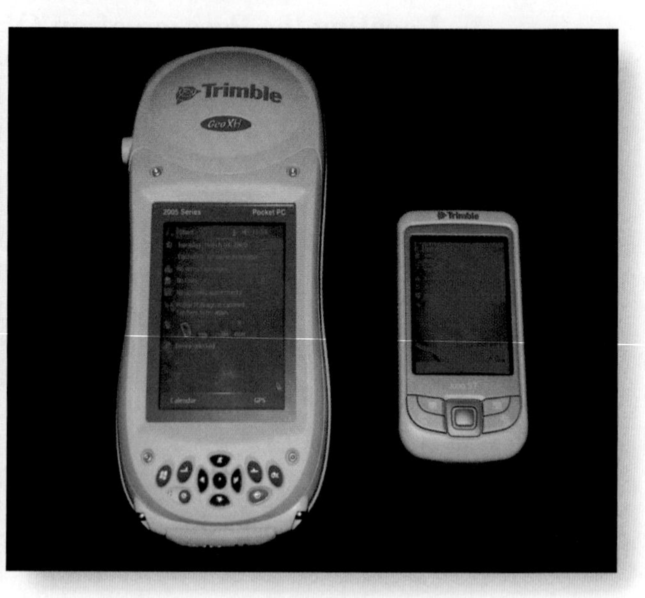

b. Two hand-held GPS receivers.

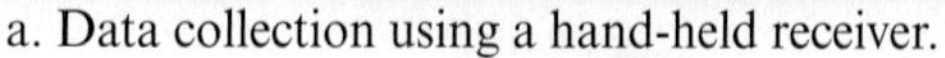

c. A GPS receiver installed on a tractor used for precision agriculture.

FIGURE 3–4 Ground-based GPS receivers come in many shapes and sizes with associated differences in capability and cost. a) A hand-held GPS receiver. b) Two different hand-held GPS receivers. The one on the left is more expensive but has much greater capability. c) A GPS receiver mounted on a tractor used in precision agriculture to prepare, plant, and fertilize crops in southern California.

plished by placing two GPS receivers at two desired locations (e.g., over two property boundary pins) and then accurately computing the GPS-derived distance between the points. This is referred to as *static relative positioning*.

One of the most important ways of achieving greater horizontal and vertical accuracy is to differentially correct the timing signals recorded by the GPS receiver. *Differential GPS* is also based on the use of two GPS receivers (USA, 2008). One GPS receiver is located at a geographic location with known *x*,*y*, and *z*-coordinates (e.g., a U.S. Geological Survey or National Geodetic Survey horizontal/vertical benchmark). This is called the base or reference station GPS receiver. A second mobile GPS receiver is then used to roam around the study area from one important location to another. The two units simultaneously measure the code pseudo-ranges associated with four or more GPS satellites visible to them. The roaming GPS receiver communicates its information to the base station. The base station calculates the timing corrections that need to be applied to the observed code pseudo-ranges and transmits this information back to the roaming GPS receiver. The roaming GPS receiver uses the timing correction information to obtain sub-meter positional

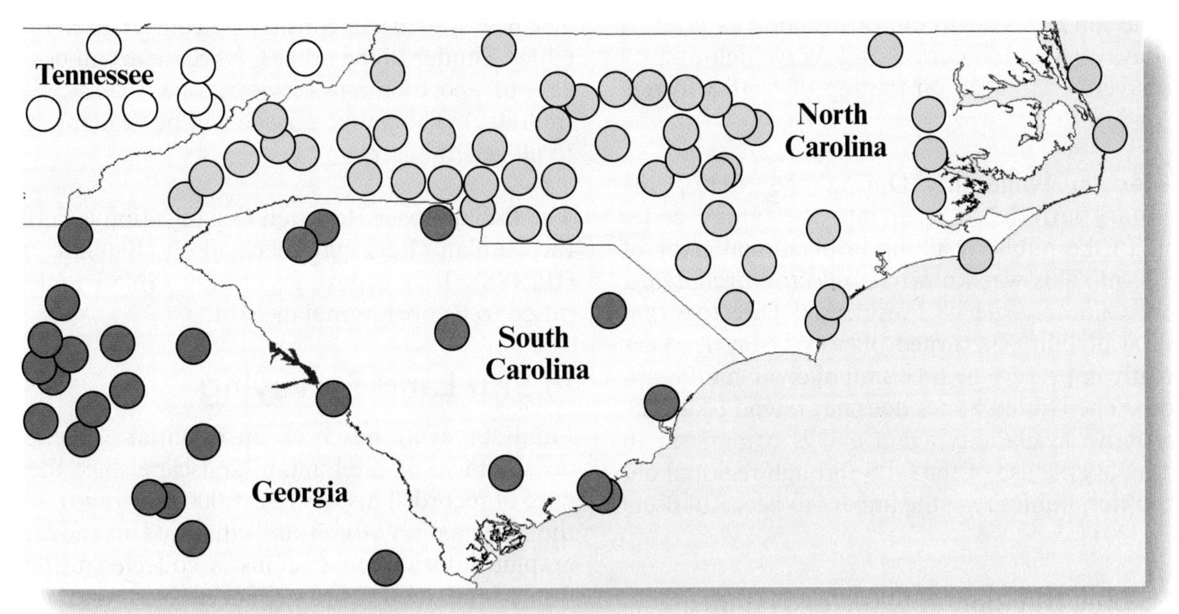

a. CORS in South Carolina, North Carolina, and parts of Georgia and Tennessee.

b. CORS located in Columbia, SC.

c. GPS receiver antenna that is placed on top of the tower.

FIGURE 3–5 a) A map of the Continuously Operating Reference Stations (CORS) in South Carolina, North Carolina and parts of Georgia and Tennessee. South Carolina has nine CORS. b) The 10 m CORS tower in Columbia, SC. c) The precision-grade GPS receiver antenna operates 24 hours a day, 7 days a week on the Columbia, SC, CORS tower. It is shown here on the ground during calibration (courtesy of the National Geodetic Survey).

accuracy in near real-time. If desired, the information from the base station GPS can be saved and the information obtained by the roaming GPS receiver can be processed at the end of the day in batch mode.

In many locations it is now possible to use permanent government-sponsored base station GPS receivers for differential GPS applications. For example, *Continuously Operating Reference Stations (CORS)* are located throughout the United States and Canada, especially around harbors, waterways, and airports (NGS, 2011). Any GPS receiver within approximately 200 km of a CORS can receive timing corrections to improve its GPS measurements to approximately ±3 cm horizontally and ±5 cm vertically, relative to the National Spatial Reference System. This is a significant advance in differential GPS measurement technology. The general location of CORS stations in South Carolina, North Carolina and parts of Georgia and Tennessee are shown in Figure 3-5a. The CORS stations are usually located on towers approximately 10 m above the ground so that as many GPS satellites as possible can be seen without obstruction 24 hours a day, 7 days a week (Figure 3-5b). Very high-quality GPS receivers are placed on the top of CORS towers (Figure 3-5c).

GPS Selective Availability During the 1990s, the U.S. military introduced error into the timing codes available to the public resulting in positional error of up to 100 m. This was known as *selective availability*. President Clinton issued a Presidential Directive that selective availability be turned off as of May 1, 2000. This greatly improved the precision of civilian GPS applications. The United States does not intend to implement selective availability again and is committed to preventing hostile use of the GPS through regional denial of service, minimizing the impact to peaceful users (GPSgov, 2011).

Other Global Navigation Satellite Systems

There are several other Global Navigation Satellite Systems in the process of being deployed (Table 3-1).

The former Soviet Union developed a global navigation satellite system called the *Global'naya Navigatsionnaya Sputnikovaya Sistema* (GLONASS) which at one time was operational (Table 3-1). After the break-up of the Soviet Union, it fell into disrepair with gaps in coverage and only partial availability. In the past decade, the Russian Federation began to restore GLONASS. In 2011, GLONASS had 23 operational satellites that covered 100% of the Russian territory. The system requires 24 satellites to provide services worldwide. GLONASS is currently the most expensive program of the Russian Federal Space Agency, consuming a third of its budget in 2010. This is a good example of how important GPS is to some of the most influential countries in the world. GLONASS was made available to Russian citizens in 2007.

In 2002, the European Union and European Space Agency agreed to introduce their alternative to the United States' NAVSTAR GPS, called the *Galileo* positioning system named after the famous Italian astronomer *Galileo Galilei* (Table 3-1). One of the main objectives of the European *Galileo* system is for the European nations to be independent of the United States' GPS and the Russian GLONASS. The *Galileo* system is supposed to be operational in 2015 with 18 satellites. The goal is to eventually have 27 satellites in orbit including three spares. The first experimental satellite was launched on December 28, 2005. Users are supposed to be able to combine the signals from both *Galileo* and the United States' GPS satellites to increase positional accuracy.

China is developing its own global satellite navigation system called COMPASS (or BeiDou-2) (Table 3-1). The new system will consist of a constellation of 35 satellites. Similar to the other GNSS, there will be two levels of positioning service: open and restricted (military). The public service will be available globally to all general users.

The Indian Space Research Organization is developing the Indian Regional Navigation Satellite System (IRNSS). It is a next generation GNSS and is supposed to be operational in 2014.

In Situ Land Surveying

Land surveying has been an essential element in the development of the human landscape since the beginning of recorded history (*ca.* 5,000 years ago). Much of the information stored and analyzed in modern geographic information systems is collected using traditional land surveying or GPS-enabled land surveying instruments. In developed countries, surveys conducted by registered land surveyors are required to purchase a home; construct a home or building; build a road, bridge, or tunnel; construct a drainage network; build a dam; etc. Some of the major types of in situ land surveys and their characteristics are summarized in Table 3-2.

Surveying Instruments and Techniques

The basic principles of surveying have changed little over the centuries, but the tools used by surveyors have evolved tremendously.

Traditional Land Surveying Simple plane-table surveying instruments and procedures have been used for millennia. It is believed that they were used to map the extent of flooding along the Nile in Egypt, to layout the position of the pyramids, and to align Stonehenge in England. The *Cyclopedia*, one of the very first scientific encyclopedias for the arts and sciences published in 1729, depicts plane-table surveying instruments. Such instruments were used to produce the first relatively accurate maps of most of the world. For example, even as late as the early twentieth century, Claude Birdseye and Herbert Clarke surveyed locations in the western United States for the U.S. Geological Survey using relatively simple plane-table surveying instruments (Figure 3-6ab). Both surveyors are looking through special telescopes (called alidades) at very specific features in the terrain such as a tree or rock outcrop. The alidade is placed on a level plane-table and a line from the center of the plane table (which we will refer to as station #1) is drawn in the exact direction (bearing) toward the feature of interest, e.g., a rock outcrop. Lines to many features of interest in the terrain may also be drawn from station #1, e.g., to other

TABLE 3–2 Selected in situ land surveys conducted using traditional and GPS-assisted surveying instruments. Much of this type of detailed survey information is used in large-scale GIS analysis applications.

Type of Survey	Characteristics
Archaeological/ Anthropological Survey	Surveys that identify the geographic location (*x*, *y*, and *z*) of archaeological and/or anthropological artifacts found at a site. Artifacts may be found at the same *x,y* location but at different *z* elevations.
As-built Survey	A survey conducted after construction to document that the structures, utilities, landscaping, sidewalks, and roads originally proposed were built in the planned locations.
Bathymetric Survey	A survey that measures the elevation (i.e., depth) of surveyed points *below* streams, lakes, seas, or oceans. The elevation information may be mapped as bathymetric contours (lines of equal elevation *below* a datum such as sea level).
Boundary Survey	Locates the boundaries of a parcel of land based on its legal description. This involves locating, setting, or restoring markers (e.g., metal rods) at the corners or along the edges of a parcel. Detailed information about a surveyed parcel in Chapin, SC, is found in Figure 3-9.
Construction Survey	Identifies the geographic location (*x*, *y*, and *z*) of roads, sidewalks, utility lines, landscaping, and buildings to be constructed.
Deformation Survey	Determines if a structure has changed its shape or is moving. The 3-dimensional locations of specific points associated with the structure are determined, a period of time is allowed to pass, and these positions are then re-measured. A comparison is then made to determine if any change in structural shape or position has taken place.
Engineering Surveys	Associated with detailed engineering designs (e.g., topographic, as-built). Such surveys often require very accurate geodetic measurements.
Erosion and Sediment Control Plan	A survey used to identify how construction will effect the movement of stormwater runoff and/or sediment across the construction site. The plan documents how builders will adjust the terrain elevation, slope, and aspect to limit the flow of runoff and/or sediment onto adjoining properties.
Foundation Survey	A survey conducted to verify that the cured foundation was constructed in the location authorized in the site plan. When the location of the finished foundation is checked and approved, the remainder of the structure can be built.
Hydrographic Survey	Maps and nautical charts of the coastline, bathymetry, and important marine features (e.g., buoys, docks, shipwrecks).
Mortgage Survey	Determines existing land boundaries and building locations to verify that there are no structures encroaching on the property under consideration and that the position of any structures are within the correct county zone (e.g., single-family residential, commercial) and meet building code requirements. Title companies and lending institutions often require a mortgage survey prior to construction.
Site Plan	A construction site plan includes all existing and proposed conditions associated within a given site, including: structures, utility lines, fences, roads, sidewalks, topography, landscaping, and wetlands delineation. The plan might also include geographic data on natural vegetation distribution, hydrology, drainage flows, endangered species habitat, FEMA Flood Insurance Rate Maps, and local traffic patterns.
Subdivision Plan	A map based on a survey of a parcel of land (Cowen et al., 2008). Boundary lines are drawn inside the overall parcel to identify proposed individual lot lines and roads. Monuments such as iron rods are placed in the ground to mark lot corners and curve ends. The plat is recorded in the *cadastre* (USA) or land registry (UK). The final plan/plat becomes a contract between the developer and the city or county, determining what can be built on the property and under what conditions. Upon completion of a subdivision, an As-built Plan is usually required by the local government. This is done so that any roadway constructed will pass ownership from the developer to the local government by way of a contractual covenant. The roadways will normally be maintained by the local government when this process is completed.
Topographic Survey	A terrain survey that measures the elevation of surveyed points on a particular piece of land. The elevation information is often mapped as topographic contours (lines of equal elevation above a datum such as sea level).
Wetlands Delineation and Location Survey	A detailed environmental survey completed when construction work is to be performed on or adjacent to a site containing wetlands. Depending on local, state, and/or federal regulations, wetlands are usually classified as areas that are completely inundated with water for more than two weeks during the growing season.

Plane-Table Surveying

a. Claude Birdseye surveying the Colorado River in 1923.

b. Herbert Clark surveying using an alidade and plane-table.

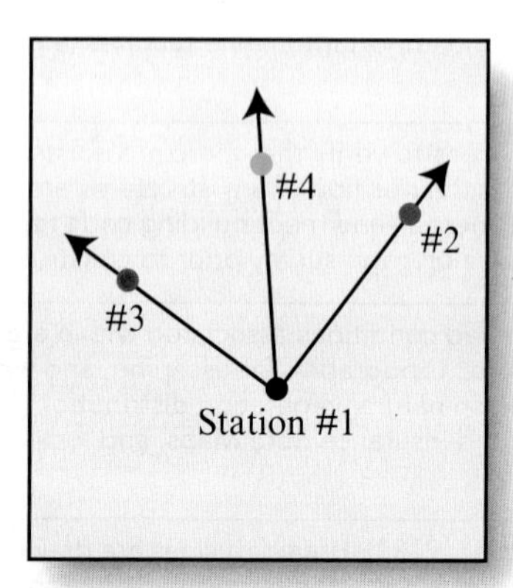

c. Rays shot from station #1.

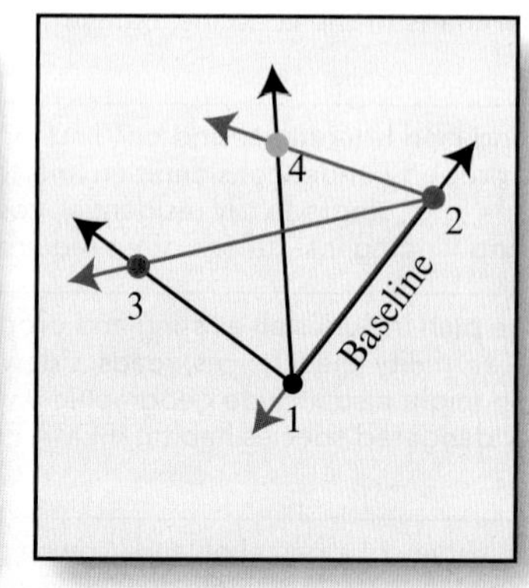

d. Rays shot from station #2.

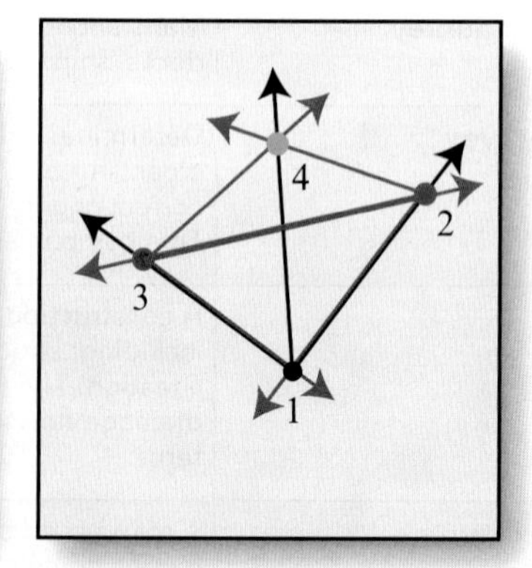

e. Rays shot from station #3.

FIGURE 3–6 a,b) U.S. Geological Survey surveyors conducted plane-table surveys of much of the United States in the nineteenth and twentieth centuries. c) A hypothetical example of shooting rays with an alidade on a plane-table to three distinct features in the landscape from station #1. d) Shooting rays to the features from station #2. e) Shooting rays to the features from station #3 (historical photographs courtesy of the U.S. Geological Survey).

rock outcrops or prominent features in the terrain (Figure 3-6c). Ideally, the plane table is situated directly over a permanent ground control point (GCP) monument that has known x, y, and z coordinates. A present-day example of a permanent survey monument (marker) in Milwaukee, WI, is shown in Figure 3-7b.

Once radiating lines were drawn to all of the features of interest from station #1, the surveyor packed up the equipment and moved to station #2, which was most likely one of the features viewed from station #1. The surveyor then oriented the plane table and sited the alidade back toward station #1. Ideally, the surveyors

Horizontal/Vertical Control Survey Monument (Marker)

a. Witness post in the Uinta Mountains of Utah.
40° 49′ 44.4″ N latitude and
110° 52′ 1.2″ W longitude.

b. U. S. Army Corps of Engineers survey
marker near Milwaukee, WI.
43° 02′ 50.4″ N latitude and
87° 52′ 46.8″ W longitude.

FIGURE 3–7 a) A witness post in the Uinta Mountains in Utah. Government permanent survey monuments are not supposed to be disturbed by the public based on a law passed in 1909. b) A horizontal/vertical ground control survey marker cemented into concrete in Milwaukee, WI, by the U.S. Army Corps of Engineers.

were able to measure the exact distance from stations #1 and #2 on the ground using a dimensionally stable chain or tape. The distance between stations #1 and #2 became the baseline (Figure 3-6d). All of the features shot from station #1 were then re-shot using the alidade from station #2. The intersecting lines from stations #1 and #2 on the plane table map identified the general location of the features. The surveyors then proceeded to pack up all the equipment and go to station #3, where the entire process was repeated (Figure 3-6e). This yielded a plane-table map with lines radiating from the three stations resulting in the intersection of three lines at each of the points of interest in the scene if they were visible from all three stations. Viewing a feature of interest from three or more locations is more accurate than viewing from just two stations.

A second member of the surveying crew would go to a station (e.g., #3) and hold a leveling rod vertically. The leveling rod (often called a stadia rod) functions like a large ruler with numbers inscribed in meters or feet. The surveyor at the home station could view the stadia rod through the alidade and determine the change in elevation in feet or meters between the home station and the station where the stadia rod was located. In this way, the surveyor could obtain accurate information about the relative difference in elevation between two stations. If the surveyor had accurate absolute elevation information (e.g., that station #1 was 100 m above sea level), then he or she could determine the absolute elevation at all of the other stations using the plane table, alidade, and stadia rod.

Traditional manual land surveying based on such techniques and instruments is time consuming. Also, it is often very difficult to get to certain locations or to have a clear line-of-sight to all the stations of interest from a given station. Fortunately, there have been major advances in electronic distance and angular measurement. Surveyors eventually had access to theodolites that could measure horizontal and vertical angles very accurately. They also had very accurate leveling capability. All of these improvements eventually resulted in the development of what is called a total station.

Surveying Using a Total Station A *Total Station* is a theodolite with an electronic distance measurement device (usually a laser) that can also be used for leveling when set to the horizontal plane. Total Stations function using an onboard computer and special-purpose software. The laser range-finding may be accurate to a few millimeters at 1,000 m. A conventional total station needs local or federal control points (e.g., Figure 3-7) over which it can be set up, from which it can tra-

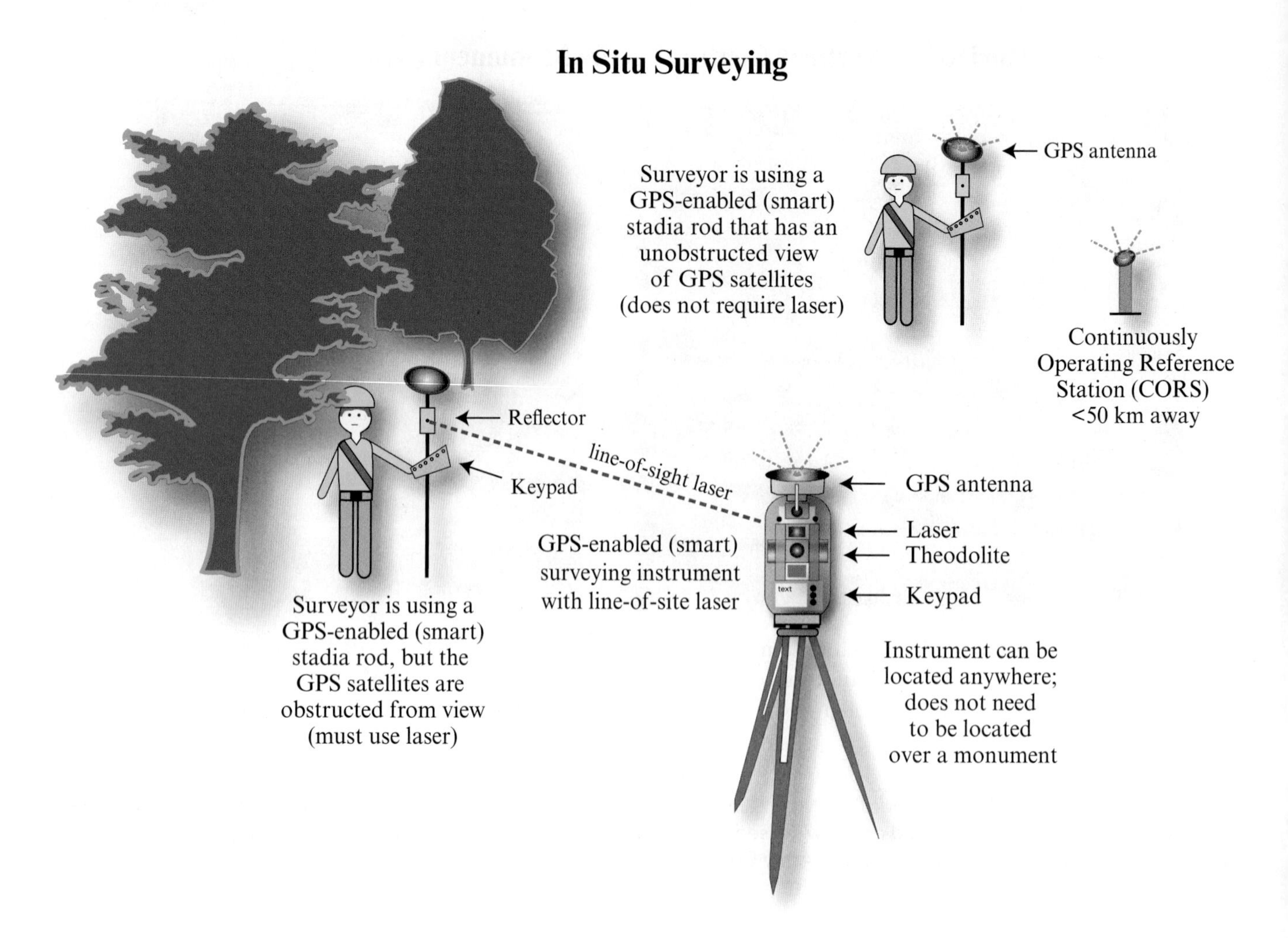

FIGURE 3–8 A GPS-enabled (smart) surveying instrument and the roving GPS-enabled (smart) stadia rod constantly communicate with GPS satellites, the Continuously Operating Reference Station (CORS), and one another. When the GPS-enabled (smart) stadia rod antenna can lock onto the required number of satellites, very accurate *x*, *y*, and *z* measurements can be obtained. However, when the smart stadia rod is obscured from viewing the GPS satellites, the surveyor can use the laser on the GPS-enabled surveying instrument to obtain accurate measurements. The ability to switch between the two technologies allows most of the important locations in a study area to be surveyed without having to move the base station too often.

verse, and to which it can measure to resect (triangulate) its position.

Surveying Using a SmartStation A *SmartStation* is a GPS-enabled Total Station that uses dual-frequency GNSS receivers and real-time kinematic (RTK) technology (Figure 3-8). A *SmartPole* is a GPS-enabled stadia rod. SmartStations and SmartPoles have revolutionized surveying (Leica, 2009). Surveyors can conduct a land survey using these instruments in a number of ways. First, both the SmartStation and the SmartPole can be used independently to obtain accurate *x*, *y*, and *z* measurements, if desired. The only requirements are that they be in contact with a Continuously Operating Reference Station (CORS) which may be up to 50 km (maximum) away, and that they can communicate with at least five GPS satellites at any moment. It is important to note that the SmartStation can be located virtually anywhere and does not have to be associated with a ground control monument. SmartStations can usually determine their position within a few seconds to centimeter-level accuracy when < 50 km from a CORS.

Normally, a surveyor will set up the SmartStation at a location that has an unobstructed view of the sky. The surveyor then takes the SmartPole and walks to important locations in the terrain to obtain measurements. When a location is out in the open and the SmartPole antenna has a clear view of the required number of satellites, then the measurement is made by communicating with the GPS satellites, the CORS, and the SmartStation as shown in Figure 3-8. One of the major time-saving advantages of such surveying is that it is only necessary to obtain measurements once at each location. It is not necessary to look back at previously surveyed points as with historical plane-table surveying. One measurement at each location is sufficient.

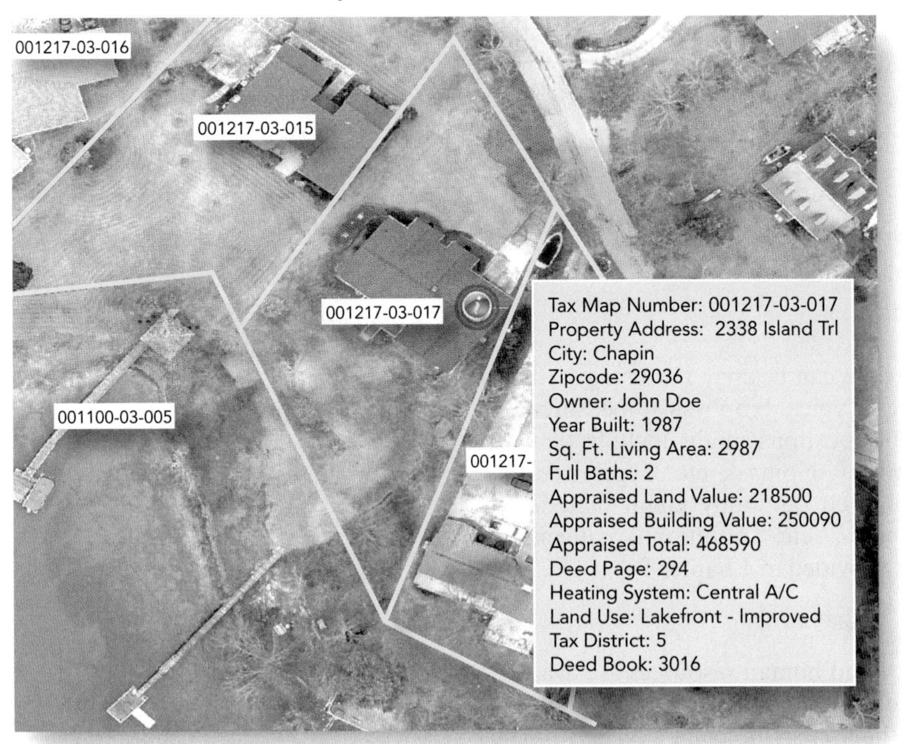

FIGURE 3–9 The surveyed parcel boundaries of the property at 2338 Island Trail, Chapin, SC, (tax map number 001217-03-017) are overlaid on 2011 natural-color vertical aerial photography. In developed countries, legal property boundaries associated with residential, commercial, and public property are almost always surveyed on the ground by a registered land surveyor. The attributes associated with a parcel are usually stored in a relational database (courtesy of Lexington County GIS Internet Property, Mapping, and Data Services).

Unfortunately, sometimes the point to be collected will be in a location that obstructs the SmartPole GPS antenna and prevents it from communicating with the required number of GPS satellites. This is common in heavily urbanized areas with tall buildings or in heavily vegetated areas. When this happens, the surveyor can sometimes collect the desired information using the laser range-finding capability associated with the SmartStation and the SmartPole as shown in Figure 3-8.

Why is it important to know about GPS-enabled surveying? Because much of the large-scale public utility, housing, hydrologic, and transportation infrastructure information stored and analyzed in a GIS is collected by land surveyors using this technology. For example, the exact boundaries of a parcel of property are almost always identified by a land surveyor (Cowen et al., 2008). Detailed information about one land-surveyed parcel in Chapin, SC, is found in Figure 3-9.

GPS-enabled SmartStations and SmartPoles allow surveyors to obtain geographic information more efficiently and accurately. The use of TotalStation and SmartStation technology is not limited to registered land surveyors. Many public employees and research scientists such as geographers, foresters, archaeologists, geologists, etc. routinely use GPS-enabled surveying equipment to obtain accurate geographic information in their study areas.

In Situ Data Sampling or the Taking of a Census

It is common for lay persons and scientists to collect cultural or biophysical geospatial data in the field using sampling or by taking a census of the population.

Sampling

Sometimes it is virtually impossible to collect the geospatial information desired for the entire study area due to cost, time, and constantly changing subject matter (e.g., the river is flowing). In such cases data may be collected using a well thought-out sampling scheme. **Sampling** is a procedure concerned with the selection of a subset of individuals from within a population to infer some knowledge about the whole population and especially to make predictions based on statistical inference.

In such cases, careful attention should be paid to obtaining a representative number of unbiased samples per category of interest using appropriate probability sampling logic within a frame. The most commonly used methods of sampling include (Lunetta and Lyon, 2005; Congalton and Green, 2009):

- simple random sampling,
- systematic sampling,
- stratified sampling, and
- cluster sampling.

Unbiased sample data can be analyzed using statistical analysis techniques. Typical biophysical measurements sampled at specific locations might include temperature, relative humidity, biomass, etc. Typical cultural measurements collected randomly might include age, sex, religion, income, etc. Additional information about sampling is provided in Chapter 5.

A Census

If sufficient money and human resources are available, it may be possible to conduct a census of the population. A **census** is the systematic collection of information about *all* the members of a given population. This means that virtually every one of the persons, places, or things of interest in the study area are investigated. It is believed that the first human census was taken in ancient Rome to identify males fit for military service.

The most common census in developed nations is the national census of population and/or housing. However, it is important to remember that it is possible to conduct a census on practically any important topic as long as time and financial resources are sufficient, e.g., census of agriculture, forestry, business, traffic, buffalo, etc.

2010 United States Census The U.S. Bureau of the Census conducts a census of the population of the United States every 10 years. The 2010 Census cost $7 billion to implement, using a short form that asked 10 basic questions. It is important to note that the detailed socioeconomic information that was collected during past censuses (e.g., 1990 and 2000 Census) will continue to be collected through the *American Community Survey.* The *American Community Survey* provides data about communities in the United States on a 1-year or 3-year cycle, depending on the size of the community, rather than once every 10 years. A small percentage of the population on a rotating basis will receive the *American Community Survey* each year. No household will receive it more than once every five years.

The 2010 Census *Demographic Profile Summary File* has been released for the entire country. The Demographic Profile contains information on topics such as name, sex, age, race, Hispanic or Latino origin, household relationship, household type, group quarters population, housing occupancy, and housing tenure. The profiles were released on a state-by-state basis for each of the 50 states, the District of Columbia and Puerto Rico (http://2010.census.gov/2010census/data/).

Quotes and two maps associated with important Demographic Profiles are found below:

- ***Population Distribution and Change: 2000 to 2010*** (Makun and Wilson, 2011). "The U.S. resident population includes the total number of people in the 50 states and the District of Columbia. The resident population of the United States on April 1, 2010, was 308.7 million, an increase of 9.7 percent over the 281.4 million counted during the 2000 Census. The increase of 9.7 percent over the last decade was lower than the 13.2 percent increase for the 1990s and comparable to the growth during the 1980s of 9.8 percent." A map of the population density of the United States by county in 2010 is shown in Figure 3-10a.
- ***Age and Sex Composition: 2010*** (Howden and Meyer, 2011). "Between 2000 and 2010, the U.S. population under the age of 18 grew at a rate of 2.6 percent. The growth rate was even slower for those aged 18 to 44 (0.6 percent). This contrasts with the substantially faster growth rates seen at older ages. The population aged 45 to 64 grew at a rate of 31.5 percent. The large growth in this age group is primarily due to the aging of the Baby Boom population. The population aged 65 and over also grew at a faster rate (15.1 percent) than the population under age 45." A map of the median age by state in 2010 is shown in Figure 3-10b. Utah remained the only state with a median age under 30. Maine had the highest median age of 42.7. All states experienced an increase in median age when compared with the 2000 Census. This is an important indication of population aging.

The U.S. Bureau of the Census provides quantitative geographic information about the spatial distribution of many important demographic and socioeconomic variables. In addition, some value-added companies take the Bureau of the Census information and adjust it to be especially compatible with the major types of GIS applications. For example, Esri (2011) provides users with the ability to generate reports and color-coded maps by Zipcode, drive time, custom polygon, and trade area, in addition to standard geographies provided by the Census Bureau such as states, counties, census tracts, and block groups. Several of the most important sources of census information are identified in the Appendix.

Examples of U.S. Census Bureau Geographic Information

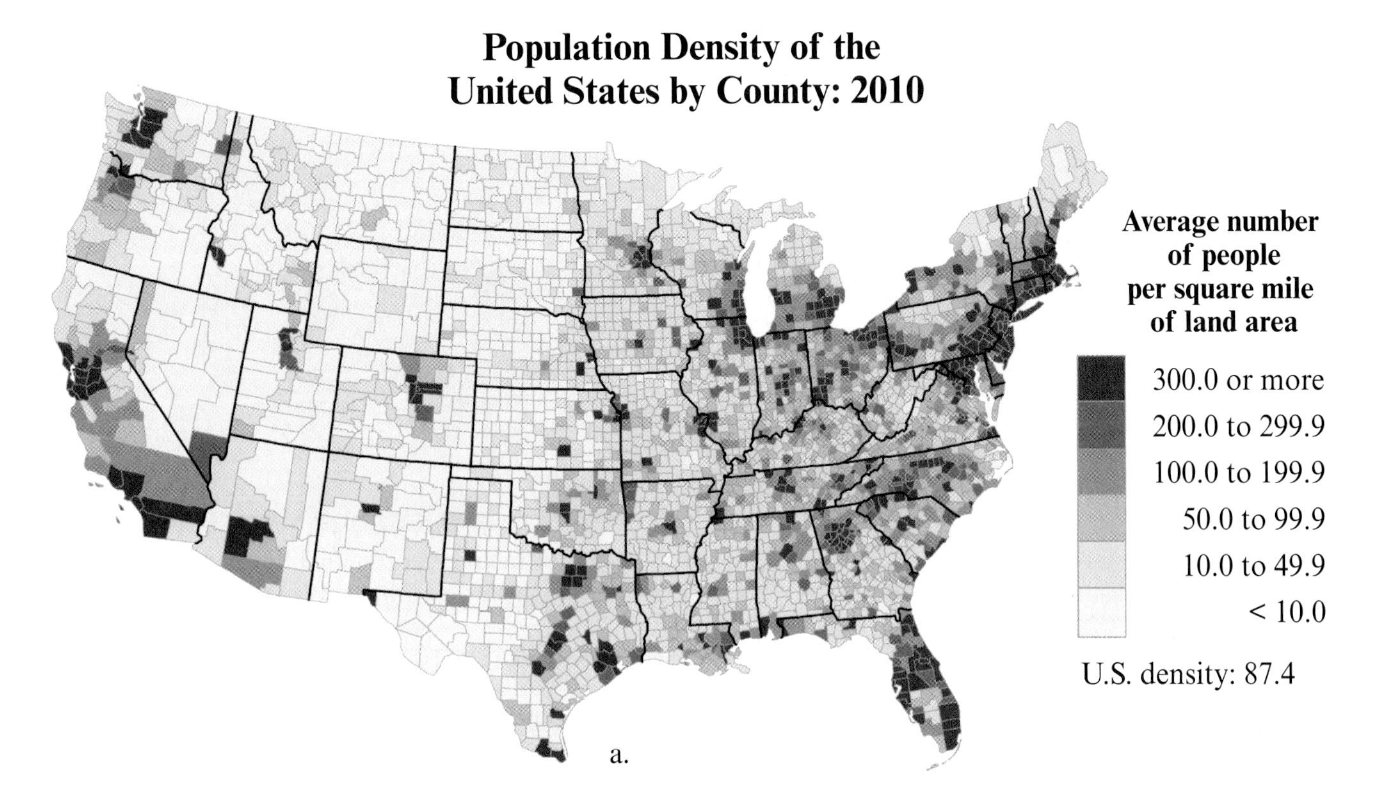

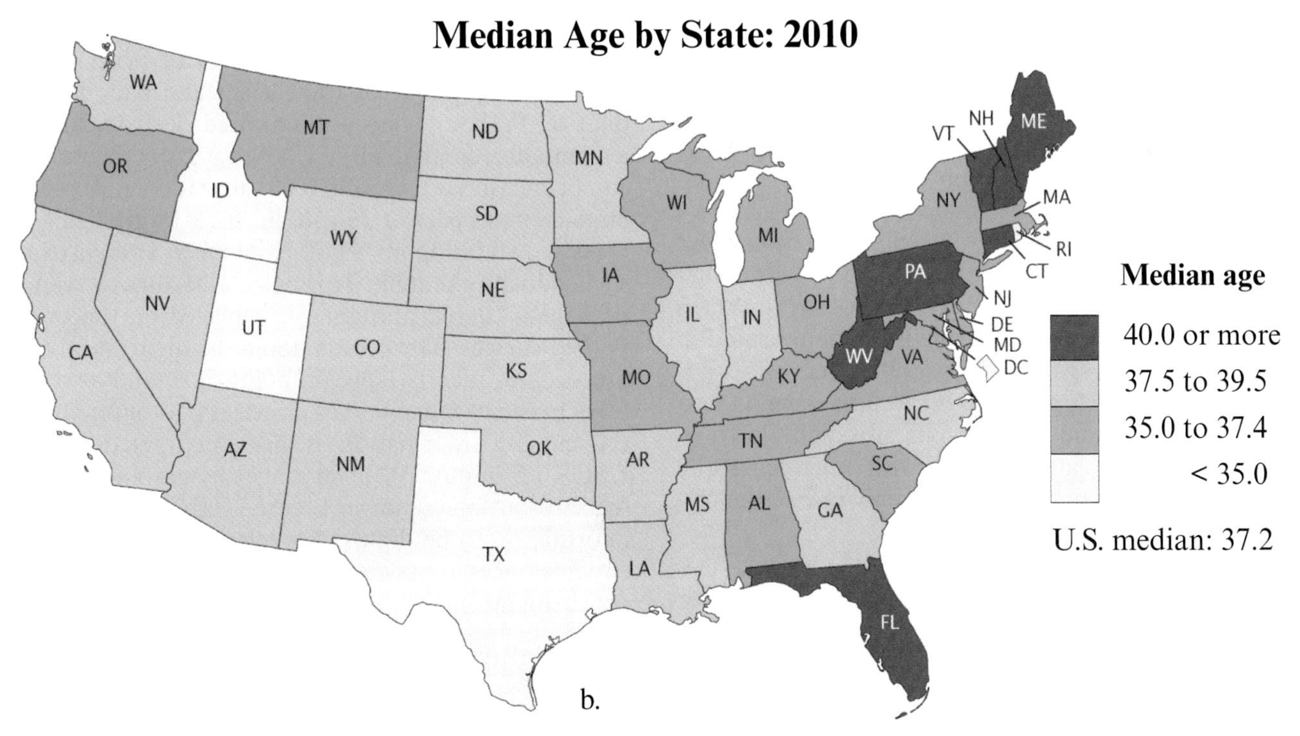

FIGURE 3–10 Two examples of geospatial information available from the U.S. Bureau of the Census for the conterminous United States (Alaska, Hawaii, and Puerto Rico results are not shown). a) 2010 Population Density of the United States by county. b) 2010 Median Age of the United States by state. The maps were extracted from the U.S. Bureau of the Census demographic profile documents *Population and Distribution and Change: 2000 to 2010* (Makun and Wilson, 2011) and *Age and Sex Composition: 2010* (Howden and Meyer, 2011).

Digitizing Table Used to Obtain New *x,y* Coordinate Information

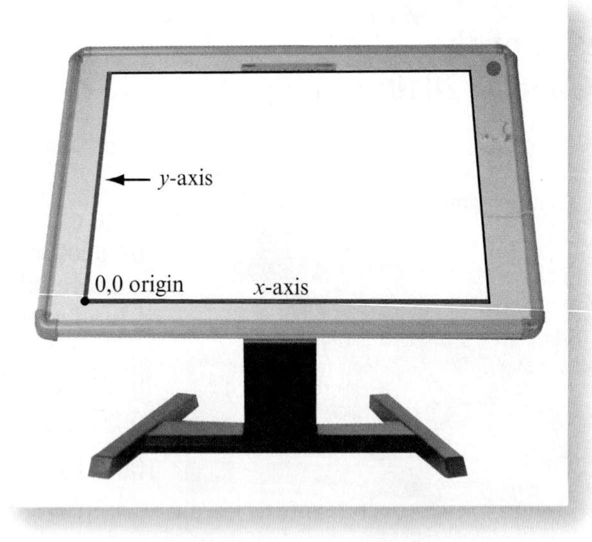

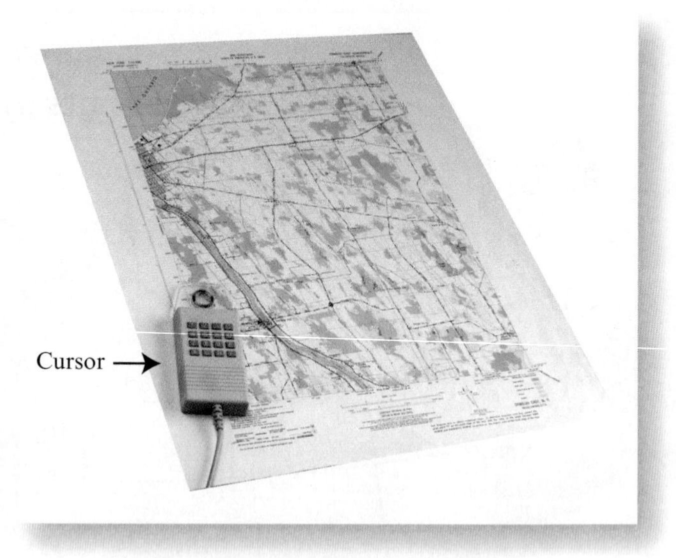

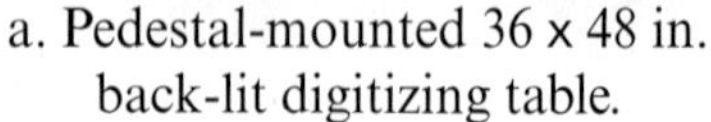

a. Pedestal-mounted 36 x 48 in. back-lit digitizing table.

b. Extracting coordinate information using a 16-button cursor.

FIGURE 3–11 a) A pedestal-mounted 36 x 48 in. back-lit digitizing table with a spatial resolution of approximately 0.001 in. Note the origin of the table and the *x*- and *y*-axis. b) The hard-copy map or aerial photograph is placed on the surface of the table. In this example, an analyst is using a hand-held 16-button cursor to obtain the *x,y* coordinates of point, line, and area features of interest on a USGS 7.5-minute quadrangle 1:24,000-scale topographic map.

Digitization of Historical Spatial Information

There are a tremendous number of historical and current maps, aerial photographs, diagrams, and other types of geospatial information that exist only in analog (hard-copy) format (i.e., there is no digital version). These resources are of great value and must be handled carefully because they are often one-of-a-kind originals that are very fragile. Consequently, they are often analyzed alone, without the benefit of being related to other types of geospatial information. Great effort has been made to develop techniques to turn these historical analog maps and photographs into digital data so that they can be related in a GIS with other geospatial information. This process is commonly called **digitization**.

Digitizing is usually performed using one of three primary devices:

- Digitizing tables or tablets using a hand-held cursor or electronic pen,
- Heads-up on-screen digitization using a cursor or electronic pen, and
- Raster scanning using a scanning densitometer.

It is useful to review each of these digitization alternatives.

Digitizing Tables and Tablets

Digitizing tables and tablets consist of a flatbed surface that may be opaque or translucent and back-lit. The digitizer flatbed surface is monitored electronically via a computer so that all *x,y* locations on the surface can be measured to within 0.001 to 0.005-in. A typical large-format pedestal 36 x 48 in. back-lit digitizing table is shown in Figure 3-11a. Note the *x*- and *y*-axis associated with the table. Normally, a hard-copy map or perhaps an aerial photograph is placed on top of the flatbed surface. The person doing the digitization then proceeds to identify specific point, line, and area features in the hard-copy map or aerial photograph using the cursor. Information is being extracted from a USGS 7.5-minute 1:24,000-scale topographic map using a 16-button cursor in Figure 3-11b. Sometimes the information to be digitized is relatively small. In such circumstances, it may be possible to use a small-format digitizing tablet.

Using digitization software, it is possible to scale the digitizing table or tablet so that the *x,y*-coordinates obtained for the point, line, and area features are as accurate as possible given the constraints of the digitization process. Normally, it is necessary to take the information derived during digitization and process it using a geometric correction algorithm found within the GIS software. Ideally, this yields digital geospatial data that

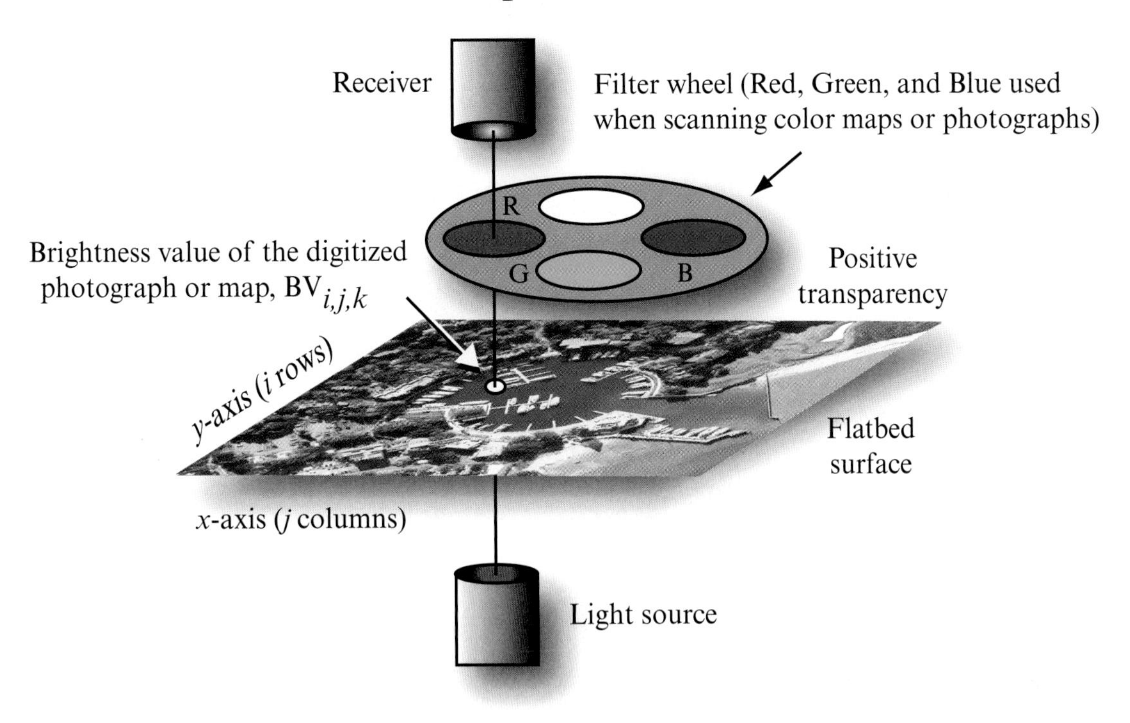

FIGURE 3–12 Schematic of a flatbed microdensitometer. A black & white negative or positive transparency is converted from an analog map or photograph into a single matrix of digital brightness values, $BV_{i,j,k}$. A color negative or positive transparency is separated into three registered matrices based on the density of the three dyes found at each location in the photograph or map. The spot size that is analyzed during the digitization process may be as small as a few micrometers; hence the term microdensitometer.

can be related to other geometrically accurate geospatial information.

Heads-up On-screen Digitization Using Scanned Maps or Images

Heads-up on-screen digitizing is performed using specialized GIS software. First, the map or image that is going to be used to extract the *x,y*-coordinates of point, line, and area features is scanned using techniques discussed in the next section. The scanned map or image is then displayed on the computer screen. Hopefully, the scanned map or image has already been geometrically rectified into a standard map projection. The analyst then uses a mouse cursor or pen to identify specific points, lines, or areas on the screen that are of particular interest. The digitization software collects the *x,y*-coordinates of these features and places them in a format that can be used by the GIS and hopefully analyzed in conjunction with other geospatial information.

Raster-Scanning

Raster-scanning systems are commonly used to digitize hard-copy maps and historical aerial photographs. Densitometry is the measurement of transmission or reflection characteristics of objects or features in photographic images or maps. The density (*D*) characteristics of a negative or positive transparency film can be measured using a densitometer. There are several types of densitometers, including flatbed and drum microdensitometers, and linear or area array charge-coupled device densitometers.

Microdensitometer Digitization The characteristics of a typical flatbed microdensitometer are shown in Figure 3-12. This instrument can measure the density characteristics of very small areas of a negative or positive transparency, down to just a few micrometers in size, hence the term microdensitometer. Basically, a known quantity of light is projected from the light source toward the receiver optics. If the light encounters a very dense portion of the film, very little light will be transmitted to the receiver. If the light encounters a very clear portion of the film, then much of the light will be transmitted to the receiver. The densitometer can output the characteristics at each *i,j* location in the map or photograph in terms of transmittance, opacity, or density. The amount of light recorded by the receiver is commonly converted into a digital brightness value, designated $BV_{i,j,k}$, which refers to the

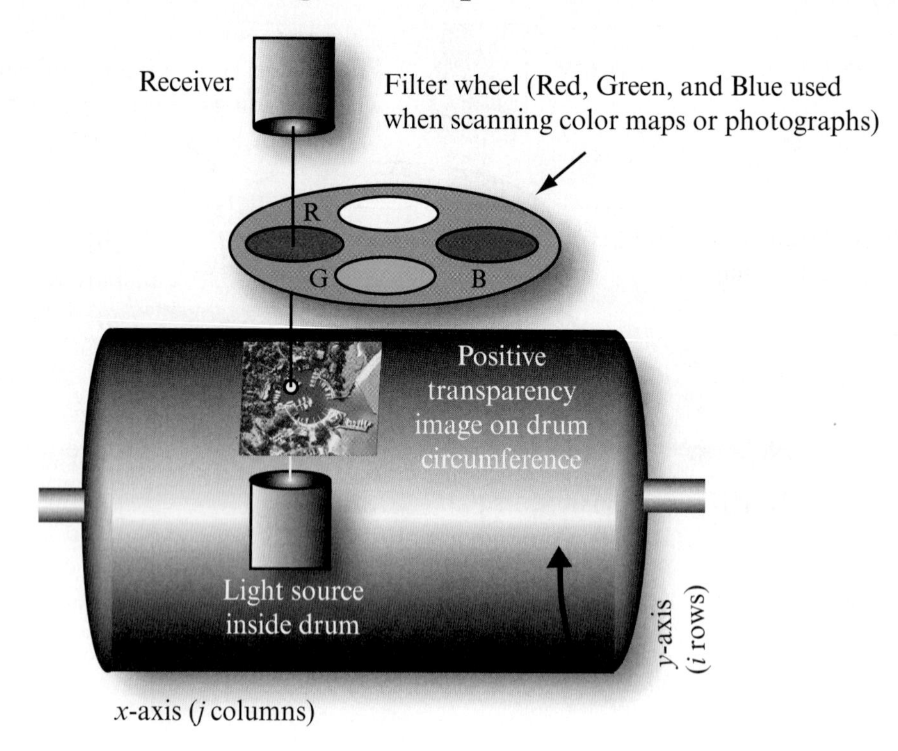

FIGURE 3–13 A rotating-drum, optical-mechanical microdensitometer works on exactly the same principle as the flatbed microdensitometer except that the map or image transparency is mounted on a rotating drum so that it forms a portion of the drum's circumference. The light source is situated in the interior of the drum, and the drum is continually rotated in the y-direction. The x-coordinate is obtained by the incremental translation of the source-receiver optics after each drum revolution.

location in the photograph or map at row i and column j and band k. At the end of each scan line, the light source steps in the y-direction some Δy to scan along a line contiguous and parallel to the previous one. As the light source is scanned across the image, the continuous output from the receiver is converted to a series of discrete numerical values on a pixel-by-pixel basis. This **analog-to-digital conversion** process results in a matrix of values that are usually recorded in 8-bit bytes (values ranging from 0 to 255) or more (e.g., 12-bit data). These data are then stored on a disk for subsequent digital analysis.

Scanning imagery at spot sizes <12 μm may result in noisy digitized data, because the spot size approaches the dimension of the film's silver halide crystals. Table 3-3 summarizes the relationship between digitizer scanning spot size (IFOV) measured in dots-per-inch (DPI) or micrometers and the pixel ground resolution at various scales. The algorithms for converting from DPI to μm and vice versa are presented in Table 3-3.

A simple black & white photograph or map has only a single band, $k = 1$. However, sometimes you may need to digitize color photography or maps. In such circumstances, three specially designed filters are used that determine the amount of light transmitted by each of the dye layers in the film (Figure 3-12). The negative or positive transparency is scanned three times ($k = 1, 2$ and 3), each time with a different filter. This extracts spectral information from the respective dye layers found in color and color-infrared aerial photography or maps and results in a registered three-band digital data set for subsequent image processing.

The characteristics of a typical rotating-drum microdensitometer are shown in Figure 3-13. The film transparency of a map or photograph is mounted on a glass rotating drum so that it forms a portion of the drum's circumference. The light source is situated in the interior of the drum. The y-coordinate scanning motion is provided by the rotation of the drum. The x-coordinate is obtained by the incremental translation of the source-receiver optics after each drum revolution.

Some rotating-drum microdensitometers reflect light off very small areas on the surface of the hard-copy map or photograph and record the blue, green, and red reflectance characteristics associated with each picture element.

TABLE 3–3 Relationship between digitizer detector instantaneous-field-of-view (IFOV) measured in dots-per-inch (DPI) or micrometers (μm), and the pixel ground resolution at various scales.

Digitizer Detector IFOV		Pixel Ground Resolution at Various Scales (in meters)					
Dots-per-inch (DPI)	**Micrometers**	**1:40,000**	**1:20,000**	**1:9,600**	**1:4,800**	**1:2,400**	**1:1,200**
100	**254.00**	10.16	5.08	2.44	1.22	0.61	0.30
200	**127.00**	5.08	2.54	1.22	0.61	0.30	0.15
300	**84.67**	3.39	1.69	0.81	0.41	0.20	0.10
400	**63.50**	2.54	1.27	0.61	0.30	0.15	0.08
500	**50.80**	2.03	1.02	0.49	0.24	0.12	0.06
600	**42.34**	1.69	0.85	0.41	0.20	0.10	0.05
700	**36.29**	1.45	0.73	0.35	0.17	0.09	0.04
800	**31.75**	1.27	0.64	0.30	0.15	0.08	0.04
900	**28.23**	1.13	0.56	0.27	0.14	0.07	0.03
1000	**25.40**	1.02	0.51	0.24	0.12	0.06	0.03
1200	**21.17**	0.85	0.42	0.20	0.10	0.05	0.03
1500	**16.94**	0.67	0.34	0.16	0.08	0.04	0.02
2000	**12.70**	0.51	0.25	0.12	0.06	0.03	0.02
3000	**8.47**	0.33	0.17	0.08	0.04	0.02	0.01
4000	**6.35**	0.25	0.13	0.06	0.03	0.02	0.008

Useful Scanning Conversions:

DPI = dots per inch; μm = micrometers; I = inches; M = meters
From DPI to micrometers: μm = (2.54 / DPI)10,000
From micrometers to DPI: DPI = (2.54 / μm)10,000
From inches to meters: M = I × 0.0254
From meters to inches: I = M × 39.37

Computation of Pixel Ground Resolution:

PM = pixel size in meters; PF = pixel size in feet; S = photo or map scale factor
Using DPI: PM = (S/DPI)/39.37 PF = (S/DPI)/12
Using micrometers: PM = (S × μm) 0.000001 PF = (S × μm) 0.00000328
For example, if a 1:6,000 scale aerial photograph is scanned at 500 DPI, the pixel size will be (6000/500)/39.37 = 0.3048 meter per pixel or (6000/500)/12 = 1.00 foot per pixel. If a 1:9,600 scale aerial photograph is scanned at 50.8 μm, the pixel size will be (9,600 × 50.8)(0.000001) = 0.49 meter or (9,600 × 50.8)(0.00000328) = 1.6 feet per pixel.

Linear Array CCD

|← 3,000 photosites →|

a.

Area Array CCD

c.

Linear Array CCD Flatbed Scanner

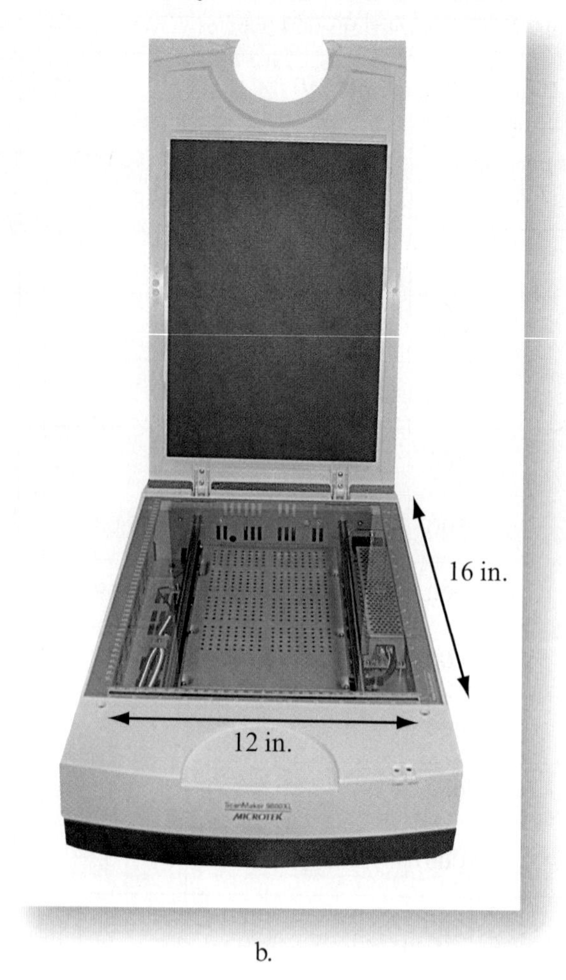

b.

FIGURE 3–14 a) A linear charge-coupled device (CCD) containing 3,000 photosites. b) An oversized flatbed scanner based on linear array CCD technology capable of digitizing hard-copy maps and aerial photographs that are up to 12 x 16 in. It is especially useful for digitizing 9 x 9 in. aerial photographs in a single pass. c) An example of an area array CCD used in an area-array scanner.

Flatbed and rotating drum microdensitometers yield the most accurate raster digitization of maps and images. Microdensitometers are often found at laboratories that conduct research to very exacting standards (e.g., soft-copy photogrammetry) or at service companies that specialize in providing customers with high-quality raster digitization.

Linear and Area Array Charge-Coupled Device (CCD) Digitization Advances in the personal computer industry have spurred the development of flatbed, desktop scanners based on linear array CCDs (Figure 3-14a) that can be used to digitize hard-copy negatives, paper prints, or transparencies at 50 to 6,000 pixels per inch (Figure 3-14ab). The hard-copy photograph or map is placed on the glass. The digitizer optical system illuminates an entire line of the hard-copy photograph or map at one time with a known amount of light. A linear array of detectors records the amount of light reflected from or transmitted through the map or photograph along the array and performs an A-to-D conversion. There are linear CCDs with >20,000 elements. The linear array is stepped in the *y*-direction, and another line of data is digitized.

It is possible to purchase useful desktop color scanners for less than $200. Many digital image processing laboratories use these inexpensive desktop digitizers to convert hard-copy remotely sensed data and maps into a digital format. Desktop scanners provide surprisingly good spatial precision. An optional "transilluminator" can be purchased for back-lighting any film that needs to be scanned. Unfortunately, most desktop scanners are designed for 8.5 × 14 in. originals, and most aerial photographs are 9 × 9 in. Similarly, most hard-copy maps are greater than 8.5 × 14 in. Under such conditions, the analyst must digitize the 9 × 9 in. photograph or map in two multiple sections (e.g., 8.5 × 9 in. and

Gray Scale and Color Control Patches Placed Adjacent to Photographs or Maps to Be Scanned

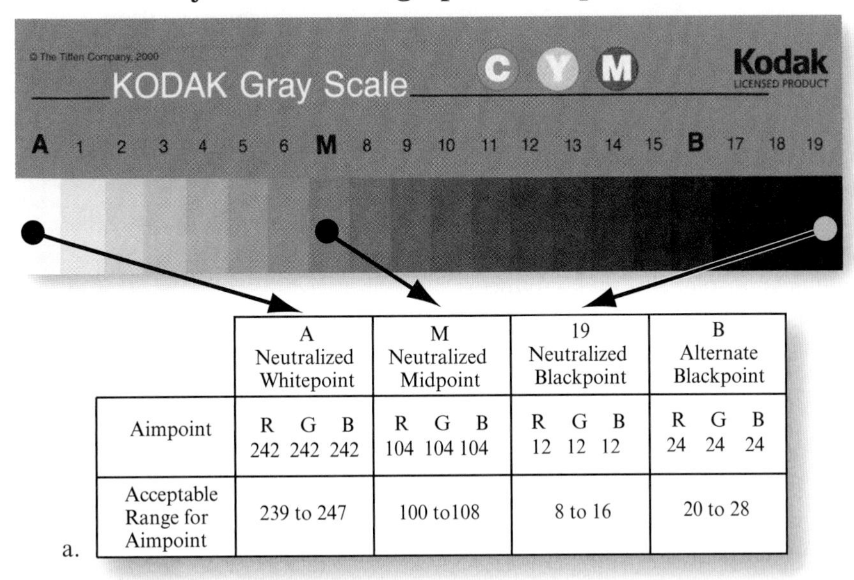

	A Neutralized Whitepoint	M Neutralized Midpoint	19 Neutralized Blackpoint	B Alternate Blackpoint
Aimpoint	R G B 242 242 242	R G B 104 104 104	R G B 12 12 12	R G B 24 24 24
Acceptable Range for Aimpoint	239 to 247	100 to108	8 to 16	20 to 28

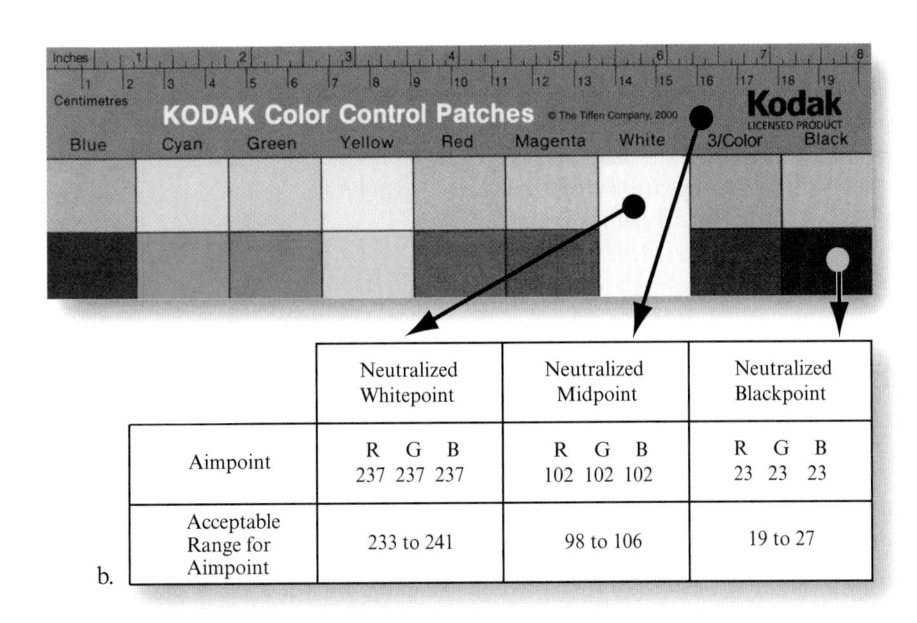

	Neutralized Whitepoint	Neutralized Midpoint	Neutralized Blackpoint
Aimpoint	R G B 237 237 237	R G B 102 102 102	R G B 23 23 23
Acceptable Range for Aimpoint	233 to 241	98 to 106	19 to 27

FIGURE 3–15 a) A Gray Scale card is placed adjacent to a black & white aerial photograph or map to be scanned. The goal is to have the RGB values in the digital output file match as close as possible the aimpoint RGB values specified in the table for white, mid, and black points. b) The Color Control Patch card is placed adjacent to the color map or color aerial photograph to be scanned (courtesy of U. S. National Archives and Records Administration; Puglia et al., 2004).

0.5 × 9 in. for a 9 × 9 in. aerial photograph) and then digitally *mosaic* the two pieces together. The mosaicking process can introduce both geometric and radiometric error. Therefore, it is always better to use as high-quality and as large a digitizer as possible to minimize the amount of mosaicking required. A high-quality 12 × 16 in. scanner is shown in Figure 3-14b.

Some digitizing systems utilize area array CCD technology (Figure 3-14c). These systems scan the film (the original negative or positive transparency) as a series of rectangular image segments or tiles. Radiometric calibration algorithms are then used to compensate for uneven illumination encountered in any of the tile regions. When scanning a color image, the scanner stops on a rectangular image section and captures that information sequentially with each of the color filters (blue, green, red) before it moves to another section.

When scanning black & white or color images or maps, it is good practice to use special Gray Scale and Color Control Patches such as those shown in Figure 3-15ab.

The U.S. National Archives and Records Administration (NARA) recommends that these cards be laid next to the map or image that is to be digitized (Puglia et al., 2004). After digitizing, the analyst looks at the quality of the red, green, and blue (RGB) values of the white, gray, and black parts of the gray scale or color control patches on the computer screen. If the values of the RGB values for the white, gray, and black test areas lie within the "aimpoint" range, then it is likely that the digitization has been successful. If the values fall outside the aimpoint range, then adjustments should be made and the image or map should be redigitized until aimpoint values are achieved.

Remote Sensing Data Collection

A large proportion of the geospatial information analyzed using geographic information systems is originally extracted by analyzing remotely sensed data, e.g., land use, land cover, building footprints, transportation and utility networks, digital terrain models (topographic and bathymetric), slope, and aspect (Figure 3-16). Many GIS practictioners assume that such information comes from other sources. They are surprised to learn how much geospatial information comes from the processing of remotely sensed data (Miller et al., 2003).

Remote sensing is defined by the American Society for Photogrammetry & Remote Sensing as:

> the measurement or acquisition of information of some property of an object or phenomenon by a recording device that is not in physical or intimate contact with the object or phenomenon under study.

Remote sensing instruments such as cameras, multispectral and hyperspectral scanners, thermal-infrared detectors, Radio Detection and Ranging (RADAR) sensors, and Light Detection and Ranging (LiDAR) instruments are flown onboard satellites or on sub-orbital aircraft such as airplanes, helicopters, and unmanned aerial vehicles (UAVs) (Figure 3-16). Sound Navigation and Ranging sensors (SONAR) are placed on board ships and submarines to map the bathymetry of subsurface terrain. Table 3-4 summarizes the remote sensing systems used to obtain many of the most important variables used by GIScientists.

This chapter provides an overview of several of the most important remote sensing systems and the types of information that can be extracted from the remote sensor data. More detailed information about how

FIGURE 3–16 A remote sensing instrument collects information about an object or phenomenon within the instantaneous-field-of-view (IFOV) of the sensor system without being in direct physical contact with it. The instrument is usually located onboard an aircraft or satellite platform.

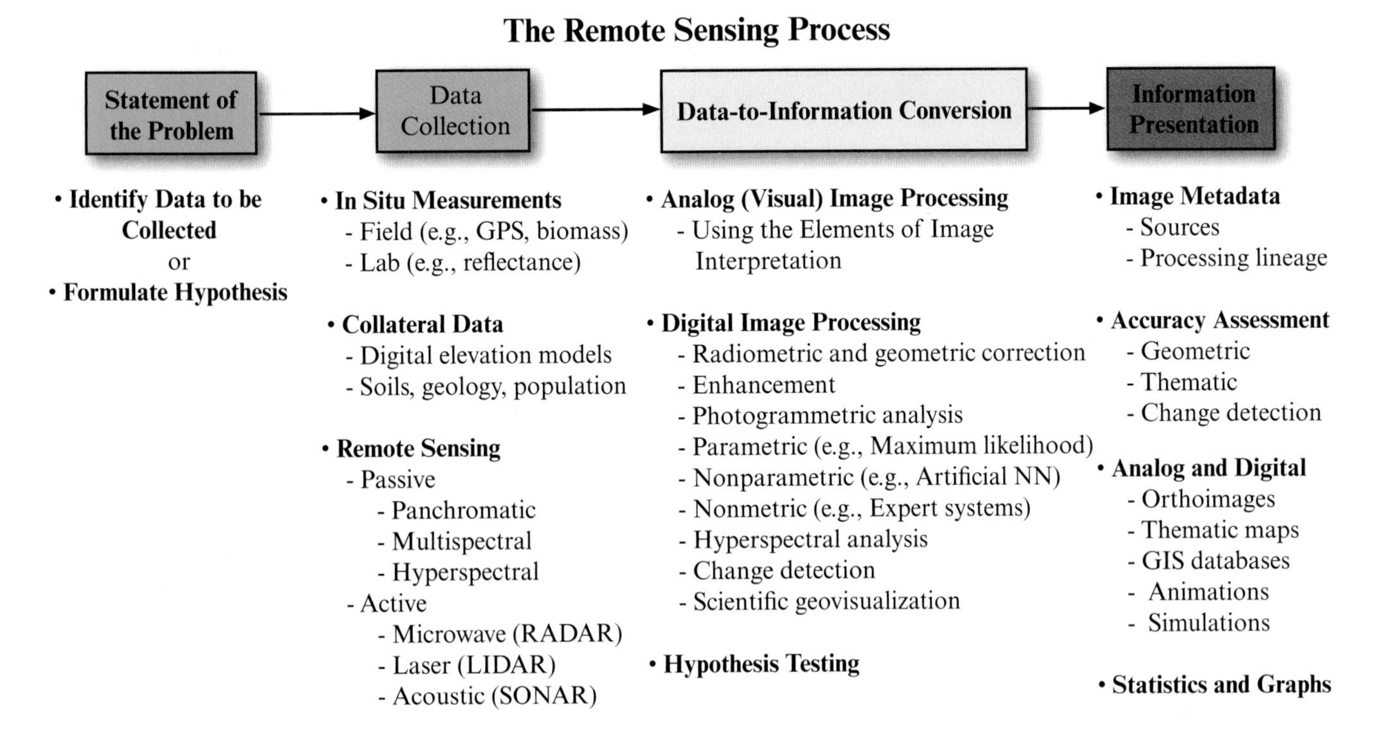

FIGURE 3–17 GIScientists generally use the remote sensing process when extracting geospatial information from remotely sensed data. The goal is to turn the remote sensor data into accurate and useful information.

these remote sensing systems operate and how to interpret the imagery using analog and digital image processing techniques are found in Jensen (2005; 2007).

The Remote Sensing Process

Remote sensing is not new. Laypersons and scientists have been collecting and analyzing remotely sensed data since the first aerial photography was obtained from captive balloons over Paris, France, by Gaspard Felix Tournachon in 1858. The remote sensing data-collection and analysis procedures used for Earth resource and urban applications are often implemented in a systematic fashion called the **remote sensing process**. The procedures in the remote sensing process include (Figure 3-17):

- Identifying the data to be collected or the hypothesis to be tested.
- Collecting the in situ, collateral, and remote sensor data (McCoy, 2005).
- In situ and remotely sensed data are processed using analog or digital image processing techniques. If necessary, hypotheses are tested.
- Metadata, digital image processing lineage, and the accuracy of the derived geospatial information are provided. The results are communicated using images, maps, GIS databases, animations, simulations, statistics, and graphs.

Resolution Considerations

Remote sensing systems collect analog (e.g., hard-copy aerial photography) and/or digital data (e.g., a matrix of brightness values obtained using a scanner, linear array, or area array). The amount of radiance, L (watts $m^{-2}\ sr^{-1}$; i.e., watts per meter squared per steradian), recorded within the instantaneous-field-of-view (IFOV) of an optical remote sensing system (e.g., a picture element or pixel in a digital image), is a function of:

$$L = f(\lambda, s_{x,y,z}, t, \theta, P, \Omega) \quad \text{where} \qquad (3.1)$$

λ = wavelength (spectral response measured in various bands of the electromagnetic spectrum). For active systems such as RADAR, LiDAR, and SONAR, it is the amount of back-scattered microwave, laser light, or sound energy, respectively;

$s_{x,y,z}$ = x, y, z location of the pixel and its size (x, y);

t = temporal resolution, i.e., when and how often the remote sensor data are collected;

θ = set of angles that describe the geometric relationships between the radiation source (e.g., the Sun), the terrain target of interest (e.g., a corn field), and the remote sensing system;

P = polarization characteristics of the back-scattered energy recorded by the sensor; and

TABLE 3–4 Geospatial information and the remote sensing systems that are typically used to obtain such information.

	Useful Remote Sensing Systems						
Geospatial Information	**Ultra-violet**	**Aerial Photography (analog or digital)**	**Multispectral/ Hyperspectral**	**Thermal-Infrared**	**Light Detection & Ranging (LiDAR)**	**Radio Detection & Ranging (RADAR)**	**Sound Navi-gation & Ranging (SONAR)**
Land Use and Land Cover		Yes	Yes	Yes	Yes	Yes	
Digital Terrain Modeling **- Topographic** **- Bathymetric**		Yes	Yes		Yes	Yes	Yes
Transportation Infrastructure		Yes	Yes		Yes	Yes	
Cadastral **- Parcel Boundaries** **- Building Footprints**		Yes	Yes		Yes		
Hydrologic		Yes	Yes	Yes	Yes	Yes	Yes
Utility Infrastructure		Yes	Yes	Yes	Yes		
Water	Yes	Yes	Yes	Yes	Yes	Yes	Yes
Vegetation	Yes	Yes	Yes	Yes	Yes	Yes	Yes
Soils and Rocks	Yes	Yes	Yes	Yes	Yes	Yes	Yes
Atmosphere	Yes	Yes	Yes	Yes	Yes	Yes	
Snow and Ice		Yes	Yes	Yes	Yes	Yes	
Volcanic Effects		Yes	Yes	Yes	Yes	Yes	Yes

Ω = radiometric resolution (precision) at which the data (e.g., reflected, emitted, or back-scattered radiation) are recorded by the remote sensing system.

GIS practictioners interested in using remote sensing-derived information in their GIS should be generally knowledgeable about the parameters associated with Equation 3.1 and how they influence the nature of the remote sensing data collected.

Spectral Resolution

Most remote sensing investigations are based on developing a deterministic relationship (i.e., a model) between the amount of electromagnetic energy reflected, emitted, or back-scattered in specific bands or frequencies in the electromagnetic spectrum (e.g., such as red light) and the chemical, biological, and physical characteristics of the phenomena under investigation (e.g., a corn field). **Spectral resolution** is the number and size of specific wavelength intervals (referred to as bands or channels) in the electromagnetic spectrum to which a remote sensing instrument is sensitive.

Multispectral remote sensing systems record energy in multiple bands of the electromagnetic spectrum. For example, the bandwidths of the four multispectral bands associated with a typical digital frame camera are shown in Figure 3-18a. In this example, the camera records information in four specific regions of the electromagnetic spectrum (band 1 = 450 – 515 nm; band 2 = 525 – 605 nm; band 3 = 640 – 690 nm; and band 4 = 750 – 900 nm). Note that there may be gaps between the spectral sensitivities of the various detectors.

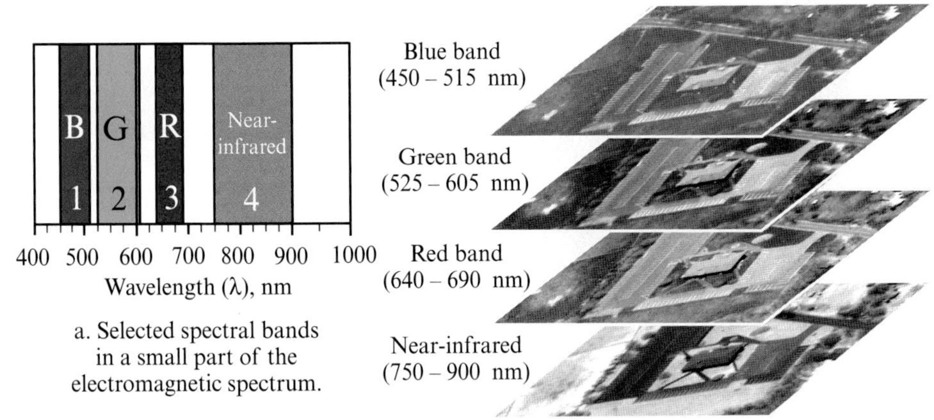

a. Selected spectral bands in a small part of the electromagnetic spectrum.

b. Individual multispectral band images.

c. Natural color-composite consisting of blue, green, and red bands.

d. Color-infrared color-composite consisting of green, red, and near-infrared bands.

FIGURE 3–18 a) The spectral bandwidths of the four bands (blue, green, red, and near-infrared) of a typical digital frame camera. b) Individual band images obtained by the multispectral digital frame camera. c) Natural color-composite made by color-combining the blue, green, and red bands. d) Color-infrared color-composite made by color-combining the green, red, and near-infrared bands.

Hyperspectral remote sensing instruments acquire data in tens to hundreds of spectral bands. **Ultraspectral remote sensing** involves data collection in many hundreds or even thousands of bands.

Certain regions or spectral bands of the electromagnetic spectrum are optimum for obtaining information about biophysical parameters. The bands are selected to maximize the contrast between the object of interest and its background (i.e., object-to-background contrast). Careful selection of the spectral bands or frequencies improve the probability that the desired information will be extracted from the remote sensor data.

Spatial Resolution

Remote sensing systems record the spatial characteristics of objects on the terrain. For example, each silver halide crystal in an analog aerial photograph and each picture element in a digital remotely sensed image is located at a specific location in the image and associated with specific *x,y*-coordinates on the ground. Once rectified to a standard map projection, the spatial information associated with each silver halide crystal or pixel is of significant value because it allows the remote sensing–derived information to be used with other spatial data in a GIS.

There is a general relationship between the size of an object or area to be identified and the spatial resolution of the remote sensing system. **Spatial resolution** is a measure of the smallest angular or linear separation between two objects that can be resolved by the remote sensing system. The spatial resolution of aerial photography may be measured by 1) placing calibrated, parallel black and white lines on tarps that are placed in the field, 2) obtaining aerial photography of the study area, and 3) computing the number of resolvable line pairs per millimeter in the photography.

Many satellite remote sensing systems use optics that have a constant instantaneous-field-of-view (IFOV) (Figure 3-16). Therefore, a remote sensing system's nominal spatial resolution is defined as the dimension in meters (or feet) of the ground-projected IFOV where the diameter of the circle (D) on the ground is a function of the instantaneous-field-of-view (β) multiplied by the altitude (H) of the sensor above ground level (AGL) (Figure 3-16):

$$D = \beta \times H. \quad (3.2)$$

Pixels are normally represented on computer screens and in hard-copy images as rectangles with equal length and width. Therefore, we typically describe a sensor's nominal spatial resolution as being 10 × 10 m

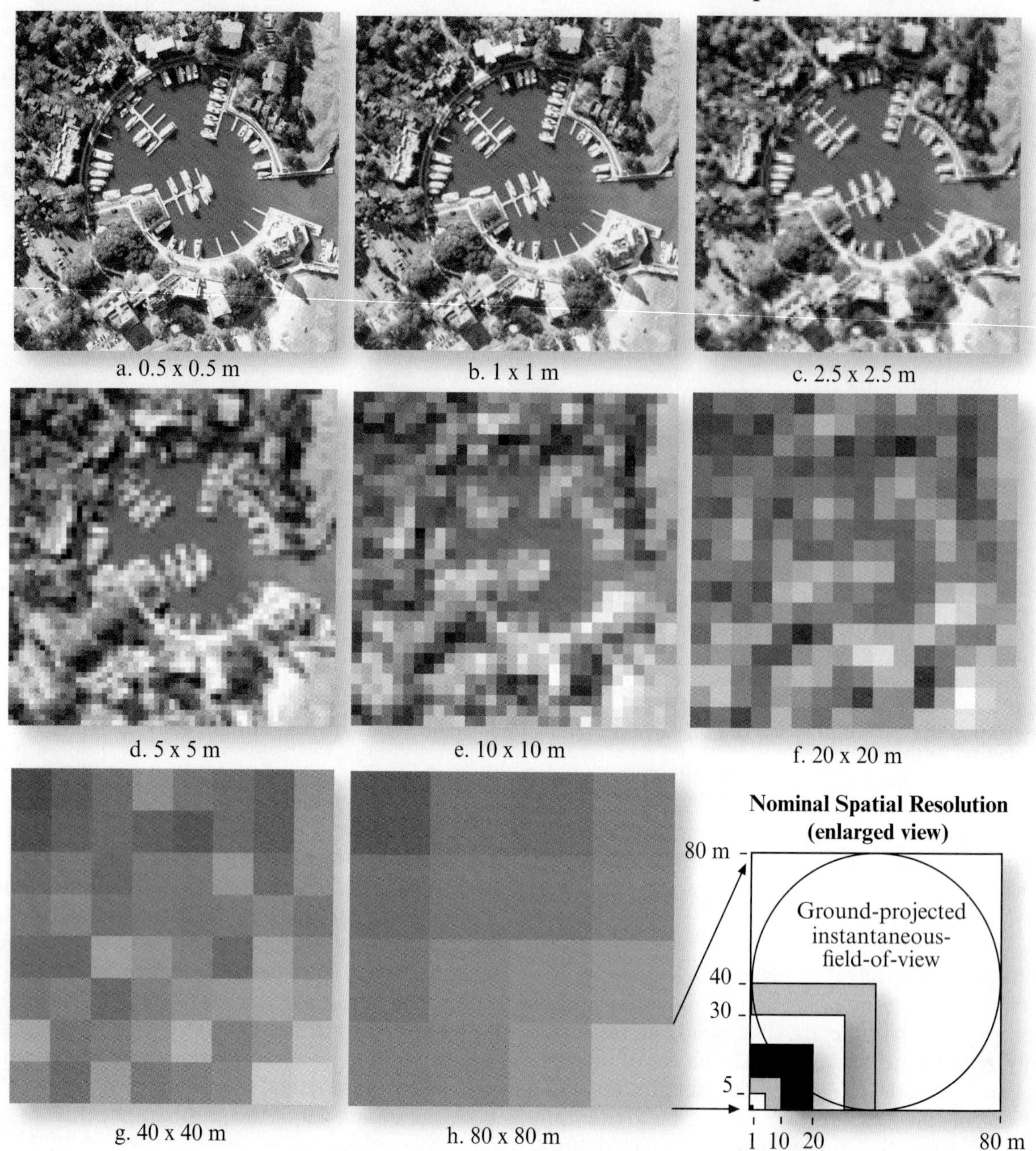

FIGURE 3–19 The original Harbor Town, SC, image was collected at a nominal spatial resolution of 0.3 × 0.3 m (approximately 1 × 1 ft.) using a digital frame camera. The original imagery was resampled to derive the imagery with the simulated spatial resolutions shown.

or 30 × 30 m, etc. For example, DigitalGlobe's QuickBird has a nominal spatial resolution of 61 × 61 cm for its panchromatic band and 2.44 × 2.44 m for the four multispectral bands. The Landsat 7 Enhanced Thematic Mapper Plus (ETM^+) has a nominal spatial resolution of 15 × 15 m for its panchromatic band and 30 × 30 m for six of its multispectral bands. Generally, the smaller the nominal spatial resolution, the greater the spatial resolving power of the remote sensing system.

Figure 3-19 depicts digital camera imagery of an area in Hilton Head, SC, at resolutions ranging from 0.5 × 0.5 m to 80 × 80 m. Note that there is not a significant difference in the interpretability of 0.5 × 0.5 m data, 1 × 1 m data, or even 2.5 × 2.5 m data. However, the urban spatial information content decreases rapidly when using 5 × 5 m imagery and is practically useless for urban analysis at spatial resolutions greater than 10 × 10 m. This is the reason historical Landsat MSS data

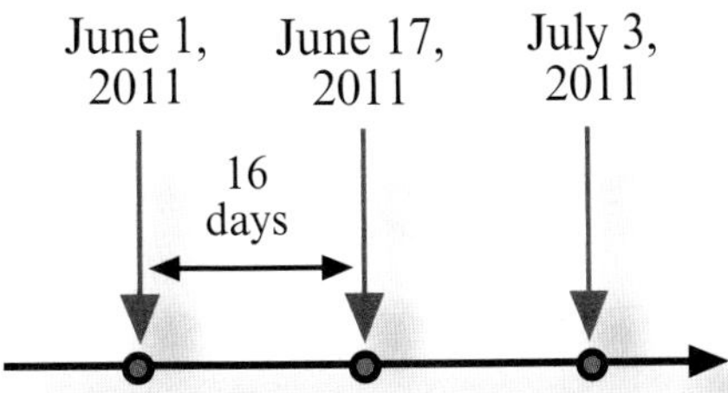

FIGURE 3–20 The temporal resolution of a remote sensing system refers to how often it records imagery of a particular area. This example depicts the systematic collection of remote sensor data every 16 days, presumably at approximately the same time of day. NASA Landsat Thematic Mappers 4 and 5 had 16-day revisit cycles. NOAA Geostationary Operational Environmental Satellites (GOES) collect new images every half-hour which are especially useful for monitoring storm events in near real-time.

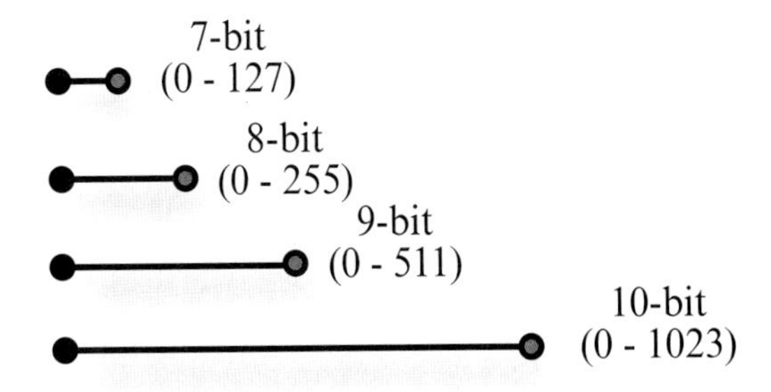

FIGURE 3–21 The radiometric resolution of a remote sensing system is the sensitivity of its detectors to differences in signal strength as they record the radiant flux reflected, emitted, or back-scattered from the terrain. The energy is normally quantized during an analog-to-digital conversion process to 8-, 9-, 10-bits or more.

(79 × 79 m) are of little value for most urban applications (Jensen and Cowen, 1999).

A useful rule of thumb is that in order to detect a feature of interest, the spatial resolution of the sensor should be less than one-half the size of the feature measured in its smallest dimension. For example, if you wanted to identify all the oak trees in a park, the minimum acceptable spatial resolution would be approximately one-half the diameter of the smallest oak tree's crown. Even this spatial resolution, however, will not guarantee success if there is no difference between the spectral response of the oak tree (the object) and the soil or grass surrounding it (i.e., its background).

Some sensor systems, such as LiDAR, do not completely "map" the terrain surface. Rather, the surface is "sampled" using laser pulses sent from the aircraft at some nominal time interval (Raber et al., 2002). The ground-projected laser pulse may be very small (e.g., 10 to 15 cm in diameter) with samples spaced approximately every 1 to 6 m on the ground. Spatial resolution would appropriately describe the ground-projected laser pulse (e.g., 15 cm) but sampling density would describe the number of laser returns per square meter (Hodgson et al., 2003; 2005).

Temporal Information and Resolution

A remotely sensed image is recorded at a unique moment in time. Multiple records of the same landscape obtained through time can be used to identify processes at work, identify change, and to make predictions. The **temporal resolution** of a remote sensing system generally refers to how often the sensor records imagery of a particular area. The temporal resolution of the sensor system shown in Figure 3-20 is every 16 days. Ideally, the sensor obtains data repetitively to capture unique discriminating characteristics of the object under investigation (Jensen, 2007). For example, agricultural crops have unique phenological cycles in each geographic region. To measure specific agricultural variables, it is necessary to acquire imagery at critical dates in the phenological cycle. Change information provides insight into processes influencing the development of the crop (Jensen et al., 2002). Fortunately, several satellite sensor systems such as SPOT, IKONOS, ImageSat, and QuickBird are pointable, meaning that they can acquire imagery off-nadir. Nadir is the point directly below the spacecraft. This increases the probability that imagery will be obtained during a growing season or during an emergency.

Radiometric Resolution

Some remote sensing systems record electromagnetic radiation with more precision than others. **Radiometric resolution** is the sensitivity of a remote sensing detector to differences in signal strength as it records the radiant flux reflected, emitted, or back-scattered from the terrain. It defines the number of just discriminable signal levels. The Landsat 1 Multispectral Scanner launched in 1972 recorded reflected energy with a precision of 6-bits (values ranged from 0 to 63). Landsat 4 and 5 Thematic Mapper sensors launched in 1982 and 1984, respectively, recorded data in 8-bits (values from 0 to 255) (Figure 3-21). Thus, the Landsat TM sensors had improved radiometric resolution (sensitivity) when compared with the original Landsat MSS. QuickBird and IKONOS sensors record data in 11-bits (values from 0 to 2,047). High radiometric resolution generally increases the probability that phenomena will be remotely sensed more accurately.

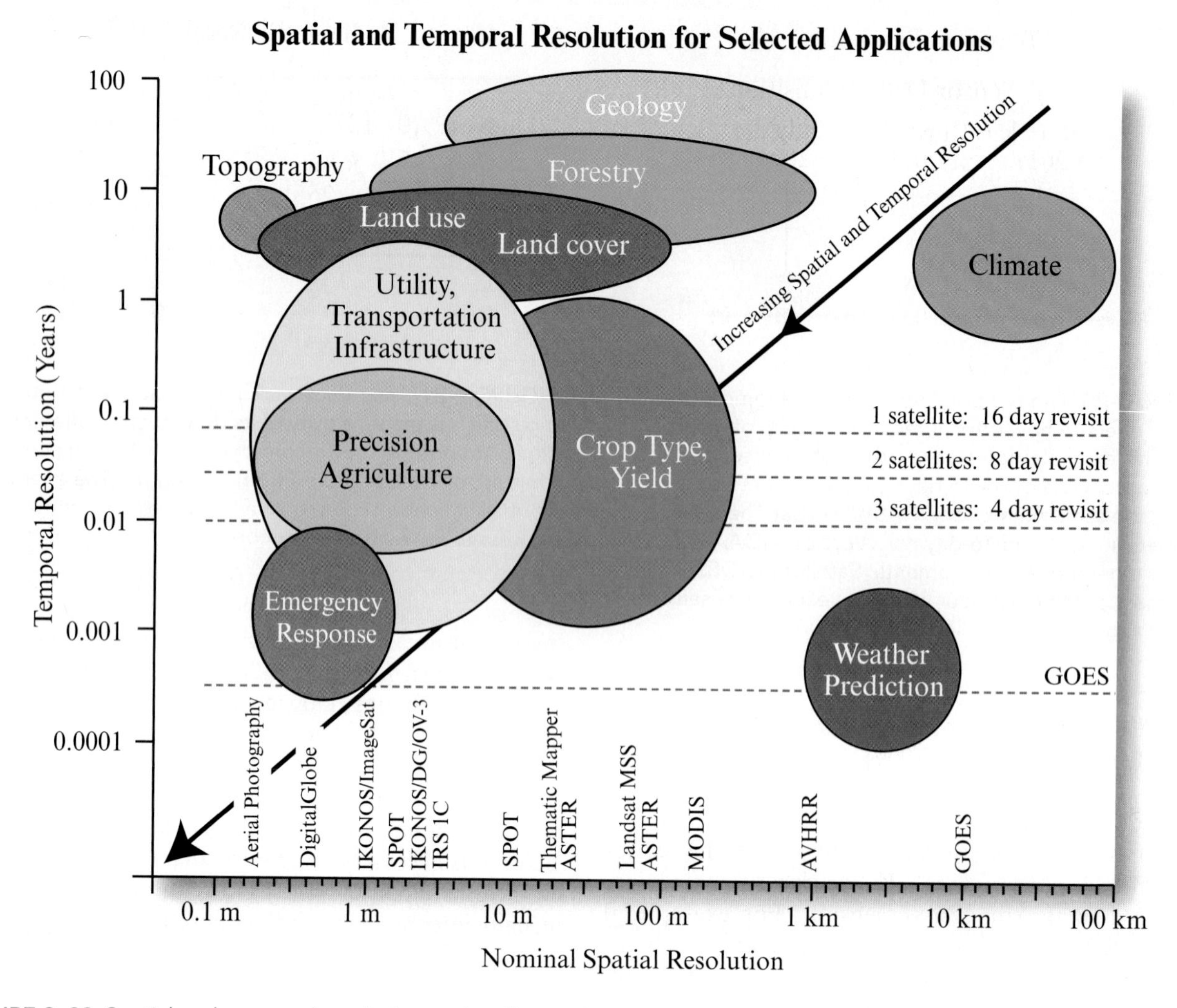

FIGURE 3–22 Spatial and temporal resolution trade-offs must be made when collecting remote sensor data for selected applications. For example, applications such as land use mapping generally require high spatial resolution imagery (e.g., 1 to 5 m) at relatively low temporal resolution (e.g., 1 to 10 years). Conversely, for weather prediction we are generally content with lower spatial resolution imagery (e.g., 5 x 5 km) if it can be collected frequently (e.g., every half-hour).

Trade-offs between Spatial and Temporal Resolution

There are often trade-offs associated with the various resolutions that must be decided upon when collecting remote sensing data (Figure 3-22). Generally, the higher the temporal resolution requirement (e.g., monitoring hurricanes every half-hour), the lower the spatial resolution requirement (e.g., the NOAA GOES weather satellite records images with 4 × 4 to 8 × 8 km pixels). Conversely, the higher the spatial resolution requirement (e.g., monitoring urban land-use with 1 × 1 m data), the lower the temporal resolution requirement (e.g., every 1 to 5 years). Some applications such as agricultural crop type or yield estimation might require relatively high temporal resolution data (e.g., multiple images obtained during a growing season) and moderate spatial resolution data (e.g., 80 × 80 m pixels). Transportation studies and emergency response applications may require very high spatial (e.g., 0.5 × 0.5 m) and high temporal resolution (e.g., daily) data collection which generates tremendous amounts of data.

Polarization Information

The polarization characteristics of electromagnetic energy recorded by a remote sensing system are important variables that can be used in many Earth resource investigations. Sunlight is polarized weakly. However, when sunlight strikes a non-metallic object (e.g., grass, forest, or concrete) it becomes depolarized and the incident energy is scattered differentially. Generally, the more smooth the surface, the greater the polarization. It is possible to use polarizing filters on aerial cameras to record polarized light at various angles. It is also possible to selectively send and receive polarized energy using active sensor systems such as RADAR (e.g., horizontal send, vertical receive – HV; vertical send, horizontal receive – VH; vertical send, vertical receive – VV; horizontal send, horizontal receive – HH). Multiple-polarized RADAR imagery is an especially useful application of polarized energy.

Angular Information

Remote sensors record specific angular characteristics associated with each exposed silver halide crystal or pixel. The angular characteristics are a function of:

- the location of the illumination source (e.g., the Sun for a passive system or the sensor itself in the case of RADAR, LiDAR, and SONAR), and
- the orientation of the terrain facet (pixel) or terrain cover (e.g., vegetation) under investigation.

There is always an angle of incidence associated with the incoming energy that illuminates the terrain and an angle of exitance from the terrain to the sensor system. This bidirectional nature of remote sensing data collection influences the spectral and polarization characteristics of the at-sensor radiance, *L*, recorded by the remote sensing system. Viewing the same terrain from two different angles introduces stereoscopic parallax, which is the foundation for all stereoscopic photogrammetric and radargrammetric analysis.

Remote Sensing Terminology

The primary remote sensing systems used to obtain analog and digital aerial photography and multispectral and hyperspectral imagery are shown in Figure 3-23. Remote sensor data may be obtained using analog (e.g., film) and digital remote sensing systems. Digital remote sensor data are usually stored as a matrix (array) of numbers. Each digital value is located at a specific row (*i*) and column (*j*) in the matrix (Figure 3-24). A **pixel** is defined as a 2-dimensional picture element that is the smallest nondivisible element of a digital image. Each pixel at row (*i*) and column (*j*) in the image has an original brightness value (*BV*) associated with it. Some scientists call it a digital number (*DN*) value. The dataset may consist of *n* individual bands, each band denoted as (*k*) in the multispectral or hyperspectral imagery. Thus, it is possible to identify the brightness value (*BV*) of a particular pixel in the dataset by specifying its row (*i*), column (*j*), and band (*k*) coordinate, i.e., $BV_{i,j,k}$. It is important to understand that the *n* bands are all geometrically registered to one another. Therefore, a road intersection in band 1 at row 4, column 4 (i.e., $BV_{4,4,1}$) should be located at the same row and column coordinate in the fourth band (i.e., $BV_{4,4,4}$). Ideally, the brightness values at the two locations are different; otherwise, the information content of the two images at that location is redundant.

The analog-to-digital conversion that takes place onboard the sensor system usually creates pixels with a range of 8 to 12 bits. This is called the radiometric resolution or quantization level of the remote sensor data. As previously mentioned, the greater the range of possible brightness values, the more precise we may be able to measure the amount of radiance recorded by the detector. One can think of quantization as if it were a ruler. We can obtain more accurate measurements of an object using a ruler that has 1,024 subdivisions (e.g., 10-bit data) than with a ruler that only has 256 subdivisions (e.g., 8-bit data).

Aerial Photography

Both analog (film) and digital aerial photography are obtained using high-quality, metric cameras that obtain aerial photographs along a flightline (Figure 3-23ab). The aerial photographs usually have 60% endlap and 30% sidelap. This results in a block of aerial photography covering the study area of interest. The 60% endlap introduces stereoscopic parallax which allows stereoscopic analysis to take place and is the basis for photogrammetric information extraction. A high proportion of the land use and land cover information processed in most GIS are extracted from analog or digital aerial photography.

Analog Vertical Aerial Photography

Analog vertical aerial photography uses film with various emulsions and special filters. The three major types of film are: 1) black & white panchromatic, 2) normal color, and 3) color-infrared film. Table 3-5 summarizes several of the characteristics of normal color aerial photography and color-infrared aerial photography. For example, an object that is pure red in reality (i.e., the object reflects lots of red light but very little blue and green light) will appear red on normal color film. Conversely, the same pure red object will appear green in the false-color, color-infrared film (assuming it does not reflect near-infrared energy). Vegetation reflects a substantial amount of near-infrared energy and relatively little green and red light. Therefore, healthy vegetation appears red in false-color, color-infrared film. Many of the older analog (film) cameras are being replaced with digital frame cameras.

Digital Vertical Aerial Photography

Most city, county, state, and federal agencies now request digital aerial photography that can easily be turned into orthophotography. An **orthophotograph** is a special type of vertical airphoto with the geometric distortion and the effects of relief displacement removed. An orthophotograph has all the geometric qualities of a planimetric map and the spectral detail found in the vertical aerial photograph. Distances and angles can be accurately measured using orthophotography. Orthophotography in a standard map projection can be easily ingested into geographic information systems. Orthophotography is one of the framework

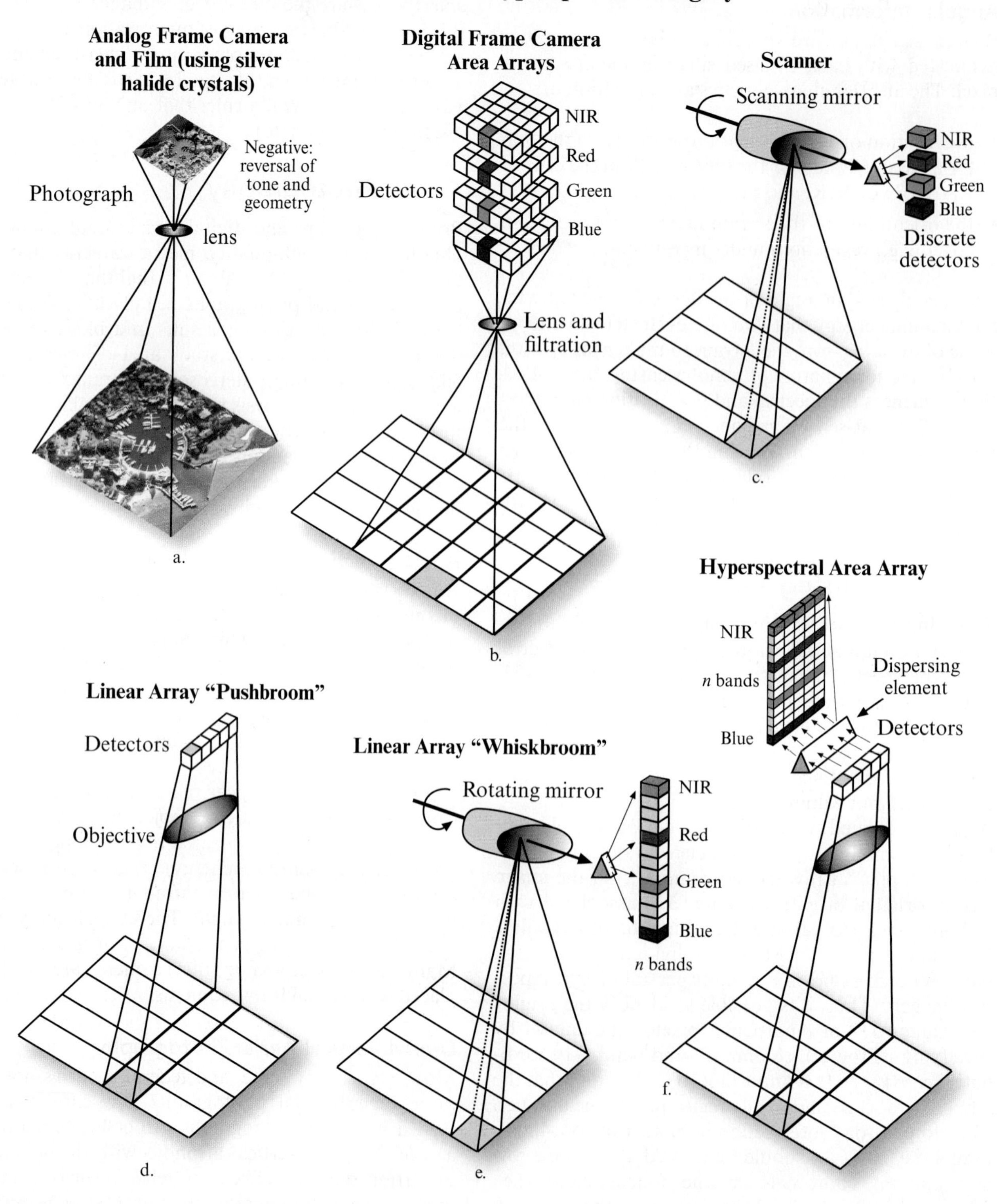

FIGURE 3–23 Six types of remote sensing systems used for multispectral and hyperspectral data collection: a) traditional analog (film) aerial photography, b) digital frame camera aerial photography based on area arrays, c) imaging using a scanning mirror and discrete detectors, d) multispectral imaging using linear arrays (often referred to as "pushbroom" technology), e) imaging with a scanning mirror and linear arrays (often referred to as "whiskbroom" technology), and f) imaging spectrometry using linear and area arrays.

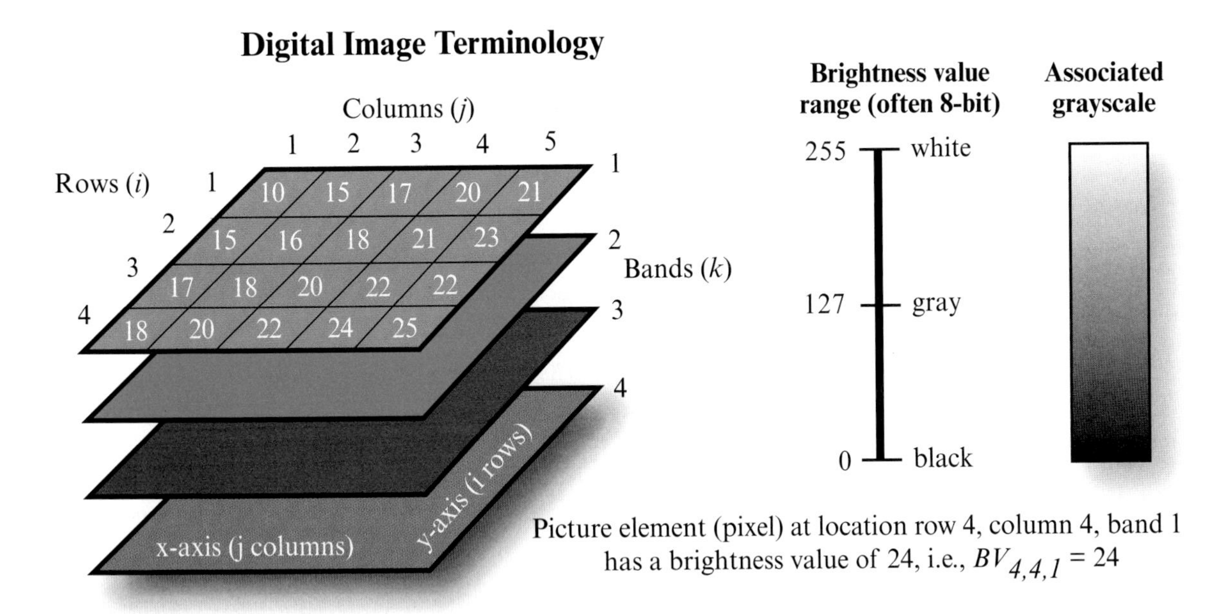

FIGURE 3–24 Digital remote sensor data are stored in a matrix format. Picture element (pixel) brightness values (*BV*) are located at row *i*, column *j*, and band *k* in the multispectral or hyperspectral dataset. The digital remote sensor brightness values are normally stored as 8-bit bytes with values ranging from 0 to 255. However, some remote sensing systems now routinely collect 10-, 11-, or 12-bit data.

datasets of the National Spatial Data Infrastructure discussed in Chapter 1. Large-scale normal color and color-infrared orthophotography of Beaufort, SC, are shown in Figure 3-25.

The U.S. Department of Agriculture contracts with photogrammetric firms to collect either 1 x 1 or 2 x 2 m spatial resolution digital aerial photography for most of the agricultural land in the United States every year or two during the growing season as part of its National Agriculture Imagery Program (NAIP). This program has been so successful that the National States Geographic Information Council (NSGIC) and other groups have proposed the *Imagery for the Nation Program* whereby 6 x 6 in., 1 x 1 ft., and 1 x 1 m digital aerial photography may be collected for the entire nation (including urbanized areas) every 1 to 3 years, often during leaf-off periods. Detailed characteristics of the proposed *Imagery for the Nation* are summarized in Table 3-6. Most of the aerial photography will be turned into orthophotography.

Digital Oblique Aerial Photography

Sometimes people feel more comfortable looking at and analyzing oblique aerial photography rather than vertical aerial photography (Figure 3-26). Several vendors now provide users with the option of obtaining vertical as well as oblique aerial photography. For example, Pictometry International, Inc., uses a five-camera arrangement whereby every time a vertical aerial photograph is collected, four additional oblique photographs are obtained in the North, East, South, and West directions (Pictometry, 2011). Because the flightlines overlap by 20 to 30 percent, this allows each feature in the landscape such as a building to be recorded and viewed from many different vantage points. The image analyst can simply select the view that is most pleasing and provides the most useful thematic information. Pictometry aerial photography of a portion of Columbia, SC, is shown in Figure 3-26. Innovations in digital image processing make it possible to register the oblique aerial photography in a GIS where horizontal and vertical measurements of structures and the terrain can be made while viewing the oblique photography.

Multispectral Remote Sensing

Multispectral remote sensing is the collection of remote sensor data in multiple bands of the electromagnetic spectrum. So, technically speaking, all color and color-infrared aerial photography are really multispectral remote sensing products. Most multispectral remote sensing systems strive to collect imagery with several bands in the optical portion of the spectrum (e.g., blue, green, red, and near-infrared), in the middle-infrared, and sometimes in the thermal-infrared regions. Four of the most important satellite multispectral remote sensing systems are:

- NASA's Landsat MSS and Thematic Mapper sensor systems,
- the French SPOT system,

TABLE 3–5 Spectral sensitivity characteristics of normal color and color-infrared aerial photography.

	Spectral Sensitivity			
Type of Aerial Photography	**Blue 400 – 500 nm**	**Green 500 – 600 nm**	**Red 600 – 700 nm**	**Near-infrared 700 – 1100 nm**
Natural Color Film	Yes	Yes	Yes	No sensitivity
Color appearance in image	Blue	Green	Red	None recorded
Color-infrared Film – filtered with a yellow (minus-blue) filter	Not sensitive to blue light when a yellow filter is used	Yes	Yes	Yes
Color appearance in image		Blue	Green	Red

FIGURE 3–25 a) Natural color vertical aerial orthophotography obtained in 2007 at a spatial resolution of 0.25 x 0.25 m (RGB = red, green, and blue bands). b) Color-infrared aerial orthophotography (RGB = near-infrared, red, and green bands) (photography courtesy of Beaufort County GIS).

Pictometry
Digital Aerial Photography
of Columbia, SC

Photography was obtained
from multiple flightlines

FIGURE 3–26 Natural color vertical and oblique aerial photography of the Strom Thurmond Wellness Center in Columbia, SC, obtained at four cardinal directions (North, East, South, West) and at Nadir (i.e., vertical). The nominal spatial resolution was 6 x 6 in. (photography courtesy of Pictometry International, Inc).

- the IKONOS-2 and GeoEye-1 systems by GeoEye, Inc., and
- QuickBird and WorldView-2 by DigitalGlobe, Inc.

Characteristics of these multispectral remote sensing systems are summarized in Table 3-7.

Landsat

The United States has progressed from multispectral scanning systems (Landsat MSS launched in 1972) to more advanced scanning systems (Landsat 7 Enhanced Thematic Mapper Plus launched in 1999). A diagram of how a scanning system functions is shown in Figure 3-23c. A mirror scans the terrain perpendicular to the direction of flight. Electromagnetic energy reflected or emitted from within the IFOV of the sensor system is projected onto a bank of detectors. An analog-to-digital conversion transforms the electrical measurements into radiance ($W\ m^{-2}\ sr^{-1}$).

The Land Remote Sensing Policy Act of 1992 specified the future of satellite land remote sensing programs in the United States. Unfortunately, Landsat 6 with its Enhanced Thematic Mapper did not achieve orbit when launched on October 5, 1993. Landsat 7 was launched on April 15, 1999, to relieve the United States' land remote sensing data gap. Unfortunately, Landsat 7 now has scan-line correction problems. A Landsat Data Continuity Mission is scheduled for launch sometime in the future.

SPOT Image, Inc. HRV

The French pioneered the development of linear array multispectral remote sensing technology with the launch of SPOT satellites 1 through 5 in 1986, 1990, 1993, 1998, and 2002. SPOT satellite characteristics are summarized in Table 3-7. Note the relatively high spatial resolution (e.g., 2.5 × 2.5 m) and the moderate spectral resolution. A diagram of how a linear array "pushbroom" remote sensing system functions is

TABLE 3–6 Characteristics of the proposed *Imagery for the Nation* program based on suborbital, vertical digital aerial photography.

Proposed *Imagery for the Nation* Program			
Federal Program Steward	**U.S. Geological Survey**	**U.S. Geological Survey**	**U.S. Dept. of Agriculture (except Alaska which is USGS)**
Nominal Spatial Resolution	6 in.	1 ft.	1 meter
Image Type	Natural color	Natural color	Natural color
Leaf Condition	Off	Off	On
Cloud Cover	0%	0%	10%
Orthophotography Horizontal Accuracy	2.5 ft. @ 95% NSSDA	5 ft. @ 95% NSSDA	25 ft. @ 95% NSSDA
Location and Threshold	U.S. Census Bureau Urbanized Areas with populations >50,000 and >1,000 people per square mile	Areas east of the *Mississippi River* and all counties west of the *Mississippi River* with >25 people per square mile	Entire nation, including all islands and territories, enhancing existing USDA NAIP program.
Frequency	Every 3 years	Every 3 years	- Every year in 48 states - Every 5 years in Alaska - Every 3 years in Hawaii, islands, and territories
Local Cost Share	50%	None	None
Buy-up Options Improvements over the standard base products can be selected by local, state, regional, and tribal agencies. *Buy-ups* require the organization to pay the differential costs above the standard base product for each buy-up requested.	1) 100% for CIR or 4-band data 2) 100% for > frequency 3) 100% for > footprint 4) 100% for > *x,y* accuracy 5) 100% for 3-inch resolution 6) 100% for improved elevation data products 7) 100% for removal of building lean (true orthophoto)	1) 100% for CIR or 4-band digital product 2) 100% for > frequency 3) 100% for > footprint 4) 100% for > *x,y* accuracy 5) 100% for 3-inch resolution 6) 100% for improved elevation data products 7) 100% for removal of building lean (i.e., the creation of a true orthophoto)	1) 100% for CIR or 4-band digital product 2) 100% for > frequency 3) 100% for > footprint

shown in Figure 3-23d. A linear array containing many detector elements (e.g., 3,000) is pointed at the terrain perpendicular to the direction of flight. Individual detector elements in the linear array record the amount of electromagnetic energy reflected or emitted from within each IFOV. Note that there are no moving parts such as a scanning mirror. This results in the collection of more geometrically accurate remote sensor data.

GeoEye, Inc. IKONOS-2 and GeoEye-1

Space Imaging, Inc. (now called GeoEye, Inc.) launched IKONOS-2 on September 24, 1999. The IKONOS-2 sensor system has an 1 × 1 m panchromatic band and four 3.28 × 3.28 m multispectral bands (Table 3-7). IKONOS-2 images of the World Trade Center obtained on June 30, 2000 and September 15, 2001 are shown in Figure 3-27. GeoEye-1 was launched on September 6, 2008. It has a 41 × 41 cm panchromatic band and four multispectral bands at 1.65 × 1.65 m spatial resolution (Table 3-7) (GeoEye, 2011).

DigitalGlobe, Inc. QuickBird and WorldView-2

DigitalGlobe, Inc., launched QuickBird on October 18, 2001, with a 61 × 61 cm panchromatic band and four 2.44 × 2.44 m multispectral bands (Table 3-7). DigitalGlobe launched WorldView-1 on September 18, 2007, with a 0.5 × 0.5 m panchromatic band. WorldView-2 was launched on October 8, 2009, with a 46 × 46 cm

IKONOS Imagery of the World Trade Center

a. June 30, 2000.

b. September 15, 2001.

FIGURE 3–27 Before and after IKONOS-2 satellite imagery of the World Trade Center. The spatial detail comes from the 1 × 1 m panchromatic data and the spectral (color) information comes from the 4 × 4 m multispectral data (satellite images courtesy of GeoEye, Inc.).

panchromatic band and eight multispectral bands at 1.85 × 1.85 m spatial resolution (DigitalGlobe, 2011).

NASA *Terra* and *Aqua* Multispectral Sensors

NASA's Earth Observing System (EOS) *Terra* satellite was launched on December 18, 1999. It contains five remote sensing instruments (MODIS, ASTER, MISR, CERES, and MOPITT). The EOS *Aqua* satellite was launched in May, 2002. One of the most interesting multispectral sensors onboard is the Multiangle Imaging SpectroRadiometer (MISR) which has nine separate charge-coupled device (CCD) pushbroom cameras to observe the Earth in four spectral bands and at nine view angles. It provides data on clouds, atmospheric aerosols, and multiple-angle views of the Earth's deserts, vegetation, and ice cover.

Hyperspectral Remote Sensing

Hyperspectral remote sensing systems collect data in tens to hundreds of bands in the electromagnetic spectrum often using the "whiskbroom" technology shown in Figure 3-23e. The NASA Jet Propulsion Laboratory (JPL) Airborne Visible Infrared Imaging Spectrometer (AVIRIS) collects 224 bands of hyperspectral data in this manner (NASA, 2011). An example of an AVIRIS hyperspectral datacube of Sullivan's Island, SC, is shown in Figure 3-28.

NASA's Moderate Resolution Imaging Spectrometer (MODIS) onboard the EOS *Terra* and *Aqua* satellites has 36 bands from 0.405 to 14.385 μm and collects data at 250 × 250 m, 500 × 500 m, and 1 × 1 km nominal spatial resolutions. MODIS views the entire surface of the Earth every one to two days, making observations in 36 spectral bands to inventory land and ocean surface temperature, primary productivity, land-surface cover, clouds, aerosols, water vapor, temperature profiles, and fires.

New hyperspectral remote sensing systems often use the combined linear and area array technology shown in Figure 3-23f. Energy detected from within each IFOV (e.g., pixel) along the linear array is dispersed using a prism onto an area array of detectors. The result is hyperspectral imagery with less geometric distortion (because there is no scanning mirror) and high radiometric fidelity because each detector along the linear array can dwell longer at each particular IFOV (e.g., pixel) on the Earth's surface. The Canadian Airborne

TABLE 3–7 Characteristics of several of the most widely used satellite multispectral remote sensing systems.

	Resolution			
Sensor	**Spatial (meters)**	**Spectral (micrometers, μm)**	**Temporal (days)**	**Radiometric (bits)**
Landsat (NASA)				
- Multispectral Scanner 1, 2 and 3	79 x 79	0.50 - 0.60	18	6
	79 x 79	0.60 - 0.70		
	79 x 79	0.70 - 0.80		
	79 x 79	0.80 - 1.10		
	240 x 240 (3)	10.4 - 12.6		
- Thematic Mapper 4 and 5, and Enhanced Thematic Mapper^{+} 7	15 x 15 PAN (7)	0.52 - 0.90	16	8
	30 x 30	0.45 - 0.52		
	30 x 30	0.52 - 0.60		
	30 x 30	0.63 - 0.69		
	30 x 30	0.76 - 0.90		
	30 x 30	1.55 - 1.75		
	120 (4,5), 60 (7)	10.4 - 12.5		
	30 x 30	2.08 - 2.35		
SPOT Image, Inc.				
- HRV 1, 2, 3 and HRVIR 4 and 5	10 x 10 PAN	0.51 - 0.73	Pointable	8
	10 x 10 PAN (4)	0.61 - 0.68		
	2.5 x 2.5 PAN (5)	0.48 - 0.71		
	20 x 20 (4); 10 x 10 (5)	0.50 - 0.59		
	20 x 20 (4); 10 x 10 (5)	0.61 - 0.68		
	20 x 20 (4); 10 x 10 (5)	0.79 - 0.89		
	20 x 20 (4,5)	1.58 - 1.75		
- Vegetation Sensor 4 and 5	1150 x 1150	0.50 - 0.59	1	8
	1150 x 1150	0.61 - 0.68		
	1150 x 1150	0.79 - 0.89		
	1150 x 1150	1.58 - 1.75		
GeoEye, Inc.				
- IKONOS-2 (1999)	1 x 1 PAN	0.526 - 0.929	Pointable	11
	3.28 x 3.28	0.445 - 0.516		
	3.28 x 3.28	0.506 - 0.595		
	3.28 x 3.28	0.632 - 0.698		
	3.28 x 3.28	0.757 - 0.853		
- GeoEye-1 (2008)	0.5 x 0.5 PAN	0.450 - 0.800		
	1.65 x 1.65	0.450 - 0.510		
	1.65 x 1.65	0.510 - 0.580		
	1.65 x 1.65	0.655 - 0.690		
	1.65 x 1.65	0.780 - 0.920		
DigitalGlobe, Inc.				
- QuickBird (2001)	0.61 x 0.61 PAN	0.405 - 1.053	Pointable	11
	2.44 x 2.44	0.430 - 0.545		
	2.44 x 2.44	0.466 - 0.620		
	2.44 x 2.44	0.590 - 0.710		
	2.44 x 2.44	0.715 - 0.918		
- WorldView 1 (2007)	0.50 x 0.50 PAN	0.40 - 0.90		
- WorldView 2 (2009)	0.46 x 0.46 PAN	0.45 - 0.80		
	1.85 x 1.85	0.40 - 0.45		
	1.85 x 1.85	0.45 - 0.51		
	1.85 x 1.85	0.51 - 0.58		
	1.85 x 1.85	0.585 - 0.625		
	1.85 x 1.85	0.630 - 0.690		
	1.85 x 1.85	0.705 - 0.745		
	1.85 x 1.85	0.770 - 0.895		
	1.85 x 1.85	0.860 - 1.040		

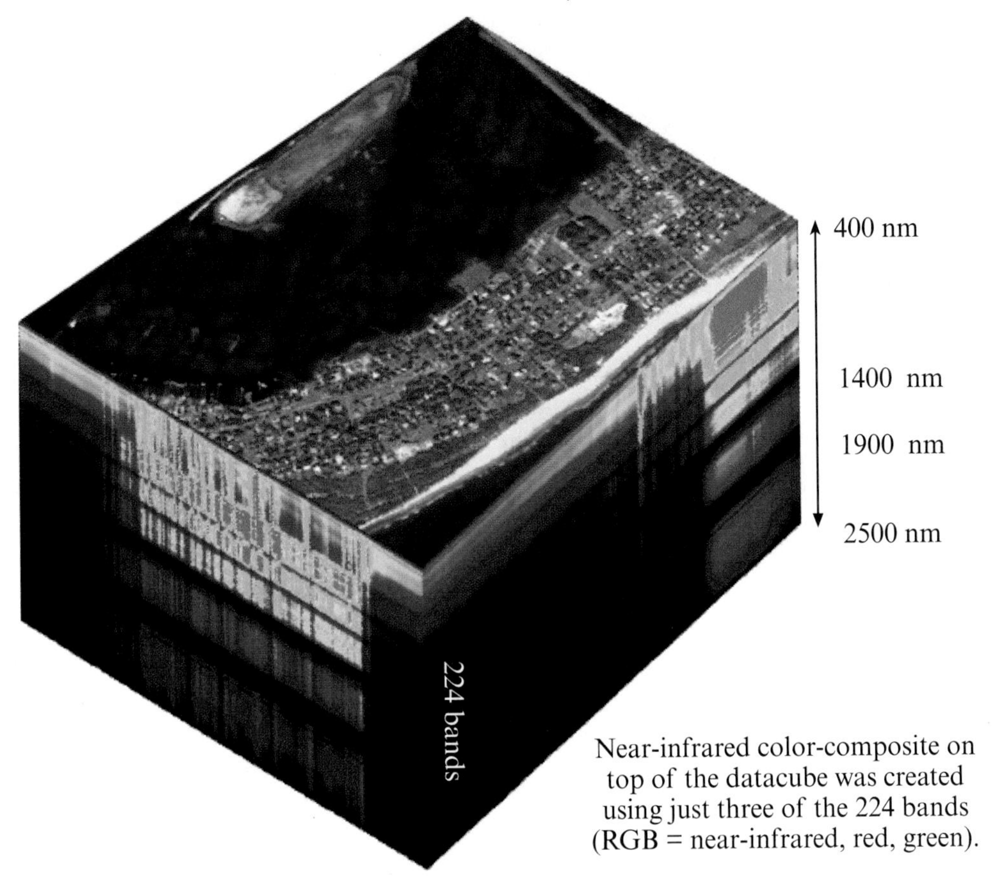

FIGURE 3–28 AVIRIS hyperspectral imagery of Sullivan's Island, SC, obtained on October 26, 1998. The spatial resolution was 3 × 3 m. The atmosphere absorbs most of the electromagnetic energy near 1,400 and 1,900 nm, causing the dark bands in the hyperspectral datacube.

Imaging Spectrometer (CASI-2) and the Australian HyMap systems use this technology.

Hyperspectral remote sensing systems mounted on aircraft provide high spatial and spectral resolution remotely sensed data. These sensors can collect data on demand when disaster strikes (e.g., oil spills or floods) if cloud-cover conditions permit (e.g., Karaska et al., 2004).

Thermal-infrared Remote Sensing

The temperature of an object is often one of its most diagnostic biophysical characteristics. For example, a human's temperature is so diagnostic that when it departs even slightly from 98.6°F, we often rush the person to the doctor. Water, vegetation, soils and rocks, snow and ice, and human structures all exhibit relatively predictable temperatures. When the temperatures of these objects change, it is often a signal that something important is happening.

It is time-consuming and tedious to walk about the terrain measuring the temperature of objects with a thermometer. Fortunately, it is possible to map the temperature of the terrain using thermal-infrared remote sensing systems. In fact, more GIS databases are including geospatial temperature information that are useful for a variety of applications, including: the identification of urban heat islands (Figure 3-29), the allocation of firefighting resources during a forest fire, residential and commercial heat-loss insulation studies, searching for missing persons or criminal activity, etc. Many government agencies (e.g., police, drug enforcement, immigration border-patrol officers) now routinely use hand-held thermal-infrared sensors or forward-looking infrared sensors (FLIR) mounted in aircraft. Thermal-infrared remote sensing will become more important in the future as additional orbital and suborbital sensors obtain thermal data and costs decrease.

Thermal-infrared Energy

All objects having a temperature above absolute zero (0 K; -273.16°C; -459.69°F) exhibit random motion.

a. Landsat 7 Enhanced Thematic Mapper Plus (ETM$^+$) image obtained on September 28, 2000 (RGB = bands 3,2,1; 30 x 30 m pixels).

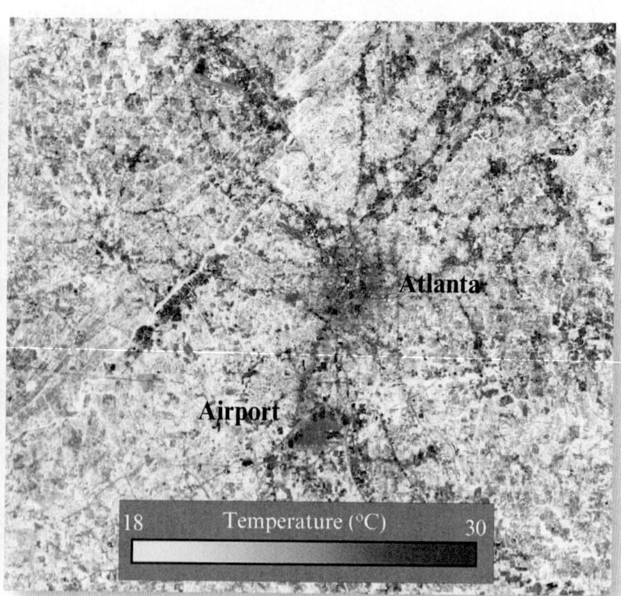

b. Temperature map derived from Landsat 7 ETM$^+$ thermal-infrared image.

FIGURE 3–29 a) Natural color image of Atlanta, GA, obtained by the Landsat 7 Enhanced Thematic Mapper Plus (ETM$^+$) sensor on September 28, 2000. b) A temperature map of the Atlanta, GA, urban heat island derived from the analysis of Landsat ETM$^+$ thermal-infrared imagery (courtesy of NASA Earth Observatory).

The energy of particles of molecular matter in random motion is called kinetic heat (also referred to as internal, real, or true heat). When these particles collide, they change their energy state and emit electromagnetic radiation. We can measure the true kinetic temperature (T_{kin}) or concentration of this heat using a thermometer. We perform in situ (in-place) temperature measurement by placing the thermometer in direct physical contact with a plant, soil, rock or water body.

Fortunately, an object's internal kinetic heat is also related to the amount of radiant energy leaving the object, which allows us to utilize remote sensing technology. The electromagnetic radiation exiting an object is called radiant flux (Φ) and is measured in Watts. The concentration of the amount of radiant flux exiting (emitted from) an object is its radiant temperature (T_{rad}). For most real-world objects (except those composed of glass and metal) there is usually a high positive correlation between the true kinetic temperature of the object (T_{kin}) and the amount of radiant flux radiated from the object (T_{rad}). Relationships such as these allow us to place thermal-infrared detectors some distance from an object to measure its radiant temperature, which ideally correlates well with the object's true kinetic temperature. This is the basis of remote sensing temperature measurement.

Remote Sensing Thermal Characteristics

Beyond the *visible* region of the electromagnetic spectrum from 0.4 – 0.7 μm, we encounter the *reflective infrared region* from 0.7 – 3 μm and the **thermal-infrared** *region* from 3 – 14 μm (Figure 3-30). The only reason we can use remote sensing instruments to detect infrared energy in the region from 3 – 14 μm is because the atmosphere allows a portion of the infrared energy to be transmitted from the terrain to the detectors. Regions that pass energy are called atmospheric windows. Conversely, the black areas in Figure 3-30 are regions of the electromagnetic spectrum in which the atmosphere absorbs most of the infrared energy present. These regions are called absorption bands. Water vapor (H_2O), carbon dioxide (CO_2), and ozone (O_3) are responsible for most of the absorption. The atmosphere "closes down," making it almost impossible to perform remote sensing of the environment in these regions. For example, atmospheric water vapor (H_2O) absorbs most of the energy exiting the terrain in the region from 5 – 7 μm, making it almost useless for thermal-infrared remote sensing. Fortunately, remote sensing instruments can be engineered to be sensitive to the infrared energy present within just the atmospheric windows. The region from 3 – 5 μm is used to measure the temperature of hot targets like forest fires. The region from 8 – 14 μm is used to measure the typi-

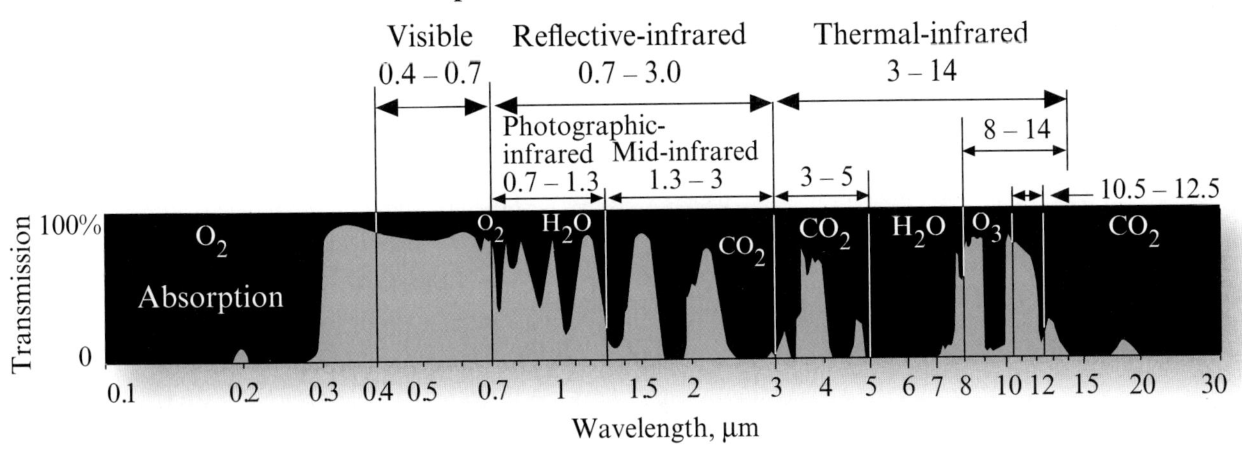

FIGURE 3–30 Atmospheric windows in the electromagnetic spectrum shown here are of significant value for remote sensing reflective and thermal-infrared energy. Photographic films can be made sensitive to reflective energy from 0.4 – 1.3 μm. Electro-optical sensing systems can record infrared energy from 0.4 – 14 μm. The 3 – 5 μm region is especially useful for monitoring hot targets such as forest fires and geothermal activity. Vegetation, soil, and rock thermal characteristics are best monitored using the 8 – 14 μm region for suborbital data collection. The 10.5 – 12.5 μm region is used when thermal imagery is acquired from orbital sensors above the Earth's ozone layer.

cal temperature of soils, rocks, water, and urban-suburban phenomena.

The basic principles of operation and components of a thermal-infrared across-track scanning system are shown in Figure 3-31. The diameter of the circular ground area viewed by the sensor, D, is a function of the instantaneous-field-of-view, β, of the scanner measured in milliradians and the altitude of the scanner above ground level, H (refer to Equation 3-1).

The mirror scans the terrain at a right angle (perpendicular) to the direction of flight. The mirror also views internal hot and cold calibration sources (targets) during each scan. The exact temperature of these calibration sources is known.

Photons of thermal-infrared radiant flux, Φ, emitted by the terrain, are routed to a mirror that focuses the photons onto the detector. The detector converts the incoming radiant energy into an analog electrical signal. The greater the number of photons impacting the detector, the greater the signal strength. The most commonly used infrared detectors are:

- *In:Sb* (indium antimonide) with a peak sensitivity near 5 μm for measuring hot targets in the 3 – 5 μm region; and
- *Ge:Hg* (mercury-doped germanium) with a peak sensitivity near 10 μm; or *Hg:Cd:Te* (mercury-cadmium-telluride) sensitive from 8 – 14 μm.

Many agencies now use forward-looking infrared (FLIR) sensors that focus emitted thermal-infrared radiation from the terrain onto an array (matrix) of heat-sensitive detectors.

NASA's EOS Advanced Spaceborne Thermal Emission and Reflection Radiometer (*ASTER*) is one of the most useful satellite thermal-infrared remote sensing systems. It has five bands in the thermal-infrared region between 8 and 12 μm with 90 × 90 m spatial resolution. It also has three broad bands between 0.5 and 0.9 μm with 15 × 15 m pixels and stereo capability and six bands in the shortwave-infrared region (1.6 – 2.5 μm) with 30 × 30 m spatial resolution. ASTER is the highest spatial resolution sensor system on the EOS *Terra* platform and provides detailed information on surface temperature.

The first hyperspectral thermal sensor was the Canadian Thermal Airborne Spectrographic Imager 600 (TASI), which uses linear array pushbroom technology to collect 32 bands in the electromagnetic spectrum from 8 – 11.5 μm (ITRES, 2006).

It is important to remember that you should not interpret a thermal-infrared image as if it were an aerial photograph or multispectral image. Cameras and multispectral sensors normally record *reflected* short-wavelength energy from the terrain. Conversely, thermal-infrared images record *emitted* long-wavelength radiant energy from the terrain. To interpret a thermal-infrared image one must think thermally, i.e., why is this object emitting more energy than a nearby object? To think thermally, the analyst must be aware of several thermal radiometric principles that are beyond the

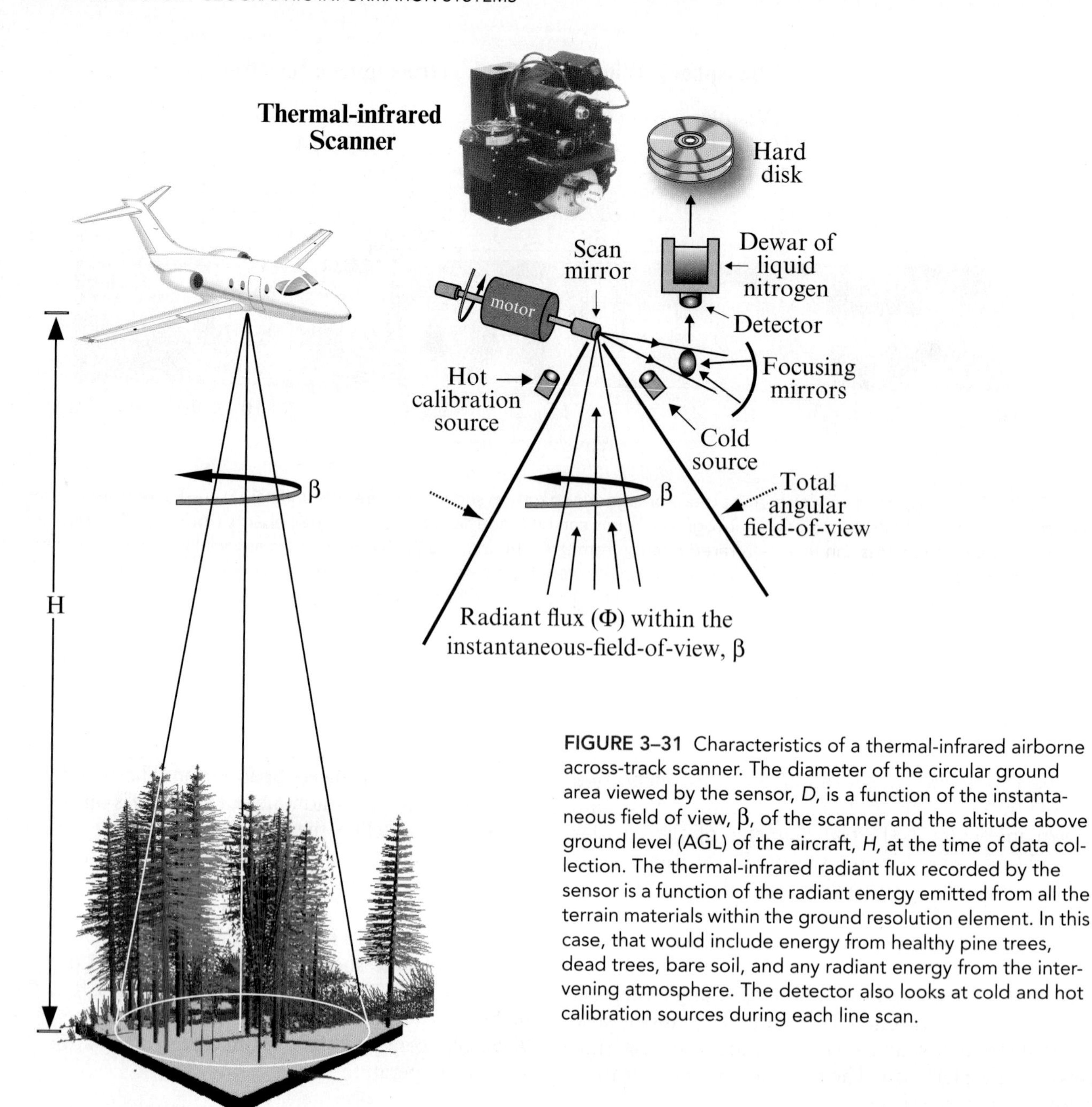

FIGURE 3–31 Characteristics of a thermal-infrared airborne across-track scanner. The diameter of the circular ground area viewed by the sensor, *D*, is a function of the instantaneous field of view, β, of the scanner and the altitude above ground level (AGL) of the aircraft, *H*, at the time of data collection. The thermal-infrared radiant flux recorded by the sensor is a function of the radiant energy emitted from all the terrain materials within the ground resolution element. In this case, that would include energy from healthy pine trees, dead trees, bare soil, and any radiant energy from the intervening atmosphere. The detector also looks at cold and hot calibration sources during each line scan.

scope of this book such as emissivity, the Stefan-Boltzmann Law, Wein's Displacement Law, and the diurnal temperature characteristics of materials. Please refer to the thermal-infrared remote sensing chapter in Jensen (2007) for additional information.

LiDAR Remote Sensing

One of the most important advances in remote sensing has been the development of **LiDAR** (light detection and ranging) technology. LiDAR has revolutionized our ability to obtain accurate digital surface models (DSMs) that contain detailed *x*, *y*, and *z* location information about buildings, vegetation (trees, shrubs, grass), telephone poles, etc. In addition, innovative vegetation removal algorithms have been developed that produce detailed bare-Earth digital terrain models (DTMs). According to the National Research Council, LiDAR is now the sensor of choice for the creation of high resolution DTMs, especially for FEMA-related floodplain mapping (Maidment et al., 2007). Many GIS databases contain bare-Earth DTMs derived from LiDAR data.

Laser Remote Sensing

The LiDAR remote sensing instrument consists of a controller and a laser transmitter and receiver. As the aircraft moves forward along the line-of-flight, a scanning mirror directs pulses of laser light across-track perpendicular to the line-of-flight (Figure 3-32a).

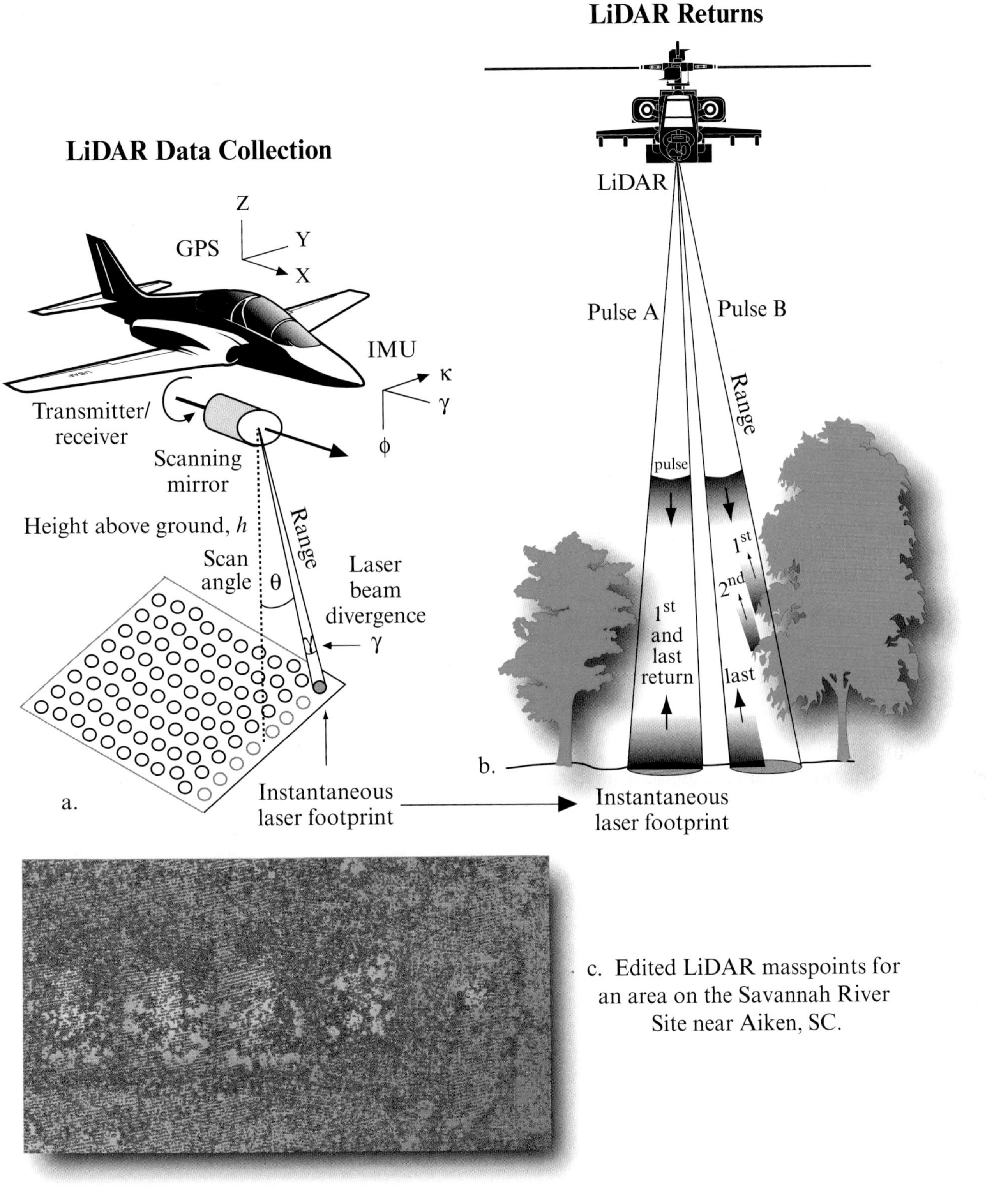

FIGURE 3–32 a) A LiDAR remote sensing instrument transmits pulses of laser light toward the ground using a scanning mirror. Some of this energy is scattered back toward the aircraft and recorded by the receiver electronics. Onboard GPS and an Inertial Measurement Unit (IMU) document the exact location of the aircraft and the roll, pitch, and yaw at the instant the laser pulse is sent and received. b) Multiple returns may be generated from a single pulse of laser light. In this example, the first and last return from pulse A represent the bare-Earth. There are three returns from pulse B; two from tree branches and one from the bare-Earth. The intensity of each return is a function of the amount of energy back-scattered toward the LiDAR. c) An example of individual LiDAR masspoints obtained from multiple flightlines over the Savannah River Site.

LiDAR systems for topographic mapping use eye-safe, near-infrared laser light (1040 to 1060 nm). Blue-green lasers centered at approximately 532 nm are used for bathymetric mapping due to their water penetration capability. LiDAR data can be collected at night if desired because it is an active system that is not dependent on sunlight. LiDAR systems can emit pulses at rates >200,000 pulses per second. This is the equivalent of sending 200,000 surveyors into the field every second to obtain an accurate *x, y,* and *z* measurement.

A pulse of laser light travels at *c*, the speed of light (3×10^8 m s^{-1}). LiDAR technology is based on the accurate measurement of the laser pulse travel time from the transmitter to the terrain and back to the receiver. The range measurement process results in the collection of elevation data points (called **masspoints**) arranged systematically in time across the flightline (Figure 3-32a). The laser footprint is approximately circular on the ground and varies with the scan angle and the topography encountered. LiDAR data are collected along with a) aircraft location information obtained from the onboard GPS unit, and b) aircraft roll, pitch, and yaw information obtained from the Inertial Measurement Unit (IMU) at the exact instant that each laser pulse is sent and received.

Each laser pulse illuminates a near-circular area on the ground called the instantaneous laser footprint, e.g., 30 cm in diameter (Figure 3-32a). A single pulse can generate one return or multiple returns. Figure 3-32b depicts how multiple returns might be produced from a single pulse. The energy within laser pulse *A* interacts with the ground. One might assume that this would generate a single return. However, if there are any materials whatsoever with local relief within the instantaneous laser footprint (e.g., grass, small rocks, twigs), then there may be multiple returns. The *first-return* will come from these materials that have local relief (even on the order of 3 to 5 cm) and the *second-return* and perhaps *last-return* will come from the bare-Earth. Although not identical, the range (distance) associated with the first- and last-returns would be very similar.

Conversely, laser pulse *B* encounters two parts of a tree at different elevations and then the bare-Earth. In the example, part of pulse *B* encounters a branch at 3 m AGL, causing some of the incident laser pulse to be back-scattered toward the LiDAR receiver. This is recorded as the *first-return* (Figure 3-32b). The remainder of the pulse continues until at 2 m AGL it hits another branch that scatters some energy back toward the LiDAR receiver. This is recorded by the LiDAR receiver as the *second-return*. In this example, approximately one-half of the pulse finally reaches the ground, and some of it is back-scattered toward the LiDAR receiver. This is the *last-return*. If we wanted information about the height of the tree and its structural characteristics then we would be interested in the first- and second-returns associated with pulse *B*. If we are only interested in creating a bare-Earth digital terrain model then we would be very interested in the last-returns associated with pulses *A* and *B*.

Thus, each laser pulse transmitted from an aircraft can yield multiple returns. This is referred to as *multiple-return LiDAR* data. Post-processing the original data results in several LiDAR data files commonly referred to as:

- first-return,
- intermediate-returns,
- last-return, and
- intensity.

Each of the individual masspoints in each of these files consists of the following information: time of day, *x*-coordinate, *y*-coordinate, *z*-coordinate, and intensity.

The masspoints associated with each return file (e.g., first return) are distributed throughout the landscape at various densities depending upon the scan angle, the number of pulses per second transmitted (e.g., 200,000 pps), aircraft speed, and the materials that the laser pulses encounter (Young, 2011). Areas on the ground that do not yield any LiDAR-return data are called data voids.

Extraction of Digital Surface Models (DSMs)

Masspoints associated with the last-returns from a LiDAR mission flown over the Savannah River Site on October 10, 2004, are shown in Figure 3-32c. Each masspoint has a unique *x*, *y* and *z* location. The individual masspoints are usually processed using inverse-distance-weighting (IDW) interpolation to create a raster (grid) of elevation values or the masspoints may be processed to create a triangular-irregular-network (TIN). The interpolation process creates a digital surface model (DSM) which contains the elevation characteristics of all the trees, shrubs, and man-made structures. The brighter the pixel in the DSM, the greater the elevation. For example, the buildings in the first return LiDAR data shown in Figure 3-33a are higher than the surrounding ground, therefore the buildings are brighter than the ground.

The LiDAR-derived inverse-distance-weighted DSM can be made even easier to interpret by applying a shaded-relief algorithm that highlights the terrain as if it were illuminated by the Sun from a specific direction (e.g., from the northwest). An example is presented in Figure 3-33d. The last-return digital surface model for the same area is shown in Figure 3-33b and in shaded-relief format in Figure 3-33e.

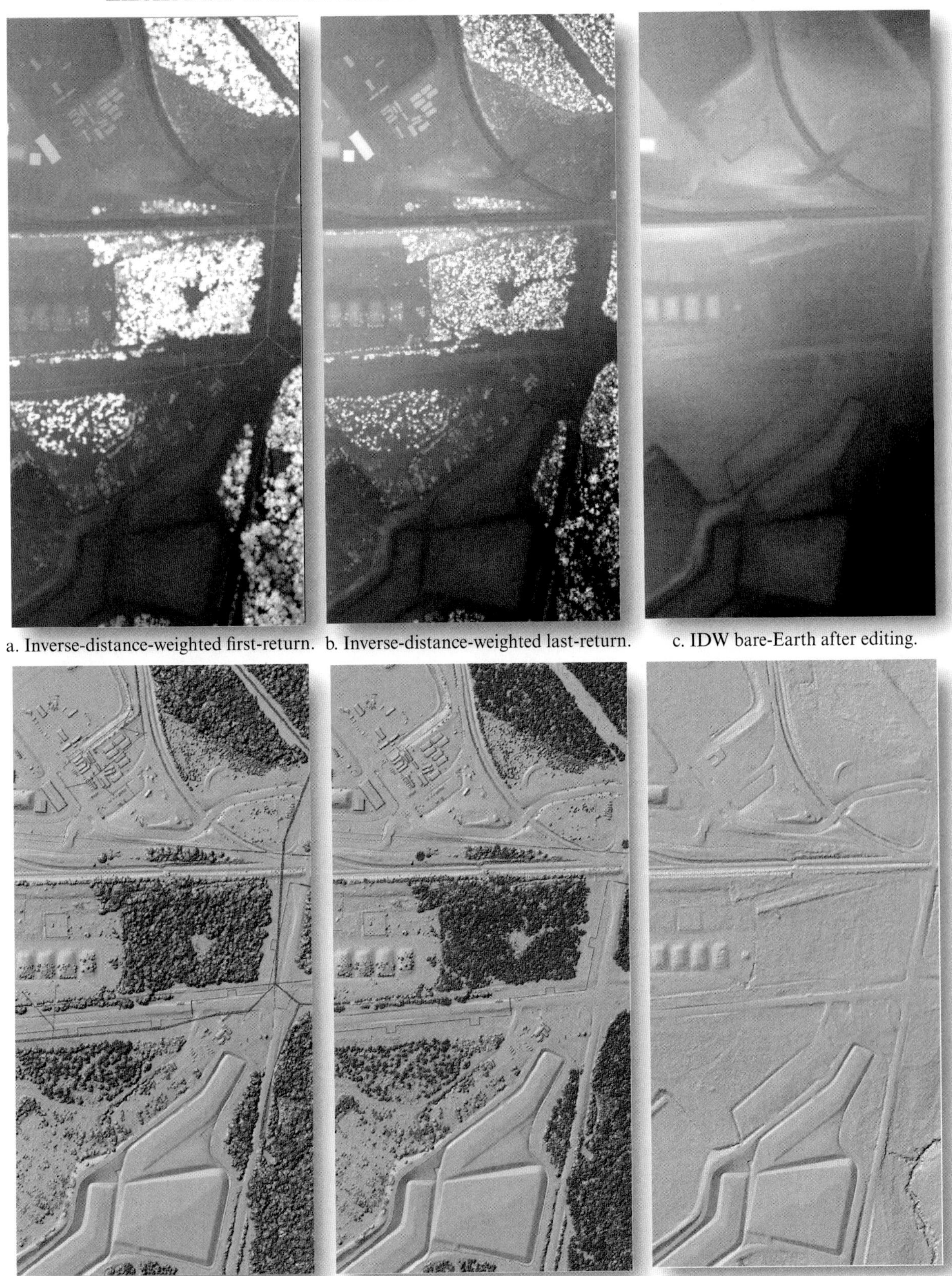

FIGURE 3–33 a) Inverse-distance-weighting (IDW) applied to first-return LiDAR data to create a digital surface model (DSM). b) IDW applied to last-return LiDAR data. c) IDW applied to edited masspoints to create a bare-Earth digital terrain model (DTM). d–f) Shaded-relief versions of a–c.

Comparison of Last-return LiDAR Data and the Bare-Earth Digital Terrain Model

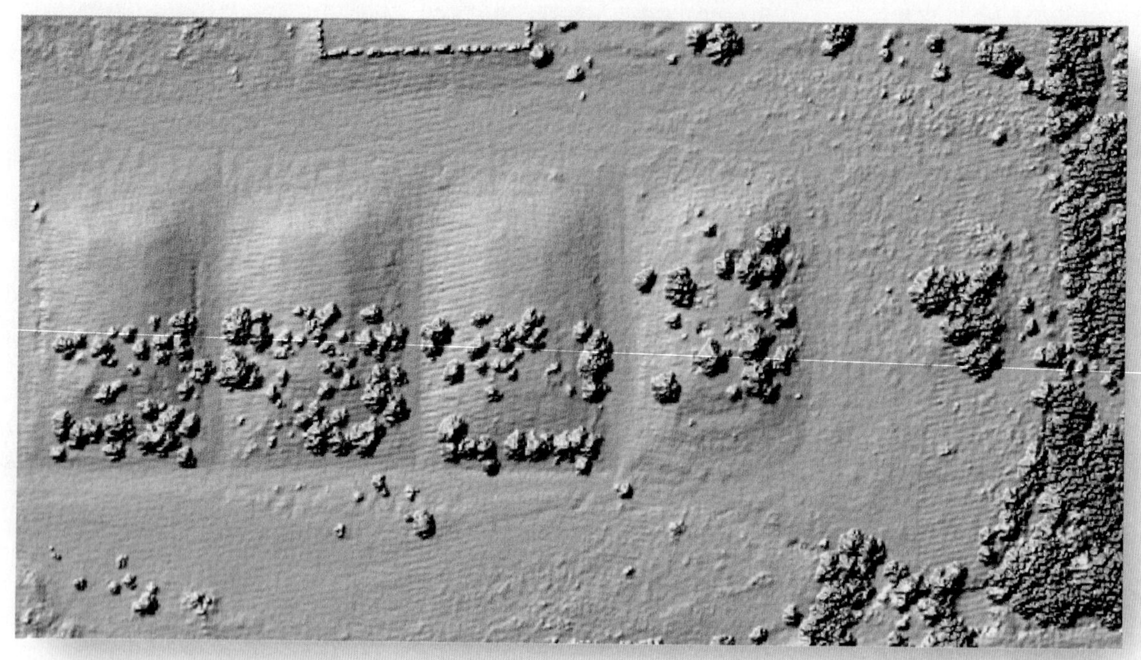

a. Last-return LiDAR data displayed in shaded-relief.

b. LiDAR-derived bare-Earth digital terrain model overlaid with 25 cm contours.

FIGURE 3–34 a) Inverse-distance-weighting (IDW) applied to last-return LiDAR data to create a digital surface model (DSM) displayed using shaded-relief. b) IDW applied to edited masspoints to create a bare-Earth digital terrain model (DTM) overlaid with 25 cm contours.

Extraction of a Bare-Earth DTM

Digital surface models (DSM) are of significant value for many applications such as the extraction of vegetation height and biomass and building height information. However, if the goal is to create a digital terrain model (DTM), the presence of vegetation (and other surface features) can be a nuisance. In areas covered by dense vegetation, the majority of the LiDAR returns will be from the canopy, with only a few pulses reaching the ground.

A bare-Earth DTM may be created by systematically removing masspoints in the first-, intermediate-, and/

or last-return LiDAR data that come from trees, shrubs, and even grass that extend above the bare ground. This is done using a filtering algorithm that passes through the LiDAR dataset examining each masspoint and the elevation characteristics associated with its *n* nearest neighbors. The filter then identifies those points that are a) bare ground, b) scrub-shrub, c) trees, and/or d) man-made structures. Only the bare ground masspoints are used to create the bare-Earth DTM. A bare-Earth DTM is shown in Figures 3-33c and 3-33f. A detailed examination of a small portion of the study area is shown in Figure 3-34a with 25 cm contours overlaid on the bare-Earth DTM in Figure 3-34b.

LiDAR remote sensing technology is improving rapidly. For example, the number of laser pulses transmitted every second by LiDAR systems increases dramatically every year resulting in greater LiDAR masspoint density from the same flight altitude.

RADAR Remote Sensing

RADAR (Radio Detection and Ranging) imagery is becoming more important as a source of geospatial information. RADAR remote sensing can be performed both day and night because it is not dependent upon solar radiation. RADAR sensors actively transmit pulses of microwave electromagnetic energy that interact with the terrain. The back-scattered energy is then recorded by the system electronics to produce a dataset that can be processed to yield a RADAR image. The RADAR system is especially sensitive to changes in terrain surface roughness and the amount of water present in the vegetation and/or soil. The long-wavelength energy can penetrate through clouds. Consequently, RADAR is often the sensor of choice for tropical areas of the world that are perennially shrouded in clouds.

RADAR Sensor Characteristics

RADAR sensors transmit much longer wavelength energy than LiDAR sensors (Table 3-8). The band designations are based on the use of RADAR during wars when it was necessary to keep the exact nature of the wavelength or frequency a secret.

The characteristics of a typical active microwave remote sensing system are shown in Figure 3-35. A pulse of microwave energy is transmitted toward the ground perpendicular to the line-of-flight of the aircraft (called the look direction) and at a certain depression angle (γ). The pulse of energy illuminates a strip of land to the side of the aircraft; hence the term side-looking-airborne-radar (SLAR). The microwave energy interacts with the terrain in the geographic area between the near- and far-range. The RADAR system

TABLE 3–8 Selected RADAR wavelengths and frequencies.

RADAR Band Designations (common wavelengths in parentheses)	Wavelength (λ) in cm	Frequency (υ) in GHz
K_a (0.86 cm)	0.75–1.18	40.0–26.5
K	1.19–1.66	26.5–18.0
K_u	1.67–2.39	18.0–12.5
X (3.0 and 3.2 cm)	2.40–3.89	12.5–8.0
C (7.5, 6.0 cm)	3.90–7.49	8.0–4.0
S (8.0, 9.6, 12.6 cm)	7.5–14.99	4.0–2.0
L (23.5, 24.0, 25.0 cm)	15.0–29.99	2.0–1.0
P (68.0 cm)	30.0–100	1.0–0.3

electronics record the amount of energy that is back-scattered from the terrain toward the RADAR antenna onboard the aircraft or spacecraft. It keeps track of the amplitude and phase history of the pulses of microwave energy recorded and is able to synthesize a very narrow beam width. This produces what is commonly referred to as Synthetic Aperture Radar (SAR) data. It is possible to send and receive like polarized microwave energy (i.e., vertical send, vertical receive = VV; horizontal send, horizontal receive = HH) or to send and receive cross-polarized energy (i.e., VH and HV).

Characteristics of selected satellite SARs are summarized in Table 3-9. The European Remote Sensing satellites ERS-1 and ERS-2 collect 26 × 30 m spatial resolution C-band (5.6 cm) RADAR imagery of much of Earth. Similarly, the Canadian Space Agency RADARSAT-1 and RADARSAT-2 collect C-band active microwave imagery at many spatial resolutions, the finest being 3 × 3 m. Suborbital RADARs, such as Intermap's Star-3*i*, can be flown day and night, in inclement weather to obtain very high spatial resolution RADAR imagery.

RADAR Environmental Considerations

RADAR imagery cannot be interpreted as if it were an aerial photograph or a multispectral image. The tones in a black & white RADAR image have nothing to do with blue, green, red, or near-infrared energy reflected from the scene. Rather, the shades of gray in a black & white RADAR image are primarily a function of a)

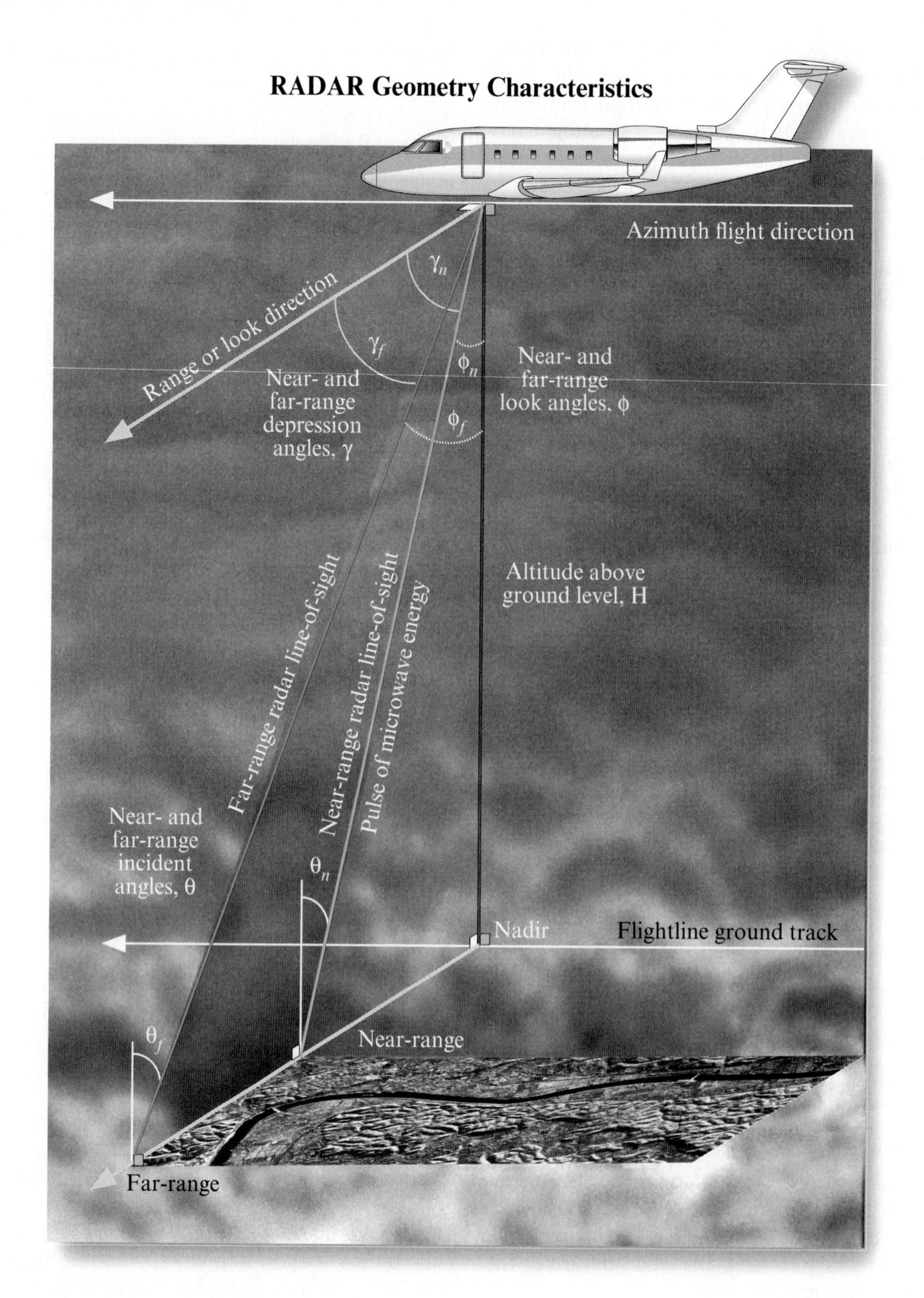

FIGURE 3–35 Geometric characteristics of RADAR imagery acquired by a side-looking-airborne-radar (SLAR) through cloud cover. All the nomenclature assumes that the terrain is flat.

terrain surface roughness, b) water content, and c) how the terrain polarizes or depolarizes the incident microwave energy.

Depending on the wavelength and depression angle of the incident microwave energy, it is relatively easy to discriminate between surfaces with just a few centimeters of difference in their surface roughness (e.g., between grassland, a field containing small cobblestones, and asphalt pavement). Generally, the greater the surface roughness, the stronger (brighter) the radar return. Thus, a field of small cobblestones usually generates a much stronger (brighter) return than an adjacent asphalt road. Large features such as buildings and mountains act as corner reflectors back-scattering a significant amount of energy toward the RADAR

TABLE 3–9 Characteristics of selected satellite Synthetic Aperture Radars (SARs).

Synthetic Aperture Radar (SAR)	Launch	Origin	Wave-length μ, cm	Depression angle, γ (near–far range) [Incident angle]	Polari-zation	Azimuth Resolu-tion, m	Range Resolu-tion, m	Swath width- km	Alti-tude km	Cover-age	Dura-tion
ERS-1,2	1991 1995	ESA	C - (5.6)	67° [23°]	W	30	26	100	785	polar orbit	--
JERS-1	1992	Japan	L - (23.5)	51° [39°]	HH	18	18	75	568	polar orbit	6.5 yr.
RADARSAT-1	1995	Canada	C - (5.6)	70° – 30° [10° – 60°]	HH	8 – 100	8 – 100	50 – 500	798	polar orbit	--
SRTM	2000	USA	X - (9.6) C - (5.3)	--	HH W,HH	30 30	30 30	X-50 C-225	225	60° N – 56°S	11 d
Envisat ASAR	2002	ESA	C - (5.3)	[15° – 45°]	Quad-pol	30 – 1000	30 – 1000	5 – 150	786	polar orbit 98°	--
RADARSAT-2	2007	Canada	C - (5.4)	70° – 30° [10° – 60°]	Quad-pol	3 – 100	2.4 – 100	20 – 500	798	polar orbit	--

sensor and generating extremely strong (bright) returns.

A RADAR sensor transmits a pulse of microwave electromagnetic energy that interacts with the terrain. Different types of terrain conduct this energy better than others. One measure of a material's electrical characteristics is the complex dielectric constant, defined as a measure of the ability of a material (e.g., vegetation, soil, rock, water, ice) to conduct electrical energy. Dry surface materials such as soils, rocks, and vegetation have dielectric constants from 3 to 8 in the microwave portion of the spectrum. Conversely, water has a dielectric constant of approximately 80. As expected, water conducts electricity very well. The most significant parameter influencing a material's dielectric constant is its moisture content. Therefore, the amount of moisture in a soil, on a rock surface, or within vegetative tissue has a significant impact on the amount of backscattered radar energy.

Moist soils reflect more radar energy than dry soils, which absorb more of the radar wave, depending on the dielectric constant of the soil material. Therefore, radar images may be used to estimate bare-ground soil-moisture content when the terrain is devoid of most other material, such as plants and rocks, and has a uniform surface roughness. The amount of soil moisture also influences how deep the incident electromagnetic energy penetrates into the material. If the soil has a high surface-soil moisture content, then the incident energy will only penetrate a few centimeters into the soil column and will be scattered more at the surface producing a stronger, brighter return.

Plant canopies (forest, agriculture, grassland, etc.) are water-bearing structures consisting of foliage (leaves) and woody materials (stems, trunk, stalks, and branches). Remote sensing systems such as the Landsat Thematic Mapper, SPOT, or aerial photography sense reflected optical wavelength energy measured in micrometers that is reflected, scattered, transmitted, and/or absorbed by the first few layers of leaves and stems of a healthy canopy. We typically get little information about the internal characteristics of the canopy, and much less information about the surface soil characteristics lying below the canopy. Conversely, active microwave energy can penetrate the vegetation canopy to varying depths depending upon the frequency, polarization, and incident angle of the radar system. Microwave energy sometimes responds to objects in the plant's tissues that are measured in centimeters.

If a radar sends a pulse of vertically or horizontally polarized microwave energy toward a stand of trees, it interacts with the components present and scatters some of the energy back toward the sensor. The amount of energy received is proportional to the nature of the energy sent (its frequency and polarization) and is dependent upon whether or not the canopy components depolarize the signal, how far the signal penetrates into the canopy, and whether it eventually interacts with the ground soil surface.

Shuttle Radar Topography Mission (SRTM) Data of Mt. Kilimanjaro

a. Color-coded display of SRTM-derived elevation of Mt. Kilimanjaro.

b. Landsat Thematic Mapper image of Mt. Kilimanjaro draped over SRTM-derived elevation data.
The look-direction is from the South to the North.

FIGURE 3–36 a) SRTM-derived elevation data (30 × 30 m) of Mt. Kilimanjaro in Tanzania, Africa. b) Landsat TM data (RGB = bands 7,4,2) draped over SRTM-derived elevation data (images courtesy of NASA Jet Propulsion Laboratory).

Water bodies function like mirrors, directing almost all of the incident energy away from the radar, resulting in water appearing very dark on radar imagery. Unlike aerial photography, there is no information whatsoever in the shadow areas of radar images. Thus, great care must be exercised when interpreting RADAR imagery. For additional information, the reader is encouraged to read the active microwave remote sensing chapter in Jensen (2007).

RADAR Interferometric Topographic Mapping

RADAR interferometry is the process whereby radar images of the same location on the ground are recorded by a) two radar antennas on the same platform, or by b) a single antenna on an aircraft or spacecraft on two different occasions. Analysis of the resulting two interferograms allows precise measurements of the range to any specific x,y,z point found in each image of the interferometric pair.

Two measurements obtained from two radars placed on the same platform separated by a few meters is called single-pass interferometry. The first single-pass interferometric SAR was the Shuttle Radar Topography Mission (SRTM) launched on February 11, 2000. It had a C-band and an X-band antenna in the cargo bay and a C-band and an X-band antenna at the end of a 60 m mast. The SRTM data yielded the world's most accurate digital surface model between 60° N and 56° S during its 11-day mission. For example, digital elevation information derived from the SRTM over Mt. Kilimanjaro in Tanzania, Africa, is shown in Figure 3-36. Interferometry may also be conducted using a single radar that obtains two measurements on different orbital tracks that are closely spaced but a day or so apart. This is the methodology used for the ERS-1,2 interferometry and is called multiple-pass or repeat-pass interferometry.

In many instances, interferometric SAR data can provide topographic information (x,y,z) that is just as accurate as digital elevation models derived using traditional optical photogrammetric techniques. However, interferometry can operate through clouds, day or night. This is important for cloud-shrouded tropical or arctic environments or when disasters strike and it is not possible to wait for an atmospheric window to obtain optical (photographic) data.

Remote Sensing Data Analysis

Remote sensor data are analyzed using image processing techniques, including: analog (visual) image processing and digital image processing.

Analog (Visual) Image Processing

Humans use the fundamental elements of image interpretation, including: grayscale tone, color, height (depth), size, shape, shadow, texture, site, association, and arrangement. The human mind is very good at recognizing and associating these complex elements in an image or photograph because we constantly process: a) profile views of Earth features every day, and b) images seen in books, magazines, television, and the Internet. Furthermore, we are adept at bringing to bear all the knowledge in our personal background and collateral information. We then converge all this evidence to identify phenomena in images and judge their significance. Precise measurement of objects (length, area, perimeter, volume, etc.) may be performed using photogrammetric techniques applied to either monoscopic (single-photo) or stereoscopic (overlapping) images.

There is a resurgence in the art and science of visual image interpretation as the digital sensor systems provide increasingly higher spatial resolution imagery. For example, many people display IKONOS-2 82 × 82 cm and QuickBird 61 × 61 cm panchromatic imagery on the computer screen and then visually interpret the data. These and other types of high spatial resolution image data are also often used as base maps in GIS projects. Jensen (2007) provides detailed information about how to visually interpret remote sensing images.

Digital Image Processing

Scientists have made significant advances in digital image processing of remotely sensed data. Digital image processing now makes use of many of the elements of image interpretation. The major types of **digital image processing** include image preprocessing (radiometric and geometric correction), image enhancement, pattern recognition, photogrammetric image processing of stereoscopic imagery, expert system (decision-tree) and neural network image analysis, hyperspectral data analysis, and change detection (Im and Jensen, 2005). A discussion of these methods is beyond the scope of this book. Detailed information on digital image processing techniques is found in Jensen (2005) and Jensen et al. (2009).

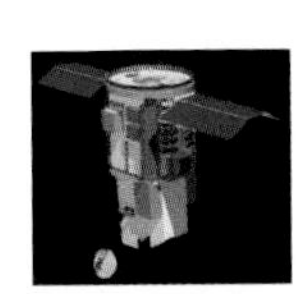

Summary

High-quality in situ and remote sensing-derived geospatial data are of critical importance for GIS analysis. This chapter reviewed the fundamental techniques used to collect in situ geospatial data using GPS, traditional and GPS-assisted land surveying, ground-based sampling, and the digitization of historical hard-copy maps and photographs.

The chapter then reviewed how geospatial information can be obtained using selected remote sensing systems, including: aerial photography, multispectral, hyperspectral, and thermal-infrared imagery, and LiDAR and RADAR imagery. The quality of the geospatial data analyzed using a GIS has a tremendous impact on the quality of the output products.

Review Questions

1. Why is it important to track as many GPS satellites as possible when collecting GPS-derived geographic coordinate information?

2. Describe the characteristics of three of the most important Global Navigation Satellite Systems (GNSS). Which of these is most likely to have a significant impact on your life?

3. Why are Continuously Operating Reference Stations (CORS) important when collecting GPS-derived geographic coordinate information?

4. How is most parcel boundary coordinate information obtained? How would you obtain the building footprint information that is often associated with parcel information?

5. Describe how a typical SmartStation and SmartPole work when performing in situ land surveying.

6. What type of digitization techniques would you use to convert an 1864 hand-drawn color map into digital information? How would you convert a historical U.S. Department of Agriculture 1932 black & white 1:20,000-scale aerial photograph into a digital dataset with 1 × 1 m pixels?

7. Describe the difference between multispectral and hyperspectral remote sensing.

8. Why is it still necessary to develop analog (visual) image-processing skills in addition to digital image processing skills in the twenty-first century?

9. Compare and contrast LiDAR and RADAR remote sensing data collection.

10. Describe how a thermal-infrared remote sensing system functions and the types of geospatial information that can be extracted with it.

11. What is the difference between a LiDAR-derived digital surface model (DSM) and a LiDAR-derived digital terrain model (DTM)? Describe several uses of digital surface models and digital terrain models in a GIS context.

12. Describe four technologies that can be used to obtain accurate elevation information for input to a GIS.

13. Describe several types of geospatial information readily available in the 2010 Census.

14. Why is knowing about in situ data collection, digitizing, and remote sensing data collection important to a person learning about GIS?

Glossary

Analog-to-Digital Conversion: The transformation of analog (hard-copy) data such as a historical map or aerial photograph into digital information.

Census: The systematic collection of information about the members of a population. Each of the persons, places, or things of interest in the study area are investigated.

Crowd Sourcing: The outsourcing of tasks traditionally performed by an employee or contractor to an undefined, large group of people or community (i.e., a crowd), through an open call usually via the Internet.

Digital Image Processing: The analysis of digital remote sensor data using special-purpose software for preprocessing (radiometric and geometric), enhancement, classification, and change detection.

Digitization: The process of converting information found in hard-copy (analog) maps, images, and diagrams into digital information. Hopefully, the digitized information can then be rectified and analyzed with other geospatial information using a GIS.

Geotagging: The process of adding geographical identification metadata to various media such as terrestrial photographs, videos, etc.

Global Navigation Satellite System (GNSS): The generic term for various constellations of satellites used to determine the geographic location of features on the surface of the Earth. Important GNSS include the United States' GPS, the European *Galileo* system, the Russian GLONASS, and the Chinese COMPASS.

Global Positioning System (GPS): The NAVigation System using Timing And Ranging (NAVSTAR) Global positioning System is a U.S.-owned utility that provides users with position, navigation, and timing services. It consists of a constellation of 24 to 32 satellites that operate in six different orbits.

Hyperspectral Remote Sensing: The collection of spectral data in tens or hundreds of bands in the electromagnetic spectrum. NASA's AVIRIS and MODIS are hyperspectral remote sensing systems.

LiDAR: Remote sensing using Light Detection and Ranging technology where near-infrared laser energy is transmitted toward the terrain or blue-green laser energy is transmitted into a water body and the characteristics of the back-scattered energy are recorded and processed.

Masspoints: LiDAR-derived elevation datapoints located systematically across flightlines.

Multispectral Remote Sensing: Sensors that collect data in several bands in the electromagnetic spectrum. The Landsat Enhanced Thematic Mapper Plus, QuickBird, and GeoEye-1 are multispectral sensor systems.

NAVigation System using Timing And Ranging (NAVSTAR) Global Positioning System (GPS): The primary navigation system for the U.S. government. NAVSTAR GPS consists of a constellation of 24 to 32 satellites.

Orthophotograph: A special type of vertical aerial photograph with the geometric distortion and relief displacement effects removed.

Pixel: A 2-dimensional picture element that is the smallest nondivisible element of a digital image.

RADAR: Remote sensing using Radio Detection and Ranging technology in which microwave energy is transmitted toward the terrain and the characteristics of the back-scattered energy are recorded and processed.

RADAR Interferometry: The process whereby radar images of the same location on the ground are recorded by a) two radar antennas on the same platform, or by b) a single antenna on a platform on two different occasions.

Radiometric Resolution: The sensitivity of a remote sensing detector to differences in signal strength as it records the radiant flux reflected, emitted, or back-scattered from the terrain.

Remote Sensing: The measurement or acquisition of information of some property of an object or phenomenon by a recording device that is not in physical or intimate contact with the object or phenomenon under study.

Remote Sensing Process: The process of extracting useful information from remotely sensed data by: 1) identifying the in situ and remote sensing data to be collected, 2) collecting the data, 3) extracting information from the data, and 4) presenting the information.

Sampling: A procedure concerned with the selection of a subset of individuals from within a population to yield some knowledge about the whole population and especially to make predictions based on statistical inference.

Spatial Resolution: A measure of the smallest angular or linear separation between two objects that can be resolved by a remote sensing system.

Spectral Resolution: The number and size of specific wavelength intervals (referred to as bands or channels) in the electromagnetic spectrum to which a remote sensing instrument is sensitive.

Thermal-infrared Remote Sensing: Remote sensing technology that measures energy emitted from the terrain in two primary regions of the electromagnetic spectrum: 3 – 5 μm for hot targets and 8 – 14 μm for general terrain and water bodies.

Temporal Resolution: How often in situ or remotely sensed data are collected for a particular area.

Ultraspectral Remote Sensing: Data collection in many hundreds or even thousands of bands in the electromagnetic spectrum.

References

Congalton, R. G. and K. Green, 2009, *Assessing the Accuracy of Remotely Sensed Data: Principles and Practices*, Boca Raton: CRC Press, 180 p.

Cowen, D., Coleman, J., Craig, W., Domenico, C., Elhami, S., Johnson, S., Marlow, S., Roberts, F., Swartz, M. and N. Von Meyer, 2008, *National Land Parcel Data: A Vision for the Future*, Washington: National Academy Press, 158 p.

DigitalGlobe, 2011, *QuickBird Specifications*, (www.digitalglobe.com).

Esri, 2011, "Census 2010 Data is Instantly Usable in Maps and Easy-to-Read Reports," *Esri News*, Redlands: Esri, Inc., May 23, 2011.

GeoEye, 2011, *GeoEye Home Page*, (http://www.geoeye.com).

GPSgov, 2011, *Official U.S. Government Information about the Global Positioning System (GPS) and Related Topics*, (http://www.gps.gove/systems/gps/).

Hodgson, M. E., Jensen, J. R., Raber, G., Tullis, J., Davis, B., Thompson, G. and K. Schuckman, 2005, "An Evaluation of LiDAR derived Elevation and Terrain Slope in Leaf-off Conditions," *Photogrammetric Engineering & Remote Sensing*, 71(7):817–823.

Hodgson, M. E., Jensen, J. R., Schmidt, L., Schill, S. and B. A. Davis, 2003, "An Evaluation of LiDAR- and IFSAR-derived Digital Elevation Models in Leaf-on Conditions with USGS Level 1 and Level 2 DEMS," *Remote Sensing of Environment*, 84(2003):295–308.

Howden, L. M. and J. A. Meyer, 2011, *Age and Sex Composition: 2010*, Census Briefs #C2010BR-3, Washington: U.S. Census Bureau, 15 p.

Howe, J., 2006, "The Rise of Crowd Sourcing," *Wired* (http://www.wired.com/wired/archive/14.06/crowds.html).

Im, J. and J. R. Jensen, 2005, "Change Detection Using Correlation Analysis and Decision Tree Classification," *Remote Sensing of Environment*, 99:326–340.

Itres, 2006, *Thermal Airborne Spectrographic Imager (TASI)*, Alberta, CN: Itres Research (http://www.itres.com).

Jensen, J. R., 2005, *Introductory Digital Image Processing: A Remote Sensing Perspective*, Upper Saddle River: Pearson Prentice-Hall, 525 p.

Jensen, J. R., 2007, *Remote Sensing of the Environment: An Earth Resource Perspective*, Upper Saddle River: Pearson Prentice-Hall, Inc., 592 p.

Jensen, J. R. and D. C. Cowen, 1999, "Remote Sensing of Urban/Suburban Infrastructure and Socioeconomic Attributes," *Photogrammetric Engineering & Remote Sensing*, 65(5):611–622.

Jensen, J. R., Botchway, K., Brennan-Galvin, E., Johannsen, C., Juma, C., Mabogunje, A., Miller, R., Price, K., Reining, P., Skole, D., Stancioff, A. and D. R. F. Taylor, 2002, *Down to Earth: Geographic Information for Sustainable Development in Africa*, Washington: National Academy Press, 155 p.

Jensen, J. R., Im, J., Hardin, P., and R. R. Jensen, 2009, "Chapter 19: Image Classification," in *The SAGE Handbook of Remote Sensing*, Warner, T. A., Nellis, M. D. and G. M. Foody (Eds.), Los Angeles: SAGE Publications, 269–296.

Karaska, M. A., Huguenin, R. L., Beacham, J. L., Wang, M., Jensen, J. R., and R. S. Kaufman, 2004, "AVIRIS Measurements of Chlorophyll, Suspended Minerals, Dissolved Organic Carbon, and Turbidity in the Neuse River, N.C.," *Photogrammetric Engineering & Remote Sensing*, 70(1):125–133.

Leica, 2009, *Combining TPS and GPS: SmartStation and SmartPole High Performance GNSS Systems*, Switzerland: Leica Geosystems AG, 44 p.

Liverman, D., Moran, E. F., Rindfuss, R. R. and P. C. Stern, 1998, *People and Pixels: Linking Remote Sensing and Social Science*, Washington: NRC, 244 p.

Lunetta, R. and J. G. Lyon, 2005, *Remote Sensing and GIS Accuracy Assessment*, Boca Raton: CRC Press, 380 p.

Maidment, D. R., Edelman, Heiberg, E. R., Jensen, J. R., Maune, D. F., Schuckman, K. and R. Shrestha, 2007, *Elevation Data for Floodplain Mapping*, Washington: National Academy Press, 151 p.

Makun, P. and S. Wilson, 2011, *Population Distribution and Change: 2000 to 2010*, 2010 Census Briefs #C2010BR-01, Washington: U.S. Census Bureau, 11 p.

McCoy, R., 2005, *Field Methods in Remote Sensing*, New York: Guilford, 159 p.

Miller, R. B., Abbott, M. R., Harding, L. W., Jensen, J. R., Johannsen, C. J., Macauley, M., MacDonald, J. S. and J. S. Pearlman, 2003, *Using Remote Sensing in State and Local Government: Information for Management and Decision Making*, Washington: National Academy Press, 97 p.

NASA, 2011, *Airborne Visible/Infrared Imaging Spectrometer (AVIRIS)* home page, (http://aviris.jpl.nasa.gov/).

NGS, 2011, *Continuously Operating Reference Stations (CORS)*, Washington: National Geodetic Survey (http://www. ngs.noaa.gov/CORS/).

Pictometry, 2011, *Pictometry Data Products* (http://www.pictometry.com).

Puglia, S., Reed, J. and E. Rhodes, 2004, *Technical Guidelines for Digitizing Archival Materials for Electronic Access: Creation of Production Master Files – Raster Images: For the Following Record Types – Textual, Graphic Illustrations/Artwork/Originals, Maps, Plans, Oversized, Photographs, Aerial Photographs, and Objects/Artifacts,* Washington: U. S. National Archives and Records Administration (NARA), 87 p. (available at http://www.archives.gov/preservation/technical/guidance.pdf).

Raber, G. T., Jensen, J. R., Schill, S. R. and K. Schuckman, 2002, "Creation of Digital Terrain Models using an Adaptive LiDAR Vegetation Point Removal Process," *Photogrammetric Engineering & Remote Sensing*, 68(12):1307–1315.

Sorrell, C., 2008, "How to GeoTag Your Photos," *Wired*, May 12, 2008 (http://www.wired.com/gadgetlab/2008/05/how-to-geotag-y/).

USA, 2008, "Chapter 11: Satellite Navigation," in *The American Practical Navigator,* Washington: U.S. Government (http://en.wikisource.org/wiki/The_American_Practical_Navigator/Chapter 11).

Young, J., 2011, *LiDAR for Dummies*, New York: Wiley Publishing, 24 p.

4 Data Quality

Geographic information systems rely on spatial data for analysis. Unfortunately, whenever data about the real world are collected and placed in a geospatial database it is likely that there will be some error and uncertainty associated with the database. The categorical (attribute) and/or positional error in the dataset may make it inappropriate or unusable for a particular project. Therefore, it is necessary to assess the attribute and positional quality of the data very early in a GIS project. This is very important in this age of free geospatial data that are shared so easily via the Internet.

In previous decades, much of the GIS analysis was performed by a relatively small number of persons that were well-trained in geographic information science (GIScience). With the proliferation of GIScience short courses, it is now quite common for people with limited geospatial knowledge to import spatial data files that have not been carefully evaluated into a GIS for a variety of applications (Devillers et al., 2005).

Overview

Data quality assessment is an important part of GIS analysis. This chapter describes common types of categorical and spatial error in geospatial data and how the error can be measured, and in certain instances corrected. Concepts of metadata, attribute and positional accuracy, and topological error are discussed. Finally, the concept of ecological fallacy and the modifiable area unit problem are introduced.

Metadata

Metadata are "data about the data" and are an important characteristic of quality geospatial data. Metadata describe the characteristics of the dataset and can be evaluated to determine if the geospatial data are appropriate for a particular study. Metadata describes:

- who collected the data,
- what data were collected,
- where the data were collected,
- when the data were collected,
- why the data were collected,
- how the data were collected,
- the scale of the data, and ideally any
- algorithms or transformations applied to the data.

Metadata should be provided for any dataset that is downloaded from the Internet or acquired from an external source (especially from friends). Without metadata, GIS users typically have meager information about the origin of the data and its history. Metadata files are often created using an extensible markup language (XML). XML allows users to easily create and modify documents and post them on the Internet.

Elements of Metadata

Metadata standards are defined by the groups or people that use them. However, there are certain elements that should be present in most metadata, including:

- spatial data structure (e.g., raster or vector),
- projection,

- coordinate system,
- datum conversion or transformation (e.g., NAD27 to NAD83),
- scale of the original data,
- when the data were created,
- how the data were collected,
- database field names and properties (e.g., values and value limits, data types, formats),
- data quality/errors and any error reports, and
- accuracy and precision of the instruments used to collect the data.

When these elements are present in the metadata, a decision can usually be made regarding the quality and utility of the data for a given GIS-related project.

Federal Geographic Data Committee (FGDC) Metadata Standards

As noted above, different organizations may have different metadata standards. Fortunately, the U.S. Federal Geographic Data Committee created the *Content Standard for Digital Geospatial Metadata* in 1998 to standardize metadata terminology, definitions, and protocols (FGDC, 1998a). This effort was in response to the tremendous variety of methods being used to prepare metadata. The FGDC identified ten content areas, including:

1. Identification information—describes the information in the other sections.

2. Data quality information—provides an assessment of the quality of the dataset including an in-depth description of the various methods used to assess the accuracy of the dataset.

3. Spatial data organization information—describes the types of spatial data features in the dataset.

4. Spatial reference information—data about the coordinate system, projection, datum, elevation, and other geographic information are contained in this section. For example, information about the map projection's standard parallels and standard meridians is included.

5. Entity and attribute information—describes the attributes in the dataset. Information such as data types, precision, and field length are provided for each attribute in the dataset.

6. Distribution information—describes how the data may be obtained, distributed, and the data copyright policies.

7. Metadata reference information—description of the metadata and how up-to-date it is.

8. Citation information—describes how the geospatial dataset should be cited.

9. Time period information—lists the time period in which the data were collected and analyzed.

10. Contact information—describes how to contact the owners or custodians of the data.

Metadata and GIS Software

Most high-quality GIS software packages contain metadata modules that allow users to create and edit metadata. In addition, the metadata modules allow for metadata files to be imported and help GIS users to remember what metadata should be maintained. For example, Figure 4-1 displays the ArcGIS® metadata user interface. Each tab corresponds to a major body of metadata information. The completed metadata information should be included as part of the entire geodatabase when sharing geospatial data with others.

Other Metadata Issues

Individuals, companies, and/or organizations may add other items to the standard metadata that are relevant to a particular project. This can sometimes create a problem when one company's metadata does not contain all of the information needed by another company. In this case, the second company may not know enough about the data to be able to make an informed decision about whether or not the data are suitable for a particular project. In general, it is advisable that there be more information in the metadata rather than too little information. Unfortunately, metadata can also contain errors. Therefore, metadata must be quality checked to ensure that everything contained therein is accurate.

Accuracy and Precision

Accuracy and precision are two concepts that GIS analysts and users need to understand. **Accuracy** refers to the extent that both attribute and positional (x,y-location) data correspond to their real-world counterparts. For example, a network dataset that contains road centerlines that are within ± 0.25 m of their true planimetric (x,y) location is said to have good positional accuracy. If all of the roads in the network dataset have accurate place names (e.g., "Main Street," "Maple Street," etc.), then the dataset is said to have good attribute accuracy.

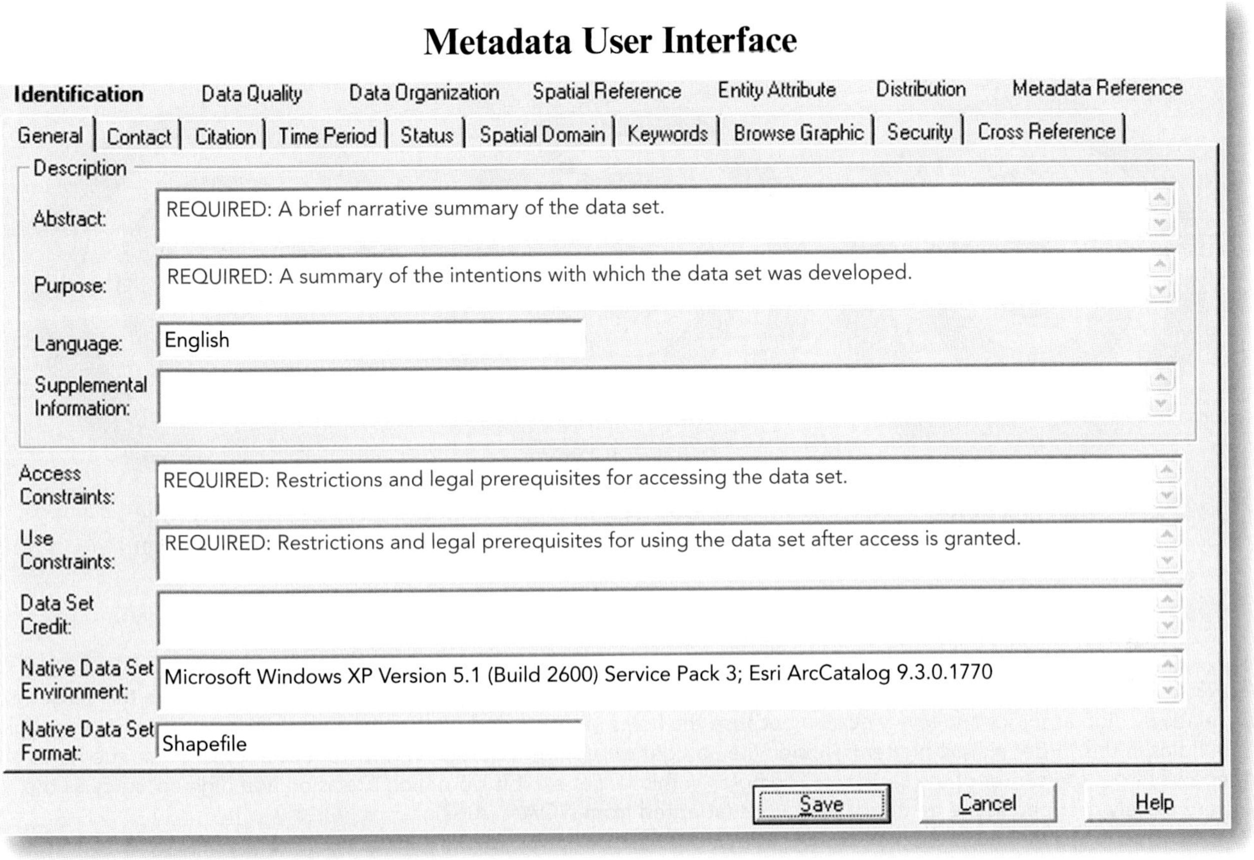

Metadata User Interface

Identification | Data Quality | Data Organization | Spatial Reference | Entity Attribute | Distribution | Metadata Reference

General | Contact | Citation | Time Period | Status | Spatial Domain | Keywords | Browse Graphic | Security | Cross Reference

Description

Abstract: REQUIRED: A brief narrative summary of the data set.

Purpose: REQUIRED: A summary of the intentions with which the data set was developed.

Language: English

Supplemental Information:

Access Constraints: REQUIRED: Restrictions and legal prerequisites for accessing the data set.

Use Constraints: REQUIRED: Restrictions and legal prerequisites for using the data set after access is granted.

Data Set Credit:

Native Data Set Environment: Microsoft Windows XP Version 5.1 (Build 2600) Service Pack 3; Esri ArcCatalog 9.3.0.1770

Native Data Set Format: Shapefile

Save | Cancel | Help

FIGURE 4–1 The Esri ArcGIS® metadata user interface allows analysts to efficiently enter metadata about a spatial data layer. Note all of the different metadata categories at the top of the interface. Also note that some metadata information is mandatory. Most sophisticated GIS software packages provide metadata modules (interface courtesy of Esri, Inc.).

Precision refers to the "exactness" of the measurements. Sometimes people think of precision as the number of decimal places that a device is capable of measuring. For example, assume you want to measure air temperature in the central business district of a city and you have two different thermometers. One thermometer measures air temperature every other degree (e.g., 94°, 96°, and 98° F, etc.) while the other thermometer measures air temperature every one-half degree (e.g., 94°, 94.5°, and 95° F, etc.). Which of these thermometers is more precise? Certainly, the thermometer that measures air temperature to every one-half degree is more precise.

Good accuracy does not necessarily guarantee good precision, and good precision does not necessarily guarantee good accuracy. Just because an instrument measures with greater precision does not mean that it is more accurate. For example, in the thermometer discussion above, assume that there is a systematic error of 3° associated with the thermometer that measures air temperature to every one-half degree, and that there is no systematic error in the other thermometer. In this case, the less-precise thermometer is actually more accurate than the more-precise thermometer. Similarly, consider a GPS instrument that is able to measure locations to within ±25 cm. This would probably be considered to be a very precise instrument. However, what if for some reason the same GPS unit had a systematic error of ±2.5 m?

In Figure 4-2a, the spatial distribution of the holes in the target exhibits high accuracy and relatively low precision. The holes are in the center of the target but the pattern is not very tight. Conversely, in Figure 4-2b, the holes exhibit relatively low accuracy and high precision. The holes are located some distance from the center but are very tightly clustered. The holes in Figure 4-2c exhibit high accuracy and high precision because the holes are located in the very center of the target in a very tight cluster.

The accuracy and precision of geospatial data should help determine the level of confidence that GIS users have when analyzing the data and reporting their results. Often, GIS users assume that their geospatial data are either more accurate or more precise than they actually are. The use of inaccurate or imprecise geospa-

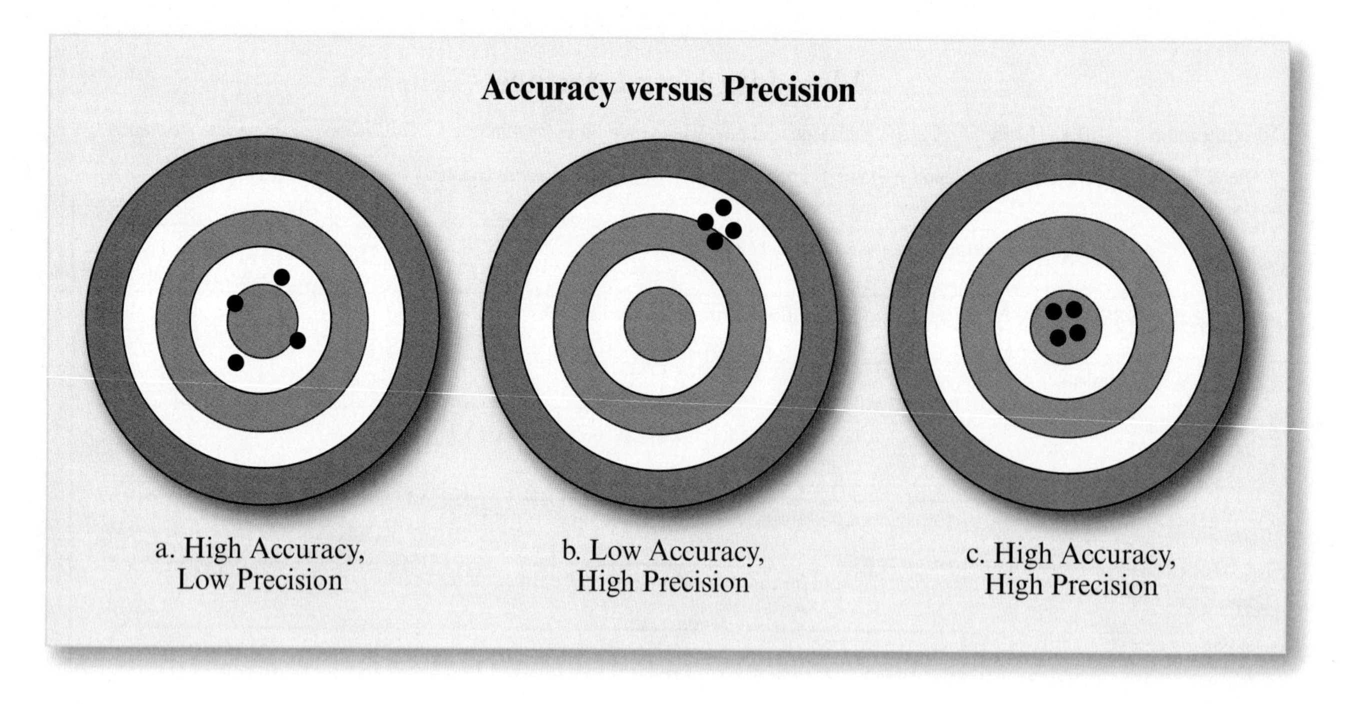

FIGURE 4–2 These three targets demonstrate the difference between accuracy and precision. a) The holes in this target exhibit relatively high accuracy and low precision because the holes are centered on the target, but the pattern is not very tight. b) The holes in this target exhibit higher precision (i.e., a tight grouping), but relatively lower accuracy because the holes are farther away from the center of the target. c) The holes in this target exhibit both high precision and high accuracy as the holes are closely grouped in the center of the target (adapted from NOAA, 2007).

tial data will most likely result in inaccurate or imprecise results. Unsubstantiated confidence in the results (e.g., a map) can result in unwise or inappropriate decisions.

Types of Error in Geospatial Data

It is almost impossible to collect real-world measurements without introducing some type of error. Common types of error include:

- attribute error (including logical consistency and completeness),
- positional error (*x*,*y*,*z*),
- topological geometric error,
- temporal error,
- interpretation error due to ecological fallacy, and
- error due to the modifiable areal unit problem.

Each of these types of error can negatively impact the results of a GIS study. Therefore, the ability to recognize the types of error that may be present in the data and how to minimize the error is an important part of a GIS project.

Attribute Error

Each of the road segments in a transportation network could contain attribute information such as the segment name, average daily traffic, age of pavement, number of lanes, direction of travel, etc. The attribute information may be accurate or inaccurate. Unfortunately, attribute error is usually not checked as well as many of the other types of error because it is tedious to check for attribute error in large spatial databases. However, these errors can be very troublesome. For example, assume there is a field titled "Last_Name" in the geodatabase of a county tax assessor. Assume that there is a family with the last name "Smith" who owns one of the parcels of land. Unfortunately, a mistake was made and the name of "James" was entered into the "Last_Name" field in the database instead of "Smith" for the parcel of land. Any inquiry about this particular parcel using the "Last_Name" field will generate inaccurate information. Mr. Smith will not appreciate receiving his tax assessment with Mr. James' name on the envelope.

Acceptable Level of Accuracy

As a GIS user, you should have in mind a target level of accuracy for each of the layers of geospatial information you use in the GIS analysis. Government agencies often identify a specific minimum level of accuracy for selected datasets. GIS users may also set their own *ad hoc* levels of accuracy.

For example, for many years the U.S. Geological Survey used the following minimum accuracy specifications for the creation of land use and land cover maps derived from remote sensor data (Anderson, et al., 1976):

- The minimum attribute accuracy level per class was 85%.
- The land use or land cover classes on a map were required to have similar levels of accuracy (i.e., no one class was to be exceptionally accurate [e.g., 99%] while the majority of the other classes were 85% accurate).
- Sometimes different image interpreters were responsible for extracting land use or land cover information for different parts of a map. When this occurred, all of the results had to meet the minimum attribute accuracy standard.

To ensure that a rigorous level of attribute accuracy is maintained in spatial data, attribute accuracy must be determined and reported. Two of the most common methods used to determine attribute accuracy are database random spot-checking and spatial sampling.

Random Spot-checking

Determining attribute accuracy can be difficult when the database contains a tremendous number of records (e.g., crop attributes for hundreds of thousands of agricultural fields in a county). Consequently, it is sometimes useful to conduct a random 'spot-check' to determine attribute accuracy. In a large database, perhaps only 2% or fewer of the records need to be spot-checked for attribute accuracy. These records are usually randomly selected so that there is no bias in the attribute accuracy assessment.

Spatial Sampling

The goal of sampling is to collect an unbiased representative sample of the population (Jensen and Shumway, 2010). In the case of a GIS geodatabase, an unbiased spatial sample can be completed using several different methods. A **random sample** with replacement occurs when every observation has an equal chance of being selected. This is one of the most simple sampling schemes, and it usually ensures that there is no bias in the sample. For example, consider the agricultural field in Figure 4-3a that has two crops growing in it. Corn occupies 2/3 of the field and soybeans are planted in the remaining 1/3 of the field. If the farmer wanted to measure the pH throughout the entire field to make sure that the soil was not acidic, then a random distribution of sample points (e.g., 9) may be sufficient to obtain a good measure of average soil pH.

In some cases, a stratified sample should be used. A **stratified random sample** should be implemented when the GIS analyst knows that the dataset contains different sub-populations and he or she makes an effort to sample within each sub-population (i.e., stratum). This helps ensure that all of the variation present in the spatial dataset is accounted for (Jensen and Shumway, 2010). In Figure 4-3b, the sample points are randomly located in either the corn or soybean section of the field based on the known area of the two crops. In this agricultural example, 1/3 of the points (3) were randomly located in the soybean section of the field, and 2/3 of the points (6) were randomly located in the corn section of the field.

Finally, a **systematic sample** can be implemented according to a predetermined system. In Figure 4-3c, the nine points were systematically located every 40 m in the x,y-direction. This ensured that the entire field was systematically sampled.

To be of value, the information obtained during random spot-checking or spatial sampling is often input to an error matrix for statistical evaluation.

Creation of an Error Matrix and the Computation of Overall Accuracy, Producer's Accuracy, User's Accuracy, and Kappa Coefficient of Agreement

A useful way to determine the attribute accuracy of nominal- and ordinal-scale data is through the construction and statistical analysis of an **error matrix** (sometimes referred to as a confusion matrix or contingency table) (Congalton and Green, 2009). Examples of nominal data to be checked for attribute accuracy include land use or land cover, soil type, etc. Ordinal data, such as low, medium, and high income, can also be checked for accuracy using an error matrix. Additional information about measurement levels (e.g., nominal, ordinal, interval, ratio) is provided in Chapters 8 and 10.

The error matrix is populated with information derived from the random spot-checking or spatial sampling methods previously discussed (Table 4-1). In the case of land cover, each checkpoint observation consists of two types of information: the class it was assigned to (e.g., Forest) and its actual class based on ground reference information (e.g., Urban). For example, the error matrix shown in Table 4-1 depicts the attribute accuracy of a three-class land cover map. Seventy-six (76) random observations were selected within the classification map. The land cover at these 76 locations was then compared with the ground reference information available for these locations. Twenty-seven (27) points were classified as Urban. Of those 27 points, 22 were classified correctly, two were misclassified as Forest,

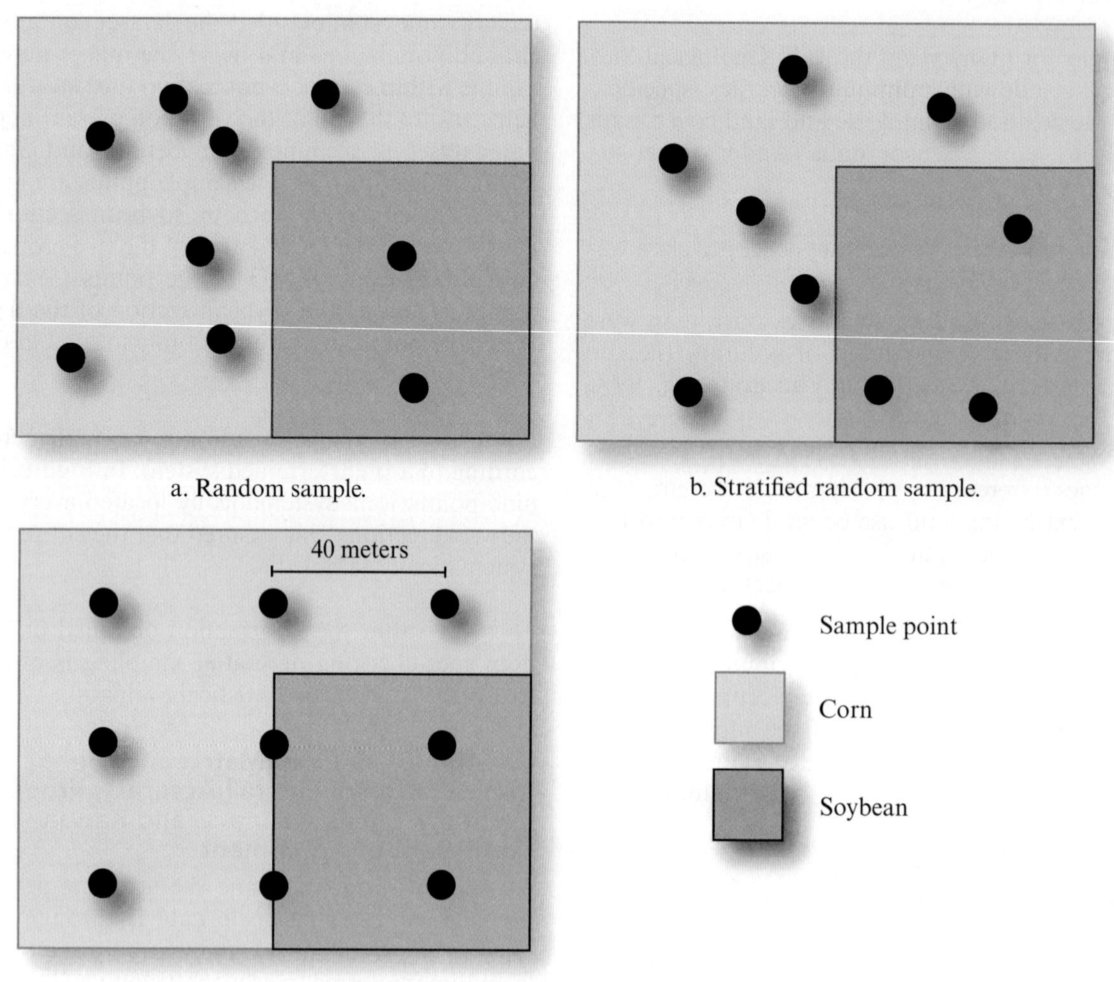

FIGURE 4–3 Three sampling schemes: random, stratified-random, and systematic. In each case, nine points are overlaid on a hypothetical field where 1/3 of the field has been planted with soybeans and 2/3 of the field has been planted with corn. The goal of the sampling is to accurately measure the pH of the soil in the field to make sure it is not too acidic. a) A map of a random distribution of the nine points. Unfortunately, only two points fall within the soybean field. It may be under-sampled. b) The placement of the nine points using stratified-random sampling. Because soybeans occupy 1/3 of the study area, three of the nine points are allocated to this strata. Corn occupies 2/3 of the study area and therefore receives six randomly distributed points within this strata. c) The placement of the nine points using systematic sampling criteria. Each point is systematically located every 40 m in the *x* and *y* directions. Unfortunately, two of the systematic points are located at the edge (interface) of the corn and soybean areas. The location of these two sample locations may need to be adjusted.

and three were misclassified as Agriculture. Therefore, one can determine how many points were correctly classified and the other categories that were mistakenly classified as that land cover type by simply examining individual columns in the error matrix. Conversely, one can examine the rows of the error matrix to see the categories that points were incorrectly classified into. For example, two points were incorrectly classified as Forest that should have been Urban (Table 4-1).

The overall accuracy may be computed after all of the values have been placed in the error matrix. Overall accuracy is calculated by adding up the number of observations that were classified correctly (i.e., the x_{ii} found in the diagonal of the matrix) for each class, k, and dividing by the total number of observations (N) in the error matrix (Jensen, 2005; Congalton and Green, 2009):

$$\text{Overall accuracy} = \frac{\sum_{i=1}^{k} x_{ii}}{N} \tag{4.1}$$

TABLE 4–1 Determining the classification attribute accuracy of a nominal scale land cover map containing three land cover classes using an error matrix.

	Urban	Forest	Agriculture	Row Total
Urban	**22**	2	2	26
Forest	2	**19**	2	23
Agriculture	3	4	**20**	27
Column Total	27	25	24	**76**
Overall Accuracy	$= \frac{\sum_{i=1}^{k} x_{ii}}{N} = \frac{22+19+20}{76} = 80.2\%$			
Producer's Accuracy	Urban = 22/27 = 81%	Forest = 19/25 = 76%	Agriculture = 20/24 = 83%	
User's Accuracy	Urban = 22/26 = 85%	Forest = 19/23 = 83%	Agriculture = 20/27 = 74%	
Kappa Coefficient of Agreement (κ)	$= \frac{N\sum_{i=1}^{k} x_{ii} - \sum_{i=1}^{k}(x_{i+} \times x_{+i})}{N^2 - \sum_{i=1}^{k}(x_{i+} \times x_{+i})} = \frac{76(61) - 1925}{5776 - 1925} = 70\%$			

There were a total of 61 observations in Table 4-1 that were classified correctly (22 + 19 + 20 = 61), and the total number of points evaluated was 76. Therefore, the overall percent accuracy of this thematic map was 61/76 = 80.2%. The user must decide if this value is acceptable. For example, assume you require ≥85% overall accuracy. In this case, the overall accuracy is <85% and does not meet the criteria. Therefore, the land cover data would need to be discarded and a new land cover map prepared and then checked again.

There are several other accuracy measures that can be extracted from the error matrix, including: producer's accuracy, user's accuracy, and the Kappa Coefficient of Agreement. Producer's accuracy is computed for each class by analyzing the columns in the error matrix. It is measured using the total number of correct observations in a category divided by the total number of observations assigned to that category (i.e., the *column* total). This statistic indicates the probability of a reference observation being correctly classified and is a measure of omission error. The producer's accuracy for the three classes is summarized in Table 4-1.

User's accuracy is computed by analyzing the rows of the error matrix. It is measured using the total number of correct observations in a category divided by the total number of observations assigned to that category (i.e., the *row* total). The result is a measure of commission error. This user's accuracy or reliability is the probability that an observation actually represents that category in reality. The user's accuracy for the three classes is summarized in Table 4-1.

The Kappa Coefficient of Agreement is a measure of agreement or accuracy between the classified observations and the reference data as indicated by a) the major diagonal, and b) the chance agreement, which is obtained by evaluating the row and column totals in the error matrix (referred to as *marginal* information) (Congalton and Green, 2009). The algorithm is provided in Table 4-1. In the example, the marginal information consisted of (26 x 27), (23 x 25), and (27 x 24). The sum of these values is 1925.

The Kappa Coefficient of Agreement for the simple land cover dataset was 70% (Table 4-1). Kappa values

TABLE 4–2 Computation of root-mean-square-error (RMSE) using actual ground reference information and observed remote sensing-derived leaf-area-index (LAI) measurements.

Actual Ground Reference LAI	Remote Sensing-derived LAI
3.65	3.52
4.25	4.00
2.37	3.40
1.64	1.62
2.89	3.01
4.12	4.08
RMSE = 0.44	

between 0.40 and 0.80 (i.e., 40 to 80%) represent moderate agreement. Kappa values <0.40 (i.e., <40%) represent poor agreement (Jensen, 2005).

Attribute Root-Mean-Square-Error (RMSE)

A RMSE computation may be used when checking the accuracy of interval and ratio-scale attribute data. In this case, the analyst selects a number of observations in the dataset and compares the values of those observations with actual ground reference information. The RMSE is computed using the equation:

$$RMSE = \sqrt{\frac{\sum_{i=1}^{n} (X_{Act_i} - X_{Obs_i})^2}{N}} \quad (4.2)$$

where X_{Act_i} is the actual value of the observation and X_{Obs_i} is the observed value. An acceptable RMSE value will vary depending on error limits set forth at the beginning of the project. For example, consider the six leaf-area-index (LAI) measurements found in Table 4-2. The table consists of remote sensing-derived LAI measurements (i.e., observed) compared with LAI measurements made on the ground using a hand-held ceptometer. Biophysical measurements such as LAI are usually measured with a precision of one or two decimal places.

In the LAI example, the RMSE is determined by computing the differences between the remote sensing derived LAI (i.e., observed) and the actual LAI ground reference value and then squaring them:

$$(3.65 - 3.52)^2 = 0.0169$$

$$(4.25 - 4.00)^2 = 0.0625$$

$$(2.37 - 3.40)^2 = 1.0609$$

$$(1.64 - 1.62)^2 = 0.0004$$

$$(2.89 - 3.01)^2 = 0.0144$$

$$(4.12 - 4.08)^2 = 0.0016$$

The sum of these values (1.1567) is then divided by the number of observations, N, i.e., (1.1567 / 6 = 0.1928). RMSE is the square root of this value:

$$RMSE = \sqrt{0.1928} = 0.44$$

Therefore, the RMSE of LAI for this dataset is equal to 0.44 LAI units. This value may or may not be acceptable depending on the error limits originally specified for the project.

Attribute Logical Consistency

Logical consistency is defined as having the same rules and logic applied throughout a dataset. If one-half of the data were collected by one person and the other half of the data were collected by another person, you need to make sure the logic used to collect the data is consistent throughout the entire dataset — regardless of which person collected the data. In some instances, part of a spatial dataset may contain more precise data than other parts.

Attribute and Spatial Completeness

Completeness is the degree to which the data exhaust the universe of all possible items (Brassel et al., 1995). Completeness consists of two parts: spatial and thematic (i.e., attribute). If a dataset is spatially complete, it covers all of the area of interest with the same level of detail. Unfortunately, sometimes a greater level of attribute detail may be collected in areas where it is easy to obtain information (e.g., near roads), and a lower level of attribute detail may be collected in hard to access areas (e.g., the headwaters of a rugged watershed). This disparity in detail is permissible only if a subset of the map is required to have greater detail.

Thematic (attribute) completeness ensures that the data contain all the thematic information necessary for a given project and that it was collected with the same level of precision. Incomplete fields, partial records, or missing records can play havoc with GIS analysis, especially if statistics must be calculated.

Positional Error

Positional accuracy measures how close the geographic coordinates of features in a spatial data layer are to their real-world geographic coordinates (both horizontally and vertically). This is a very important measurement because if a spatial data layer has poor positional accuracy, you will likely obtain poor or inaccurate results based on your GIS analysis.

Positional accuracy can be determined by examining the *x,y,z* position of features in the spatial database (i.e., a map of the data) and comparing those positions with actual real-world location measurements based on the use of a more accurate measuring device (e.g., a survey-grade GPS unit). Positional accuracy is dependent on the scale at which the data were acquired. Generally, larger-scale spatial databases (e.g., scales >1:20,000) have better positional accuracy than smaller-scale spatial databases (e.g., 1:50,000 or 1:100,000).

Unfortunately, many GIS users make the error of combining two or more spatial databases (e.g., maps) with vastly different scales and different amounts of positional error. One inaccurate spatial database can cause the entire project to have inaccurate final results. In fact, a GIS analysis is only as geometrically accurate as the least accurate map used in the project. This phenomenon is discussed further in the Error Propagation section.

Several not-for-profit organizations and government agencies have developed positional accuracy standards for paper and/or digital maps. These standards are guidelines that enable users to be sure they are using accurate spatial data. Three different data standards are presented to help you understand the positional error characteristics of paper and digital maps.

Map Accuracy Standards

Three main positional accuracy standards have been used during the past 70 years: the U.S. Geological Survey *United States National Map Accuracy Standards*, the American Society for Photogrammetry & Remote Sensing *Map Accuracy Standards for Large-Scale Maps*, and the FGDC *National Standard for Spatial Data Accuracy*.

***United States National Map Accuracy Standards* (NMAS)** The U.S. Geological Survey published the *United States National Map Accuracy Standards* to help cartographers, geographers, map-users, and others understand the spatial error in maps. The USGS published these accuracy standards in 1941 and modified them in 1947 (United States Bureau of the Budget, 1947). These standards helped ensure that maps met minimum positional accuracy criteria. The NMAS were based on the scale of maps, and their tolerances were divided into horizontal and vertical accuracy.

Maps that met NMAS printed the following text in their legends:

> This map complies with National Map Accuracy Standards.

Many historical cartographic datasets that are placed in GIS geodatabases were compiled to NMAS specifications. Therefore, it is important to know about this accuracy standard.

TABLE 4–3 The allowable horizontal error for several different map scales according to *ASPRS Accuracy Standards for Large-Scale Maps* (ASPRS, 1989).

Scale	Error ± ft.	Error ± m
1:1,200	1	0.305
1:2,400	2	0.601
1:4,800	4	1.22
1:6,000	5	1.52
1:9,600	8	2.44
1:20,000	16.7	5.09

ASPRS Map Accuracy Standards for Large-Scale Maps The American Society for Photogrammetry and Remote Sensing (ASPRS) published the *ASPRS Accuracy Standards for Large-Scale Maps* (>1:20,000 scale) in 1989. These standards effectively replaced the previous U.S. Geological Survey standards. The ASPRS standards set horizontal and vertical accuracy limits based on calculated RMSE values. This calculation of RMSE incorporates both the X and Y dimensions of the checkpoints:

$$RMSE = \sqrt{\frac{\sum_{i=1}^{n}[(X_{Act_i} - X_{Obs_i})^2 + (Y_{Act_i} - Y_{Obs_i})^2]}{N}} \quad (4.3)$$

where the RMSE is the square root of the average squared differences between actual (true) locations and locations observed on the map or in the spatial database (ASPRS, 1989). Table 4-3 lists the allowable horizontal error limits for maps at various scales using these standards. If maps adhere to the *ASPRS Accura-*

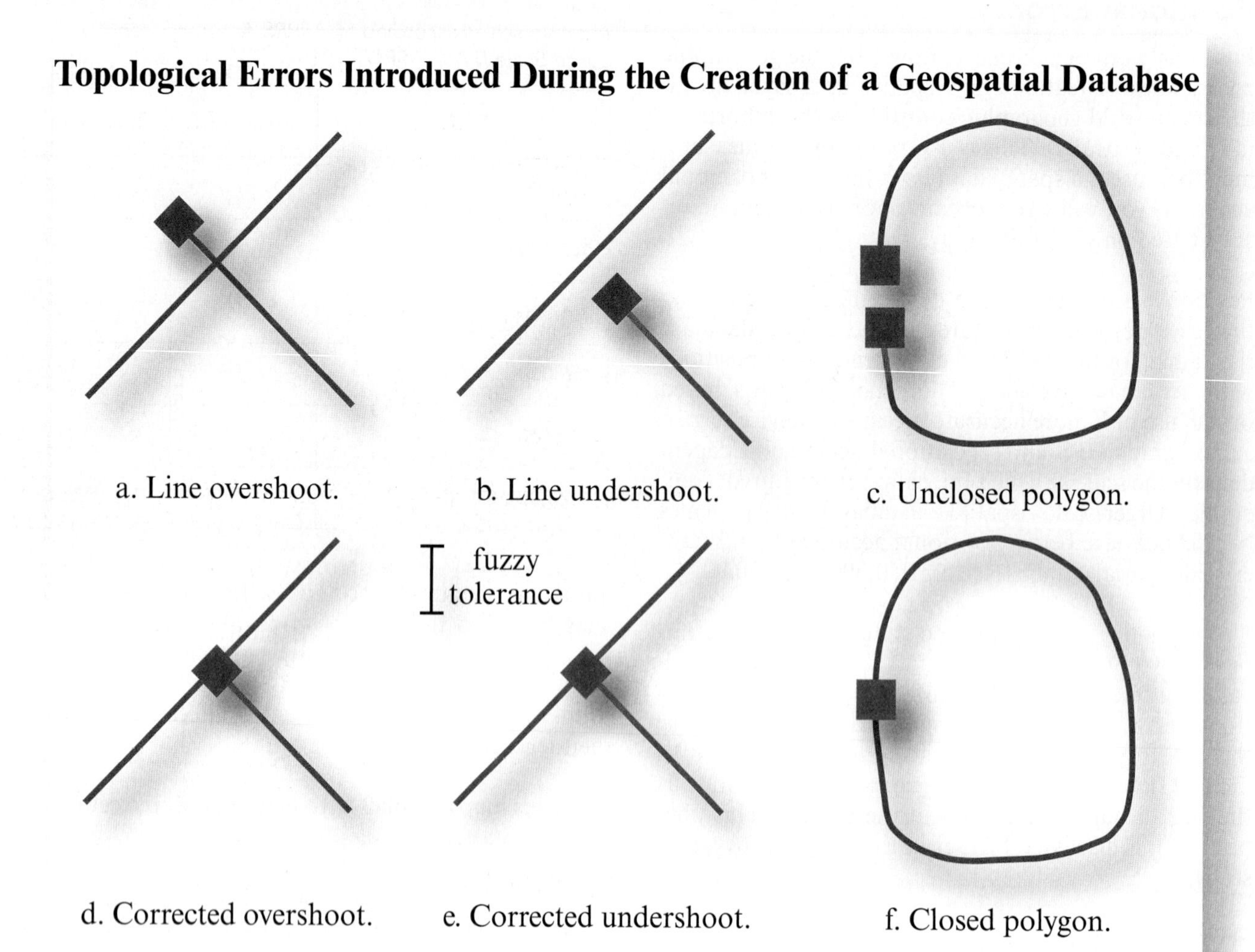

FIGURE 4–4 Example of topological error in a typical GIS geodatabase. a) Lines can be overshot causing an overshoot error. This kind of error can be corrected using a fuzzy tolerance value. b) Line undershoot errors occur when lines do not connect where they are supposed to connect. This error can be corrected by applying a fuzzy tolerance value. c) This polygon is not closed. It will not be regarded as a polygon unless the ends are snapped together. This can be accomplished using a fuzzy tolerance value. d-f) Corrected overshoot, undershoot, and closed polygon after the application of a fuzzy tolerance value.

cy Standards for Large-Scale Maps, the following text may be printed on the map:

> This map was checked and found to conform to the ASPRS standard for Class 1 map accuracy.

FGDC *National Standard for Spatial Data Accuracy* (NSSDA) In 1998, the Federal Geographic Data Committee established the *National Standard for Spatial Data Accuracy* to replace National Map Accuracy Standards (FGDC, 1998b). NSSDA uses the ASPRS accuracy standards for large-scale maps and extends the standards to maps smaller than 1:20,000-scale. The NSSDA uses RMSE Equation 4.3 to estimate accuracy with respect to true location. Accuracy is reported in ground distances at the 95% confidence level. This means that 95% of the positions in a dataset have an error that is equal to or smaller than the error standards at any particular scale (FGDC, 1998b). To convert the RMSE to 95 percent confidence, multiply the RMSE by 1.7308 (the standard error of the mean at 95% confidence). This value can then be reported on the map or in the metadata.

As with database sampling to determine accuracy, there are many different methods to sample for horizontal and vertical accuracy. As noted above, these methods include random sampling of the entire mapped area, systematic sampling to ensure that all areas on the map are represented, and stratified sampling to ensure that areas with greater variance (e.g., areas with extreme local relief) are included in the error assessment.

Topological Error

There are other kinds of errors that may be present in a geodatabase. These errors are often created at the time the geodatabase is "built". For example, the analyst creating lines and polygons in a vector geodatabase may introduce several types of topological error. Lines in the dataset may be overshot (Figure 4-4a) or undershot (Figure 4-4b) resulting in geometric errors. Polygons may not be closed resulting in polygon errors (Figure 4-4c). When polygons are not closed, they are not recognized as polygons. Instead, they are recognized as lines.

These types of errors are often introduced when creating new point, line, or area data using GIS editing tools. To correct these errors, GIS users can: a) apply an appropriate fuzzy tolerance value, or b) delete the point, line, and area data and recreate the features. **Fuzzy tolerance** is the distance within which individual discrete points are snapped to form a single point during editing (Lo and Yeung, 2007). Setting a correct fuzzy tolerance value is very important when building geospatial vector databases because a value too large can result in features being combined (snapped together) that should not be combined. Conversely, if the fuzzy tolerance is too small, some important features that need to be joined may not be snapped together. Correct application of a fuzzy tolerance results in corrected overshoots, corrected undershoots, and closed polygons as shown in Figure 4-4d-f).

Polygons often share the same *x,y*-coordinates along common borders. Unfortunately, sometimes the creation and/or editing process results in shared polygon boundaries that contain geometric error. This can introduce spurious polygons called slivers such as the ones shown in Figure 4-5a. A carefully selected fuzzy tolerance value can be applied that results in a clean linear border between adjacent polygons (Figure 4-5b). Additional information about topology is provided in Chapter 5.

Geometric Error between Two Adjacent Polygons

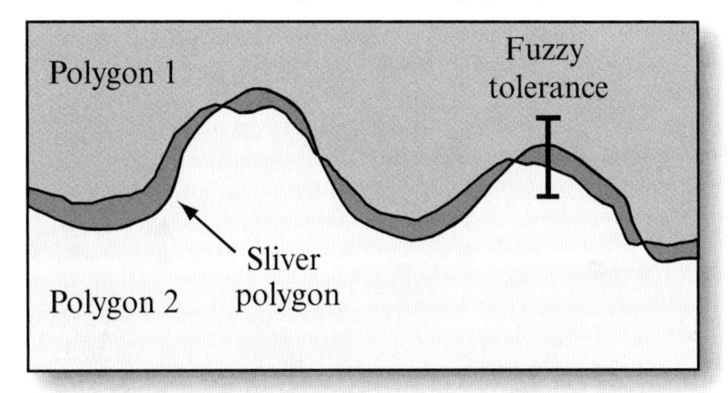

a. Geometric error along the common border of two adjacent polygons.

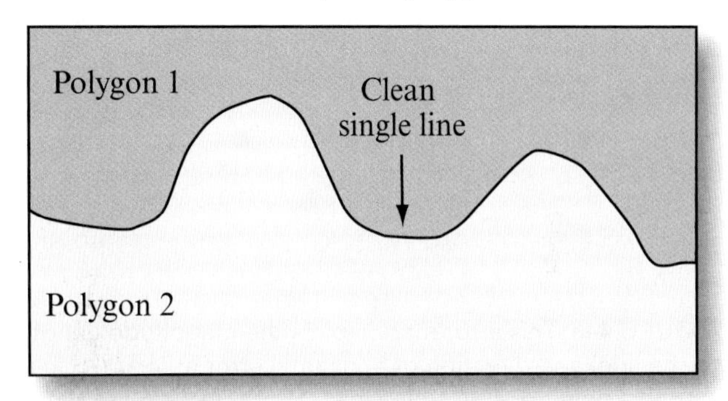

b. Clean single line shared by both polygons after use of a fuzzy tolerance.

FIGURE 4–5 a) Polygon 1 and Polygon 2 are supposed to share the same *x,y*-coordinates along their common border. Unfortunately, the two polygons have geometric error along their common border. The error has resulted in the creation of five entirely new polygons referred to as slivers (shown in red). b) The geospatial error associated with the two boundaries was corrected by selecting an appropriate fuzzy tolerance value which snapped the two lines together resulting in the single black line whose *x,y*-coordinates are shared by Polygon 1 and Polygon 2.

Temporal Accuracy

Geospatial databases may be current for a time and then become outdated. **Temporal accuracy** refers to how up-to-date a geospatial database is. Some geospatial data need to be updated every half-hour or at even shorter time increments. For example, assume you are commuting home from your job and you are trying to avoid heavy traffic. A passenger in your car has a navigation device with traffic information. The traffic information should be updated very frequently (e.g., every 1 to 2 minutes) for it to be useful. Another example would be Doppler radar images that are used to predict storm tracks and precipitation amounts. If the animated maps are more than a few hours old, they may not be useful. In other situations, data that are several years old may be appropriate for a particular project. For example, monitoring the change in land cover in a county is often performed using remotely sensed data that are five to ten years old.

Error Visualization

Error in a geospatial database is usually reported using standardized accuracy measures as previously discussed. However, it is often difficult to appreciate the

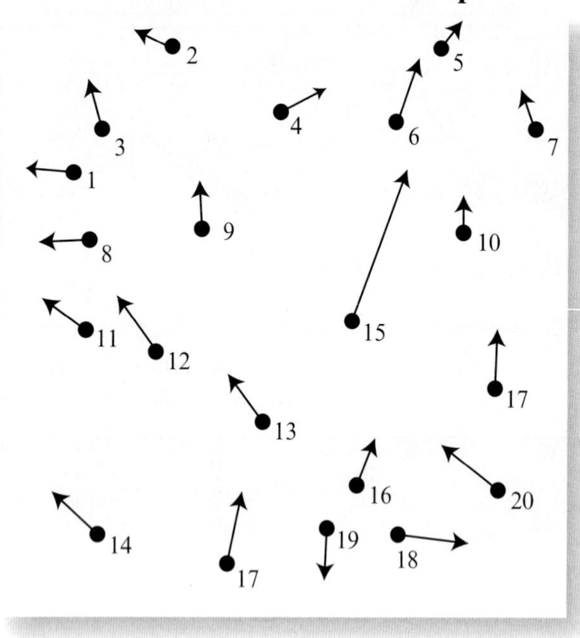

FIGURE 4–6 This error map depicts the magnitude (length of the line) and direction of horizontal error associated with 20 checkpoint locations on a map. After creating an error map, it is common to examine the errors to make sure that the errors are random and not systematic throughout the map. Checkpoints in the western half of the map appear to have a systematic bias toward the west-northwest. If the errors are systematic, this may be an indication that there are data collection or instrument calibration problems.

amount of error and its spatial distribution and pattern without visualizing the error. Therefore, scientists have developed methods to visualize error. One way to visualize errors in spatial data is to create an error map. For example, the direction and magnitude of horizontal error associated with 20 checkpoints is shown in Figure 4-6.

Another effective way to visualize error is to create a shadow map that defines the confidence that you have in certain portions of the map. For example, a land cover map consisting of cropland and deciduous forest is shown in Figure 4-7a. The accuracy associated with the deciduous forest polygons is shown in Figure 4-7b. Note how the interior of the polygons are more accurate than those areas close to the polygon boundaries. Shadow map figures are useful when describing error to those who may not be familiar with spatial data.

Error Propagation

If attribute or positional errors are not known, corrected, or accounted for at the beginning of a GIS project, they will propagate throughout the study and accumulate in interim or final products. For example, assume you have a GIS data layer that has some attribute or positional error in it. As this layer is processed with other data layers and new data are created, the error will propagate (i.e., cascade) throughout the subsequent datasets.

An example of error propagation in a GIS analysis is shown in Figure 4-8. A homogeneous field of corn that has been mapped accurately is shown in Figure 4-8a. The soil texture of the same field (sand and clay) is mapped accurately in Figure 4-8b. Unfortunately, geometric error was introduced when mapping the irrigation characteristics of the same field (Figure 4-8c). The overlay of the crop type, soil texture, and inaccurate irrigation data resulted in an inaccurate map (Figure 4-8d). Note how the use of a single inaccurate file (irrigation) caused all of the spatial information in the final map to be inaccurate. The irrigation data are mapped accurately in Figure 4-8e. The overlay of crop type, soil texture, and irrigation data resulted in an accurate map shown in Figure 4-8f that can be used to make wise land use decisions.

Ecological Fallacy

Ecological fallacy is the belief that all observations within an area will exhibit the same or similar values for a particular characteristic. In other words, it is the belief that the characteristics or relationships of a group are the same for each individual within the group (Freedman, 1999). For example, assume you live in a school district where the average standardized test score is 75 out of 100. Your friend lives in a school district where the average score for the same test is 65 out of 100. Ecological fallacy refers to the tendency that most people would have that any given student in your school district would score higher on the test than any given student in your friend's school district.

Similarly, when examining the median income in adjacent census block groups, one may incorrectly assume that individual families in a block-group with a high median income are more wealthy than individual families in a block group with a lower median income. For example, Figure 4-9 shows the median income for all California counties. Santa Clara County (A) near San Francisco has a much greater median income than rural Modoc County (B) in the northeast corner of the state. Ecological fallacy occurs if you assume that any one randomly selected individual in Santa Clara County is wealthier than any one randomly selected individual in Modoc County. This may not be the case.

Accuracy Visualization Using a Shadow Map

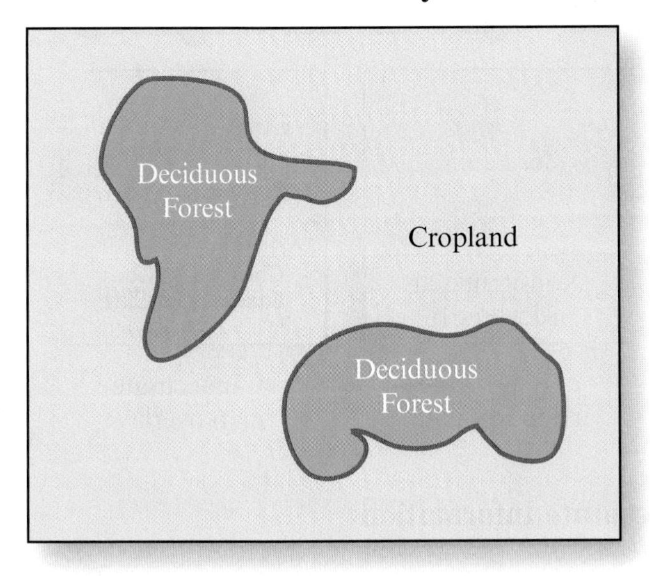

a. Land cover classification map.

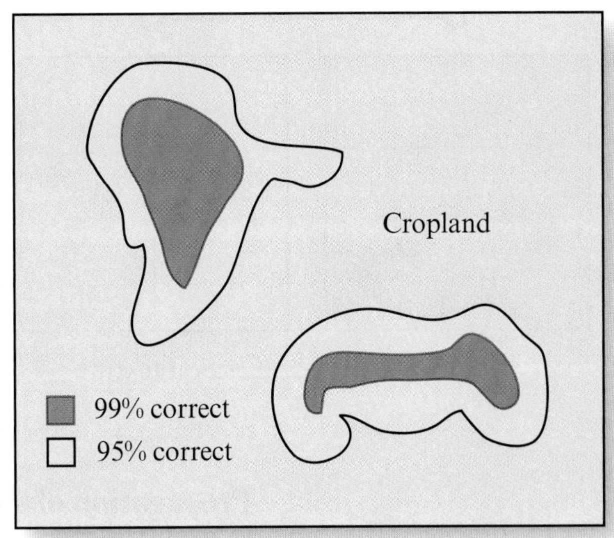

b. Shadow map of deciduous forest classification accuracy.

FIGURE 4–7 a) A land cover classification map consisting of cropland and two patches of deciduous forest. b) A shadow map depicting the accuracy of the deciduous forest class. Note that the areas close to the edges of the deciduous forest patches are less accurate than the interior of the patches.

Modifiable Areal Unit Problem

Spatial data may be reported, mapped, and analyzed using enumeration units or districts of various sizes, including countries, states, counties, cities, census block groups, census blocks, police precincts, school districts, Zipcode boundaries, etc. When smaller areal units are combined into fewer, larger units, the variation present in the smaller units may decrease (Dark and Bram, 2007). The scale effect causes variation in statistical results between different levels of aggregation. Therefore, the degree of association or correlation between variables depends on the size of the areal units being analyzed. Generally, the correlation between variables increases as the size of the areal unit increases. Consequently, it is possible for researchers to "modify" the areal units that are being mapped, introducing bias into the project. This is typically referred to as the **modifiable areal unit problem** (Openshaw, 1984).

For example, a researcher may find a "better" or "higher" correlation between two variables when the variables are analyzed at the census block level rather than at the census tract level. Both census tracts and census blocks of downtown Chicago, IL, are shown in Figure 4-10. Depending on what is being studied, either enumeration unit may be appropriate. Modifiable areal unit problems like this should be considered carefully so that the proper level of spatial aggregation is used for a particular project.

Summary

This chapter introduced several concepts that should help you understand spatial data quality. Spatial metadata is one of the most important types of information that can be used to assess the quality of spatial data. Spatial metadata information is the first file you should request when purchasing spatial data or receiving spatial data from a person or organization. You should keep the metadata up to date as you modify or change the spatial dataset in any substantial way.

Knowledge of any attribute error and horizontal and/or vertical position error will help you determine if the spatial data are of value for use in a particular study. Topological geometric errors (e.g., undershoots, overshoots, polygon closure problems, edge-match problems, etc.) must be corrected prior to data analysis. Sometimes it is useful to create error maps or shadow maps to visualize error. GIS analysts should use the most appropriate size of enumeration district (i.e., avoiding the modifiable areal unit problem) because the use of progressively larger enumeration districts

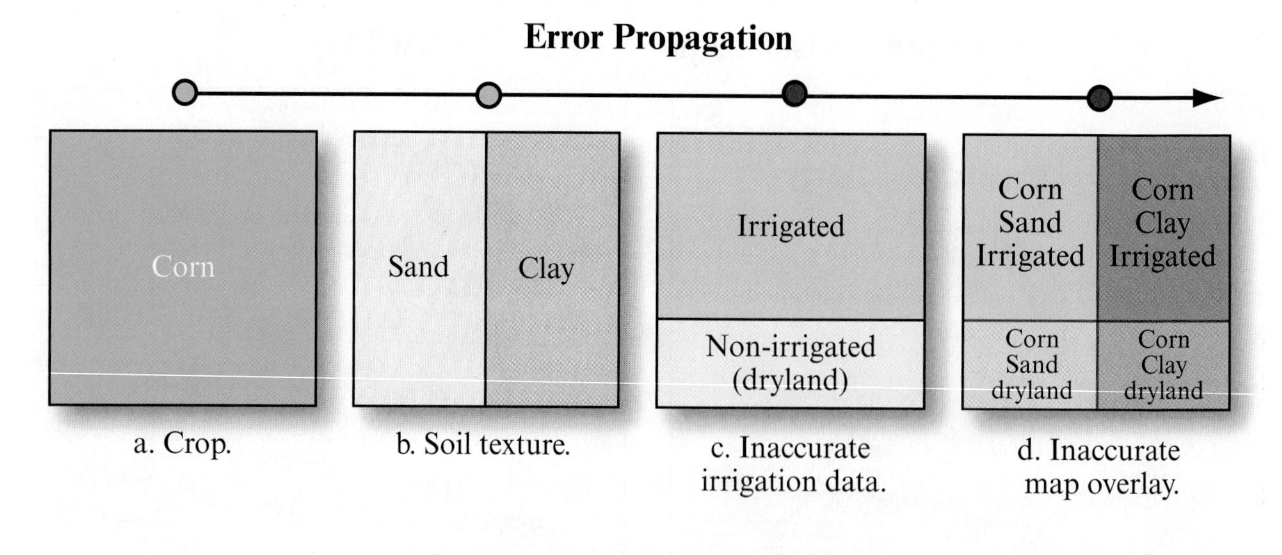

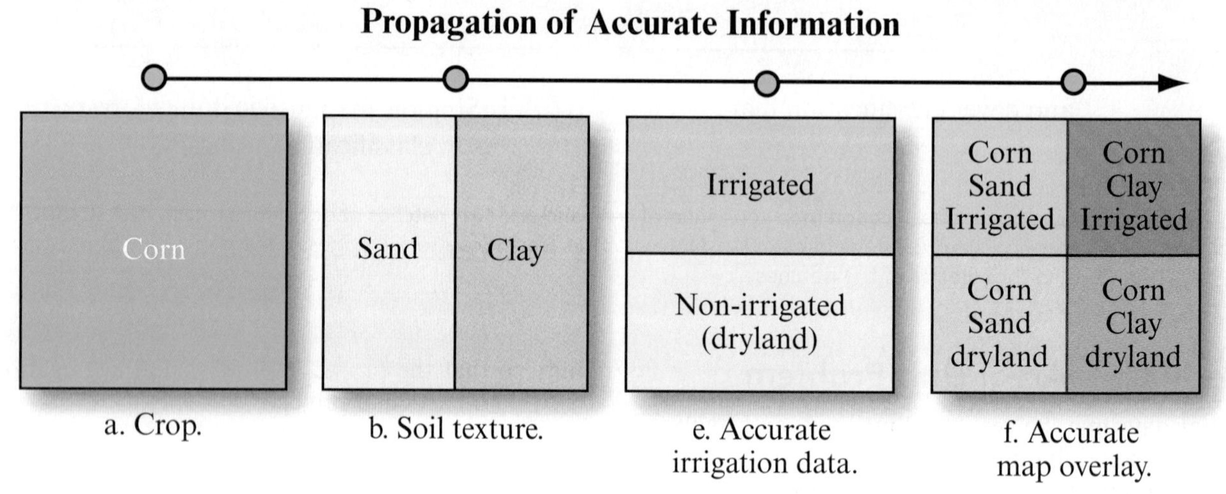

FIGURE 4–8 Error propagates during GIS analysis when inaccurate data are introduced. a) A homogeneous field of corn is mapped accurately. b) The soil texture of the same field (sand and clay) is mapped accurately. c) Unfortunately, the irrigation data were mapped inaccurately. d) The overlay of the crop type, soil texture, and inaccurate irrigation data results in an inaccurate map that could lead to unwise decisions. In this particular example, note how the use of a single inaccurate file causes all of the spatial information in the final map to be inaccurate. e) The irrigation data are mapped accurately. f) The overlay of crop type, soil texture, and accurate irrigation data results in an accurate map that can be used to make wise land use decisions.

can lead to increased association or correlation between variables.

Review Questions

1. Describe the modifiable areal unit problem and provide an example.

2. Describe ecological fallacy and provide an example.

3. Describe the various statistics that can be extracted from an error matrix to quantitatively assess the accuracy of nominal scale data.

4. What are the most common types of topological error?

5. Briefly review the history of spatial data standards in the United States.

6. How are attribute and positional error propagated in a GIS study?

7. How can you visualize the error in a geospatial dataset?

8. Describe how root-mean-square-error (RMSE) is computed when working with a) ratio-scaled data such

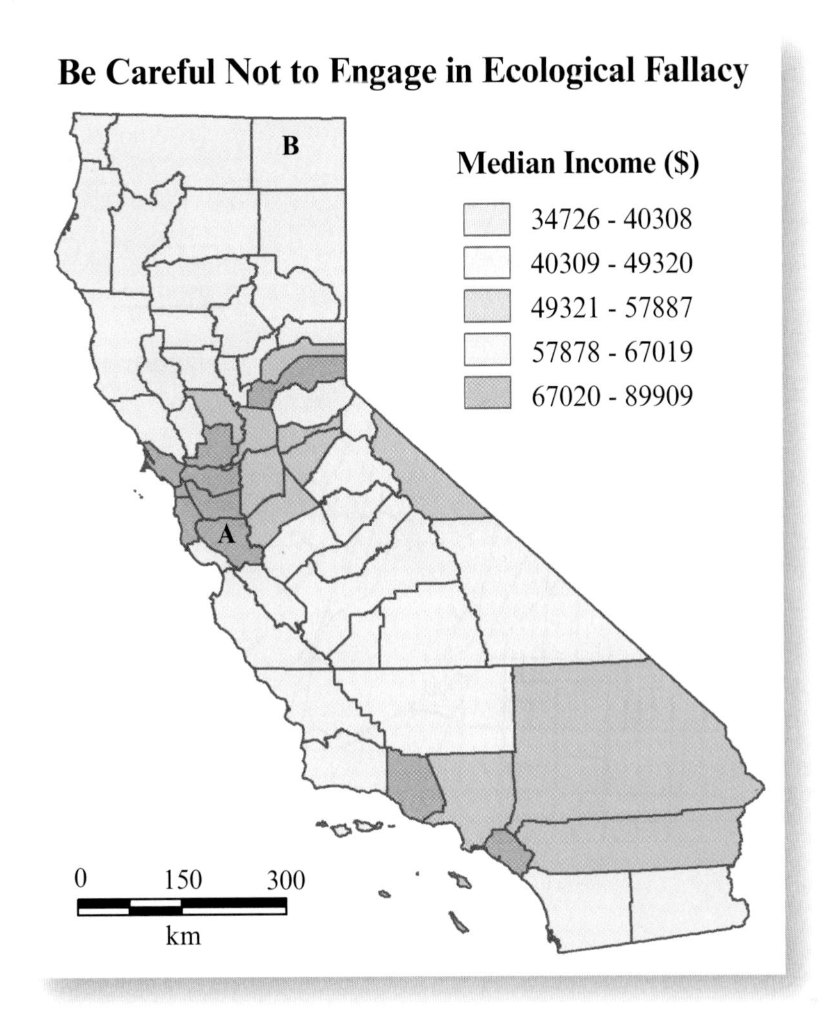

FIGURE 4–9 Ecological fallacy occurs when we assume that the characteristics of a particular area or group are associated with every person or thing that is within that area or group. For example, consider two individuals; one lives in Santa Clara county (A) near San Francisco and the other lives in rural Modoc county (B). Would you automatically assume that the person living in Santa Clara county has a higher income? Making this assumption would be an example of ecological fallacy (data courtesy of U.S. Census Bureau).

as temperature or biomass, and b) positional x, y, and z data.

9. Describe both accuracy and precision. How are they similar? How are they different?

10. Is metadata really that important? Justify why so much time and effort is spent on the creation and maintenance of metadata.

Glossary

Accuracy: The extent to which the attribute and positional (x,y-location) data correspond to their real-world counterparts.

Completeness: The extent to which the data exhaust the universe of all possible items.

Ecological Fallacy: The belief that all observations within an area will exhibit the same or similar values for a particular characteristic.

Error Matrix: A table used to calculate producer's and user's accuracies, overall accuracy, and Kappa Coefficient of Agreement.

Fuzzy Tolerance: The distance within which individual discrete points are snapped to form a single point during geographic editing.

Logical Consistency: Careful application of the same rules and logic throughout a dataset.

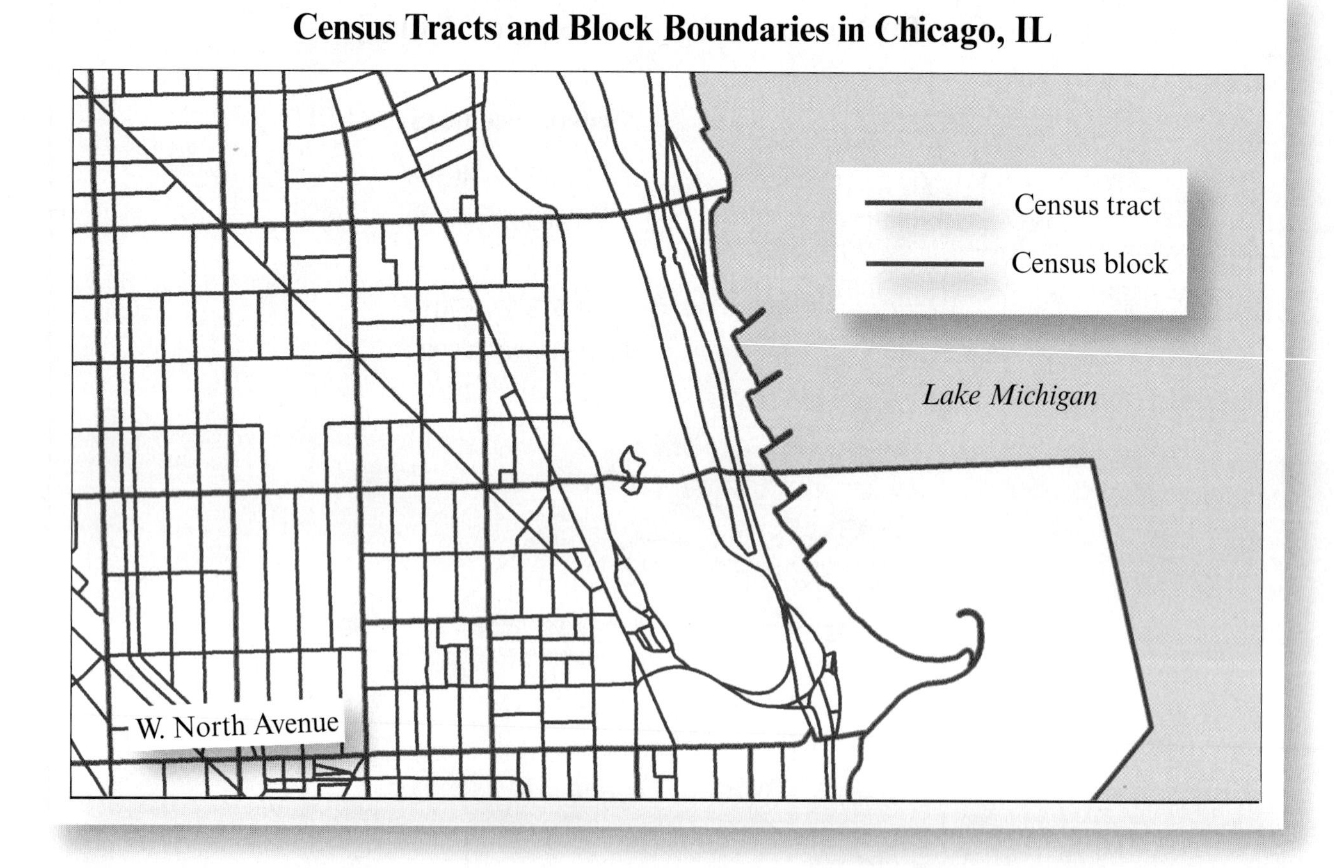

FIGURE 4–10 This figure shows United States census tracts for Chicago, IL, in blue and census blocks in red. Depending on what is being studied, either enumeration unit may be appropriate. The modifiable areal unit problem suggests that, in general, the greater the size of the enumeration unit, the greater the correlation between variables (data courtesy of the U.S. Bureau of the Census).

Metadata: Describes the basic characteristics of the spatial datasets often analyzed in a GIS.

Modifiable Areal Unit Problem: Occurs when spatial areas are analyzed using enumeration units that are poorly suited for what is being studied.

Positional Accuracy: A measure of how close the geographic coordinates of features in a spatial dataset are to their real-world geographic coordinates (both horizontal and vertical).

Precision: A measure of the "exactness" of a measurement.

Random Sample: A sample where every observation has an equal chance of being selected.

Stratified Random Sample: A sample where the observations are stratified to account for the known variation in the population.

Systematic Sample: A sample that is implemented according to a predetermined system.

Temporal Accuracy: Refers to how up to date a dataset is.

References

Anderson, J. R., Hardy, E. E., Roach, J. T. and R. E. Witmer, 1976, "A Land Use and Land Cover Classification System for Use with Remote Sensor Data," *Professional Paper #964,* Reston: U.S. Geological Survey, 60 p.

ASPRS, 1989, "ASPRS Accuracy Standards for Large-Scale Maps," *Photogrammetric Engineering & Remote Sensing,* 55:1068–1070.

Brassel, K., Bucher, F., Stephan, E. and A. Vchovski, 1995, "Completeness," in *Elements of Spatial Data Quality,* by Guptill, S. C. and J. L. Morrison (Eds.), New York: Oxford Elsevier Science, 81–108.

Congalton, R. G. and K. Green, 2009, *Assessing the Accuracy of Remotely Sensed Data: Principles & Practices,* Boca Raton: CRC Press, 183 p.

Dark, S. J. and D. Bram, 2007, "The Modifiable Areal Unit Problem (MAUP) in Physical Geography," *Progress in Physical Geography*, 31:471–479.

Devillers, R., Bedard, Y. and R. Jeansoulin, 2005, "Multidimensional Management of Geospatial Data Quality Information for its Dynamic Use within GIS," *Photogrammetric Engineering & Remote Sensing*, 17:205–215.

Freedman, D. A., 1999, "Ecological Inference and the Ecological Fallacy," *International Encyclopedia for the Social & Behavioral Sciences,* Technical Report No. 549.

FGDC, 1998a, *Content Standard for Digital Geospatial Metadata*, Washington: Federal Geographic Data Committee, Publication FGDC-STD-001-1998.

FGDC, 1998b, *Geospatial Positioning Accuracy Standards Part 3: National Standard for Spatial Data Accuracy,* Washington: Federal Geographic Data Committee, Publication FGDC-STD-007.3-1998.

Jensen, J. R., 2005, *Introductory Digital Image Processing: A Remote Sensing Perspective*, New Jersey: Pearson Prentice-Hall, 526 p.

Jensen, J. R. and J. M. Shumway, 2010, "Sampling Our World," in B. Gomez and J. P. Jones III (Eds.), *Research Methods in Geography,* New York: Wiley Blackwell, 77-90.

Lo, C. P. and A. K. W. Yeung, 2007. *Concepts and Techniques of Geographic Information Systems,* 2nd Ed., New Jersey: Pearson Prentice-Hall, 532 p.

NOAA, 2007, "Accuracy Versus Precision," in *NOAA Celebrates 200 Years of Science, Service, and Stewardship*, Washington: National Oceanic and Atmospheric Administration (http://celebrating200years.noaa.gov/magazine/tct/tct_side1.html).

Openshaw, S., 1984, *The Modifiable Areal Unit Problem*, Norwich: Geo Books, 41 p.

United States Bureau of the Budget, 1947, *United States National Map Accuracy Standards*, Washington: United States Bureau of the Budget.

5 Spatial Data Models and Databases

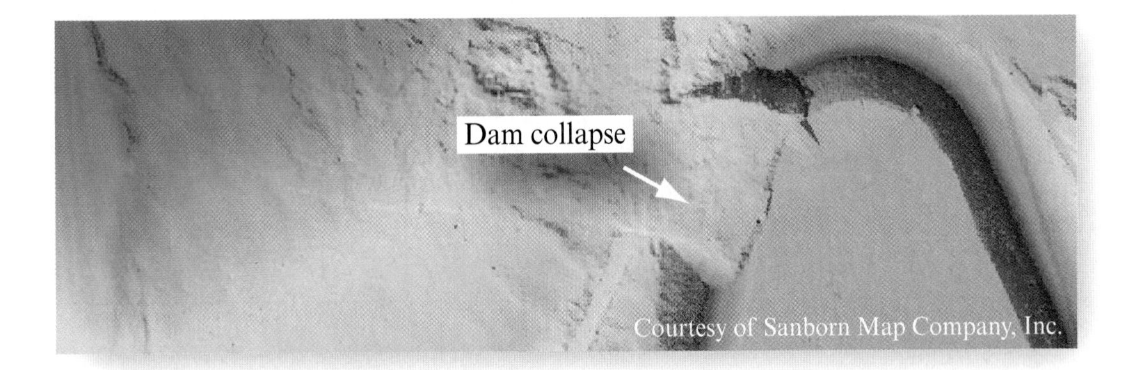

Geographic information systems typically store spatial data in one of two formats: vector or raster. These data formats are practical and efficient. Databases are often used to store the attribute data associated with these two data structures.

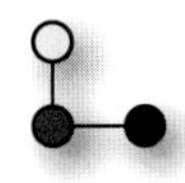

Overview

This chapter first reviews the characteristics of the two main data models that are used to represent spatial data and some common file formats. The chapter then describes some of the ways that geographic information systems store, query, and relate attribute data to these data structures through the use of databases. Students should gain a good understanding of these concepts to effectively structure, edit, and analyze spatial data.

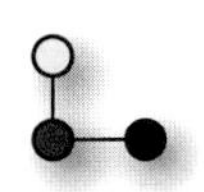

GIS Data Models

Data models define how real-world spatial features are represented in a GIS (Bolstad and Smith, 1992). Geospatial data are typically represented by two main data models (also called data structures): vector and raster. The representation of real-world spatial information in vector and raster format is shown in Figure 5-1. The vector representation consists of points, lines, and polygons created using beginning and ending nodes and intervening vertices, each with detailed *x,y* coordinate information. The raster representation stores the spatial information in a user-defined grid where every cell (picture element or pixel) has a unique geographic location and attribute value. Vector data models can be further subdivided into georelational and object-based data models.

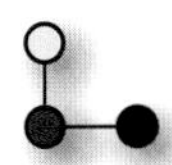

Vector Data

Vector maps represent the most common form of maps that you typically use. For example, almost all road atlases, GPS navigation devices, and Internet mapping engines display vector maps. The vector data structure uses points, lines, and polygons to represent spatial features. As stated in Chapter 2, projected points are addressed using simple *x,y* coordinates; lines consist of connected *x,y* coordinates called nodes or vertices; and polygons (areas) are simply enclosed lines where the beginning and ending nodes have the same coordinate value (Figure 5-1b).

Points

A point is the most basic vector feature and has location properties (e.g., *x,y* coordinate values). Examples of points include petroleum or freshwater wells, historic landmarks, horizontal and vertical benchmarks, utility manhole covers, telephone poles, fire hydrants, ATMs, post office deposit boxes, and police and fire stations. For example, all of the weather stations in Utah are displayed as points in Figure 5-2. Note that the *x* and *y* coordinates are in degrees of longitude and latitude. The coordinates could also be in feet or meters in a State Plane Coordinate System or in meters in a Universal Transverse Mercator (UTM) map projection. The user decides the units the *x,y* locations are stored in.

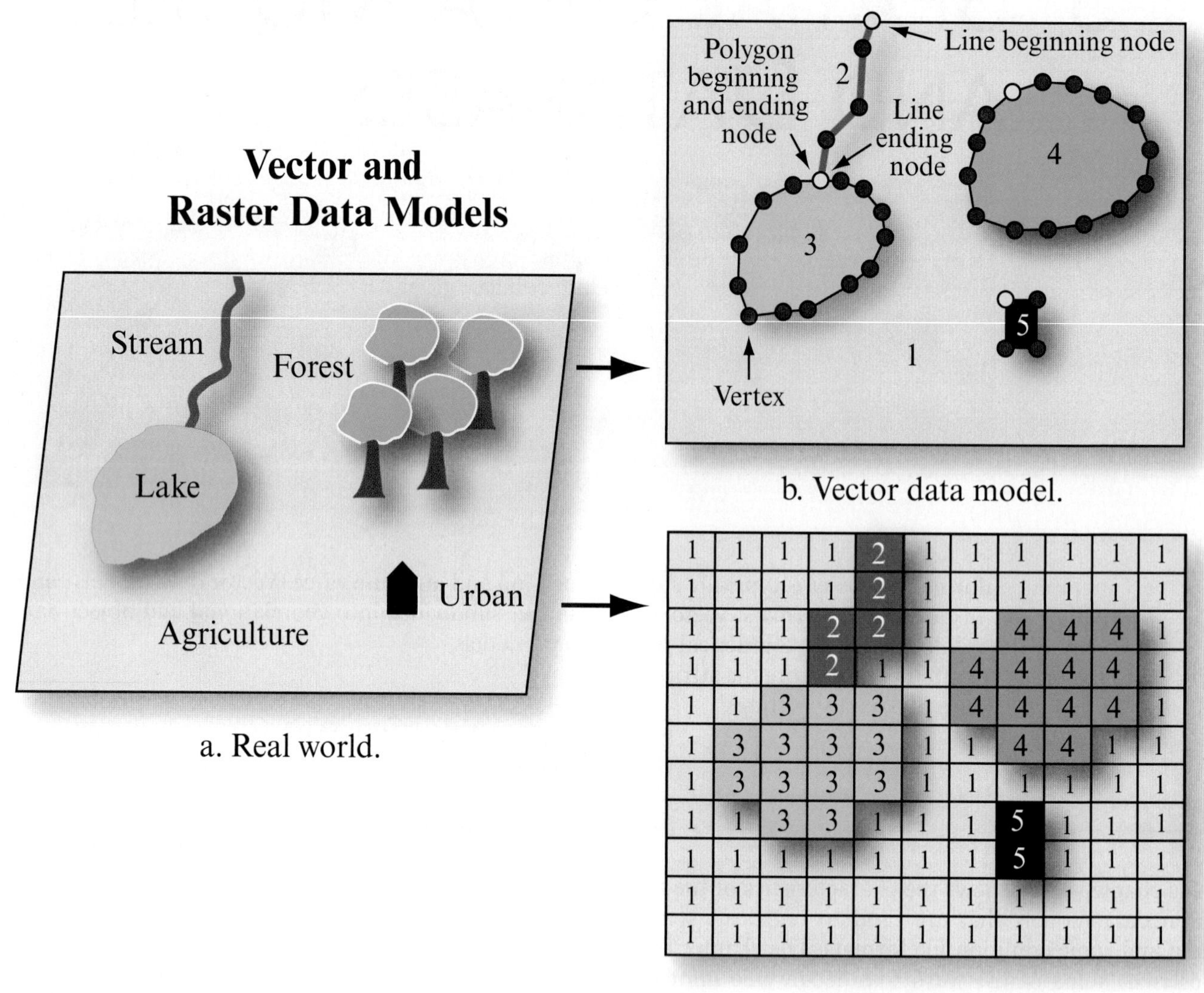

FIGURE 5–1 Features in the real world can be represented using vector and raster data models. a) The real world. b) The real world portrayed in vector format. c) The real world portrayed in raster format.

Lines

Lines are one-dimensional features that have both location and length properties. All lines have a minimum of two points, a beginning and an ending point, often referred to as **nodes**. Nodes are also located at the intersection of two or more lines. Additional points may be placed between the beginning and ending nodes to give shape to the line. These points are often called **vertices** (Figures 5-1 and 5-3). The shape of the line between the beginning and ending nodes may also be stored as a mathematical equation, e.g., a spline. Straight lines often represent anthropogenic (human-made) features such as roads, property boundaries, and administrative boundaries. Nature tends to create landscapes that consist of curved lines, such as rivers, streams, and shorelines. The major roads in Utah are shown as line segments in Figure 5-3 with Interstates 70 and 80 highlighted.

Areas (Polygons)

Areas are two-dimensional objects bounded by a continuous line. For a stand-alone area (polygon), a single node defines the beginning and ending point as shown in Figures 5-1b and 5-4. Polygons that share common boundaries share common nodes where two or more lines intersect (Figure 5-4).

Areas have both size and perimeter properties. Areas can be used to represent many different kinds of spatial phenomena such as counties, states, parcels, land cover, soil type, etc. For example, all of the county boundaries in Utah are displayed in Figure 5-4. Each county has unique perimeter and area characteristics.

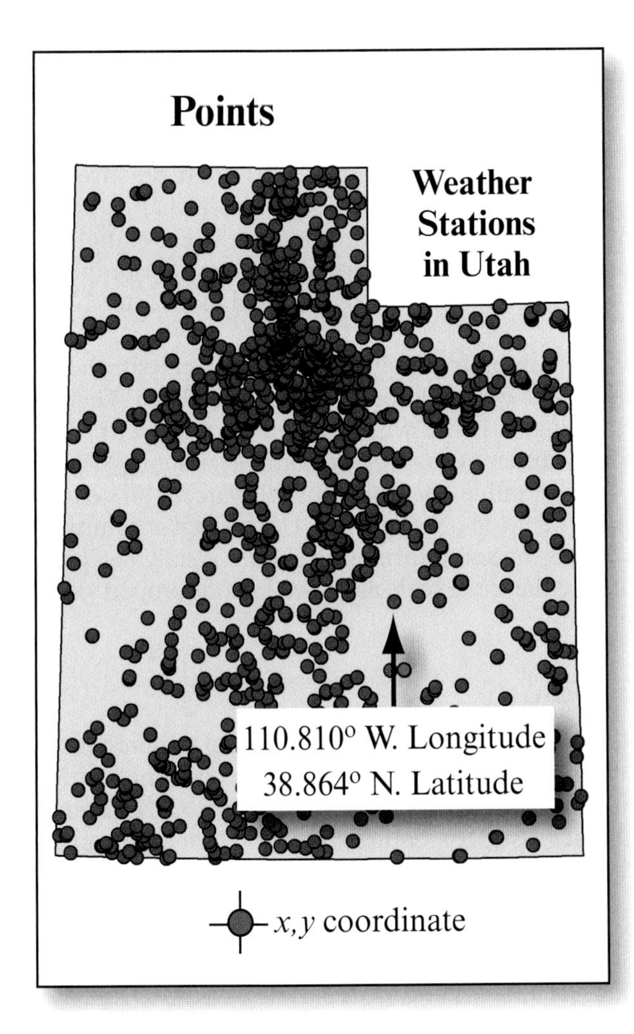

FIGURE 5–2 The points in this map represent the location of all the weather stations in Utah. Each weather station has a unique x (longitude) and y (latitude) location. The geographic coordinates of the Ghost Rocks Weather Station in Emery County are provided (courtesy State of Utah).

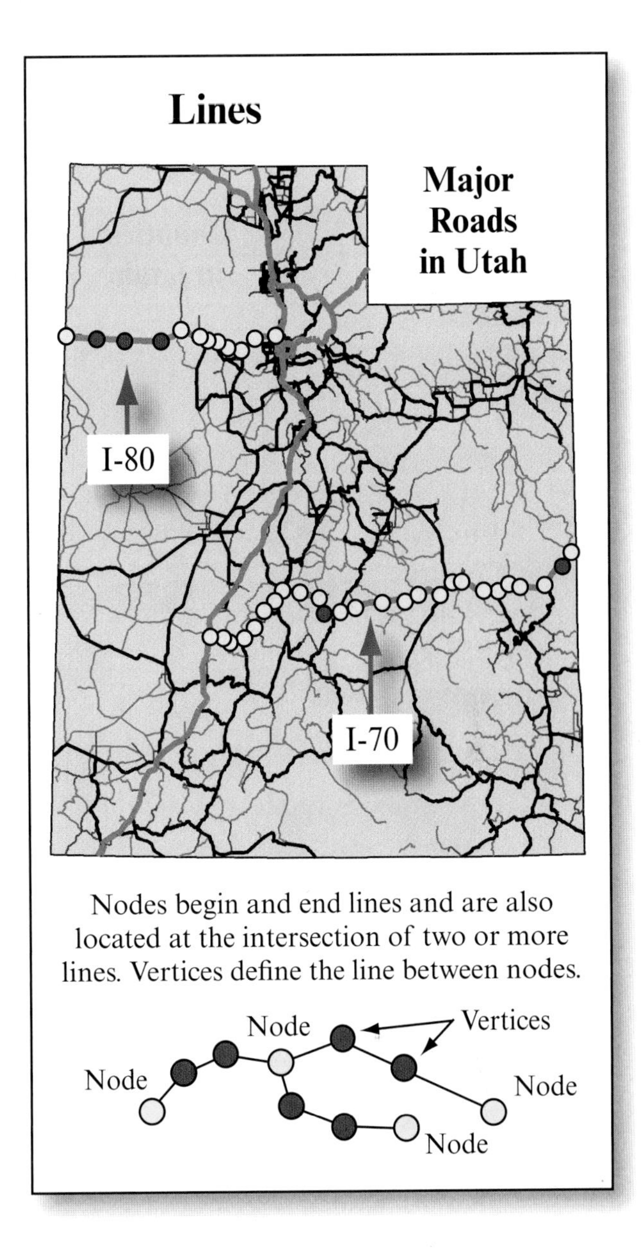

FIGURE 5–3 The lines in this map represent the major roads in Utah. Each line segment consists of a beginning and an ending node and intervening points (vertices) that give shape to the line. Nodes are also located whenever two or more lines intersect. All points in a line have unique x,y coordinates. The nodes and vertices associated with Interstates 70 and 80 are highlighted (data courtesy State of Utah).

Scale Considerations

Map scale is the ratio of the distance on the map to the distance on the Earth. A common map scale is 1:24,000. This scale means that one unit of anything measured on the map (centimeter, meter, inch, etc.) is equal to 24,000 of those same units in the real world on the ground. Map scale plays an important role in the representation of spatial features when digital spatial information is output to a hard-copy map or digital map displayed on a computer screen. For example, Figure 5-5 represents the same spatial feature (the city of Terre Haute, IN) displayed at two different scales. In the larger-scale display, Terre Haute is symbolized as a polygon whereas in the smaller-scale display it is symbolized as a point that does not include perimeter or area information.

Scale is usually described in one of three ways on a map:

- as a *representative fraction* (sometimes referred to as a dimensionless ratio): 1/24,000 or 1:24,000,
- *verbal* or *unit equivalent*: e.g., 1 in. = 24,000 in. or 1 in. = 2,000 ft., and/or
- *graphically*: e.g., a bar scale.

The GIS analyst should be aware that representative fractions and verbal scales placed on the original map

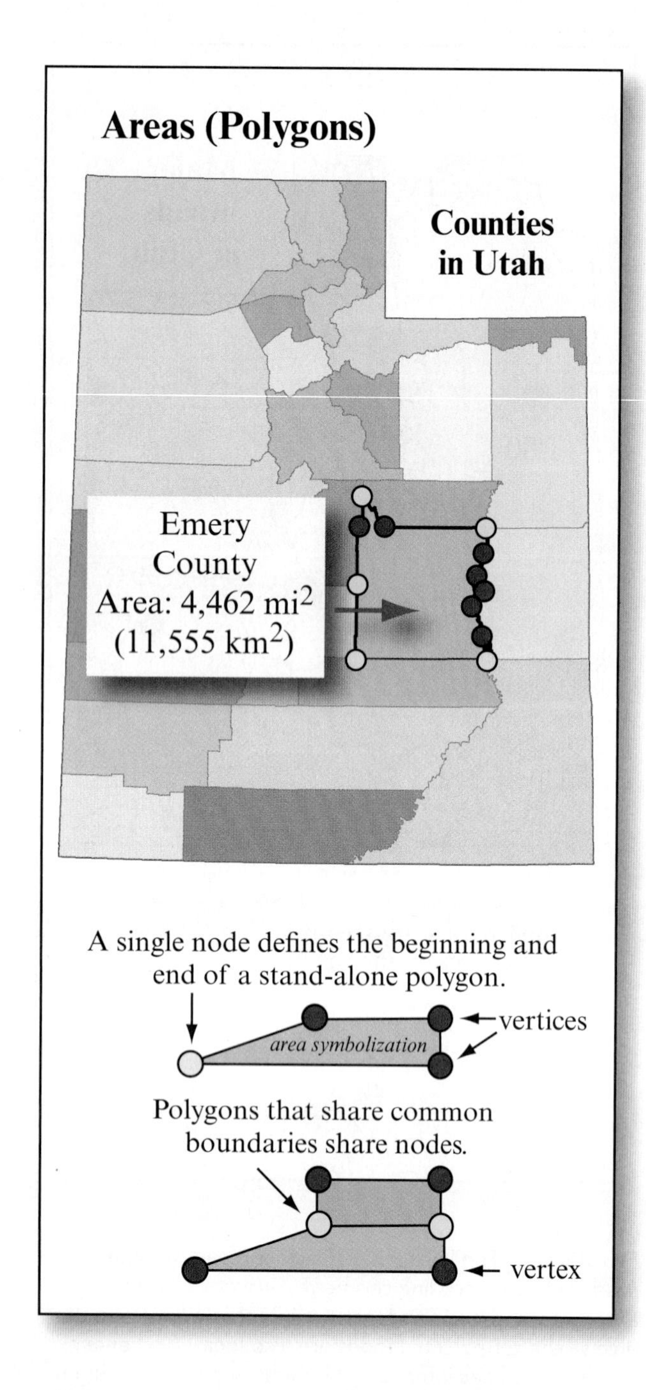

FIGURE 5–4 The polygons in the map represent the 29 counties in Utah. Each county polygon has unique perimeter and area properties. Polygons that share common boundaries share nodes. Stand-alone polygons have a single node (courtesy State of Utah).

or image change whenever the original map or image is enlarged or reduced. This is because the actual map scale has changed but the "written" representative fraction or verbal scale description is not updated. Conversely, graphical bar scales placed on hard-copy maps or displayed on the computer screen usually contain a line with hash marks placed at user-specified intervals, e.g., 0, 5, 10 km as shown in Figure 5-5. Graphical bar scales are particularly useful when maps are reduced or enlarged because the graphical bar scale changes size in proportion to the enlargement or reduction. Therefore, when creating map compositions from digital geospatial data, it is good practice to always place a graphical bar scale on the map to help the map user understand the scale of the geospatial information. Additional information about the proper cartographic use of bar scales is found in Chapter 10.

When combining multiple maps for analysis, the scale of each map should be carefully considered. Generally speaking, it is not wise to combine maps with significantly different scales. For example, assume you wanted to examine the soil type of parcels on relatively small farms in a midwestern United States county. The scale of the soil information should ideally be approximately the same scale as the cadastral (property) information.

Topology

Topology is the mathematical study of the properties of objects that are not distorted under continuous deformations (Longley et al., 2011). In a GIS, geometric characteristics of features that have topology cannot be changed regardless of how the data may be altered through projection or data transformation (Shellito, 2012). Spatial data that have topology require additional data files that define the topology. Topology information is also used to detect errors in spatial data. For example, when using a GIS we want the topology to be "correct" where lines connect with other lines, all polygons must be closed, and there should not be any space between adjacent polygons. Topology documents the relationship between features, and it describes how spatial data share geometry (Hoel et al., 2003).

Most GIS have the ability to examine and automatically correct topological errors. This is important because few (if any) spatial data layers are either created or imported with absolutely correct topology. Therefore, a GIS must be able to identify any polygons that are not closed, points that need to be snapped together, lines that need to intersect, and other topological errors. Examples of overshooting, undershooting, and polygon closure problems were discussed in Chapter 4. In addition, a GIS should be able to construct topology from new digitized information. Correct topology allows data layers to be combined and spatially analyzed.

Some of the most commonly used topologically correct vector data files are the U.S. Census Bureau's TIGER (Topologically Integrated Geographic Encoding and Referencing system) line files. These vector files are available free from the United States Census website (www.census.gov).

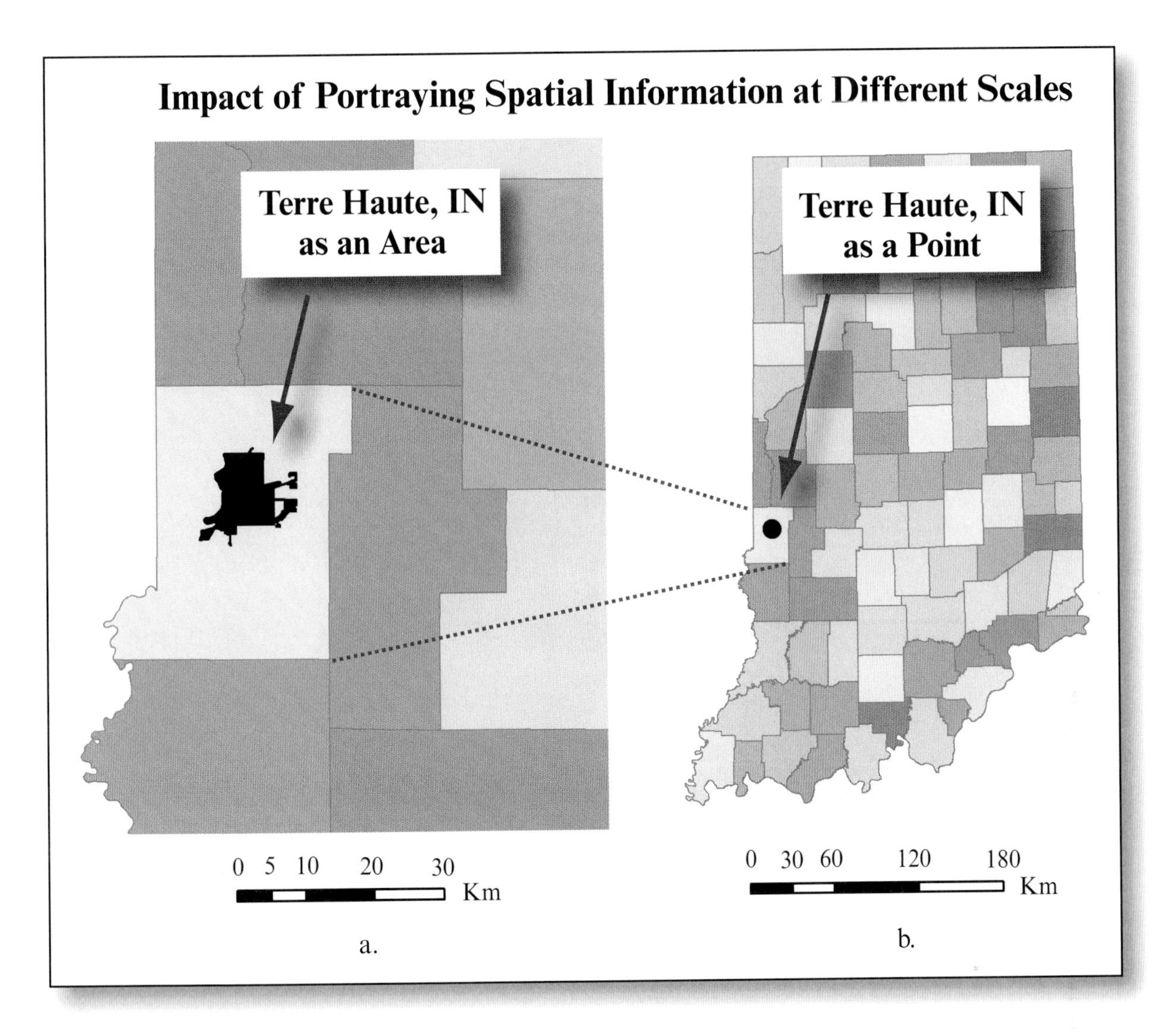

FIGURE 5–5 The scale of the map display often dictates whether a feature is displayed as an area or as a point symbol. a) The spatial extent of the city of Terre Haute, IN, is represented as an area (polygon) in this relatively large-scale map. b) The city of Terre Haute, IN, is represented as a point symbol in this smaller-scale map. All of the counties in Indiana are shown in this map. The bar scale is accurate in each map irrespective of how much magnification or reduction takes place (data courtesy of IndianaMap).

Adjacency, Enclosure, and Connectivity

Topology is also relevant when using a GIS because of three basic elements: 1) **adjacency**—information about the neighborhoods of different objects; 2) **enclosure**—information about spatial features that enclose other spatial features; and 3) **connectivity**—information about the links between spatial objects. The use of each of these three elements is central to the vector data structure. For example, a tax assessor may be interested in determining the adjacency relationship between a parcel that increased in value over 25% during the past 5 years and the parcels that immediately surround it. Enclosure can be used to determine the presence of an island within a lake.

Connectivity is central to all network analysis. For example, common GPS navigation devices use the connectivity of the road network to suggest navigation routes from one location to another. At first glance, the issue of navigation and connectivity is simple. However, it is actually more difficult than you might think. In a non-topologically correct vector layer it may appear that there are many intersections of county roads with a limited access highway such as an interstate. If this layer were used for routing or navigation, it would not be possible to know that only a few of the county roads that appear to intersect the interstate are allowed access to it. This would be very frustrating if you were constantly being directed to roads that either pass under or over an interstate highway.

Topologically correct vector line data also contain important information that allows people to find specific address numbers along a street; even the correct side of

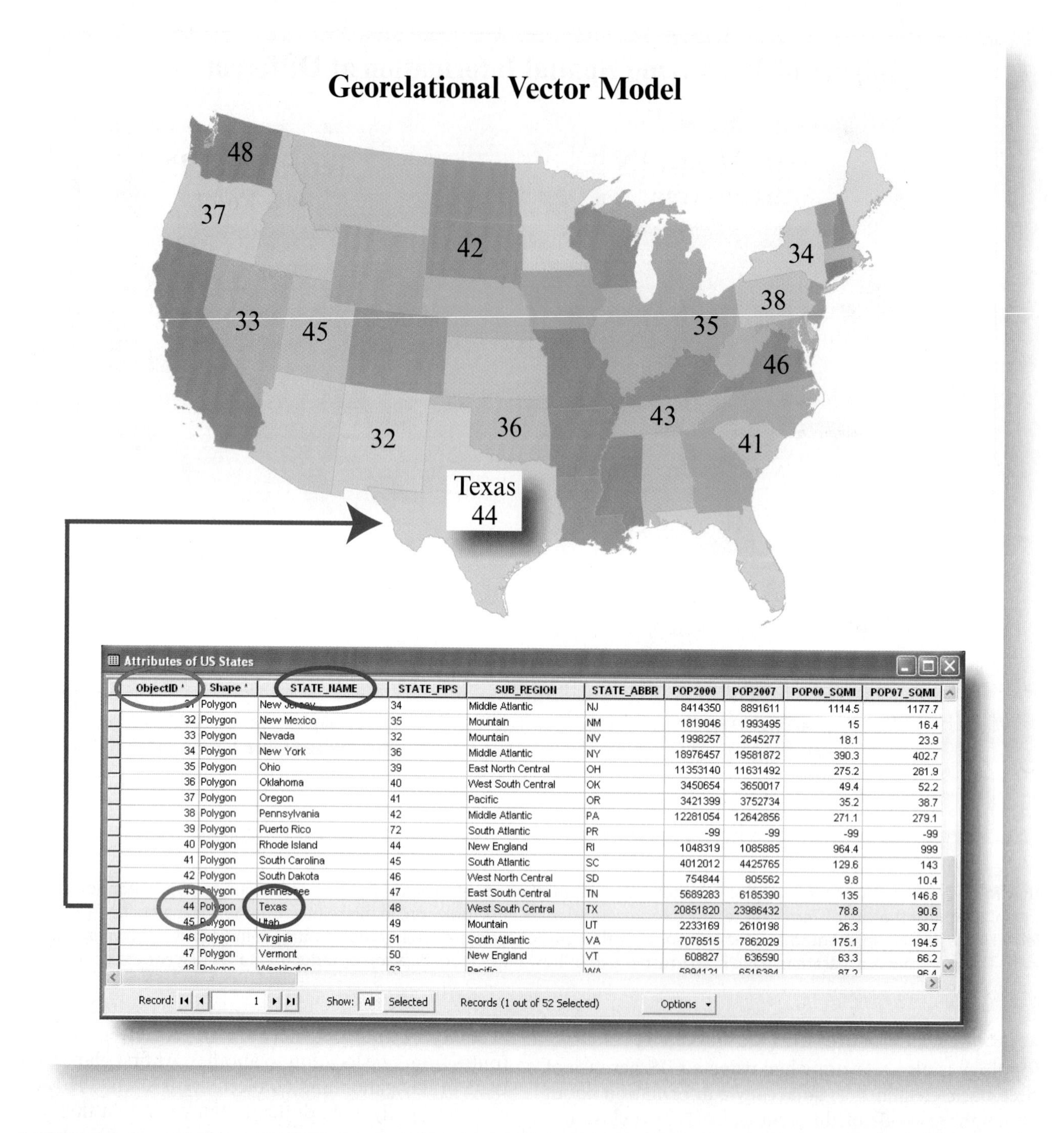

ObjectID *	Shape *	STATE_NAME	STATE_FIPS	SUB_REGION	STATE_ABBR	POP2000	POP2007	POP00_SQMI	POP07_SQMI
31	Polygon	New Jersey	34	Middle Atlantic	NJ	8414350	8891611	1114.5	1177.7
32	Polygon	New Mexico	35	Mountain	NM	1819046	1993495	15	16.4
33	Polygon	Nevada	32	Mountain	NV	1998257	2645277	18.1	23.9
34	Polygon	New York	36	Middle Atlantic	NY	18976457	19581872	390.3	402.7
35	Polygon	Ohio	39	East North Central	OH	11353140	11631492	275.2	281.9
36	Polygon	Oklahoma	40	West South Central	OK	3450654	3650017	49.4	52.2
37	Polygon	Oregon	41	Pacific	OR	3421399	3752734	35.2	38.7
38	Polygon	Pennsylvania	42	Middle Atlantic	PA	12281054	12642856	271.1	279.1
39	Polygon	Puerto Rico	72	South Atlantic	PR	-99	-99	-99	-99
40	Polygon	Rhode Island	44	New England	RI	1048319	1085885	964.4	999
41	Polygon	South Carolina	45	South Atlantic	SC	4012012	4425765	129.6	143
42	Polygon	South Dakota	46	West North Central	SD	754844	805562	9.8	10.4
43	Polygon	Tennessee	47	East South Central	TN	5689283	6185390	135	146.8
44	Polygon	Texas	48	West South Central	TX	20851820	23986432	78.8	90.6
45	Polygon	Utah	49	Mountain	UT	2233169	2610198	26.3	30.7
46	Polygon	Virginia	51	South Atlantic	VA	7078515	7862029	175.1	194.5
47	Polygon	Vermont	50	New England	VT	608827	636590	63.3	66.2
48	Polygon	Washington	53	Pacific	WA	5894121	6516384	87.2	96.4

FIGURE 5–6 Example of a georelational vector data model. The spatial features in the map layer are linked to the database via the ObjectID field. The ObjectIDs of selected states are identified on the map with Texas highlighted (#44) (data courtesy of U.S. Bureau of the Census; interface courtesy of Esri, Inc.).

the street. Additional information about topologically correct network geodatabases is presented in Chapter 7.

Georelational Vector Model

A **georelational data model** stores spatial and attribute data in separate files. The spatial data (geo) are stored in graphics files and the attribute data (relational) are stored in a relational database. A georelational dataset uses a feature ID or label to link the spatial data with the attribute data. The spatial features in the map layer are linked to the database via the ObjectID field in the database (Chang, 2010a). An example of a georelational data model is shown in Figure 5-6. The spatial information associated with 48 states is stored in one file while the attribute information about each of the states is found in a separate attribute file. The attribute information about

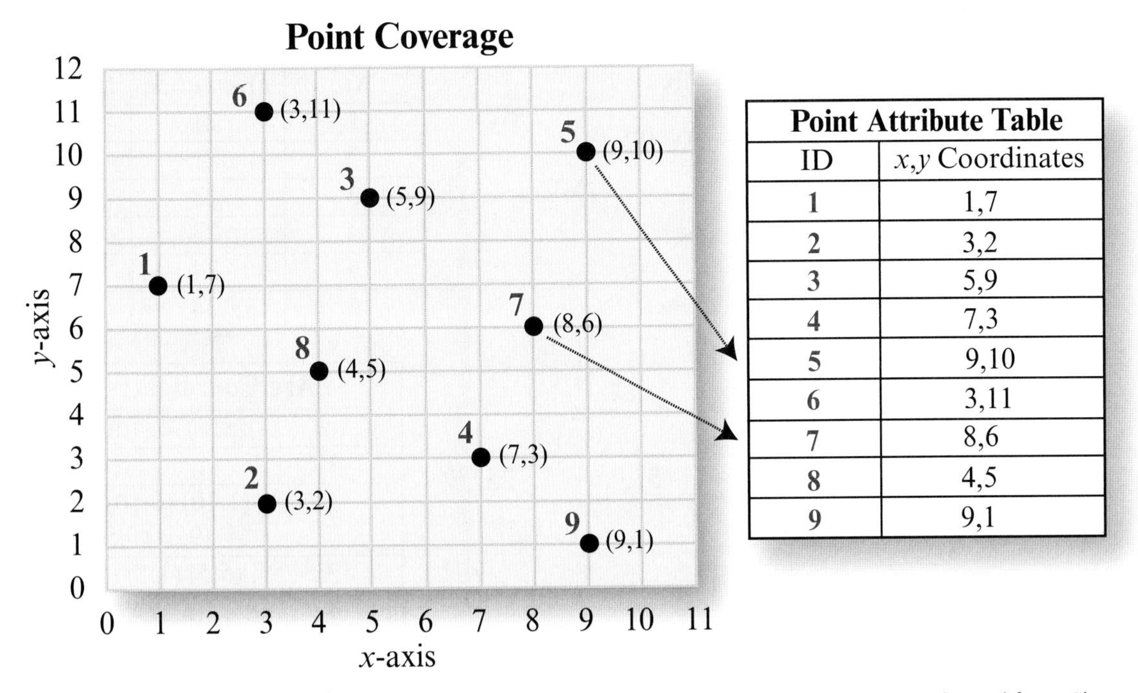

ID	x,y Coordinates
1	1,7
2	3,2
3	5,9
4	7,3
5	9,10
6	3,11
7	8,6
8	4,5
9	9,1

FIGURE 5–7 A point coverage attribute table contains the ID and *x,y* coordinates of each point (adapted from Chang, 2010a).

state #44 (Texas) is highlighted in this example. Data stored in this kind of vector model require the software to go back and forth between the spatial data and the attribute data. With large datasets, this can become cumbersome and inefficient.

The georelational data model has been used in GIS for several decades. Both the Esri ArcINFO coverage and Esri ArcGIS® shapefile formats are examples of vector georelational models. Although this data format is gradually being replaced by the object-based vector model to be discussed, the georelational data model continues to be very popular.

Arc Coverage

The Arc **coverage** is a digital vector storage framework with built-in topology that was introduced by Esri in the 1980s (USGS, 2011). The coverage is a framework—not a single file that can be copied and pasted using file management tools such as Window's File Explorer or Macintosh OS Finder. Rather, the framework consists of a collection of files and directories that are linked together to create a cohesive vector layer. Because of this, coverages are usually maintained (e.g., copied, moved, etc.) within the confines of a special program in the GIS (e.g., ArcCatalog). If distribution of a coverage is necessary, the coverage is usually converted to a single export file that can be imported back into a coverage.

Points, lines, and areas can all be represented in a coverage (Chang, 2010a). A point coverage simply relates the feature IDs and pairs of *x,y* coordinates with a point feature attribute table. The feature attribute table contains information that describes the individual points as shown in Figure 5-7.

In a coverage, lines are called arcs. The information about an arc (line) is summarized in an Arc-Node list that specifies the *from* node (starting point) and *to* node (ending point) of each arc. In Figure 5-8, Arc 2 begins at node 22 and ends at node 23. Note that this list does not define the vertices that determine the shape of the arc. This information is contained within the Arc-Coordinate List that defines the beginning and ending points (*from* node and *to* node) and all of the vertices that define the line. In Figure 5-8, Arc 2 has five coordinates that define the arc. This consists of one *from* node, one *to* node, and three vertices.

Polygon coverages (Figure 5-9) contain additional information such as the polygon Left-Right List that defines the left and right polygons of every arc (line) in the coverage according to the arc's direction. In addition, the Polygon-Arc List defines the arcs that make up each polygon. In the special case of Polygon 151, an arc with a value of 0 is listed to note that there is a Polygon (154) enclosed by Polygon 151, and the 0 value is used to separate the internal and external boundaries.

Shapefiles

Shapefiles contain non-topological vector data and attribute information in a dataset. The geometry of features is stored as shapes that comprise a set of vector coordinates. Shapefiles lack topological information found in coverages, they do not have the processing requirements of a topological dataset, and they are gen-

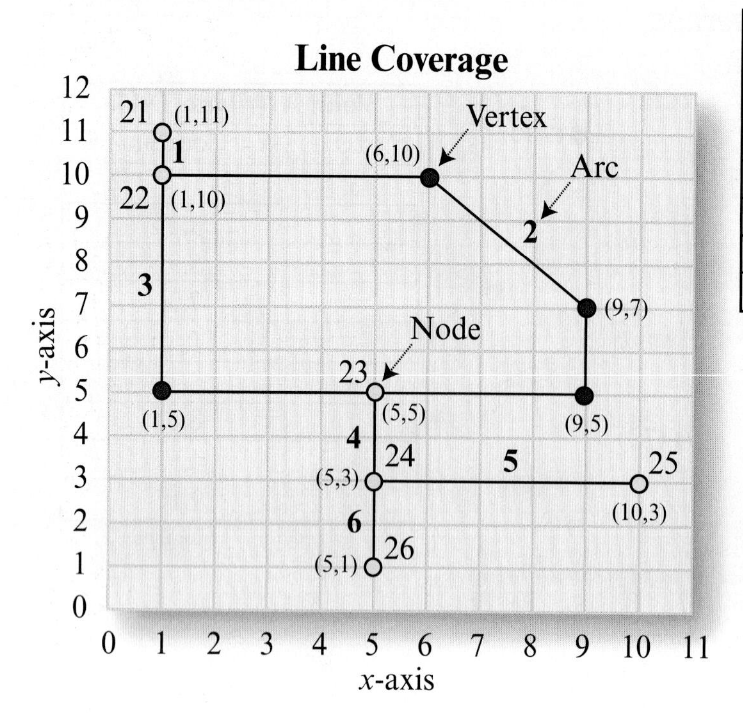

Arc Nodes		
Arc	*From* node	*To* node
1	21	22
2	22	23
3	23	22
4	23	24
5	24	25
6	24	26

Arc Coordinates	
Arc	*x,y* Coordinates
1	(1,11) (1,10)
2	(1,10) (6,10) (9,7) (9,5) (5,5)
3	(5,5) (1,5) (1,10)
4	(5,5) (5,3)
5	(5,3) (10,3)
6	(5,3) (5,1)

FIGURE 5–8 A line coverage contains an Arc-Node list that describes the *from* and *to* nodes for each arc. All points (nodes and vertices) that define the arcs are found in the Arc-Coordinate list (adapted from Chang, 2010a).

erally able to be read, displayed, and analyzed more quickly and take up less disk space. Shapefiles are actually defined by several separate files, including the following three essential files (Esri, 2011a):

1. *.shp—the main file that contains the geometric shapes,

2. *.shx—the index file that links the main file with a dBASE table, and

3. *.dbf—the dBASE table that stores feature attributes.

Some shapefiles may also contain other files besides these three essential files. Therefore, as with a coverage, care must be taken when copying, moving, or otherwise manipulating the data as all files associated with a single shapefile must be copied or moved together.

Object-Based Vector Model

Advances in computer technology have made it possible for both spatial and attribute data to be stored in a single system called an **object-based vector model**. In this model, spatial data are treated as objects. These objects can represent a spatial feature such as a river, a park, a road, or almost anything (Chang, 2010a). These objects hopefully contain all of the information and properties necessary to define the object.

While the object-based vector model is more efficient than the georelational model because of its ability to store all the objects in a single system, there are still many people who do not use it. This is probably because some users are more comfortable with the georelational data model and are unwilling to change to the new nomenclature and use of the object-based model. Fortunately, the new geodatabase file format in ArcGIS® makes it easy to transition to the object-based vector model. The object-based data model is linked closely with Esri's ArcObjects, a development environment for Esri's products, that consists of thousands of classes and objects. This enables users to modify or create code and provides an integrated environment for Esri products.

Classes

A **class** is a collection of objects with the same attributes (Lo and Yeung, 2007). Classes can be grouped into superclasses or divided into subclasses. For example, if you wanted to map information about all of the counties in the United States the following logic would apply. The entire United States is the superclass. The individual states are the classes. Individual counties within each state would be subclasses. Each county

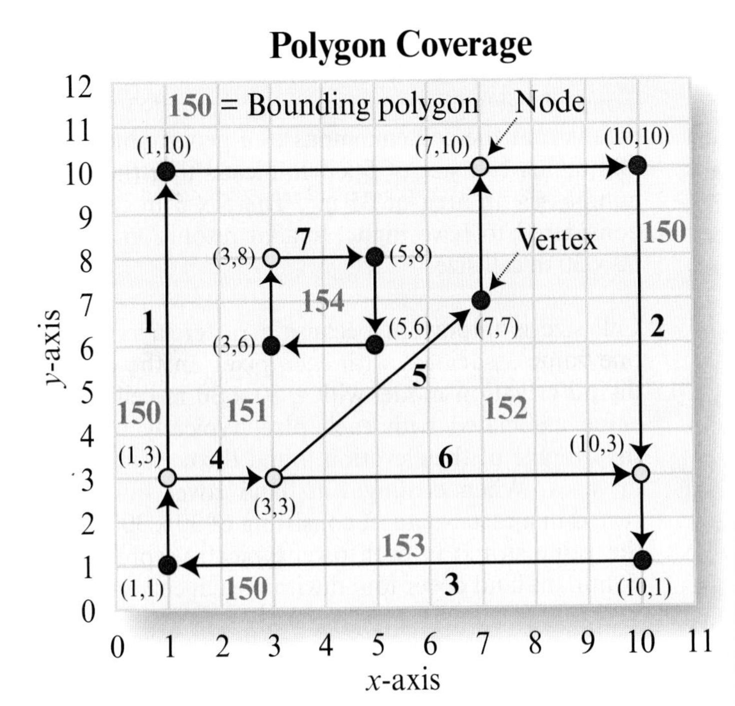

Left-Right Polygons		
Arc	Left Polygon	Right Polygon
1	150	151
2	150	152
3	150	153
4	151	153
5	151	152
6	152	153
7	151	154

Polygon Arcs	
Polygon	Arc
151	1,4,5,0,7
152	5,2,6
153	6,3,4
154	7

Arc Coordinates	
Arc	x,y Coordinates
1	(1,3) (1,10) (7,10)
2	(7,10) (10,10) (10,3)
3	(10,3) (10,1) (1,1) (1,3)
4	(1,3) (3,3)
5	(3,3) (7,7) (7,10)
6	(3,3) (10,3)
7	(3,8) (5,8) (5,6) (3,6) (3,8)

FIGURE 5–9 Polygon coverages contain a polygon Left-Right list for each arc. This information allows for studies of adjacency. Arcs that make up each polygon are found in the Polygon-Arc list. All points (nodes and vertices) that define the arcs are found in the Arc-Coordinate list (adapted from Chang, 2010a).

could then have multiple attributes associated with it such as location (latitude and longitude coordinates), population, area, etc.

Geodatabases

The **geodatabase** is an object-based vector model that maintains topologically integrated spatial datasets. One may think of a geodatabase as a collection of geographic datasets (e.g., vector data, tabular data, etc.). The geodatabase extends the abilities of the coverage model with support of complex networks, relationships among feature classes, and object-oriented features (MacDonald, 2001). The geodatabase is a part of ArcObjects.

In a geodatabase, vector data can be stored as points, lines, and polygons. The geodatabase organizes vector data into feature classes and feature datasets. Although ArcGIS® is able to edit and maintain multiple file formats (e.g., coverage and shapefile), the geodatabase is the native data structure for ArcGIS®. As such, ArcGIS® is now designed to most effectively work with geodatabases. Finally, geodatabases allow users to define specific topology rules to be used for a specific dataset.

There are three kinds of geodatabases that ArcGIS® supports (Esri, 2011b):

1. File geodatabase: stored as folders in a file system. It is ideal for single users or small workgroups.

2. Personal geodatabase: stored in a Microsoft Access data file. Personal geodatabases are best used when

there is a single data author/editor and a small number of users.

3. ArcSDE geodatabase: stored using ORACLE, Microsoft SQL Server, IBM DB2, or IBM Informix. They can be unlimited in size [or limited by the size restrictions of the data base management system (DBMS)] and number of users.

The selection of the appropriate geodatabase depends on the size of the data files, number of users, and authoring/editing considerations. Both file and personal geodatabases are freely available to all ArcGIS® users. Use of an ArcSDE geodatabase usually requires additional DBMS software and licenses.

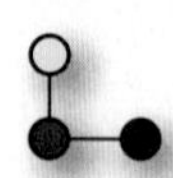

Raster Data

Raster data have a more simple data structure than vector data as discussed in Chapters 1 and 3. Raster data are represented in space by an array (or grid) of cells (Figure 5-1c). A raster layer contains cells arranged in rows and columns. Each cell contains a value that describes the phenomena being examined. The cells in the array are commonly called picture elements or pixels, and they are usually square (i.e., the sides of a pixel have the same dimension). Unlike the vector data model, the raster data model has remained relatively unchanged since its inception.

Raster data are especially useful to describe spatial phenomena that vary continuously across the landscape. Such phenomena include elevation above sea level, precipitation, temperature, etc. For example, a digital elevation model (DEM) of the Wasatch Front in Utah in raster format is shown in Figure 5-10. The DEM consists of pixels that are 30 x 30 m in size.

Raster Cell Value

Every cell in a raster layer has a unique nominal, ordinal, or interval/ratio-scaled value associated with the phenomena being mapped at that particular location. Raster cells usually contain a number in either integer or floating point format. Integer data typically represent nominal-scale categorical data such as land use or land cover type. Using this logic, the numbers can represent different land cover types as in the U.S. Geological Survey *Land Use and Land Cover Classification System for Use with Remote Sensor Data* (Anderson et al., 1976) where 1 = Urban or Built-up Land, 2 = Agricultural Land, 3 = Rangeland, etc.

Raster cells may also contain floating point data that represent continuous data. For example, a raster temperature file can store the temperature in degrees associated with each cell (e.g., 27.2° C). Raster data stored as floating point numbers require more space and computing power to store, query, and analyze.

Cell Size

Cell size in a raster layer refers to the x and y dimensions of each pixel. A raster cell size of 30 x 30 m means that the cell encompasses a geographic area of 900 m^2. A cell size of 5 x 5 m means that the cell encompasses an area of 25 m^2. The 5 x 5 m cell size is considered to have higher spatial resolution than the 30 x 30 m cell size.

Cell size is important because a raster layer has just one value associated with each pixel. In the case of a digital elevation model with a 30 x 30 m cell size, the value associated with each pixel typically represents the average of the elevation found throughout the 900 m^2 area. When dealing with land cover information stored in a raster dataset consisting of 30 x 30 m pixels, the value stored in each pixel typically represents the dominant land cover found within each cell.

Raster Georeferencing

Raster data need to be georeferenced to relate them with other spatial datasets. Typically, raster layers are referenced using a coordinate system that is related to the number of rows and columns in the layer. For example, a raster layer may have the following spatial characteristics in UTM Zone 12 North (Figure 5-11a):

Upper left easting X = 405,135

Upper left northing Y = 4,425,560

Rows = 11

Columns = 11

Cell size = 30

Using this spatial information it is possible to determine the spatial dimensions of the entire layer. The lower right UTM coordinates of the dataset would be 405,465 X and 4,425,230 Y. The lower right X value was calculated by multiplying the number of columns by 30 meters and then adding this to the upper X value:

405,135 + (11 x 30) = 405,465

The lower right Y point was calculated by multiplying the number of rows by 30 meters and subtracting this value from the upper left Y value:

Raster Digital Elevation Model

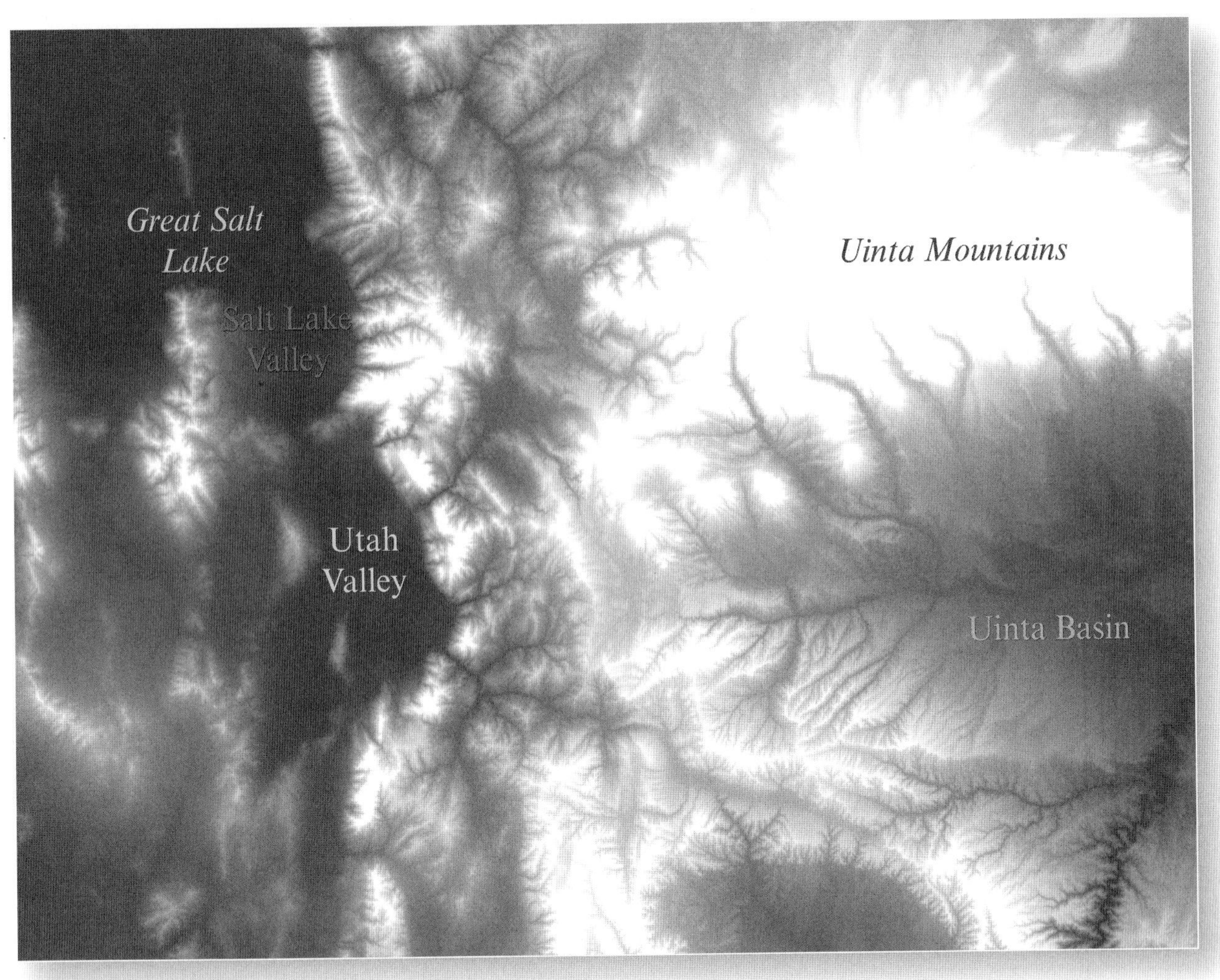

FIGURE 5–10 A digital elevation model (DEM) of the southern Wasatch Front in Utah. In this raster dataset, every cell (pixel) has the value of the elevation above sea level in meters. Areas with high elevation (e.g., the *Uinta Mountains*) are bright white. Areas with lower elevations (e.g., the *Great Salt Lake*) are dark. Continuous data such as these are efficiently stored in a raster data format. The elevation data would most likely be displayed as contour lines if they were stored as vector data (data courtesy of U.S. Geological Survey).

4,425,560 - (11 x 30) = 4,425,230

Using this method, all of the upper left values for each cell can be interpolated throughout the layer.

Finally, the georeferenced values can be interpolated within individual pixels. For example, the georeferenced value of the midpoint (centroid) of a pixel in the middle of the raster grid in Figure 5-11a is shown in Figure 5-11b. The centroid's coordinates are 405,300 X and 4,425,395 Y. The centroid was determined using the value of the upper-left location 405,285 X and 4,425,410 Y.

Raster File Formats

There are many different raster file formats that are available to use in a GIS. Two of the more common formats are the ARC GRID and GeoTIFF.

Vector and Raster Data Model Conversion

Vector and raster data are often used together in GIS projects. For example, it is quite common to overlay vector information (e.g., all of the buildings and par-

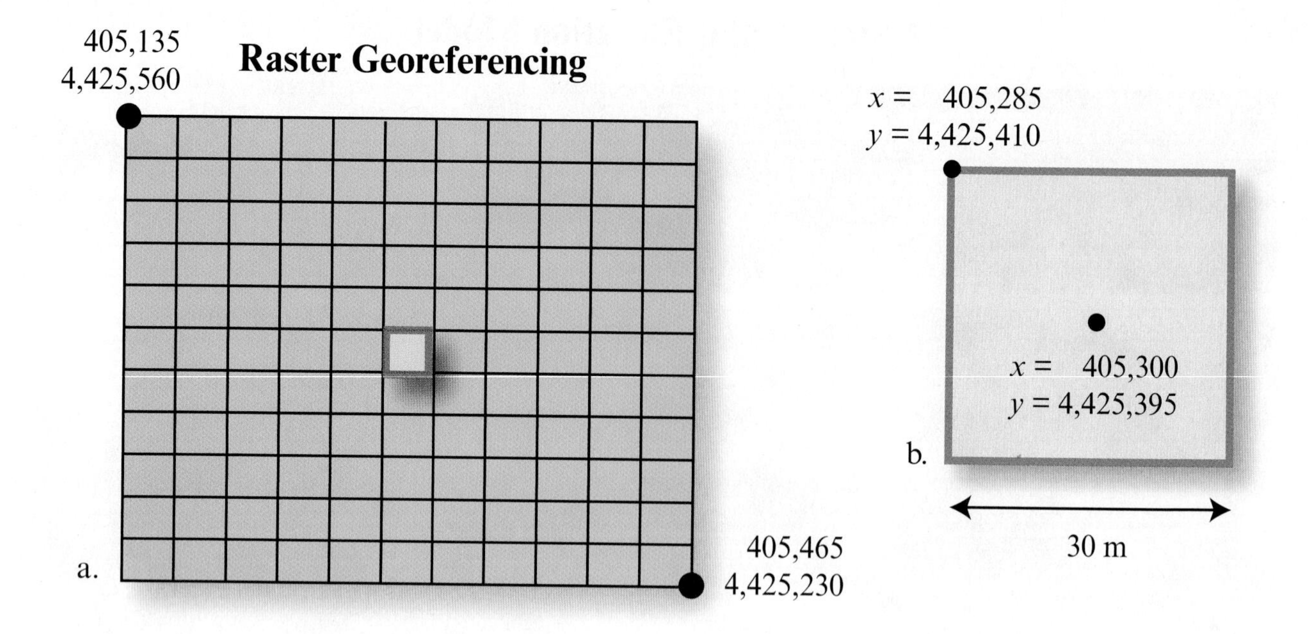

FIGURE 5–11 a) The raster layer contains 11 rows and 11 columns and each cell is 30 x 30 m in dimension. Using this information, it is possible to estimate spatial reference values for individual pixels within the raster. b) The yellow pixel in the middle of the raster is greatly enlarged. This 30 x 30 m raster pixel has an upper left *x,y* coordinate pair of 405285, 4425410. Georeferenced values can be interpolated throughout the pixel. The centroid of the pixel has an *x,y* coordinate pair of 405300, 4425395.

cels in a community) on top of a hill-shaded raster digital elevation model or onto a digital aerial photograph. You will probably encounter a time when you need to convert vector data into a raster format and raster data into a vector format.

Vector-to-Raster Conversion

Point, line, and polygon data stored in a vector data structure can be converted into a raster data structure using a **vector-to-raster conversion**. The new raster data are based on one of the attributes in the vector layer. So, for multiple attributes in a vector dataset you would need to create multiple raster layers. For example, part of the transportation network for downtown Salt Lake City, UT, is shown in vector format in Figure 5-12a. The vector transportation layer was converted into raster data using the codes associated with three different types of roads in the vector attribute table. The vector attribute data were converted to a raster grid with 250 x 250 m cells in Figure 5-12b. The vector attribute data were converted to a raster grid with 500 x 500 m cells in Figure 5-12c. Line weight and color are used to discriminate between the three types of roads in the original vector dataset. The only way to distinguish between the three types of roads in the raster dataset is by varying the color. Also note that the more coarse 500 x 500 m cell size results in a much more blocky (often referred to as pixelated), generalized rendition of the original road network.

Congalton (1997) noted two challenges encountered when performing a vector-to-raster conversion: polygon fill and cell size. Polygon fill refers to the filling of each newly created raster pixel with the correct value. This requires careful selection of the spatial interpolation algorithm used such as nearest-neighbor or bilinear interpolation discussed in Chapter 9. Cell size (e.g., 1 x 1 m, 5 x 5 m) is an important consideration as it must be balanced between the overall size of the new raster file and the level of detail desired by the user. Being able to select appropriate values for these parameters helps ensure that the polygon-to-raster conversion is successful.

Raster-to-Vector Conversion

Raster data can be converted to point, line, and polygon vector data using a **raster-to-vector conversion**. The resolution of the original raster layer (e.g., 10 x 10 m, 100 x 100 m, 1000 x 1000 m) will determine the usefulness (and the accuracy) of the data in the new vector layer. For example, consider a raster dataset that contains information about the location of all the wells in a county. When converting this raster layer to a vector point layer, the points will be placed in the vector layer based on the pixel that contained well information in

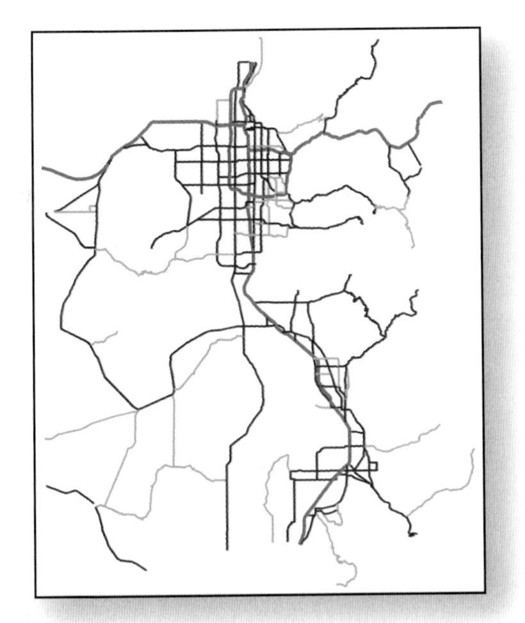

Vector-to-Raster Conversion

Interstate highway
State highway
Paved local road

a. Vector road network information.

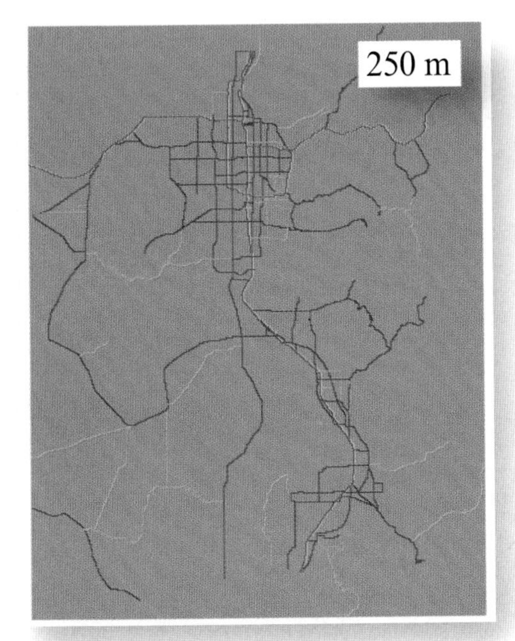

b. Vector-to-raster conversion with a pixel size of 250 x 250 m.

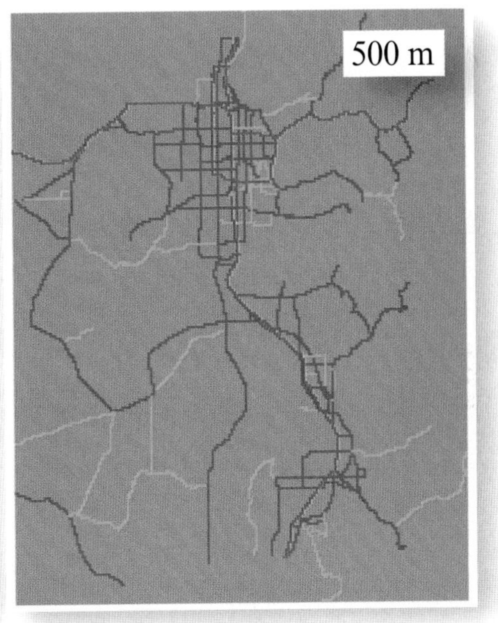

c. Vector-to-raster conversion with a pixel size of 500 x 500 m.

FIGURE 5–12 It is possible to convert vector data to raster data using a vector-to-raster data conversion. a) Three types of roads in downtown Salt Lake City, UT, are displayed in vector format. b) A map of the same road information after a vector-to-raster conversion with output pixel resolution of 250 x 250 m. c) A map of the road information after a vector-to-raster conversion with output pixel resolution of 500 x 500 m. Note how "blocky" or "stair-stepped" the 500 x 500 m data are compared to the 250 x 250 m data (data courtesy of State of Utah).

the raster layer. Very rarely will the well actually be in the middle of a raster cell. For example, if the cell size of the raster layer was 30 x 30 m, there are 900 m^2 in a pixel where the well could actually be located. If the cell size were 5 x 5 meters, there would only be 25 m^2 where the well could be. Similarly, when converting from a raster layer to a line layer, the vector file will contain lines that existed in the middle of raster cells. If the original raster data had a large cell size, then the resulting vector layer will probably not be very accurate and may look "blocky."

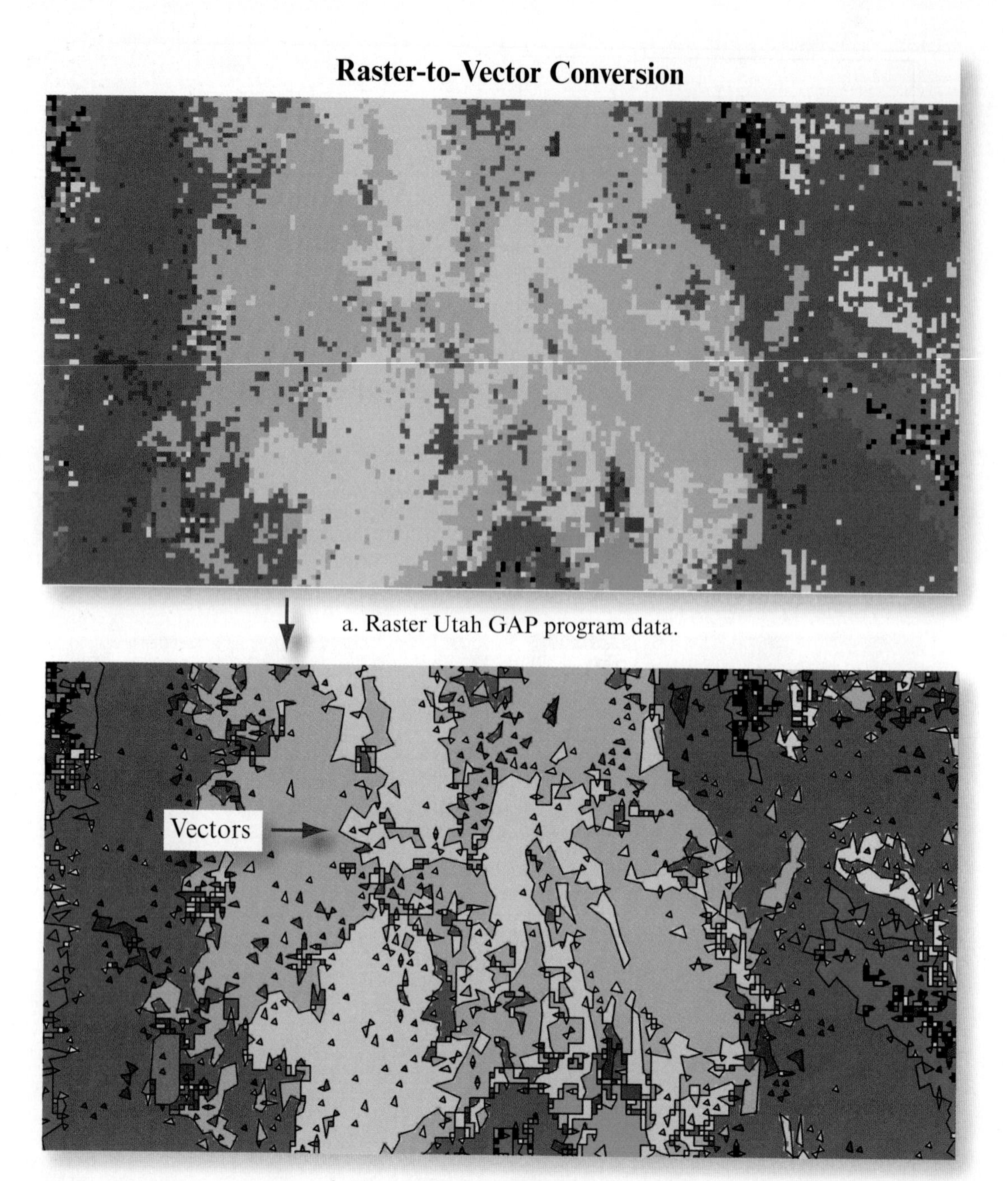

FIGURE 5–13 It is possible to convert raster data to vector data using a raster-to-vector data conversion. a) The raster data are part of Utah's GAP analysis program. b) Note that single-cell raster areas were converted to triangular-shaped vector polygons and that larger areas were converted into various different shapes. This occurs when the "Simplify Polygons" is selected when converting from raster-to-vector. When "Simplify Polygons" is not selected the vector polygons rigidly conform to the original area of the raster cells (data courtesy of State of Utah).

There is an excellent GAP dataset for the state of Utah in raster format (Figure 5-13a). A raster-to-vector conversion was applied to a portion of these data (Figure 5-13b). The resulting vector database may be used just like any other vector database. Unfortunately, it may contain some undesirable artifacts created during the raster-to-vector conversion.

Several processing steps can be performed to minimize raster-to-vector conversion problems. It is quite common in raster datasets to have many individual pixels that have values completely different from surrounding values. This is especially prevalent in raster land cover datasets where individual pixels of a particular class may appear like islands. Each of these "island" pixels

TABLE 5–1 The contents of a typical flat-file database, where all of the data records are contained in a single file that can be queried, analyzed, and reported. Columns are often referred to as fields and rows as records.

Parcel #	Name	Address	Assessed Property Value
750123	James W. Smith	123 Davenport Boulevard	$150,000
750125	Paul K. Wells	125 Davenport Boulevard	$165,000
750127	Howard M. Boggs	127 Davenport Boulevard	$155,000
750129	Samuel F. Fraser	129 Davenport Boulevard	$158,000

will typically result in separate and distinct island polygons in the vector data layer, which can be visually unpleasant (Figure 5-13b). Therefore, preprocessing of the raster data can be performed to remove the isolated, island cells. This can be done by filtering the raster data prior to conversion to remove isolated individual pixels with unique values. For example, a 3 x 3 maximum dominant GIS function could be applied to the raster data that looks at the eight pixels surrounding a pixel and assigns the pixel the value of the dominant value found in the surrounding eight neighbors.

Enhancement of the most important parts of the raster layer may be performed to make sure that those features are converted accurately to the vector file. For example, a researcher may want to extract roads from a raster file. To ensure that the roads are extracted as accurately as possible, the researcher could first apply an edge enhancement to the raster layer before performing the conversion. The converted data can be further processed to remove "blocky" or "stair-stepped" characteristics (Congalton, 1997).

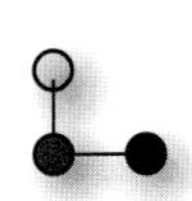

Databases

Databases typically store the attribute data associated with the spatial data in a GIS. Attribute databases are often called the "heart" of a GIS because they make spatial data query possible based on attributes. A **database management system (DBMS)** is used to add, edit, query, analyze, and report on the attributes contained in the database.

Database management systems have been around for many years and have their foundations in computer science. The DBMS user community is tremendously diverse and the use of DBMS in GIS is just one of many DBMS applications. Examples of people and organizations who typically use DBMS include accountants, banks, retail chains, brokerage firms, etc. The unifying theme of each of these organizations and people is that they need to store, query, and analyze information. For example, your bank probably has a database with all of the bank's clients names, their addresses, and much more information. This information can be accessed on demand by bank employees.

In a GIS, the attributes in the DBMS (e.g., population density) associated with a spatial object such as a county can be analyzed to address important questions. Most common computer-aided design (CAD) programs do not have this capability.

Flat Files

Flat files store all the information in the database in a single file. An example of a flat-file database is a spreadsheet that contains all the information in a series of columns and rows (Table 5-1). Columns are often referred to as fields and rows are often referred to as records. This kind of database is sufficient for smaller datasets where analysis speed and storage space requirements are not significant issues.

Relational Databases

Extremely large databases may require substantial amounts of mass storage and significant computer processing resources. Also, not everyone in every department may need to have access to all of the data stored in the entire database. One way to solve this problem is to use a relational database. **Relational databases** are related to one another by unique identifiers that allow users to link two or more databases or tables together. For example, a county government might have one database that contains information about all of the parcels in the county, another database associated with tax assessment, and another containing information about delinquent tax payments. The public might be allowed to have access to the parcel and tax assessment information but not to the information about delinquent payments.

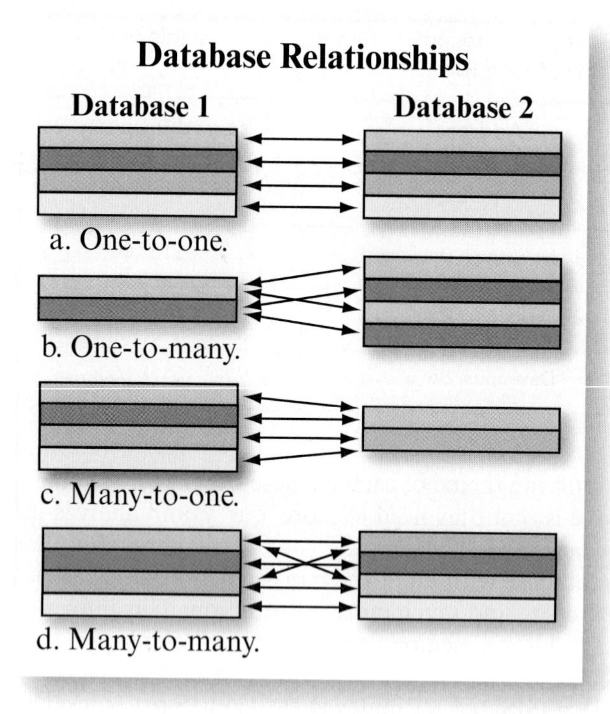

FIGURE 5–14 The types of relationships that may exist between two databases (adapted from Chang, 2010b). In each case, identifying fields relate the two databases together. a) The two databases have a one-to-one relationship where every record in one database corresponds to one (and only one) record in another database. b) Single records in the first database may correspond to multiple records in the second database. c) Conversely, multiple records in the first database only correspond to a single record in the second database. d) Records in both databases may correspond to multiple records in either database.

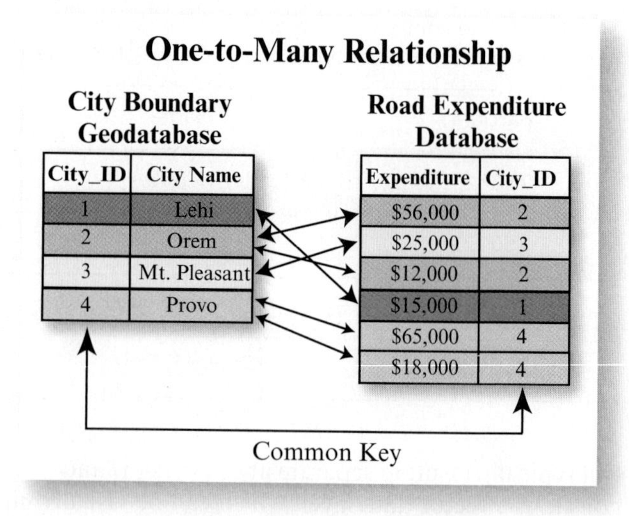

FIGURE 5–15 This figure demonstrates a one-to-many database relationship. The City Boundary geodatabase contains a unique identifier for each city within a county (City_ID). This identifier relates this database to the hypothetical Road Expenditure Database using the same unique identifier. Thus, the City_ID is the common key between the two databases. In this example, the city of Provo had two road expenditures that totaled $83,000.

The unique identifier used to relate databases is sometimes called a **primary key**. This same field in the adjoining database is called a **foreign key**. If the primary key and the foreign key have the same field name in each database, they are called the **common key**.

Sometimes a feature dataset and its accompanying database contain a field that is designed to be related to external databases. This is commonly the case when using census data where a polygon feature (map) dataset is designed to be related to a database that contains socioeconomic data. For example, Jensen et al. (2004a) related a polygon dataset of a city's block groups with a database that contained socioeconomic data for the same block groups. The two datasets were related by a unique block group identifier.

Different Database Relationships

Databases can be joined using several different kinds of relationships: one-to-one, one-to-many, many-to-one, and many-to-many (Figure 5-14). In a **one-to-one** relationship, one record in each database corresponds to one record in another database (Figure 5-14a) (Chang, 2010b). An example of this kind of relationship might be if you were mapping crime rates in census block groups throughout a city. You might have one layer that contains the spatial information and features and another layer that contains the crime information.

Another kind of relationship between databases is **one-to-many** (Figure 5-14b). An example of this relationship is a geodatabase that contains the city boundaries for a given county where each city has a unique identifier (City_ID in Figure 5-15). Another database contains road expenditures for each city during the first three months of the year. This database also uses the unique city identifier City_ID. The two databases may be linked in a one-to-many relationship based on the common key City_ID.

Databases may also be related in a **many-to-one** relationship where many records in a table or database may be related to one record in another database (Figure 5-14c) (Chang, 2010b). Figure 5-16 demonstrates how a many-to-one relationship might be configured. The land cover polygon data are coded as numbers (LUCODE) in the database on the left. These numbers are then linked to their description in the second database through the field USGS_Code. This relationship

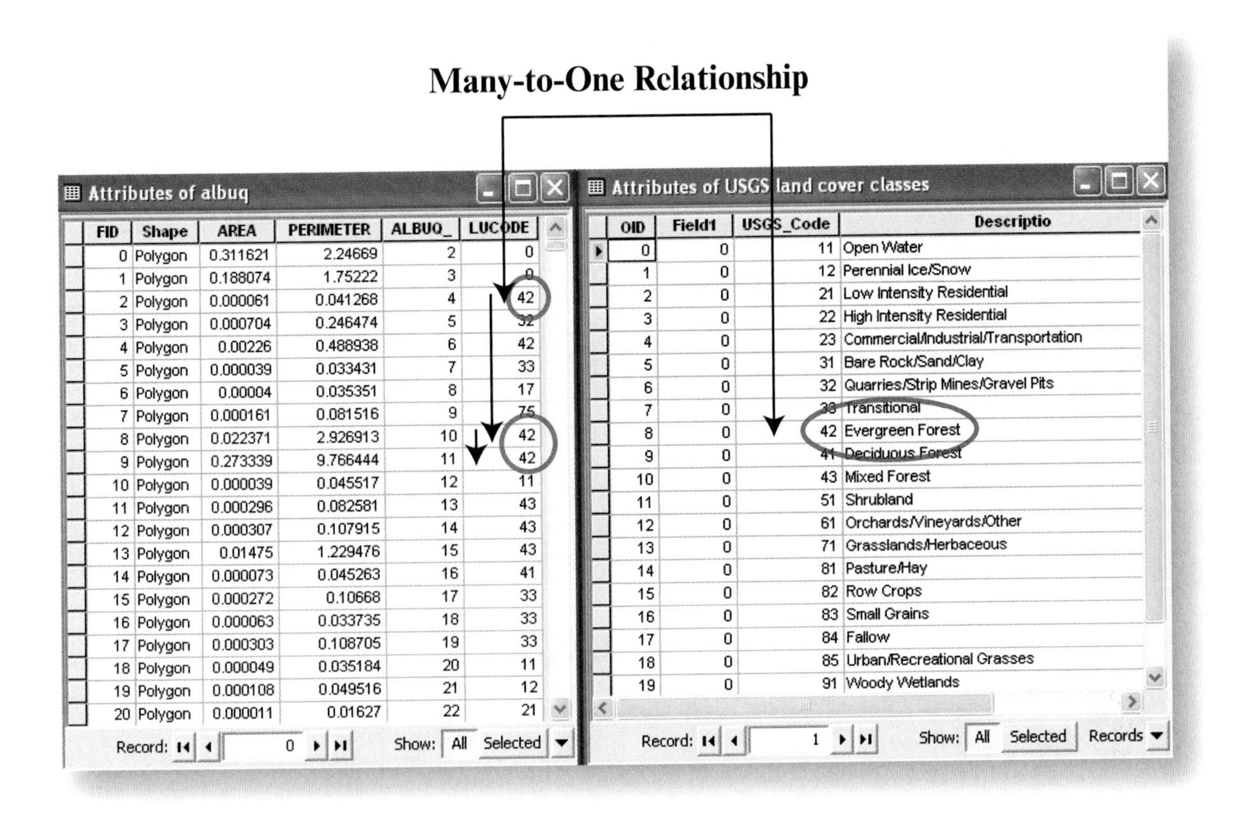

FID	Shape	AREA	PERIMETER	ALBUQ_	LUCODE
0	Polygon	0.311621	2.24669	2	0
1	Polygon	0.188074	1.75222	3	0
2	Polygon	0.000061	0.041268	4	42
3	Polygon	0.000704	0.246474	5	32
4	Polygon	0.00226	0.488938	6	42
5	Polygon	0.000039	0.033431	7	33
6	Polygon	0.00004	0.035351	8	17
7	Polygon	0.000161	0.081516	9	75
8	Polygon	0.022371	2.926913	10	42
9	Polygon	0.273339	9.766444	11	42
10	Polygon	0.000039	0.045517	12	11
11	Polygon	0.000296	0.082581	13	43
12	Polygon	0.000307	0.107915	14	43
13	Polygon	0.01475	1.229476	15	43
14	Polygon	0.000073	0.045263	16	41
15	Polygon	0.000272	0.10668	17	33
16	Polygon	0.000063	0.033735	18	33
17	Polygon	0.000303	0.108705	19	33
18	Polygon	0.000049	0.035184	20	11
19	Polygon	0.000108	0.049516	21	12
20	Polygon	0.000011	0.01627	22	21

OID	Field1	USGS_Code	Descriptio
0	0	11	Open Water
1	0	12	Perennial Ice/Snow
2	0	21	Low Intensity Residential
3	0	22	High Intensity Residential
4	0	23	Commercial/Industrial/Transportation
5	0	31	Bare Rock/Sand/Clay
6	0	32	Quarries/Strip Mines/Gravel Pits
7	0	33	Transitional
8	0	42	Evergreen Forest
9	0	41	Deciduous Forest
10	0	43	Mixed Forest
11	0	51	Shrubland
12	0	61	Orchards/Vineyards/Other
13	0	71	Grasslands/Herbaceous
14	0	81	Pasture/Hay
15	0	82	Row Crops
16	0	83	Small Grains
17	0	84	Fallow
18	0	85	Urban/Recreational Grasses
19	0	91	Woody Wetlands

FIGURE 5–16 This figure demonstrates a many-to-one relationship. The land cover polygon data are coded as numbers (LUCODE) in the database on the left. These numbers are then linked to their description in the second database through the field USGS_Code. This relationship provides the qualitative description of the different land cover types that can be used in the key or legend for the map, i.e., LUCODE 42 = Evergreen Forest. Storing the qualitative description in a separate database also decreases the amount of storage space needed for the original database (interfaces courtesy of Esri, Inc.).

provides the qualitative description of the different land cover types that can be used in the map legend.

Finally, a **many-to-many** relationship exists where many (or more than one) records in one database can be related to many (or more than one) records in a different database (Figure 5-14d) (Chang, 2010b). For example, different soil types can grow more than one crop species and a crop can grow in more than one soil type.

Relate and Join

When using a GIS, databases are combined using either "relate" or "join" commands. A *relate* operation temporarily connects two tables based on a common key, but the tables remain physically separate. Relate enables users to combine two or more tables at the same time. Relate is appropriate for all four kinds of relationships shown in Figure 5-14. While databases are related, it is possible to save the related database into a permanent database with all the attributes from the original databases.

A *join* operation is useful to combine two tables with a common key. Join is often used in one-to-one or many-to-one relationships. Whereas "relate" provides a temporary union of two or more databases, "join" physically combines the databases.

Raster Databases

Raster data layers do not have the same kind of databases as vector data layers. Raster datasets have **Value Attribute Tables** that are similar to histograms because they describe the number of times that a cell value occurs in a dataset. For example, most states have land cover data that are in raster format. These data have raster Value Attribute Tables that list each of the different land cover types and the number of times that each land cover type occurs in the layer. The Value Attribute Table associated with the Utah GAP Analysis Program raster habitat data are shown in Figure 5-17. Area can be calculated using the Value Attribute Table by multiplying the number of times each value occurs by the area of each cell.

Types of Attribute Data

There are four kinds of attribute data that can be input into a database: nominal, ordinal, interval, and ratio.

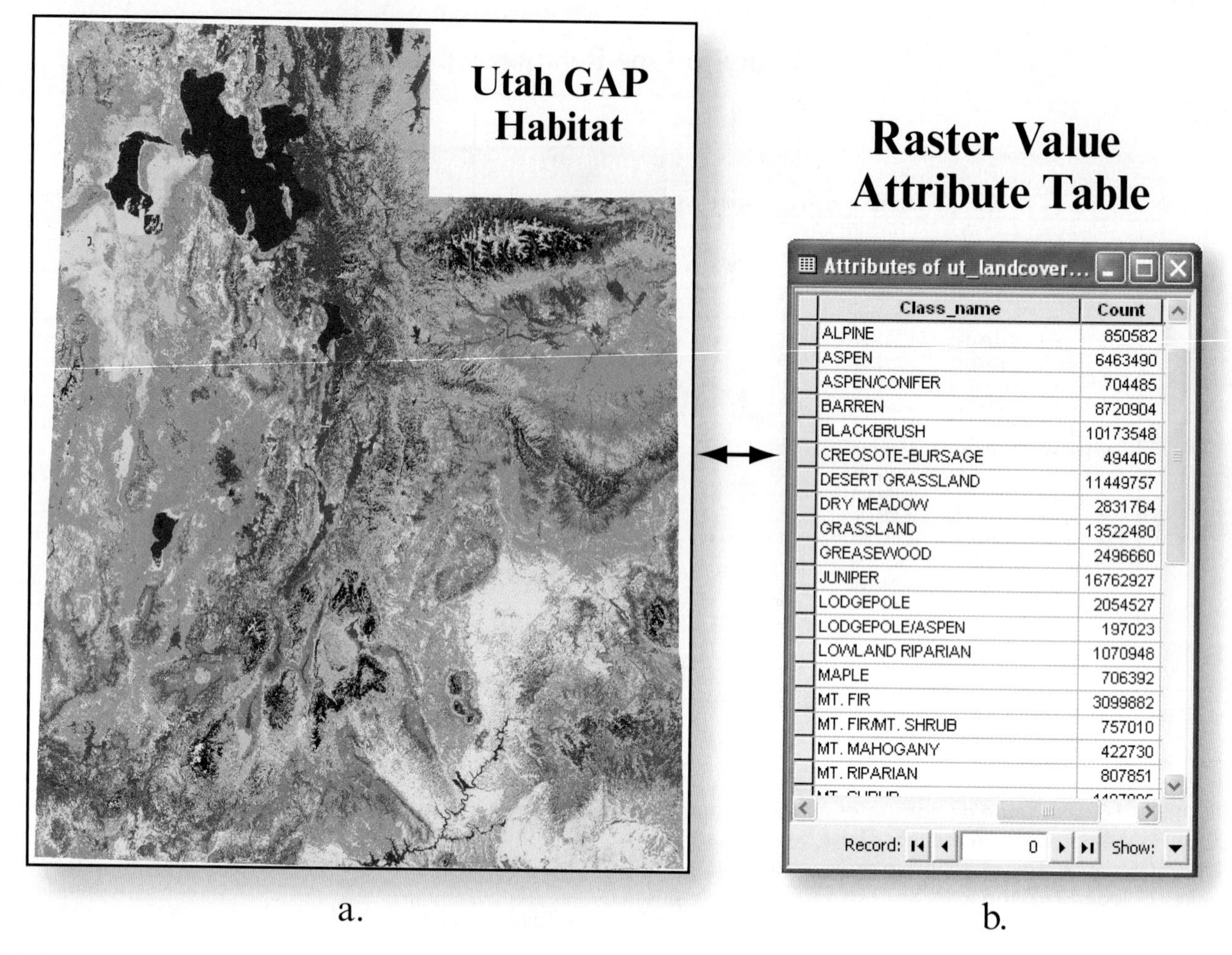

Class_name	Count
ALPINE	850582
ASPEN	6463490
ASPEN/CONIFER	704485
BARREN	8720904
BLACKBRUSH	10173548
CREOSOTE-BURSAGE	494406
DESERT GRASSLAND	11449757
DRY MEADOW	2831764
GRASSLAND	13522480
GREASEWOOD	2496660
JUNIPER	16762927
LODGEPOLE	2054527
LODGEPOLE/ASPEN	197023
LOWLAND RIPARIAN	1070948
MAPLE	706392
MT. FIR	3099882
MT. FIR/MT. SHRUB	757010
MT. MAHOGANY	422730
MT. RIPARIAN	807851

FIGURE 5–17 Raster Utah GAP habitat spatial data and its associated Value Attribute Table. a) Each of the different colors represents a different habitat type (Class_name). b) The number of pixels in each of the habitat classes is summarized in the "Count" column. The area in each habitat class can be calculated by multiplying the count in this table by the area of each pixel (data courtesy of State of Utah; interface courtesy of Esri, Inc.).

The data may be input as numbers or text. Nominal data represent different kinds or categories of data. These data are class names and do not have any rank or other value associated with them. Examples include land cover categories, race, gender, and many others. Ordinal data are ranked (or ordered). Examples of ordinal data include low, medium, and high income, or low, medium, and high rates of a virus infection. Interval data are numeric data without an absolute zero value. However, these data have known intervals between their values. A good example of this is temperature measured in Fahrenheit where a value of 30° is 10° cooler than 40°, but a value of 0° has no bearing on other values. Ratio data are numeric data with an absolute zero value. Two examples of this kind of data are actual annual income or house values where zero values are meaningful. Additional information about measurement levels is found in Chapter 8.

All of these types of data can be input, queried, and analyzed in a GIS. However, only certain statistical measures can be used to describe each of the different attributed data types. The only descriptive statistical measure available to nominal data is the mode, the most frequently occurring observation. Ordinal data can be described by the mode and median. The median is the midpoint of ranked data. Interval and ratio data can be described using the mode, median, mean, standard deviation, and variance. These statistical measures are discussed in Chapter 8.

Adding and Deleting Attribute Fields

The DBMS should allow you to quickly add and delete fields within the database. Adding fields is necessary to input the result of a classification or computation. When you add a field to a database you usually specify what kind of data the field will have (e.g., numeric, text) and the length of the field. These are important characteristics because if you select "text" as the data type then you will not be able to perform any numerical operations on the field. Also, if you specify that the field is 30 characters long, you are allocating space in the file, and files can get very large when there are many thousands of records. So, when adding a field in a database, make sure that you select the data type that is most appropriate and then determine an appropriate length for the field.

Deleting entire fields is often performed when there are useless or redundant fields in a database. This can occur when you acquire a database from an external source. In this case, you should delete all of the unnecessary fields because they occupy storage space and can increase processing and query time. You may want to delete fields when you share databases with other people. You should only share data that are necessary.

Data Entry

Data can be input into a GIS database in multiple ways. A single attribute can be entered by simply selecting a specific field in a record and then typing in the value. In addition, multiple values can be input using the "calculate" command where records are first selected and then calculated to a specific value. All of the records that are selected will have a specific value placed in the field that is being manipulated.

Data entry in a database can be a time-consuming task. For example, if you have a database with 10,000 polygons and 30 fields of attribute data, this represents 300,000 attribute values. Therefore, it is useful to first determine if reliable data are already available. Government data repositories, such as www.census.gov, contain database and tabular data that are relatively easy to integrate into a GIS database. Finding existing data can dramatically decrease the amount of time and money spent on database development.

A quick way to add or modify data in a specific field is through the use of the calculate command. The calculate command can be used to populate the field of every record, or selected records, in a database. For example, assume you had a field called "Inches" in a database that contained the amount of rainfall in inches for a group of weather stations. It would be very simple to convert inches to other units, such as centimeters, using the calculate command. In this example, you would create a new field called "CM" for centimeters and then recalculate the values using the formula:

$$CM = \text{Inches} \times 2.54$$

This would place the value in centimeters into the "CM" field in the database. Another use of the calculate command could be computing the adjusted income for every record in a database based on a cost of living adjustment.

It is always important to check the accuracy of your new input data. You can do this by checking each individual record or, if you have many records in the database, by selecting several records at random.

Integration with External Databases

Sometimes it may be necessary to integrate GIS feature and database data with external databases such as Oracle or Access. For example, Jensen et al. (2004b) integrated vector and raster data with the Oracle database engine to create a comprehensive GIS analysis engine with equal vector and raster capabilities. The final product, called the *Amazon Information System*, was used as a repository and analysis engine for use with data acquired in an Amazon forest research project. This kind of integration is common in GIS when multiple organizations need to dynamically use, analyze, query, and otherwise manage data. The ability to integrate spatial data with external databases can save much time, effort, and resources.

Data Query

Data are usually queried in two ways in a GIS. First, specific data may be queried using Structured Query Language to examine attributes in a table. Second, data may be queried by spatial location.

Selection by Attribute

Virtually all databases can be queried by attribute using **Structured Query Language** (SQL). SQL is used by many commercial database packages including Oracle and Access. When using a GIS, SQL is usually implemented in a command line type of interface such as the one shown in Figure 5-18. In this example, note that a field is ready for a value to be entered to build the query.

The syntax of SQL usually requires that a field name be given and then a set of attributes defined. For example, here are several SQL statements:

"Age" = 34

"Income" >= 24000

Last_name = "Adams"

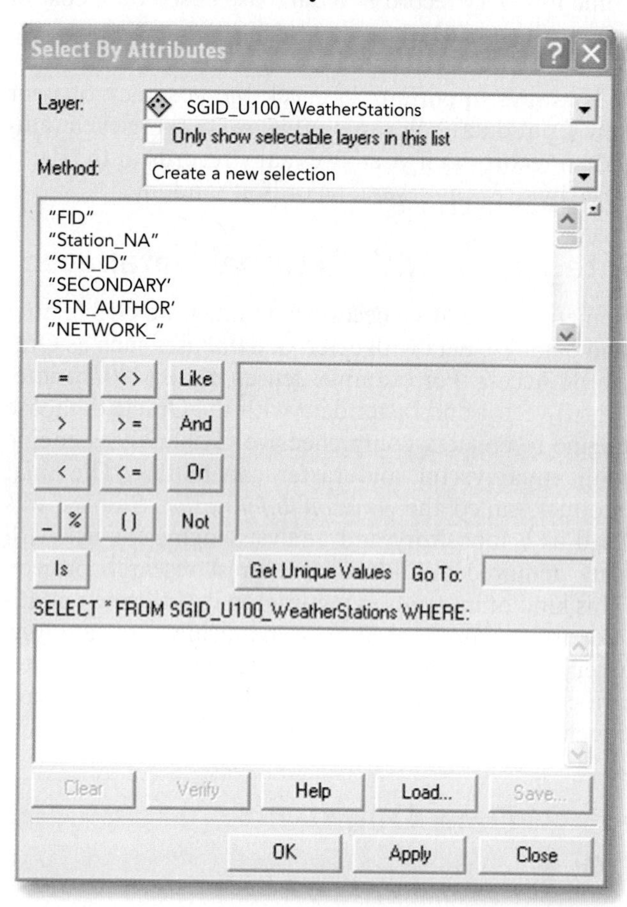

FIGURE 5–18 Geospatial databases may be queried using a Structure Query Language (SQL) interface (interface courtesy of Esri, Inc.). In this example, features may be selected from a file containing all the weather stations in Utah.

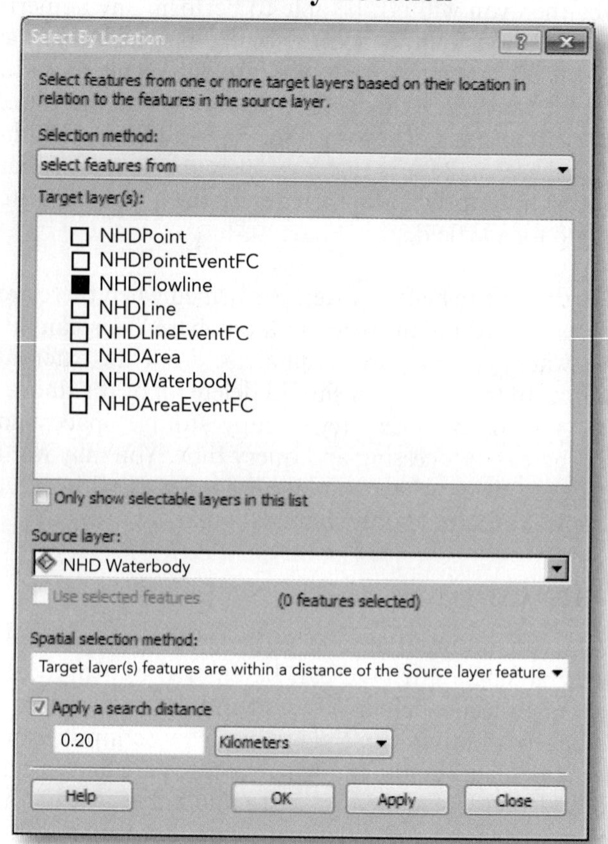

FIGURE 5–19 A Selection by Location interface allows users to select features based on their position relative to other features. In this example, all the National Hydrography Dataset NHDFlowline segments (i.e., *StreamRiver*) in the study area that are within 0.2 km of existing NHDWaterbody features (i.e., *LakePonds*) will be selected. The selection results are shown in Figure 5-20b (interface courtesy of Esri, Inc.; data courtesy of the National Hydrography Dataset).

SQL query statements can also contain Boolean connectors:

"Income" >= 30000 AND "Income" < 40000

"Income" >= 30000 OR "Income" < 20000

and multiple fields:

"Income" >= 30000 AND "County" = "Richland"

"Income" >= 30000 OR "Last_Name" = "Adams"

Selection by Location

Data can be selected by their spatial location. One way this can be done is through drawing a box around a group of features. This is useful if you know the specific area where the elements of interest are located.

Data can also be selected based on their position relative to other features in the database. Usually you can specify different parameters that define what features should be selected. The Esri ArcGIS® Selection by Location interface is shown in Figure 5-19. In this example, all National Hydrography Dataset NHDFlowline *StreamRiver* segments within 0.2 km of existing NHD Waterbody *LakePonds* will be selected. The results of the selection are displayed in Figure 5-20b. The OBJECTID, Shape, and Identifier of the selected *StreamRiver* segments are listed in Figure 5-20c.

Combinations of Data Queries

It is common for both attribute and spatial data queries to be used in a project. For example, a city tax assessor may want to see all of the homes that are currently appraised at a value >$250,000 and are locat-

Selection by Location

a. NHDFlowline *StreamRiver* and NHDWaterbody *LakePond* features.

b. *StreamRiver* segments selected within 0.2 km of *LakePonds*.

NHDFlowline

OBJECTID	Shape	Identifier
213	Polyline	83610207
306	Polyline	83610077
433	Polyline	83610157
645	Polyline	83610417
681	Polyline	83610261
748	Polyline	83610079
1626	Polyline	83610309
1761	Polyline	83610311
2184	Polyline	83610201
....	....	....

c. A list of nine NHDFlowline *StreamRiver* segments within this geographic area that are within 0.2 km of *LakePonds*.

FIGURE 5–20 Features in a database can be selected based on their location relative to other features in space. a) All of the NHDFlowline *StreamRiver* and NHDWaterbody *LakePond* features in the National Hydrography Dataset within this small study area are mapped. b) Using the Select by Location information provided in Figure 5-19, all of the *StreamRiver* segments within 0.2 km of *LakePonds* are selected. Note that the dashed line stream segment just north of segment 748 was not selected because it is classified as a *Connector* in the database, not a *StreamRiver*. c) The OBJECTID, Shape, and Identifier of the nine *StreamRiver* segments are listed (data courtesy of National Hydrography Dataset).

ed within specific neighborhoods. This operation would contain an SQL statement and a select by spatial location request.

New Data Layers

After using selecting features by attribute or by location, you can output just the selected features to an entirely new file. This allows you to extract a subset of the original dataset for analysis. For example, assume you have a county-wide property ownership layer that contains socioeconomic data of Portland, OR. You are only interested in the location of all households making >$200,000. You could simply implement the following SQL statement:

"Income" > 200000 AND "City" = "Portland"

This would select all of those records in Portland with incomes >$200,000. After selecting these records, you could export them to a new spatial data layer. Then, you would perform spatial analysis on the new dataset. This procedure is often useful to create a new dataset to ensure that you do not unintentionally modify the original spatial dataset.

Summary

This chapter described the basic principles of vector and raster spatial data models, how vector and raster data are stored, the topology associated with Georelational and Object-based Vector Models, and how to convert between vector and raster data structures. The fundamental characteristics of databases were introduced. Attribute databases represent the heart of GIS data, and the ability to create, modify, and analyze databases is essential to successful GIS use. Finally, the ability to relate and join databases and to query spatial data based on attributes and/or location was discussed.

Review Questions

1. Differentiate between vector and raster data structures.

2. Describe the role of scale in the representation of cities as either points or areas.

3. Give an example of spatial data especially well suited for vector and raster data structures.

4. Define topology. Why is topology important?

5. What are some of the challenges when converting between vector and raster data?

6. Differentiate between the different kinds of database relationships.

7. Provide an example of when you might use each kind of database relationship.

8. What is the difference between "relate" and "join" operations?

9. Describe two of the ways in which data are entered into a database.

10. What is SQL? Provide an example of how it is used to perform "Selection by Attribute."

11. Provide an example of when you might use a "Selection by Location" operation.

Glossary

Adjacency: Information about the neighborhoods of different objects.

Class: A collection of objects with the same attributes. Especially useful in geodatabases.

Common Key: When the primary key and the foreign key have the same field name in each database.

Connectivity: Information about the links between spatial objects.

Coverage: A georelational vector storage framework developed by Esri with built-in topology for geographic information.

Data Models: Define how real world spatial features are represented in a GIS.

Database Management System (DBMS): Computer software used to add, edit, query, analyze, and report on the attributes contained in the database.

Enclosure: Information about spatial features that enclose other spatial features.

Foreign key: The primary field in a second database that links with the primary key to combine two or more databases.

Geodatabase: An object-based vector model that maintains topologically integrated spatial datasets.

Georelational Data Model: A vector data model that stores spatial and attribute information in separate files.

Many-to-many: A database relationship where many records in one database can be related to many records in another database.

Many-to-one: A database relationship where many records in a database may correspond to one record in another database.

Node: The beginning and ending points of an arc.

Object-Based Vector Model: A vector data model that uses objects to store both spatial and attribute data in a single system.

One-to-many: A database relationship where one record in a database may correspond to many records in another database.

One-to-one: A database relationship where one record in each database corresponds to one record in another database.

Primary Key (Key Field): A unique identifier used to relate databases.

Raster Data Structure: A data structure that uses a grid consisting of rows, columns, and cells to represent spatial data.

Raster-to-Vector Conversion: The act of converting raster data to points, lines, or polygons.

Relational Database: A database where unique identifiers are used to link two or more databases or tables together.

Shapefile: A georelational vector dataset developed by Esri that contains non-topological attribute and spatial data.

Structured Query Language (SQL): A unique database computer language commonly used for data query.

Topology: The mathematical study of the properties of objects that are not distorted under continuous deformations. The geometric characteristics of features in a GIS that have topology cannot be changed regardless of how the data may be altered through projection or data transformation.

Value Attribute Table: A table associated with a raster dataset that describes the number of times that a cell value occurs in a dataset.

Vector Data Structure: A data structure that uses points, lines, and polygons to represent spatial features.

Vector-to-Raster Conversion: The act of converting points, lines, or polygons into a raster data format.

Vertices: Points along a line (between the beginning and ending node) that define a line.

References

Anderson, J. R., Hardy, E. E., Roach, J. T. and R. E. Witmer, 1976, "A Land Use and Land Cover Classification System for use with Remote Sensor Data," *Professional Paper #964,* Reston: U.S. Geological Survey, 60 p.

Bolstad, P. V. and J. L. Smith, 1992,"Errors in GIS Assessing Spatial Data Accuracy," *Journal of Forestry*, 90:21–29.

Chang, K., 2010a, "Chapter 3: Vector Data Model," in *Introduction to Geographic Information Systems*, New York: McGraw Hill, 41–58.

Chang, K., 2010b, "Chapter 8: Attribute Data Management," in *Introduction to Geographic Information Systems*, New York: McGraw Hill, 155–157.

Congalton, R. G., 1997, "Exploring and Evaluating Vector-to-Raster and Raster-to-Vector Conversion," *Photogrammetric Engineering & Remote Sensing*, 63:425–434.

Esri, 2011a, *Esri Shapefile Technical Description*, Redlands: Esri (http://www.Esri.com/library/whitepapers/pdfs/shapefile.pdf).

Esri, 2011b, *Types of Geodatabases*, Redlands: Esri (http://resources.arcgis.com/content/geodatabases/9.3/types-of-geodatabases).

Hoel, E., Menon, S. and S. Morehouse, 2003, "Building a Robust Relational Implementation of Topology," *Advances in Spatial and Temporal Databases—Lecture Notes in Computer Science,* 2750:508–524.

Jensen, R. R., Gatrell, J., Boulton, J., and B. Harper, 2004a, "Using Remote Sensing and Geographic Information Systems to Study Urban Quality of Life and Urban Forest Amenities," *Ecology & Society*, 9(5):5 [online at URL: http://www.ecologyandsociety.org/vol9/iss5/art5/].

Jensen, R. R., Yu, G., Mausel, P., Lulla, K., Moran, E. and E. Brondizio, 2004b, "An Integrated Approach to Amazon Research–the Amazon Information System," *Geocarto International*, 19(3):55–59.

Lo, C. P. and A. K. W. Yeung, 2007, *Concepts and Techniques of Geographic Information Systems,* 2nd Ed., Upper Saddle River: Pearson Prentice-Hall.

Longley, P. A., Goodchild, M. F., Maguire, D. J. and D.W. Rhind, 2011, *Geographic Information Systems and Science*, 3rd Ed., Sussex, England.

MacDonald, A., 2001, *Building A Geodatabase*, Redlands, CA: Environmental Systems Research Institute.

Shellito, B. A., 2012, *Introduction to Geospatial Technologies*, New York: W. H. Freeman, 500 p.

USGS, 2011, *Coastal and Marine Geology InfoBank*, U. S. Geological Survey (http://walrus.wr.usgs.gov/infobank/programs/html/definition/arc.html) last accessed October 2011.

6 SPATIAL ANALYSIS OF VECTOR AND RASTER DATA

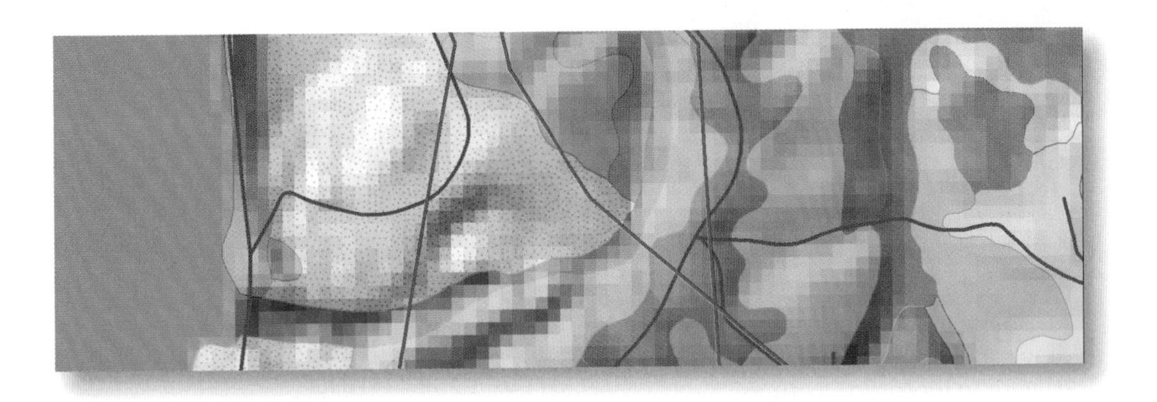

Analysts process vector and raster data in a GIS to understand important spatial relationships and to gain new knowledge (Madden, 2009). The relationships may involve biophysical data (e.g., fauna, vegetation, soil, water) and/or human-related data (e.g., population density, education, income, building value, religion, zoning, etc.). The goal is to extract as accurate information as possible from the data so that new knowledge is acquired and wise decisions can be made (Clarke, 2011).

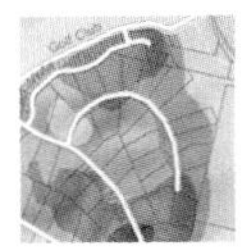

Overview

This chapter introduces vector and raster data analysis. Vector data analysis is introduced first with an emphasis on buffering point, line, and area features and on principles of vector overlay. Raster data analysis is then introduced with a focus on physical distance measurement (including buffering), local operations applied to single rasters, local operations applied to multiple rasters, neighborhood operations (e.g., spatial filtering), and regional (zonal) operations.

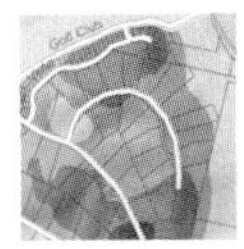

Vector Data Analysis

Buffering involves the creation of a special-purpose polygon that is a specified distance (e.g., 100 m) around a point, line, or area (polygon) feature. The buffering process actually creates two geographic areas: 1) the geographic area that lies within the specified buffer distance, and 2) the geographic area beyond the buffer limit. Buffers around point, line, and area features may be created from vector or raster data.

Buffering Using Vector Data

GIScientists often perform buffering of point, line, and area vector data during spatial analysis. The GIS buffering algorithm identifies the geometric coordinates of a line exactly n units away from the point, line, or area (polygon) feature. This is called *positive buffering*. The buffering algorithm identifies the x,y coordinates of the beginning node, intermediate points (vertices), and ending node of the encompassing buffer polygon.

Buffering Point Features

There is a tremendous variety of point-type features in the world. Common examples include the centroid of a residential building (Figure 6-1a), condominium, school, fire station, or church, utilities (e.g., a fire hydrant, telephone pole, power pole, cell tower, post office box), or a single point representing an entire central business district or city.

Buffering around a point feature creates a perfectly circular buffer zone some n units from the point feature. For example, a 10 m buffer around the centroids of selected residential houses in Port Royal, SC, is shown in Figure 6-1b. Note that when a 10 m buffer is used, that none of the buffers intersect, i.e., none of the building centroids are within 10 m of one another. However, when the buffer threshold is enlarged to 20 m, some of the buffer zones overlap (Figure 6-1c). Some GIS investigations require that the buffer zone of each individual point feature retain its unique buffer characteristics. Other studies might be content with

Buffering Point Features

a. Point (building centroids), line (road network), and area (building footprint) features.

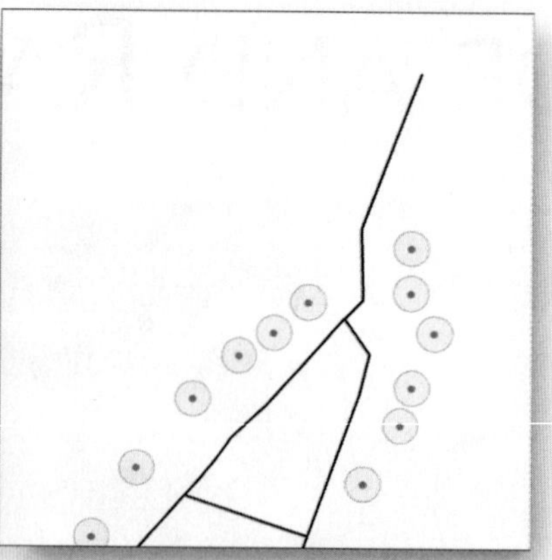

b. 10 m buffer around building centroids.

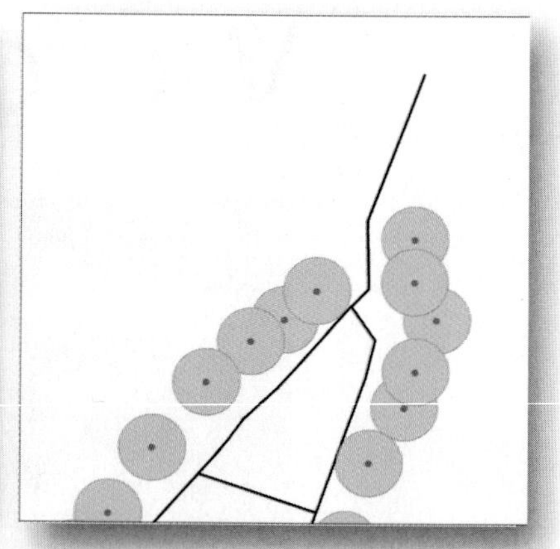

c. 20 m buffer around building centroids with no dissolve.

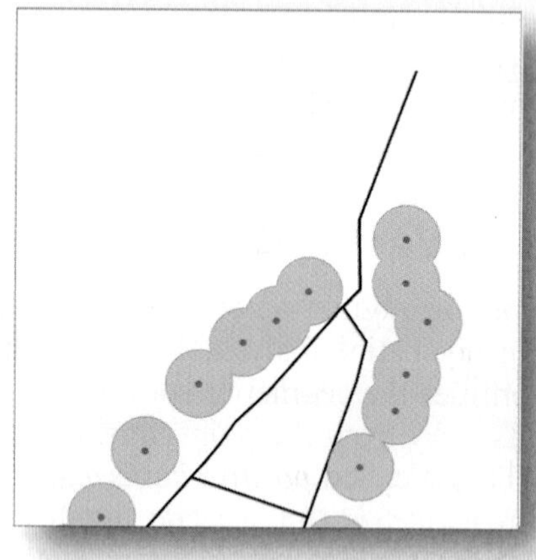

d. 20 m buffer around building centroids with dissolve.

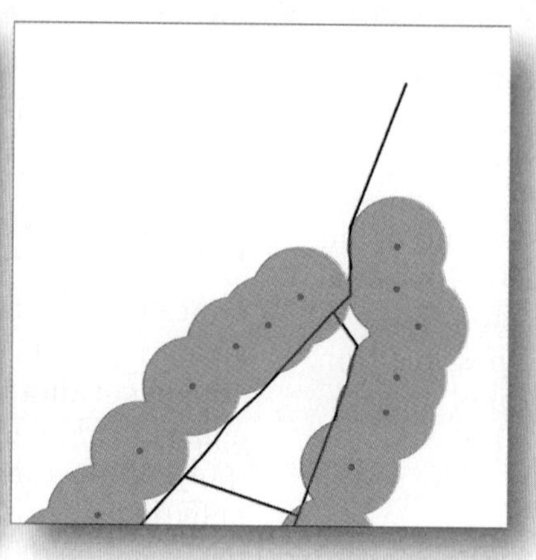

e. 30 m buffer around building centroids with dissolve.

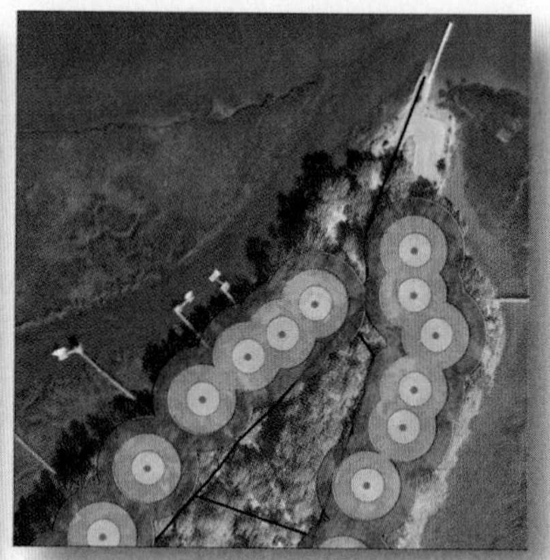

f. 10 m, 20 m, and 30 m buffers around building centroids with dissolve.

FIGURE 6–1 a) Point (residential building centroid), line (road network), and area (residential building footprint) features overlaid on color-infrared orthophotography of a part of Port Royal, SC. b) A 10 m buffer around building centroids. c) A 20 m buffer around the building centroids with no dissolve. d) A 20 m buffer around the building centroids with dissolve. e) A 30 m buffer around the building centroids with dissolve. f) Concentric 10 m, 20 m, and 30 m buffers around the building centroids with dissolve (data courtesy of Beaufort County GIS Department and USGS).

combining all the overlapping buffer zones. This is called *buffer dissolving*. For example, Figure 6-1d shows the 20 m buffers around the residential building centroids after being dissolved. A 30 m buffer around the building centroids with dissolve is shown in Figure 6-1e.

Some spatial investigations may utilize the information contained in several buffer zones. For example, the 10 m, 20 m, and 30 m buffers around the building centroids can be superimposed upon one another as shown in Figure 6-1f. In this example the buffer regions are symbolized using colors that are 50% transparent so that the underlying detail in the color-infrared orthophoto can still be seen.

For illustrative purposes, Figure 6-2 depicts an enlarged view of what takes place if an analyst requests thirty 1 m buffers around several of the most northern building centroids shown in Figure 6-1e.

Buffering Linear Features

Some common examples of linear spatial features that are often buffered include: transportation networks (e.g., highway, railroad, subway), utility networks (e.g., water, power, cable, sewer), and hydrologic networks (e.g., stream, river, storm water).

Buffering around linear features creates a buffer zone that has approximately the same shape as the original

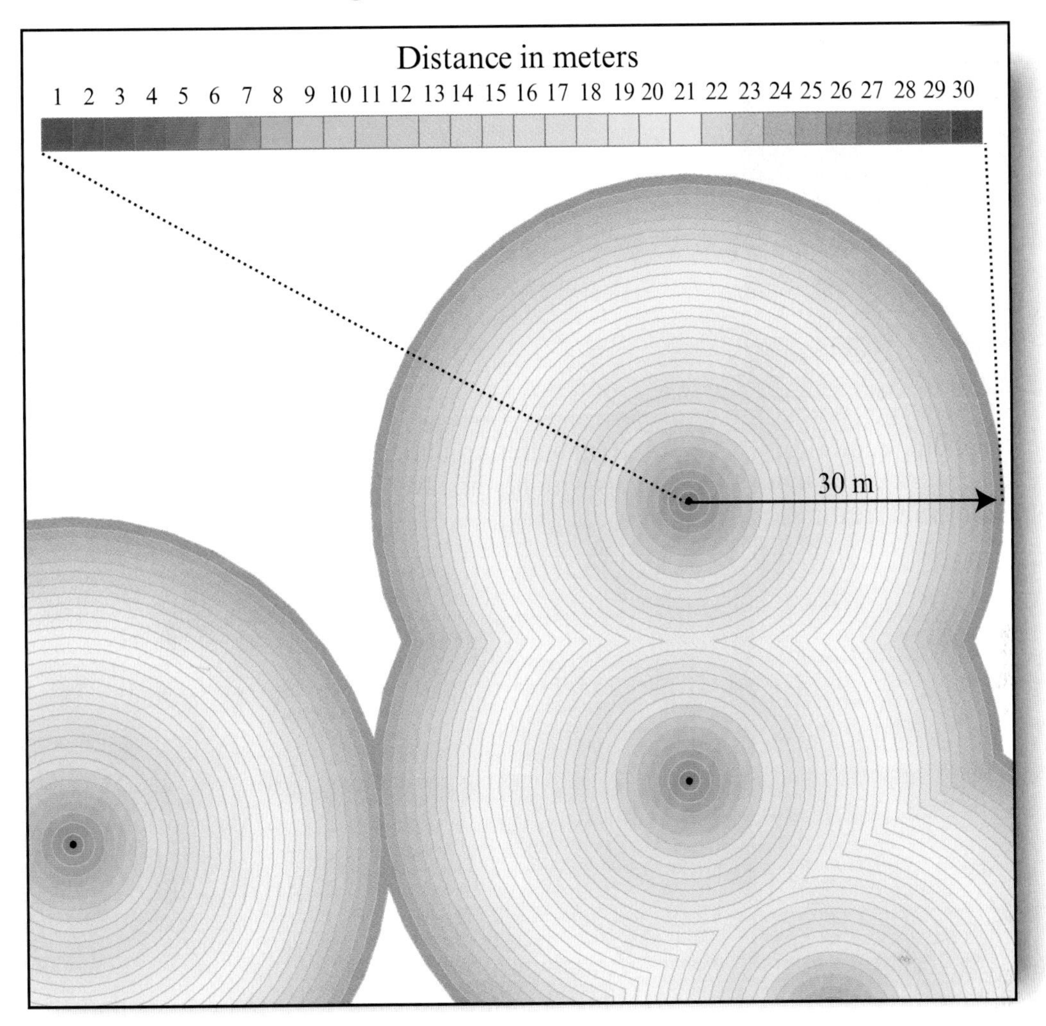

FIGURE 6–2 An enlargement of 30 m vector buffering around several of the most northern building centroids found in Figure 6-1e (data courtesy of Beaufort County GIS Department).

linear feature extended out *n* units from the original linear feature. For example, Figure 6-3b displays a 10 m buffer around selected street segments in Port Royal, SC. Note how the 10 m street segment buffers overlap. Once again, these individual 10 m buffer regions can be collapsed using a dissolve function as shown in Figure 6-3c. Twenty- and 30-meter buffer zones around the street network are shown in Figures 6-3d,e. If desired, the analyst can also request that the buffering be applied to only one side of a line segment (e.g., to the left or right of the line).

Some investigations will utilize the information contained in several buffer zones created around the same linear feature. For example, the 10 m, 20 m, and 30 m buffer zones around the street network are shown in Figure 6-3f.

Buffering Area Features

Some common examples of area (polygonal) features that might be buffered include: building footprints [e.g., residential (Figure 6-4a), commercial, and public], administrative units (e.g., counties, states, countries), polygons of land cover or land use area (e.g., forest, urban, water, wetland, National Parks).

Buffering around area features creates a buffer zone that has approximately the same shape as the original polygon extended out *n* units from the original polygon boundary. For example, Figure 6-4b displays a 10 m buffer around selected building footprints in Port Royal, SC. Note that some of the buildings in this area were constructed very close to one another. Consequently, some of the building footprint buffers intersect when using a 10 m buffer. These individual 10 m

Buffering Linear Features

a. Point (building centroid), line (road network), and area (building footprint) features.

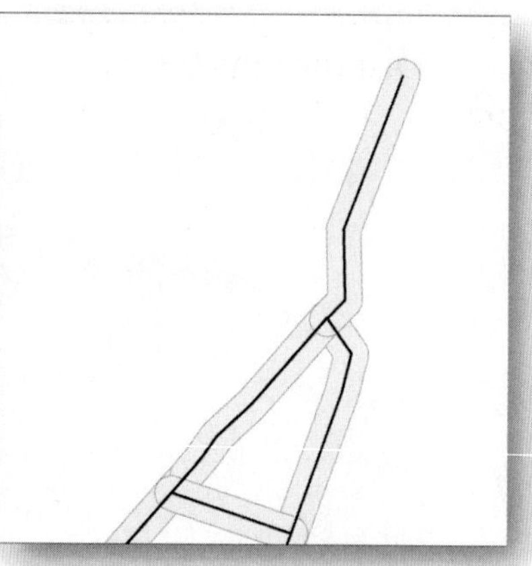

b. 10 m buffer around streets with no dissolve.

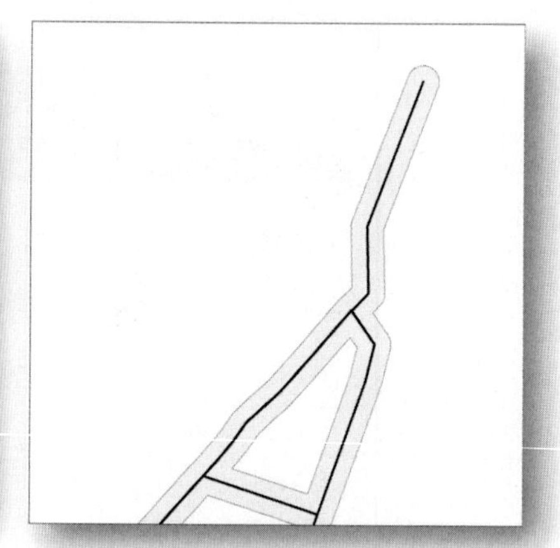

c. 10 m buffer around streets with dissolve.

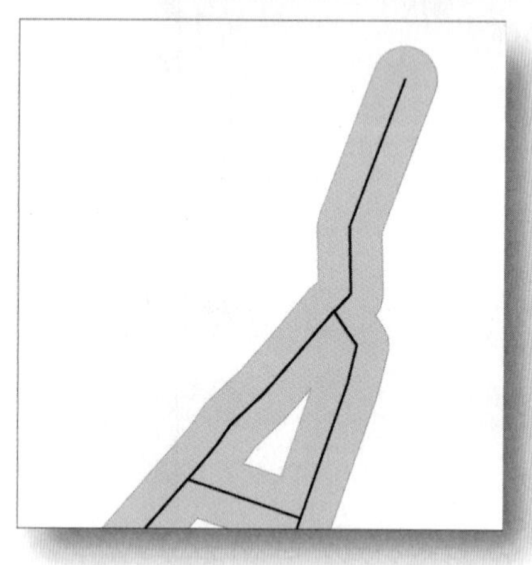

d. 20 m buffer around streets with dissolve.

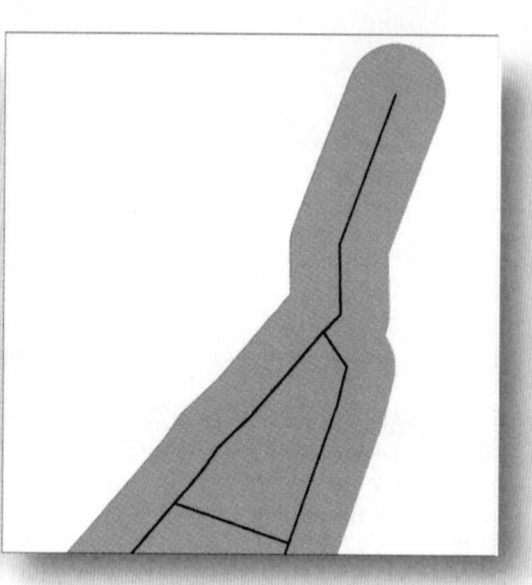

e. 30 m buffer around streets with dissolve.

f. 10 m, 20 m, and 30 m buffers around streets with dissolve.

FIGURE 6–3 a) Point (residential building centroid), line (road network), and area (building footprint) features overlaid on color-infrared orthophotography of a part of Port Royal, SC. b) A 10 m buffer around the street segments with no dissolve. c) A 10 m buffer around the street segments with dissolve. d) A 20 m buffer around the street segments with dissolve. e) A 30 m buffer around the street segments with dissolve. f) Concentric 10 m, 20 m, and 30 m buffers around the street segments with dissolve (data courtesy of Beaufort County GIS Department and USGS).

buffer regions can be collapsed using a dissolve function as shown in Figure 6-4c. Twenty- and 30-meter dissolved buffer zones around the building footprints are shown in Figures 6-4d,e.

Some investigations may require information contained in several buffer zones created around the same area feature. For example, the 10 m, 20 m and 30 m buffers around the building footprints are shown in Figure 6-4f.

It is also possible to buffer an area feature using negative buffering logic. *Negative buffering* (sometimes referred to as *set-back buffering*) creates a buffer interior to the original area polygon feature. A good example of negative buffering is the identification of building set-back dimensions associated with a single parcel of land. Most city and/or county building departments require that the as-built building footprint be some distance (e.g., 5 m) away from the parcel property line. In such cases, a 5 m negative buffer (set-back) can be circumscribed *inside* the original property parcel. This makes it perfectly clear where the builder must place the building so that it is in compliance with the city or county building code. The geographic location of selected residential parcels for a portion of Port Royal, SC, are shown in Figure 6-5a (in blue) overlaid with residential building footprints (in yellow). A 5 m set-

Buffering Area Features

a. Point (building centroid), line (road network), and area (building footprint) features.

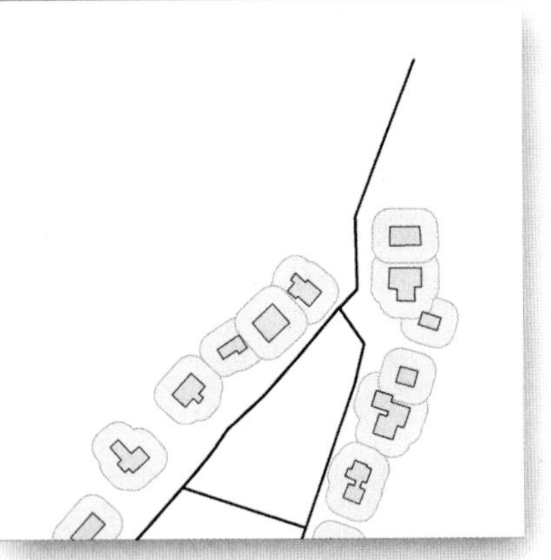

b. 10 m buffer around building footprints with no dissolve.

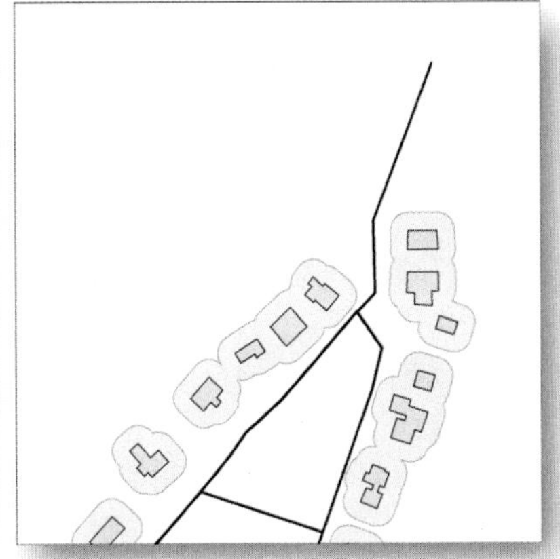

c. 10 m buffer around building footprints with dissolve.

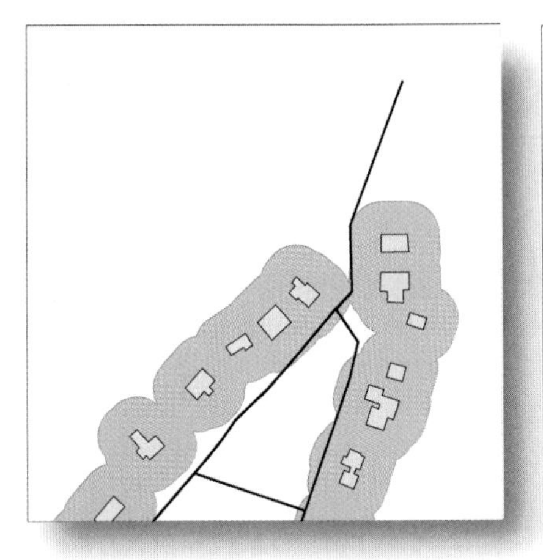

d. 20 m buffer around building footprints with dissolve.

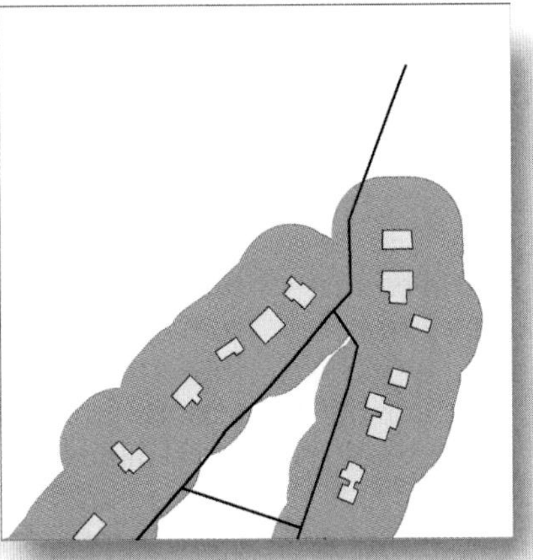

e. 30 m buffer around building footprints with dissolve.

f. 10 m, 20 m, and 30 m buffers around building footprints with dissolve.

FIGURE 6–4 a) Point (residential building centroid), line (road network), and area (building footprint) features overlaid on color-infrared orthophotography of a part of Port Royal, SC. b) A 10 m buffer around the building footprints with no dissolve. c) A 10 m buffer around the building footprints with dissolve. d) A 20 m buffer around the building footprints with dissolve. e) A 30 m buffer around the building footprints with dissolve. f) Concentric 10 m, 20 m, and 30 m buffers around the building footprints with dissolve (data courtesy of Beaufort County GIS Department and USGS).

back buffer polygon was determined for each parcel (Cowen et al., 2007) as shown in Figure 6-5b. Note that most of the single family building footprints lie within the negative 5 m (set-back) buffer region. Both 5 m and 10 m negative set-back buffer regions are shown in Figure 6-5c in blue and dark green, respectively.

Buffer Dimensions

Each of the previous point (residential building centroid), line (street), and area polygons (building footprints) were buffered using systematically larger buffers, e.g., 10 m, 20 m, and 30 m. However, this is not mandatory. For example, if there were two types of streets in the study area (e.g., main and secondary) it might be logical to buffer the more important main streets with a 20 m buffer and the less important secondary streets with a 10 m buffer for a specific application. The nature of the spatial-analysis questions dictates the size of the buffer dimensions and whether or not they are systematic.

Types of Buffering

One of the most important considerations when performing buffering around point, line, and area features using either raster or vector data is how large the buffer zone should be. The GIS analyst should select the buffer dimension (threshold) based on the best infor-

Negative (Set-back) Buffering of Area Features

a. Parcels overlaid with building footprints.

b. 5 m negative (set-back) buffer within each parcel.

c. 5 m and 10 m negative (set-back) buffer within each parcel.

FIGURE 6–5 a) Registered land parcels (in blue) overlaid with building footprints (yellow) for an area in Port Royal, SC. b) The application of a 5 m negative (set-back) buffer *inward* from each parcel boundary is shown in blue. c) Display of both 5 m and 10 m negative set-back buffers within each parcel are shown in blue and dark green, respectively (data courtesy of Beaufort County GIS Department and USGS).

mation available so that the buffer is logical and defendable. Fortunately, there are some guidelines that can be followed when deciding on the distance to buffer. DeMers (2005) identifies several basic types of buffering, including arbitrary, causative, and mandated.

Arbitrary Buffering

Arbitrary buffering is just that, arbitrary. It is based on the GIS analyst's best estimate or guess of what size the buffer should be. His or her decision may not be based on scientific principles, political mandates, or laws. For example, perhaps you are responsible for making a map of an active construction site and the map must include information on where to place fences around the property so that the general public is not harmed while construction is taking place. You would probably first create a map with a polygon around all of the active construction area. Then, you might arbitrarily decide that the public should not be allowed to be closer than 50 m of the construction area. When in doubt, however, it is good practice to err on the side of caution when selecting arbitrary buffer distances. Perhaps it would be more appropriate to specify a 100 m buffer around the active construction site.

Causative Buffering

Sometimes the landscape or conditions surrounding the point, line, or area of interest are non-uniform (i.e., heterogeneous). If you know *a priori* (before the fact) about these conditions, then you may want to apply causative buffering logic to identify buffer distances. For example, suppose you are asked to create a map that will be used to protect a pristine wetland from becoming polluted from watershed runoff. At the present time the wetland is surrounded by forest. However, various groups want to utilize part of the surrounding forest land for agriculture and part of it for a large parking lot. Runoff from both the proposed agricultural development and the proposed parking lot will drain into the wetland.

You know from previous experience that the impermeable parking lot will generate more runoff into the wetland than the surrounding forest or agricultural land with permeable soil. The parking areas also generate runoff that contains petroleum distillates. Therefore, it would be logical for the buffer boundary between the proposed parking areas and the wetland to be greater (e.g., 400 m) than the buffer boundary between the wetland and the proposed agricultural area (e.g., 200 m). It should be noted, however, that agricultural runoff also contains significant amounts of pesticides and herbicides that can also severely impact wetlands. Therefore, the analyst has to carefully investigate the characteristics of the individual phenomena and then make the most logical decision about the buffer distances to be used.

Mandated Buffering

Mandated buffering is the most straightforward type of buffering. Federal, state, local, and community government agencies routinely mandate rigorously defined buffer dimensions for specific types of features. For example, the Federal Emergency Management Agency

(FEMA) identifies 50- or 100-year flood boundaries on Digital Flood Insurance Rate Maps (DFIRMs) so that people who desire to live in or near flood zones can receive or be denied property flood insurance (Maidment et al., 2007). Similarly, almost every one of the U.S. coastal states has detailed development set-back lines that define where you can build in the coastal zone. For example, if you build a home that extends into the 40 ft. set-back line from the tidal mean-high-high water line in South Carolina, the building may not be insurable for loss due to storm surge or flooding.

Transportation departments, utilities, and conservation groups require developers to adhere to strict set-back lines. For example, there are very strict guidelines about how close building development can occur adjacent to highways, powerlines, telephone lines, pipelines, etc. These are sometimes referred to as transportation and utility easements. Similarly, almost every county has strict building easement rules that dictate how close a building can be constructed to the property line (e.g., 3 m). When analyzing such data, it is important that the GIS practictioner be aware of mandated buffer dimensions and carefully incorporate them into the GIS analysis.

Overlay Using Vector Data

Overlay is one of the most important functions in a geographic information system. The overlay (comparison) of two or more thematic features (maps) can be performed using either vector (topological) overlay or raster overlay logic. The feature layers to be overlaid must be spatially registered to a defined map projection and coordinate system.

Topological overlay involves comparing two or more vector feature layers (e.g., A and B) that have been topologically structured. The overlay process results in a new topologically structured vector feature layer (e.g., C) which includes the geometric and attribute characteristics of each of the input feature layers based upon the overlay operations that are applied.

Types of Topological Overlay

Vector GIS data layers basically consist of three types of data—points, lines, and polygons. Therefore, there are three major types of topological vector overlay that may be performed:

1. overlay of a point layer on a polygon layer, referred to as **point-in-polygon overlay**,
2. overlay of a line layer on a polygon layer, referred to as **line-in-polygon overlay**, and
3. overlay of a polygon layer on a polygon layer, referred to as **polygon-on-polygon overlay**.

The following discussion is based on the input layer being a point, line, or polygon file and the base layer being a polygon layer. The types of topological overlay and associated operations will be introduced first conceptually in Figure 6-6 and then demonstrated using real-world data of Irmo, SC.

Point-in-Polygon Overlay This type of overlay operation is performed using an input point file and a base layer polygon file. For example, in Figure 6-6a there are 14 point features in the input point layer and two polygons (A and B) in the base layer. Note that the base layer polygon file does not cover exactly the same area as the input point layer. Therefore, only those points found within the base layer polygon are included in the new output layer. Points 1, 2, 12, 13, and 14 are not found in the new output layer. Most importantly, the point features in the new output layer now contain additional attribute information about the polygon within which they reside, e.g., points 3–6 shown in red now have attribute A characteristics, and points 7–11 shown in green now have attribute B characteristics.

An example of point-in-polygon overlay would be overlaying a point feature layer containing the centroids of all the residential housing in the county (the input point layer) with a polygon feature layer of all the school districts in the county (base layer). In the new output dataset, each of the residential housing points would have both residential and school district attribute information. This information could be very important when parents are trying to determine which school district their children will attend.

Line-in-Polygon Overlay This overlay operation is applied to an input line file and a base layer overlay polygon file. In the example shown in Figure 6-6b, there is only one linear feature (e.g., a road) in the line input layer and two polygons (A and B) in the base layer. Again, the base layer polygon file does not cover exactly the same geographic area as the input line layer. Therefore, only those parts of line 1 found within the base layer polygons are included in the new output layer. Most importantly, there are now two linear features in the new output layer that contain additional attribute information about the polygon within which they reside, e.g., line segment 1A now has the attribute characteristics of polygon A, and line segment 1B has the attribute characteristics of polygon B.

An example of line-in-polygon overlay would be overlaying a linear feature layer containing the county powerline network (the input line layer) with a base polygon feature layer containing information about the forest types (e.g., pine and oak). In the output dataset, each of the subdivided powerline segments would have

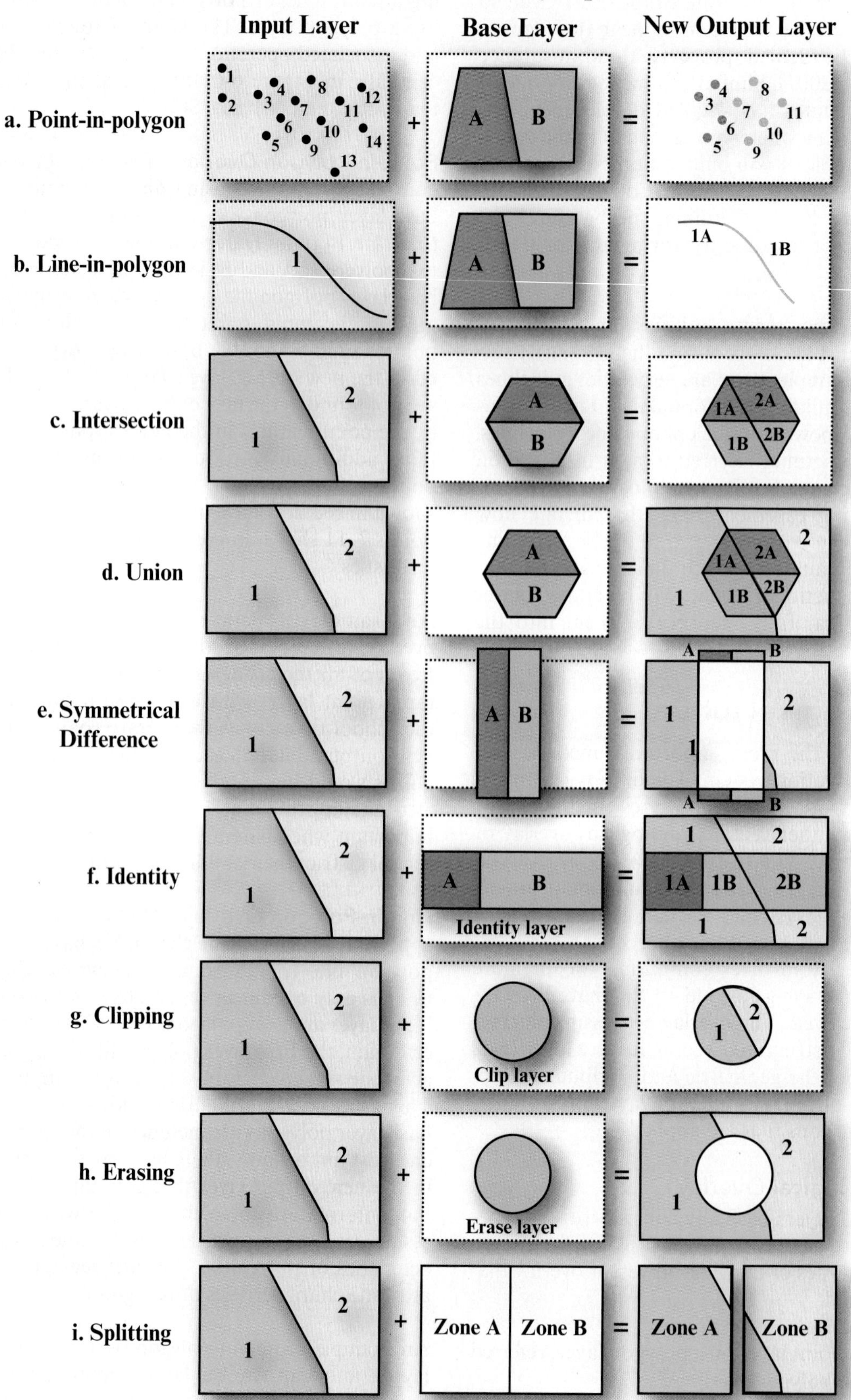

FIGURE 6–6 Selected types of vector overlay operations.

forest-type attribute information. This could be very valuable information when trying to predict those powerlines in the county that might be especially vulnerable to problems during an ice storm or snowstorm. Deciduous trees typically do well during severe ice storms or snowstorms because the leaves are not present to collect ice and/or snow. Conversely, evergreen pines retain their needles throughout the year. Individual pine needles can become encased with ice during an ice storm, causing tree limbs to become extremely heavy and break off, destroying powerlines. This situation often results in the loss of electrical power for millions of people each year.

Polygon-on-Polygon Overlay This type of overlay operation is applied to an input vector polygon feature file and a base polygon file. Overlay operations are based on Boolean logic using AND, OR, and XOR connectors. Each new polygon in the resultant output polygon file has attributes associated with both layers. The output feature layer always has more polygons than the original polygon layers (Figure 6-6c-i). Polygon-on-polygon overlay is often a complex and computationally intensive type of map overlay operation.

A good example of a polygon-on-polygon overlay application would be overlaying a polygonal feature layer containing all of the parcels in the county (the input polygon layer) with a polygon feature layer of the expected sea-level rise in the county (base layer). In the output dataset, each of the parcel polygons would have both parcel and sea-level-rise attribute information.

The **intersection** of two map layers is based on the use of the Boolean AND connector, which computes the geometric intersection of the input layer and the base feature layer (Figure 6-6c). Only those features or portions of features that overlap in both the input layer and the base layer are written to the output layer (Esri, 2011).

The **union** of two map layers is based on the use of the OR connector (Figure 6-6d). It preserves all of the features in both the input polygon layer and the base layer. The geographic extent of the output layer is a combination of both the input layer and the base layer.

The XOR connector is used when one wants to detect differences between layers. The **Symmetrical Difference** operation computes a geometric intersection of the input layer features and the base layer features (Figure 6-6e). Features or portions of features in the input and update features that do *not* overlap are written to the output layer (Esri, 2011). The output polygon file has a geographic extent that is the opposite of using the intersection operator.

The **identity** operation uses an input layer containing points, lines, or polygons.The base layer is called the identity layer and must be a polygon file (Figure 6-6f). The operation computes a geometric intersection of the input layer features and identity layer features. The input features or portions thereof that overlap the identity layer features will get the attributes of the identity layer features (Esri, 2011). The operation produces an output file that has the same geographic extent as the input layer.

Clipping extracts a geographic piece of the input layer using the base layer as a cookie cutter template (Figure 6-6g). Clipping uses the outside boundary of the polygon in the base layer to cookie-cut features and attributes from the input coverage (Esri, 2011). None of the attributes from the two datasets are combined. It is very useful for *masking-out* unwanted geographic area(s) in a GIS database. For example, one might want to display only the geographic extent within a specific school district. In this case, the input layer might be a map of the county and the base layer would be a polygon of the school district.

Erasing deletes a part of the input layer using the base layer as a template for the geographic area to be deleted (Figure 6-6h). Similar to clipping, none of the attributes from the two datasets are combined. The output layer contains only those input layer features that are *outside* the erasing region.

Splitting divides the input layer into a number of smaller layers based on the characteristics of the base layer (Figure 6-6i). Each new output coverage contains only those portions of the input layer features overlapped by the split coverage polygons. In the example, two new coverages are created consisting of Zones A and B.

Overlay Analysis Example

Several of the aforementioned vector overlay types and operators will be demonstrated using a real-world dataset centered on the Lake Murray Dam located near Irmo, SC. The vector overlay techniques will be demonstrated in the general order they might be used in a typical GIS project.

First, the clipping overlay operator will be used to refine the geographic extent of the study area. Figure 6-7a depicts the extended coverage of a color-infrared USGS Digital Orthophoto Quarter Quadrangle (DOQQ) of an area centered on *Lake Murray* and the *Saluda River*, which flows from it. The illustration also shows the clipping mask that was applied to extract a more selective study area. The geographic extent of the clipped USGS DOQQ 1×1 m spatial resolution orthophoto is shown in Figure 6-7b. The clipped USGS digital elevation model (DEM) and the derived 10 ft.

Clipping Raster and Vector Data Using Polygon Overlay

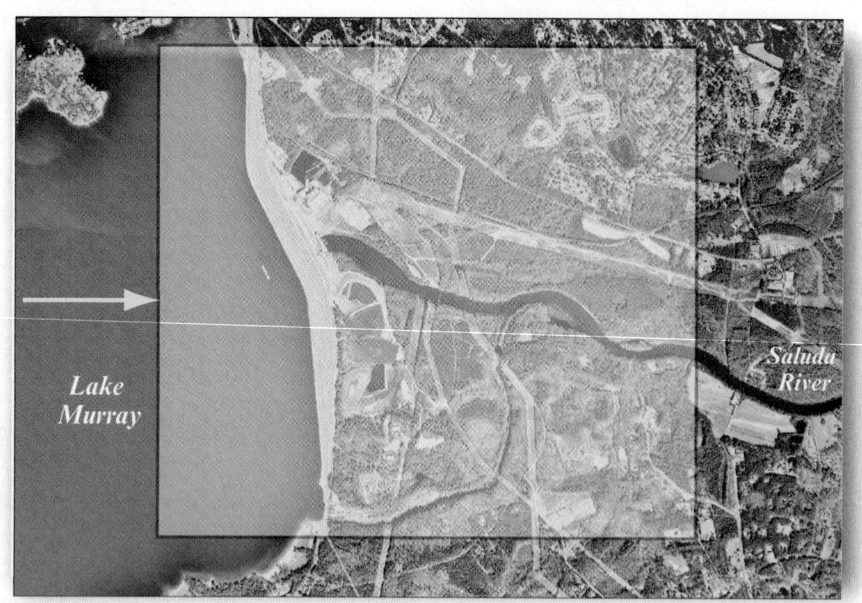

a. USGS Digital Orthophoto Quarter Quad (DOQQ) of Lake Murray Dam overlaid with clipping file.

b. Clipped color-infrared DOQQ.

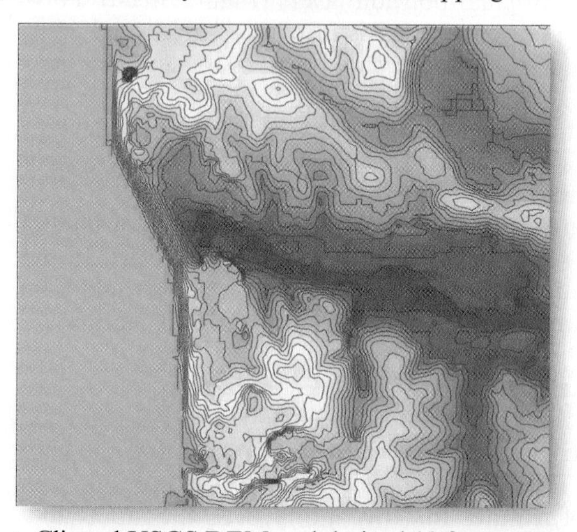

c. Clipped USGS DEM and derived 10 ft. contours.

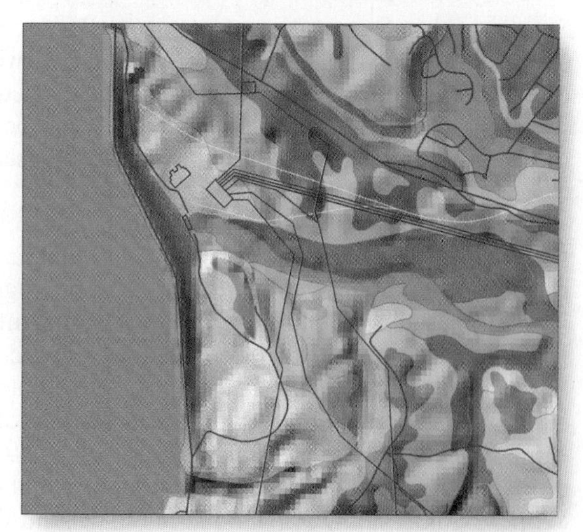

d. Clipped roads, powerlines, railroad, soil, and water polygons overlaid on hill-shaded DEM.

FIGURE 6–7 a) Color-infrared USGS Digital Orthophoto Quarter Quadrangle (DOQQ) at 1 x 1 m spatial resolution overlaid with a clipping mask. b) The clipped DOQQ. c) A USGS digital elevation model (DEM) of the clipped study area. The 10 ft. contour lines were derived from the clipped DEM. d) Linear roads, powerlines, railroad lines, and soil and water polygons are overlaid onto a hill-shaded version of the DEM shown in (c) (data courtesy of USGS).

Point-in-Polygon Overlay

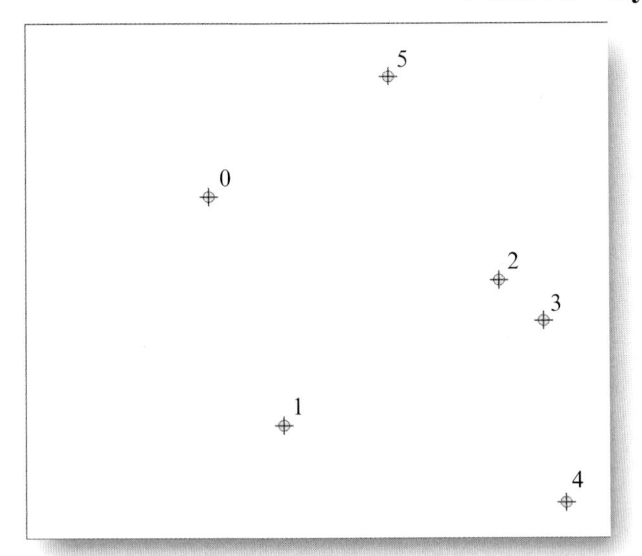

a. Six point locations identified for analysis.

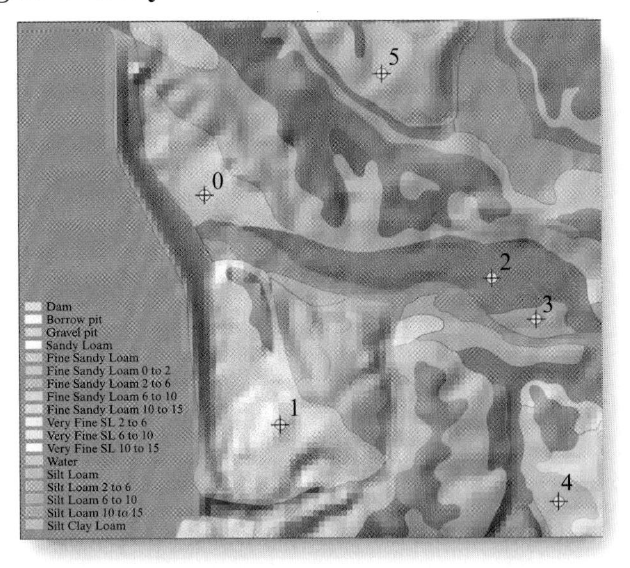

b. Six points intersected with soil polygons.

Attribute Table before Point-in-Polygon Overlay

FID	*Label*
0	A
1	B
2	C
3	D
4	E
5	F

Attribute Table after Point-in-Polygon Overlay

FID	*Label*	*Soil Type*	*Slope* (%)
0	A	Borrow pit	–
1	B	Borrow pit	–
2	C	Silt loam	–
3	D	Fine Sandy Loam	–
4	E	Very Fine Sandy Loam	6–10
5	F	Fine Sandy Loam	6–10

FIGURE 6–8 Application of point-in-polygon intersection at six locations to extract detailed soil-type and slope (%) information. a) Location of the six points before intersection and the characteristics of the attribute table. b) The six points intersected with the soils polygons and the characteristics of the resultant attribute table (data courtesy of USGS).

contours are shown in Figure 6-7c. Several clipped linear features (primary roads, powerlines, railroad lines) and the clipped soil type and water polygons are shown in Figure 6-7d. These data are overlaid on a hill-shaded version of the DEM to help the map reader appreciate the local relief of the area.

This dataset can be used for a number of interesting applications. For example, suppose we are conducting a study at the six geographic locations shown in Figure 6-8a and we need to know the soil type at each of the locations. This is a classic point-in-polygon problem. We simply need to intersect the point coverage containing the six points (Figure 6-8a) with the soil polygon coverage shown in Figure 6-8b. This results in a new output point coverage file with the six points that now contain soil attribute information. Note the content of the attribute table before and after the intersection. Each of the six points now contains information about the soil type and percent slope (e.g., 6–10%) that was previously associated with every soil polygon. It is important to note that the intersection of a point file with a polygonal file always results in the creation of an output-point file coverage. This point-in-polygon operation greatly increased the information content of the six points under consideration.

Now let us consider road segment #2436 shown in Figure 6-9a. Suppose that we want to improve the quality of this primary road segment (Type 170) but first want to determine the characteristics of the underlying soil so that good engineering decisions can be made. This is a line-in-polygon problem. We simply need to intersect the road-segment coverage (Figure 6-9a) with the soil polygon coverage. This results in a new output line segment coverage file with the original line segment subdivided into three line segments associated with the three soil type polygons encountered (Figure 6-9b). Note

Line-in-Polygon Overlay

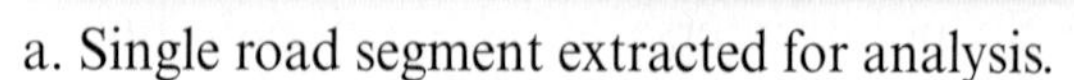

a. Single road segment extracted for analysis.

b. Road segment intersected with soil polygons.

Attribute Table before Line-in-Polygon Overlay

FID	*Segment #*	*Road Type*
0	2436	170

Attribute Table after Line-in-Polygon Overlay

FID	*Segment #*	*Road Type*	*FID_Soil*	*Soil Type*	*Slope* (%)
0	2436	170	37	Borrow pit	
1	2436	170	38	Fine Sandy Loam	6-10
2	2436	170	41	Fine Sandy Loam	2-6

FIGURE 6–9 Application of line-in-polygon intersection of road segment #2436 with soil type and slope (%) information. a) Location of road segment #2436 before intersection. b) After intersection with soils information, road segment #2436 is broken into three sub-segments that contain road type, soil type, and slope (%) attributes (data courtesy of USGS).

that the original line segment attribute information consisted of only the feature ID, segment number, and road type. After intersection with the soil polygon data, there are three line segments associated with road segment number #2436. Each of these line segments has a unique feature ID soil number as well as soil type and slope (%) information. It is important to point out that the intersection of a line file with a polygonal file always results in the creation of an output line file coverage.

Now let us consider what we would do if there was a particular area within the overall study area that was to be excluded from further analysis due to privacy or administrative reasons. This is an erase overlay problem. The area to be excluded (erased) can be applied to raster as well as vector data. For example, suppose it was necessary to exclude the polygonal boundary of the Saluda Hydroelectric Power Plant adjacent to the Lake Murray Dam from further analysis. The GIS analyst would first create a polygonal erase file and then apply the erase overlay operation to the raster and/or vector data. Figure 6-10a depicts the results of using a polygonal erase file associated with the Saluda Hydroelectric Power Plant applied to the USGS DOQQ imagery. The result is a digital orthophoto with a hole in it. All raster digital numbers within the excluded (erased) region are shown as white with an RGB value of 255, 255, 255, instead of their original digital number values.

The polygonal erase file was also used to erase the road, railroad, powerline, and soil information that fell within the boundaries of the erase polygon file (Figure 6-10b). Note how the road, railroad, powerline, and soil information abruptly stop at the boundary of the erase polygon. It is important to point out that the application of a polygonal erase operator will dramatically change the content of the original vector files to which it is applied. It will completely erase (remove) points within the exclusion area, erase parts of line segments within the excluded area, and parts of polygons

Erasing Raster and Vector Data Using Polygon Overlay

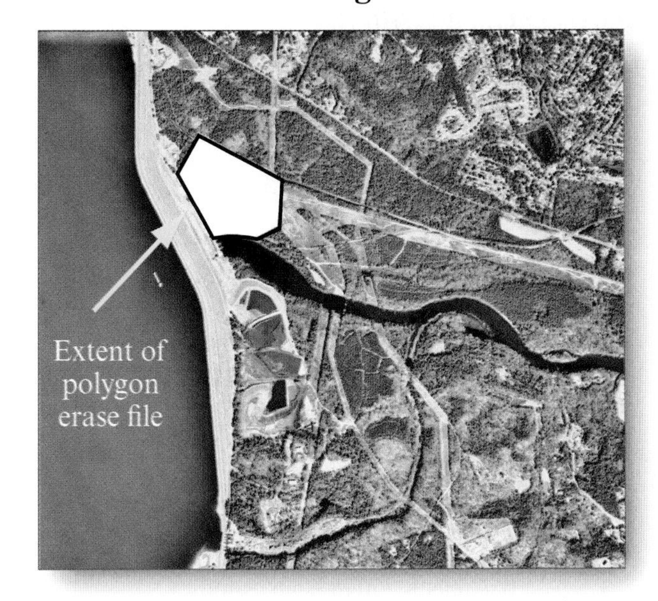

a. Part of USGS DOQQ imagery erased.

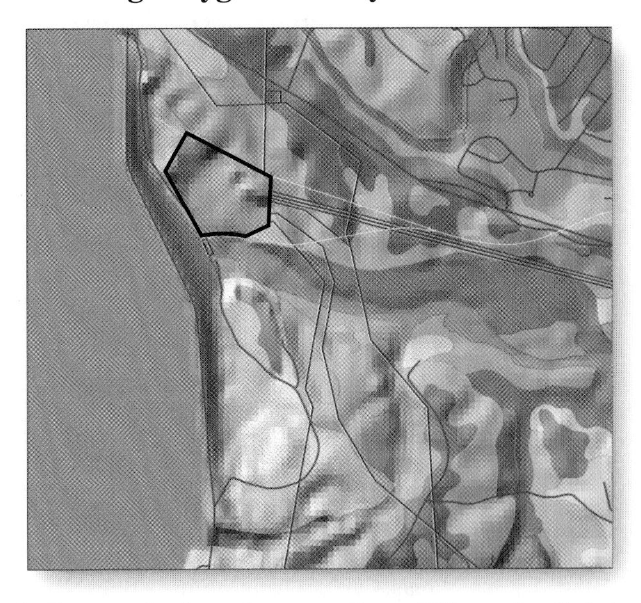

b. Removal of roads, powerlines, RR, and soil data within the extent of a polygon erase file. Hill-shaded DEM is allowed to show through for clarity.

FIGURE 6–10 a) A polygonal erase file was used to remove the area occupied by the Saluda Hydroelectric Power Plant adjacent to the Lake Murray Dam from further analysis. b) The roads, powerlines, railroad, and soil information were also erased (removed) within the extent of the polygon erase file (data courtesy of USGS).

within the excluded area. The new truncated line segments and polygons will have entirely new geometric characteristics.

Finally, let us consider the use of the Irmo, SC, geospatial data to identify suitable locations for a new upscale detached single-family residence within the study area. This will require the use of **intersection, union,** and **erase overlay** analyses and the use of spatial buffering. We will keep the location criteria relatively simple for demonstration purposes. The following "good" and "bad" criteria will be applied:

Good Criteria: Potential terrain for the new upscale single-family residence must be

- < 200 m from existing primary roads so that the cost of new paved road construction is not excessive;
- < 250 m from water for access and aesthetics.

Bad Criteria: Potential terrain must

- not be located within the river or lake;
- > 150 m from all railroad lines for noise abatement and child safety considerations;
- > 75 m from all powerlines for safety and to minimize electromagnetic interference with household electronics;
- > 200 m from all nearby borrow pits (excavations) for aesthetic and child safety considerations.

All of the information required to identify terrain that meet these criteria can be derived from the geospatial data previously described.

First, it is necessary to find the terrain within the study area that meets both of the "good" criteria. The terrain < 200 m from all primary roads is shown in Figure 6-11a and all land < 250 m from water is shown in Figure 6-11b. Of course, these data were created using buffering. Both of these criteria must be present or the terrain cannot possibly be suitable for locating the single-family residence. Therefore, this requires the *intersection* of the buffered primary road and water files. The intersection of the two files is shown in Figure 6-11c. It is clear at this point that any area outside of the intersection of these two files can never be acceptable for locating the single-family residential area based on the criteria. However, we must still refine the potential locations by incorporating the "bad" criteria into the investigation.

Locating A Single-Family Residence Using Line and Polygon Buffering and Overlay Intersection – Part A: "Good" Criteria

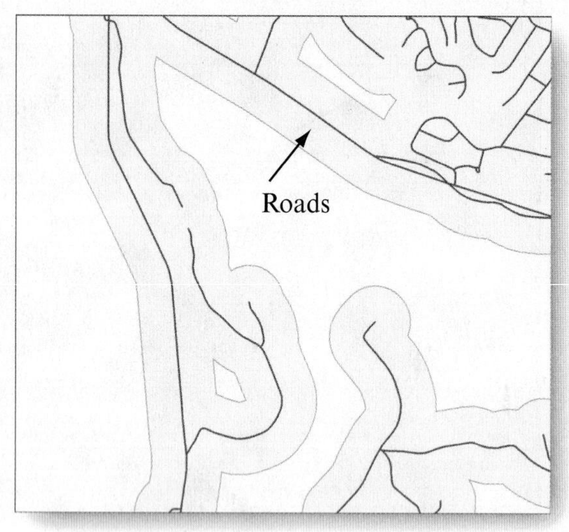

a. Areas < 200 m from primary roads.

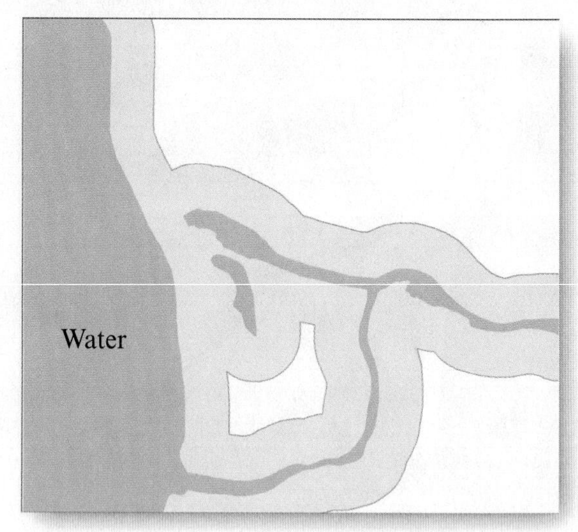

b. Areas < 250 m from water.

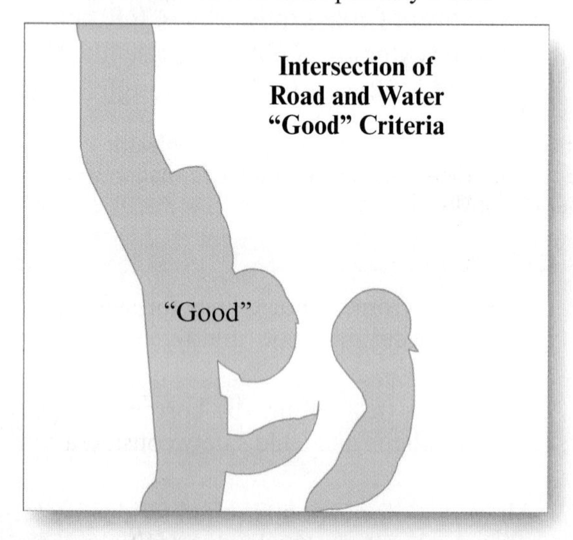

c. Intersection of (a) and (b) above. Areas < 200 m from a primary road and < 250 m from water.

FIGURE 6–11 a) Areas in the study area that are < 200 m from all primary roads. b) Areas in the study area that are < 250 m from any type of water. c) The intersection of (a) and (b) identifies areas that are < 200 m from a primary road and < 250 m from water.

It is not possible to build a home in a water body. Therefore, Figure 6-12a depicts the spatial distribution of all water in the study area, which will be excluded from analysis. All terrain < 150 m of a railroad track is shown in Figure 6-12b. All terrain < 75 m of a powerline is shown in Figure 6-12c. Note the large number of powerlines radiating away from the Saluda Hydroelectric Power Plant which will certainly remove a substantial portion of the study area from consideration. All terrain < 200 m from a borrow pit is shown in Figure 6-12d. The *union* of these four "bad" criteria is shown in Figure 6-12e. It is clear that the "bad" criteria rule out a substantial portion of the study area.

To identify the terrain that satisfies both the "good" and the "bad" criteria, it was necessary to erase all of the terrain identified using the "good" criteria by the terrain that was cumulatively recognized as inappropriate using the "bad" criteria. The result of this erase overlay operation is shown in Figure 6-12f. These geographic areas satisfy all of the criteria and appear to be suitable for locating an upscale, detached single-family residence.

Overlay Analysis Using an Interactive Model-building Program

Because overlay operations are often some of the most important tools applied in GIScience, this is an appropriate time to introduce the use of interactive object-oriented modeling to perform overlay analysis. All of the previous modeling was performed one step at a time using the fundamental buffering, intersection,

Locating a Single-Family Residence Using Polygon Buffering and Overlay Intersection, Union, and Erase – Part B: "Bad" Criteria and Results

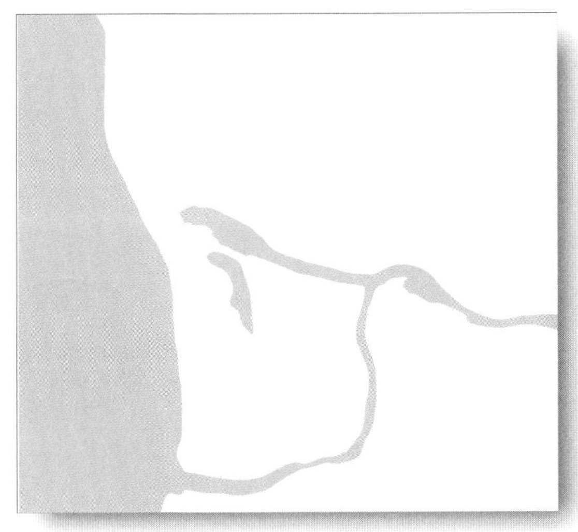

a. Lake and river water bodies.

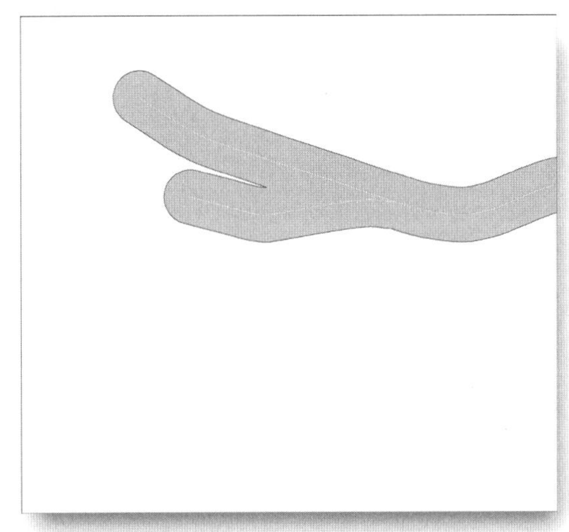

b. Areas <150 m from a railroad track.

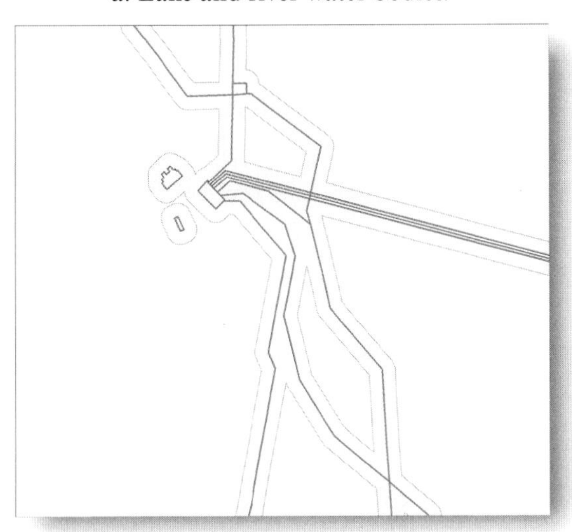

c. Areas < 75 m from a powerline.

d. Areas < 200 m from a borrow pit.

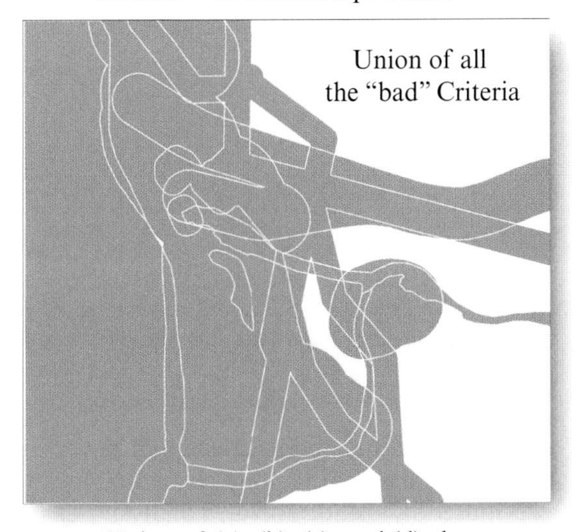

e. Union of (a), (b), (c), and (d) above.

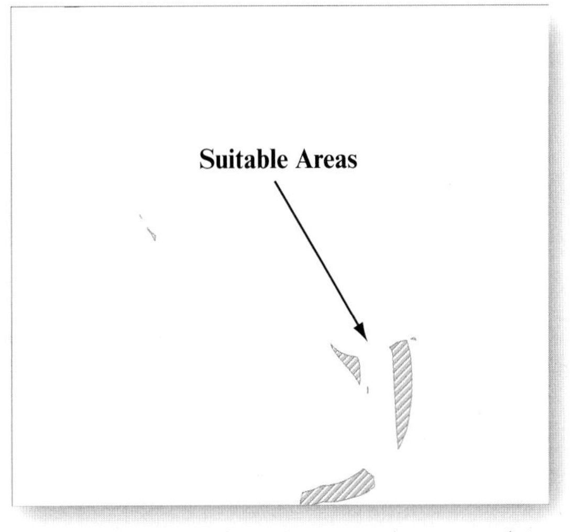

f. Suitable areas after (e) was used to erase the "good" geographic areas found in Figure 6-11c.

FIGURE 6–12 a) Lake and river water-body areas. b) Areas < 150 m from railroad tracks. c) Areas < 75 m from powerlines. d) Areas < 200 m from a borrow pit. e) The union of (a), (b), (c), and (d). f) Areas suitable for the new single-family residence.

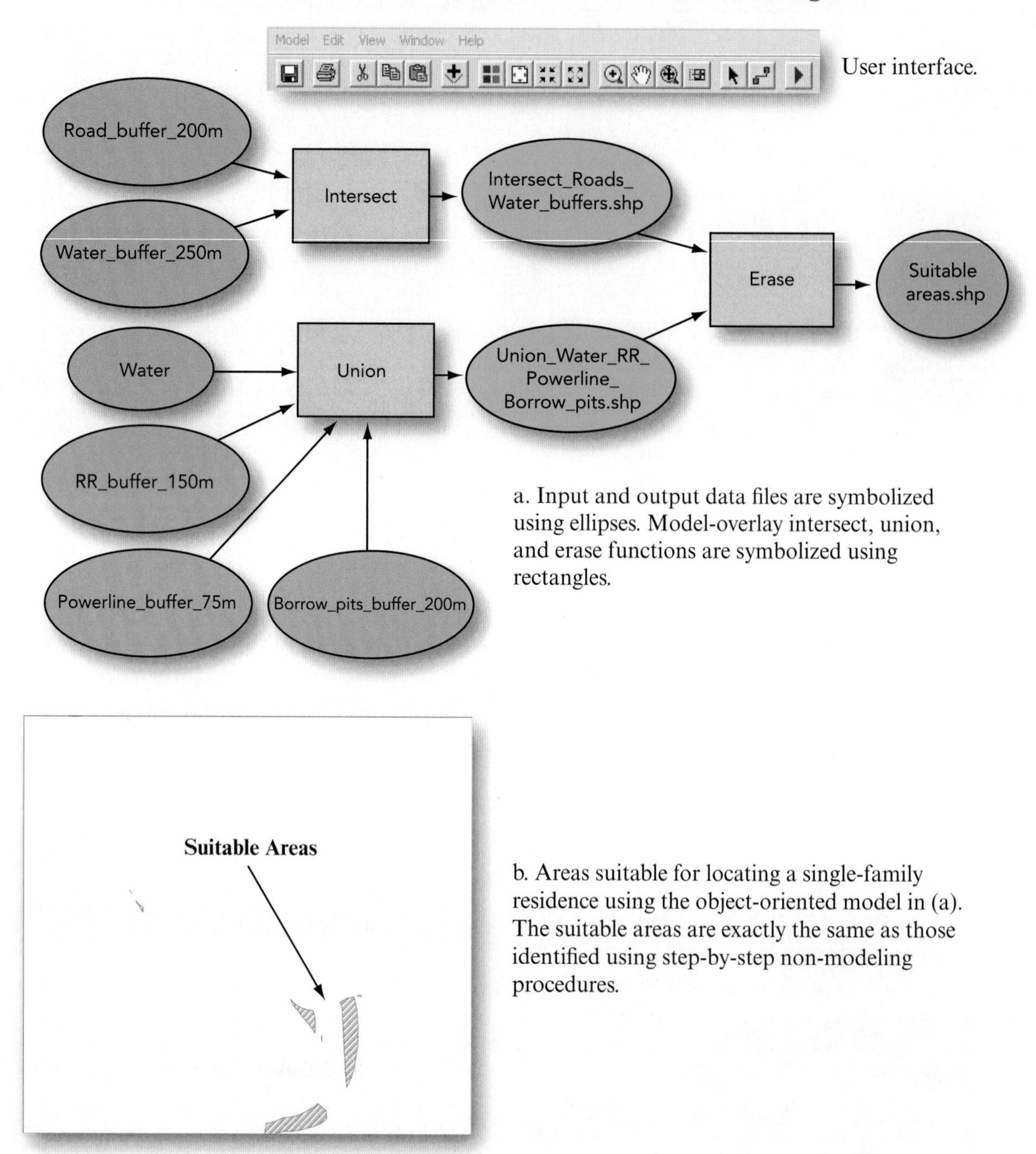

FIGURE 6–13 Application of the single-family residential location model using the ArcGIS® modeling system. a) The user interface and model components (interface courtesy of Esri, Inc.). b) The suitable areas. Compare the suitable areas with those shown in Figure 6-12f.

union, and erase operations. While this produces very accurate and repeatable results, it is often easier to conduct the analysis using a relatively simple interactive modeling system.

For example, consider the ArcGIS® Model user interface shown in Figure 6-13a. It consists of a number of icons that can be used to create and run a GIS model, in this case the single-family residential location model previously discussed. The GIS analyst uses the user interface tools to simply drag and drop the intersection tool, the union tool, and the erase tool onto the workspace below the user interface. The overlay operations are depicted as yellow rectangles. The user then clicks on a tool and the program requests the name of all of the input files associated with the operation. In this case the intersection operation requires two files:

- Road_buffer_200m and
- Water_buffer_250m,

which are displayed in blue ellipses. These files were prepared beforehand using traditional tools. They could also have been created using modeling tools. The intersect tool also requests the name of the output file and displays it in a green ellipse.

The user then clicks on the union rectangle and identifies the four input files:

- Water,
- RR_buffer_150m,
- Powerline_buffer_75m, and
- Borrow_pits_buffer_200m.

All of these files were prepared prior to running the union operation. The output file for the union operation is specified and shown in a green ellipse.

The user clicks on the erase overlay tool and then provides the input files that are the output files for the intersection and union operations. The erase output file contains the results associated with the intersection, union, and erase operations.

The results from the model (Figure 6-13b) are of course exactly the same as the results produced when the operations were processed in a traditional step-by-step fashion (refer to Figure 6-12f). However, it is much easier to perform the analysis using the modeling interface. Also, the model-building process creates a useful work-flow diagram (Figure 6-13a) that communicates to others what procedures were used to produce the final results. The diagram also represents a robust form of metadata about the project. In addition, it is straightforward to modify the input criteria to investigate various "what-if" scenarios for decision making.

Map overlay analysis can also be performed using raster data (DeMers, 2002). This will be demonstrated in the next section, which summarizes several key raster data analysis functions, including raster map overlay.

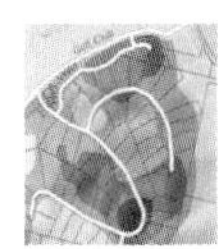

Raster Data Analysis

Geographic data in a raster (grid) format can be analyzed using at least four fundamental types of operations, including:

- Distance measurement operations,
- Local operations on single and multiple rasters,
- Neighborhood operations, and
- Zonal operations.

It is instructive to provide information about these important raster data processing operations. Several of the raster data analysis algorithms are adapted from Jensen (2005).

Raster Distance Measurement Operations

The straight-line, or Euclidean distance, across the terrain is called the physical distance. It is also possible to compute the cost distance associated with traveling over other types of surfaces, including socio-economic cost surfaces. Cost distance is discussed in Chapter 7: Network Analysis.

Earlier in this chapter you were introduced to buffer measurements from point, line, and area vector features. Most GIS software can also calculate physical distance and buffer measurement using raster data. For example, the euclidean physical distance between the centroids of two pixels in a raster can be measured using the Pythagorean theorem. To measure the distance between the centroids of cell 2,2 and cell 4,4 in the following diagram, we use the Pythagorean theorem and determine that

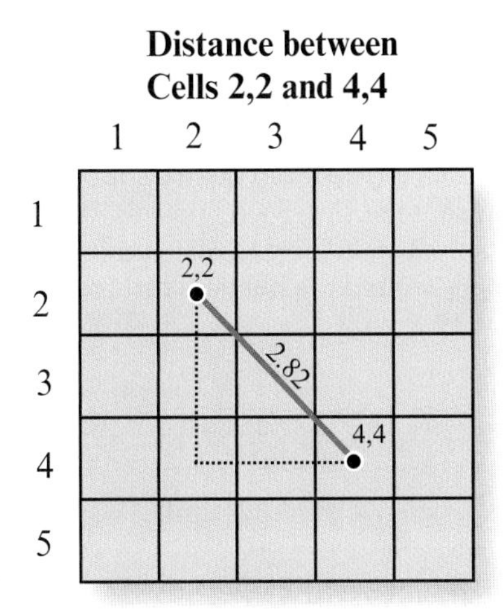

$$c^2 = a^2 + b^2 \tag{6.1}$$

$$c = \sqrt{a^2 + b^2}$$

$$c = \sqrt{(4-2)^2 + (4-2)^2}$$

Raster Buffering of Point Features

a. Building centroids at 1 x 1 m spatial resolution.

b. Building centroids at 3 x 3 m spatial resolution.

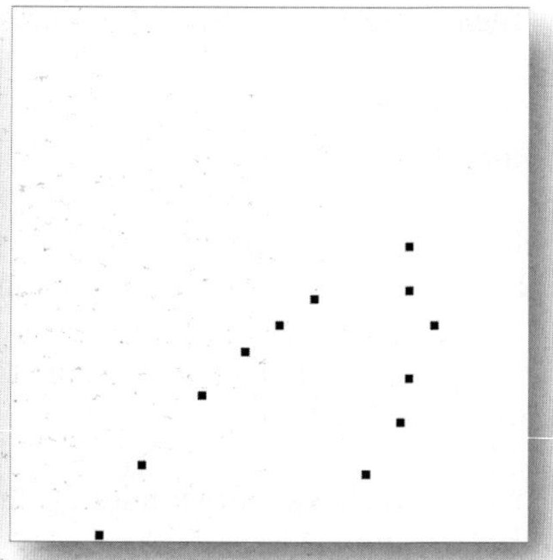

c. Building centroids at 5 x 5 m spatial resolution.

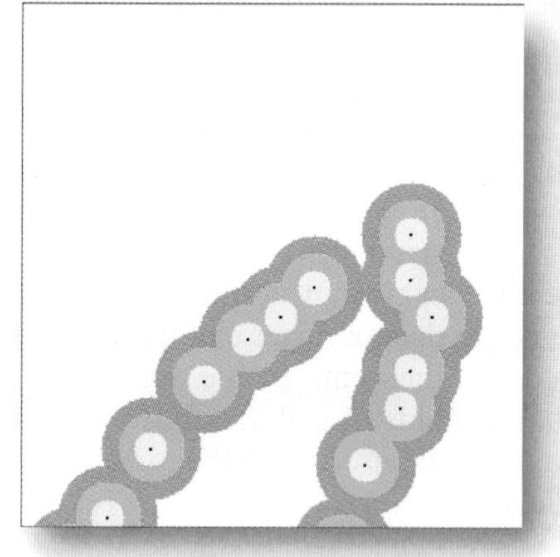

d. 1 x 1 m building centroid pixels buffered to 10 m, 20 m, and 30 m.

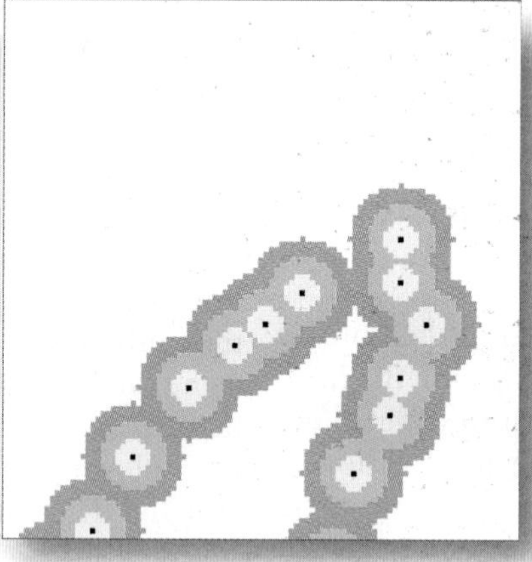

e. 3 x 3 m building centroid pixels buffered to 10 m, 20 m, and 30 m.

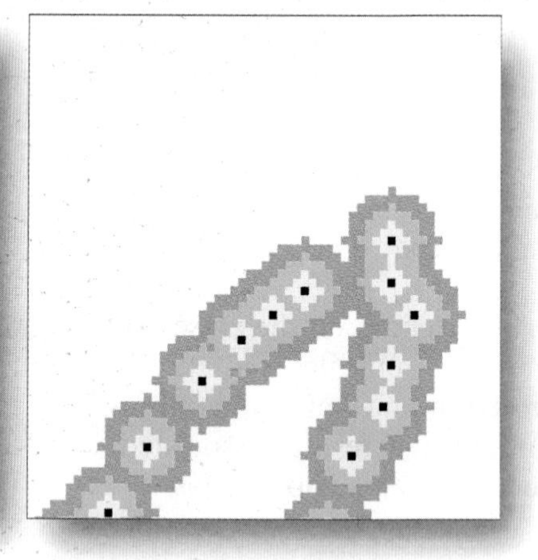

f. 5 x 5 m building centroid pixels buffered to 10 m, 20 m, and 30 m.

FIGURE 6–14 a) Point (building centroid) features of a part of Port Royal, SC, represented using 1 x 1 m pixels. It is very difficult to see the building centroid point symbols at this scale. b) Building centroids represented using 3 x 3 m pixels. c) Building centroids represented using 5 x 5 m pixels. d) 10 m, 20 m, and 30 m buffers around the building centroids represented using 1 x 1 m pixels. e) 10 m, 20 m, and 30 m buffers around the building centroids represented using 3 x 3 m pixels. f) 10 m, 20 m, and 30 m buffers around the building centroids represented using 5 x 5 m pixels (data courtesy of Beaufort County GIS Department).

$$c = \sqrt{4+4}$$

$$c = 2.82 \text{ units.}$$

Buffering Using Raster Data

Using such simple computation, buffering around point, line, and area features in a raster dataset is relatively straightforward. The buffering algorithm simply searches a specific distance away from the point, line, or area feature of interest and recodes all of these pixels to a user-specified value or to a value commensurate with the distance from the point, line, or area feature. For example, assume that a particular raster dataset consists of 10 m pixels. Also assume that a specific pixel in the dataset represents a school. If we wanted to create a 100 m buffer around this single pixel point feature (e.g., the school), then the algorithm would search the equivalent of 10 pixels north, south, east, and west away from the central pixel. All pixels $\leq$ 100 m away from the central pixel in diagonal directions (e.g., northeast, southeast, southwest, northwest) would be identified by taking into consideration the Pythagorean theorem and the hypotenuse of right triangles.

The same point (building centroid), line (street network), and area (building footprint) features used to demonstrate vector buffering earlier in the chapter will be used to demonstrate raster buffering. Figure 6-14a-c demonstrates the rasterization of the building centroid

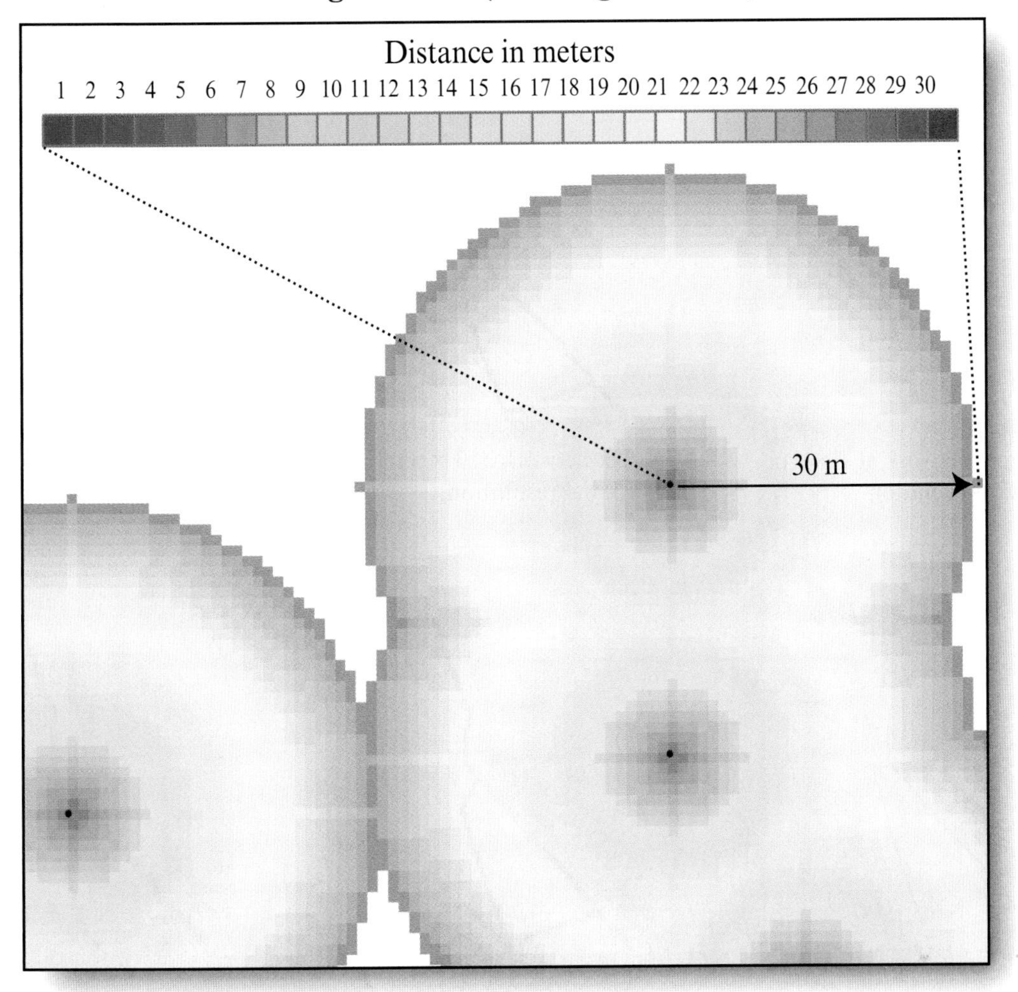

FIGURE 6–15 An enlargement of 30 m raster buffering of the 1 x 1 m pixel building centroids. Compare this figure with the vector buffering of the same building centroids in Figure 6-2 (data courtesy of Beaufort County GIS Department).

information into a grid with 1 × 1 m, 3 × 3 m, and 5 × 5 m pixels, respectively. Representation of the building centroids at 1 × 1 m spatial resolution makes it very difficult to even identify the building centroid location in Figure 6-14a. Centroids rasterized to 3 × 3 m and 5 × 5 m are shown in Figure 6-14b,c, respectively. Each building centroid pixel in the three raster datasets was buffered using 10 m, 20 m, and 30 m distance criteria (Figure 6-14d-f). Buffering the 1 × 1 m data resulted in relatively smooth concentric circles that are very similar in appearance to the vector point buffering of the building centroids shown previously in Figure 6-1b. The 10 m, 20 m, and 30 m buffering of the 3 × 3 m and 5 × 5 m building centroid data, however, becomes increasingly blocky (often referred to as being *pixelated*). For illustrative purposes, Figure 6-15 depicts an enlarged view of what takes place if an analyst requests thirty 1 m buffers around selected building centroids in a raster environment. Compare Figure 6-15 with Figure 6-2 to appreciate the level of detail associated with vector buffering and the generalization that must be considered when performing raster buffering.

The rasterization of the street network using 1 × 1 m, 3 × 3 m, and 5 × 5 m pixels is shown in Figure 6-16a-c. The 1 × 1 m spatial resolution data effectively captures the spatial detail associated with the street network. Note the loss of detail in the street network as the pixel size increases. The 3 × 3 m and 5 × 5 m representation of the street network becomes increasing pixelated. Each street pixel in the three raster datasets was buffered using 10 m, 20 m, and 30 m distance criteria (Figure 6-16d-f).

The rasterization of the building footprint area data using 1 × 1 m, 3 × 3 m, and 5 × 5 m pixels is shown in Figure 6-17a-c. The 1 × 1 m spatial resolution data effectively captures the spatial detail associated with

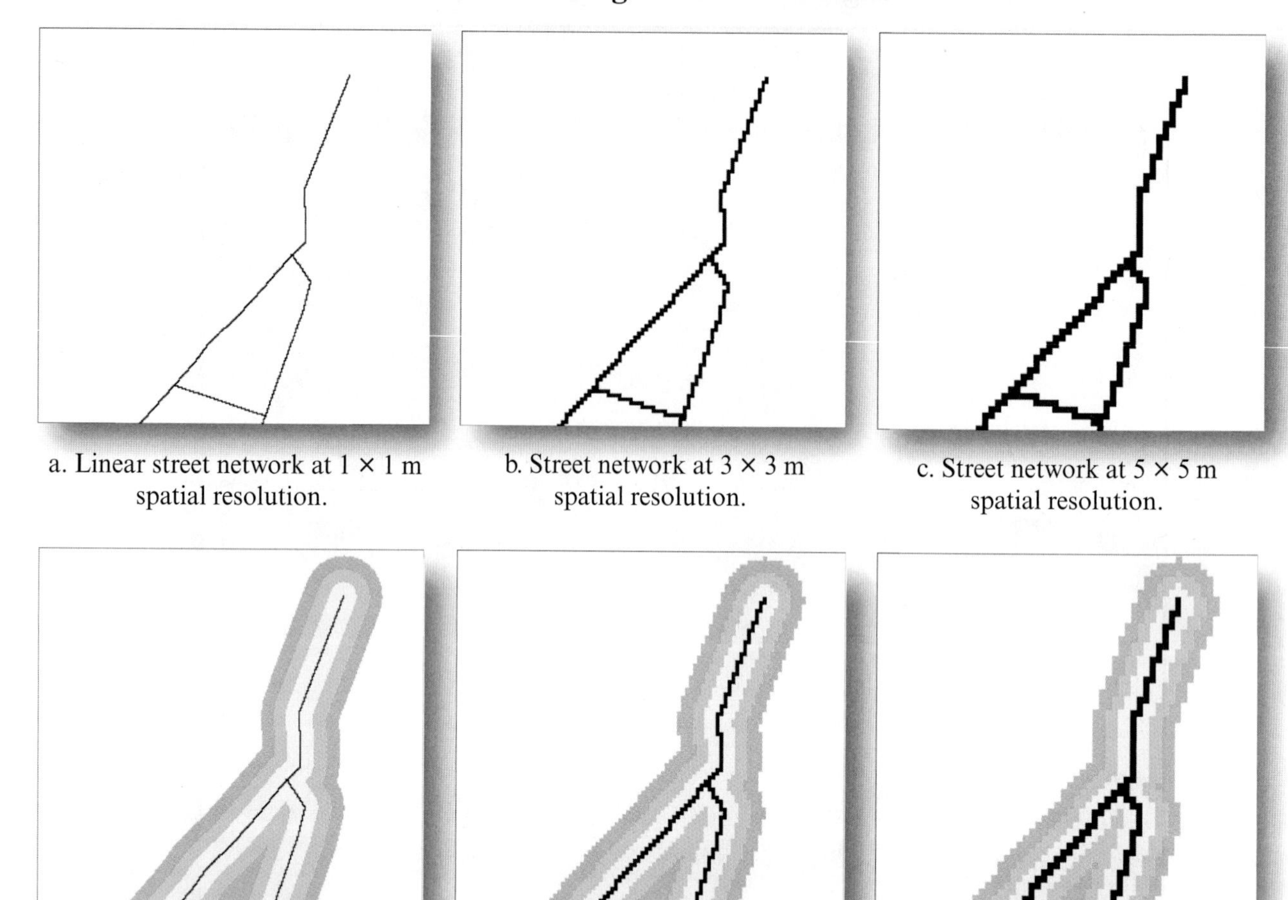

FIGURE 6–16 a) Linear (street) features of a part of Port Royal, SC, represented using 1 x 1 m pixels. b) Streets represented using 3 x 3 m pixels. c) Streets represented using 5 x 5 m pixels. d) 10 m, 20 m, and 30 m buffers around the streets represented using 1 x 1 m pixels. e) 10 m, 20 m, and 30 m buffers around the streets represented using 3 x 3 m pixels. f) 10 m, 20 m, and 30 m buffers around the streets represented using 5 x 5 m pixels (data courtesy of Beaufort County GIS Department).

most of the building footprints (compare with the vector representation in Figure 6-4). However, the 3 × 3 m and 5 × 5 m representation of the building footprints becomes increasingly pixelated. Each group of building footprint pixels in the three raster datasets were buffered using 10 m, 20 m, and 30 m distance criteria (Figure 6-17d-f). It is obvious that the most accurate buffering of the building footprints in this part of Port Royal, SC, would be produced using raster data at ≤1 × 1 m spatial resolution.

Local Raster Operations

Each pixel (cell) at location *i,j* in a raster dataset may be considered a *local* object. The value of this pixel can be operated upon independent of neighboring pixels (cells). This is typically referred to as a **local raster operation**.

Local Operations Applied to a Single Raster Dataset

Local operations can be applied to individual pixels associated with a single raster dataset. For example, the pixel at location row 2, column 2 in Figure 6-18a has a floating-point value of 45.5. It is possible to apply numerous mathematical operations to this local pixel value, including arithmetic (e.g., +, -, /, ×, absolute value, conversion to integer), logarithmic (e.g., logarithms, exponents), trigonometric (e.g., sin, cosine, tangent, arctangent, arccosine, arctangent), and power functions (e.g., square, square root, other powers) (Chang, 2010). For example, we could operate on the value 45.5

Raster Buffering of Area Features

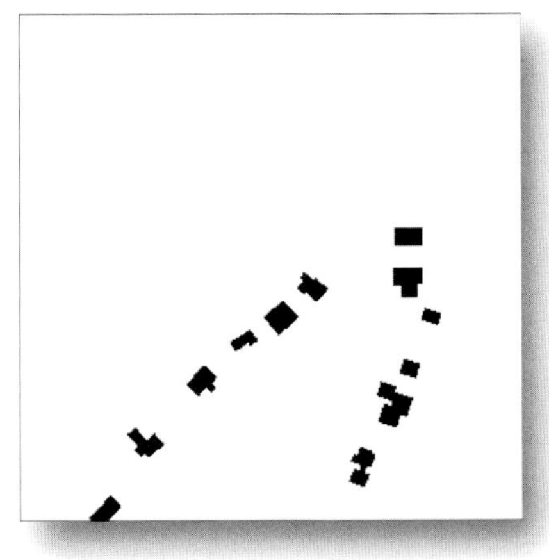

a. Building footprints at 1 x 1 m spatial resolution.

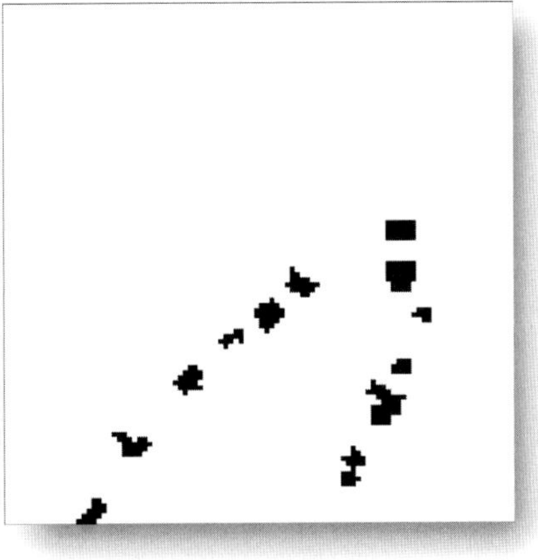

b. Building footprints at 3 x 3 m spatial resolution.

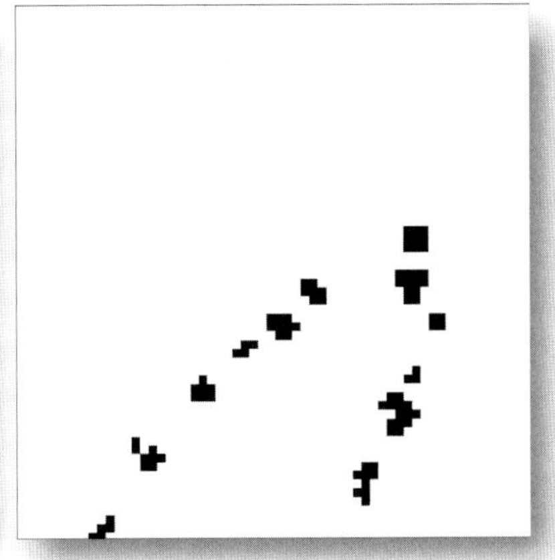

c. Building footprints at 5 x 5 m spatial resolution.

d. 1 x 1 m building footprint pixels buffered to 10 m, 20 m, and 30 m.

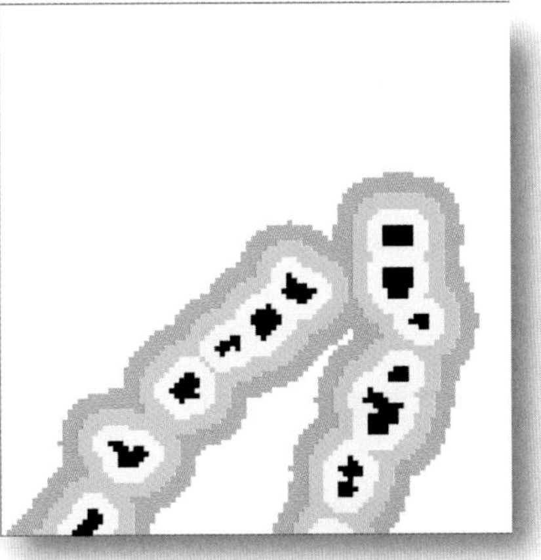

e. 3 x 3 m building footprint pixels buffered to 10 m, 20 m, and 30 m.

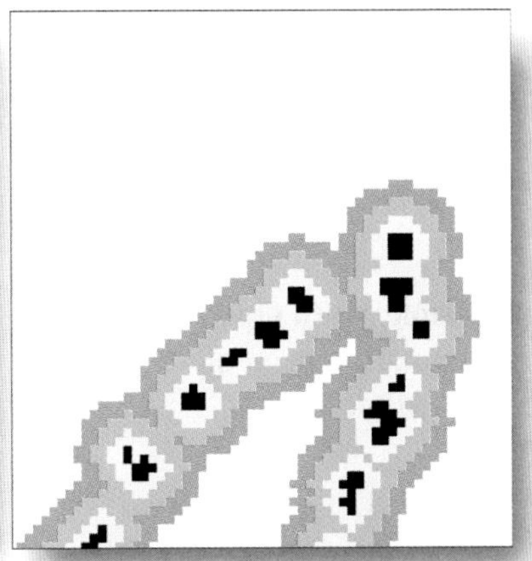

f. 5 x 5 m building footprint pixels buffered to 10 m, 20 m, and 30 m.

FIGURE 6–17 a) Area (building footprint) features of a part of Port Royal, SC, represented using 1 x 1 m pixels. b) Footprints represented using 3 x 3 m pixels. c) Footprints represented using 5 x 5 m pixels. d) 10 m, 20 m, and 30 m buffers around the footprints represented using 1 x 1 m pixels. e) 10 m, 20 m, and 30 m buffers around the footprints represented using 3 x 3 m pixels. f) 10 m, 20 m, and 30 m buffers around the footprints represented using 5 x 5 m pixels (data courtesy of Beaufort County GIS Department).

at location 2,2 using the following operators to obtain new results:

$$\text{integer}\ (45.5) = 45$$

$$\sin\ (45.5) = 0.713$$

$$\log_{10}\ (45.5) = 1.66$$

$$(45.5)^2 = 2070.25$$

Reclassification (Recoding) Using a Single Raster Dataset Sometimes it is necessary to reclassify or recode the individual pixel values in a single raster dataset. For example, perhaps the value of 45.5 used above represented feet above sea level (ASL). Maybe it is important to generalize this elevation dataset into just two numeric classes, e.g.,

Class 1 = 0 to < 50 ft. above sea level, and

Class 2 = 50 to 100 ft. above sea level.

In this case we would reclassify the pixel with a value of 45.5 as being in Class 1, i.e., the new value at location 2,2 is "1." The application of this logic to all of the values in the input raster is shown in Figure 6-18b.

Reclassification does not have to result in only integers or floating-point numbers. For example, we could re-

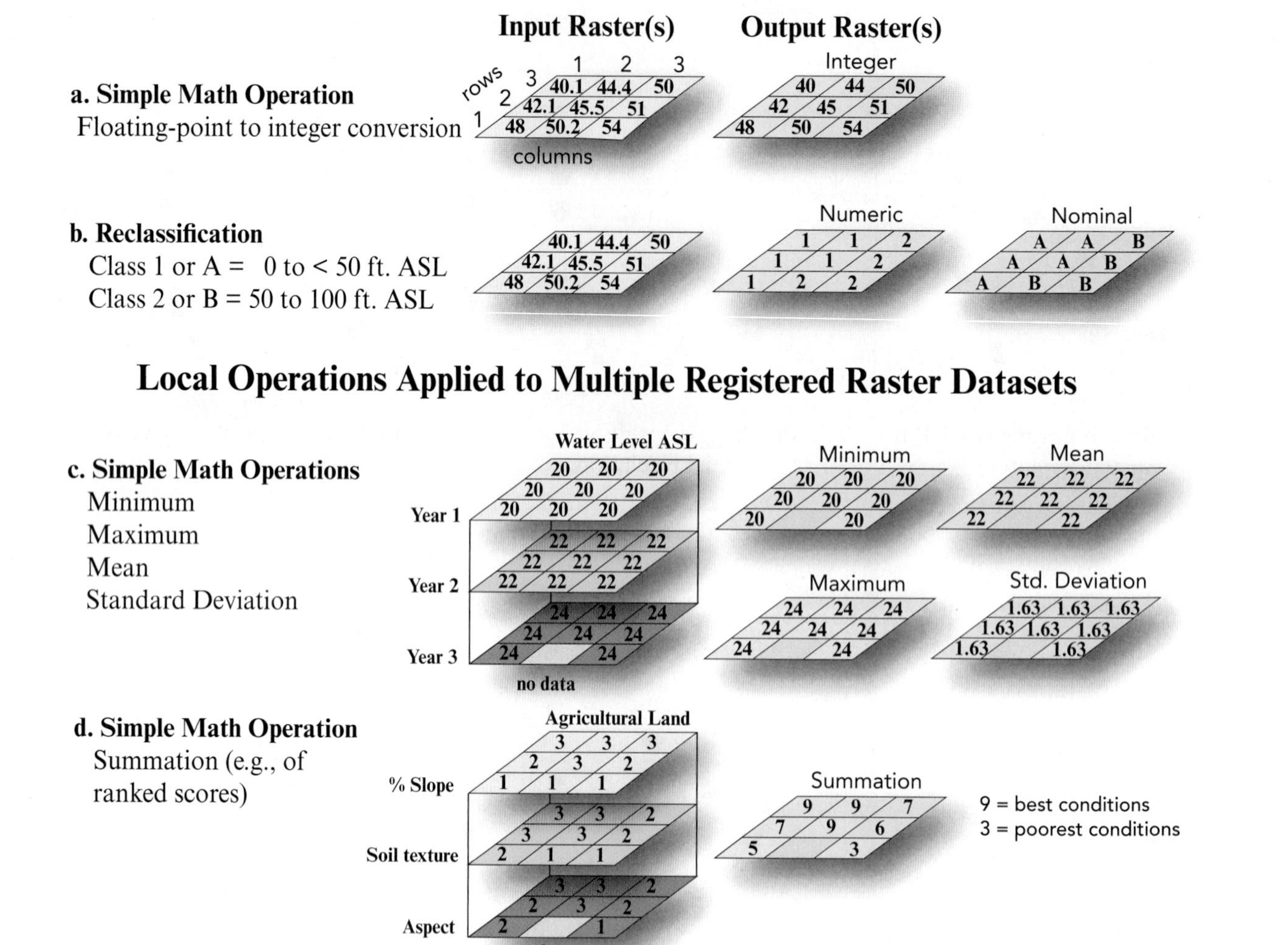

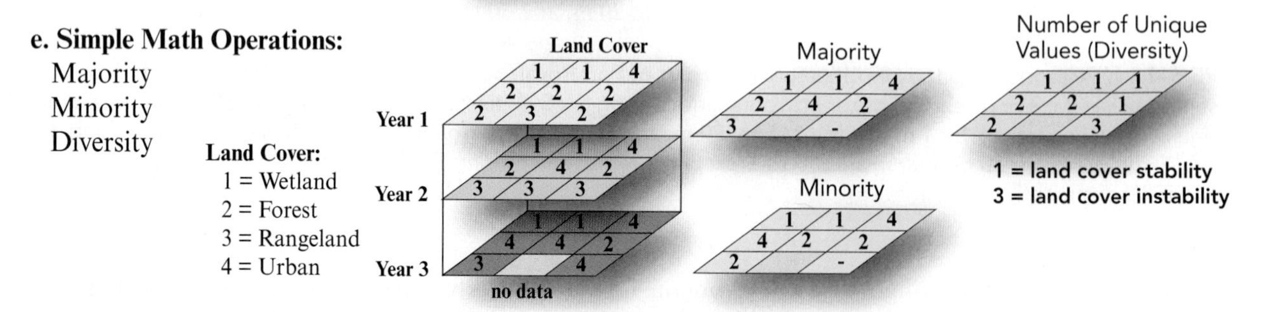

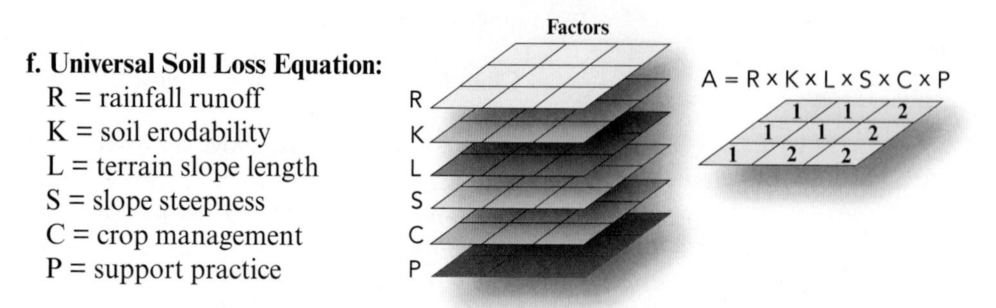

FIGURE 6–18 Local operations applied to a single raster dataset (a-b). Local operations applied to multiple registered raster datasets (c-f).

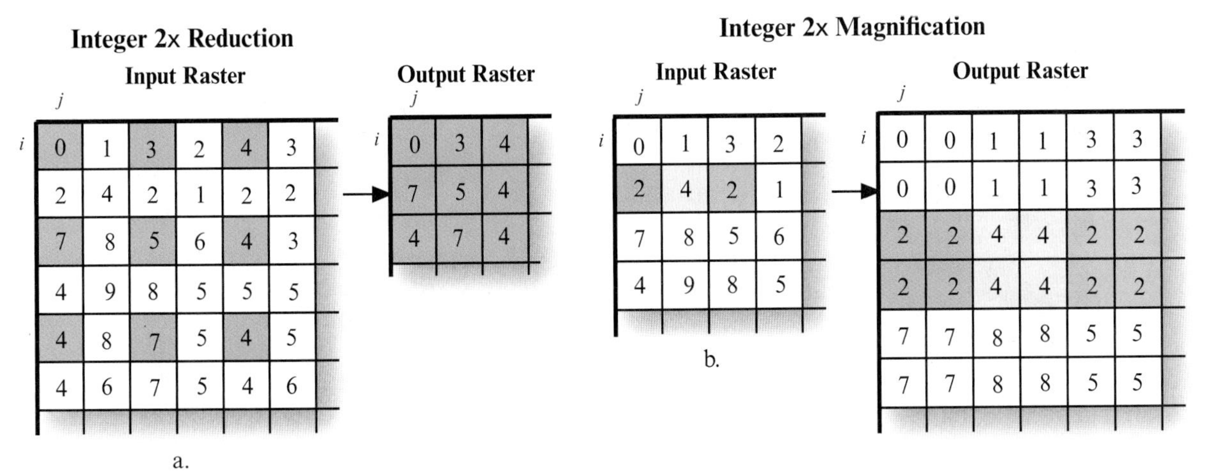

FIGURE 6–19 a) The logic associated with 2x map or image integer reduction using local pixel operations. b) The logic of 2x map or image magnification.

code all elevations between 0 to < 50 ft. above sea level as being in nominal Class A and those from 50 to 100 ft. above sea level as being in nominal Class B, i.e.

A = 0 to < 50 ft. above sea level, and

B = 50 to 100 ft. above sea level.

The results of applying this reclassification logic are also shown in Figure 6-18b.

Ordinal ranking (e.g., Poor, Good) is also permissible:

(P)oor = 0 to < 50 ft. above sea level, and

(G)ood = 50 to 100 ft. above sea level.

Reclassification, or "recoding," is one of the most important GIS local raster operations. It is used in many GIScience raster analysis projects.

Raster Reduction and Magnification Analysts routinely view maps or images that have been reduced in size or magnified during the map or image interpretation process. *Reduction* techniques allow the analyst to zoom out and obtain a regional perspective of the map or remotely sensed data. Raster map or image *magnification* allows the analyst to zoom in and view very site-specific pixel characteristics.

For example, in the early stages of a remote sensing project it is often useful to view the entire image in order to locate the row and column coordinates of a subimage that encompasses the study area. Most commercially available remote sensor data are composed of more than 3,000 rows x 3,000 columns in a number of bands. It is useful to have a simple procedure for reducing the size of the original image dataset down to a smaller dataset that can be viewed on the screen for orientation purposes. To *reduce* a digital image or map to just $1/m^2$ of the original data, every mth row and mth column of the imagery are systematically selected and displayed (Figure 6-19a).

For example, consider the Advanced Spaceborne Thermal Emission and Reflection Radiometer (ASTER) image of Oahu, HI, originally composed of 4,104 rows x 3,638 columns shown in Figure 6-20. The size of the original image was reduced by using every other row and every other column (i.e., $m = 2$) in the dataset. The sampled image shown consists of just 2,052 rows x 1,819 columns. This reduced dataset contains only one fourth (25%) of the pixels found in the original scene. The logic associated with a simple 2x integer reduction is shown in Figure 6-19a.

If you were to compare the original ASTER data with the reduced ASTER data, there is an obvious loss of detail because so many of the pixels are not present. Therefore, we rarely analyze image reductions. Instead, they are used for orienting within a scene and locating the row and column coordinates of specific areas of interest (AOI) that can then be extracted at full resolution for analysis.

Digital image *magnification* (often referred to as *zooming in*) is usually performed to enlarge the scale of an image or map for visual interpretation or, occasionally, to match the scale of another image or map. Just as row and column deletion is the simplest form of image or map reduction, row and column replication represents the simplest form of digital magnification. To magnify a digital image or map by an integer factor mx, each pixel in the original image or map is usually

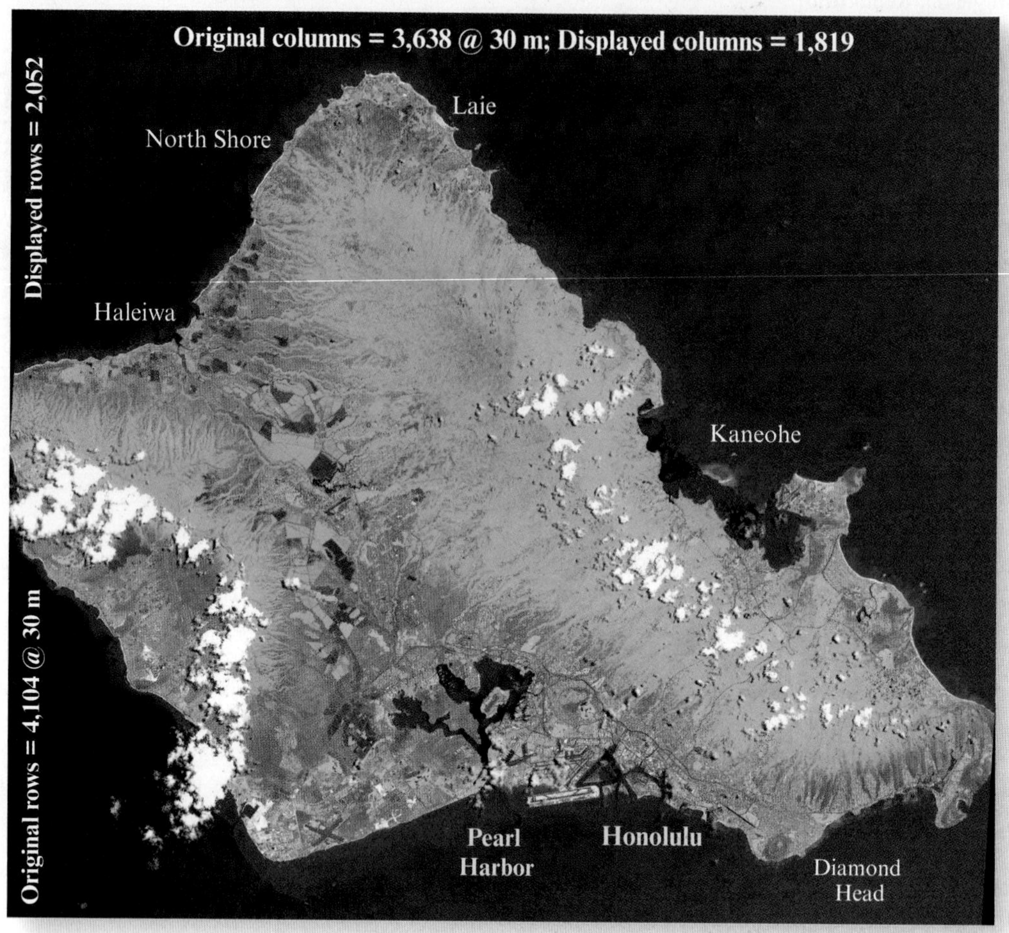

FIGURE 6–20 The 2,052 row × 1,819 column image represents only 25% of the data found in the original 4,104 row × 3,638 column NASA Advanced Spaceborne Thermal Emission and Reflection Radiometer (ASTER) image. It was created by sampling every other row and column (courtesy NASA/GSFC/METI/ERSDAC/JAROS and U.S./Japan ASTER Science Team).

replaced by an *m* x *m* block of pixels, all with the same value as the original input pixel. The logic of a 2x magnification is shown in Figure 6-19b. This form of magnification is characterized by visible square tiles of pixels in the output display. Image magnifications of 1x, 2x, and 3x applied to the ASTER image of Oahu, HI, is shown in Figure 6-21.

Most sophisticated digital image processing systems allow an analyst to specify floating-point magnification (or reduction) factors (e.g., zoom in 2.75×). This requires that the original remote sensor or map data be resampled in near real time using one of the standard resampling algorithms (e.g., nearest-neighbor, bilinear interpolation, or cubic convolution discussed in Chapter 9). This is a very useful technique when the analyst is trying to obtain detailed information about the characteristics of a relatively small geographic area of interest.

In addition to magnification, virtually all GIS and digital image processing systems provide a mechanism whereby the analyst can *pan* or *roam* about a much larger geographic area (e.g., 2,048 x 2,048) while viewing only a portion (e.g., 512 x 512) of this area at any one time. This allows the analyst to view parts of the database much more rapidly.

Local Operations Applied to Multiple Registered Raster Datasets

Raster map overlay occurs when local operations are applied to multiple raster layers. Tomlin (1990) referred to this as **map algebra** when the multiple raster layers are processed using arithmetic and algebraic operations. When high-quality multiple raster layers are

Magnification of ASTER Imagery of Oahu, HI

a. 1x magnification (original resolution).

b. 2x magnification.

c. 3x magnification.

FIGURE 6–21 NASA ASTER imagery of Oahu, HI, magnified 1x, 2x, and 3x (courtesy NASA/GSFC/METI/ERSDAC/JAROS and U.S./Japan ASTER Science Team).

involved, raster map overlay will yield geospatial information equivalent to that produced using vector overlay operations.

Map Algebra A variety of arithmetic and algebraic local operations can be applied to multiple registered raster datasets. For example, it is possible to compute or determine the minimum, maximum, range (maximum-minimum), sum (Σ), mean ($\bar{x}$), median, mode, and standard deviation (σ) associated with the individual pixel values found at the same geographic location (e.g., row and column) in multiple raster layers. For example, assume that the input raster layers in Figure 6-18c represent lake water levels above sea level recorded on three dates. The minimum, maximum, mean ($\bar{x}$), and standard deviation (σ) of the water level at each pixel over this time period were computed from the three datasets for each pixel and placed in the respective output rasters. Note that the Year 3 raster dataset is missing a data value, which resulted in no value at that location in the output raster file.

The data analyzed in the multiple rasters may be numeric or categorical. For example, let us assume that the three input raster layers in Figure 6-18d represent terrain percent slope, soil texture, and aspect. However, instead of each raster variable being represented by the actual numeric value (e.g., percent slope), each variable has been ordinally scaled (i.e., rank-ordered) to have values ranging from 1 to 3 where 1 = poor, 2 = good, and 3 = best, based on a farmer's local corn cultivation knowledge. In this case, the simple arithmetic sum (Σ) of the three raster values per pixel yields a new output raster with values ranging from 3 (poorest condition) to 9 (best condition) for corn growth. Any pixel with a value of 9 in the new output dataset should be an ideal geographic location for corn production.

Sometimes it is useful to determine how frequently or infrequently a given numeric or categorical value occurs. In such cases, local operations applied to multiple raster datasets can be used to identify the *majority*, *minority*, and/or the *number of unique values* encountered (i.e., *diversity*). For example, Figure 6-18e depicts three-raster layers that contain information on the land cover present on three successive dates. Four identical land cover classes are mapped on each date (classes 1-4). The most prevalent land cover class encountered (i.e., the majority) within each pixel over the three years is placed in the raster output map in Figure 6-18e. The least encountered land cover class (i.e., the minority) is identified per pixel in Figure 6-18e. The number of unique land cover classes encountered during the three-year period is shown in Figure 6-18e. A value of "1" in an output pixel suggests that the land cover was relatively stable through time. A value of "3" suggests land cover instability or diversity through time.

Examples of Map Overlay Using Local Operations Applied to Multiple Registered Raster Datasets

Some of the most useful GIS models are based on the use of simple map algebra local operations applied to multiple registered raster datasets.

Universal Soil Loss Prediction Using Map Overlay Local Operations Applied to Multiple Raster Datasets The well-respected *Revised Universal Soil Loss Equation* Version 2 (*RUSLE2*) was originally developed by Wischmeier and Smith (1960; 1978) of the U.S. Department of Agriculture and then revised by Renard et al. (1997). The model is available at NRCS (2010) and computes the potential long-term average annual soil loss in tons per acre per year (A) for a geographic area (e.g., a pixel) using the equation (Figure 6-18f):

$$A = R \times K \times L \times S \times C \times P \qquad (6.2)$$

where

R is the rainfall and runoff factor (the greater the intensity and duration of a rainstorm, the higher the erosion potential),

K is a soil erodability factor (influenced heavily by soil texture),

L is the terrain slope length,

S is the slope steepness (the longer and steeper the slope, the greater the risk for erosion),

C is a crop/vegetation management factor used to determine the relative effectiveness of soil and crop management systems in terms of preventing soil loss, and

P is a support practice factor which weights practices that will reduce the amount and rate of the water runoff and thus reduce the amount of erosion.

The *RUSLE2* only predicts the amount of soil loss that results from sheet or rill erosion on a single slope and does not account for additional soil losses that might occur from gully, wind or tillage erosion (Stone, 2010).

Spatial information about each of these six variables is stored in separate raster layers as shown in Figure 6-18f. The potential long-term average annual soil loss in tons per acre per year (A) in the output file for each pixel is computed by multiplying each of the six factor values by one another. The *RULSE2* is a simple, but very robust local operator model based on multiple input rasters. It has been used worldwide to predict the amount of erosion that will occur given accurate information on the aforementioned six variables. This simple model has been used to prevent soil erosion, increase the productivity of farmlands, and generally improve the quality of life for millions of people.

FIGURE 6–22 High-spatial-resolution (1 x 1 ft.) digital color-infrared aerial photography of a portion of the May River estuary near Bluffton, SC (aerial photography courtesy of Beaufort County GIS Department; from Jensen and Hodgson [2011] courtesy of The Nature Conservancy).

Sea-level-Rise Prediction Using Map Overlay Local Operations Applied to Multiple Raster Datasets Sea-level rise is occurring at a rate of approximately 1.0 ft. per century (Gutierrez et al., 2007). It is important to know what impact sea-level rise will have on natural ecosystems and human-made features (USGS and FWS, 2004). The following case study uses map overlay local operations applied to multiple raster datasets to predict how 1.0 ft. of sea-level rise might impact the land cover for a geographic area along the shoreline of the May River near Bluffton, SC (west of Hilton Head, SC) (Figure 6-22).The sea-level-rise prediction is based on the use of rules derived from the intersection of remote sensing-derived raster land cover data and LiDAR-derived raster elevation data (Jensen and Hodgson, 2011).

The elevation of the study area was extracted from LiDAR data obtained at a posting density of approximately 1 point per m^2. The LiDAR data were acquired at low tide, therefore there were returns from exposed tidal flats that are typically below sea level. Masspoints above ground level (e.g., in the trees) were systematically removed prior to the creation of the bare-earth digital terrain model (DTM). Deep, non-turbid water typically absorbs most of the incident LiDAR laser pulses of energy resulting in data voids (i.e., blank areas in the masspoint coverage). The LiDAR masspoints were interpolated to a 1 x 1 m grid (Figure 6-23) using inverse-distance-weighting (IDW) logic (discussed in Chapter 9). The elevation in Figure 6-23 ranged from –2.4 ft. below sea level to 41 ft. above sea level.

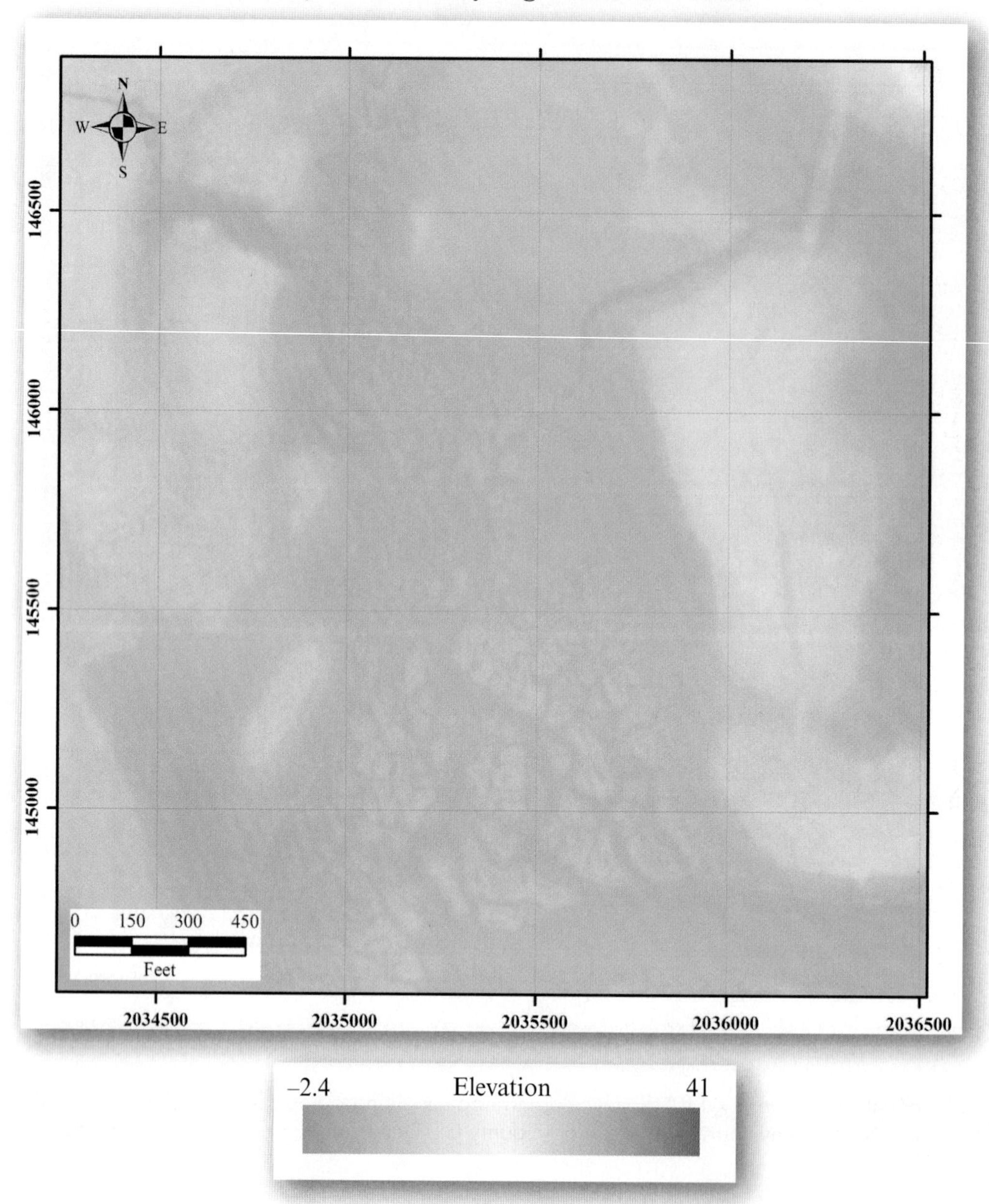

FIGURE 6–23 The digital terrain model (DTM) was derived from LiDAR data acquired at low tide with a posting density of approximately 1 point per m^2. Masspoints above ground level (e.g., in the trees) were systematically removed prior to creation of the DTM. The raster DTM contains continuous data that ranges from –2.4 to 41 ft. above sea level (original LIDAR data courtesy of Beaufort County GIS Department; from Jensen and Hodgson [2011] courtesy of The Nature Conservancy).

The land cover information was extracted from 2006 high-spatial-resolution (1 x 1 ft.) color-infrared digital aerial photography obtained by EarthData, Inc. A combination of supervised object-oriented image segmentation classification and human visual interpretation resulted in a land cover map with 12 classes (Figure 6-24). Characteristics and photographs of the marine land cover classes are found in Figure 6-25.

Spartina alterniflora (smooth cordgrass) is a very important component of the coastal South Carolina ecosystem, capable of supporting numerous species of fish, animals, and birds. Studies have documented that the health of the *Spartina*-dominated ecosystem is closely related to the health of the offshore fishing industry as most of the detritus (dissolved organic matter) supporting the food chain comes from the *Spartina* and other estuarine species. Interestingly, people along the Pacific coast of the United States (e.g., California, Ore-

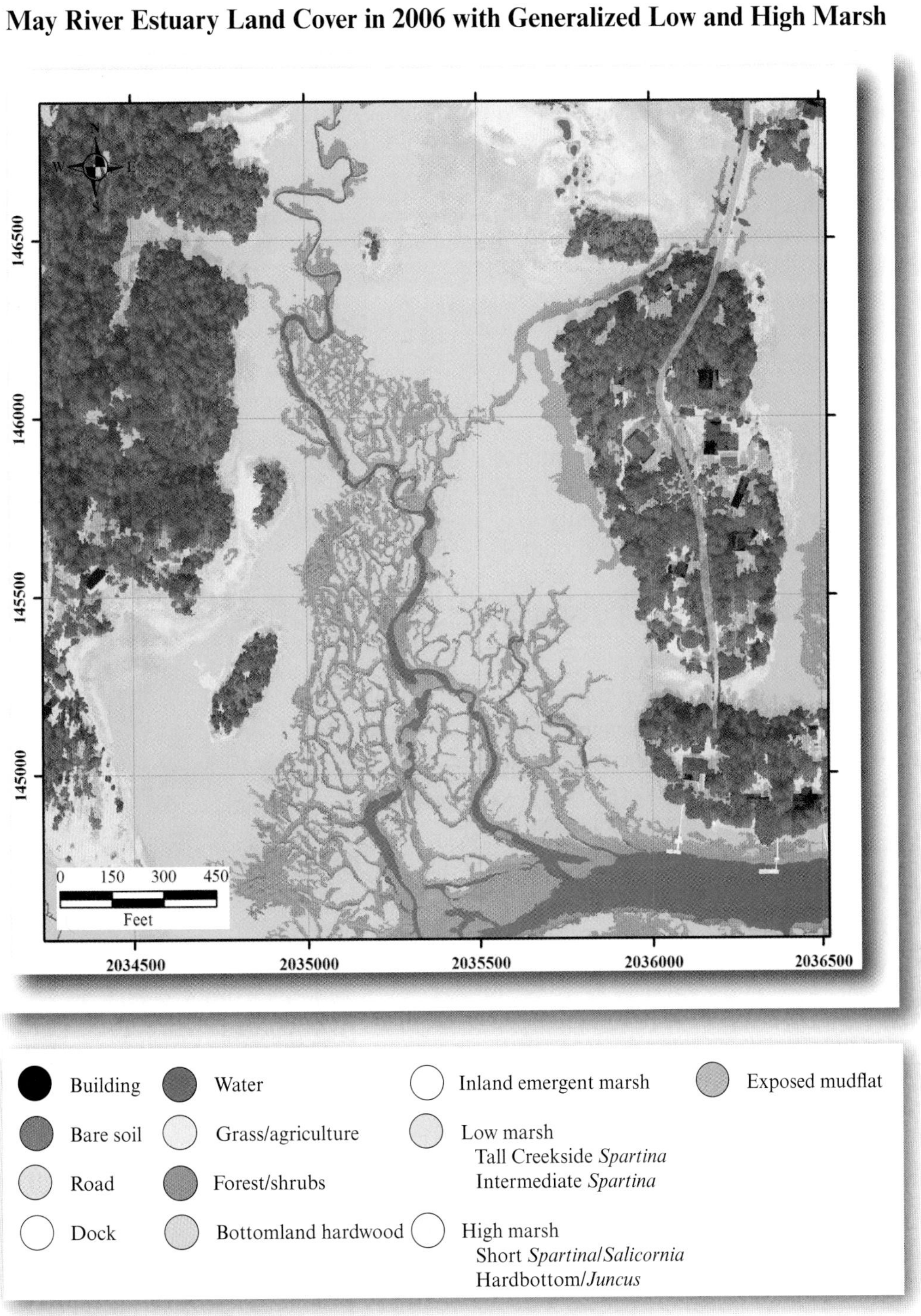

May River Estuary Land Cover in 2006 with Generalized Low and High Marsh

FIGURE 6–24 Land cover information derived from the 2006 1 x 1 ft. digital color-infrared aerial photography (original aerial photography provided by Beaufort County GIS Department; adapted from Jensen and Hodgson [2011] courtesy of The Nature Conservancy).

gon, Washington) consider *Spartina alterniflora* to be an invasive species and are trying to eradicate it.

Forest consists primarily of evergreen loblolly pine (*Pinus taeda*) and evergreen southern live oak (*Quercus virginiana*). Sea-level rise may impact buildings and docks so they were also identified. Sea-level rise will impact deciduous, bottomland hardwood which was not present within this part of the study area.

To predict the impact of future sea level on the terrain it was first necessary to determine the current elevation characteristics of the land cover in the study area. This is especially important for the marine environment,

Land Cover Class

Tall Creekside *Spartina alterniflora* (Smooth Cordgrass) is more dense on the creekbanks where diurnal tidal flushing deposits nutrients and maintains reasonable levels of salinity. Over time, the creekside *Spartina* may trap suspended sediments, resulting in a gradual increase in the elevation of the tidal creek berm.

Intermediate *Spartina alterniflora* (Smooth Cordgrass) grows in a more stressed environment behind the creekbank, where nutrients are not as plentiful and there may be increased salinity levels in the substrate because of reduced tidal flushing.

***Salicornia spp.* (Glasswort)** and **Short** *Spartina* are often interspersed in more saline environments, usually some distance from the tidal creek channels. Patches of Short *Spartina* and *Salicornia* are often associated with **hardbottom** material. It is possible to walk relatively easily on this less-frequently flooded hardbottom terrain. Sometimes the hardbottom is devoid of vegetation.

***Juncus roemerianus* (Black Needlerush)** generally is able to tolerate more saline conditions than *Spartina* or *Salicornia*. In the May River watershed, *Juncus* typically exists at the higher elevations in the marsh.

Exposed Mudflat consists of unconsolidated sediment and detritus (decomposed organic material). Ephemeral sandbars and oysterbars may also be present.

Water
The May River experiences twice daily tides. The water is often heavily laden with suspended sediment.

FIGURE 6–25 May River estuarine land cover characteristics and terrestrial photographs (Jensen and Hodgson, 2011).

TABLE 6–1 Rules determined by examining the intersection of LiDAR-derived elevation (Figure 6-23) with the remote sensing-derived land cover (Figure 6-24). The rules were then applied to a new DTM with –1.0 ft. of elevation simulating an increase of 1.0 ft. in sea-level rise, resulting in the predicted land cover shown in Figure 6-26 (Jensen and Hodgson [2011] courtesy of The Nature Conservancy).

Rules
if the land cover in 2006 (LC_{2006}) is > 4.96 ft. after sea-level rise (SLR), then $LC_{slr\_model} = LC_{2006}$
if LC_{2006} = Dock then LC_{slr_model} = Dock
if LC_{2006} = Water then LC_{slr_model} = Water
if LC_{2006} <–1.0 ft. after SLR, then LC_{slr_model} = Water
if LC_{2006} ≥–1.0 and ≤0.32 ft. after SLR, then LC_{slr_model} = Exposed mudflat
if LC_{2006} >0.32 and ≤2.76 ft. after SLR, then LC_{slr_model} = Low marsh
if LC_{2006} >2.76 and ≤4.96 ft. after SLR, then LC_{slr_model} = High marsh

where twice-daily tidal inundation of the terrain by salt water has a significant impact on the type and geographic distribution of vegetation found in the study area.

To obtain this information, the LiDAR-derived digital elevation information (Figure 6-23) was intersected with the remote sensing-derived raster land cover information (Figure 6-24). Statistics were computed and histograms of the elevation of individual land cover types were created. The statistics and histograms provided information about the relationship between estuarine vegetation type and elevation. It was assumed that these same biophysical relationships will exist in the future as sea level changes. Therefore, these data can be used to predict the change in land cover that may exist under various sea-level-rise scenarios.

The mean ±1 standard deviation for each marine land cover class and the mean ±2 standard deviations for the upland land cover classes were used to create the rules used in the sea-level-rise predictive model (Table 6-1).

To predict the impact of sea-level rise in the future, it was necessary to create a digital terrain model (DTM) that reflected a specific sea-level-rise scenario. A 1.0 ft. rise in sea level was selected for demonstration purposes. This required the creation of a modified DTM. This was accomplished by subtracting 1.0 ft. of elevation from every pixel in the original bare-earth DTM.

An ArcGIS® raster data model was then constructed using 1) the original land cover information, 2) the –1.0 ft. adjusted DTM simulating 1.0 ft. of sea-level rise, and 3) the heuristic rules derived from the histograms summarized in Table 6-1. Note that the rules are in the format of conditional "IF-THEN" statements that can be easily applied to the original land cover map and the modified DTM.

The predicted land cover associated with a 1.0 ft. rise in sea level in the study area based on locally derived rules is shown in Figure 6-26. In many instances, the land cover was stable, i.e., it was not influenced by a positive 1.0 ft. change in sea level. In other instances, the original land cover was allocated to another land cover because it could not logically exist given future sea-level conditions. In particular, note the increase in the amount of open water and exposed mudflat predicted. Substantial changes are predicted to occur in the spatial distribution of Low and High marsh. Buildings and docks were not impacted with just 1.0 ft. of sea-level rise.

This scenario predicts the impact of a relatively modest amount of sea-level rise. It is a simple matter to adjust the elevation of the original raster DTM (e.g., subtract 2- or 3-ft. from the DTM) and rerun the model using the original raster land cover data and the rules.

It is important to note that this sea-level-rise predictive model did not take into consideration any sedimentation buildup in the estuarine environment through time or any future erosion in the upland environment. It also did not take into consideration any changes in ocean salinity that may or may not accompany sea-level rise.

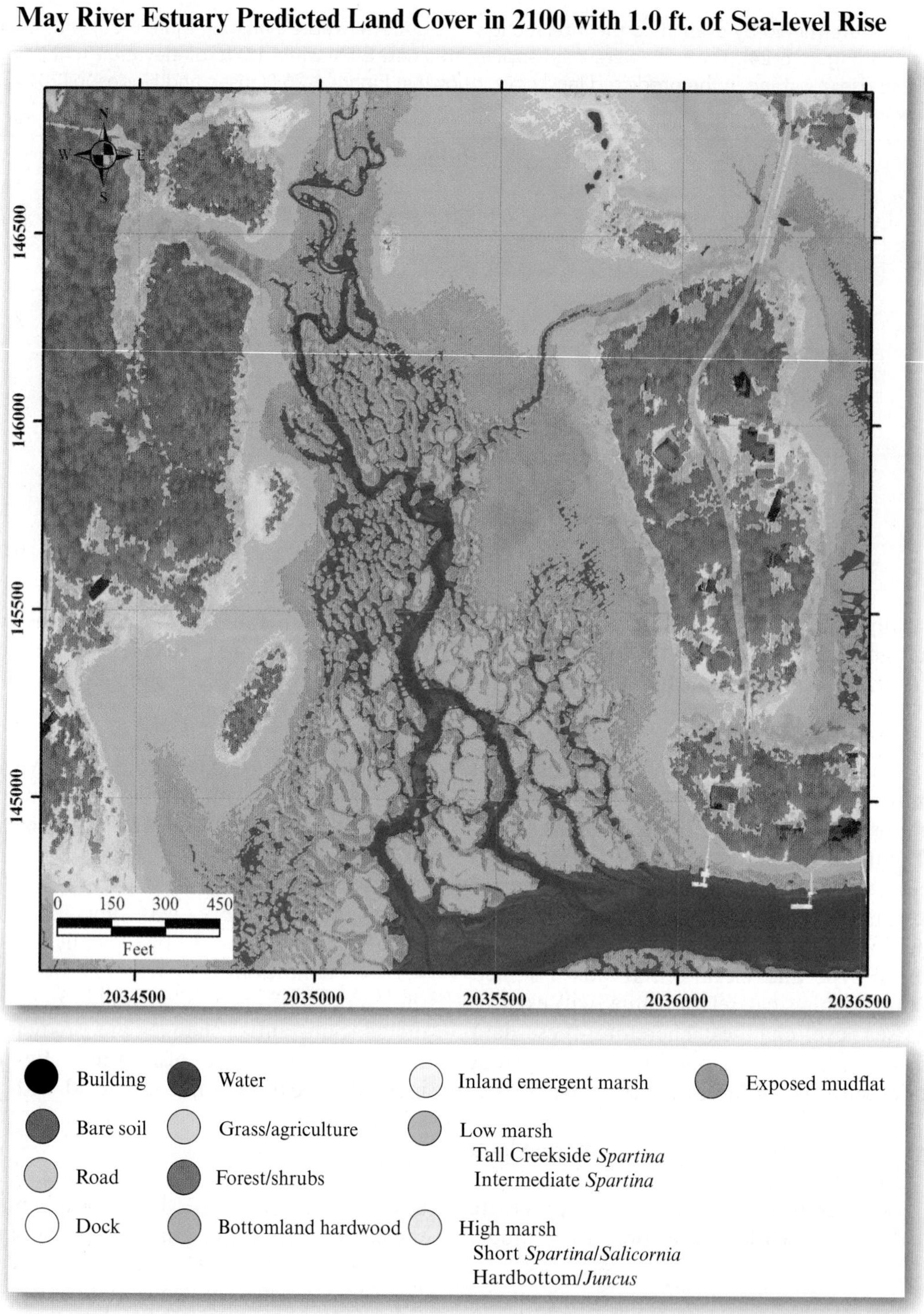

May River Estuary Predicted Land Cover in 2100 with 1.0 ft. of Sea-level Rise

146500
146000
145500
145000

0 150 300 450
Feet

2034500 2035000 2035500 2036000 2036500

Building
Water
Inland emergent marsh
Exposed mudflat
Bare soil
Grass/agriculture
Low marsh
Tall Creekside *Spartina*
Intermediate *Spartina*
Road
Forest/shrubs
Dock
Bottomland hardwood
High marsh
Short *Spartina*/*Salicornia*
Hardbottom/*Juncus*

FIGURE 6–26 Predicted land cover after sea level has risen by 1.0 ft. The rules used to create this prediction are listed in Table 6-1. A 1.0 ft. rise in sea level may have an impact on the spatial distribution of the estuarine land cover and to a limited extent the upland land cover in this area (adapted from Jensen and Hodgson [2011] courtesy of The Nature Conservancy).

Neighborhood Raster Operations

As previously discussed, local raster operations modify the values of each pixel in an image or map dataset independent of the characteristics of neighboring pixels. Conversely, **neighborhood raster operations** modify the value of each focal pixel in the context of the values of the pixels surrounding it. Some of the most commonly used raster neighborhood types are shown in Figure 6-27, The *focal cell* (f) is usually at the center of the neighborhood being examined, as shown in Figure 6-27a.

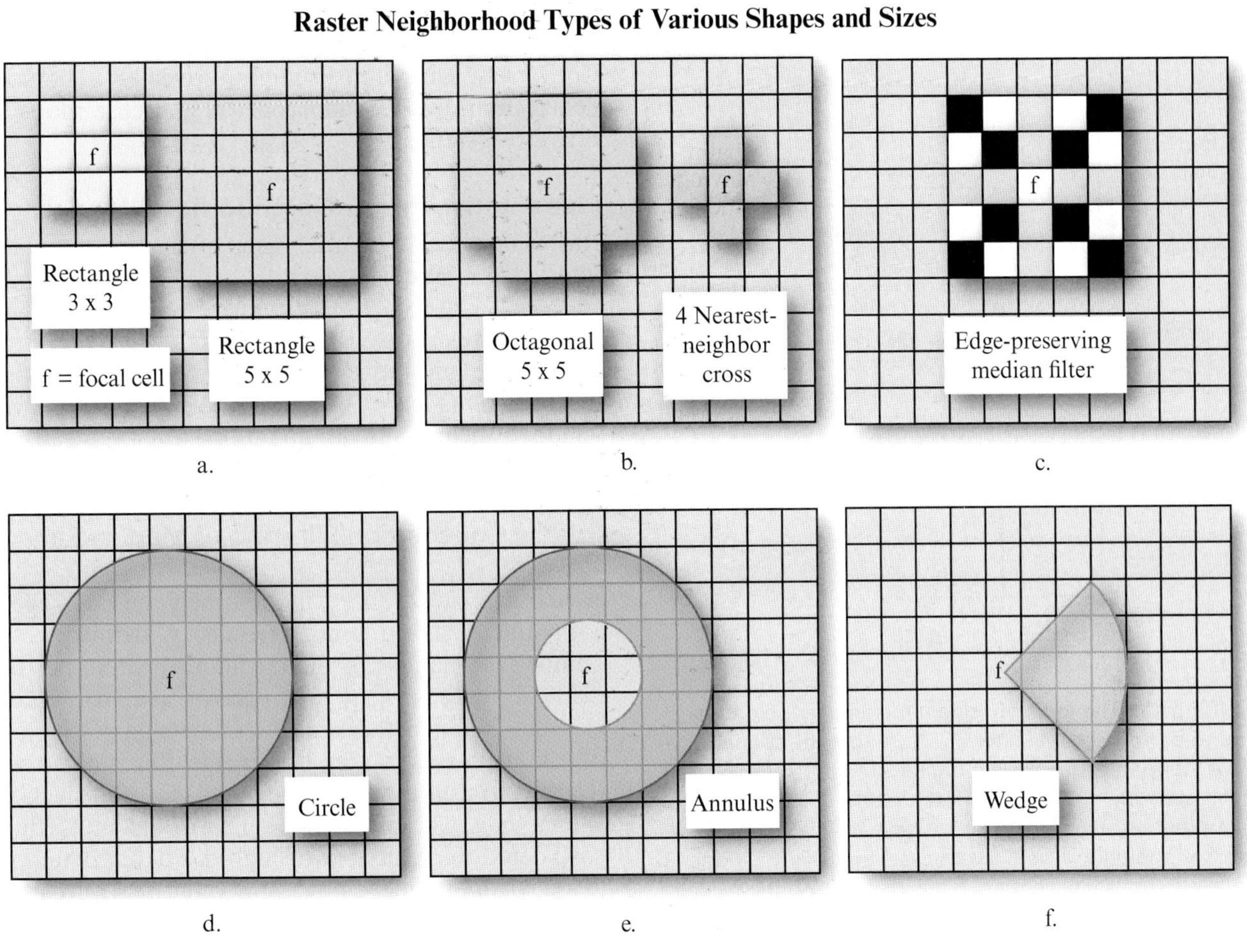

Raster Neighborhood Types of Various Shapes and Sizes

FIGURE 6–27 Examples of various raster neighborhood types. The most common convolution masks used to filter maps and images are found in a, b, and c.

The raster rectangular neighborhood operators are probably the most heavily used, with 3 x 3 and 5 x 5 being the most prevalent (Figure 6-27a). The 5 x 5 octagonal and 4 nearest-neighbor cross and edge-preserving median filter neighborhoods are also used when filtering images (Figure 6-27bc). Rectangular neighborhoods usually have an odd number of rows and columns so that there is always a central, focal pixel that is being evaluated. It is important to remember, however, that users can specify virtually any size of rectangular neighborhood, e.g., 17 x 17, 25 x 25, etc.

The logic of using a rectangular neighborhood to perform spatial filtering is shown in Figure 6-28. Note that in this example the 3 x 3 spatial moving window is stepped sequentially from left to right through the input raster dataset, line by line. Also note that the first row and column of the output matrix may not have any values when using a 3 x 3 neighborhood. In this case, the user must decide whether or not to leave the rows and columns blank or replicate the values from an adjacent row or column.

The circle neighborhood extends a user-specified radius away from the focal cell (Figure 6-27d). An annulus neighborhood centered on the focal cell includes the geographic area (i.e., pixels) bounded by the outer circle and the inner circle (Figure 6-27e). Pixels within the innermost circle are *not* included in the annulus computation. The wedge neighborhood encompasses a piece of a circle radiating out from the focal cell (Figure 6-27f).

Note that often only a part of a given pixel (cell) is included within the boundaries of a circular, annulus, or wedge neighborhood. When this occurs, the pixels are included if their centroids (i.e., the exact center of the pixels) lies within the neighborhood.

Qualitative Raster Neighborhood Modeling

Some of the most important uses of raster neighborhood analysis involves nominal-scale data such as land cover (e.g., Class A, B, and C) or ordinal-scaled data (e.g., Good =1, Adequate =2, and Poor = 3). However, unlike the previous section which only involved the examination of individual pixels in a single file or in mul-

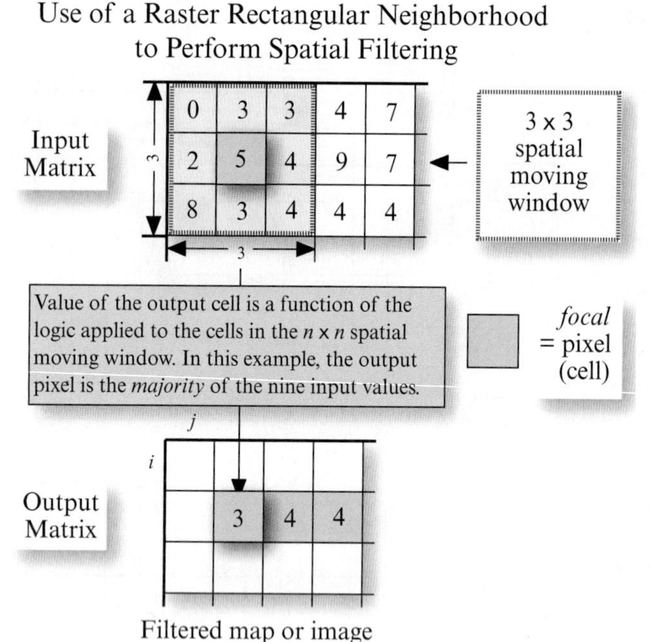

FIGURE 6–28 The logic of using a rectangular neighborhood to perform spatial filtering. Note that the spatial window is stepped sequentially from left to right through the input raster, line by line. Also note that the first row and column of the output matrix may not have any values when using a 3 x 3 neighborhood. In this case, the user must decide whether or not to leave them blank or replicate the values from an adjacent row or column.

tiple registered files, raster neighborhood analysis usually examines a focal cell as well as a predetermined number of pixels surrounding the focal cell and uses this information to assign a new value to the focal cell in a new output file. A few of the qualitative measures that can be determined are shown in Figure 6-29a.

The application of a simple 3 x 3 window majority filter is shown in Figure 6-29a. Majority filters are often used to remove the salt-and-pepper noise associated with remote sensing-derived land cover maps. The result is a land cover thematic map that is much more pleasing to look at because an isolated pixel (e.g., water) that is totally surrounded by a majority of other types of land cover (e.g., forest) is assigned to the majority land cover class that surrounds it. Sometimes it is good to determine the majority or minority of digital number values within a spatial moving window (Figure 6-29a).

Perhaps it is important to determine the diversity of values found within the spatial moving window (Figure 6-29a). For example, a high diversity value for a pixel might indicate the presence of a large number of land cover types in a relatively small region (i.e., within the 3 x 3 window). Such diversity might be especially important for certain animals that require a diverse (heterogeneous) land cover habitat for survival. Conversely, some animals might thrive best in homogeneous (non-diverse) land cover (e.g., dense monoculture forest stands).

Quantitative Raster Neighborhood Modeling

Raster neighborhood analysis is often used to analyze interval and ratio-scaled data.

Simple Univariate Statistics Some of the most common quantitative univariate descriptive statistic measurements extracted from $n \times n$ spatial moving windows include the minimum, maximum, mean, and standard deviation (Figure 6-29b).

Spatial Convolution Filtering of Map and Image Data

A characteristic of maps and remotely sensed images is a parameter called **spatial frequency**, defined as the number of changes in digital number value per unit distance for any particular part of a map or image (Jensen, 2005). If there are very few changes in value over a given area in a map or image, this is commonly referred to as a low-frequency area. Conversely, if the values change dramatically over short distances, this is considered to be an area of high-frequency detail. Because spatial frequency by its very nature describes the values over a spatial *region*, it is possible to adopt a spatial approach to extracting quantitative spatial information. This is done by looking at the local (neighboring) values rather than just an independent value. This perspective allows the analyst to extract useful spatial frequency information from maps or images.

Spatial frequency in raster thematic maps or remotely sensed imagery may be enhanced or subdued using two different approaches. The first is spatial convolution filtering based on the use of convolution masks (Lo and Yeung, 2007). The procedure is relatively easy to understand and can be used to enhance low- and high-frequency detail, as well as edges. Another technique is Fourier analysis, which mathematically separates a raster map or image into its spatial frequency components. Fourier analysis is discussed in Jensen (2005).

A **linear spatial filter** is a filter for which the value ($V_{i,j}$) at location i,j in the output image or map is a function of some weighted average (linear combination) of values located in a particular spatial pattern around the i, j location in the input image or map (Figure 6-28). This process of evaluating the weighted neighboring pixel values is called two-dimensional convolution filtering (Jensen, 2005; Pratt, 2007).

Sophisticated geographic information systems and remote sensing digital image processing software (e.g.,

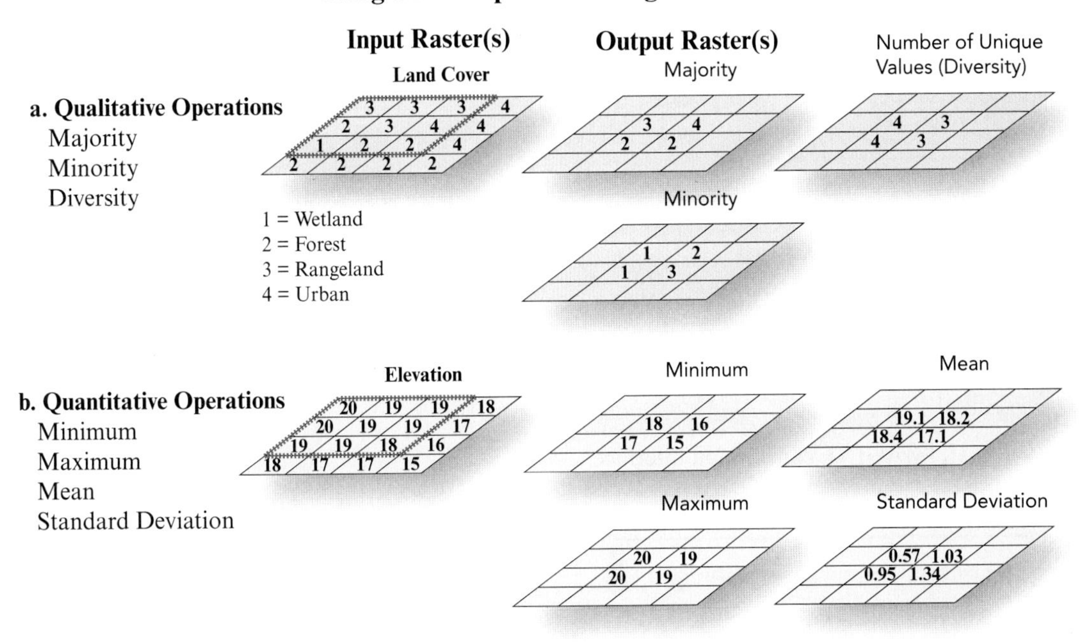

FIGURE 6–29 Neighborhood operations applied to a single raster dataset using a 3 x 3 spatial moving window. a) Simple qualitative operations. b) Simple quantitative operations.

ERDAS IMAGINE, ENVI) provide simple user interfaces that allow the analyst to specify the size of the convolution kernel (e.g., 3 x 3, 5 x 5) and the coefficients to be placed in the convolution kernel. Examples of ERDAS IMAGINE and ArcGIS® ArcMap™ convolution filtering user interfaces are shown in Figure 6-30.

Spatial convolution filtering can be used to enhance low-frequency detail, high-frequency detail, and edges in both raster thematic maps and digital images. The following discussion of spatial convolution filtering will be based on the application of various filters to a high-spatial-resolution color aerial photograph. It is important to remember, however, that the filters can also be applied to continuous raster thematic map data such as elevation, temperature, humidity, population density etc. (Warner et al., 2009).

Low-frequency Filtering in the Spatial Domain

Raster enhancements that block or minimize high-spatial frequency detail are called **low-frequency** or **low-pass** filters. The simplest low-frequency filter evaluates a particular input value, V_{in}, and the pixels surrounding the input pixel, and outputs a new value, V_{out}, that is the mean of this convolution. The size of the neighborhood convolution mask or kernel (n) is usually 3 x 3, 5 x 5, 7 x 7, or 9 x 9. Examples of symmetric 3 x 3 and 5 x 5 convolution masks are shown in Figure 6-27a. The following discussion will focus primarily on the use of 3 x 3 convolution masks with nine coefficients, c_i, defined at the following locations:

$$\text{Convolution mask template} = \begin{bmatrix} c_1 & c_2 & c_3 \\ c_4 & c_5 & c_6 \\ c_7 & c_8 & c_9 \end{bmatrix} \tag{6.3}$$

For example, the coefficients in a low-frequency convolution mask are usually set equal to 1 (e.g., Figure 6-30a,b and Table 6-2):

$$\text{Low-frequency filter} = \begin{bmatrix} 1 & 1 & 1 \\ 1 & 1 & 1 \\ 1 & 1 & 1 \end{bmatrix} \tag{6.4}$$

The coefficients, c_i, in the mask template are multiplied by the following individual values (V_i) in the input digital image or raster map (Jensen, 2005):

$$\text{Mask template} = \begin{matrix} c_1 \times V_1 & c_2 \times V_2 & c_3 \times V_3 \\ c_4 \times V_4 & c_5 \times V_5 & c_6 \times V_6 \\ c_7 \times V_7 & c_8 \times V_8 & c_9 \times V_9 \end{matrix} \tag{6.5}$$

Spatial Convolution Filtering User Interfaces

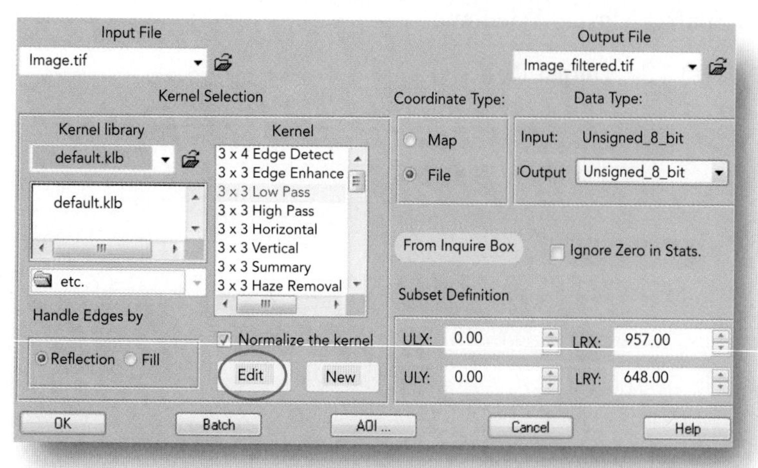

a. ERDAS IMAGINE convolution interface.

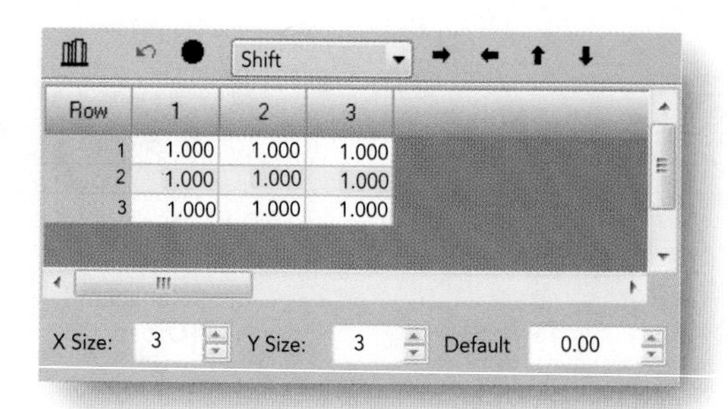

b. ERDAS IMAGINE 3 x 3 low-pass filter.

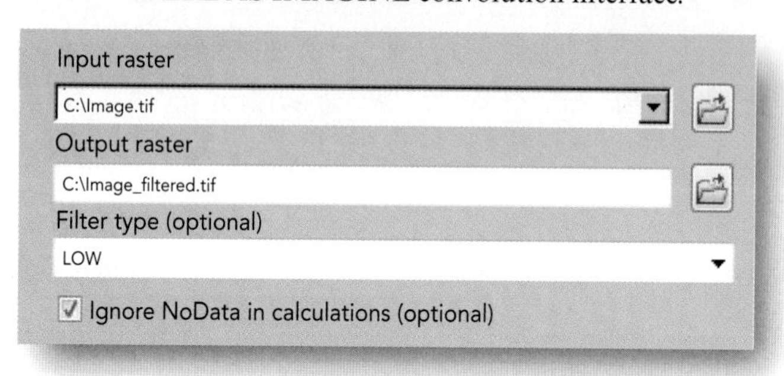

c. ArcGIS® ArcMap™ filter interface.

FIGURE 6–30 a) An example of the ERDAS IMAGINE convolution user interface. b) The analyst can use the edit menu to input the desired coefficients in an *n* x *n* kernel. In this case, a 3 x 3 low-pass filter is being prepared (interfaces courtesy of Intergraph Corporation). c) Spatial filtering using the ArcGIS® ArcMap™ spatial analyst filtering interface. A low-pass filter has been selected (interface courtesy of Esri, Inc.).

The primary input pixel under investigation at any one time is $V_5 = V_{i,j}$. The convolution of the low-frequency filter (with all coefficients equal to 1) and the original data will result in a low-frequency filtered image or map, where (Jensen, 2005):

$$LFF_{5,\text{out}} = \text{Int}\frac{\sum_{i=1}^{n=9} c_i \times V_i}{n} = \text{Int}\left(\frac{V_1 + V_2 + V_3 + \cdots + V_9}{9}\right) \quad (6.6)$$

The spatial moving average then shifts to the next pixel, where the average of all nine digital number values is computed. This operation is repeated for every pixel in the input image (Figure 6-28). Image smoothing is useful for removing "salt and pepper" noise in raster data. This simple smoothing operation will, however, blur the image, especially at the edges of objects. Blurring becomes more severe as the size of the kernel increases.

A high-spatial-resolution (6 x 6 in.) normal color digital aerial photograph of a residential area in Germany is shown in Figure 6-31a. It was obtained by an unmanned aerial vehicle (UAV) developed by SenseFly, Inc. Application of a **low-frequency filter** (Equation 6.4 and Table 6-2) to the red band of the residential image is shown in Figure 6-31b. Note how the image becomes blurred, suppressing the high-frequency detail. Only the general trends are allowed to pass through the low-pass filter. In a heterogeneous, high-frequency urban environment, a high-frequency filter usually provides superior results.

Three spatial filtering algorithms (median, minimum/maximum, and Olympic) do not use coefficients within the *n* x *n* neighborhood being examined. The **median filter** simply ranks the pixel values found within the *n* x *n* neighborhood from lowest to highest and selects the median value, which is then placed in the central value of the mask. Common neighborhood patterns used in median filters are shown in Figure 6-27a,b. The application of a median filter to the residential scene is shown in Figure 6-31c. Median filters allow fine detail to be erased and large regions to take on the same digital number value (referred to as posterization). Note how Figure 6-31c appears to be posterized.

Minimum or **maximum filters** examine the digital number values of adjacent pixels in a user-specified region (e.g., 3 x 3 pixels) and then replace the value of the cen-

TABLE 6–2 Selected low- and high-frequency filters and linear and nonlinear edge enhancement filters with their convolution mask coefficients.

$$\text{Convolution mask template} = \begin{bmatrix} c_1 & c_2 & c_3 \\ c_4 & c_5 & c_6 \\ c_7 & c_8 & c_9 \end{bmatrix} \qquad \text{Example: Low-frequency filter} = \begin{bmatrix} 1 & 1 & 1 \\ 1 & 1 & 1 \\ 1 & 1 & 1 \end{bmatrix}$$

	c_1	c_2	c_3	c_4	c_5	c_6	c_7	c_8	c_9	Example
Spatial Filtering										
Low-frequency	1	1	1	1	1	1	1	1	1	Figure 6-31b
High-frequency	1	-2	1	-2	5	-2	1	-2	1	Figure 6-31d
Linear Edge Enhancement										
Emboss Northwest	0	0	1	0	0	0	-1	0	0	Figure 6-32a
Emboss East	0	0	0	1	0	-1	0	0	0	---
ArcGIS® Edge Enhancement	-0.7	-1	-0.7	-1	6.8	-1	-0.7	-1	-0.7	---
Compass North	1	1	1	1	-2	1	-1	-1	-1	---
Compass NE	1	1	1	-1	-2	1	-1	-1	1	Figure 6-32b
Compass East	-1	1	1	-1	-2	1	-1	1	1	---
Compass SE	-1	-1	1	-1	-2	1	1	1	1	---
Compass South	-1	-1	-1	1	-2	1	1	1	1	
Compass SW	1	-1	-1	1	-2	-1	1	1	1	
Compass West	1	1	-1	1	-2	-1	1	1	-1	
Compass NW	1	1	1	1	-2	-1	1	-1	-1	
Vertical Edges	-1	0	1	-1	0	1	-1	0	1	
Horizontal Edges	-1	-1	-1	0	0	0	1	1	1	
Diagonal Edges	0	1	1	-1	0	1	-1	-1	0	
Nonlinear Edge Enhancement										
Laplacian 4	0	-1	0	-1	4	-1	0	-1	0	Figure 6-32c
Laplacian 5	0	-1	0	-1	5	-1	0	-1	0	Figure 6-32d
Laplacian 8	-1	-1	-1	-1	8	-1	-1	-1	-1	

Spatial Filtering of Raster Data

a. Original contrast stretched.

b. Low-frequency filter applied to the red band.

c. Median filter.

d. High-frequency sharp edge filter applied to the red band.

FIGURE 6–31 a) High-spatial-resolution color digital aerial photography of a residential area in Germany. b) Low-frequency filter (LFF) applied to the red band. c) Median filter applied to the red, green, and blue bands. d) High-frequency sharp edge filter applied to the red band (original digital aerial photography courtesy of Sensefly, Inc.).

ter pixel with the minimum or maximum value encountered.

The **Olympic filter** is named after the system of scoring in Olympic events. Instead of using all nine elements in a 3 x 3 matrix, the highest and lowest values are dropped and the remaining values are averaged.

High-frequency Filtering in the Spatial Domain

High-frequency filtering is applied to raster maps or images to remove the slowly varying components and enhance the high-frequency local variations (Jensen, 2005). One type of **high-frequency filter** that accentuates or sharpens edges uses the coefficients summarized in Table 6-2. The application of this high-frequency sharp edge filter to the residential aerial photograph red band is shown in Figure 6-31d.

Edge Enhancement in the Spatial Domain

Often, the most valuable information that may be derived from an image or map is contained in the edges surrounding objects of interest (Jensen, 2005). **Edge enhancement** delineates these edges in an image or map and makes them more conspicuous and often easier to understand. Generally, what the eyes see as pictorial edges are simply sharp changes in digital number value between two adjacent pixels. The edges may be enhanced using either linear or nonlinear edge enhancement techniques.

Linear Edge Enhancement Edge enhancement is often performed by convolving the original data with a weighted mask or kernel, as previously discussed. One of the most useful edge enhancements causes the edges to appear in a plastic shaded-relief format. This is often referred to as embossing. Embossed edges may be

Spatial Filtering of Raster Data

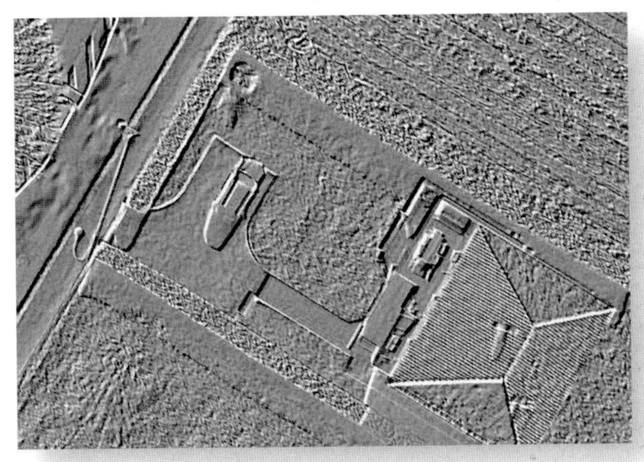

a. Emboss Northwest filter.

b. Compass Northeast filter.

c. Laplacian 4 filter.

d. Laplacian 5 filter.

FIGURE 6–32 Application of various convolution masks and logic to the red band of high-spatial-resolution imagery of a residential area in Germany. a) Emboss Northwest filter. b) Compass Northeast directional filter. c) Laplacian 4 edge enhancement contains information about the edges. d) Laplacian 5 edge enhancement adds the edge data back onto the original image (original digital aerial photography courtesy of Sensefly, Inc.).

obtained by using embossing filters such as the Emboss Northwest and the Emboss East enhancements summarized in Table 6-2.

The direction of the embossing is controlled by changing the value of the coefficients around the periphery of the mask. The plastic shaded-relief impression is pleasing to the human eye if shadows are made to fall toward the viewer. The red band of the residential image processed using the Emboss Northwest filter is shown in Figure 6-32a.

The ArcGIS® high-pass edge enhancement coefficients are provided in Table 6-2. This filter removes low-frequency variation and highlights the boundary (edges) between different regions (Esri, 2011).

Compass gradient masks may be used to perform two-dimensional, discrete differentiation directional edge enhancement (Pratt, 2007). Table 6-2 lists the coefficients used in eight commonly used compass gradient masks. The compass names suggest the slope direction of maximum response. For example, the east gradient mask produces a maximum output for horizontal digital number value changes from west to east. The gradient masks have zero weighting (i.e., the sum of the mask coefficients is zero) (Pratt, 2007). This results in no output response over regions with constant brightness values (i.e., no edges are present). A Compass Northeast gradient mask applied to the residential image is shown in Figure 6-32b.

Richards and Xiuping (2006) identified four additional 3×3 filters that may be used to detect edges in images

Spatial Filtering of Raster Data

a. Sobel edge enhancement.

b. Roberts edge enhancement.

FIGURE 6–33 Application of two nonlinear edge enhancements to the red band of the high spatial resolution residential imagery. a) A Sobel edge enhancement. b) A Roberts edge enhancement (original digital aerial photography courtesy of Sensefly, Inc.).

(vertical, horizontal, and diagonal). Thee filter coefficients are listed in Table 6-2.

Laplacian filters may be applied to imagery or continuous surface maps to perform edge enhancement. The Laplacian filter is a second derivative (as opposed to the gradient, which is a first derivative) and is invariant to rotation, meaning that it is insensitive to the direction in which the discontinuities (e.g., edges) run. The coefficients associated with three important 3 x 3 Laplacian filters are listed in Table 6-2 (Jahne, 2005; Pratt, 2007):

Sometimes by itself, the Laplacian image may be difficult to interpret. For example, consider the Laplacian 4 filter applied to the residential scene shown in Figure 6-32c. Therefore, some analysts prefer using a Laplacian edge enhancement that adds the edge information back onto the original map or image using the Laplacian 5 algorithm. The result of applying this enhancement to the residential scene is shown is Figure 6-32d.

Nonlinear Edge Enhancement Nonlinear edge enhancements are performed using nonlinear combinations of pixels. For example, the Sobel edge detector is based on the 3 x 3 window numbering scheme previously described and is computed according to the relationship (Jensen, 2005):

$$\text{Sobel}_{5,out} = \sqrt{X^2 + Y^2} \qquad (6.7)$$

where

$$X = (V_3 + 2V_6 + V_9) - (V_1 + 2V_4 + V_7)$$

and

$$Y = (V_1 + 2V_2 + V_3) - (V_7 + 2V_8 + V_9)$$

This procedure detects horizontal, vertical, and diagonal edges. A Sobel edge enhancement of the residential scene is found in Figure 6-33a.

The Roberts edge detector is based on the use of only four elements of a 3 x 3 mask. The new pixel value at pixel location $V_{5,out}$ (refer to the 3 x 3 numbering scheme in Equation 6.3) is computed according to the equation (Jensen, 2005):

$$\text{Roberts}_{5,\,out} = X + Y \qquad (6.8)$$

where

$$X = |V_5 - V_9|$$
$$Y = |V_6 - V_8|$$

A Roberts edge filter is applied to the residential scene in Figure 6-33b.

Other types of spatial filters may be applied to raster data. For example, there are filters that can extract the texture of surfaces. Several of these filters are described in Jensen (2005).

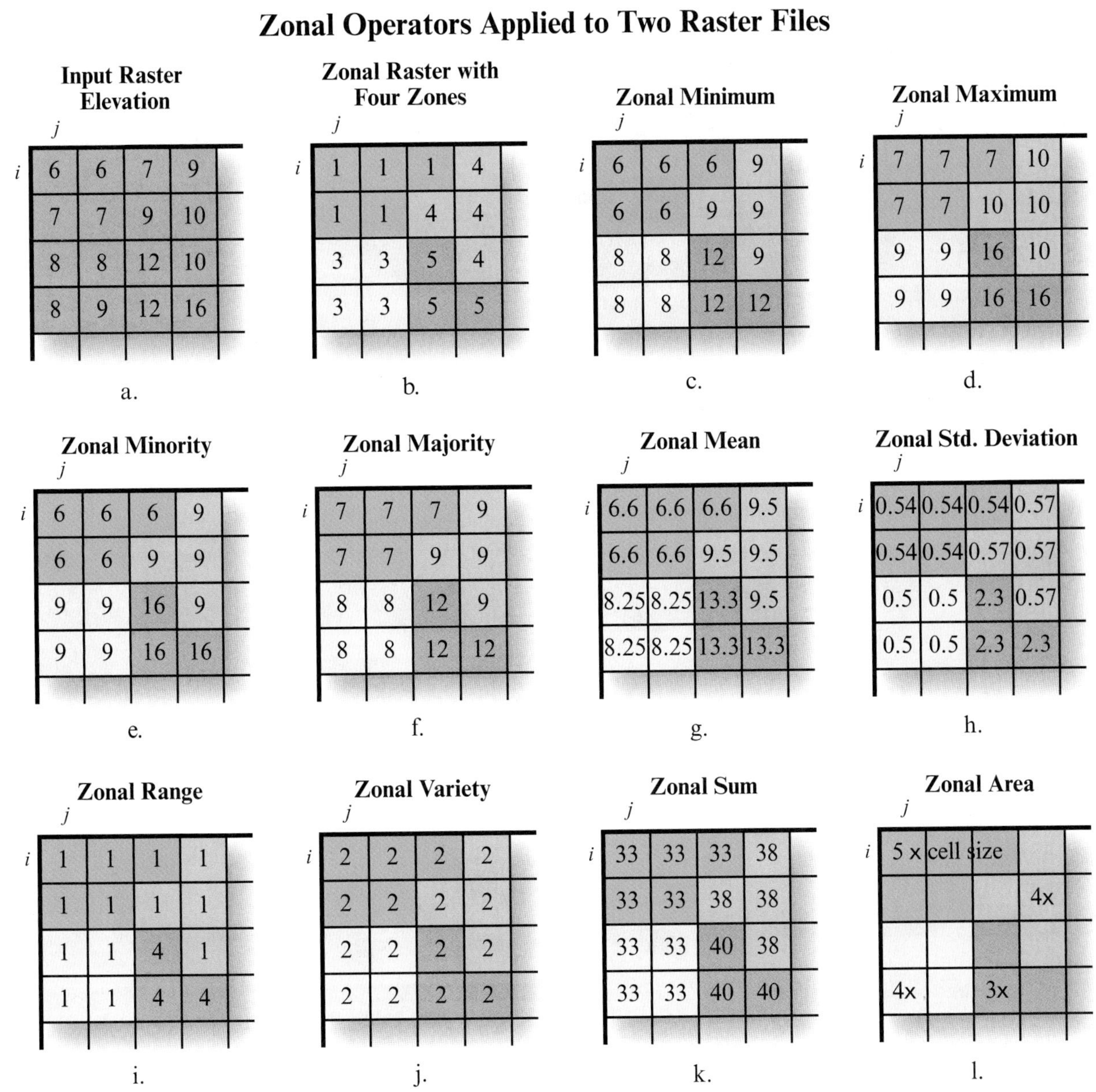

Zonal Operators Applied to Two Raster Files

Input Raster Elevation

6	6	7	9
7	7	9	10
8	8	12	10
8	9	12	16

a.

Zonal Raster with Four Zones

1	1	1	4
1	1	4	4
3	3	5	4
3	3	5	5

b.

Zonal Minimum

6	6	6	9
6	6	9	9
8	8	12	9
8	8	12	12

c.

Zonal Maximum

7	7	7	10
7	7	10	10
9	9	16	10
9	9	16	16

d.

Zonal Minority

6	6	6	9
6	6	9	9
9	9	16	9
9	9	16	16

e.

Zonal Majority

7	7	7	9
7	7	9	9
8	8	12	9
8	8	12	12

f.

Zonal Mean

6.6	6.6	6.6	9.5
6.6	6.6	9.5	9.5
8.25	8.25	13.3	9.5
8.25	8.25	13.3	13.3

g.

Zonal Std. Deviation

0.54	0.54	0.54	0.57
0.54	0.54	0.57	0.57
0.5	0.5	2.3	0.57
0.5	0.5	2.3	2.3

h.

Zonal Range

1	1	1	1
1	1	1	1
1	1	4	1
1	1	4	4

i.

Zonal Variety

2	2	2	2
2	2	2	2
2	2	2	2
2	2	2	2

j.

Zonal Sum

33	33	33	38
33	33	38	38
33	33	40	38
33	33	40	40

k.

Zonal Area

5 x cell size			
			4x
4x		3x	

l.

FIGURE 6–34 Examples of various zonal operators applied to two raster files. a) The input raster data consists of elevation values. b) The zonal raster consists of pixels belonging to four soil types, 1-4. c) Zonal minimum. d) Zonal maximum. e) Zonal minority. f) Zonal majority. g) Zonal mean. h) Zonal standard deviation. i) Zonal range. j) Zonal variety. k) Zonal sum. l) Zonal area = number of cells in zone x cell size.

Zonal Operations

Think of a group of pixels in a portion of a raster (matrix) dataset that all have the same value, i.e., 10. Now think about an adjacent group of pixels that have the value of 11. These two groups of pixels may be considered to be "zones" in the raster dataset. Perhaps they are associated with counties #10 and #11 in a specific state or watersheds #23 and #24. These two zones are considered to be contiguous zones.

Conversely, now visualize a group (zone) of pixels with the value of 100 on one side of a lake. The lake consists of a zone of pixels with values of 1. On the other side of the lake there is a separate and distinct zone of pixels also with the value of 100. The pixels with values of 100 might be a specific soil or land cover type on each side of the lake. In this case, we would have two noncontiguous zones separated by the lake zone.

Zonal Statistics

Zonal statistics may be extracted from individual raster datasets or from two raster datasets (Figure 6-34).

Examples of Selected Zonal Operations

a. May River watershed overlaid on a digital terrain model (DTM) that is the input raster from which statistics are computed.

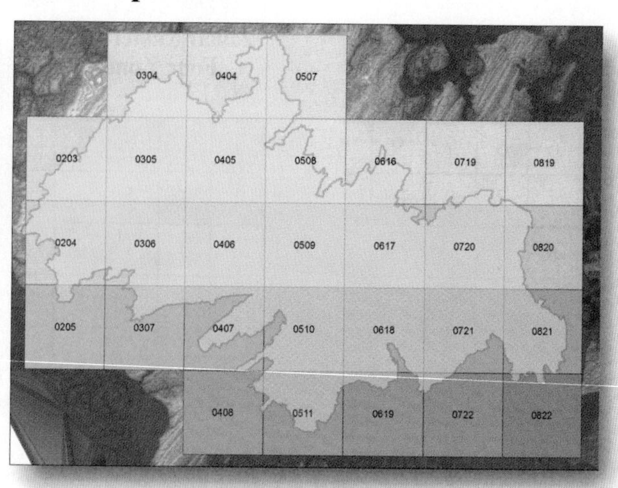

b. The zonal dataset consists of 29 input raster zones (tiles).

c. Zonal Mean: The maximum elevation value in each zone is assigned to all the pixels in the zone.

d. Zonal Minimum: The minimum elevation value in each zone is assigned to all the pixels in the zone.

FIGURE 6–35 Examples of zonal operations. a) The input raster consists of elevation values found within the watershed boundary. b) The zone raster consists of 29 tiles. c) The result of applying a zonal mean operator on the raster DTM in (a) and the 29 raster zones in (b). d) The result of applying a zonal minimum operator on the raster DTM in (a) and the 29 raster zones in (b) (LiDAR-derived elevation data courtesy of Beaufort County GIS Department).

Zonal Statistics from a Single Raster Some of the most important zonal measurements extracted from a single raster dataset are geometric in nature, including the area, perimeter, thickness, and the location of the centroid of each zone.

The geographic *area* of all of the cells within a specific zone is computed by summing the number of pixels in the zone and multiplying it by the size of the cell (e.g., in m^2). The *perimeter* of a contiguous zone is the length of all the boundary pixels. The perimeter of a noncontiguous zone is the sum of the length of all the pixels in all of the related noncontiguous zones. The radius of the largest circle that be inscribed in a zone is called the zone *thickness*. The *centroid* (geometric center) of a zone is located at the intersection of the major and minor axis of an ellipse that is best-fit to individual zone.

Zonal Statistics from Two Raster Datasets Zonal statistics are often computed using two raster datasets: 1) an input raster and 2) a zonal raster. The input raster usually consists of thematic values such as land cover type, temperature, elevation, population, etc. The zonal raster usually contains some regularized group of zones that consist of contiguous or noncontiguous zones of pixels. For example, the zonal raster dataset could be individual counties in a state, individual watersheds, school districts, or arbitrary subdivisions such as rectangular tiles, etc.

The zonal operation creates a new output raster dataset that summarizes the cell values in the input raster for each zone in the zonal raster. The most common zonal summary statistics include minimum, maximum, minority, majority, mean, standard deviation, range, variety, sum, and zonal geographic area as demonstrated in Figure 6-34. In this example, the input raster dataset consists of elevation values in integer format. The zonal dataset consists of pixels belonging to one of four soil types. Zonal area is the sum of the cells within the zone multiplied times the cell size. The input values must be integers to compute the median (not shown), minority, majority, and variety.

A practical example of zonal analysis is shown in Figure 6-35. The May River watershed in South Carolina is overlaid on a LiDAR-derived digital elevation model in Figure 6-35a. The DTM elevation data represents the input raster values that will be used to compute various statistics by zone. Twenty-nine (29) user-defined zones (tiles) are identified in Figure 6-35b. Elevation statistics were extracted from the DTM pixels within each of the zones. The mean elevation value of each zone was determined by computing the *zonal mean*. The mean values are color-coded in Figure 6-35c. The higher elevation is in the northwest portion of the watershed with mean elevation values ranging up to 31 ft. above sea level.

The minimum elevation value of each zone was determined by computing the *zonal minimum*. The minimum values for each zone are color-coded in Figure 6-35d. The minimum values are typically found along the May River and its tributaries. The dark-blue anomaly in zone #304 in the northwest part of the watershed is caused by a 15 ft. deep pit.

It is important to note that all the pixel values within a zone have exactly the same value. Information summarized by zone is very important in many GIS investigations.

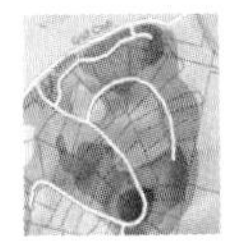

Summary

This chapter provided examples of selected types of vector and raster data analysis. Vector buffering of point, line, and area features is an important part of many GIS studies. Vector-overlay analysis is one of the most important types of GIS analysis and includes point-in-polygon, line-in-polygon, and polygon-on-polygon analysis. Point, line, and area features in raster data can also be buffered. Raster local operations can be used to analyze individual pixels using local operations applied to single or multiple registered raster datasets. Raster neighborhood operations can be applied to individual pixels and surrounding neighborhood pixels to perform spatial filtering and regional (zonal) analysis.

Review Questions

1. Describe how you would identify the location of a 300 m buffer around all the wetland adjacent to a proposed development. What type of geospatial information would you use and how would you conduct the analysis?

2. You are planning on purchasing a lot that is 70 x 80 m in size. Local building codes require that your house be constructed ≥ 3 m away from the existing property lines. You have access to a high-resolution cadastral dataset of the study area that includes detailed property line spatial information. How would you go about deciding if your proposed home will fit on the property under consideration?

3. Describe two types of buffering that can be applied to vector area (polygonal) data.

4. Provide an example of a typical point-in-polygon overlay analysis problem.

5. What type of raster filter would you use to enhance the high-frequency characteristics in a remotely sensed image?

6. What filter would you use to emphasize the low-frequency, slowly varying characteristics in a raster map or image?

7. Describe a typical spatial analysis problem that requires zonal analysis.

8. Why is texture in an image or map important? What algorithm would you use to extract texture information from a high-spatial-resolution digital aerial photograph? Why did you select this particular algorithm?

9. You have a high-spatial-resolution digital aerial photograph of an area with an extremely dense stream network. What edge enhancement algorithm would you

use to identify the detailed structure of the stream network in the image? Why did you select this particular edge enhancement?

10. Describe how the Universal Soil Loss Equation works and how it can be implemented using raster local operations in a GIS.

11. Describe how raster convolution filtering works. What coefficients would you use in a 3 x 3 convolution kernel to enhance edges in a raster map or image that run north–south?

12. Provide an example of a typical line-in-polygon overlay analysis problem.

Glossary

Buffering: The creation of a polygon that is a specified distance (e.g., 100 m) around a point, line, or area (polygon) feature.

Clipping: An operation that extracts a geographic area of the input layer using the outside boundary of a polygon in the clip base layer.

Edge Enhancement: The process of enhancing edges in an image or map to make them more identifiable.

Erasing: Deletes a part of the input layer using the erase base layer as a template for the geographic area to be deleted. The output layer contains only those input layer features that are *outside* the erase region.

High-frequency Filter: A raster image–enhancement that emphasizes the high-spatial-frequency detail in a map or image.

Identity: An operation that computes the geometric intersection of the input layer features and identity layer features. The input features or portions thereof that overlap the identity layer features receive the attributes of the identity layer features.

Intersection: The intersection of two map layers is based on the use of the AND connector, which computes the geometric intersection of the input layer and the base feature layer. Only those features or portions of features that overlap in both the input layer and the base layer are written to the output layer.

Laplacian Edge Enhancement: A second derivative filter (as opposed to the gradient, which is a first derivative) that is invariant to rotation, meaning that it is insensitive to the direction in which the edges run.

Linear Spatial Filter: A filter for which the value ($V_{i,j}$) at location *i,j* in the output image or map is a function of some weighted average (linear combination) of values located in a particular spatial pattern around the *i,j* location in the input image or map.

Line-in-polygon Overlay: The overlay of a line layer on a polygon layer.

Local Raster Operation: Each pixel (cell) at location *i,j* in a raster dataset may be considered to be a local object. The value of this pixel can be operated upon independent of neighboring pixels (cells).

Low-frequency Filter: A raster image-enhancement that de-emphasizes or blocks the high-spatial frequency detail in the map or image.

Map Algebra: Arithmetic and algebraic local operations applied to multiple registered raster datasets.

Median Filter: Ranks the pixel values found within the $n \times n$ neighborhood from lowest to highest and selects the median value, which is then placed in the central value of the neighborhood.

Minimum/Maximum Filter: Examines the values of adjacent pixels in a user-specified region (e.g., $n \times n$ pixels) and then replaces the value of the central pixel with the minimum or maximum value.

Neighborhood Raster Operation: Modifies the value of each focal pixel in the context of the values of the pixels surrounding it.

Olympic Filter: Using all the values in an $n \times n$ region, the highest and lowest values are dropped and the remaining values are averaged.

Point-in-Polygon Overlay: The overlay of a point layer on a polygon layer.

Polygon-on-Polygon Overlay: The overlay of a polygon layer on a polygon layer.

Raster Map Overlay: Occurs when local operations are applied to multiple raster layers.

Spatial Frequency: The number of changes in value per unit distance for any particular part of a raster map or image.

Splitting: Divides the input layer into a number of smaller layers based on the characteristics of the base layer. Each new output coverage contains only those portions of the input layer features overlapped by the split coverage polygons.

Symmetrical Difference: An operation that computes the geometric intersection of the input-layer features and the base layer features. Features or portions of features in the input and update features that do *not* overlap are written to the output layer.

Union: The intersection of two map layers based on the use of the OR connector, which preserves all of the features in both the input-polygon layer and the base-polygon layer.

References

Chang, K., 2010, *Introduction to Geographic Information Systems*, New York: McGraw Hill, 5th Ed., 224–268 p.

Clarke, K. C., 2011, *Getting Started with Geographic Information Systems*, Upper Saddle River: Pearson Prentice-Hall, Inc., 369 p.

Cowen, D. J., Coleman, D. J., Craig, W. J., Domenico, C., Elhami, S., Johnson, S., Marlow, S., Roberts, F., Swartz, M. T. and N. Von Meyer, 2007, *National Land Parcel Data: A Vision for the Future*, Washington: National Academy Press, 158 p.

DeMers, M. N., 2002, *GIS Modeling in Raster*, New York: John Wiley & Sons, 208 p.

DeMers, M. N., 2005, *Fundamentals of Geographic Information Systems*, 3rd Ed., New York: John Wiley & Sons, 467 p.

ENVI, 2011, *Environment for Visualizing Images*, Boulder: ITT Visual Information Solutions (www.ittvis.com/default.aspx).

Esri, 2011, *ArcGIS® DeskTop Help*, Redlands: Esri, Inc. (www.Esri.com).

Gutierrez, B.T., Williams, S. J. and E. R. Thieler, 2007, "Potential for Shoreline Changes Due to Sea-level Rise Along the U.S. Mid-Atlantic Region," *U.S. Geological Survey Open-File Report #2007-1278*, Washington: USGS (http://pubs.usgs.gov/of/2007/1278).

Jahne, B., 2005, *Digital Image Processing*, New York: Springer-Verlag, 630 p.

Jain, A. K., 1989, *Fundamentals of Digital Image Processing*, Inglewood Cliffs, NJ: Prentice-Hall, Inc., 342-357.

Jensen, J. R., 2005, *Introductory Digital Image Processing: A Remote Sensing Perspective*, Upper Saddle River: Pearson Prentice-Hall, Inc., 592 p.

Jensen, J. R. and M. E. Hodgson, 2011, *Predicting the Impact of Sea Level Rise in the Upper May River in South Carolina Using an Improved LiDAR-derived Digital Elevation Model, Land Cover Extracted from High Resolution Digital Aerial Imagery, and Sea Level Rise Scenarios*, Charleston: The Nature Conservancy, 75 p.

Lo, C. P. and A. K. W. Yeung, 2007, *Concepts and Techniques in Geographic Information Systems*, Upper Saddle River: Pearson Prentice-Hall, Inc., 532 p.

Madden, M. (Ed.), 2009, *Manual of Geographic Information Systems*, Bethesda: American Society for Photogrammetry & Remote Sensing, 1352 p.

Maidment, D. R., Edelman, S., Heiberg, E. R., Jensen, J. R., Maune, D. F., Schuckman, K. and R. Shrestha, 2007, *Elevation Data for Floodplain Mapping*, Washington: National Academy Press, 151 p.

NRCS, 2010, *Revised Universal Soil Loss Equation, Version 2 (RUSLE2): Official NRCS RUSLE2 Program*, West Lafayette: Purdue University (http://fargo.nserl.purdue.edu/rusle2_dataweb/RUSLE2_Index.htm).

Pratt, W. K., 2007, *Digital Image Processing*, 4th Ed., New York: John Wiley & Sons, 782 p.

Renard, K. G., Foster, G. R., Weesies, G. A., McCool, D. K. and D. C. Yoder, 1997, *Predicting Soil Erosion by Water: A Guide to Conservation Planning with the Revised Universal Soil Loss Equation (RUSLE)—Agricultural Handbook 703*, Washington, DC: U. S. Department of Agriculture.

Richards, J. A. and J. Xiuping, 2006, *Remote Sensing Digital Image Analysis*, Heidelberg: Springer-Verlag, 439 p.

Russ, J. C., 2006, *The Image Processing Handbook*, 5th Ed., Boca Raton: CRC press, 817.

Stone, R. P., 2010, *Universal Soil Loss Equation (USLE)*, Ontario: Ministry of Agriculture, Food, and Rural Affairs (http://www.omafra.gov.on.ca/english/engineer/facts/00-001.htm).

Tomlin, C. D., 1990, *Geographic Information Systems and Cartographic Modeling*, Upper Saddle River: Pearson Prentice-Hall, Inc.

USGS and FWS, 2004, *Habitat Displacement and Sea Level Change—The Blackwater Model*, Washington: U.S. Department of the Interior (http://geology.usgs.gov/connections/fws/landscapes/blackwater_model.htm).

Warner, T. A., Nellis, M. D. and G. M. Foody, 2009, *The SAGE Handbook of Remote Sensing*, London: SAGE Publications Ltd., 504 p.

Wischmeier, W. H., and D. D. Smith, 1960, "A Universal Soil-loss Equation to Guide Conservation Farm Planning," *Transactions International Congress Soil Science*, (7):418–425.

Wischmeier, W. H. and D. D. Smith, 1978, *Predicting Rainfall Erosion Losses: A Guide to Conservation Planning—Agricultural Handbook #537*, Washington: U. S. Department of Agriculture, 58 p.

7 Network Analysis

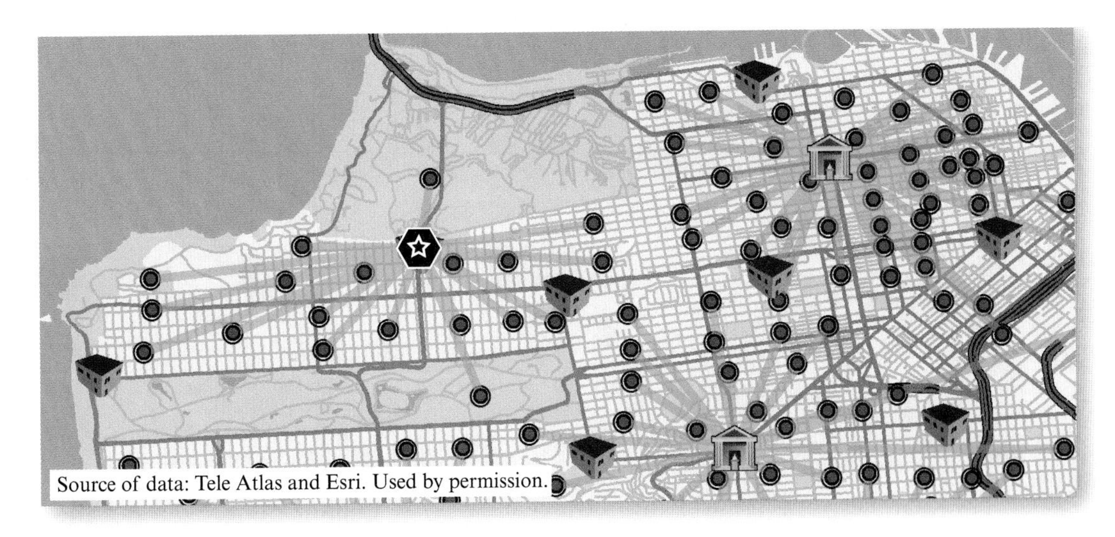
Source of data: Tele Atlas and Esri. Used by permission.

A **network** is a system of interconnected lines (edges) and intersections (junctions) that represent possible routes from one location to another. There are human-made and natural networks. Cars, trucks, subways, taxis, and school buses travel on paved and unpaved transportation networks (Figure 7-1a). Trains travel on railroad networks (Figure 7-1b). Airplanes traverse carefully controlled ground transportation networks (Figure 7-1c) and usually fly on pre-determined flight path networks. We walk and ride bicycles on trail and sidewalk networks (Figure 7-1d). Animals travel on trail networks to and from nesting and foraging habitats. Water and sewage flow in both natural and human-made networks.

Humans are very interested in the movement of goods, services, animals, and resources traveling on networks (e.g., Maidment, 2002; Salah and Atwood, 2010). They are also interested in identifying the optimum path through a network and/or locating new facilities at the optimum location within a network. Therefore, it is not surprising that a great amount of research has gone into developing GIS functions that can be used to analyze the spatial characteristics of networks to address some very important problems (e.g., Lemmens, 2010). Some typical network applications include:

- Personal: locate the closest facility (e.g., market, dentist, hospital).
- Personal: find the geographic location of a friend who lives at the address 1010 N. Main Street.
- Government: optimize the daily routes for hundreds of mail carriers.
- Education: identify the optimum school bus routes that honor right-side curb approach and do not have U-turns.
- Public Safety: route emergency response vehicles (e.g., ambulance, fire engines, police) to incidents.
- Public Works: determine the best route for weekly trash collection in a city or county.
- Business: determine the optimum route to deliver new appliances including the time window and distance restrictions.
- Business: identify the optimum location for a new store that captures 60% of the market share given the presence of three existing stores and two competitor stores.

Overview

The reader is first introduced to geocoding and address matching. Then, two general types of geodatabase networks are reviewed: Transportation (undirected) and Geometric Utility (directed). The general process of creating a topologically correct network geodatabase from geographic information stored in a GIS is considered. Potential sources of network information are discussed. Fundamental network elements such as edges, junctions, and turns are described. The concepts of network cost (e.g., impedances such as time, distance, or visibility), restrictions (e.g., barriers, temporary road closures, accidents, road weight limitations), and hierarchy are presented.

Transportation (Undirected) Networks

a. Road network in Sao Paulo, Brazil.

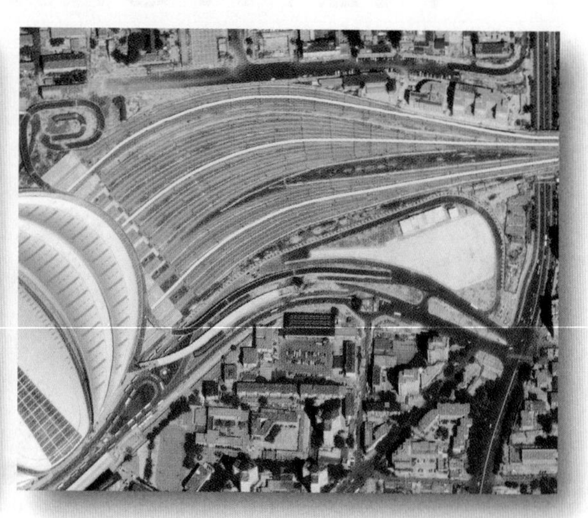

b. Beijing, China South Railway Station.

c. Ground transportation network at Tokyo International Airport.

d. Pedestrian network surrounding the *Pyramid of Peace* in Kazakhstan.

FIGURE 7–1 Examples of selected transportation (undirected) networks. a) Octavio Frias de Oliveira Bridge and road transportation network in Sao Paulo, Brazil (20 July 2010). b) Beijing, China South Railway Station and railroad network (11 August 2009). Three of 24 tracks in the network are highlighted. c) Airline ground transportation network at Tokyo International Airport (21 March 2009). d) Walking trails surrounding the *Pyramid of Peace* in Kazakhstan (20 October 2009) (satellite images courtesy of GeoEye, Inc.).

Much of this chapter is concerned with describing the various types of analyses that can be performed on transportation networks, including identifying the optimum route to a location or the optimum delivery route, generating travel directions, finding the closest facility, identifying a service area, and location-allocation modeling. The network analysis procedures are demonstrated using topologically correct network datasets. The reader is then introduced to geometric network analysis with an emphasis on stream network analysis, including determining flow direction, tracing edges or junctions upstream or downstream, and the use of barriers in a utility network.

Geocoding

Geocoding is the process of finding a geographic location from an address (Esri, 2011f). Geocoded information is used by businesses to determine where their customers are located, by police departments to see spatial patterns of crime (Andresen, 2006; Ratcliffe, 2004), by biologists to examine the distribution of animal vehicle collisions (Gonser et al., 2009), and by state health departments to determine the extent and

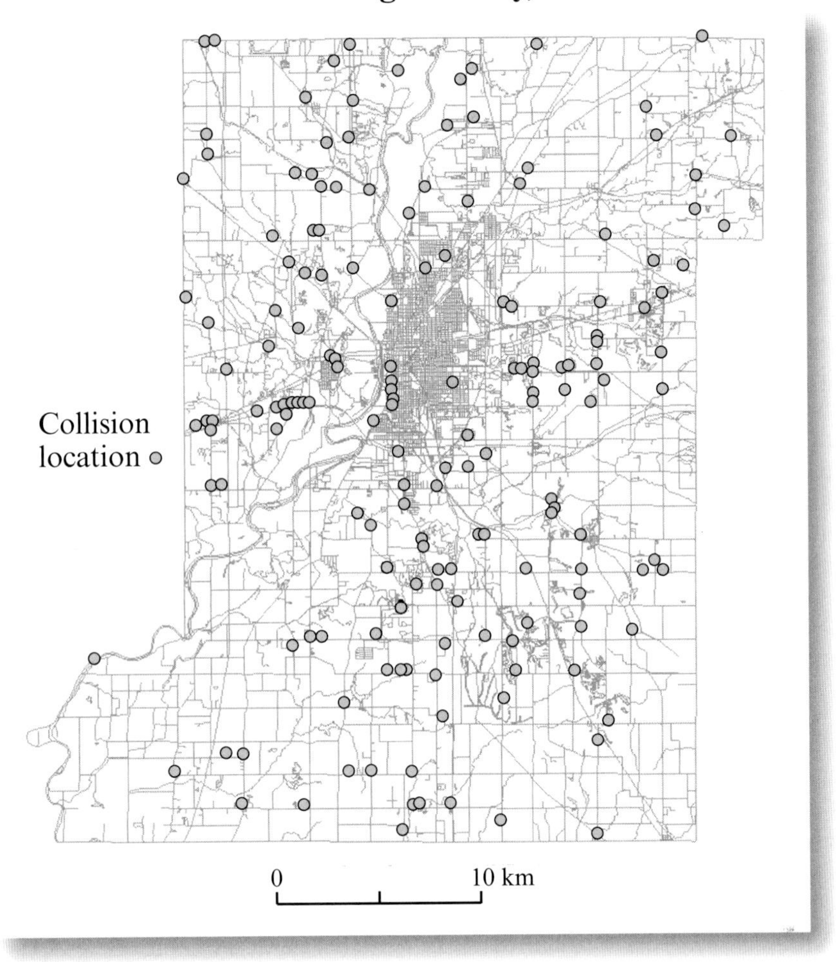

FIGURE 7–2 The location of deer and vehicle collisions in 2001 in Vigo County, IN. Law enforcement officers recorded the approximate address of each collision (e.g., 1010 N. Main Street) in text format in a spreadsheet. This address information was then geocoded (address matched) to identify the geographic location of each collision within the U.S. Bureau of the Census MAF/TIGER line file reference geodatabase (adapted from Gonser et al., 2009).

spatial dimensions of disease (Kreiger et al., 2003). Each of these applications is especially suited for geocoding because each tends to occur at specific point locations. For example, the locations of all recorded deer and vehicle collisions in Vigo County, IN, in 2001 are shown in Figure 7-2. The address of each of these collisions was noted by a law enforcement officer (e.g., 1010 N. Main Street). The information was then geocoded to its approximate geographic location in a U.S. Bureau of the Census MAF/TIGER line file network geodatabase.

The most common type of geocoding is **address matching,** which plots street addresses as points on a map. During the mapping process, the locations of addresses are interpolated along road segments based on the attributes stored in the geocoded database. For example, you have probably input an address into a navigation device and instructed the device to direct you to the location using the shortest or fastest route. Before the navigation device can begin to calculate your route, it must first determine where the desired street address is located. It does this using geocoded information. You may have noticed that the actual destination point displayed on your personal navigation device may not always be exactly where it should be. This is because the device must interpolate the address location along the road segment and the interpolation process is only as good as the quality of the geospatial information in the geocoded database.

Geocoding Components

Geocoding can be characterized in terms of its fundamental components: the input dataset, the output dataset, the processing algorithm, and the reference dataset (Goldberg et al., 2007). The *input dataset* contains the records that the user wishes to have geocoded. These records are usually addresses (e.g., 1010 N. Main Street). The *output dataset* contains the geographically referenced code generated from the input dataset. The accuracy of the output dataset depends on the quality of the input dataset (i.e., the input addresses should be as accurate as possible) and the processing algorithm that is used. The *processing algorithm* determines the appropriate position of the input data (e.g., an address) in the output dataset based on the values of each record's attributes and the values of the attributes in the reference dataset. The *reference dataset* contains the geographically coded information that can be used to find the correct locations of the data in the input dataset using the processing algorithm (Goldberg et al., 2007). The reference dataset is typically called a geocoding reference database, and it is very similar to the topologically correct transportation network geodatabase described in this chapter.

One of the most widely used geocoded geodatabases is the U.S. Bureau of the Census **MAF/TIGER/Line File** (*Master Address File/Topologically Integrated Geographic Encoding and Referencing database*). The MAF/TIGER line files contain the following detailed information for each street segment: street name, beginning and ending address for each side of the street, and the postal code on each side of the road. These fields, including their standard names, are described in Table 7-1.

TABLE 7–1 Basic components of U.S. Bureau of the Census MAF/TIGER/Line files. These fields allow input addresses to be found (matched) in the reference database.

Variable	Description
FEDIRP	Any direction that precedes a street name, e.g., N, E, S, W.
FENAME	The name of the street.
FETYPE	The type of road or street (e.g., boulevard, street, road, lane)
FRADDL	The beginning address on the left side of the street.
TOADDL	The ending address on the left side of the street.
FRADDR	The beginning address on the right side of the street.
TOADDR	The ending address on the right side of the street.
ZIPL	The Zip code on the left side of the street.
ZIPR	The Zip code on the right side of the street.

Preprocessing

Before geocoding can begin, preprocessing must occur where both the input dataset and the reference dataset are analyzed and a processing algorithm is constructed. The processing algorithm (sometimes called an address locator) is generally created by a geocoding engine that is embedded in the GIS. The geocoding engine constructs the address locator by examining the addresses and parses them to standardize their characteristics. For example, consider the following address: 15 N Oakley Boulevard, Chicago, IL 60612.

This address has the following components:

- Street number = 15
- Direction that precedes the street name = N
- Street name = Oakley
- Street type = Boulevard
- City = Chicago
- State = Illinois
- Zip code = 60612

The parsing process separates the individual components above and enables the address to be found in the reference dataset. For an entire input dataset, parsing results in individual records where there is a value for each of the components that are present in the original address. Many address variations are possible. For example, apartment numbers can be added to street numbers, suffixes such as "NE" or "South," can be added to either the street name or street type, and so forth. Also, many addresses may be missing information or the information may be in a different order. To remedy this, the addresses are standardized in the input dataset and are placed in a particular order that can be read by the processing algorithm. During standardization, street types such as "BLVD" and "Boulevard" or "Street" and "St" are given the same notation.

Address Matching

The addresses are matched to the geocoding database to determine what percentage are able to be used (i.e., plotted). The actual percentage can vary greatly based on the parameters that the user defines. A user may determine that only 60% of the parameters must match before the address can be mapped. A user may do this

MAF/TIGER Data for a Street Network in Chicago, IL

Street Segment Information

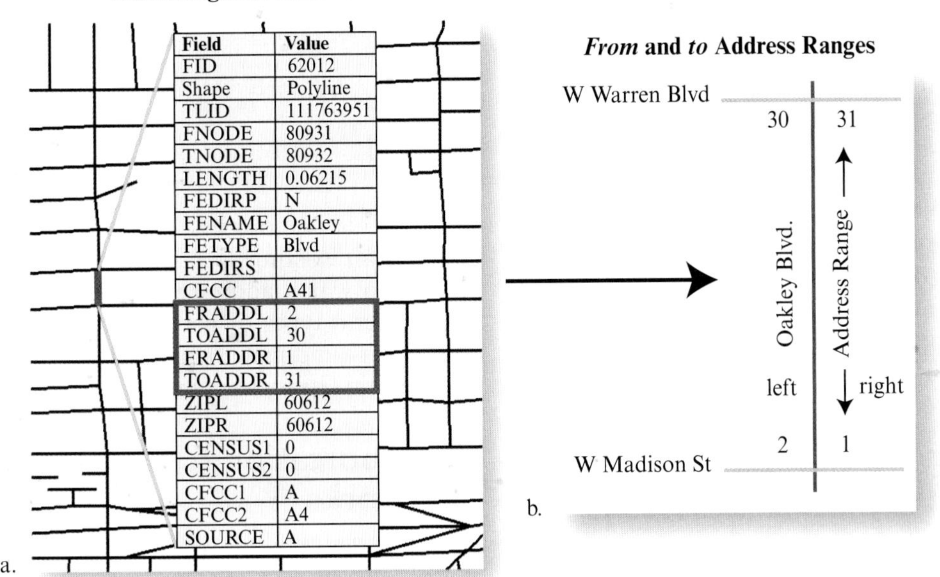

Field	Value
FID	62012
Shape	Polyline
TLID	111763951
FNODE	80931
TNODE	80932
LENGTH	0.06215
FEDIRP	N
FENAME	Oakley
FETYPE	Blvd
FEDIRS	
CFCC	A41
FRADDL	2
TOADDL	30
FRADDR	1
TOADDR	31
ZIPL	60612
ZIPR	60612
CENSUS1	0
CENSUS2	0
CFCC1	A
CFCC2	A4
SOURCE	A

Interpolated Address Locations

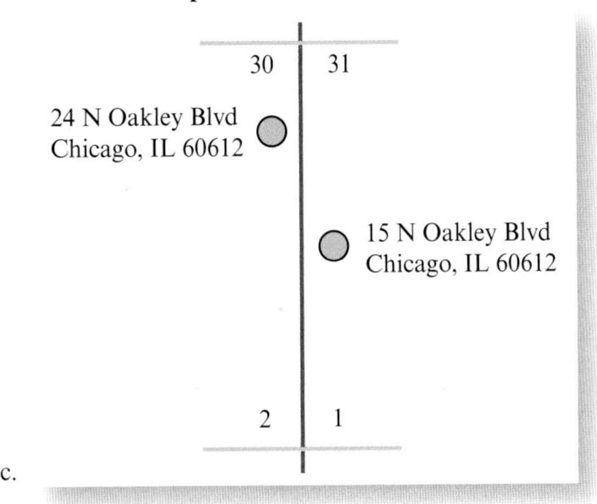

FIGURE 7–3 a) A street segment from a MAF/TIGER line file of Cook County, IL. The red street segment is associated with North Oakley Boulevard. Note the information about the street segment in the "Identify" yellow box to the right. In particular, note the "*from*" and "*to*" address information in the blue outlined box. b) The possible *from* and *to* address ranges of the Oakley Boulevard street segment. Even and odd addresses are on the left- and right-hand sides of the street, respectively. c) Numeric addresses along Oakley Boulevard can be interpolated to their approximate locations. In this example, 15 N Oakley Boulevard is interpolated to be midway between West Madison Street and West Warren Boulevard along the right side of the street. Conversely, an address at 24 N Oakley Boulevard would be much closer to West Warren Boulevard along the left side of the street (data courtesy U.S. Bureau of the Census).

because many of the addresses do not have the Zip code or the city noted in their records. Relaxing the parameters generally enables a greater percentage of addresses to be located, but some of them may contain errors. Conversely, strict address matching criteria will match fewer addresses, but the matched addresses should have a higher probability of being accurate. The key is to find the right kind of parameters for address matching that provide the level of accuracy needed while also matching a larger percentage of the original addresses. This process usually takes some experimentation.

To understand the geocoding process, it is useful to go through an example of how addresses are matched. A small part of the U.S. Bureau of the Census MAF/TIGER line dataset of Cook County, IL, is shown in Figure 7-3a. The red street segment and its associated characteristics are provided. The street address used previously (15 N Oakley Boulevard, Chicago, IL, 60612) lies along the street segment in red.

In this example, the *from* and *to* addresses on the right side of the road range from 1 to 31 (Figure 7-3b). This lets the address matching algorithm know that odd-numbered addresses are on the right side of the road and the values range from 1 to 31. Conversely, the left side of the street has address values that range from 2 to 30. Using these values, an individual street number can be interpolated to its approximate location along the road segment and placed on the correct side of the road. In this example, the address "15 N Oakley Blvd" would be located at approximately the midpoint of the road segment and placed on the right side of the street. A different address at "24 N Oakley Blvd" would be placed much closer to West Warren Blvd along the left side of the street (Figure 7-3c).

Geocoding Quality

Although geocoding is a straightforward process, there is great potential for error (Kreiger et al., 2003; Goldberg et al., 2007). The quality of geocoding is often measured by the address match rate. Many researchers are often surprised at lower-than-expected address-matching rates. Below are some common contributors to low address-matching rates:

- Misspelled street names,
- Incorrect city name (e.g., inputting the name of an adjacent city),
- Incorrect directional identifier (N instead of S; E instead of W),
- Out-of-range street number,
- Incorrect street type (e.g., Boulevard, Avenue, Road, Trail),
- Using an abbreviation that is not recognized (e.g., Blvd, Av, Rd), and
- Missing data (e.g., street name, number, directional identifier, Zip code).

The key is to determine the minimum "match rate" that is acceptable for a given project and then exceed that rate, if possible.

Positional accuracy is another geocoding concern. Positional accuracy is the measure of how close the geocoded address is to the actual location of the address. As noted above, address geocoding is done using interpolation of an address along a street segment based on the *from* and *to* address values. If these *from* and *to* values are incorrect, address points will be placed at incorrect locations. Also, addresses in the real world do not always follow a strict "linear" progression along a road. For example, in the example above, there is no guarantee that the address "15 N Oakley Blvd" is located precisely in the middle of the street segment.

Types of Networks

The geocoding process just described assumes that there is an existing specially prepared network geodatabase to which addresses can be matched. There are two general types of network geodatabases: 1) Transportation (undirected) networks (Figure 7-1), and 2) Geometric Utility (directed) networks.

Transportation (Undirected) Networks

Road, railroad, subway, and pedestrian networks can be traversed along edges (lines) in *any* direction that is allowed (Butler, 2008). In many instances it is permissible to even make U-turns within the network. These are usually referred to as transportation or undirected networks (DeMers, 2002). Transportation networks are used by dispatchers to route fire equipment to a home or send police to an incident. People use transportation network information accessed with their cellphones to determine the fastest or shortest route to a location.

Geometric Utility (Directed) Networks

Some materials in the real world flow in only one direction within a network, unless manipulated by people. These materials or phenomena move within what is referred to as a **geometric utility** or **directed network**. Examples of geometrically directed networks include water, sewer, natural gas, and electrical networks. Natural forces such as gravity and pressure act on these fluid, electromagnetic, and gaseous materials. If desired, managers or engineers can manipulate the rate of flow of the materials within the network by adjusting external forces, such as the terrain slope (gravity) or pressure.

Transportation (Undirected) Network Analysis

Sophisticated geocoding and undirected network analysis requires a specially prepared, topologically correct network geodatabase.

Building a Topologically Correct Transportation (Undirected) Network Geodatabase

The topologically correct (undirected) transportation network is created using the procedures listed in Figure 7-4. It includes a collection of source network information related to the problem to be solved, building the network dataset elements, specifying the network analysis procedures to be performed, and solving the network analysis problem and presenting the results. It is useful to review characteristics of these procedures.

Collect Source Network Information

Typical digitized road networks, railroad networks, and so on, stored in a standard GIS database are useful for numerous relatively simple network visualization problems. For example, you might want to identify all of the major roads and railroads within the network and color code them accordingly. Or, you might want to compute a 200 m buffer around all the four-lane roads. The fundamental network source information consists of the geographic coordinates (x,y) of point and linear features and their attributes. The source network information can be obtained using GPS, remote sensing (primarily photogrammetric and LiDARgrammetric), or digitization of network information from existing maps (Figure 7-4a). The original source information is usually stored in a standard GIS database.

When more complex or sophisticated network analysis is required, such as finding the shortest distance or fastest route from Point A to an address at Point B, then a specially prepared type of network geodatabase must be built (Butler, 2008). This is because in a typical source-network file, simple line features like roads in the database are not aware of one another and do not have knowledge about individual street or intersection turn or barrier characteristics. The line segments don't know that they are connected or in what manner they are connected. In other words, there is no topology associated with the various line and point features in the network.

Build Topologically Correct Network Dataset Elements

A topologically correct network database contains information about the relationships between the following network elements: *edges* (lines), *junctions* (intersections), and *turns* (Figures 7-4b and 7-5). Lines in the original source materials are converted to edges in the topologically correct network dataset. Cars, trucks, animals, and people travel along the edges. Intersection points in the original source materials are converted to junctions in the topologically correct network dataset. Junctions exist wherever two or more edges connect in a network. Turn attribute information determines the direction of travel that can take place along an edge or when two or more edges intersect.

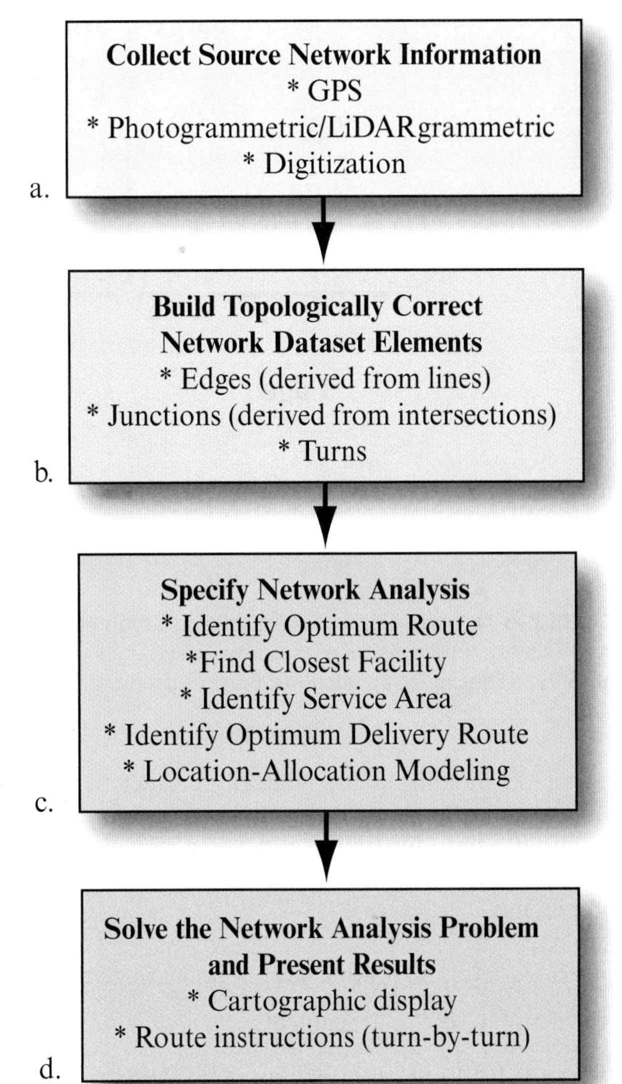

FIGURE 7–4 General network creation and analysis procedures for transportation (undirected) networks. a) Network source materials (lines, intersections, attributes) may be acquired using a variety of techniques. b) The topologically correct network database is built consisting of edges, junctions, turns, and network cost characteristics. c) The type of network analysis is specified. d) The network problem is solved and results presented in cartographic or other formats.

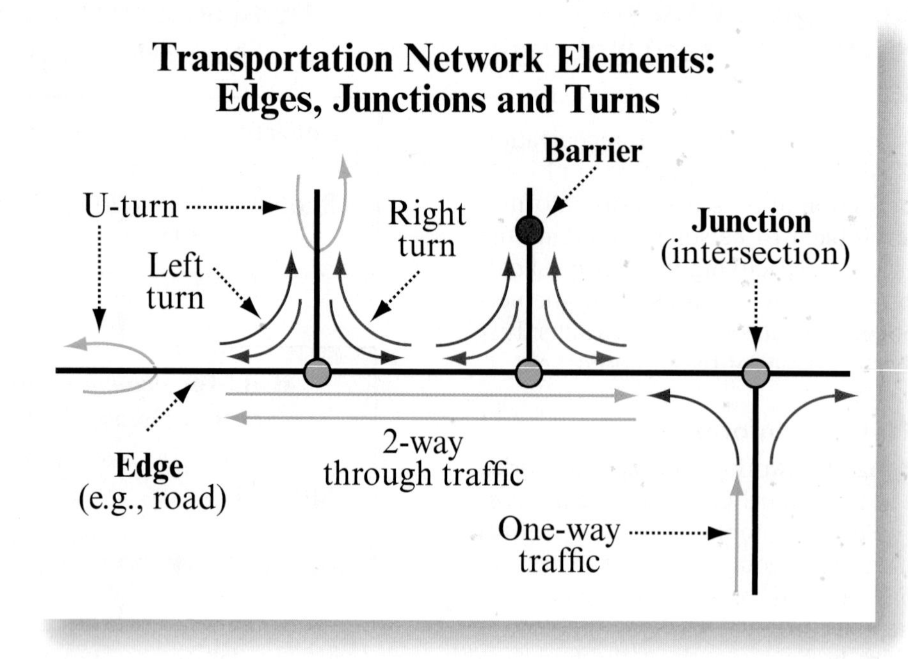

FIGURE 7–5 A topologically correct transportation network consists of network elements, including: edges, junctions, and turns. This example consists of three two-way edges (roads) and a one-way edge (road). Various types of turns are allowed where the edges meet at junctions. Barriers prohibit movement along an edge (adapted from Esri, 2011g).

The person building a topologically correct network database typically includes detailed attribute information about edges, junctions, and turns. For example, the attribute information about a road segment (edge) might include

- the x,y coordinates of the edge segment (e.g., road),
- the length of the road segment,
- two-way traffic is permitted along the edge, or
- only one-way traffic in a certain direction is permitted.

Road junctions can be coded to provide information about

- one-way complete stop,
- two-way complete stop,
- three-way complete stop,
- four-way complete stop,
- four-way warning signals (e.g., yellow),
- four-way traffic signals (e.g., red, green, yellow), and/or
- dead ends (barrier restriction).

The type of turns allowed when two or more edges meet may be specified, such as

- right turns,
- left turns,
- U-turns,
- yield, and/or
- through traffic.

A topologically correct network geodatabase will also include **network cost** (often referred to as **impedance**) information. For example, speed limits can be attributed to network elements such as road segments (edges). Similarly, the time required to pass through an intersection (junction) when turning left, going through the intersection, or turning right can also be specified. Whenever something such as a bus travels over a network element (e.g., a road) and/or passes through an intersection (junction), it accumulates network costs. The network cost can be estimated in terms of distance, time spent, or other calculated variables. Such information is required when trying to determine the shortest distance or most efficient way to get from Point A to Point B, and in other network analysis problems.

This is the type of detailed topological information that must be included in a topologically correct network dataset to perform sophisticated network analysis. For this reason, it is usually necessary to use specialized GIS software to "build" a network dataset that contains correct connectivity policy and appropriate attributes.

The *building process* creates the network elements (edges, junctions, and turns), defines connectivity, and assigns values to the element attributes (Figure 7-4b). GIS software vendors often provide network dataset construction wizards to assist users to prepare network datasets in the appropriate format (e.g., the Esri Network Dataset Wizard; Esri, 2011b,e). Topologically correct network geodatabases may be used to model a single mode of transportation (e.g., a road network) referred to as *unimodal network analysis* or to model multiple modes of transportation at one time (e.g., road, subway, railroad) referred to as *multimodal network analysis.*

Specify the Network Analysis to be Performed and Solve the Problem

Once the topologically correct network geodatabase is constructed, it is possible to specify the type of network analysis to be performed (Figure 7-4c). Network analysis is typically used to solve relatively specific network problems. Examples include:

- selecting the optimum route between two points, i.e., what is the optimum route from my current location to the closest hospital emergency room? This assumes that the addresses of all of the hospitals in the region have been accurately geocoded and placed in a specially-prepared network geodatabase.
- determining the service area of a particular activity or location;
- selecting the optimum route(s) to pick up or deliver at n locations using k vehicles; and
- location/allocation modeling, e.g., given the existence of five pizza restaurants in the city, what would be the ideal location for a new pizza restaurant that minimizes customer travel time? Where can I locate the pizza restaurant to capture 50% of the market share given the existence of two competitors in the area?

The network analysis problem is then solved and the results displayed in cartographic or other formats (Figure 7-4d).

It is useful to review some of the major geospatial questions or problems that can be answered using transportation network analysis.

Network Analysis Problem: What Is the Optimum Route (Shortest Path)?

The path (edge) from one location to another is generally referred to as a **route**. A route consists of a minimum of two points, a starting point and an ending (termination) point. The most simple route starts at Point 1 and terminates at Point 2. You have probably already performed this function by inputting two addresses into an online map server to determine the best route between the two addresses. You have also probably used this to determine the best route from your car's current location to an address or point of interest using a GPS navigation device. Conversely, a complex route begins at Point 1, stops at numerous intervening points, and ends at a terminating point.

There are several important parameters that should be considered when determining the optimum route, including the source of the network, edge and turn impedance, the method of computing the minimum network cost, display of straight line versus the true shape of the optimum route (shortest path), incorporation of barriers or other restrictions, the incorporation of time information, and whether or not to provide written directions.

Source of the Network

The network that is used to determine the optimum route (shortest path) may come from a variety of sources. The analyst could build the topologically correct network geodatabase from original source materials following the steps described in Figure 7-4 using specially prepared GIS network-building software.

The analyst could use a topologically correct network provided by a government agency. For example, a U.S. Bureau of the Census MAF/TIGER/Line network file of downtown Columbia, SC, will be used to demonstrate several route-finding applications in this chapter. As noted earlier, the MAF/TIGER/Line network database includes spatial data for geographic features such as roads, railroads, rivers, and lakes, as well as legal and statistical geographic areas that correspond to the 2009 American Community Survey, 2009 Population Estimates, 2007 Economic Census, and Census 2000 and 2010. The MAF/TIGER/Line Shapefiles do not contain any demographic or economic data. Such data must be downloaded separately from the Bureau of the Census (refer to Chapter 3 and the Appendix). The MAF/TIGER/Line files contain edge, node (junction), and turn information such as that shown in Figures 7-3 and 7-5.

Sometimes the topologically correct network is produced by a commercial firm that specializes in the collection of source materials and building network databases.

Edge and Turn Impedance

Examples of the edges (e.g., roads), junctions (intersections or nodes), and possible turn options found in a typical transportation network are shown in Figure 7-5. The cost of traversing the network edge segments (e.g., roads) is referred to as **edge impedance**. The impedance can refer to the physical distance associated with each edge segment (e.g., 100 m). It can also be translated into edge time impedance if the speed limit of each segment is present in the network database. For example, if we assume the speed limit is 60 mph and a line segment is one mile long, then the edge segment can be traversed in one minute. Impedance information is used in personal navigation devices and other routing programs to estimate the time to the destination.

It should be noted that edge impedance does not have to be associated with just distance or time. The individual edges in a network could be rank-ordered according to how scenic they are, e.g., each edge segment could have a "scenic" ordinal-scale attribute value from 1 to 10. This would allow the least and most scenic routes to be identified. Similarly, each road segment could be attributed with information about how "bumpy" it is, allowing the most smooth or comfortable route to be determined.

Normally, the movement of vehicles or materials must slow down when edges (lines) meet at a junction (intersection). Therefore, it is common for topologically correct network datasets to incorporate **turn impedance** information. For example, Figure 7-5 depicts three two-way edges (e.g., roads) and a one-way edge (road). The edges meet at three formal junctions (intersections). Various types of turns are allowed where the edges meet at the junctions, including left turns, right turns, and U-turns. The time associated with making these types of turns can be stored as turn impedance values in the network database. Normally, left turns and U-turns take more time (e.g., 60–120 seconds) than right turns (e.g., 5 seconds) on two-way streets. GIS network analysis software allows the analyst to specify the exact cost associated with left, right, and U-turns in the networks.

Computing the Minimum Network Cost (e.g., Distance) Using an Impedance Matrix

Now that you appreciate that the actual distance traveled or time consumed can be measured and stored as impedance values, it is important to understand how we compute the minimum cost to travel from various point locations in the network dataset irrespective of the impedance values used (e.g., distance, time, scenic value). This is typically referred to as finding the optimum route or shortest-path analysis.

Shortest-path analysis requires the creation of an impedance matrix. The impedance matrix is computed using the edge information stored in the network database. For example, consider the simple network consisting of the five junctions (nodes) and seven edges (e.g., roads) shown in Figure 7-6a. In this example, the impedance is the distance between two nodes in the network. Note that some of the nodes are not directly connected, i.e., it is not possible to get from Node 1 to Node 5 without passing through Nodes 2, 3, and/or 4. The ~ symbol in the impedance matrix means that there is no direct connection between two of the nodes.

The most common algorithm used to determine the shortest distance to nodes in a network was developed by Dijkstra (1959). The algorithm uses the information stored in an impedance matrix to calculate the shortest distance from Node 1 to all other nodes. It is an interactive process and is the one used in ArcGIS® Network Analysis to solve optimum route problems (Esri, 2011a). We will use an iterative method to determine the shortest path from Node 1 to the other four nodes shown in Figure 7-6a using methods discussed in Lowe and Moryadas (1975) and Chang (2010).

We begin by first filling in the impedance matrix shown in Figure 7-6b. Node 1 is 20 units from Node 2 and 11 units from Node 3. There is no direct connection between Node 1 and Nodes 4 and 5, hence the ~ symbol. Note that the impedance matrix is symmetrical about the diagonal of the matrix. The process continues until the impedance matrix is complete.

The goal is to identify the shortest distance from Node 1 to Nodes 2, 3, 4, and 5 in the network. Some of the required information is already available in the impedance matrix (i.e., Node 1 is 20 units from Node 2 and 11 units from Node 3). However, some of the information required (i.e., the shortest distance from Node 1 to Node 4 and the shortest distance from Node 1 to Node 5) can only be determined using the iterative process described below.

Step 1: We first identify the minimum impedance distance among the two paths that are directly connected to Node 1, i.e., Nodes 2 and 3, as shown in the map (Figure 7-6a) and in the impedance matrix in Figure 7-6b:

$$\min(\text{Path}_{12}, \text{Path}_{13}) = \min(20, 11)$$

Path_{13} is chosen because it has the minimum impedance value (11 units) among the two possible paths. This information is placed in the first line of the shortest-path matrix shown in Figure 7-6c. Node 3 is now part of the solution list associated with Node 1.

Step 2: A new list of potential paths that are directly or indirectly connected to nodes in the solution list (i.e., Nodes 1 and 3) is created:

$$\min(\text{Path}_{12}, \text{Path}_{13}+\text{Path}_{34}, \text{Path}_{13}+\text{Path}_{35}) = \min(20, 26, 31)$$

Path_{12} is chosen because it has the minimum impedance value (20 units) among the possible paths. This information is placed in line 2 of the shortest-path matrix

Shortest-Path Analysis Using an Impedance Matrix Based on Distance

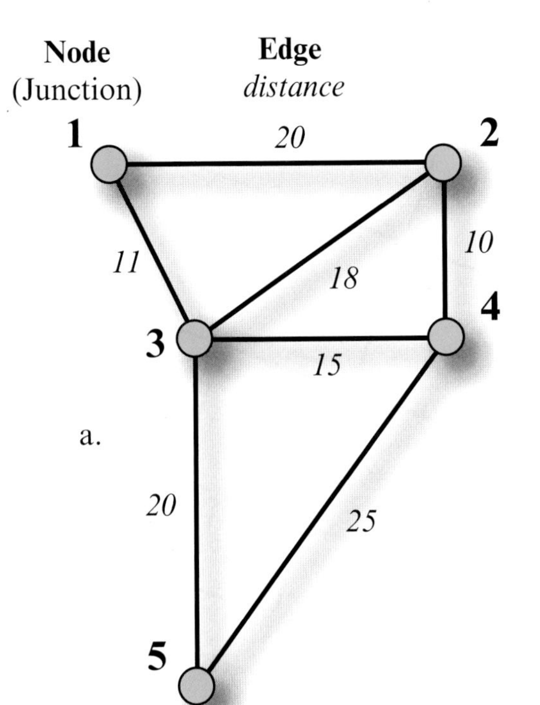

b.

Impendance Matrix for Five Nodes					
	1	2	3	4	5
1	~	20	11	~	~
2	20	~	18	10	~
3	11	18	~	15	20
4	~	10	15	~	25
5	~	~	20	25	~

c.

Shortest Path from Node 1 to All Other Nodes			
From-Node	To-Node	Shortest Path	Minimum Cumulative Impedance
1	3	$Path_{13}$	11
1	2	$Path_{12}$	20
1	4	$Path_{13}$ + $Path_{34}$	26
1	5	$Path_{13}$ + $Path_{35}$	31

FIGURE 7–6 a) The cost impedance (e.g., distance in this example) for seven edges associated with five junctions (nodes). b) The impedance matrix values for each of the five nodes. c) The shortest path from Node 1 to all five of the nodes (adapted from Chang, 2010).

(Figure 7-6c). Nodes 3 and 2 are now part of the solution list associated with Node 1.

Step 3: A new list of potential paths that are directly or indirectly connected to nodes in the solution list (i.e., Nodes 1, 3 and 2) is created:

$$\min(Path_{12}+Path_{24}, Path_{13}+Path_{34}, Path_{13}+Path_{35}) =$$

$$\min(30, 26, 31)$$

We select $Path_{13}$+$Path_{34}$ because it has the minimum impedance value (26 units) among the possible paths and add Node 4 to the solution list (Figure 7-6c).

Step 4: A new list of potential paths that are directly or indirectly connected to nodes in the solution list (i.e., Nodes 1, 3, 2, and 4) is created:

$$\min(Path_{12}+Path_{24}+Path_{45}, Path_{13}+Path_{35}) = \min(55, 31)$$

We select $Path_{13}$+$Path_{35}$ because it has the minimum impedance value (31 units) among the possible paths and add Node 5 to the solution list. The shortest paths from Node 1 to all of the other nodes are now stored in the shortest path matrix (Figure 7-6c). Information such as this could be used in a cell phone or other personal navigation device to identify the optimum route from Node 1 to any of the other nodes. Please note that it would be necessary to create an entirely new shortest path matrix if we wanted to determine the shortest path from Node 2 to all the other nodes, and so on.

Display of Straight Line or True Shape of the Optimum Route (Shortest Path)

The distance from Point 1 to Point 2 in a simple route-finding problem can be computed using a) a straight line or b) the cumulative true distance that takes into account the road network. The network analyst usually has to decide if he or she wants to display the straight-

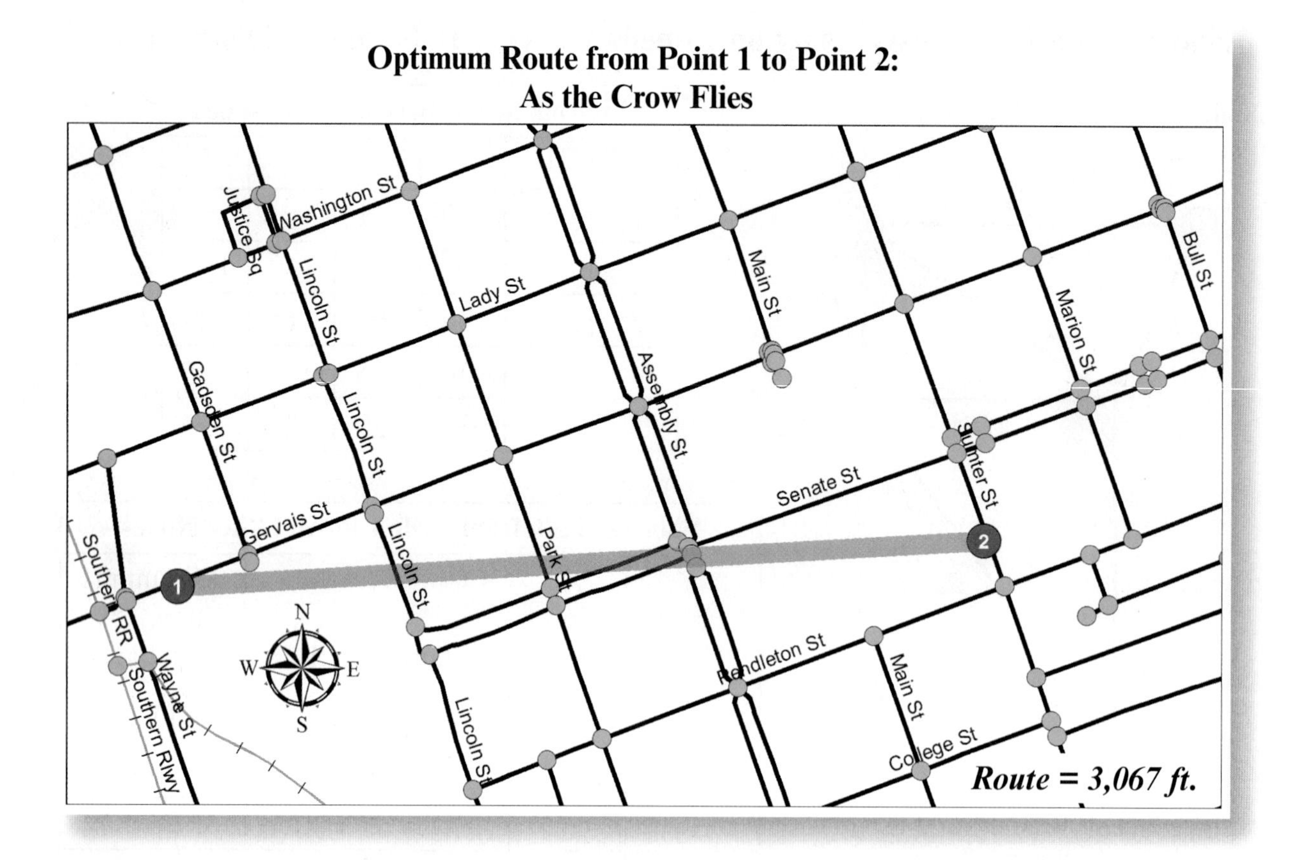

FIGURE 7–7 The transportation network in downtown Columbia, SC, consists of road line segments (edges) and intersections (junctions shown in green) derived from the U.S. Bureau of the Census MAF/TIGER/Line 2009 dataset. The straight-line optimum route (as the crow flies) between Point 1 (origin) and Point 2 (destination) is 3,067 ft. While somewhat informative, the straight line route disregards the existing street network and intervening buildings and other structures (e.g., parks, water bodies) that could be encountered along the route (data courtesy U.S. Bureau of the Census).

line distance between origin and destination points or the true shape of the optimum route.

Displaying the optimum route from the Point 1 origin to the Point 2 termination in a straight line (as the crow flies) is sometimes of value. The determination of the shortest route as a straight line does not require the creation of an impedance matrix. The algorithm simply computes the distance between Points 1 and 2 using the Pythagorean theorem.

The straight-line distance from origin to destination has no regard for the existing road network or the buildings or other features that would be encountered along the route. For example, the straight-line distance from Point 1 to Point 2 in downtown Columbia, SC, based on the Bureau of the Census MAF/TIGER/Line 2009 network data is shown in Figure 7-7. In this case, the optimum straight-line (as the crow flies) route is 3,067 ft. Unfortunately, the route cuts diagonally across the street network and passes through many buildings, parks, and other structures. In fact, this particular route passes directly through the South Carolina State Capitol and office buildings.

Most optimum-route (shortest-path) network-analysis problems display the route from the origin (Point 1) to the destination (e.g., Point 2) in its true shape. For example, the shape of the shortest network path from Point 1 to Point 2 in the downtown Columbia, SC, example is shown in Figure 7-8. This shortest path was determined using the impedance distance information previously described. The length of the optimum route is 3,745 ft. The route follows the existing street network, minimizing the distance from Point 1 to Point 2.

Barriers and Other Restrictions

Unfortunately, the route shown in Figure 7-8 has a serious flaw. The government MAF/TIGER/Line 2009 network database contains a non-existent portion of Senate St. that passes directly through the South Carolina State Capitol grounds as shown in the digital orthophoto in Figure 7-8. In order to create a correct optimum route (shortest path), it would be necessary to a) edit the Senate St. edge or b) include a barrier in

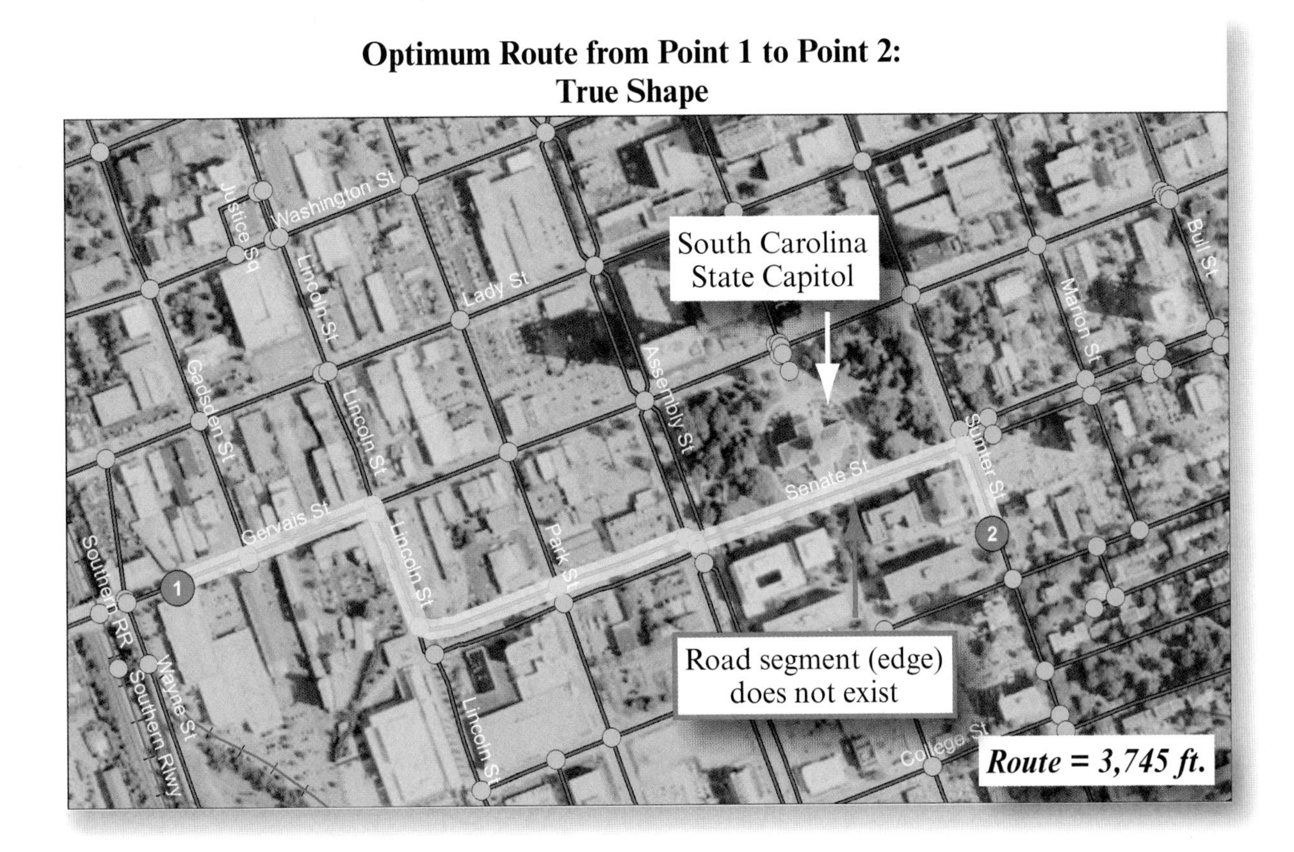

FIGURE 7–8 The true shape of the optimum route from Point 1 to Point 2 in downtown Columbia, SC, based on analysis of MAF/TIGER/Line 2009 network data. Unfortunately, there is an error in the MAF/TIGER/Line network dataset on a portion of Senate St. on the State Capitol grounds. The road segment does not exist. Therefore, the optimum route is incorrect. This flaw demonstrates why it is so important that the network database be as accurate as possible (data courtesy U.S. Bureau of the Census and City of Columbia).

the network database. For illustrative purposes, a barrier was placed at the intersection of Assembly and Senate streets. The optimum route was then recomputed. The result is the correct optimum route shown in Figure 7-9. If desired, there are other types of restrictions that can be included in the optimum-route analysis, including polygonal areas such as parks and water bodies or linear restrictions such as a road under construction. For example, the bad road segment on Senate St. in Figure 7-8 could be designated as a linear restriction instead of using the point barrier at the intersection of Assembly and Senate streets as shown in Figure 7-9.

Network Analysis Problem: Traveling Salesperson Optimum Route

One of the most widely used applications of network analysis is the traveling salesperson problem. A traveling salesperson typically must make several stops during a day. Given knowledge of the location of the several stops, the question becomes "What is the optimum route to take that will minimize the total impedance value (cost)?" The impedance value is typically the distance traveled or time required.

Traveling Salesperson Optimum-Route Considerations

The salesman typically starts at the office, makes the required stops, and returns to the office. For example, let's consider Point 1 in the previous example as being the location of the company office. During the day, the salesman must stop at the five locations identified in Figure 7-10. After considering the previously placed barrier and the location of the required stops, the network solver identified the route shown in Figure 7-10 with the business stops labeled from 2 to 6. The salesman returns to the company office (Point 7) after all five stops have been made.

Note that the MAF/TIGER/Line network database allows U-turns. The route to and from Points 5 and 6 require the vehicle to make a U-turn and travel over the same road segment (edge) previously traversed. The total length of the optimum route to visit the five locations and return home is 10,306 ft. (1.95 mi.).

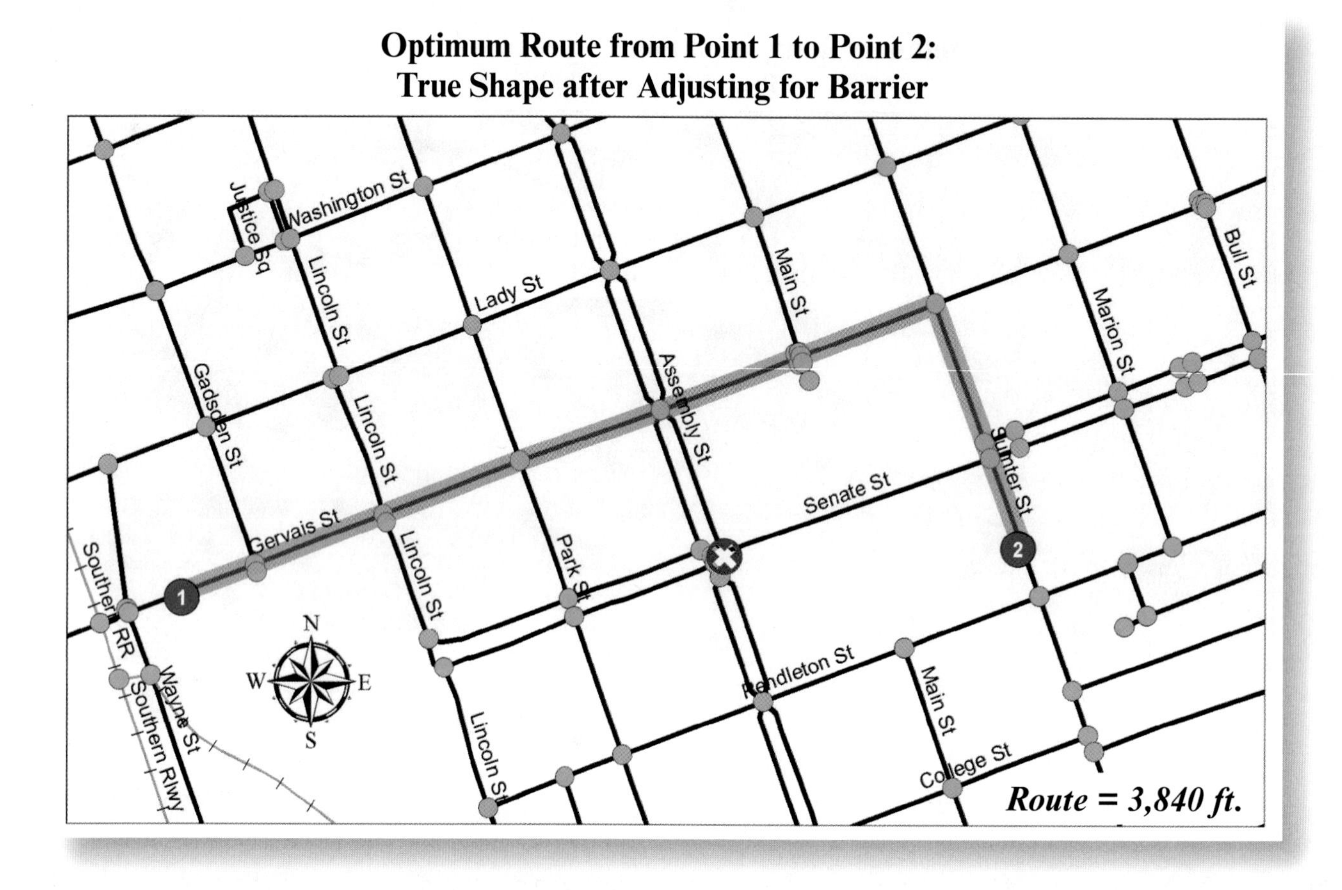

FIGURE 7–9 The true shape of the optimum route from Point 1 to Point 2 after placing a barrier at the corner of Assembly and Senate streets (data courtesy U.S. Bureau of the Census).

Optimum Route Written Directions

Directions are turn-by-turn instructions on how to navigate the route. They can be created for any route that is generated from a network analysis as long as the network dataset supports them. For example, the network directions for the traveling salesperson route shown in Figure 7-10 are

- Proceed 0.05 mile (265 ft.) northeast along Gervais St. and then turn left onto Gadsden St.
- Proceed 0.2 mile (1,041 ft.) northwest on Gadsden St. and then turn right onto Washington St.
- Proceed 0.1 mile (522 ft.) northeast on Washington St. and then turn right on Lincoln St.
- Proceed southeast 0.09 mile (510 ft.) on Lincoln St. and then turn left on Lady St., and so on.

The public generally enjoys written or spoken route directions in addition to map directions. Spoken directions are especially useful and more safe when a person is driving a motor vehicle to the chosen location.

Network Analysis Problem: Where Is the Closest Facility?

One of the most often used network analysis applications is locating the shortest path to a facility such as a police station, fire department, emergency room, grocery store, gas station, automated teller machine (ATM), fast food restaurant, or bank (Boyles, 2002). Sometimes there are hundreds of places to choose from, e.g., fast food restaurants or ATMs, in a city.

Closest-Facility Analysis

When conducting a closest-facility analysis, the analyst usually needs to provide the following information: a) the origin of the search (usually the current location), b) the maximum number of facilities that may be considered (e.g., 20), c) how far away you are willing to search (i.e., a cutoff distance value such as 5 miles) or maximum time to the facility (e.g., 3 minutes), d) the direction of search (i.e., from the origin to each of the selected facilities or from the facilities to the origin), and e) the location of any known barriers that exist at the present time (e.g., a closed road intersection). The network cost can be in whatever units the user desires.

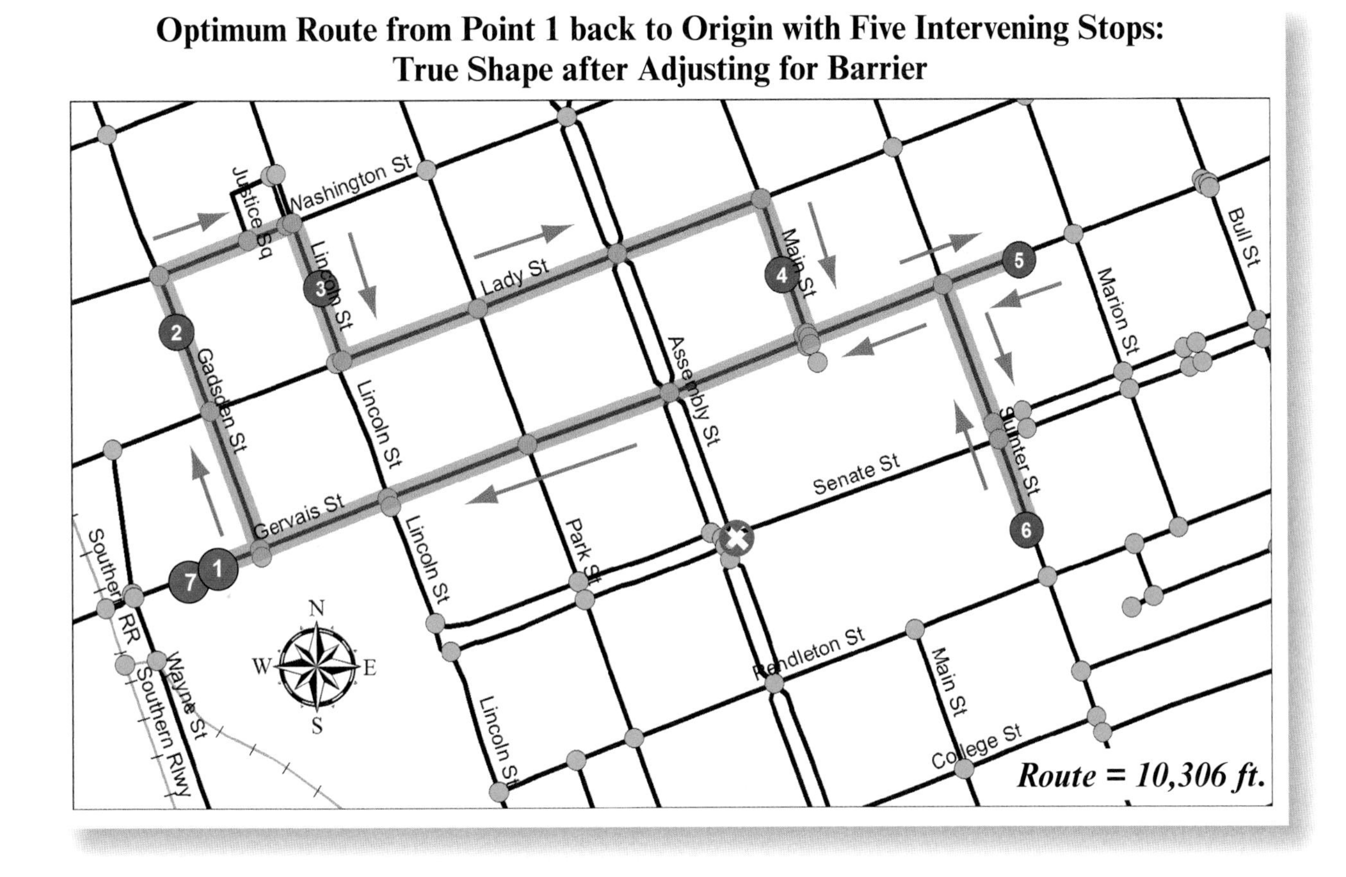

FIGURE 7–10 An example of the traveling salesperson problem. The goal is to determine the optimum route from the company office (Point 1) back to the origin with five intervening stops. The solution takes into consideration a barrier at the corner of Assembly and Senate streets. Note that the network turn criteria allows U-turns after visiting Point 5 and Point 6. Point 7 is back at the origin (Point 1) (data courtesy U.S. Bureau of the Census).

However, it is typically measured in units of distance or time. The closest facility algorithm then typically computes the round-the-block cost from the origin to each of the candidate facilities that meet the criteria. The facility with the minimum cost is the closest facility. The route is identified and mapped, and written and/or verbal instructions created.

Consider the closest-facility network-analysis problem shown in Figure 7-11. The yellow ball is the origin (e.g., your current location in an automobile). You are running short of money and need to locate the closest ATM from your current location. There are numerous ATMs in the vicinity but you do not want to travel more than one mile because you have upcoming business downtown. Note that there is one barrier in place because you are not allowed to drive across the State Capitol grounds to get to the facility. The closest-facility algorithm computes the distance from your location and identifies the ATM located on Washington St. near Assembly St. as the closest facility (0.62 mile; 3,265 ft.). If desired, the algorithm can be instructed to provide detailed turn-by-turn directions so that you can navigate to the ATM using verbal or written instructions.

Locating the closest-facility application is one of the most heavily used GIS network applications on mobile phones (Fu and Sun, 2010). Users typically use their current location as the origin and let the software locate the closest facilities. Ideally, the database is robust and contains location and attribute information about all of the possible facilities.

Network Analysis Problem: What Is the Service Area of a Particular Facility?

Facilities such as ATMs, gas stations, or fast-food restaurants serve a certain geographic area associated with a certain clientele. The dimensions of the service areas are usually specified according to travel distance or travel time away from the facility.

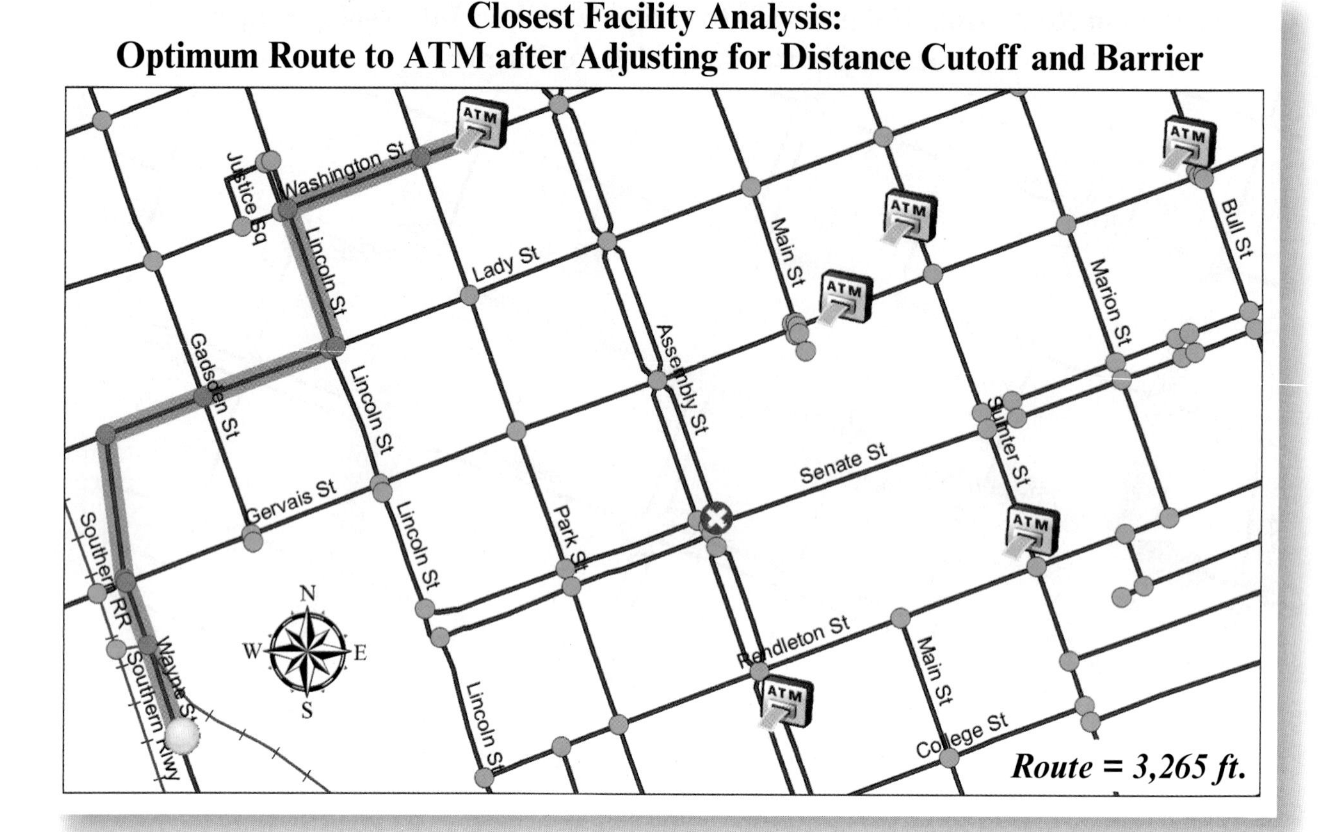

FIGURE 7–11 Example of the closest facility problem. The algorithm computes the distance from the origin to each of the six ATMs in the network. It then selects the route with the minimum distance. In this example, a cutoff value of 1 mile was used, i.e., the algorithm did not consider ATMs greater than 1 mile from the origin. The solution took into consideration the barrier at the intersection of Assembly and Senate streets. Therefore, the ATM at the corner of Pendleton and Assembly streets was not selected (data courtesy U.S. Bureau of the Census).

Network Service Area Analysis

The **network service area** is the geographic region that encompasses all parts of the network that can be reached within a certain impedance (cost) value. This is often referred to as allocation modeling, which identifies the parts of the network that meet the minimum or maximum impedance criteria specified by the user either from or to a facility, such as a fire station (Lo and Yeung, 2007). For example, if distance is selected as the impedance value, then it is possible to identify all parts of the transportation network that are less than 1 mile from the fire station. If time is selected as the impedance value, it is possible to identify all parts of the network within 5 minutes of the fire station. Service area can be calculated based on all types of networks, including road, subway, bus, pedestrian, railroad, airline, water supply, sewer, etc. Once service areas are identified, they can be used to estimate how many people or other phenomena lie within the service areas.

It is straightforward to identify the service areas of facilities using a topologically correct network database. The user simply needs to identify the type of network to be evaluated (e.g., road); the locations of the existing facilities (e.g., fast-food restaurants); type of impedance (e.g., distance or travel time); any point, line, or area barrier restrictions within the region (e.g., closed streets), and the type of display desired (e.g., polygonal service area or the service area along edges [e.g., roads] in the network).

Service areas can be created in two directions: a) the direction away from the facility or b) the direction toward the facility. This is important because the network may contain impedance values that result in travel time being different depending upon whether you are going toward or away from the facility. For example, the service area for a pizza delivery restaurant would normally be created "away from the facility" since pizzas are delivered from the store to the customer. Conversely, an emergency room analysis should

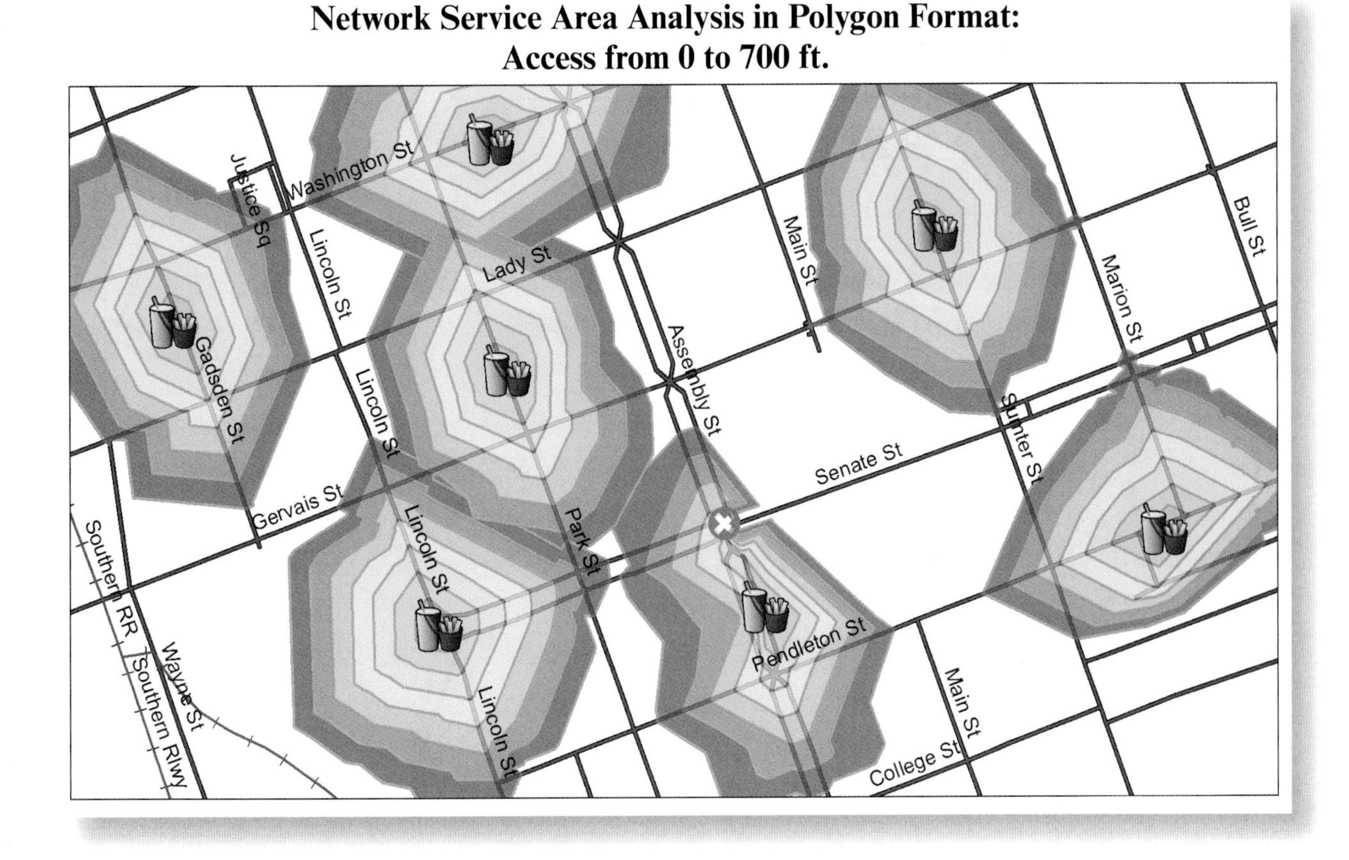

FIGURE 7–12 An example of service area analysis in polygon format. In this example, the algorithm computes the distance from the seven fast-food restaurants outward to a distance of 700 ft. The algorithm takes into consideration a barrier at the corner of Assembly and Senate streets (data courtesy U.S. Bureau of the Census).

choose "toward the facility" because the most important part of the trip for the patient may be from their location to the emergency room or hospital.

Network service area delineation will be demonstrated using the location of seven fast-food restaurants that can be walked to at lunch time in downtown Columbia, SC. The fast-food restaurants are typically found on the first floor of buildings that house other uses (e.g., corporate offices and apartments). People walk to these fast-food restaurants. Therefore, walking distance is more important than driving distance. Normally, people do not want to walk a great distance to a fast-food restaurant for lunch, e.g., >700 ft. In this example we will use distance measured in feet as the impedance value.

The service area surrounding each of seven existing fast-food restaurants from 0 to 700 ft. is shown in polygon format in Figure 7-12. The seven color-coded class intervals from green to red (0 to 700 ft., respectively) that intersect the road network around each fast-food restaurant are what is important. Note that there is a substantial amount of geographic area in downtown Columbia that is not within 700 ft. of a fast-food restaurant. Such information will be of value when we determine where a new fast-food restaurant should be located in the subsequent section.

The service area of the seven fast-food restaurants from 0 to 700 ft. is shown in linear format in Figure 7-13. The linear display shows the true distance from each restaurant along each road in the network. It is less cluttered and quite informative. Any dark orange or red portion of a road is >500 ft. from a fast-food restaurant.

Joining Service Area and Point Information to Identify Candidate Locations

Service area information can be especially useful for locating potential sites for new establishments such as schools, distribution centers, or retail stores like fast-food restaurants. For example, Figure 7-14 displays the seven aforementioned fast-food restaurants plus five potential fast-food sites selected by the analyst. The goal is to identify which of the potential fast-food sites would be the best place to locate a new restaurant. A major assumption will be that the optimum new fast-

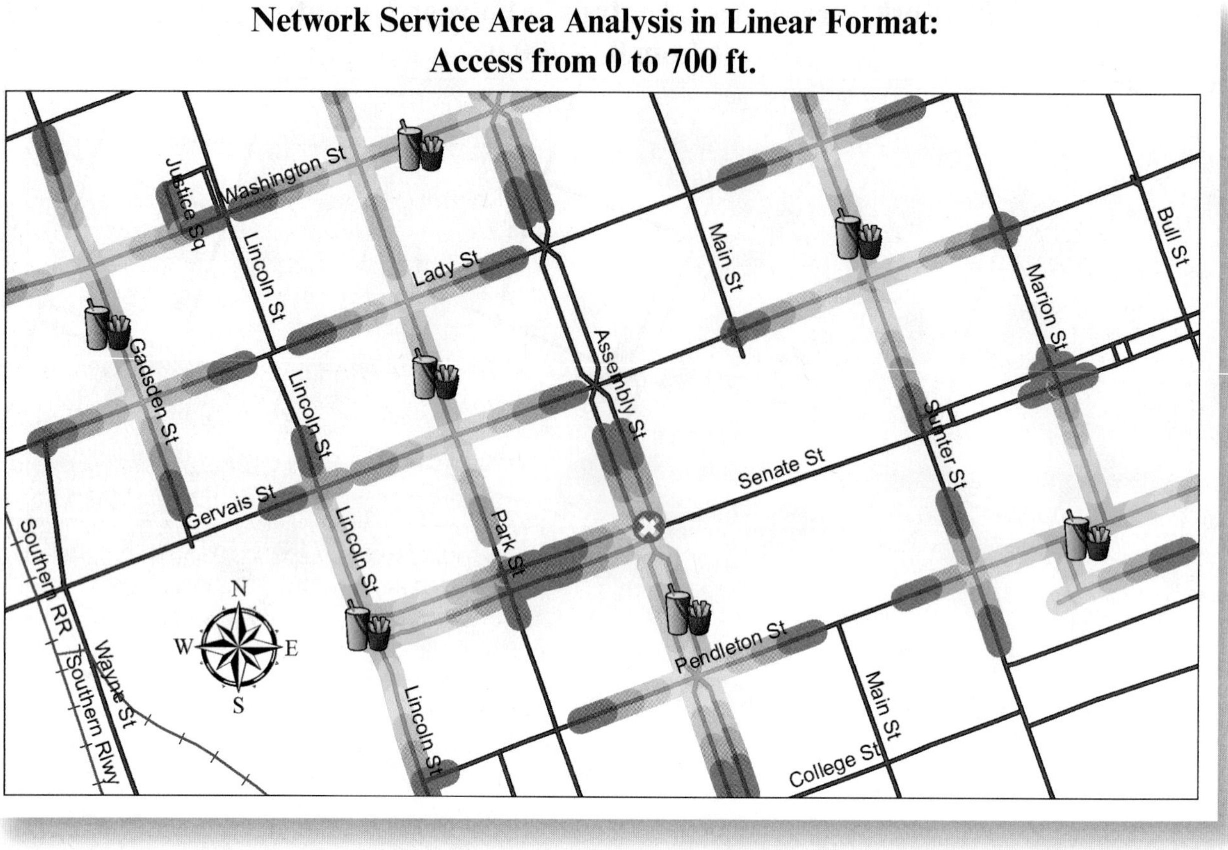

Network Service Area Analysis in Linear Format: Access from 0 to 700 ft.

FIGURE 7–13 An example of service area analysis in linear format. In this example, the algorithm computes the distance from the fast-food restaurant outward to a distance of 700 ft. The algorithm takes into consideration a barrier at the corner of Assembly and Senate streets (data courtesy U.S. Bureau of the Census).

food sites should not reside within 700 ft. of an existing fast-food restaurant.

The service areas of the seven existing fast-food restaurants and the five potential sites are displayed in Figure 7-15. Although this graphic is informative, it doesn't provide the more detailed information required to identify the best locations for the new restaurant.

Therefore, the service areas of the existing seven fast-food restaurants were "joined" with the location of the five potential fast-food sites. The result was a new file containing attribute information that identified only two of the potential sites as being >700 ft. away from existing fast-foot restaurants. The two good potential sites are located at #4P and #5P in Figure 7-15. This analysis only considered distance as the major cost impedance factor. The user could now use other factors (e.g., access, parking, monthly lease, client economic status) to determine which of the two locations is most suitable for a new restaurant.

Use of Origin–Destination (O-D) Cost Matrix Information

It is also possible to identify the optimum location(s) for the new fast-food restaurants using an origin-destination matrix. An **origin–destination matrix** consists of the cost (usually measured in distance or time) from each of the *n* origins to each of the *m* destinations. For example, the 35 origin–destination connections between the seven existing fast-food restaurants (origins) and five potential fast-food locations (destinations) are shown in Figure 7-16. It is important to note that although there is a straight line between each origin and destination, the actual length of the line stored in the network database is based on the "round-the-block" distances associated with the edges (lines) for each origin–destination (O–D) pair. The distances for each of the origin–destination pairs are summarized in Table 7-2.

It is a straightforward matter to determine if a potential fast-food location is within *x* feet of an existing fast-foot location by evaluating the origin–destination matrix. For example, let's use the same criteria as be-

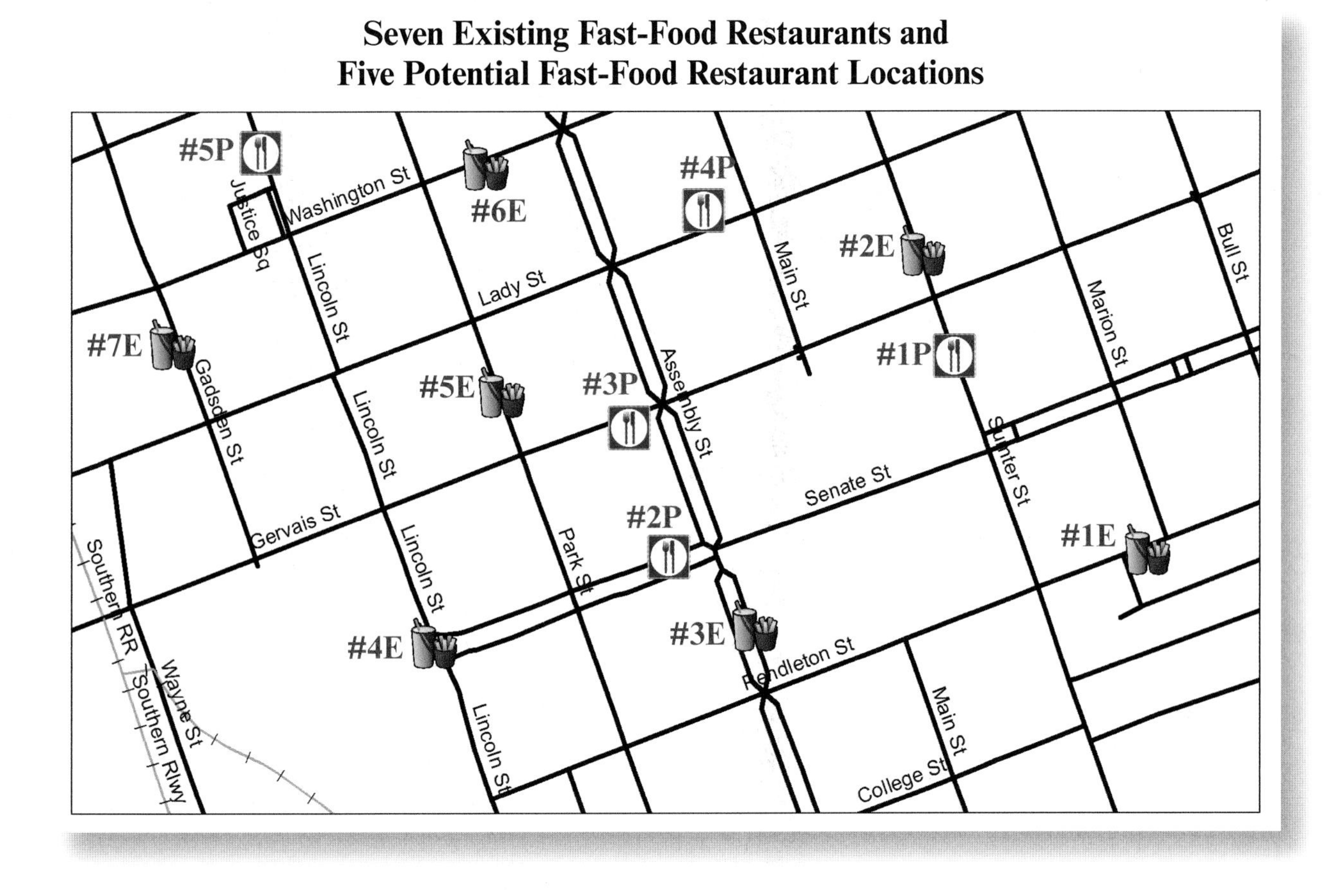

FIGURE 7–14 Location of seven existing fast-food restaurants (labeled #1E to #7E) and five potential fast-food restaurants (labeled #1P to #5P) (data courtesy U.S. Bureau of the Census).

fore where the potential fast-food restaurant must be >700 ft. from existing fast-foot restaurants. The O–D distance from #2E to #1P equals 388 ft. (Table 7-2; Figure 7-16). The O–D distance from #3E to #2P equals 496 ft. The O–D distance from #5E to #3P equals 633 ft. Examination of Table 7-2 reveals that only two of the potential fast-food locations, #4P and #5P, are >700 ft. from all existing locations. The results are substantiated in map format in Figure 7-17, where three of the potential restaurant O–D line segments (#1P, 2P, and 3P) lie within the existing 0–700 ft. restaurant service area.

Network Analysis Problem: Location-Allocation Modeling for Facility Location

Location-allocation modeling is defined as finding the best locations for one or more new facilities that will service a given set of points and then assigning those points to the facilities, taking into account factors such as the number of facilities available, their cost, and the maximum impedance (e.g., distance or time) from a facility to a point (Kennedy, 2001). Location-allocation modeling can help answer important spatial problems such as:

- Given the geographic distribution of *n* police stations in a city, where would be the best place to locate a new police station?
- If a retail petroleum company that operates gas stations has to close one or two of its stores, which store(s) should it close to maintain the greatest overall demand for its products?
- Given the location of existing furniture distribution centers, where should a new furniture factory be built to minimize the distance to the furniture distribution centers?

Some location-allocation problems can be organized according to the following criteria (Esri, 2011c,d):.

- Maximize attendance,
- Minimize impedance,
- Maximize market share,
- Maximize coverage, or
- Target market share.

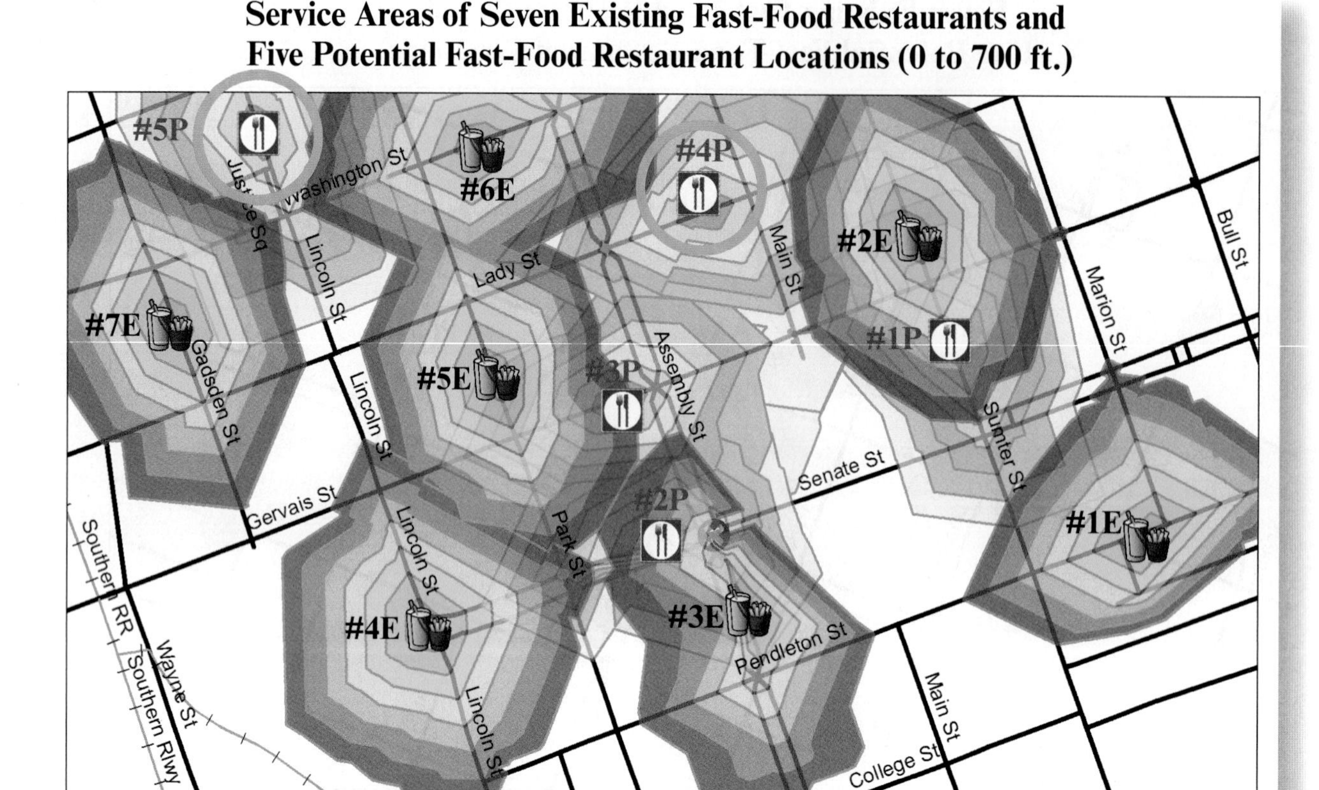

FIGURE 7–15 The service areas associated with the seven existing fast-food restaurants (labeled #1E - #7E) and five potential fast-food restaurants (labeled #1P - #5P) from 0 to 700 ft. in two contrasting color schemes. After "joining" the service area of the seven existing fast-food restaurants with the location of the five potential fast-food restaurants, only two potential locations (#4P and #5P) were outside the 0 to 700 ft. service area of the existing fast-food restaurants (data courtesy U.S. Bureau of the Census).

It is useful to demonstrate a few of these location-allocation problems using ArcGIS® Network Analyst.

Maximize Attendance Problem

Maximize attendance location-allocation modeling can be used to solve neighborhood store location problems where the proportion of demand allocated to the chosen candidate facility or facilities falls within a specified time or distance to the demand points (e.g., 5 minutes or 7 miles). The demand is usually in the form of point values that may represent a variety of characteristics such as total population within a Census Tract or school district, age of the population, per capita income, years of education, property value, etc. The best individual candidate facility or the best set of candidate facilities (e.g., three facilities) that maximize the total allocated demand are selected. This type of modeling usually requires a specific impedance cutoff beyond which demand is not considered (e.g., 5 minutes of travel time or 7 miles distance). To demonstrate maximize attendance location-allocation modeling, we will use the topologically correct geodatabase of downtown San Francisco, CA, shown graphically in Figure 7-18a (Source: Tele Atlas, Inc. and Esri [2011d]. Used by permission).

The Network The transportation network in this dataset contains detailed information about each street and major road segment including turn and U-turn characteristics. Various parks, reservoirs, and other water bodies are also included in the database.

Candidate Facilities That Provide Goods or Services There are thirteen 3-dimensional building icons present in Figure 7-18a. These gray buildings represent *candidate facilities* (stores) that could provide the goods or services of interest, i.e., they are potentially good places for locating a new store. The placement of these initial candidate facilities must be given very careful consideration by the user. Their location usually must take into account many types of information. Distributing the initial candidate facility locations based on faulty logic will invariably cause the location-allocation modeling procedures to yield inaccurate or

TABLE 7–2 Origin–Destination (O–D) Matrix for the seven existing fast-food restaurants (E), and the five potential restaurants (P) shown in Figure 7-16.

Origin–Destination Pair	Round-the-block Distance	O–D Pair	Round-the-block Distance	O–D Pair	Round-the-block Distance	O–D Pair	Round-the-block Distance
1E–1P	1300	3E–2P	496	5E–3P	633	7E–3P	2239
1E– 2P	2181	3E–3P	1026	5E–2P	1124	7E–2P	2258
1E–3P	2712	3E–1P	1738	5E–4P	1197	7E–4P	2688
1E–4P	2714	3E–4P	1809	5E–5P	1614	7E–1P	3664
1E–5P	4921	3E–5P	3235	6E–5P	1061		
2E–1P	388	4E–2P	959	6E–4P	1217		
2E–4P	1025	4E–3P	1448	6E–3P	1512		
2E–3P	1370	4E–5P	1864	6E–2P	2028		
2E–2P	1886	4E–4P	2475	6E–1P	2607		
2E–5P	3280	4E–1P	2555	7E–5P	1036		

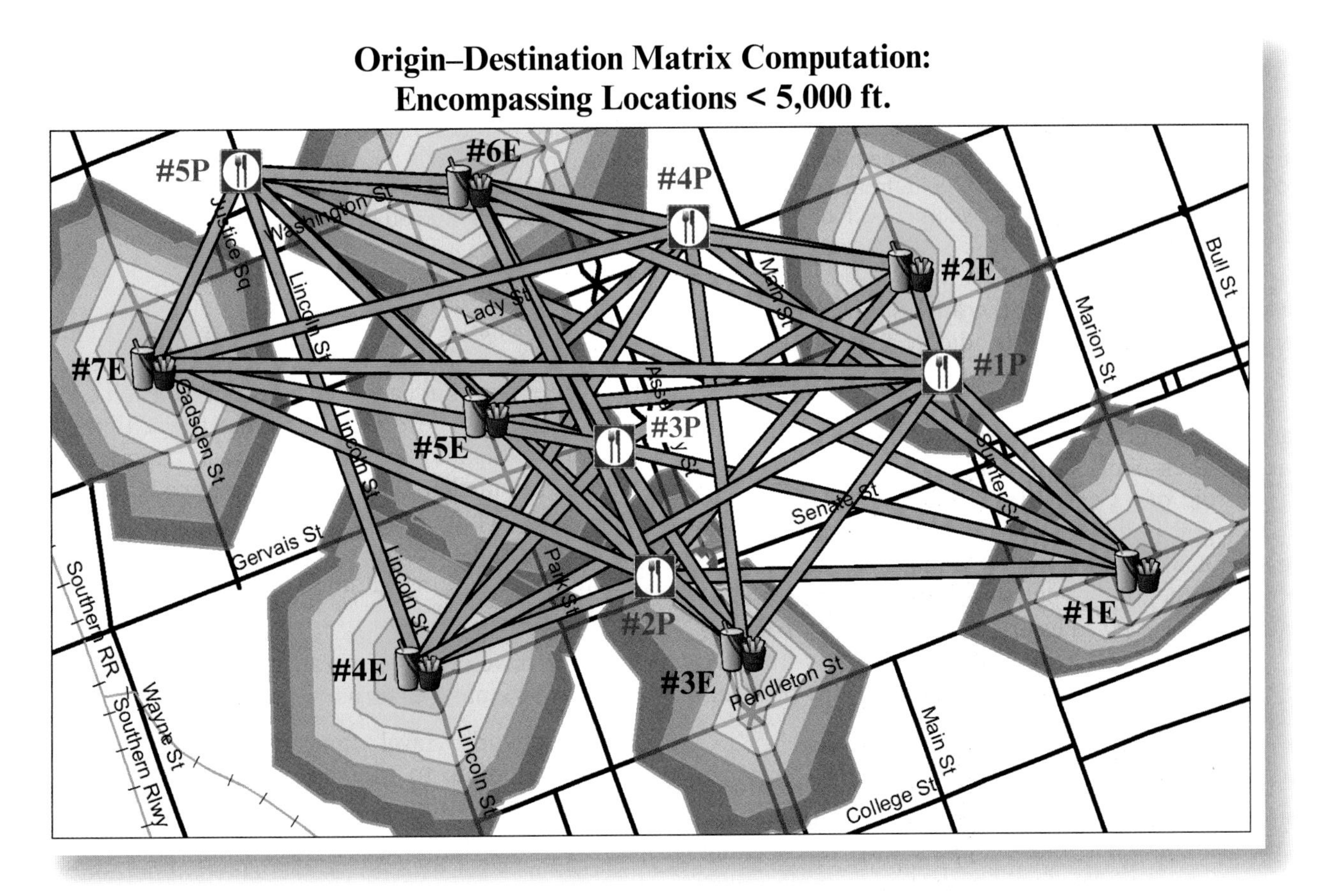

FIGURE 7–16 Connections between seven existing fast-food restaurants (origins) and five potential fast-food locations (destinations). All relationships are shown because the origin–destination distance criteria cutoff was set at 5,000 ft. The "round-the-block" distance for each origin–destination (O–D) segment is found in Table 7-2 (data courtesy U.S. Bureau of the Census).

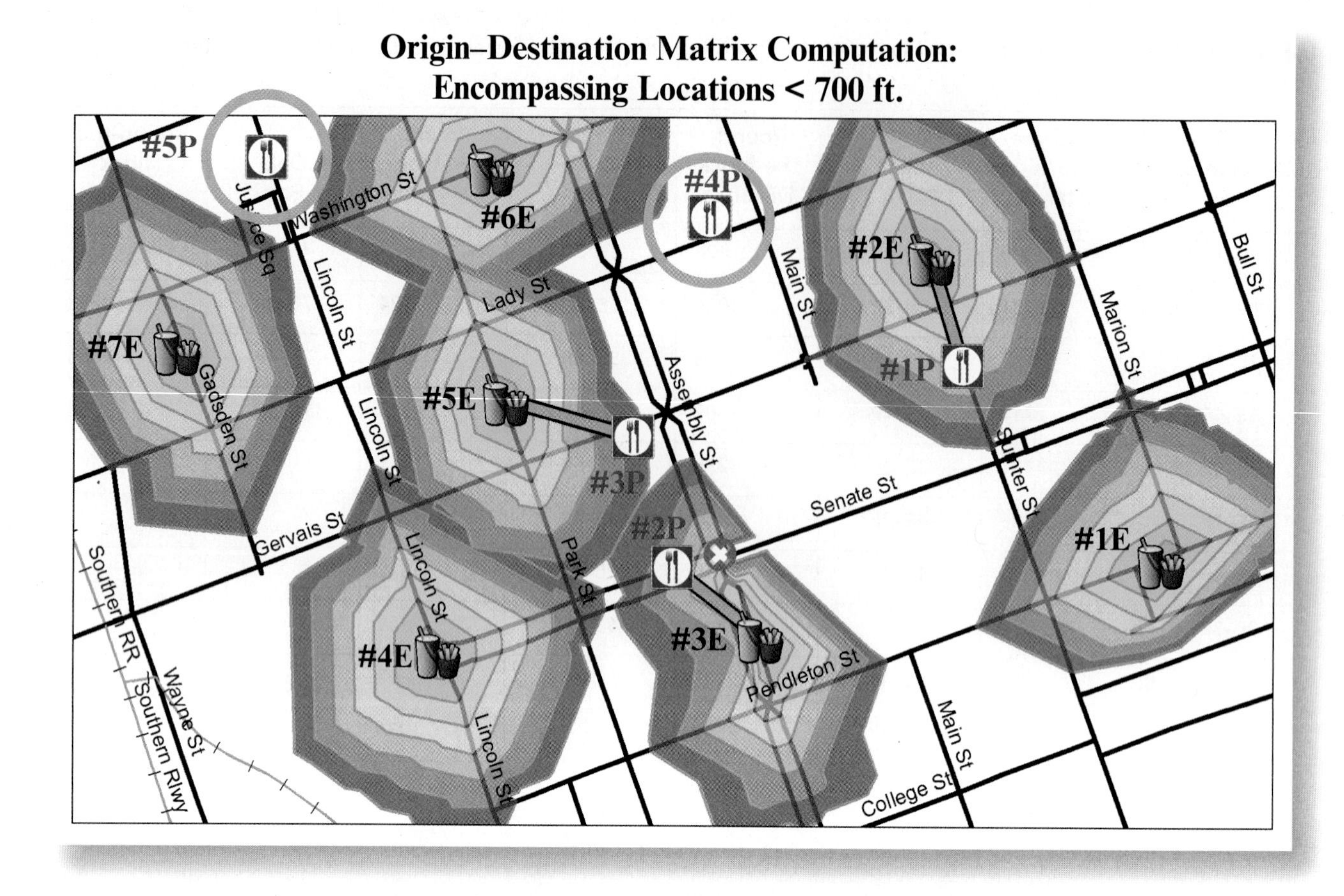

FIGURE 7–17 Origin–destination (O–D) connections between seven existing fast-food restaurants (origins) and five potential fast-food locations (destinations). The three origin-destinations < 700 ft. are identified in blue (#1P, #2P, and #3P). Two of the potential fast-food locations are >700 ft. from existing fast-food restaurants (#4P and #5P). The "round-the-block" distances for each origin-destination (O–D) segment is found in Table 7-2 (data courtesy U.S. Bureau of the Census).

unsatisfactory results. So, the analyst should be very careful when locating the candidate facilities that are to be evaluated.

Demand Points for the Goods and Services In this example, each circle symbol in the database represents the centroid of a Census Tract (Figure 7-18a). The actual polygon boundaries of the Census Tracts are not shown. Each centroid point location contains information about the total population living within each Census Tract in 2000. This is often referred to as the *demand* information because it is the people within the Census Tract who demand (i.e., purchase) the products or services.

Model Assumptions and Results Modeling location-allocation is a twofold problem that simultaneously locates candidate facilities and allocates demand points to the candidate facilities. In this example, several important parameters were set to determine the best location for one, two, and three new retail stores among the candidate stores:

- The impedance value selected was travel time in minutes (not distance) from each demand point (i.e., the population in each Census Tract) to each candidate facility. The direction of the travel time was from the demand point (i.e., Census Tract) to the candidate facility. The travel time impedance value was set at 6 minutes, meaning that people within the Census Tracts are not willing to travel more than 6 minutes from their home to shop at these retail stores.
- People traveling on the transportation network are allowed to make U-turns.
- The network travel time in minutes from the demand points to the selected candidate facilities are shown as straight lines on the maps. It is important to remember, however, that although they are shown as straight lines, the actual computation was based on the "round-the-block" travel times from each demand point to each candidate facility within the network.

Location-Allocation: Neighborhood Store Location Problem Using *Maximize Attendance* Logic

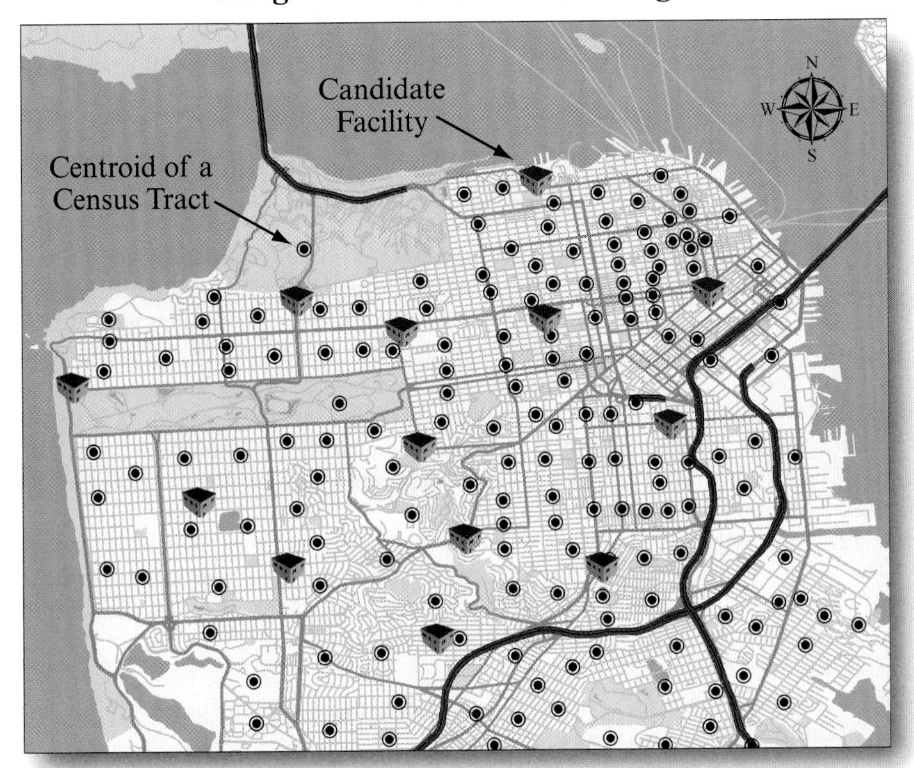

a. The buildings represent candidate facilities and the circular symbols represent the centroids of Census Tracts with population estimated in 2000.

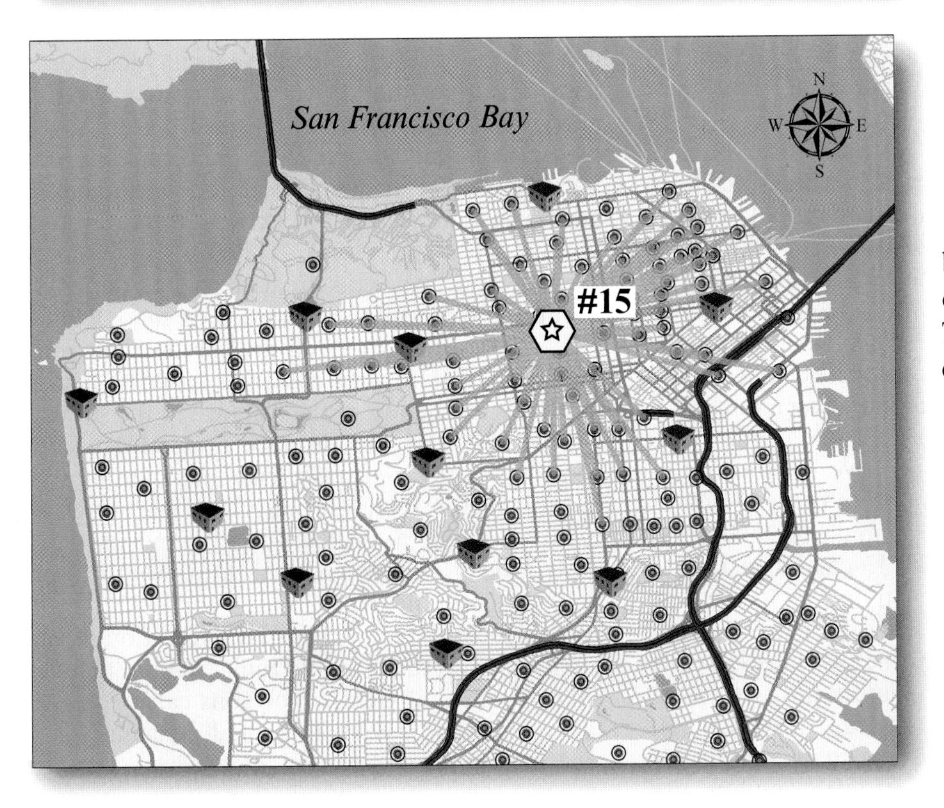

b. Optimum location for one new facility (#15). The travel-time impedance cutoff was 6 minutes.

FIGURE 7–18 An example of identifying the optimum location for one new facility in downtown San Francisco, CA. a) The U.S. Bureau of the Census population in each of the Census Tracts is represented by a circle. The 13 candidate facility locations are shown as 3-dimensional gray buildings. b) The optimum location for one new store that takes into account the surrounding population and travel time in minutes (Source of data: Tele Atlas and Esri. Used by permission).

- The location-allocation model was run multiple times to identify the best single, two, and three candidate facility locations for the new retail stores.

The single best candidate facility is shown in Figure 7-18b. Lines radiate from the selected facility to each of the demand points that are < 6 minutes away from the chosen facility. In this model run, seventy-three (73) Census Tract centroids were allocated to candidate facility #15. There are 133,129 people within the 73 Census Tracts. The travel time and/or distance traveled from each demand centroid to the candidate facility is also available.

The two best candidate facilities (#14 and #15) are shown in Figure 7-19a. Lines radiate from the two selected facilities to each of the demand points that are <6 minutes away from the facilities. The chosen retail store location #14 would service 89,959 people and the chosen location #15 would service 125,563 people, respectively.

The three best candidate facilities chosen (#4, #14, and #15) are shown in Figure 7-19b. Lines radiate from the three selected facilities to each of the demand points that are <6 minutes away from the facilities. Store #14 is associated with 49 Census Tracts with a total of 88,594 people. Store #15 is associated with 65 Census Tracts with a total of 125,426 people. Store #4 is associated with 34 Census Tracts and a total of 60,317 people.

Incorporating Existing Facilities in the Modeling Process School districts usually have schools already in existence when they try to identify the optimum location for a new school. Companies often have stores already in the area when they try to identify the optimum location for a new store. When such conditions exist, it is possible to incorporate the existing facility information during the location-allocation modeling.

For example, two existing stores have been added to the candidate facility dataset shown in Figure 7-20a. It is logical that these two stores should be taken into consideration in addition to the 13 candidate facility locations previously used when trying to locate new stores in the neighborhood. Let us assume that we hold the assumptions constant from the previous example (e.g., impedance cutoff is <6 minutes) and attempt to identify the optimum location for three new facilities. The difference is, however, that we also include the location of the two existing facilities in the analysis. By doing so we should be able to identify which Census Tracts are already allocated to the two existing facilities plus identify three new facilities that do not compete with the two existing facilities.

The market areas associated with the two existing facilities are clearly identified in Figure 7-20b. People from the census tract centroids connected to these stores are expected to shop at these two stores. The most northern existing store in Figure 7-20a is allocated 43 Census Tracts with a total population of 100,787. The most southern existing store in Figure 7-20a is allocated 27 of the Census Tracts with a total population of 68,352.

Three additional candidate facilities are identified (#3, #4, and #14) as shown in Figure 7-20b. Note that these are not the same candidate facilities chosen during the previous example that did not have information about existing stores. Candidate facility #15 was not selected because it was too close in proximity to the two existing stores. Instead, candidate facility #3 was chosen, which services 19 census tracts with a total population of 45,330.

This is a very practical type of location-allocation network analysis because it takes into consideration both existing and candidate facilities.

Network Analysis Problem: Maximize Market Share

Maximize market share location-allocation modeling can be used to solve competitive facility location problems. The algorithms select the optimum location for new facilities that maximize market share given the presence of competitors. Thus, the competing facilities must be present in the network dataset in addition to candidate facilities and any existing stores.

Gravity model concepts are used to determine the proportion of demand allocated to each candidate facility (e.g., 45%). Gravity models are based on the principle that the probability of a customer shopping at a specific store is a function of the distance to the store, its attractiveness, and the distance and attractiveness of competing sites. Generally, customers are more likely to shop at stores that are closer to home, which can be modeled using a distance-decay function, i.e., the greater the distance from home, the lower the probability that a consumer will shop at a particular store (Esri, 2011c,d). Gravity model spatial interaction research is often based on the work of Huff (1966). In practice, the characteristics of Census polygons can be substituted for information about individual consumers. This is true in the examples used here where the demand points represent the total number of people living within each Census Tract. The socioeconomic variable associated with the Census Tracts could just as well be per capita income or highest academic degree obtained. The set of facilities is chosen that maximizes the total allocated demand.

Location-Allocation: Neighborhood Store Location Problem Using *Maximize Attendance* Logic

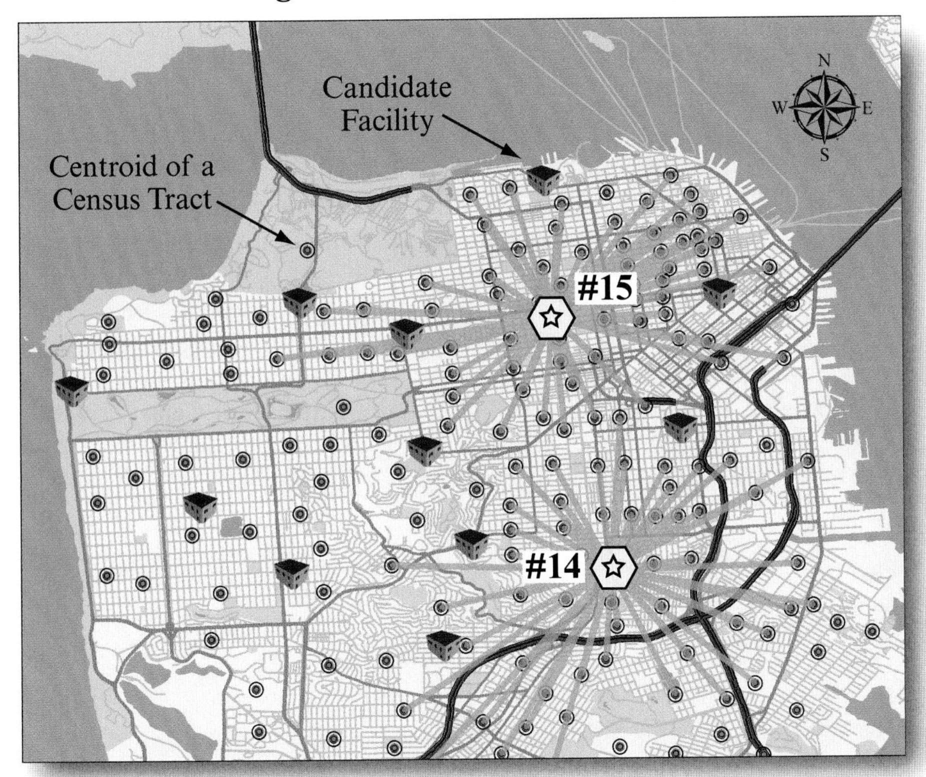

a. Optimum location for two new facilities (#14 and #15). The travel-time impedance cutoff was 6 minutes.

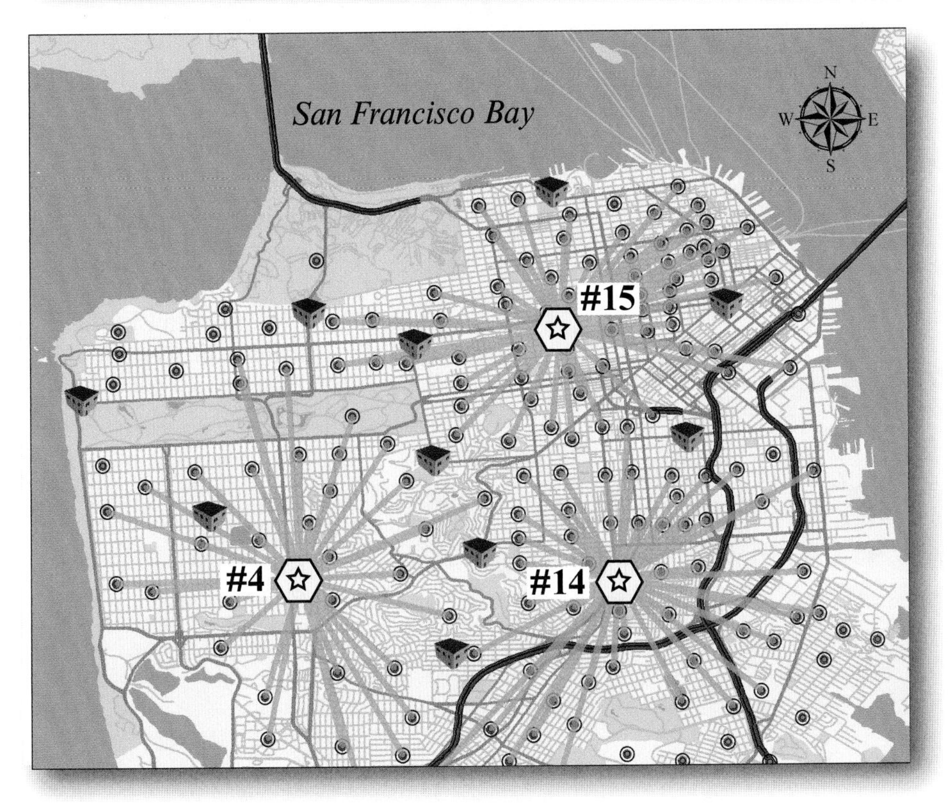

b. Optimum location for three new facilities (#4, #14, and #15).

FIGURE 7–19 a) The optimum locations for two new stores that take into account the surrounding population and travel time in minutes. b) The optimum locations for three new stores (Source of data: Tele Atlas and Esri. Used by permission).

Location-Allocation: Neighborhood Store Location Problem Using *Maximize Attendance* and *Existing Facility* Logic

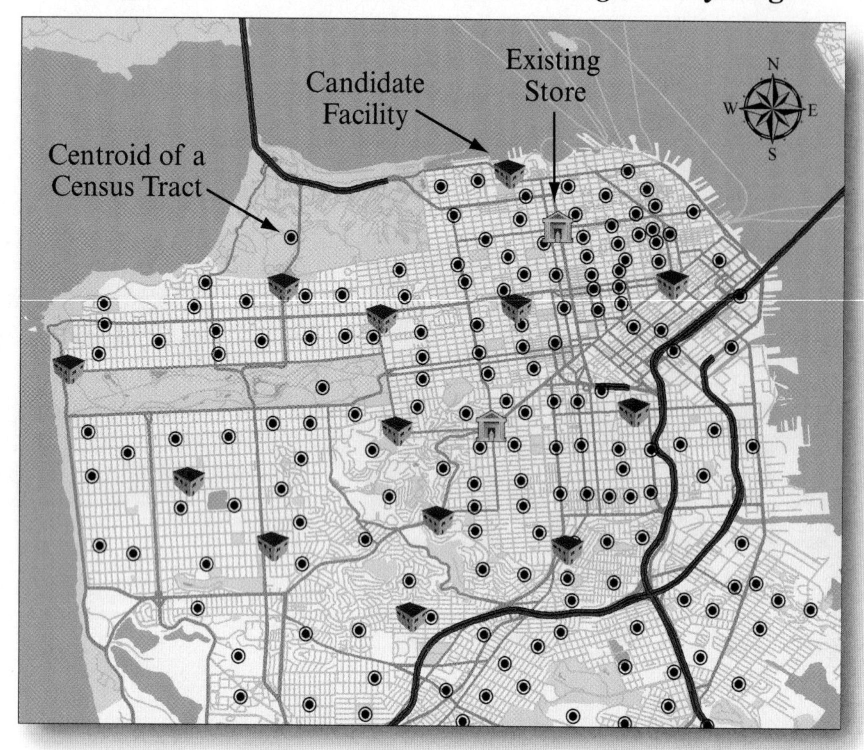

a. Two existing stores are identified. The same 13 candidate facilities are shown. The circle symbols represent the centroids of Census Tracts with population estimated in 2000.

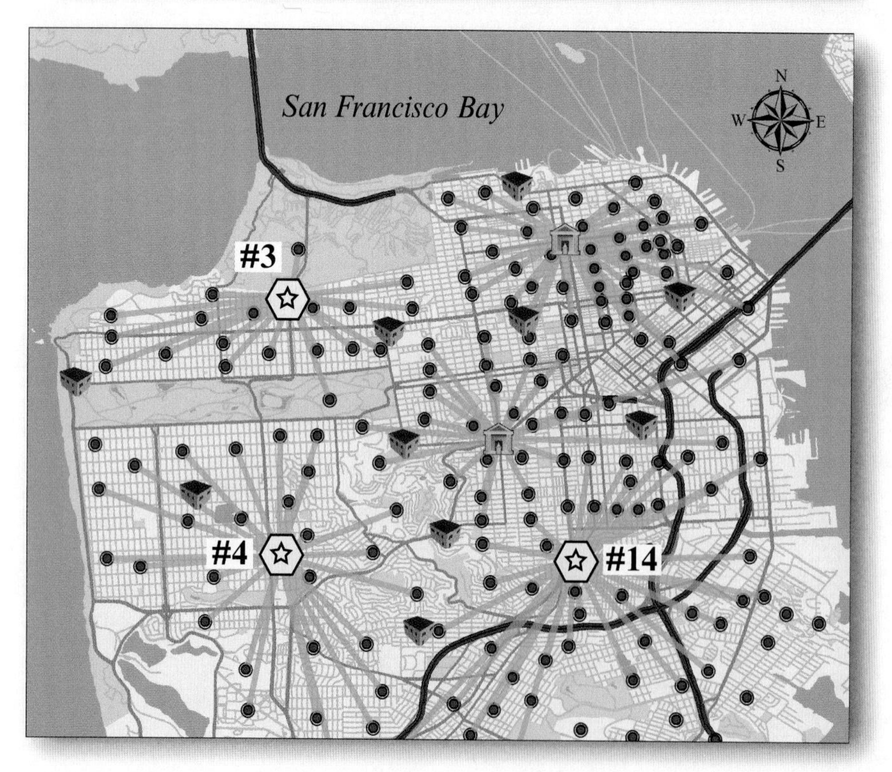

b. The optimum location for three new facilities (#3, #4, and #14) with two stores in existence. The travel-time impedance cutoff was 6 minutes.

FIGURE 7–20 An example of using maximize attendance and existing facility logic to locate three new stores. a) Two existing facilities are identified in addition to the Census Tract centroids. The 13 candidate facility locations are shown as buildings. b) The optimum locations for three new stores that take into account two existing stores, the surrounding population, travel time in minutes, and existing stores (Source of data: Tele Atlas and Esri. Used by permission).

Location-Allocation: Competitive Facility Location Problem and Facility Location Modeling to Capture Market Share

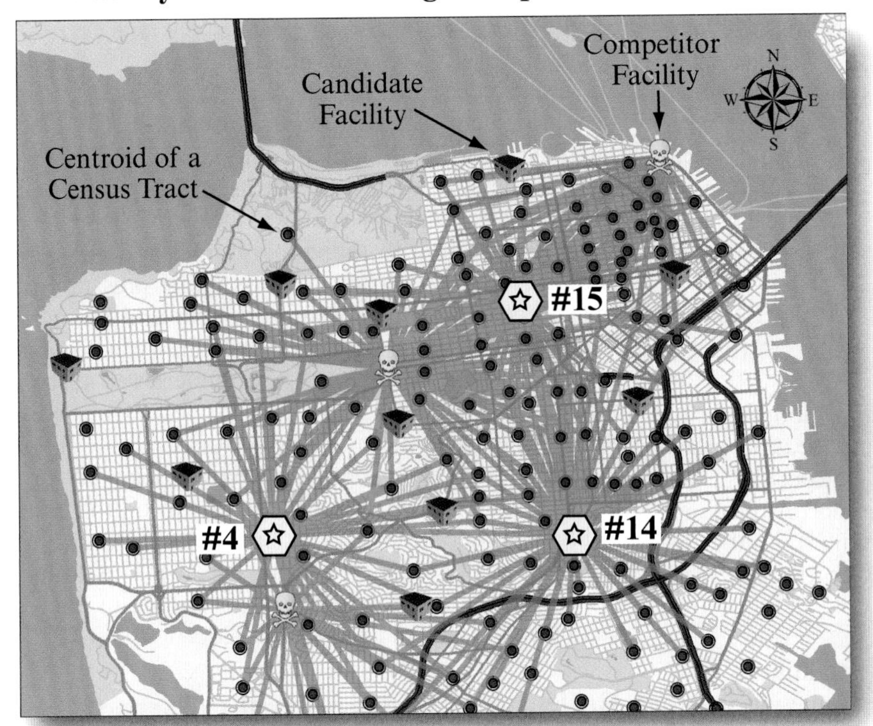

a. The optimum location for three new facilities (# 4, #14 and #15) in the presence of three competing stores. The travel-time impedance cutoff was 6 minutes. This accounts for 43% of the market share.

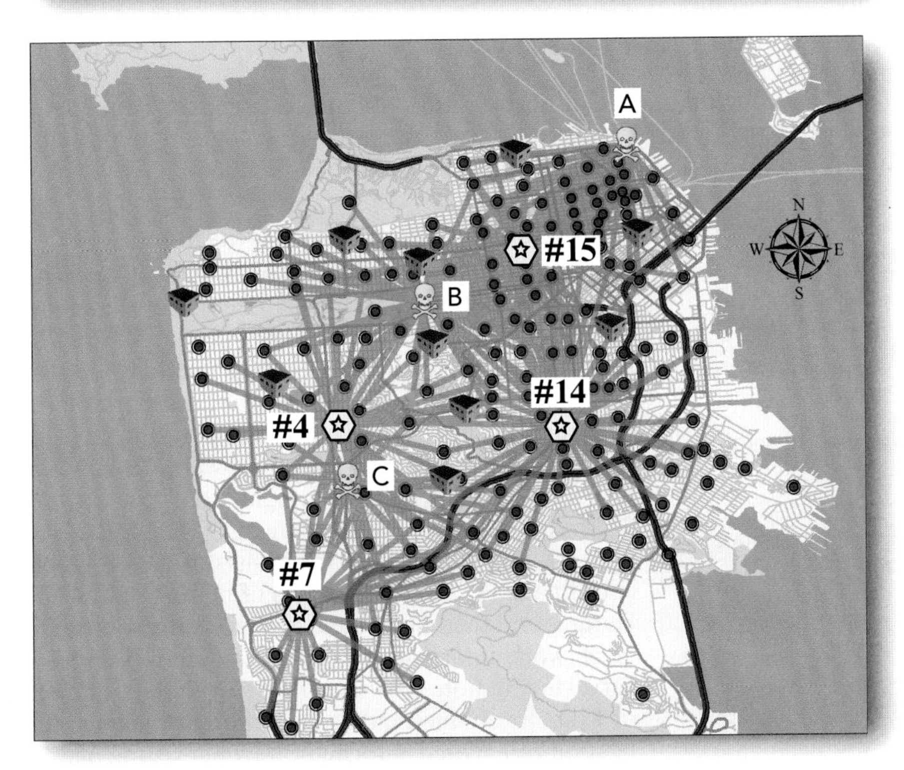

b. To capture 55% of the market share, four stores (#4, #7, #14 and #15) were selected. The travel-time impedance cutoff was 6 minutes.

FIGURE 7–21 An example of using maximize market share and capture market share logic to locate facilities. a) In addition to the 13 candidate facilities, three competitor facilities are included (shown as skull and cross-bone symbols). The optimum three facilities identified (stars) account for 43% of the market share in the region. b) It is quite a different problem to identify how many stores should be used to capture a specific percentage of the market share and where these stores should be located. Here the goal was to find both the number of stores and the geographic location of the stores to capture 55% of the market share. The model identified four stores that accounted for 55% of the market share (Source of data: Tele Atlas and Esri. Used by permission).

For example, consider the San Francisco study area database with 13 candidate stores plus the existence of three competitor stores shown using skull and crossbone point symbols in Figure 7-21a. In this problem, we are looking for the optimum places to locate three new stores with an impedance cutoff time of 6 minutes. The optimum three locations are shown as stars with radiating lines to the Census Tracts they would serve. The three facilities chosen (#4, #14, and #15) capture 43% of the market share in the region taking into account competitive store locations.

Network Analysis Problem: Target Market Share

Target market share location-allocation modeling can also be used to solve competitive facility location problems. In this case, the user can identify a specific target market share to be reached in the presence of the competitive facilities (e.g., 55%). The minimum number of candidate facilities are chosen to reach the specified target market share.

For example, let us hold the previous conditions constant (i.e., candidate facilities, three competing facilities, census demand points, and 6-minute travel-time-impedance cutoff) and specify a total market share of 55%. The model chose four candidate locations to reach the 55% market share in the face of competing facilities (Figure 7-21b). The four candidate-facility locations chosen had the following characteristics:

- Candidate facility #4 serves 41 census tracts and 110,108 people,
- Candidate facility #7 serves 24 census tracts and 98,267 people,
- Candidate facility #14 serves 64 census tracts and 182,627 people, and
- Candidate facility #15 serves 73 census tracts and 144,046 people.

The three competing stores using this scenario had the following characteristics (Figure 7-21b):

- Competing store A serves 41 census tracts and 72,190 people,
- Competing store B serves 70 census tracts and 142,424 people, and
- Competing store C serves 23 census tracts and 40,753 people.

This type of competitive location modeling is very useful for a variety of business applications.

Geometric Utility (Directed) Network Analysis

As discussed earlier in this chapter, geometric utility (directed) networks represent a special kind of geodatabase specifically designed to model the flow of materials in one direction, i.e., U-turns are not allowed. For example, electrical power flows outward from a source generating station to individual homes and businesses (Figure 7-22a). Natural gas flows under pressure from the source generating station to homes and businesses. Petroleum generally flows in one direction from the source to refineries or from the refineries to distribution points (Figure 7-22b). Sewage flows from homes and businesses to a central sewage disposal site (Figure 7-22c). Water in tributary streams (e.g., 1st-order streams) flows downhill under gravity into progressively higher-order streams (e.g., 2nd- and 3rd-order) and then into a river (e.g., 4th-order stream). The drainage network associated with the Goosenecks of the San Juan River is shown in Figure 7-22d.

Building a Topologically Correct Geometric Utility (Directed) Database

Sophisticated utility (geometric) network analysis requires a specially prepared, topologically correct network geodatabase.

Collect Source Network Information

Standard utility (e.g., electrical, natural gas, water) network information may be digitized and stored in a standard GIS database format (e.g., an ArcGIS® shapefile). These data are useful for numerous relatively simple network visualization problems. For example, you might want to simply identify all of the river and tributary stream segments within a watershed and color code them blue. Or, you might want to compute a 200-m buffer around all the streams. The fundamental network source information consists of the geographic coordinates (*x*, *y*, and perhaps *z*) of point, line, and area features and their attributes. As before, the source utility network information may be obtained using GPS surveying, remote sensing (primarily photogrammetric or LiDARgrammetric data collection), or manual digitization of network information from existing maps or diagrams (Figure 7-23a). The original utility network source information is usually stored in a standard GIS database.

When more sophisticated utility network analysis is required, a specially prepared type of geometric utility network geodatabase must be built (Maidment, 2002; Maidment et al., 2007; Price, 2008). This is because in

Geometric Utility and River (Directed) Networks

a. Electric power transmission line.

b. Petroleum refinery pipeline network in Texas.

c. Sewage treatment plant network in Newport Beach, CA.

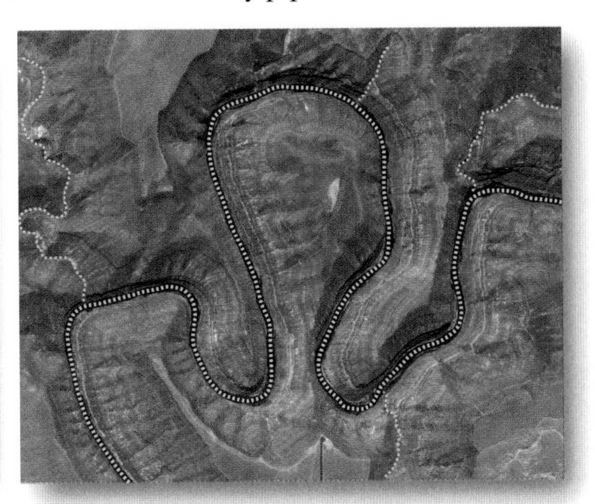

d. Drainge network: Goosenecks of the *San Juan River*, UT.

FIGURE 7–22 Examples of selected utility and river (directed) networks. a) Power transmission lines that are part of a regional energy network. b) A dense network of pipes at a petroleum refinery in Texas. c) Sewage disposal plant in Newport Beach, CA. d) Goosenecks of the *San Juan River* (image courtesy of GeoEye, Inc.).

a typical source utility network file (e.g., an ArcGIS® shapefile), simple line features like individual stream segments are not aware of one another or have knowledge about how the stream segments intersect or whether barriers to flow are present (e.g., dams, valves). The stream or pipeline segments don't know that they are connected or in what manner they are connected, i.e., they have no topology.

Build Topologically Correct Utility (Directed) Network Elements and Attributes

A topologically correct utility network database contains information about the relationships between the following network elements: *edges* (lines), *junctions* (source points and edge intersections), *sink points*, and *barriers* (Figure 7-23 and Figure 7-24). Lines in the original source materials are converted to *edges* in the topologically correct network database (Figure 7-23b and Figure 7-24). Water, electricity, and sewage travels along the edges in channels, cables, and pipes.

Intersection points in the original source materials are converted to *junctions* in the topologically correct network dataset (Figure 7-24). The junctions can also contain information about valves present at the junction and their condition (e.g., open, closed).

A *source junction* point provides the material to the network and pushes the material away from itself (Price, 2008). For example, an electrical power plant generates power and pushes the power away from itself

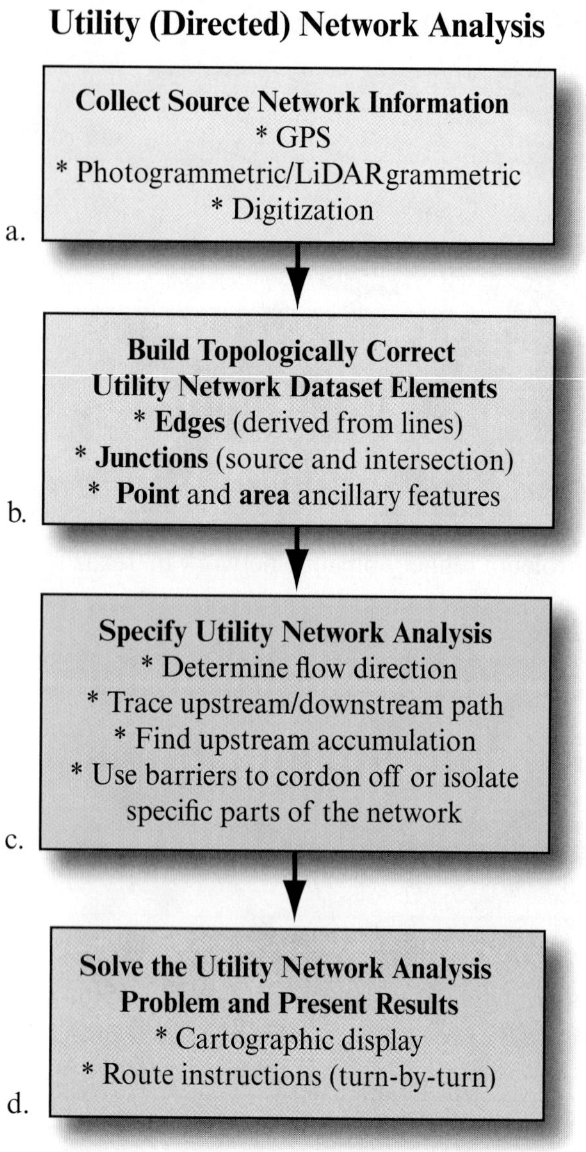

Utility (Directed) Network Analysis

a.
Collect Source Network Information
* GPS
* Photogrammetric/LiDARgrammetric
* Digitization

b.
Build Topologically Correct Utility Network Dataset Elements
* **Edges** (derived from lines)
* **Junctions** (source and intersection)
* **Point** and **area** ancillary features

c.
Specify Utility Network Analysis
* Determine flow direction
* Trace upstream/downstream path
* Find upstream accumulation
* Use barriers to cordon off or isolate specific parts of the network

d.
Solve the Utility Network Analysis Problem and Present Results
* Cartographic display
* Route instructions (turn-by-turn)

FIGURE 7–23 General network creation and analysis procedures for a geometric utility (directed) network. a) Network source materials (lines, source junction points, intersections, sink points, barriers, and attributes) may be acquired using a variety of data collection techniques. b) The topologically correct utility network database is built. c) Various types of utility network analysis may be performed. These are typical examples. d) The utility network problem is solved and the results presented in cartographic or other formats.

to consumers via transmission lines. Similarly, a source junction point might be the sewage coming from a single house or the most upstream point in stream tributary.

A *sink point* is the location where the material or commodity is used, collected, or actually leaves the network. For example, all of the sewage in a community of homes typically flows to a sewage disposal plant sink point. The point where all of the water flows from a watershed into a river is a sink point. The electric power meter at your home represents the sink point for the electricity sent to your home. This means that sometimes individual points in the network database can be source junction points (e.g., they create sewage or water) or sink points (e.g., they receive electrical power). The user determines whether it is a source or sink point in the utility network.

Barriers may be introduced into the utility network by the network analyst to highlight or isolate a specific part of a network for special types of analysis (Figure 7-24). Some utility network datasets also include other point features (e.g., a spring or well) and area features (e.g., a lake or pond) for completeness (Figure 7-24). These ancillary point and area features may not be connected topologically with the edge or junction features in the utility network geodatabase.

The person building a topologically correct utility network database typically includes detailed attribute information about the edges and junctions and the source and sink points. For example, attribute information about a stream segment (edge) might include

- the x,y- and perhaps z-coordinates of the source junction point (e.g., a spring in the side of a mountain),
- the x,y- and perhaps z-coordinates of the end of the stream segment (e.g., where the stream intersects another stream segment),
- the length of the stream segment,
- the width of the stream segment or the diameter of the water pipe, and/or
- the slope of the stream segment assuming digital elevation information is present to compute the slope.

Attribute information about the intersection of two stream segments might include:

- valve condition (open, closed, intermediate), and/or
- restriction (e.g., a dam, damaged water main valve, damaged power pole).

A topologically correct utility network database will also include utility network cost (impedance) information. As before, this could be a) the distance or time it takes the material (e.g., water, petroleum, sewage) to pass through the edge segment, b) information about the speed and/or time it takes for the material to flow into the next stream or pipeline segment based on the impedance characteristics of the valve at the intersection, or c) some other characteristic such as river segment scenic beauty. Whenever a material such as electricity travels over the network element (e.g., a

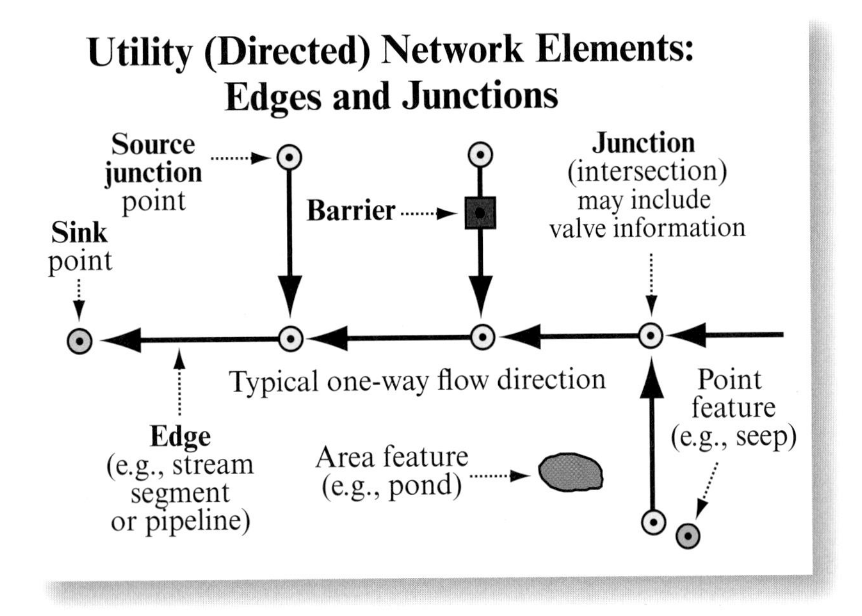

FIGURE 7–24 A topologically correct utility (directed) network consists of network elements, including: edges, junctions (source junction points and intersections), and sink points. This example consists of seven one-way edges (e.g., stream segments or pipes) that intersect at three junctions. In this example, only downstream movement of the material is permitted. A barrier prohibits movement along one of the edges. All of the materials in the network flow to a sink point.

transmission line segment) and/or passes through an intersection (junction), it is charged a network cost. The utility network cost can be specified in terms of distance, time spent, or other calculated variables.

This is the type of detailed topological utility information that may be included in a topologically correct utility network dataset to perform sophisticated utility network analysis. For this reason, it is necessary to use specialized GIS software to *build* a utility network dataset that contains accurate connectivity information and appropriate attributes.

The *building process* creates the network elements (consisting of edges, junctions, source points, sink points, barriers), defines connectivity, and assigns values to the element attributes (Figure 7-23b). Topologically correct utility network geodatabases may be used to model a single utility (e.g., an electrical network) referred to as unimodal utility network analysis or to model multiple utilities at one time (e.g., electrical, water, sewer), referred to as multimodal utility network analysis.

Specify the Network Analysis to Be Performed and Solve the Problem

Once the topologically correct utility network geodatabase is constructed, it is possible to specify the type of utility network analysis to be performed (Figure 7-23c). The utility network analysis problem is then solved and the results displayed in cartographic or other formats (Figure 7-23d).

We will use a topologically correct utility dataset extracted from the **National Hydrography Dataset (NHD)** to demonstrate utility network analysis. The NHD is maintained by the U.S. Geological Survey (USGS, 2011). It is a vector geospatial dataset for surface water hydrography created from digitized topographic maps and other sources. The dataset is available nationwide at medium resolution 1:100,000–scale and at high resolution 1:24,000–scale. In Alaska, the NHD is available at 1:63,360–scale. In a few geographic areas, the NHD is available at various "local resolutions."

The National Hydrography Dataset is organized by hydrologic units including (USGS, 2011)

- drainage areas,
- drainage subregions (4-digit Hydrologic Unit Code (HUC), and
- drainage subbasins (8-digit HUC).

High resolution NHD data are usually obtained at the subbasin level and may be downloaded in a file-based Esri geodatabase format known as "NHDinGEO" and in an Esri shapefile format known as "NHDGEOinShape." NHD data of the United States may be downloaded at no charge using the viewer at http://nhd.usgs.gov/data.html.

For demonstration purposes, we will use topologically correct NHD information for a small part of *Diamond Fork River* in the Wasatch Mountains in Utah (Figure 7-25). The edges (stream segments) are part of the "NHD_Flowline" dataset and the stream junctions are part of the "HYDRO_Net_Junctions" dataset (Figure 7-25a). For example, the attribute information for edge #1623 in Figure 7-25a includes:

- code = river,
- type = intermittent,
- river reach code = 16020202000846 (a reach is any length of stream between any two points such as gauging stations, river miles, etc.), and
- length = 2.51 km.

Point #1743 is a stream junction. Also included is NHD_Point symbol #185 which represents a spring/seep and NHD_Waterbody #304 which represents a small pond (area = 0.18 km^2) (Figure 7-25a). For illustrative purposes, the NHD data are overlaid on the National Elevation Dataset (NED) in Figures 7-25bc and on a near-infrared color composite of Landsat Thematic Mapper data (RGB = bands 4,3,2) in Figure 7-25d.

Below are some relatively straightforward problems that can be addressed using a topologically correct utility network geodatabase:

- identification of the flow direction of specific edges (e.g., stream segments, pipeline segments),
- tracing the edges or junctions above (upstream) or below (downstream) a selected edge or junction, and
- placing barriers in a utility network to highlight or isolate a specific part of the network for further analysis.

Network Analysis Problem: Flow Direction in a Utility Network

In a utility network such as the National Hydrography Dataset, the flow of the water along edges is determined by the network configuration. Network edge-flow-direction characteristics are incorporated into the database during the digitization and building process. For example, the red arrows in Figure 7-26a identify the flow direction for every edge (stream segment) in this part of the *Diamond Fork River* watershed. Note that as the edges (stream segments) intersect at junctions that the flow is always downstream.

Simple flow direction information such as this is often very valuable in more complex utility analysis operations. For example, one might be in charge of a complex network consisting of thousands of pipes within an industry (e.g., petroleum refinery) or city block (e.g., water and sewer lines). In emergency situations, it is important to know how the network is configured, which edges (e.g., pipes) flow into one another, and the direction of flow. Only then can accurate decisions be made when a problem arises along an edge or at a junction.

Network Analysis Problem: Tracing Edges and Junctions Upstream or Downstream in a Utility Network

In the past, a transparent piece of mylar was used to trace important features. **Digital tracing** functions in a similar manner, except that the computer identifies (traces) features in the utility network that are connected. A network element such as an edge or junction can only be included in a digital trace if it is in some logical way connected to other elements (e.g., edges, junctions) in the network.

Sometimes problems occur within a utility network. For example, a problem might occur along a specific edge such as a leak in a canal or a break in a power line. Similarly, a valve at the junction of two waterline edges might break or shut down. A transformer on a power pole might be destroyed during a lightning storm. These types of problems impact upstream parts of the utility network (e.g., power from the generating plant to all of the homes) or impact downstream parts of the network (e.g., a break in a major sewer line or intersection that routes sewage from individual homes to a sewage treatment plant).

When these types of problems occur, system analysts can identify the location of the incoming service calls in the utility network. The service calls typically tend to spatially congregate above or below some specific edge (e.g., stream segment, powerline segment) or junction (e.g., stream intersection or power pole). The analyst can then run a trace function to identify all of the edges or source points above (upstream) or below (downstream) the problem edge or junction to see what parts of the utility network are or will be impacted.

For example, let's assume that there is a problem with edge #612 in our NHD stream network. The stream bank has eroded somewhere along this stream segment, resulting in zero water entering the next stream junction. In the example shown in Figure 7-26b, the analyst has identified edge #612 and then requested an *upstream trace.* All of the segments upstream are now highlighted in red. The analyst could then accumulate information about these upstream segments and determine from their attribute information how much water they typically yield under certain conditions. He or she could then start to prepare plans to mitigate the flood-

National Hydrography Dataset
***Diamond Fork River*, Wasatch Mountains, UT**

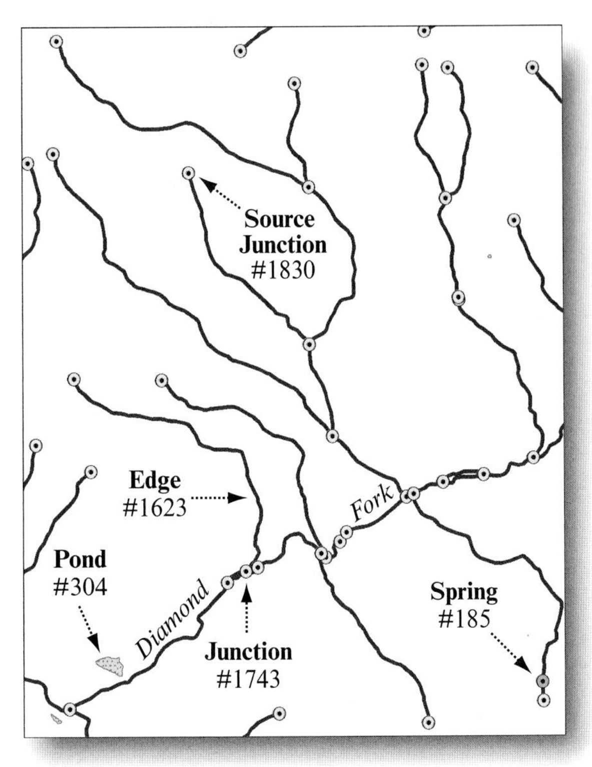

a. Edges (stream segments) and stream junctions.

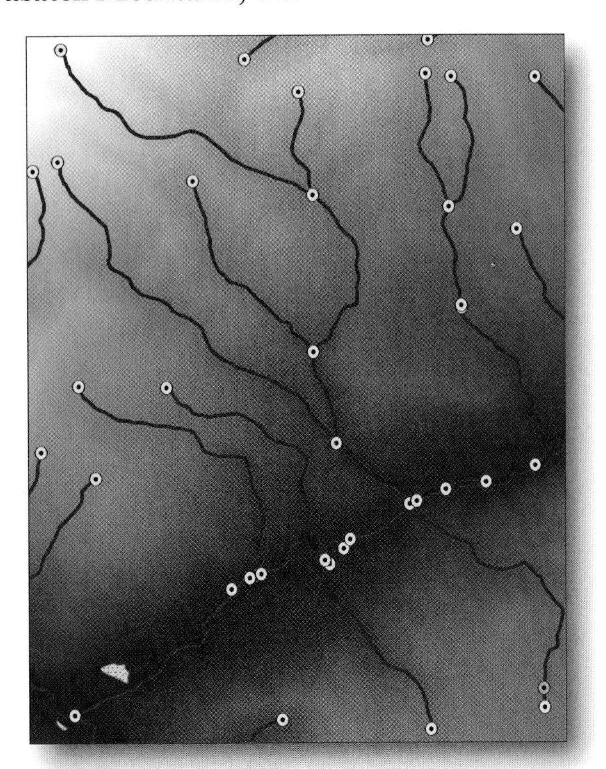

b. Overlaid on National Elevation Dataset (1 Arc Sec).

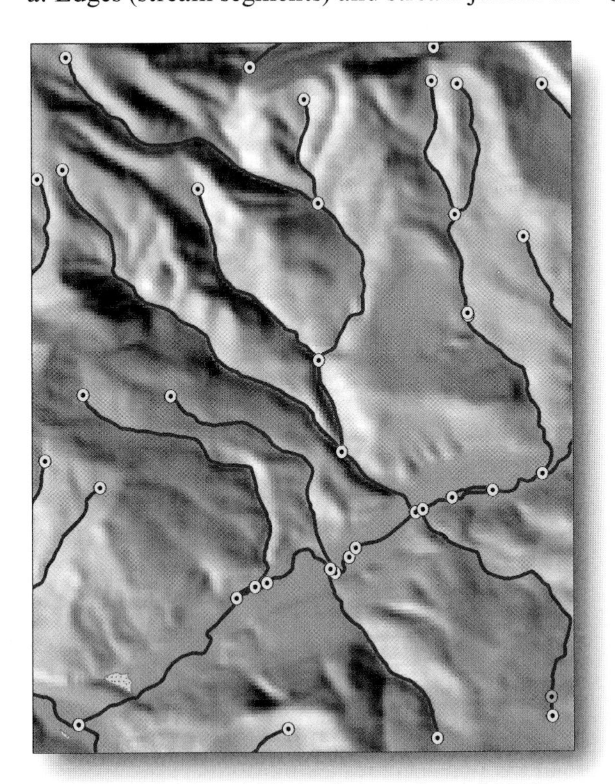

c. Overlaid on hill-shaded version of NED.

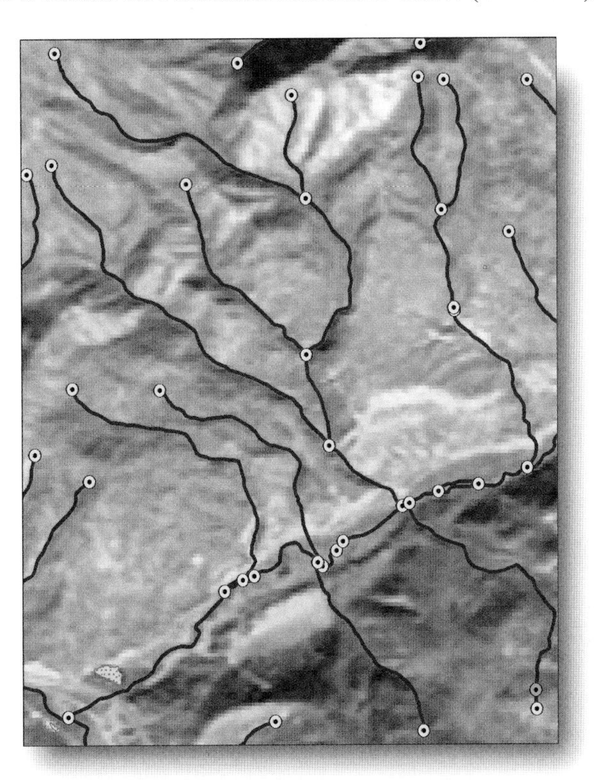

d. Overlaid on Landsat Thematic Mapper data.

FIGURE 7–25 Example of a portion of a topologically correct stream network dataset of *Diamond Fork River* in the Wasatch Mountains of Utah. a) Edges, junctions and other features are from the National Hydrography Dataset. b-d) The NHD stream network overlaid on the National Elevation Dataset and on Landsat Thematic Mapper imagery (RGB = bands 4, 3, 2). (Data courtesy of the National Elevation Dataset and the National Hydrography Dataset.)

Edge Flow Direction and Upstream Trace
***Diamond Fork River*, Wasatch Mountains, UT**

a. Edge flow direction.

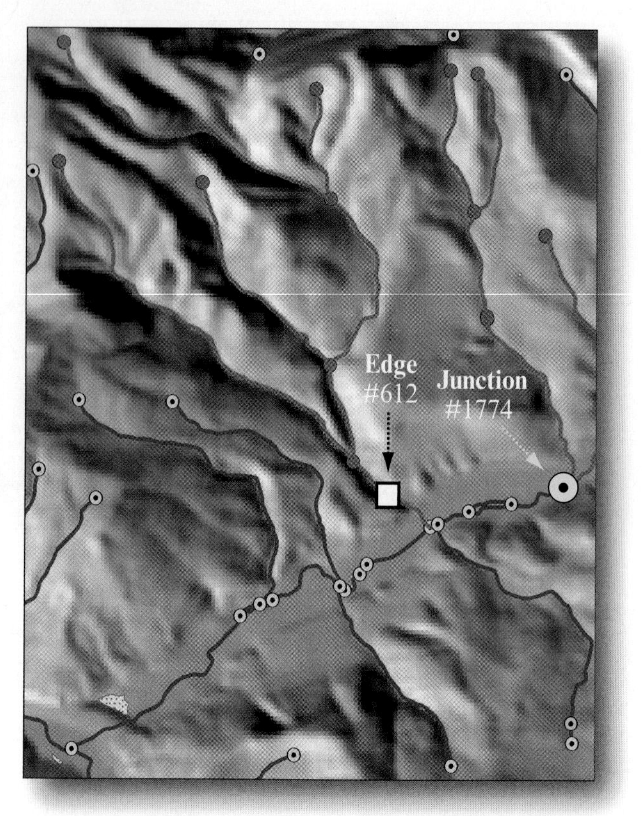

b. Trace upstream from an edge and a junction.

FIGURE 7–26 a) The red arrows identify the flow direction of individual stream segments (edges). b) Stream junctions and edges (stream segments) traced upstream from edge #612 and upstream from junction #1774 (data courtesy of the National Elevation Dataset and the National Hydrography Dataset).

ing that might occur at edge #612 while repairs take place.

Similarly, perhaps a large valve at junction #1774 is broken (Figure 7-26b). In this case, all of the stream segments upstream of junction #1774 are highlighted in red.

The stream segments and source points identified in this water network example could just as well be powerlines or homes in an electrical utility network, respectively. In this case, the analyst could run a trace to identify all of the homes upstream of the powerline or power pole problem to determine the number of people out of power and get extra help to repair the powerlines or poles if necessary.

Network Analysis Problem: Using Barriers in a Utility Network

Barriers in a transportation network are usually used to identify problem junctions or edges in the network that are to be avoided. Conversely, barriers are often placed in a utility network by an analyst to highlight or isolate a specific part of the network (Figure 7-24). For example, suppose there is a problem at Junction #1805 in the *Diamond Fork* watershed (Figure 7-27). The control floodgate is broken and cannot be closed. The analyst wants to know which of the junctions and edges downstream of the problem might be impacted by the increased water flow. In particular, he or she wants to know which junctions and edges will be impacted from the source of the problem at junction #1805 to junction #1707 where the *Diamond Fork River* enters the *Spanish Fork River*. Therefore, the analyst has placed an artificial barrier shown as a red box at junction #1707 where the *Diamond Fork River* flows into the *Spanish Fork River* (Figure 7-27). In this case, the artificial barrier becomes a sink point.

The solution identified 13 downstream junctions and 14 downstream segments (edges) that will be impacted (Figure 7-27). Note that because of the inherent flow-direction information contained in the utility network,

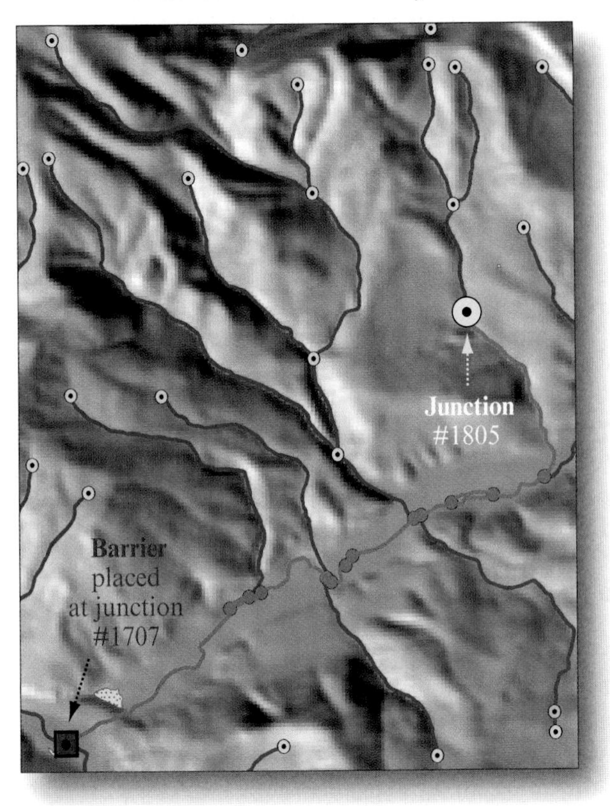

FIGURE 7–27 The downstream trace from a problem at junction #1805 to an artificial barrier placed at junction #1707 where the *Diamond Fork River* enters the *Spanish Fork River*. All of the intervening junctions and edges (stream segments) are identified (data courtesy of the National Elevation and Hydrography Datasets).

none of the tributary stream segments that flow into the *Diamond Fork River* in this area are included in the solution. Only the main downstream channel between junction #1805 and barrier junction #1707 is selected. If desired, the analyst can rapidly accumulate the attribute information associated with the stream segments and 13 junctions to determine if the system can withstand the increased water flow caused by the problem at junction #1805. This is called *upstream accumulation* and is the total cost of all network elements that lie upstream of a given point in the network, in this case the barrier (sink).

Network Analysis Problem: Network Schematic Diagrams

All of the network examples presented in this chapter have displayed the geographic distribution of edges and junctions in map format. However, sometimes people working with network information do not care if everything is cartographically correct. They often have a limited amount of space to view the entire network. Under such conditions, analysts often use simple schematic diagrams of the network which they display on large wall-mounted computer screens. Numerous water, electrical, nuclear, natural gas, subway, and railroad agencies or companies use digital schematic diagrams to monitor network activities. Some geographic information systems such as ArcGIS® allow the user to display network information in its proper planimetric position as well as in schematic diagram format. Special tools are made available to create the schematic diagrams.

Summary

This chapter introduced the fundamental characteristics of geocoding and two types of networks: transportation (undirected) networks and geometric utility (directed) networks. The fundamental characteristics of geocoding and address matching were reviewed. Aspects of building topologically correct transportation and geometric utility networks were discussed. Several transportation network analysis applications were provided, including finding the optimum route, finding the closest facility, determining the service area, and location-allocation modeling. Several geometric utility network analysis applications were discussed, including: the determination of flow direction, upstream or downstream tracing, and the incorporation of barriers to cordon off specific parts of the network for more detailed analysis.

Review Questions

1. Describe why it is not possible to use a standard GIS road network coverage for sophisticated network analysis purposes. Provide information about how a topologically correct network geodatabase is prepared and its unique characteristics compared with a standard road network coverage.

2. What is geocoding and why is it important? What are some of the problems that are often encountered when performing address matching?

3. Explain the difference between directed and undirected networks and provide several examples of each.

4. Describe the characteristics of network cost (impedance) and why it is important in network analysis. Pro-

vide some examples of network cost examined during network analysis.

5. Summarize the characteristics of three types of network analysis performed on transportation (directed) networks.

6. Describe why the existence of barriers and other restrictions are so important in network analysis. Provide two examples of barriers often encountered during transportation (undirected) and utility (directed) network analysis.

7. Define location-allocation modeling and provide two examples of such modeling in transportation (undirected) networks.

8. Describe the elements of a topologically correct utility (directed) network. Identify any differences between the elements of a topologically correct utility network and a topologically correct transportation network.

9. Provide examples of the usefulness of an upstream trace- and a downstream-trace analysis applied to a power utility network.

10. Lightning has destroyed a power pole. What utility network analysis methods would you use to identify the location of the power pole and all those facilities that do not have power within the network due to the loss of the pole?

Glossary

Address Matching: The most common type of geocoding, which plots street addresses as points on a map.

Digital Tracing: A computer process that identifies (traces) features in a utility or natural network that are connected such as streams in a hydrologic network. A network element such as an edge or junction can only be included in a digital trace if it is in some logical way connected to other elements (e.g., edges, junctions) in the network.

Edge Impedance: The cost of traversing network edge segments (e.g., roads) or passing through junctions.

Geocoding: The process of finding a geographic location from an address.

Geometric Utility (Directed) Networks: A special type of network where travel along the edges (e.g., pipes, streams) is usually only allowed in one direction.

Location-Allocation Modeling The process of finding the best location(s) for one or more new facilities (e.g., a fast-food restaurant) that will service a given set of points (e.g., homes) and then assigning those points to the new facilities. The process takes into account factors such as the number of facilities available, their cost, and the maximum impedance (e.g., distance or time) from a facility to a point.

MAF/TIGER/Line File: The U.S. Bureau of the Census *Master Address File/Topologically Integrated Geographic Encoding and Referencing* network geodatabase. The files contain information about each street segment, including: street name, beginning and ending address for each side of the street, and the postal code on each side of the road.

Maximize Attendance Location-Allocation Modeling: Used to solve neighborhood store location problems where the proportion of demand allocated to the candidate facility or facilities falls within a specified time or distance to the demand points (e.g., 5 minutes or 7 miles).

Maximize Market Share Location-Allocation Modeling: Used to locate facilities that maximize market share.

National Hydrography Dataset (NHD): A topologically correct geodatabase of surface water hydrography created from digitized topographic maps and other sources. It is available nationwide at medium resolution 1:100,000–scale and at high resolution 1:24,000–scale. In Alaska, the NHD is available at 1:63,360–scale. In a few geographic areas, the NHD is available at various "local resolutions."

Network: A system of interconnected lines (edges) and intersections (junctions) that represent possible routes from one location to another.

Network Cost (Impedance): The cost of traversing a network. Whenever something such as a car or bus travels over a network element (e.g., a road) and/or passes through an intersection (junction), it accumulates network costs based on the impedance characteristics of the edge or intersection.

Network Service Area: The geographic region that encompasses all parts of the network that can be reached within a certain impedance (cost) value.

Origin–Destination Matrix: A matrix that contains information about the cost (usually measured in distance or time) from each of n origins to each of m destinations.

Route: The path (edge) from one location to another.

Target Market Share Location-Allocation Modeling: Used to solve targeted market share competitive facility location problems.

Transportation (Undirected) Network: A network where travel along the edges (e.g., road, railroad, subway, pedestrian walkway) may be in *any* direction that is allowed.

Turn Impedance: The cost of making a turn in the network.

References

Andresen, M. D., 2006, "Crime Measures and the Spatial Analysis of Criminal Activity," *British Journal of Criminology*, 46:258–285.

Boyles, D., 2002, *GIS Means Business*, Redlands, CA: Esri Press, 161 p.

Butler, J. A., 2008, *Designing Geodatabases for Transportation*, Redlands, CA: Esri Press, 461 p.

Chang, K., 2010, "Chapter 17: Path Analysis and Network Applications," in *Introduction to Geographic Information Systems*, New York: McGraw Hill, 367–391.

DeMers, M. N., 2002, *Fundamentals of Geographic Information Systems*, New York: John Wiley & Sons, 480 p.

Dijkstra, E. W., 1959, "A Note on Two Problems in Connexion with Graphs," *Numerische Mathematik*, 1:269–371.

Esri, 2011a, "Algorithms Used by Network Analyst," in *ArcGIS® Resource Center*, Redlands, CA: Esri, Inc. (www.Esri.com).

Esri, 2011b, "ArcGIS® Desktop 10," in *ArcGIS® Resource Center*, Redlands, CA: Esri, Inc. (www.Esri.com).

Esri, 2011c, "Exercise 9: Choosing Optimal Store Locations Using Location-Allocation," in *ArcGIS® Resource Center*, Redlands, CA: Esri, Inc. (www.Esri.com).

Esri, 2011d, "Location-Allocation," in *ArcGIS® Resource Center*, Redlands, CA: Esri, Inc. (www.Esri.com).

Esri, 2011e, "New Network Dataset Wizard," in *ArcGIS® Resource Center*, Redlands, CA: Esri, Inc. (www.Esri.com).

Esri, 2011f, "Reverse Geocoding Network Locations," in *ArcGIS® Resource Center*, Redlands, CA: Esri, Inc. (www.Esri.com).

Esri, 2011g, "Turns in the Network Dataset," *ArcGIS® Resource Center*, Redlands, CA: Esri, Inc. (www.Esri.com).

Fu, P. and J. Sun, 2010, *Web GIS: Principles and Applications*, Redlands, CA: Esri Press, 296 p.

Goldberg, D. W., Wilson, J. P. and C. A. Knoblock, 2007, "From Text to Geographic Coordinates: The Current State of Geocoding," *URISA Journal*, 19(1):33–46.

Gonser, R. A., Jensen, R. R. and S. A. Wolf, 2009, "The Spatial Ecology of Deer-Vehicle Collisions," *Applied Geography*, 29:527–532.

Huff, D., 1966, "A Programmed Solution for Approximating an Optimum Retail Location," *Land Economics*, 42(3):293.

Kennedy, H., 2001, *Dictionary of GIS Terminology*, Redlands, CA: Esri Press, 118 p.

Krieger, N., Waterman, P. D., Chen, J. T., Soobader, M. and S. V. Subramanian, 2003, "Monitoring Socioeconomic Inequalities in Sexually Transmitted Infections, Tuberculosis, and Violence: Geocoding and Choice of Area-based Socioeconomic Measures," *Public Health Reports*, 118(3): 240–260.

Lemmens, M. J., 2010, "Mobile GIS Systems (Hard and Software)," *GIM International*, 24(12):28–29.

Lo, C. P. and A. K. W. Yeung, 2007, "Chapter 10: Spatial Data Analysis, Modeling, and Mining," in *Concepts and Techniques in Geographic Information Systems*, Upper Saddle River: Pearson Prentice-Hall, 392–393.

Lowe, J. C. and S. Moryadas, 1975, *The Geography of Movement*, Boston: Houghton Mifflin, 333 p.

Maidment, D. R., 2002, *Arc Hydro: GIS for Water Resources*, Redlands, CA: Esri Press, 203 p.

Maidment, D. R., Edelman, S., Heiberg, E. R., Jensen, J. R., Maune, D. F., Shuckman, K. and R. Shrestha, 2007, *Elevation Data for Floodplain Mapping*, Washington: National Academy Press, 151 p.

Price, M., 2008, *Mastering ArcGIS®*, New York: McGraw Hill, 3rd Ed., 607 p.

Ratcliffe, J. H., 2004, "Geocoding Crime and a First Estimate of a Minimum Acceptable Hit Rate," *International Journal of Geographical Information Science*, 18(1):61–72.

Salah, A. M. and D. Atwood, 2010, "Is ONE Route Good Enough?" *ArcUser*, Spring (2010), 32–35.

USGS, 2011, *The National Hydrography Dataset*, Washington: U.S. Geological Survey, http://usgs.gov/data.html.

8 Statistics and Spatial Data Measurements

Most of the spatial data measurements that you will need to make in a typical GIS project can be performed automatically and efficiently using special-purpose algorithms that are a part of the GIS software. However, it is important that you understand the nature of the computations that take place after you push a button to perform a particular function or query using the GIS. This knowledge will enable you to properly apply various spatial analysis functions. In addition, you will be able to explain the process or function to others who may not be familiar with spatial data or spatial data analysis.

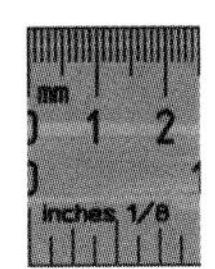

Overview

Using spatial data and GIS analysis appropriately is an important part of conducting an accurate GIS investigation. The developers and users of GIS have backgrounds in many different disciplines, including geography, geology, computer science, mathematics, engineering, forestry, landscape ecology, and others (Wright et al., 1997). Due in part to this diversity, many of the algorithms, statistics, and procedures implemented in a GIS often employ techniques that are outside of the experience or "comfort zone" of some users. This unfamiliarity may occasionally cause people to use spatial data and GIS analysis procedures incorrectly.

This chapter describes some of the basic properties of spatial data measurement and analysis used in a GIS. It also introduces some of the fundamental descriptive statistics and spatial statistics and how these can be used to enhance our understanding of spatial relationships. The chapter begins by describing how simple Euclidian and Manhattan distance measurements are made. Then, common polygon measurements are introduced. Useful descriptive and spatial statistics are discussed. These concepts are followed by a description of spatial autocorrelation and Moran's I. Finally, point pattern analysis techniques are presented.

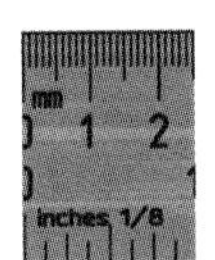

Length (Distance) Measurement

As stated in Chapter 5, a point is located using *x, y* coordinates; lines consist of connected points; and polygons (areas) are connected, enclosed lines. Linear distance measurements are usually computed using the Pythagorean theorem or Manhattan distance methods.

Linear Distance Measurement Based on the Pythagorean Theorem

One of the most common measurements you will need to calculate using a GIS is the **Euclidean distance** between two projected points. Such measurements can be used to determine the distance to nearest neighbors or the number of points within a certain buffer distance from a point under investigation.

The Euclidean distance between two points is easily computed using the Pythagorean theorem. The Pythagorean theorem is based on the relationship between the three sides of a right triangle and is typically stated as follows: In any right triangle (a triangle where one inside angle = 90°), the length of the line segment

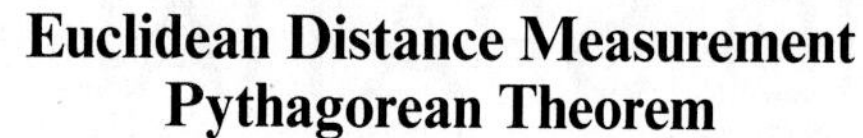

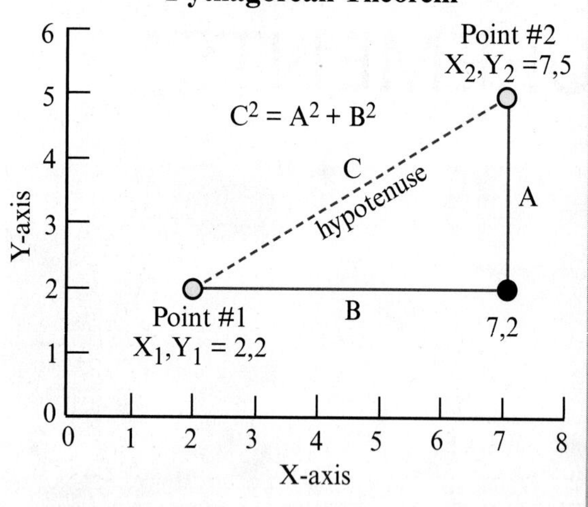

FIGURE 8–1 Calculating the Euclidean distance between two points in an *X,Y* Cartesian coordinate system using the Pythagorean theorem.

TABLE 8–1 The coordinates of Point #1 and Point #2 in Figure 8-1 in meters.

Point	X-coordinate	Y-coordinate
1	2	2
2	7	5

opposite the right angle (the hypotenuse) is equal to the square root of the squared sums of the lengths of the other two legs (i.e., the two sides other than the hypotenuse). These relationships are shown in Figure 8-1.

In mathematical terms, the equation is expressed as:

$$C^2 = A^2 + B^2 \tag{8.1}$$

where A and B are the lengths of two line segments that are not the hypotenuse (C). Therefore, if you know the projected X, Y coordinates for any two points, it is a relatively straightforward matter to determine the distance between them—you simply determine the lengths of the two legs and then calculate the length of the hypotenuse. For example, suppose you want to measure the distance between Point #1 and Point #2 in the Cartesian coordinate system shown in Figure 8-1 and listed in Table 8-1. To determine the distance between these two points it is first necessary to calculate the distance of the two sides of the triangle that form the right angle. To determine the length of line A, one of the Y values is subtracted from the other Y value ($2 - 5 = -3$). To determine the length of line B, one of the X values is subtracted from the other X value ($2 - 7 = -5$). Both values are used in Equation 8-1:

$$C^2 = (-3)^2 + (-5)^2$$

$$C^2 = 9 + 25$$

$$C^2 = 34$$

$$C = \sqrt{34}$$

$$C = 5.83 \text{ m}$$

The distance between Point #1 and Point #2 in Figure 8-1 is 5.83 m.

TABLE 8–2 The coordinates of Point #1 and Point #2 in Figure 8-2 in a Universal Transverse Mercator (UTM) Cartesian coordinate system (Zone 12 N).

Point	UTM X-coordinate	UTM Y-coordinate
1	432,860	4,426,841
2	432,966	4,427,036

Normally, the coordinates of the points that you are investigating are described in terms of their location in a particular coordinate system, e.g., the Universal Transverse Mercator (UTM) map projection. For example, suppose you wanted to compute the distance between Point #1 and Point #2 in the agricultural field shown in Figure 8-2. The coordinates of the two points are listed in Table 8-2.

In this case the computation would be

$$C^2 = (432860 - 432966)^2 + (4426841 - 4427036)^2$$

$$C^2 = (-106)^2 + (-195)^2$$

$$C^2 = 11236 + 38025$$

$$C^2 = 49261$$

$$C = \sqrt{49261}$$

$$C = 221.95 \text{ m}$$

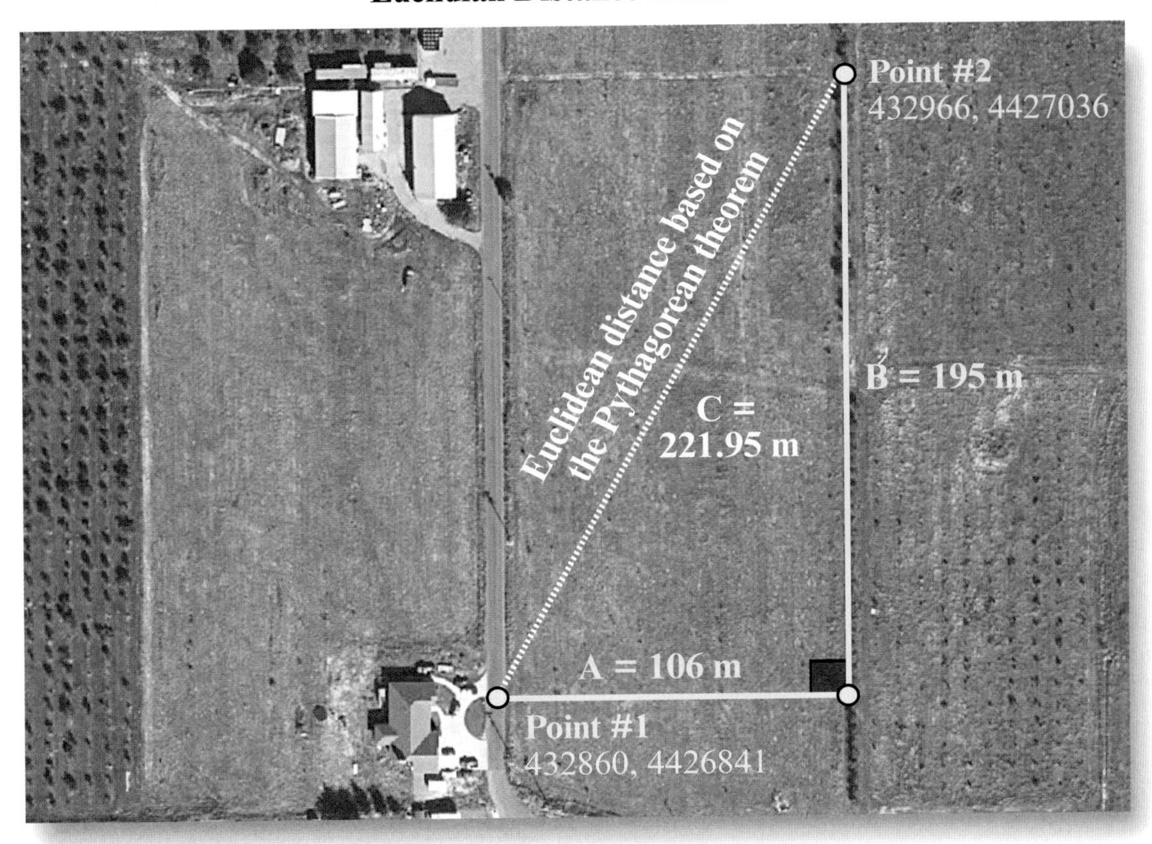

FIGURE 8–2 Euclidean distance measurements are based on the Pythagorean theorem where the lengths of lines A and B in a right triangle can be used to calculate the length of the hypotenuse, C. In this example, the distance from a point in front of the single-family residence to a corner of the adjacent field is calculated (aerial photography courtesy State of Utah).

The distance between these two UTM points is 221.95 m. A limitation of using the Pythagorean theorem is that this method only works when the points used in the measurement are comparable—that is, they are in a coordinate system based on a projection such as UTM. Also, this method will not work for latitude and longitude or for projected points that are great distances from one another because of the impact of the curvature of the Earth.

Manhattan Distance Measurement

Linear distance measurement based on the Pythagorean theorem is useful for many applications, but it does have limitations. One limitation is the fact that to get from Point #1 to Point #2 in an urban environment—and even in many natural settings—it may not be logical to measure the Euclidean distance between two points using a straight line (i.e., using the hypotenuse) "as the crow flies." To remedy this, the **Manhattan distance** between two points may be calculated, where:

$$\text{Manhattan}_{\text{distance}} = |X_1 - X_2| + |Y_1 - Y_2| \quad (8.2)$$

The Manhattan distance (sometimes referred to as "round-the-block" or "city block" distance) between two points utilizes the lengths of the two sides of the right triangle, but not the hypotenuse. This is analogous to going from Point #1 to Point #2 in a city where you cannot simply walk through buildings or climb over fences. Rather, you are required to walk around the block to get from Point #1 to Point #2. For example, the Manhattan distance between Point #1 and Point #2 in Figure 8-3 is:

$$\text{Manhattan}_{\text{distance}} = |2 - 7| + |2 - 5|$$

$$\text{Manhattan}_{\text{distance}} = 5 + 3$$

$$\text{Manhattan}_{\text{distance}} = 8 \text{ m}$$

Note that this is not the same value (5.83 m) calculated using the Pythagorean theorem in the previous section.

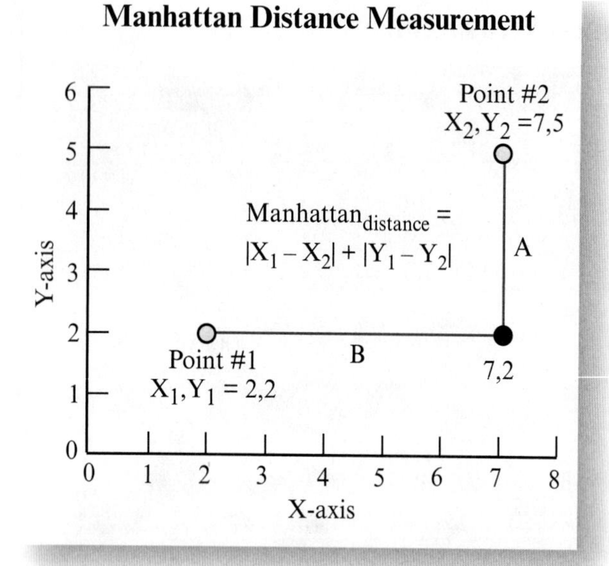

FIGURE 8–3 The calculation of the Manhattan distance between Point #1 and Point #2 in an *X*, *Y* Cartesian coordinate system.

Therefore, while it is often very useful to determine the Euclidean distance between Point #1 and Point #2 "as the crow flies" using the Pythagorean theorem, other factors must sometimes be considered before a practical distance measurement can be made. In fact, many geographic areas have features that *impede* making direct Pythagorean theorem-based distance measurements between two points.

For example, suppose we need to go from location A to location B in downtown Salt Lake City, UT (Figure 8-4). We are interested in traveling the shortest distance possible between location A and B. The white line is the hypotenuse of a right triangle and is the most direct and shortest route between the two locations. In this case, however, the Euclidean distance between location A and B is actually of little value because it would be necessary to walk through buildings, climb over fences and walk through numerous stands of vegetation to get from one location to another, even though it is the shortest distance.

A more suitable approach to obtaining an accurate measurement of the functional or practical distance between location A and B is to a) identify a route that takes into account existing roads and trails and subdivide it into *n* (e.g., 6) logical line segments, and then b) compute the distance of these *n* segments using either the Pythagorean theorem or Manhattan distance logic. The more practical distance between location A and location B would be one of the colored lines drawn in Figure 8-4.

Other Considerations

Both Euclidean and Manhattan distance measurements are useful for many applications. The decision to use one distance measurement technique versus the other is based on numerous factors. For example, it is unlikely that the terrain will be completely flat between points under investigation or that there will be no physical impediments along the route traveled. In addition, the quickest route between two points is not always the shortest route. For example, when traveling from one point to another in a car, it may be quicker to travel on limited-access highways rather than "surface" streets—even if the surface street route is shorter.

Least-cost distance uses a friction surface, such as a digital terrain model, to determine the least-cost route to get from one point to another. This kind of measurement is especially useful when a person is hiking in hilly or mountainous terrain. To get from a beginning point to an ending point, a least-cost distance would examine the topography and perhaps the slope of the terrain and determine the best route to hike. Similarly, assume you are going to ride a bike from your home to the grocery store. Both your home and the grocery store are located at approximately the same elevation. However, it is possible to ascend and descend many hills on your way to the grocery store depending on the route you select. Perhaps there is a somewhat longer route to the store that has virtually no elevation or slope change. You would probably choose the flat route if you were mainly interested in purchasing groceries. Conversely, you might select a more "hilly" route if you wanted a strenuous workout. You could also take into consideration the traffic volume or the scenic views and landmarks along the potential routes. A somewhat longer route on a less-congested highway might be superior to the shorter route on a heavily congested highway.

Given these considerations and others discussed in Chapter 7, it is easy to appreciate how complicated routing and networking can become. Users must often input many different parameters to determine the optimum route from one point to another.

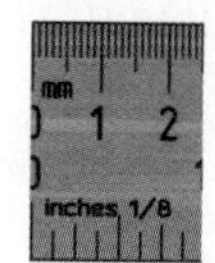

Polygon Perimeter and Area Measurements

Many geospatial projects require the measurement of polygon perimeter and area. For example, perhaps you are interested in the area of a particular stand (patch)

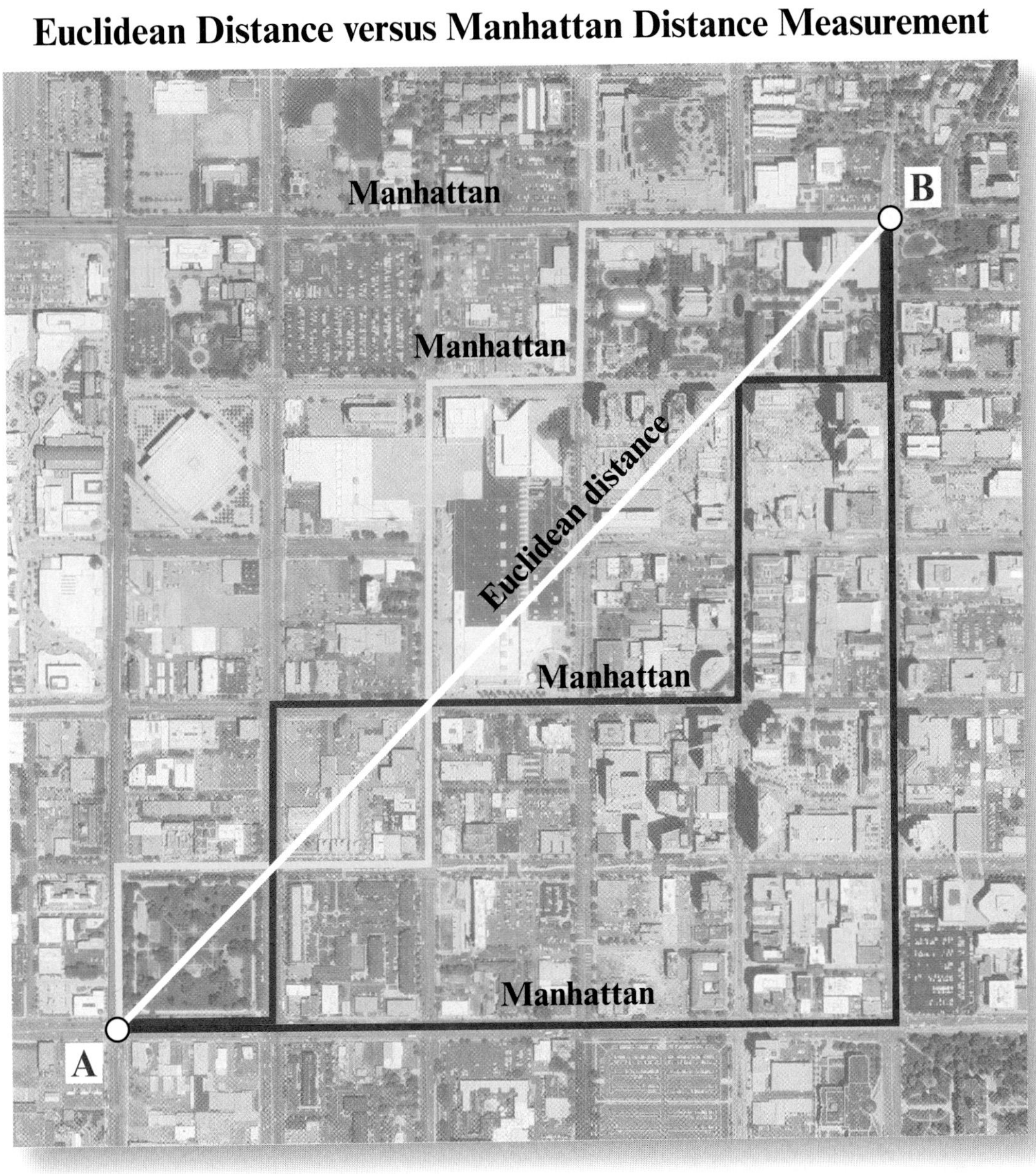

Euclidean Distance versus Manhattan Distance Measurement

FIGURE 8–4 The white line from the intersection at location A to the intersection at location B would require you to walk through commercial buildings, climb over fences, and pass through parks and natural areas. Therefore, the Euclidean distance (white line) would not be representative of the practical distance to walk from location A to location B. Conversely, it is possible to determine the Manhattan "round-the-block" distance for the same journey. In this example, all of the lines except for the white line, have exactly the same length from location A to location B as they traverse through the city (aerial photography courtesy of State of Utah).

of old-growth forest or you wish to compare the areas of forest patches from different years. You may also be interested in the perimeter of each of the patches. Other studies may be interested in the perimeter and area of U.S. Census Bureau subdivision units such as census tracts, blocks, counties, and states. These kinds of measurements are commonly required, and it is important to understand the process by which they are calculated. The following sections describe how to measure polygon perimeter and area.

Perimeter Measurement

The **perimeter** of a polygon is measured by determining the length of each of the n line segments associated with a polygon and then summing them:

$$Perimeter = \sum_{i=1}^{n} length_i \tag{8.3}$$

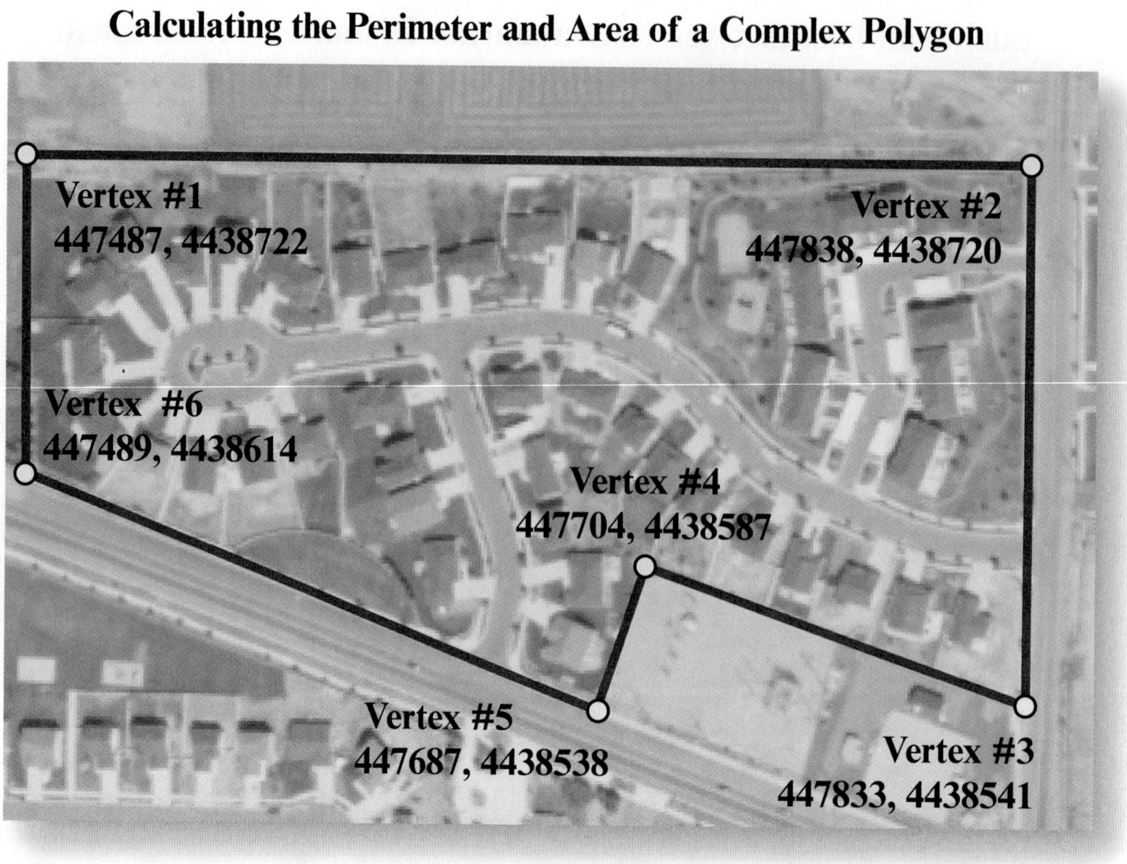

FIGURE 8–5 A six-sided polygon circumscribes a subdivision located in Spanish Fork, UT (vertex #1 is used twice to close the polygon). The perimeter and area of this polygon can be calculated using Equations 8.3 and 8.4, respectively (aerial photography courtesy of State of Utah).

The length of each line segment is usually computed using the Pythagorean theorem as previously discussed. For example, consider the six-sided polygon with six vertices circumscribing a subdivision in Spanish Fork, UT, shown in Figure 8-5. The coordinates of the six polygon vertices are listed in Table 8-3.

To determine the perimeter of this polygon, the Pythagorean theorem was used to compute the distance associated with each line segment. The perimeter of the polygon is 1,039 m.

Polygon Area Measurement

The **area** of a polygon is a measurement of the geographic region enclosed by the polygon. Calculating the area of a polygon is a simple task when the polygon has a "regular" geometric shape—such as a square, rectangle, circle, or right triangle. In these cases, standard formulas may be used to calculate area (Table 8-4).

These regular shapes are prevalent in many anthropogenic (human-made) landscapes (e.g., rectangular or square property boundaries, road networks, circular crop patterns). However, these common shapes are less prevalent in natural environments, where it becomes more complicated and computationally intense to calculate the area of an irregularly shaped polygon.

A complex polygon's area may be computed if the cartesian coordinates $(X_1, Y_1), (X_2, Y_2),..., (X_n, Y_n)$ of all its vertices, listed in order, are known. The formula is

$$Area = 0.5\left|\sum_{i=1}^{n} Y(X_{i+1} - X_{i-1})\right| \quad (8.4)$$

where Y is the y-axis (or Northing) coordinate for each vertex, X_{i+1} is the x-axis (or Easting) coordinate for the next vertex, and X_{i-1} is the x-axis (or Easting) coordinate for the previous vertex. This equation must be calculated using sequential vertices going in the same direction. Let us compare both the simple and complex formulas for computing the area of a square in a Cartesian coordinate system (Table 8-4 and Figure 8-6). We could use the simple formula listed in Table 8-4 [Area = $side^2$ = (2 x 2) = 4] to quickly determine that

TABLE 8–3 UTM coordinates of six vertices surrounding a subdivision in Spanish Fork, UT (Figure 8-5), used to demonstrate how to calculate the perimeter of the complex polygon.

Vertex	UTM X-coordinate Easting	UTM Y-coordinate Northing	Distance from Vertex to Vertex (e.g., 1 to 2)
1	447487	4438722	
2	447838	4438720	351.01
3	447833	4438541	179.07
4	447704	4438587	136.96
5	447687	4438538	51.87
6	447489	4438614	212.08
1	447487	4438722	108.02
		$Perimeter = \sum_{i=1}^{n} length_i =$	**1,039 m**

TABLE 8–4 Formulas used to compute the area of regular geometric shapes.

Shape	Area Formula
Square	$side^2$
Rectangle	$length \times width$
Circle	$\pi \times radius^2$
Right Triangle	$\frac{base \times height}{2}$

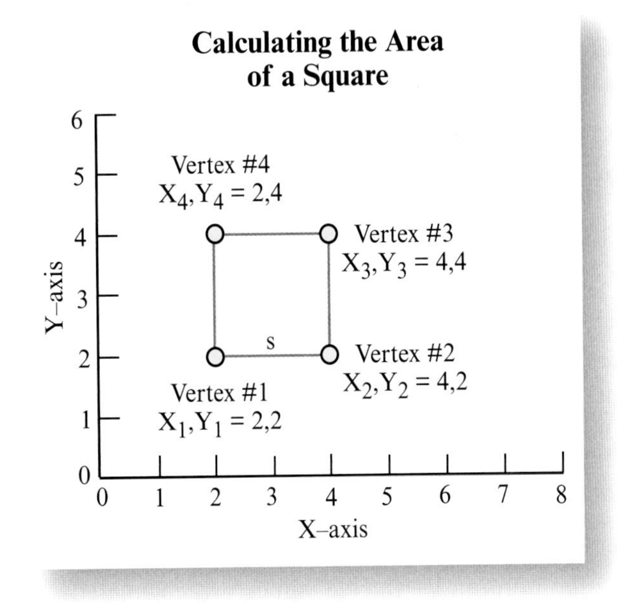

FIGURE 8–6 A square in a Cartesian coordinate system.

the area of the square is 4 m^2. Use of Equation 8.4 yields the same answer as demonstrated in Table 8-5.

Obviously, when dealing with common shapes, it is easier to use the simple equations to compute area. Equation 8.4 should be used when it is necessary to calculate the area of a complex polygon. For example, consider the use of Equation 8.4 to compute the area of the complex polygon surrounding the residential subdivision in Spanish Fork, UT (Figure 8-5). Table 8-6 presents the *X*- and *Y*-coordinates of the six vertices and the contribution calculated for each vertex. The area of the polygon is 52,216 m^2 or approximately 5.2 hectares. This example only has six vertices. As you might imagine, it is more computationally intensive to calculate the area of an extremely complex polygon that has hundreds or even thousands of vertices. Also,

TABLE 8–5 Easting and Northing values for the square shown in Figure 8-6 and the computation of its area using Equation 8.4.

Vertex	X-coordinate (Easting)	Y-coordinate (Northing)	Contribution
1	2	2	4
2	4	2	4
3	4	4	-8
4	2	4	-8
		$Area = 0.5\left\lvert \sum_{i=1}^{n} Y(X_{i+1} - X_{i-1}) \right\rvert =$	4 m^2

some polygons may have polygons inside them. In such cases, the area of the enclosed polygon needs to be calculated and then subtracted from the area of the surrounding polygon.

After calculating the basic perimeter and area properties of various polygons (patches) throughout a landscape, it is possible to use these properties to compute numerous landscape ecology metrics often used in geographic research (e.g., Frohn, 1998; Frohn and Hao, 2006).

Raster Polygon Measurement

Calculating polygon area and perimeter in raster datasets is different from measuring area and perimeter in vector datasets. To determine the area of a single patch in a raster dataset, you first isolate the polygon region by selecting the cells within it. Then, reclassify (recode) the cells so that their values are unique. Finally, sum the number of cells (e.g., 20) and multiply it by the area of each cell (e.g., 100 m^2) to determine the polygon area (2,000 m^2). Remember that a cell (pixel) that is 10 x 10 m has an area equal to 100 m^2.

Raster polygon perimeter values are calculated in a similar manner, where the outside cells of the patch are identified and summed, and then multiplied by the perimeter cell's side distance. It is important to remember that the cell's side distance can be the actual pixel cell size (e.g., 10 m) or the hypotenuse of the cell size (e.g., the hypotenuse of a 10 x 10 m pixel is 14.142 m).

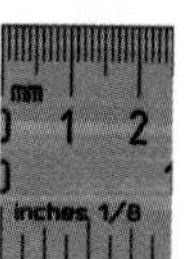

Descriptive Statistics

Before describing some of the spatial statistics that you will likely use, it is important to first introduce some basic descriptive statistics. Most GIS have the ability to quickly provide summary statistics of database fields or geographic phenomena. These statistics are often employed as a first look at the data. The first set of descriptive statistics measures central tendency including the mode, median, and mean. The **mode** is the most common value in a dataset. It can be computed using all levels of data (e.g., nominal, ordinal, interval, and ratio). The **median** is the middle value of an ordered dataset. As such, it can only be used in datasets that can be ordered or ranked. Therefore, a median can only be calculated when the data are ordinal, interval, or ratio scale. In datasets with an odd number of values, the median is the middle value. When there is an even number of values, the median is the average of the two middle-ranked values. The **mean** of a dataset is simply its average and is calculated using the equation

$$\bar{x} = \frac{\sum_{i=1}^{n} X}{n} \tag{8.5}$$

where the sum of all observation values (X) is divided by the total number of values (n). The mean is affected by outliers, or extreme values, whereas the median is not. This is why median values are often used instead

TABLE 8–6 UTM coordinates of the six vertices surrounding a subdivision in Spanish Fork, UT (Figure 8-5), used to demonstrate how to calculate the area of a complex polygon.

Vertex	UTM X-coordinate Easting	UTM Y-coordinate Northing	Contribution
6	447489	4438614	
1	447487	4438722	1549113978
2	447838	4438720	1535797120
3	447833	4438541	-594764494
4	447704	4438587	-648033702
5	447687	4438538	-954285670
6	447489	4438614	-887722800
1	447487	4438722	
	$Area = 0.5\left\|\sum_{i=1}^{n} Y(X_{i+1} - X_{i-1})\right\| =$		**52,216 m²**

of mean values when describing socioeconomic characteristics. For example, assume you are in a room with nine other people and you wanted to use the mean to describe the income of all ten people. If nine of the ten people had annual incomes of approximately $80,000, but one person had an annual income of $200,000, then the mean annual income of the group will be much larger than is representative of the group. Conversely, the median annual income of the group is not affected by the large outlier.

Where the mean, median, and mode are equal (or at least close to equal), the distribution is said to be **normal** or bell-shaped (Figure 8-7a). Where the mean, median, and mode are different, the distribution is said to be non-normal or *skewed* (Figure 8-7d,e).

Measures of dispersion about the mean include variance, standard deviation, skewness, and kurtosis. **Variance** measures the average squared variation about the mean and is calculated using

$$s^2 = \frac{\sum_{i=1}^{n} (X - \bar{x})^2}{n - 1} \tag{8.6}$$

where the mean ($\bar{x}$) is subtracted from each observation value, X, and then squared. These values are summed and divided by the number of observations minus one.

Standard deviation describes the average deviation about the mean and is calculated using

$$s = \sqrt{\frac{\sum_{i=1}^{n} (X - \bar{x})^2}{n - 1}} \tag{8.7}$$

Standard deviation is the square root of the variance, and it brings the values back to the original units. Standard deviation is used quite frequently to describe general dispersion about the mean. In fact, in normal (bell-shaped) distributions, the **empirical rule** states that about 68% of the observations will fall within one standard deviation of the mean; about 95% of the observations will fall within two standard deviations of the mean; and almost 100% (actually 99.7%) of the observations will fall within three standard deviations of the mean.

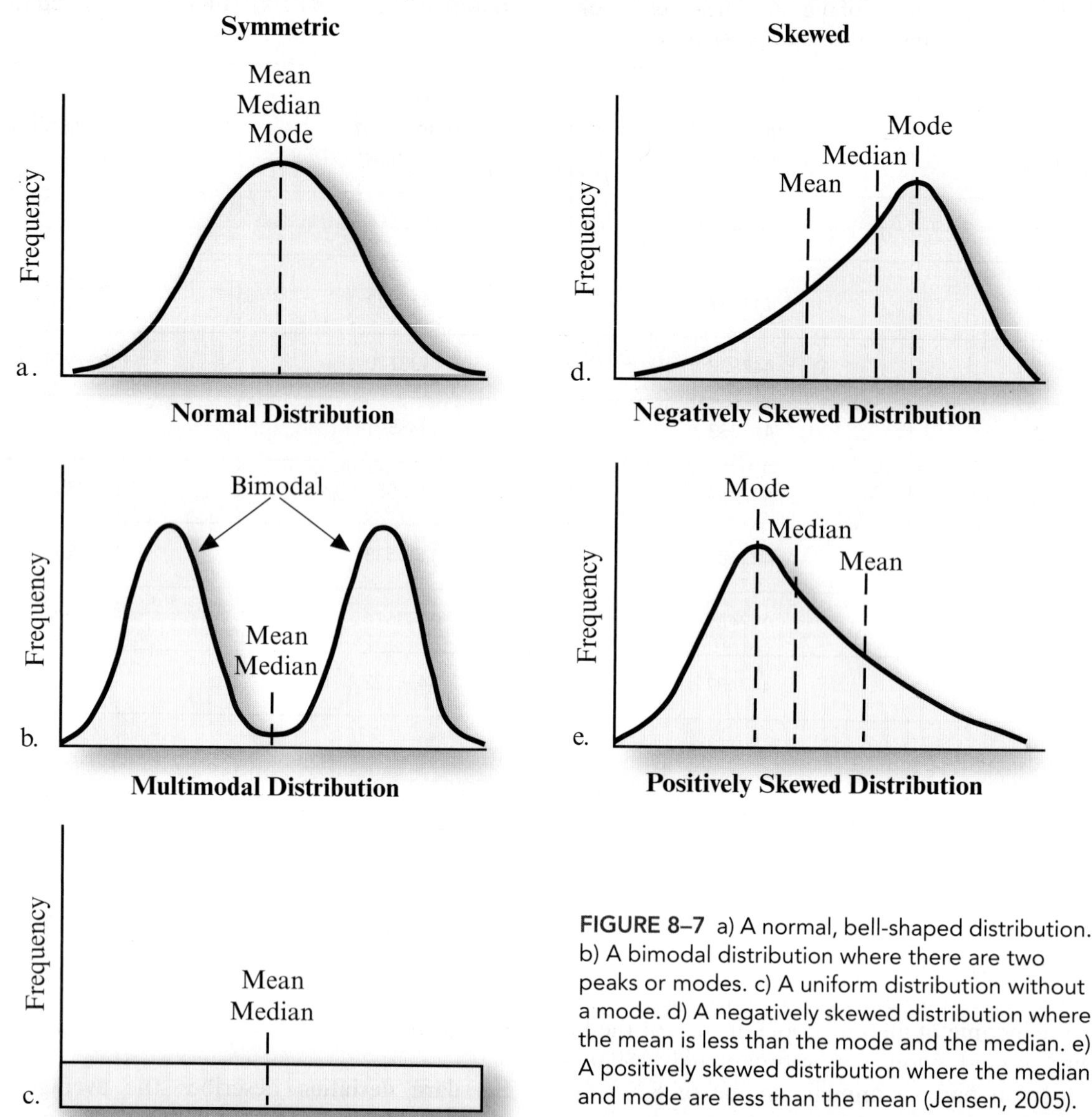

FIGURE 8–7 a) A normal, bell-shaped distribution. b) A bimodal distribution where there are two peaks or modes. c) A uniform distribution without a mode. d) A negatively skewed distribution where the mean is less than the mode and the median. e) A positively skewed distribution where the median and mode are less than the mean (Jensen, 2005).

Standard deviation is often used in thematic mapping (e.g., Krygier and Wood, 2011). The median California county income is shown using five class intervals based on natural breaks in Figure 8-8a. California's median income by county displayed using standard deviation class intervals is shown in Figure 8-8b.

Skewness measures the asymmetry of the distribution of data values and is calculated using the equation

$$skewness = \frac{1}{n}\sum_{i=1}^{n}\left(\frac{X_i - \bar{x}}{s}\right)^3 \qquad (8.8)$$

where $\bar{x}$ is the mean and s is the standard deviation. Skewness is zero for any symmetric distribution. When the median is greater than the mean it signifies that the distribution is negatively skewed (Figure 8-7d). When the median is less than the mean, the skewness is positive, indicating that the tail of the distribution extends toward larger data values (Figure 8-7e).

Kurtosis (from the Greek word *kurtos*, meaning "bulging") measures the peakedness of the distribution of data values. Kurtosis is measured using the equation

$$kurtosis = \left(\left[\frac{1}{n}\sum_{i=1}^{n}\left(\frac{X_i - \bar{x}}{s}\right)^4\right] - 3\right) \qquad (8.9)$$

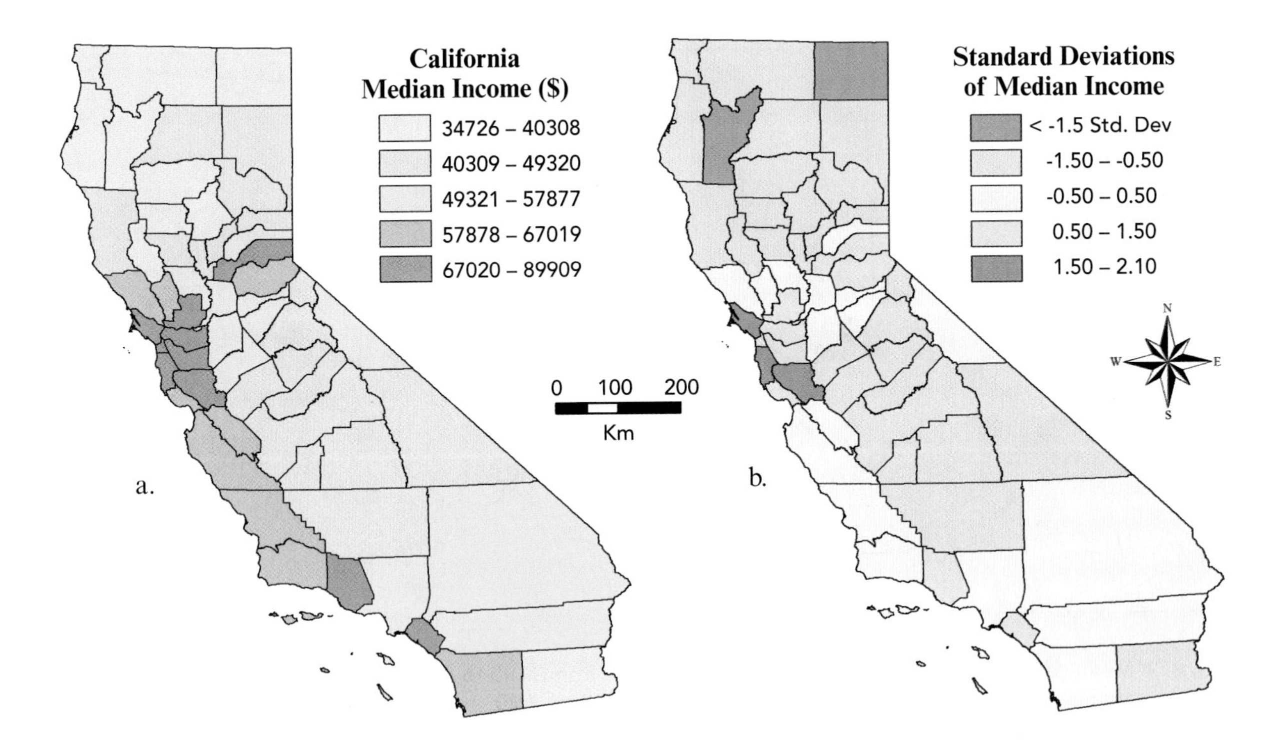

FIGURE 8–8 a) A map showing the median income of California by county using five natural break class intervals. b) A map of the median income of California created using class intervals based on standard deviations above and below the mean (data courtesy of U.S. Bureau of the Census).

where X represents the observation values, n is the total number of values in the distribution, and $\bar{x}$ is the mean of the distribution. A kurtosis value >0 suggests a pointed or peaked distribution (curve). If the value is <0, the curve is more flat or less-peaked. A value of approximately zero suggests that the data are normally distributed.

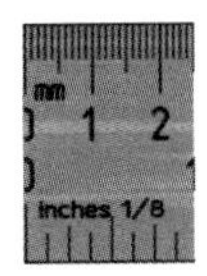

Descriptive Spatial Statistics

People have been drawing maps and looking at spatial relationships for thousands of years. Statistics play an important role in processing spatial data for mapping and discovering spatial relationships. Within statistics there is a special set of procedures that are useful when analyzing spatial data often referred to as **spatial statistics**. These statistics allow you to quantitatively describe and assess certain spatial characteristics of landscapes. They also provide a way to compare different landscapes and determine whether a given distribution of a phenomena is significantly different from a random distribution.

Mean Center

Some basic descriptive statistics can be used to describe landscapes. These statistics are very similar to their non-spatial counterparts. An example of this kind of statistic is the mean center of a geographic distribution. The **mean center** is a measure of central tendency that can be used to determine the center of a distribution plotted in geographic or Cartesian coordinates. An example of this is the identification of the mean center of the population distribution of the United States. After each decennial census, the U.S. Census Bureau calculates the place where an imaginary map of the United States would balance perfectly if all residents were of identical weight. The migration of the mean center of population in the United States from 1790 to 2010 is shown in Figure 8-9. Based on the 2010 Census of the United States, the mean center of population is near Plato, MO, in Texas County.

Another example is the identification of the mean center of all the functioning water wells in Vigo County, IN (Figure 8-10a). Knowing the mean center of this spatial distribution could help a user to determine an optimum location for a new well or help determine where the underground aquifer may be depleted.

This method might also be used to determine the mean center of a series of crimes, traffic violations, or other

Mean Center of Population of the United States from 1790 to 2010

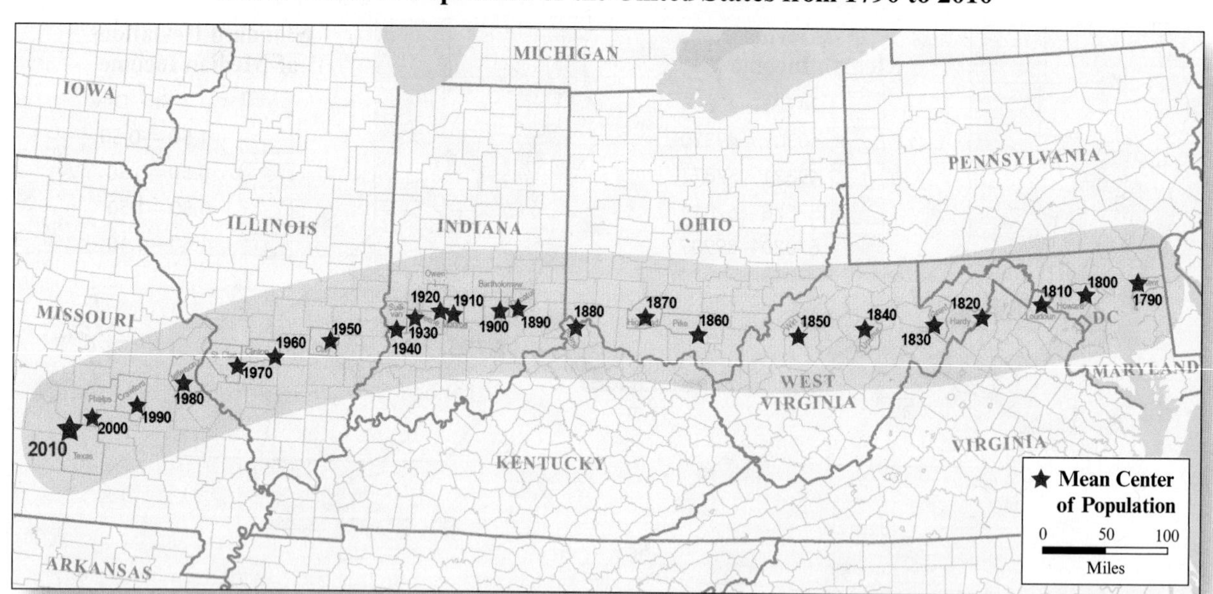

FIGURE 8–9 Mean center of the population of the United States from 1790 to 2010. Note how the center has followed a general west-southwest track. Mean center of population is near Plato, MO, in 2010 (data courtesy of Geography Division, U.S. Bureau of the Census).

kinds of data. For example, assume that similar crimes have been committed in the same area over a period of several months. Law enforcement officials could geocode each crime and then determine where the mean center of the crimes is located. This information could be used by officers to determine the best location for extra police presence. Another example would be to plot all of the people in a city or county affected by a particular lung ailment. This could help researchers determine if there is perhaps a centrally located cause to the ailment.

Standard Distance

Standard distance is another measure that can be used to describe a spatial distribution. This measure is similar to standard deviation. It determines how dispersed a distribution is about the mean center. In the Vigo County, IN, example described above, the standard distance was calculated for the distribution (Figure 8-10b). The green circle is the first standard distance about the mean center. If the points in the distribution are random, then about 68% of the points are encompassed by the first standard distance.

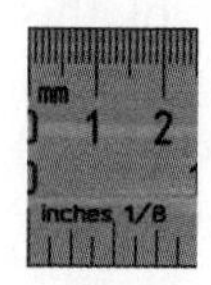

Spatial Autocorrelation

One of the most heavily used spatial statistics is spatial autocorrelation. **Spatial autocorrelation** measures the spatial ordering and spatial dependency of geographic data and indicates whether neighboring or adjacent values vary together. In other words, spatial autocorrelation is the correlation of the variable to itself through space (Burt et al., 2009). Spatial autocorrelation is based on Waldo Tobler's first law of geography where "everything is related to everything else, but near things are more related than distant things" (Tobler, 1970).

Positive spatial autocorrelation means that nearby or neighboring values are more similar than distant values. This kind of relationship is observed quite frequently in both anthropogenic (human-made) and natural systems. For example, the distribution of median house values or household income tends to be positively spatially autocorrelated in cities because more wealthy residents tend to live in neighborhoods that segregate themselves from lower income areas. As a result, lower income residents live in other areas.

In physical geography, biogeographers often find that adjacent forest patches are positively spatially autocorrelated in terms of the number and types of species present. Negative spatial autocorrelation describes patterns where neighboring values are dissimilar. This kind of pattern is not found very often, but could be very useful when mapping the effects of some artificial (anthropogenic) influence on a pattern. An example might be the selection of trees planted in home gardens. When a pattern is neither positively nor negative-

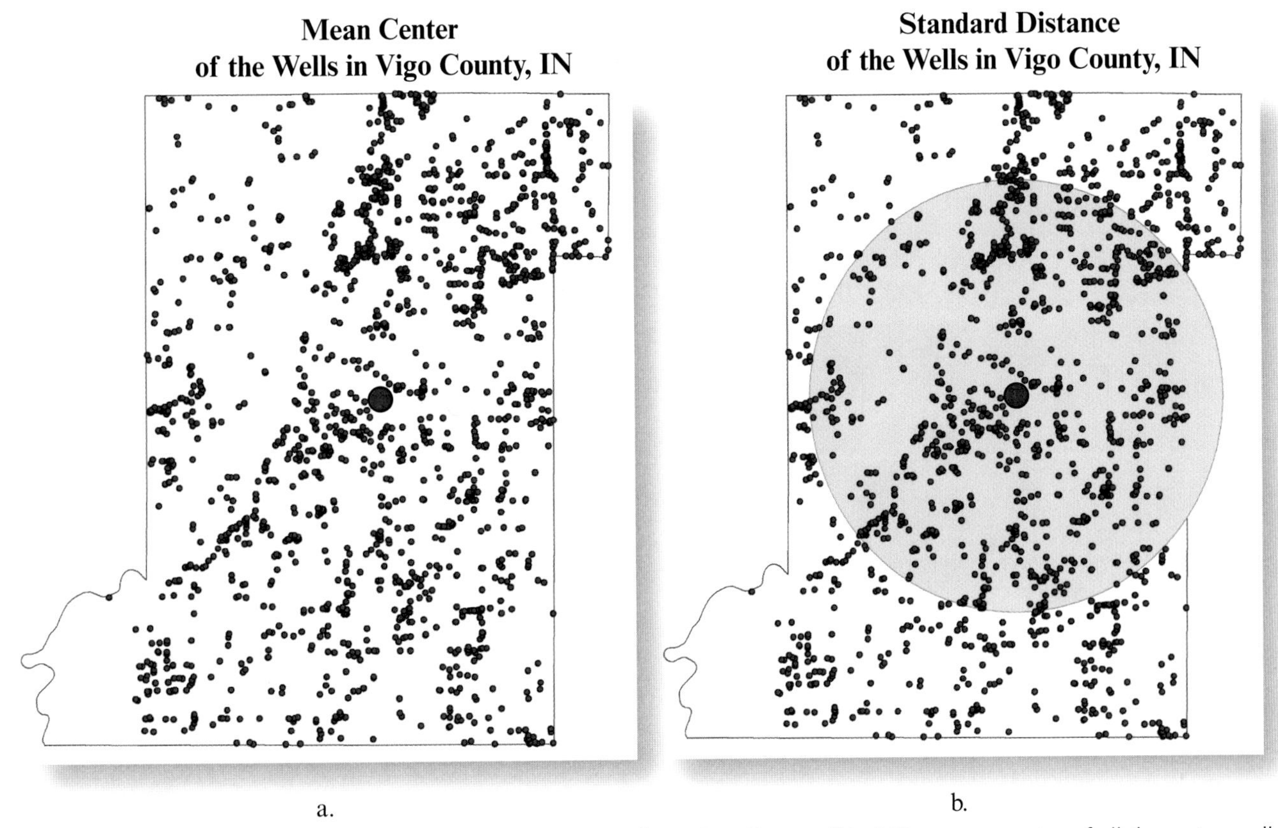

FIGURE 8–10 The location of all known functioning water wells in Vigo County, IN. a) The mean center of all the water wells is located at the red dot. b) The green circle is the first standard distance about the mean center. If the points in the distribution are random, then 68% of the points are encompassed by the first standard distance (data courtesy of IndianaMap).

ly spatially autocorrelated, the pattern is said to be random.

Finally, spatial autocorrelation measures whether similar values cluster together, and is therefore scale dependent. At one scale, a particular feature may appear to be clustered, yet that same distribution may not appear clustered at another scale. Therefore, scale must be considered before beginning a spatial autocorrelation analysis and when interpreting results.

Moran's I

The **Moran's I** measure of spatial autocorrelation has been used since 1950 (Moran, 1950). Moran's I measures the interdependence in spatial distributions and allows researchers to test hypotheses about the interdependence of spatial data. It is most often used to determine the spatial autocorrelation of interval- or ratio-scaled attribute data—although other attributes (e.g., nominal and ordinal) may also be used.

Moran's I ranges from –1 to +1. Positive values suggest that nearby areas are similar and negative values suggest that nearby areas are dissimilar. Values close to zero indicate no correlation between the attribute values. Moran's I is found in many GIS software programs and is expressed as (Paradis, 2011)

$$\text{Moran's I} = \frac{N}{S_o} \frac{\sum_{i=1}^{n} \sum_{j=1}^{n} w_{ij}(x_i - \bar{x})(x_j - \bar{x})}{\sum_{i=1}^{n} (x_i - \bar{x})^2} \tag{8.10}$$

where $\bar{x}$ is the mean of variable x; x_i is the value at point i; x_j is the value at point i's neighbor j; w_{ij} is the weight between observation i and j; and S_o is the sum of all w_{ij}.

A map of the 2000 mean family size found in Census Block Groups in several communities near Salt Lake City, UT, is shown in Figure 8-11. By visually examining the map, you can probably discern that mean family size may be spatially autocorrelated, i.e., larger families tend to occur throughout the west and southwest part of the valley. However, to quantitatively determine this relationship you could calculate Moran's I which equals 0.44. This value indicates that there is positive spatial autocorrelation of average family size in the Census Block Groups in the Salt Lake Valley. In

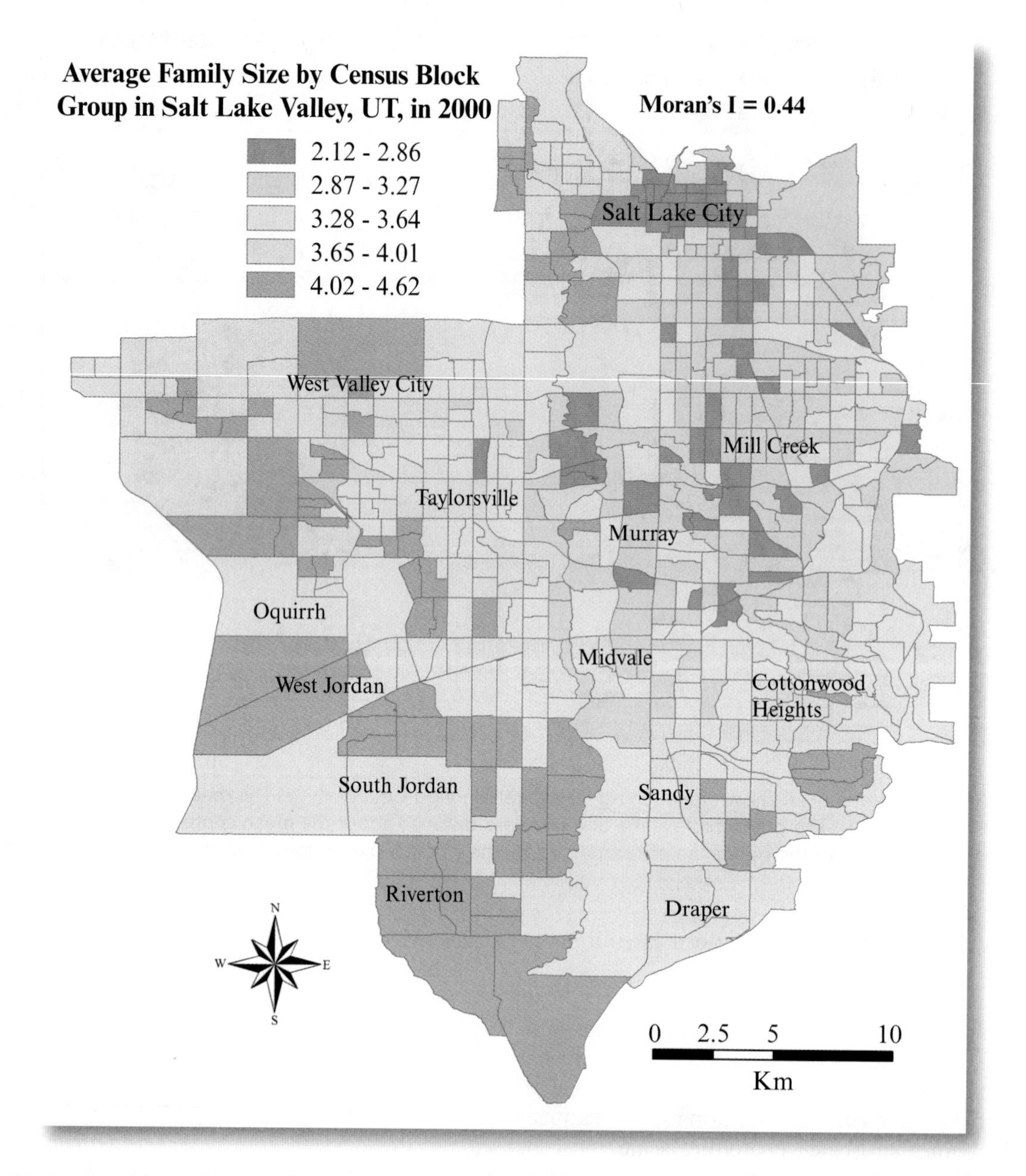

FIGURE 8–11 A map of the 2000 mean family size found within 124 Census Block Groups in communities near Salt Lake City, UT. Note the similarity of mean family size for many adjacent polygons. Moran's I value for this geographic area is 0.44 suggesting that the data are definitely clustered (see report in Figure 8-12) (data courtesy of the U.S. Bureau of the Census).

addition to the Moran's I value, a *z*-score is typically reported that helps the analyst to determine the significance of the pattern. For example, in the ArcGIS® summary report shown in Figure 8-12, the *z*-score is 69.9, which means that there is less than 1% likelihood that the clustered pattern could be the result of random chance.

Interesting geographic questions can be posed based on the Moran's I analysis. For example, why are larger families settling in block groups around the western and southern part of the valley? Could factors be adjusted that would encourage larger families to live in areas where smaller families currently live?

Applications that might use spatial autocorrelation and Moran's I include measuring broad trends in ethnic or racial segregation over time in a particular city, county, or neighborhood. In this case, Moran's I would help determine whether segregation is increasing, decreasing, or remaining the same. Another example where spatial autocorrelation would be useful is evaluating the distribution of a disease through space and time—is the disease isolated, concentrated, or becoming more diffuse?

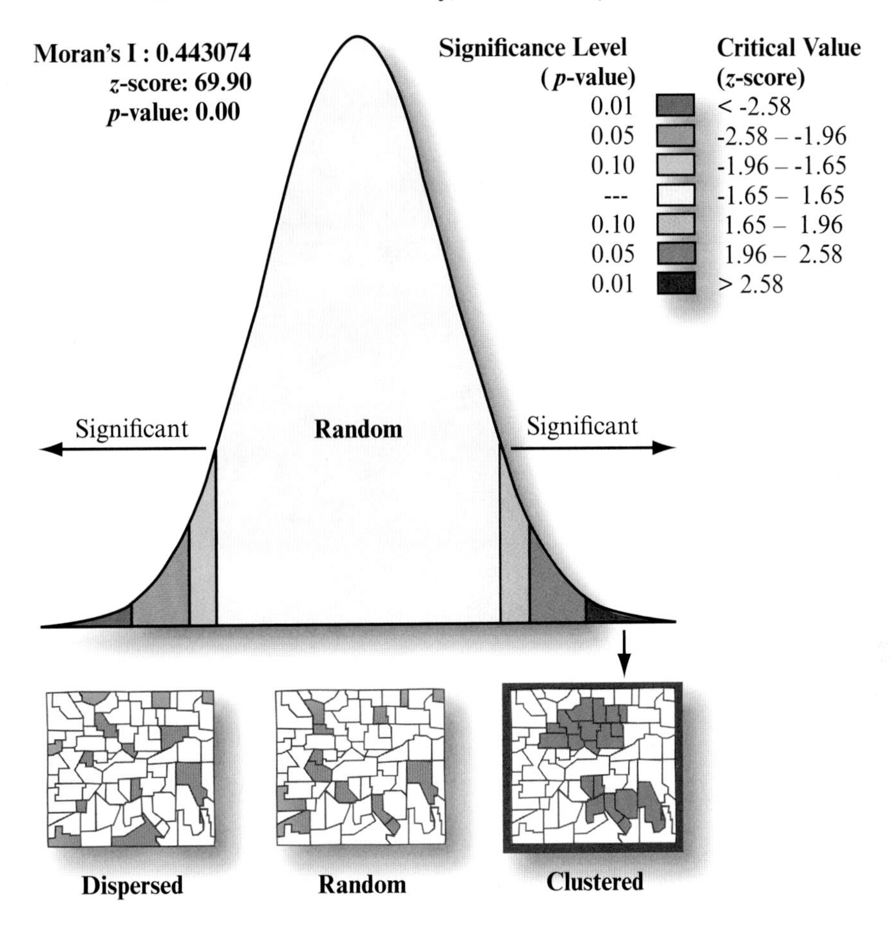

FIGURE 8–12 ArcGIS® summary report of the computation of Moran's I (0.44) for the 2000 Salt Lake Valley, UT, family size dataset shown in Figure 8-11. The z-score of 69.9 means that there is less than 1% likelihood that the clustered pattern could be the result of random chance. Therefore, the distribution is definitely clustered as opposed to being random or dispersed (summary format courtesy of Esri, Inc.).

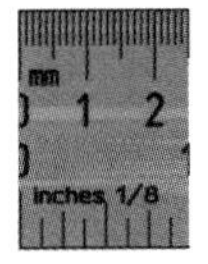

Point Pattern Analysis

Points in real life could be well locations, bird nests, oil drilling sites, crime locations, or telephone poles. When these points are placed on maps they often exhibit distinct patterns that are the result of some spatial process. This spatial process is a result of underlying forces that might be determining the way the points are distributed. Understanding what may be driving the point location process helps researchers to model and predict where other points (e.g., bird nests, potential oil drilling sites, or well locations) may be located. In point pattern analysis, the main emphasis is on the location of the points—not on any attributes that the points possess. This contrasts with spatial autocorrelation where an area's attributes are analyzed. Two methods are often used to determine point patterns: quadrat analysis and nearest-neighbor analysis.

Quadrat Analysis

A **quadrat** is a user-defined geographic area that is usually square or rectangular. **Quadrat analysis** is often used to determine the uniformity of points distributed in a number of quadrats. For example, if you were studying the nesting locations of sparrows, you would overlay your study area with quadrats and count the number of nests within each quadrat. If each quadrat contained exactly the same number of nests, the distribution would be considered to be uniform. Conversely, a landscape with all of the nests in just a few of the quadrats suggests that the nests are clustered.

A quantitative measure can be calculated to determine if the points are clustered by assuming that all quadrats should have the same number of points (nests). To calculate this, the total number of nests is divided by the number of quadrats in the study area. This number then becomes the expected distribution if the nests are normally distributed. A *Chi-square* statistical test can

FIGURE 8–13 The geographic distribution of sparrow nest sites (blue dots) near Cranberry Lake, NY. Twenty quadrats each 250 x 250 m (62,500 m^2) in size were overlaid on the nests (in white) to perform quadrat analysis. The number of sparrow nests in each quadrat (in yellow) were used to compute the *Chi-square* statistic to determine whether or not the nests were uniformly distributed (data courtesy of Elaina Tuttle; aerial photogaphy courtesy of USGS).

be applied by subtracting the expected (E) number of points found in each quadrat from the observed (O) number of points in each quadrat, squaring the result, and then dividing by the expected number for the quadrat:

$$\chi^2 = \sum_{i=1}^{n} \frac{(O-E)^2}{E} \tag{8.11}$$

This value is summed for all n quadrats. The resulting value—the *Chi square* statistic—can be compared with critical values in a standardized table.

To demonstrate the use of quadrat analysis, consider the 36 sparrow nests located near Cranberry Lake, NY, shown in Figure 8-13 and summarized in Table 8-7 (Formica et al., 2004; Tuttle et al., 2006). The sparrow nest locations (blue dots) are superimposed on a color-infrared aerial photograph of the study area. By visually examining the illustration, you can probably determine that the nests do not appear to be uniformly distributed throughout the landscape. Rather, there seems to be a pattern to the distribution of nests; they appear to be associated with water bodies. Quadrat analysis was applied to these nest locations using square quadrats that were 250 x 250 m (62,500m^2) in size (Figure 8-13). The number of nests found within each quadrat are summarized in Table 8-7.

TABLE 8–7 The number of sparrow nests observed in twenty 250 x 250 m quadrats near Cranberry Lake, NY (Figure 8-13), and the computation of the associated *Chi-square* statistic. The quadrat numbers begin in the upper left at number one and proceed left to right, top to bottom.

Quadrat	Observed Nests	Contribution
1	3	0.8
2	4	2.6889
3	0	1.8
4	0	1.8
5	2	0.0222
6	7	15.022
7	1	0.3556
8	0	1.8
9	7	15.022
10	1	0.3556
11	2	0.0222
12	0	1.8
13	0	1.8
14	0	1.8
15	3	0.8
16	3	0.8
17	0	1.8
18	0	1.8
19	3	0.8
20	0	1.8
	36	
Chi-square	$\chi^2 = \sum_{i=1}^{n} \frac{(O-E)^2}{E} =$	**52.89**

The expected count of nests for each quadrat was determined by dividing the number of nest points (36) by the total number of quadrats (20) yielding a value of 1.8. This number was subtracted from the observed count found within each quadrat, squared, and divided by 1.8. The summation of this value for each quadrat equals the *Chi-square* statistic which was 52.89 (Table 8-7). This value was compared to the value found in the *Chi-square* statistical table (degrees of freedom = *N*-2 or 34) at alpha = 0.05. The *Chi-square* statistic of 52.89 exceeded the table value of 48.6 suggesting that the nesting sites are not uniformly distributed. Conversely, if the calculated *Chi-square* value was less than the table value it would be necessary to conclude that the nests are uniformly distributed.

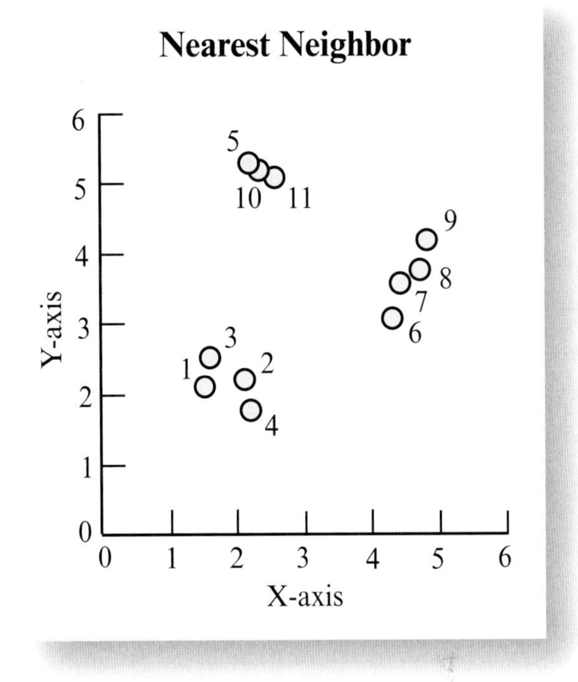

FIGURE 8–14 The geographic distribution of 11 hypothetical point observations used to demonstrate nearest-neighbor point analysis. The point coordinates and the distance to nearest neighbors are summarized in Table 8-8.

One of the shortcomings of quadrat analysis is that the size of the quadrat can dramatically affect the results of the *Chi-square* test. Therefore, care must be taken when deciding upon the size of the quadrat.

Nearest-Neighbor Point Analysis

Nearest-neighbor point analysis is commonly performed using a GIS. Nearest-neighbor analysis creates an index based on the distance of each object to its closest neighboring object. This analysis determines whether the spatial distribution of the locations is random or non-random, and is expressed as an index of the ratio of the observed distance between points divided by the expected distance (hypothetical random distribution).

One of the assumptions of nearest-neighbor point analysis is that the points are "free" to locate anywhere throughout the study area. For example, consider the geographic distribution of the 11 hypothetical points shown in Figure 8-14 and listed in Table 8-8. The distance from each point to all other points was computed using the Pythagorean theorem. Each point's nearest neighbor and the Euclidean distance to the

TABLE 8–8 The 11 points shown in Figure 8-14 with their nearest neighbor and Euclidean distance to nearest-neighbor.

Point	X	Y	Nearest Neighbor	Euclidean Distance to Nearest Neighbor
1	1.5	2.1	3	0.41
2	2.1	2.2	4	0.46
3	1.6	2.5	1	0.41
4	2.2	1.75	2	0.46
5	2.3	5.2	10	0.14
6	4.3	3.1	7	0.51
7	4.4	3.6	8	0.34
8	4.7	3.75	7	0.34
9	4.8	4.2	8	0.46
10	2.2	5.3	5	0.14
11	2.5	5.1	10	0.36
		d_a		0.37

nearest-neighbor are also summarized in Table 8-8. All of the distance to nearest neighbors are averaged together to determine d_a (or the actual nearest-neighbor distance).

To determine whether the points in this distribution are randomly distributed it is necessary to compare these values to the expected average between nearest neighbors in a random point distribution. The expected average distance between nearest neighbors for a random point distribution is:

$$d_e = \frac{1}{2\sqrt{n/A}} \quad (8.12)$$

where n is the number of points and A is the area of the study region. The area of the study in this hypothetical example is 36 (i.e., 6 x 6 = 36 square units). The ratio of the two values (d_a and d_e) will always equal one (or very close to one) if the points being analyzed are randomly distributed. Where there is a clustered pattern, distances to nearest neighbors are smaller than the expected distances; d_a is less than d_e and $R < 1$.

Therefore, in the example above, the expected random distance between each of the points in the hypothetical point pattern would be:

$$0.905 = \frac{1}{2\sqrt{11/36}}$$

This same equation can be written as:

$$Random = \frac{1}{2\sqrt{density}} \quad (8.13)$$

where density is equal to the number of points divided by the total area. In this example, the actual nearest-neighbor distance, d_a, was 0.37 (Table 8-8), which is much smaller than the expected distance (0.905). This value is also used to calculate the nearest-neighbor index described below.

Dispersed Distribution Index

Similar to determining the distance for a random point pattern, one can also calculate a value that depicts the mean nearest-neighbor values if the points were perfectly dispersed. The index for determining if the points are perfectly dispersed is calculated by dividing 1.07453 by the square root of the density:

$$Disperse = \frac{1.07453}{\sqrt{density}} \quad (8.14)$$

$$Disperse = \frac{1.07453}{\sqrt{0.31}} = 1.93$$

This index represents the distance the points would be apart if they were perfectly dispersed in the 36 units of geographic space. If the actual mean nearest-neighbor distance was close to this value we would say that the points are dispersed. Again, the actual nearest-neighbor distance in this example (0.37) is much smaller than this index (1.93). This means that the points are not dispersed throughout the landscape.

Nearest-Neighbor Ratio

The **nearest-neighbor ratio** provides a useful measure of the pattern in a single value. This ratio is simply the observed nearest-neighbor distance divided by the expected distance for a random distribution:

$$NNR = \frac{Dist_{Obs}}{Dist_{Ran}} \quad (8.15)$$

where $Dist_{Obs}$ is the mean nearest-neighbor distance and $Dist_{Ran}$ is the expected distance for a random point pattern (0.905). Based on the example data provided, the NNR would be (Figure 8-15):

$$NNR = \frac{0.37}{0.905} = 0.41$$

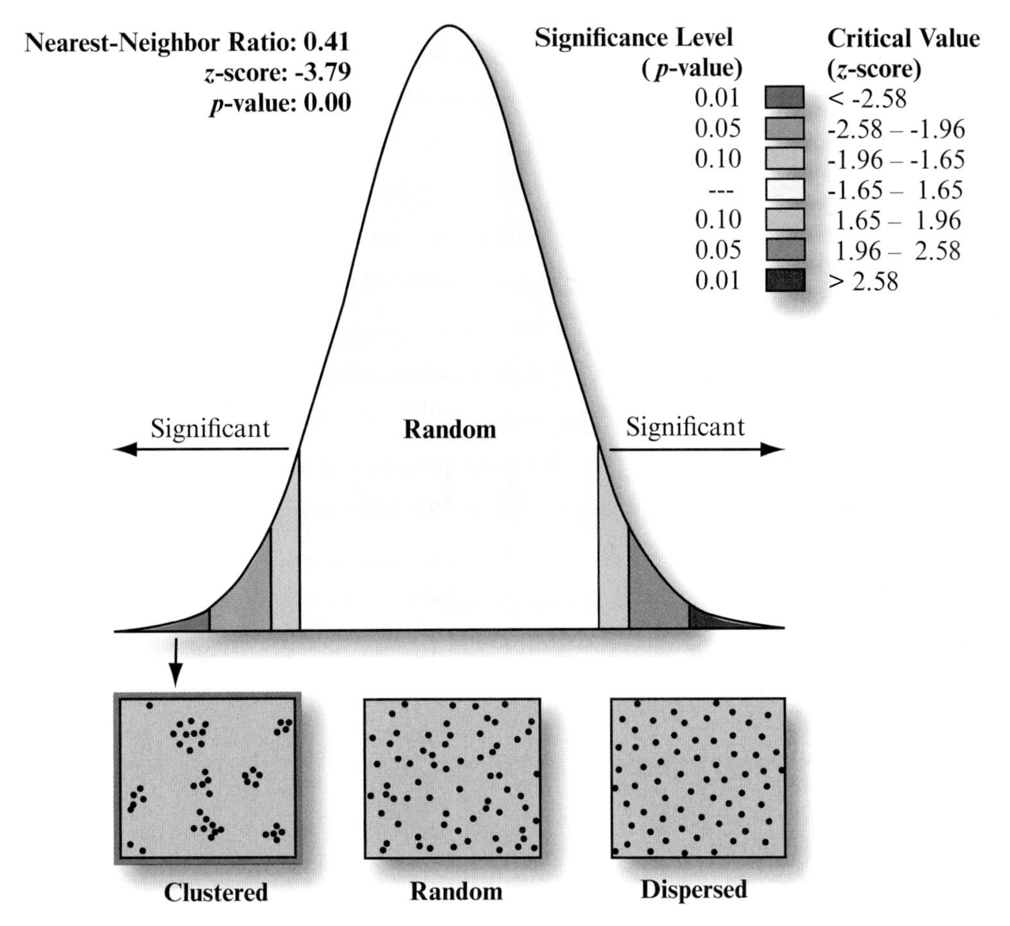

FIGURE 8–15 This report summarizes the results of the nearest-neighbor analysis of the 11 hypothetical points shown in Figure 8-14 and listed in Table 8-8. The nearest-neighbor ratio = 0.41 with a z-score of –3.79 and p-value of 0.00. Given the z-score of –3.79, there is less than 1% likelihood that this cluster pattern can be the result of random chance (summary format courtesy of Esri, Inc.).

A value of 1 indicates that the data are perfectly random (mean observed distance = expected distance for random distribution). The value of 0.41 indicates that the points are more clustered than random or dispersed.

Nearest-Neighbor Test Statistic

It is possible to determine whether the pattern is significantly different from random by performing a statistical test (Ebdon, 1985). The test statistic is very similar to a t-test, and it is based on the difference between the observed and expected random nearest-neighbor differences. It is calculated using the equation

$$c = \frac{d_{Obs} - d_{Ran}}{SE_d} \tag{8.16}$$

where c is the statistic, d_{Obs} is the mean of the observed nearest-neighbor distances, d_{Ran} is the expected nearest-neighbor distance for a random point pattern, and SE_d is the standard distance of the mean nearest-neighbor distance. The standard error of the mean nearest-neighbor distance is calculated using

$$SE_d = \frac{0.26136}{\sqrt{np}} \tag{8.17}$$

where n is the number of points in the pattern and p is the density of points per unit area. In the example, the SE_d would equal

$$SE_d = \frac{0.26136}{\sqrt{11(0.31)}} = \frac{0.26136}{\sqrt{3.41}} = 0.141$$

The test statistic can now be calculated for the point data (Figure 8-15):

$$c = \frac{0.37 - 0.904}{0.141} = \frac{-0.534}{0.141} = -3.79$$

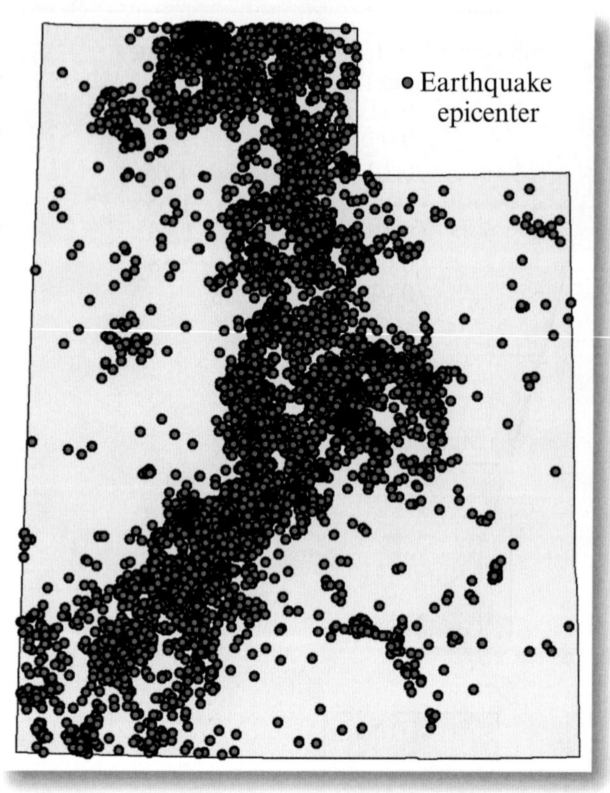

FIGURE 8–16 Earthquake epicenters in Utah from June 1962 to 2001. During this time period there were 1,431 earthquakes (data courtesy of State of Utah).

Because *c* is a standard normal deviate, the Empirical Rule (described above) applies, and there is a 68.2% chance of finding the value of *c* between –1.0 and 1.0 (one standard deviation about the mean), and a 95.4% chance of finding the value of *c* between –2.0 and 2.0 (two standard deviations about the mean). Similarly, the significance of *c* can be determined by examining the critical values of a standard normal deviate table. In the example point data pattern, we find that –3.79 is less than the critical value of –3.291 (alpha = 0.001; two tailed test). Therefore, we can conclude that there is less than a 1% chance that the clustered pattern is the result of random chance. An analysis of the eleven hypothetical points using ArcGIS® reports all of these values (Figure 8-15).

Nearest-neighbor point analysis allows us to quantitatively determine whether the points are randomly distributed. Similar to the other spatial measurements discussed in this chapter, nearest-neighbor analysis has many applications. For example, nearest-neighbor analysis may be used by geographers and geologists to study the pattern of earthquake epicenters. The distribution of earthquake epicenters in Utah from 1962 to 2001 is shown in Figure 8-16. The average nearest-neighbor analysis summary is shown in Figure 8-17. Similar to the 11 points used above, the nearest-neighbor analysis reveals that the pattern is significantly clustered, and there is less than a 1% chance that the point pattern was caused by random chance.

Nearest-neighbor point analysis can be used to determine if violent crime in a city is clustered or random (e.g., Anselin et al., 2000; Ratcliffe, 2005). Others may want to determine if deer-vehicle collisions are random or clustered around specific habitat types (Gonser et al., 2009). In each of these cases, nearest-neighbor analysis helps to determine whether the points are randomly distributed or clustered. It does not determine the factors that may be influencing the spatial pattern.The analyst must investigate and determine why the pattern is clustered. Finally, the computation of nearest-neighbor values and indices is dependent on the size of the study area because it directly impacts point density. This means that it is possible to obtain different nearest-neighbor values by changing the size of the study area.

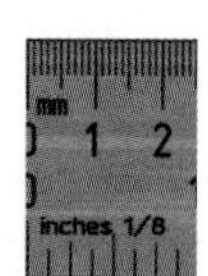

Summary

This chapter introduced some of the common descriptive statistics, spatial statistics, and distance and area measurements that you may encounter while working with a GIS. There are many more descriptive and multivariate statistics and spatial statistics that were not presented. If you are interested in learning more about these topics please consult a spatial statistics textbook (e.g., Ripley, 2004; Kalkhan, 2011).

Review Questions

1. What is the difference between Euclidean distance and Manhattan distance measurement? When would you use one type of distance measurement technique versus another?

2. Explain how a polygon perimeter is measured. Give an example of when you might need to measure a polygon's perimeter.

3. Define and describe the difference between the mode, median, and mean.

4. Give an example of a study where the mean center of a spatial distribution might be useful.

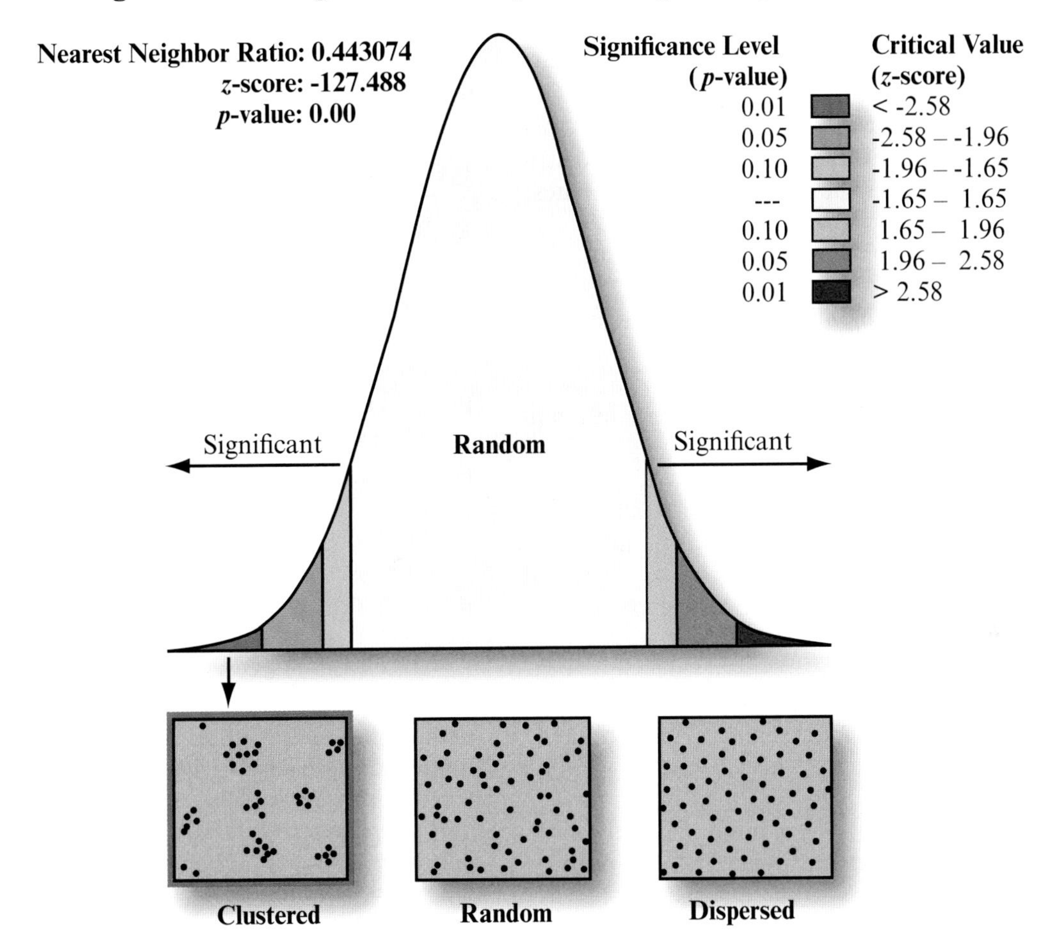

FIGURE 8–17 This summary report summarizes the results of the nearest-neighbor analysis of the earthquake epicenters in Utah from 1962 to 2001. Given the z-score of −127.488, there is less than 1% likelihood that this cluster pattern can be the result of random chance (summary format courtesy of Esri, Inc.).

5. What is spatial autocorrelation? Describe two studies where spatial autocorrelation information would be important.

6. What are the two main types of point analysis described in this chapter? Give an example of where each type of analysis might be used.

7. Why is standard distance often reported with the mean center?

8. What does skewness measure? Why is it useful to report skewness when describing a distribution?

9. How is raster polygon area measured?

10. Why is it important to have a sound understanding of the statistics and other measurements described in this chapter?

11. Why is it important to evaluate the peakedness of a distribution of observations?

Glossary

Area: Measurement of the geographic region enclosed by a polygon.

Empirical Rule: In a normal distribution, about 68% of the observations will fall within one standard deviation of the mean, about 95% will fall within two standard deviations of the mean, and almost 100% (99.7%) will fall within three standard deviations of the mean.

Euclidean Distance: The simple, straight-line distance between two projected points.

Kurtosis: A measure of the peakedness of the distribution of data values.

Manhattan Distance: The "around-the-block" measurement of distance.

Mean: The arithmetic average of a dataset.

Mean Center: A measure of central tendency that can be used to determine the center of a spatial distribution plotted in geographic or Cartesian coordinates.

Median: The middle value of an ordered dataset.

Mode: The most commonly occurring value in a dataset.

Moran's I: A measure of the spatial autocorrelation in a dataset.

Nearest-Neighbor Ratio: An analysis that determines whether the spatial distribution of points is dispersed, random, or clustered. It is the observed nearest-neighbor distance divided by the expected distance for a random distribution.

Normal Distribution: A bell-shaped distribution where the mode, median, and mean are approximately equal.

Perimeter: Measured by determining the length of each of the n line segments associated with a polygon and then summing them.

Quadrat: A user-defined geographic area that is usually square or rectangular and is used in quadrat analysis.

Quadrat Analysis: A technique used to determine the uniformity of points distributed in a number of quadrats.

Skewness: A measure of the asymmetry of a distribution of data values.

Spatial Autocorrelation: Measures the spatial ordering and spatial dependency of geographic data to indicate whether neighboring or adjacent values vary together.

Spatial Statistics: Statistics used to quantitatively describe and assess certain spatial characteristics of landscapes.

Standard Deviation: Average deviation about the mean.

Standard Distance: A measure of how dispersed a spatial distribution is about the mean center.

Variance: The average squared variation about the mean.

References

Anselin, L., Cohen, J., Cook, D., Gorr, W. and G. Tita, 2000, "Spatial Analyses of Crime," *Criminal Justice,* 4:213–262.

Burt, J. E., Barber, G. M. and D. L. Rigby, 2009, *Elementary Statistics for Geographers,* 3rd Ed., New York: Guilford Press, 653 p.

Ebdon, D., 1985, *Statistics in Geography,* 2nd Ed., Boston: Blackwell Publishing, 232 p.

Formica, V. A., Gonser, R. A., Ramsay, S. and E. M. Tuttle, 2004, "Spatial Dynamics of Alternative Reproductive Strategies: The Role of Neighbors," *Ecology,* 85:1125–1136.

Frohn, R. C., 1998, *Remote Sensing for Landscape Ecology: New Metric Indicators for Monitoring, Modeling, and Assessment of Ecosystems,* Boca Raton: Lewis Publishers, 105 p.

Frohn, R. C. and Y. Hao, 2006, "Landscape Metric Performance in Analyzing Two Decades of Deforestation in the Amazon Basin of Rondonia, Brazil," *Remote Sensing of Environment,* 100(2):237–251.

Gonser, R. A., Jensen, R. R. and S. A. Wolf, 2009, "The Spatial Ecology of Deer-Vehicle Collisions," *Applied Geography,* 29:527–532.

Jensen, J. R., 2005, *Introductory Digital Image Processing: A Remote Sensing Perspective,* Upper Saddle River: Pearson Prentice-Hall, 526 p.

Kalkhan, M. A., 2011, *Spatial Statistics: Geospatial Information Modeling and Thematic Mapping,* Boca Raton: CRC Press, 184 p.

Krygier, J. and D. Wood, 2011, *Making Maps: A Visual Guide to Map Design for GIS,* 2nd Ed., New York: Guilford Press, 256 p.

Moran, P. A. P., 1950, "Notes on Continuous Stochastic Phenomena," *Biometrika,* 37:17–33.

Paradis, E., 2011, *Moran's Autocorrelation Coefficient in Comparative Methods,* http://cran.r-project.org/web/packages/ape/vignettes/morani.pdf.

Ratcliffe, J. H., 2005, "Detecting Spatial Movement of Intra-Region Crime Patterns Over Time," *Journal of Quantitative Criminology,* 21:103–123.

Ripley, B. D., 2004, *Spatial Statistics,* New York: John Wiley & Sons, 272 p.

Tobler, W. R., 1970, "A Computer Movie Simulating Urban Growth in the Detroit Region," *Economic Geography,* 46:234–240.

Tuttle, E. M., Jensen, R. R., Formica, V. A. and R. A. Gonser, 2006, "Using Remote Sensing Image Texture to Study Habitat Use Patterns: A Case Study Using the Polymorphic White-throated Sparrow (*Zonotrichia albicollis*)," *Global Ecology & Biogeography,* 15:349–357.

Wright, D. J., Goodchild, M. F. and J. D. Proctor, 1997, "GIS: Tool or Science? Demystifying the Persistent Ambiguity of GIS as 'Tool' versus 'Science'," *Annals of the Association of American Geographers*, 87:346–362.

9 Spatial Analysis of 3-Dimensional Data

Courtesy of Sanborn Map Company, Inc.

Many important variables analyzed in a GIS exist at a particular geographic location (*x,y*) and have a unique nominal scale alphanumeric value (e.g., the value is class A, class B, class 10, or class 30). Some good examples of nominal scale variables include:

- land cover,
- land use,
- soil type, and
- surface geology.

Many of these variables are continuous in nature, i.e., they can exist everywhere on the landscape. Unfortunately, sometimes we can only collect information about these phenomena at relatively few discrete *x,y* locations on the ground. It is usually not possible for us to extend or extrapolate these data through space to create a complete continuous surface. For example, if we sample the land cover at just 20 places in a county, it would not be wise to extrapolate these data to create a map of the land cover of the entire county.

Conversely, many important variables analyzed in a GIS are located at a specific location (*x,y*) and may have a unique ordinal, interval, or ratio-scale quantitative *z*-value. These are commonly called **control points.** The *z*-value of the control point is usually associated with a recognized base value, such as topographic elevation above sea level. Some other examples include:

- bathymetry (elevation below sea level),
- terrain aspect (e.g., 0° N, 180° S),
- terrain slope (degrees or percent),
- temperature (32° Fahrenheit; 0° Celsius),
- water turbidity (secchi depth below water level),
- water salinity (practical salinity units),
- barometric pressure (millibars), and
- relative humidity (percent).

It is possible to measure some of these ordinal, interval, and ratio-scaled variables directly using remote sensing instruments (e.g., temperature, elevation). Sometimes the only way to obtain the required data is to collect the measurements at specific geographic locations (*x,y*) on the ground using transducers (e.g., a thermometer) or some other measurement device (e.g., a GPS unit to measure *x,y* location and *z*-elevation). In either case, there are algorithms that take the relatively few discrete *x,y* and *z* measurements (i.e., control points) and *interpolate* between them to create a statistical surface that contains *z*-values at each user-defined *x,y* location within the study area.

Overview

It is possible to convert control point observations (e.g., *x,y*, and *z*-elevation) into a polygonal Triangular Irregular Network (TIN) data structure and then perform surface processing. It is also possible to convert the control point data into a raster (i.e., matrix) format using spatial interpolation techniques and then perform surface processing. This chapter describes how TIN and raster datasets are created and how numerous types of surface processing are performed, such as the extraction of slope, aspect, and isolines, and the application of analytical hill-shading and color to improve the interpretability of the 3-dimensional surface.

LiDAR Masspoints Overlaid on Orthophotography of Test Plots on the Savannah River Site near Aiken, SC

a. Color-infrared orthophotography (1 x 1 m).

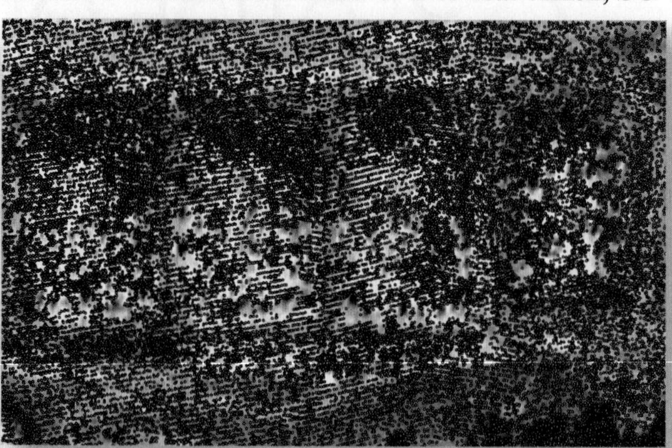

b. LiDAR masspoints overlaid on orthophotography.

c. Oblique aerial view of the test plots.

FIGURE 9–1 a) U.S. Geological Survey 1 x 1 m digital color-infrared orthophotography of the test plots on the Savannah River Site. b) The 37,150 LiDAR masspoints with a nominal posting density of 0.25 m overlaid on the color-infrared digital orthophotography. Most of the data voids are where LiDAR masspoints on trees were removed. c) An oblique aerial view of the four test plots.

The data conversion and surface processing alternatives will be demonstrated using LiDAR-derived digital elevation masspoints for a small area on the Savannah River Site (SRS) near Aiken, SC. The area under investigation consists of four engineered mounds created to test the effectiveness of hazardous waste site management. The local relief ranges from 200 to 230 ft. above sea level. A digital orthophoto of the study area is shown in Figure 9-1a. The LiDAR masspoint postings are overlaid on the orthophoto in Figure 9-1b. The nominal posting density of the masspoints is 0.25 x 0.25 m. An aerial oblique view of the test plots is shown in Figure 9-1c.

Note that although the LiDAR instrument attempts to systematically collect the data, the final location of the LiDAR-derived masspoints is somewhat random. This is caused by atmospheric turbulence at the time of data acquisition, actual data voids where the sensor did not collect data, the overlap of multiple flightlines of LiDAR data, and the manual removal of masspoints that were located on trees or buildings. Each of the 37,150 LiDAR-derived elevation postings may be considered to be discrete *x,y,z* measurements that are within ± 10 cm of their true *x,y* (location) and *z* (elevation).

The reader should keep in mind that the data interpolation and surface processing techniques applied to elevation data discussed in this chapter can be applied to most other statistical surfaces (e.g., precipitation, temperature, population, relative humidity, biomass, etc).

Vector Representation and Processing of 3-Dimensional Data

While it is possible to perform a vector-to-raster conversion on control point data, many GIScientists prefer to convert the data into a Triangular Irregular Network (TIN) data structure and then perform surface processing.

Triangular Irregular Network (TIN) Data Structure

In a **Triangular Irregular Network (TIN)**, the surface is represented by a set of triangular facets with 3-dimensional coordinates at their vertices (Mark and Smith, 2004). TINs are typically constructed from a set of

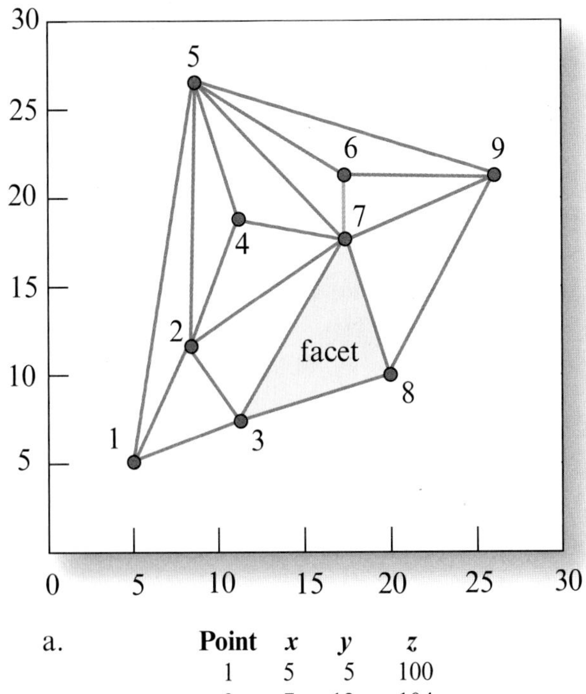

a.

Point	*x*	*y*	*z*
1	5	5	100
2	7	12	104
3	12	7	105
4	12	18	110
5	8	27	106
6	17.5	22	105
7	17.5	17.5	111
8	20	10	106
9	27	22	106

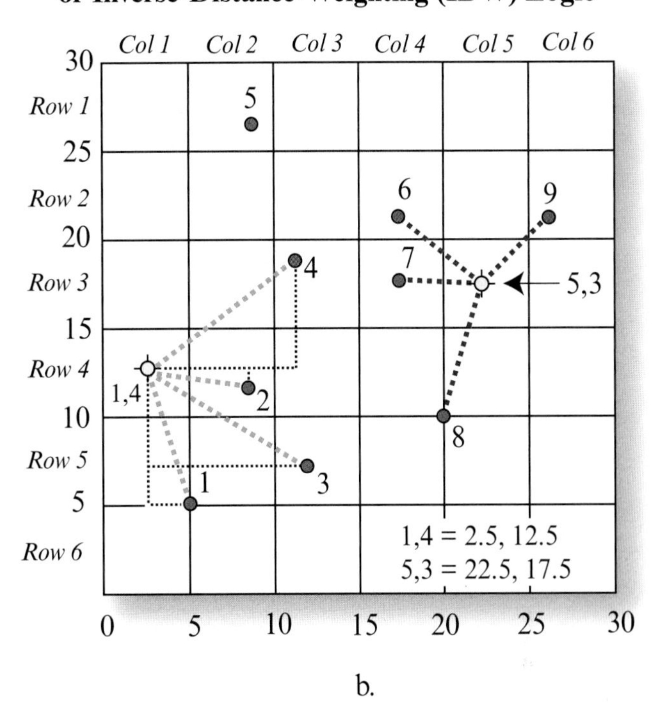

b.

FIGURE 9–2 a) The logic associated with creating a triangular irregular network (TIN) using nine elevation measurements. b) Cells 1,4 and 5,3 in the output raster dataset can be filled using Nearest-neighbor or Inverse-Distance-Weighting (IDW) logic. The computation is described in Table 9-1.

known values, called "spot heights" or "control points," that are used as the vertices in the creation of the facets. For example, consider the nine hypothetical elevation spot heights shown in Figure 9-2a. A TIN is constructed by extending vectors in all directions from an individual control point to its nearest-neighbors. This results in the creation of numerous triangular facets covering the surface. The greater the distance between a point observation and its nearest-neighbors, the greater the size of the triangular facet. It is important to note that the vertices of each facet are located at the exact x,y location of the original control point values. There is no interpolation between control points.

A TIN can also be created using linear vector information alone or in conjunction with point data. For example, if an analyst has vector contour lines in a study area, it is possible to use the individual elevation values along the contour lines to create a TIN of the study area. If point elevation values are also available, then both the point values and the points along the linear contour lines can be used at the same time to create a more accurate TIN.

Many scientists like the TIN data structure because it can adapt to the variable complexity of the topography (or other type of 3-dimensional surface such as temperature). Ideally, a TIN will have small triangles in rugged areas that require more detailed 3-dimensional information and relatively larger triangles in smooth areas. If the TIN is based on carefully selected control points that accurately capture the 3-dimensional nature of the surface, a maximum of information about the surface can be obtained with a minimum volume of data when compared to a typical raster (grid) data structure (Peucker and Chrisman, 1975; Peucker et al., 1978; Marks and Smith, 2004).

TIN Surface Processing

Most geographic information systems automatically compute three important characteristics associated with each TIN triangular facet, including elevation (or other z-value), aspect of the facet (e.g., its orientation

Triangular Irregular Network (TIN), Analytical Hill-shading, Hypsometric Tinting, and Contour Extraction from LiDAR Masspoints

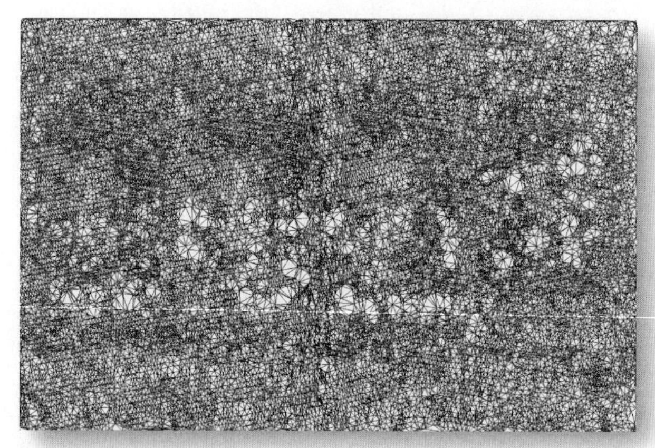

a. TIN derived from LiDAR masspoints.

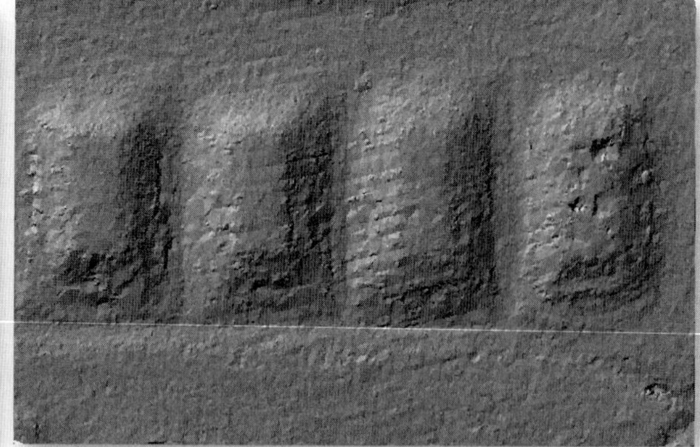

b. Analytically hill-shaded Triangular Irregular Network (TIN).

c. TIN hypsometrically tinted using 19 class intervals and overlaid with 25 cm contours.

FIGURE 9–3 a) A Triangular Irregular Network (TIN) derived from the 37,150 masspoints displayed in Figure 9-1b. b) An analytically hill-shaded version of the TIN with the artificial Sun illumination coming from the northwest (315°) at 45° above the horizon. c) The TIN color-coded using 19 class intervals and overlaid with 25 cm contours.

north, south, east, or west), and the slope of the facet (in degrees or percent).

Displaying TIN Data

One of the first useful displays of point observations using a TIN data structure is a simple display of all the TIN triangles (facets). For example, Figure 9-3a depicts thousands of TIN facets associated with the SRS LiDAR masspoints (Figure 9-1b). While this display is of interest, it is difficult to interpret or to gain very much appreciation about the 3-dimensional nature of the data.

Fortunately, each TIN facet can also be displayed as if it were illuminated from any user-specified direction using digital **analytical hill-shading** techniques. The usual convention is to highlight the surface as if the sunlight were coming from the northwest (315°) at 45° above the horizon. This causes the synthetic shadows to fall toward the reader, helping him or her to visualize the 3-dimensional surface. When shadows fall toward the reader, it minimizes the **pseudoscopic illusion** effect where the reader gets confused as to what is high or low in a 3-dimensional dataset.

An example of the elevation of the facets displayed using analytical hill shading with illumination from the northwest (315°) and at 45° above the horizon is shown in Figure 9-3b. As you can see, it is much easier to appreciate the 3-dimensional nature of the terrain and facets when analytical hill-shading is applied.

It is also possible to color-code each TIN facet according to its z-value. This requires the analyst to specify the number of class intervals and the black-and-white or color symbolization to be applied. The class interval logic used (e.g., continuous, natural breaks, equal interval) will have a significant impact on the display of the 3-dimensional information. The symbolization should be logical, with the black-and-white or color progression of colors making sense. For example, in the example shown in Figure 9-3c, the cooler colors are associated with lower elevation values and the warmer colors are associated with higher elevation values. This type of color display is sometimes referred to as hypsometric tinting.

Isoline (e.g., Contour) Mapping Using TIN Data

Isolines are lines of equal magnitude above some arbitrary datum (e.g., sea level). They can be easily constructed by interpolating between the z-values located at the vertices in the TIN data structure. In the case of elevation data, lines of equal elevation (contours) above sea level are typically created. For example, 25 cm contours were extracted from the SRS TIN dataset and overlaid on the individual facets in Figure 9-3c. The contours provide quantitative information about the 3-dimensional nature of the TIN continuous surface and can be labeled if desired.

Slope Mapping Using TIN Data

The **slope** of a statistical surface (e.g., elevation) is the change in z-value (i.e., the rise) divided by the distance travelled (i.e., the run). The slope of each facet in a TIN dataset can be used to create slope maps measured in degrees (0° = flat; 90° = vertical) or percent slope. A slope map of the SRS testpads derived from the TIN data is shown in Figure 9-4a. Each facet in the TIN slope map has a unique slope value and color. Note the increased slope on the sides of the testpads and that the depressions on the top of the fourth testpad have some steep slopes.

Aspect Mapping Using TIN Data

Aspect is the cardinal direction that each facet is facing in a TIN data structure. It is measured as a cardinal direction in degrees. Most slope maps typically display only eight class intervals associated with the most common directions (N [0°], NE [45°], E [90°], SE [135°], S [180°], SW [225°], W [270°], and NW [315°]). The aspect of each TIN facet in the SRS dataset is shown in Figure 9-5a. Note how accurately the algorithm portrays the north-, east-, south-, and west-facing slopes associated with each of the elevated test plots.

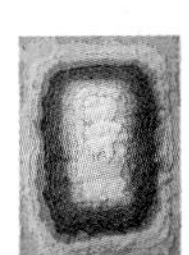

Raster Representation and Processing of 3-Dimensional Data

Many scientists prefer to process control point observations using the TIN data structure previously discussed. Others prefer to transform the individual control point observations into a matrix (raster) continuous surface using spatial interpolation techniques such as Nearest-neighbor, Inverse-Distance-Weighting (IDW), Kriging, and Splining. The continuous surface raster can then be subjected to numerous surface processing algorithms such as black-and-white or color display, and aspect, slope and isoline extraction.

Spatial Interpolation

The word *interpolation* is derived from "inter," meaning between, and "pole," which refers to control points. **Spatial interpolation** is the process of identifying the z-value (e.g., elevation above sea level) at a new location based on the characteristics of n adjacent control points. For this discussion, we assume that the control point observations have accurate x- and y-coordinate information, accurate z-values, and are associated with an appropriate map projection and datum. Performing a vector (i.e., point) to raster conversion using spatial interpolation requires three steps:

1. Select the size of the cells in the new output matrix that will be created. For example, we could specify that the output matrix contain cells that are 5 x 5 m in size such as those shown in Figure 9-2b.

2. Select the number of original data points that will be used by the spatial interpolation algorithm to compute a new value for each cell in the matrix, e.g., the four nearest points such as those shown in Figure 9-2b.

3. Select an intensity interpolation algorithm that will compute the value at the centroid of each cell (pixel) in the new matrix. Four of the most useful intensity interpolation methods are: Nearest-neighbor, Inverse-Distance-Weighting (IDW), Kriging, and Splining.

Every pixel (location) in the output matrix must contain a value. There cannot be voids in the output ma-

Slope Mapping Based on the Use of TIN, IDW, Kriged, and Splined Datasets

a. Slope derived from the TIN.

b. Slope derived from the IDW surface.

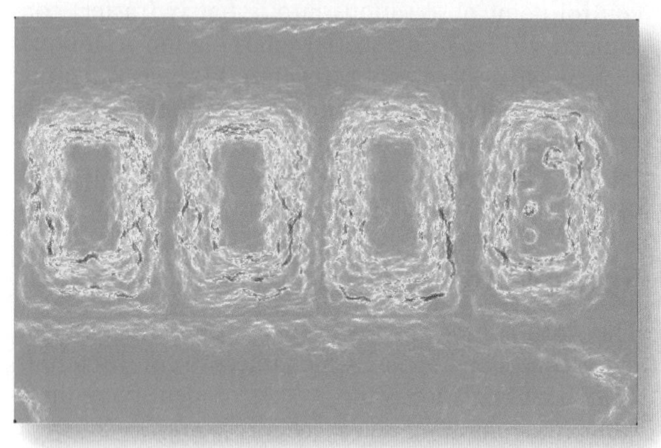

c. Slope derived from the Kriged surface.

d. Slope derived from the Splined surface.

Slope in degrees

0 - 3.32
3.33 - 6.64
6.65 - 10.2
10.3 - 14.1
14.2 - 18.3
18.4 - 23.5
23.6 - 30.7
30.8 - 43.4
43.5 - 70.5

FIGURE 9–4 a) Slope derived from the Triangular Irregular Network (TIN) displayed in Figure 9-3a. b) Slope derived from an Inverse-Distance-Weighting (IDW) interpolated surface. c) Slope derived from a Kriged surface. d) Slope derived from a Splined surface.

trix where values are not present. Therefore, the intensity interpolation part of the process systematically moves through the output matrix filling *every* pixel with a value. The value placed in each cell is derived from the original control point observations.

Nearest-neighbor Spatial Interpolation

Nearest-neighbor spatial interpolation determines the z-value at a new location using information from n nearby control points. For example, suppose we wanted to fill the cell at location column 1, row 4 in the output matrix shown in Figure 9-2b using Nearest-neighbor interpolation logic. The algorithm first determines the location of the centroid of cell 1,4 (i.e., $x = 2.5$, $y = 12.5$). It then uses the Pythagorean theorem to compute the Euclidean distance from the centroid of cell 1,4 to each of the n nearest-neighbors. In this example, $n = 4$. The four nearest-neighbors to cell 1,4 are points 1, 2, 3, and 4 with values of 100, 104, 105, and 110, respectively. The nearest-neighbor to the centroid of cell 1,4 is point 2, with a distance of 4.527 units (Table 9-1). Therefore, cell 1,4 would receive a value of 104.

The nearest-neighbors to cell 5,3 in the matrix are points 6, 7, 8, and 9 with values of 105, 111, 106, and

Aspect Mapping Based on the Use of TIN, IDW, Kriged, and Splined Datasets

a. Aspect derived from the TIN.

b. Aspect derived from the IDW surface.

c. Aspect derived from the Kriged surface.

d. Aspect derived from the Splined surface.

Aspect

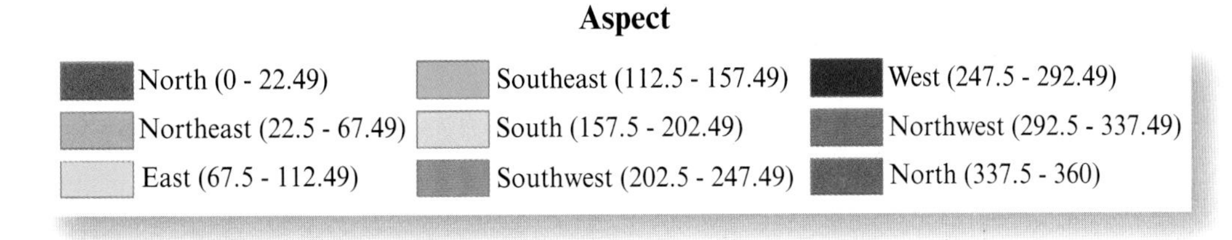

FIGURE 9–5 a) Aspect derived from the Triangular Irregular Network (TIN) displayed in Figure 9-3a. b) Aspect derived from the Inverse-Distance-Weighting (IDW) interpolated surface. c) Aspect derived from the Kriged surface. d) Aspect derived from the Splined surface.

106, respectively. The nearest-neighbor to the centroid of cell 5,3 is point 7 with a distance of 5.0 units (Table 9-1). Therefore, cell 5,3 would receive a value of 111. This process is repeated to fill each cell in the new output matrix.

Sometimes the mean of the four nearest-neighbors is used to compute the output cell z-value instead of just using the nearest-neighbor. For example, the mean of the four nearest-neighbors to cell 1,4 is 419/4 = 104.75 (Figure 9-2b; Table 9-1). Therefore, cell 1,4 would receive a z-value of 104.75 if all four nearest-neighbors were considered in the computation. Similarly, the mean of the four nearest-neighbors to cell 5,3 is 428/4 = 107 (Figure 9-2b; Table 9-1). Note that Nearest-neighbor interpolation logic gives each input point equal weight in the interpolation process.

Inverse-Distance-Weighting (IDW) Interpolation

We know from fundamental geographic principles that things that are near to us are more likely to influence us than things that are farther away from us. Therefore, if we are going to use the n nearest points to compute a z-value for the cell in question, then it would be logical to weight the closest points more heavily than the points that are farther away. This is called **Inverse-Distance-Weighting (IDW) interpolation**.

TABLE 9–1 An example of Nearest-neighbor and Inverse-Distance-Weighting (IDW) interpolation logic used to compute a new value (*Value*) at cell locations 1,4 (which has a centroid location at x = 2.5, y = 12.5 in the matrix) and cell 5,3 (with a centroid location of x = 22.5, y = 17.5), based on an analysis of the four nearest sample points shown in Figure 9-2b.

Sample Point Location	Value at Sample Point, Z	Distance from x, y to the Sample Point, D	D_k^2	$\frac{Z}{D_k^2}$	$\frac{1}{D_k^2}$
For cell 1,4					
Point #1 (5, 5)	100	$D = \sqrt{(2.5-5)^2+(12.5-5)^2} = 7.905$	62.5	1.6	0.016
Point #2 (7, 12)	104	$D = \sqrt{(2.5-7)^2+(12.5-12)^2} = \mathbf{4.527}$ **Nearest-neighbor minimum distance**	20.5	5.073	0.049
Point #3 (12, 7)	105	$D = \sqrt{(2.5-12)^2+(12.5-7)^2} = 10.977$	120.5	0.871	0.008
Point #4 (12, 18)	110	$D = \sqrt{(2.5-12)^2+(12.5-18)^2} = 10.977$	120.5	0.912	0.008
	$\bar{x} = 104.75$			Σ 8.456	Σ 0.081
				$Value_{IDW}$ =	8.456/0.081 = **104.395**
For cell 5,3					
Point #6 (17.5, 22)	105	$D = \sqrt{(22.5-17.5)^2+(17.5-22)^2} = 6.726$	45.25	2.320	0.022
Point #7 (17.5, 17.5)	111	$D = \sqrt{(22.5-17.5)^2+(17.5-17.5)^2} = \mathbf{5.0}$ **Nearest-neighbor minimum distance**	25.0	4.44	0.04
Point #8 (20, 10)	106	$D = \sqrt{(22.5-20)^2+(17.5-10)^2} = 7.905$	62.5	1.696	0.016
Point #9 (27, 22)	106	$D = \sqrt{(22.5-27)^2+(17.5-22)^2} = 6.36$	40.5	2.617	0.024
	$\bar{x} = 107$			Σ 11.073	Σ 0.102
				$Value_{IDW}$ =	11.073/0.102 = **108.55**

The distance from the x,y location of the centroid of the cell (i.e., pixel) in question to each of the n nearest points is determined using the Pythagorean theorem. The z-values for each of these points is then weighted according to how far away they are from the centroid of the cell to be filled. The weighted average of the new $Value_{IDW}$ is computed using the equation:

$$Value_{IDW} = \frac{\sum_{k=1}^{4} \frac{Z_k}{D_k^2}}{\sum_{k=1}^{4} \frac{1}{D_k^2}} \tag{9.1}$$

where Z_k are the z-values of the surrounding four data point values, and D_k^2 are the distances squared from the cell centroid in question (x, y) to these data points. In this example, the weighted average ($Value_{IDW}$) for cell 1,4 is 104.395 (truncated to 104), as shown in Table 9-1. This is different from the average value of 104.75, which was determined without inverse-distance-weighting. The $Value_{IDW}$ for cell 5,3 is 108.55 (truncated to 108). The average without weighting is 107.

An example of the application of IDW interpolation applied to the Savannah River Site LiDAR masspoints is shown in Figure 9-6. The IDW interpolation used the nearest 12 observations and created a surface with 0.25 x 0.25 m cells. An analytically hill-shaded version

Inverse-Distance-Weighting (IDW) Spatial Interpolation, Analytical Hill-shading, Hypsometric Tinting, and Contour Extraction

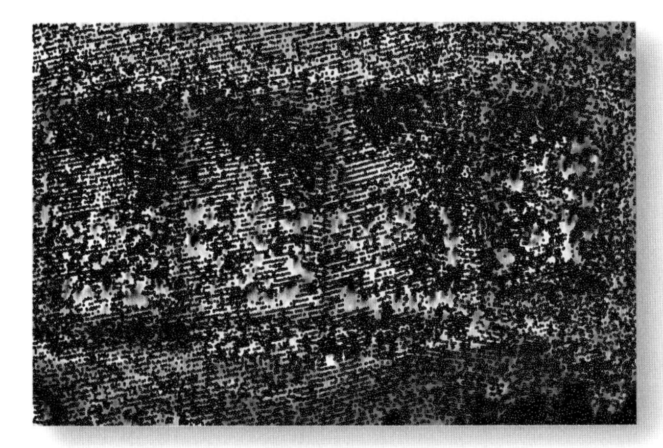

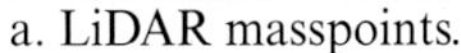

a. LiDAR masspoints.

b. Analytically hill-shaded surface created using IDW interpolation.

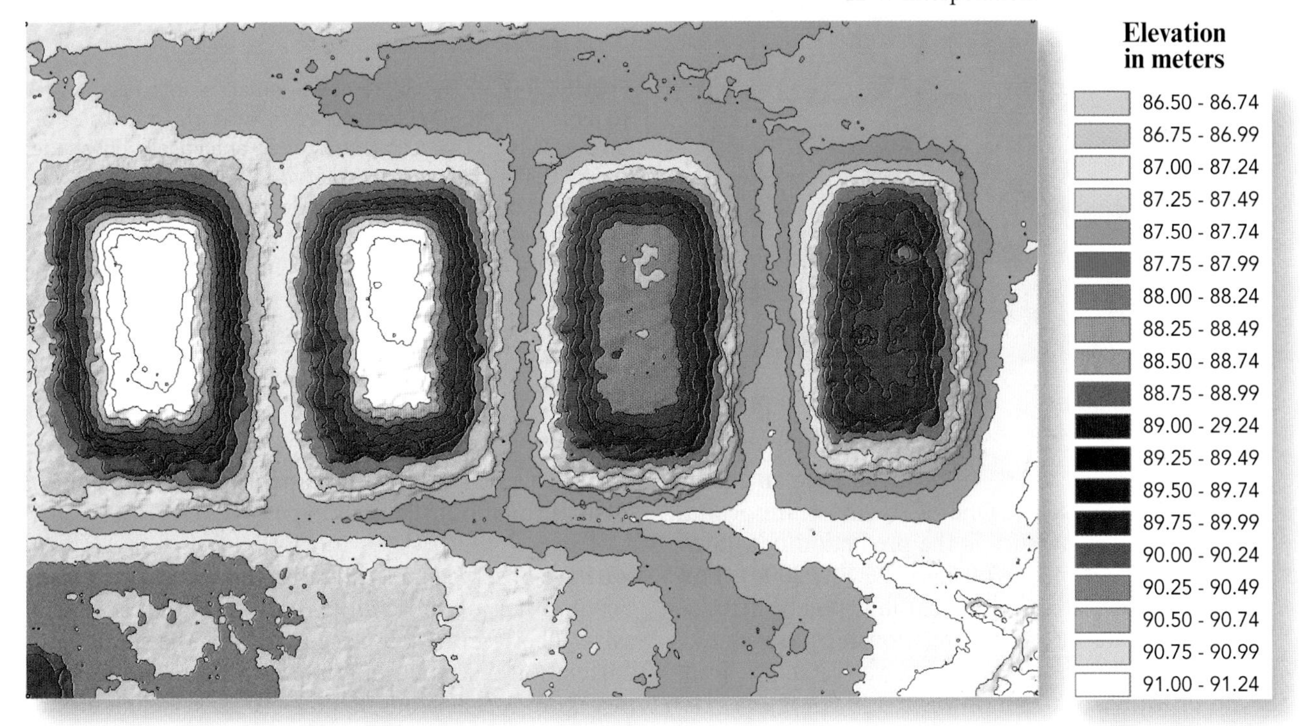

c. IDW matrix hypsometrically tinted using 19 class intervals and overlaid with 25 cm contours.

FIGURE 9–6 a) The 37,150 LiDAR masspoints overlaid on the 1 x 1 m color-infrared orthophotography. b) An analytically hill-shaded surface created using IDW interpolation. The cell size is 0.25 x 0.25 m. c) The IDW surface color-coded using 19 class intervals and overlaid with 25 cm contours.

of the statistical surface is shown in Figure 9-6b. Selecting a more coarse resolution cell size results in loss of surface topographic detail. For example, Figure 9-7 depicts the 37,150 masspoints interpolated using IDW interpolation and cell sizes of 0.25 x 0.25 m, 1 x 1 m, and 2 x 2 m, respectively.

A color-coded version of the IDW surface with 19 class intervals is shown in Figure 9-6c. IDW spatial interpolation is one of the most widely used methods of creating a continuous surface raster dataset from geographically dispersed control point observations.

Geostatistical Analysis, Autocorrelation, and Kriging Interpolation

Random variables distributed in space (e.g., elevation, temperature) are said to be *regionalized.* We can use geostatistical analysis methods to extract the spatial properties of regionalized variables (Woodcock et al., 1988ab; Jensen, 2005; Esri, 2010). Once quantified, the

Inverse-Distance-Weighting (IDW) Spatial Interpolation to 0.25, 1, and 2 Meters

a. LiDAR masspoints interpolated to 0.25 x 0.25 m pixels.

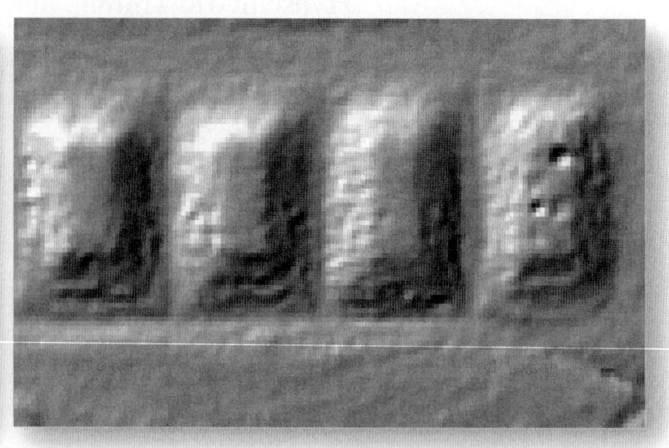

b. LiDAR masspoints interpolated to 1 x 1 m pixels.

c. LiDAR masspoints interpolated to 2 x 2 m pixels.

FIGURE 9–7 a) The 37,150 LiDAR masspoints interpolated to a raster using IDW interpolation logic and a cell size of 0.25 x 0.25 m. The surface has been analytically hill-shaded. b) LiDAR masspoints interpolated to a raster using IDW and a cell size of 1 x 1 m. Note the decrease in surface topographic detail. c) LiDAR masspoints interpolated to a raster using IDW and a cell size of 2 x 2 m.

regionalized variable properties can be used in many geostatistical applications. One of the most important applications of geostatistics is the prediction of values at unsampled locations (Wolf and Dewitt, 2000). For example, we can use geostatistical interpolation techniques to evaluate the spatial relationships associated with the LiDAR masspoints to create a systematic grid of elevation values.

Geostatistical analysis is a special branch of spatial statistics that takes into account not only the distance between control point observations but also their spatial autocorrelation (Jensen, 2005). Originally, geostatistics was synonymous with kriging—a statistical version of interpolation. **Kriging**, named after the work of Danie Krige (1951), is a generic name for a family of least-squares linear regression algorithms used to estimate the value of a continuous attribute (e.g., elevation) at any unsampled location using only the attribute data available over the study area (Lo and Yeung, 2002). However, geostatistical analysis now includes not only kriging but also the traditional deterministic spatial interpolation methods. One of the essential features of geostatistics is that the phenomenon being studied (e.g., elevation, reflectance, temperature, precipitation, a land cover class) must be capable of existing continuously throughout the landscape.

We have observed generally that things that are close to one another are more alike than those that are farther away. Therefore, as distance increases, the spatial autocorrelation discussed in Chapter 8 decreases as shown in Figure 9-8. Kriging makes use of this spatial autocorrelation information (Jensen, 2005). Kriging is similar to "distance weighted interpolation" in that it *weights* the surrounding nearby values to derive a prediction for each new location in the output raster dataset. However, the weights are based not only on the distance between the measured control points and the point to be predicted (used in Inverse-Distance-Weighting), but also on the overall *spatial arrangement* among the measured points (i.e., their autocorrelation). This is the most significant difference between deterministic (traditional) and geostatistical analysis. Traditional statistical analysis assumes the samples derived for a particular attribute are *independent* and not correlated in any way. Conversely, geostatistical analysis allows users to compute distances between observations and to model autocorrelation as a function of distance and direction. This information is then used

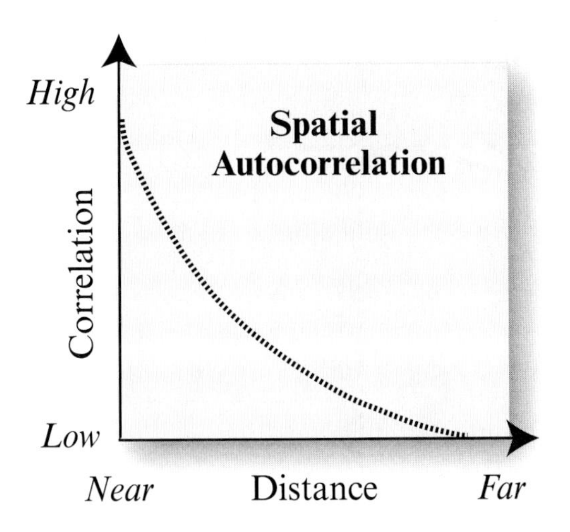

FIGURE 9–8 Phenomena that are geographically closer to one another are generally more highly correlated than things that are farther apart. Geostatistical analysis incorporates spatial autocorrelation information in the Kriging-interpolation process.

to *refine* the kriging interpolation process, making predictions at new locations more accurate than those derived using traditional methods such as Inverse-Distance-Weighting (Johnston et al., 2001; Lo and Yeung, 2002; Esri, 2010).

The Kriging process generally involves two operations (Jensen, 2005):

- quantifying the spatial structure of the surrounding data points using variography, and
- predicting a $Value_{krig}$ at each new location in the output dataset.

Variography is the process whereby a spatially dependent model is fit to the data and the spatial structure is quantified. To make a prediction for an unknown value at a specific location, Kriging uses the fitted model from variography, the spatial data configuration, and the values of the measured sample points around the prediction location (Johnston et al., 2001).

One of the most important measurements used to understand the spatial structure of regionalized variables is the **empirical semivariogram** (Figure 9-9), which can be used to relate the semivariance to the amount of spatial separation (and autocorrelation) between samples (Jensen, 2005). The semivariance provides an unbiased description of the scale and pattern of spatial variability throughout a region. For example, if elevation values of a relatively flat area are examined, there may be little spatial variability (variance), which will result in a semivariogram with predictable characteristics. Conversely, the elevation found in rugged terrain may exhibit significant spatial variability resulting in an entirely different semivariogram.

Calculating Average Semivariance Consider the hypothetical situation where we want to determine the elevation of an unknown point by evaluating the spatial characteristics of six nearby points. The six points, Z_1 through Z_6, are arranged in a line in a Cartesian coordinate system in Table 9-2a. The relationship between a pair of pixels h intervals apart (h is referred to as the *lag distance*; Table 9-3) can be given by the average variance of the differences between all such pairs. The unbiased estimate of the average semivariance of the population (γ_h) is expressed through the relationship (Curran, 1988; Isaaks and Srivastava, 1989; Slocum et al., 2005):

$$\gamma_h = \frac{\sum_{i=1}^{n-h} (Z_i - Z_{i+h})^2}{2(n-h)} \tag{9.2}$$

where Z_i is a control point value, h is the multiple of the distance between control points, and n is the number of points. The total number of possible pairs m along the transect is computed by subtracting the lag distance h from the total number of pixels present in the dataset n, that is, $m = n - h$ (Brivio and Zilioli, 2001; Johnston et al., 2001; Lo and Yeung, 2002). In this example, we are only computing the semivariance in the x-direction. In practice, semivariance is computed for pairs of observations in all directions, N, NE, E, SE, S, SW, W, and NW (Maillard, 2003). Thus, directional semivariograms are derived and directional influences can be examined.

The computation of the semivariance for the six elevation control points is summarized in Table 9-2b. The semivariance (γ_h) of the six points when $h = 1$ is 17.9 based on the following calculations:

$$\gamma_h = \frac{\sum_{i=1}^{6-1} (Z_i - Z_{i+h})^2}{2(6-1)} \quad \text{where}$$

$$\gamma_h = (Z_1 - Z_2)^2 + (Z_2 - Z_3)^2 + (Z_3 - Z_4)^2 + (Z_4 - Z_5)^2 + (Z_5 - Z_6)^2 / 10$$

$$\gamma_h = (10 - 15)^2 + (15 - 20)^2 + (20 - 30)^2 + (30 - 35)^2 + (35 - 33)^2 / 10$$

$$\gamma_h = 17.9$$

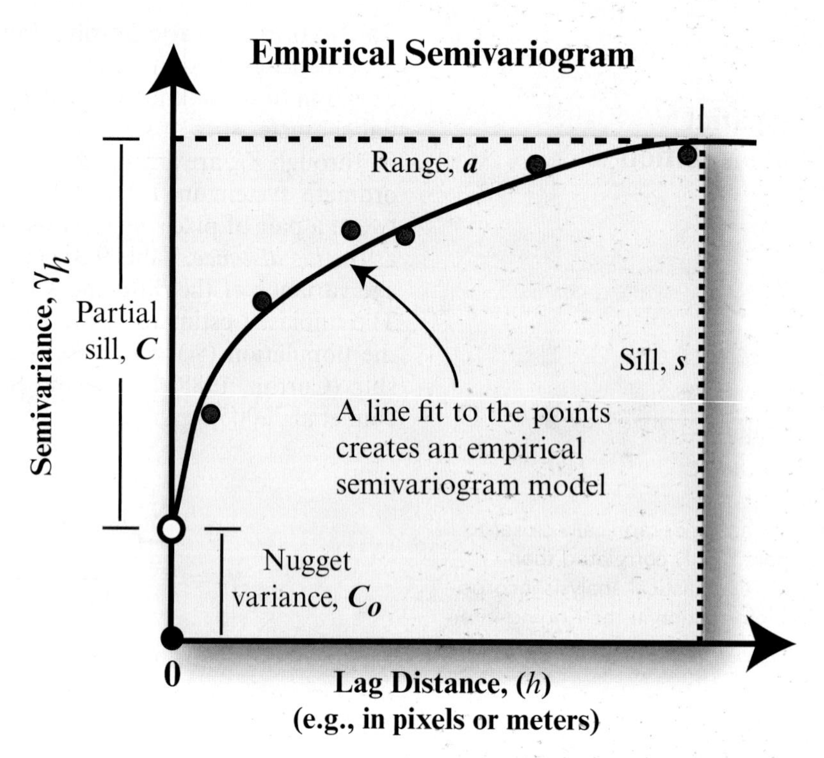

FIGURE 9–9 The *z*-values of points (e.g., pixels in an image or locations on the ground if collecting in situ data) separated by various lag distances (*h*) may be compared and their semivariance (γ_h) computed (adapted from Isaaks and Srivastava, 1989; Lo and Yeung, 2002; Jensen, 2005). The semivariance (γ_h) at each lag distance may be displayed as a *semivariogram* with the range, sill, and nugget variance characteristics described in Table 9-3.

The average semivariance is a good measure of the amount of *dissimilarity* between spatially separate control points. Generally, the larger the average semivariance (γ_h), the less similar are the point observations. In Table 9-2b we see that at a lag distance of 1, semivariance = 17.9. At a lag distance of 2, semivariance = 69.88. At a lag distance of 3, semivariance = 161.5, etc. In this hypothetical dataset, as the lag distance increases, there is greater dissimilarity among the six ground control points being examined. The greater the lag distance, the less correlated the observations.

Empirical Semivariogram The semivariogram is a plot of the average semivariance value on the *y*-axis with the various lags (*h*) investigated on the *x*-axis, as shown in Figure 9-9 and Table 9-2c. Important characteristics of the semivariogram include (Jensen, 2005):

- lag distance (*h*) on the *x*-axis,
- sill (*s*),
- range (*a*),
- nugget variance (C_o), and
- spatially dependent structure displayed graphically (e.g., Figure 9-9; Table 9-2c).

When spatial correlation exists, pairs of points that are close together (on the far left of the *x*-axis) should have less difference (be low on the *y*-axis). As points become farther away from each other (moving right on the *x*-axis), in general, the difference squared should be greater (moving up on the *y*-axis). The semivariogram model often flattens out at a certain lag distance from the origin. The distance where the model *first* flattens out is the *range*. The range is the distance over which the samples are spatially correlated. The *sill* is the value on the *y*-axis where the range is located. It is the point of maximum variance and is the sum of the structural spatial variance and the nugget effect. The *partial sill* is the sill minus the nugget (Jensen, 2005).

The semivariogram value on the *y*-axis should theoretically equal zero when lag (*h*) equals zero. However, at an infinitesimally small separation distance, the semivariogram often exhibits a *nugget effect*, which is >0. The nugget effect is attributed to measurement errors or spatial sources of variation at distances smaller than the sampling interval (or both).

A semivariogram provides information on the spatial autocorrelation of control point datasets. For this reason and to ensure that Kriging predictions have positive Kriging variances, a model is fit to the semivariogram (i.e., a continuous function or curve). This model quantifies the spatial autocorrelation in the data (Johnston et al., 2001).

TABLE 9–2 Semivariance computation (adapted from Jensen, 2005; Slocum et al., 2005).

a. Six equally spaced hypothetical elevation control points (Z_1 through Z_6).

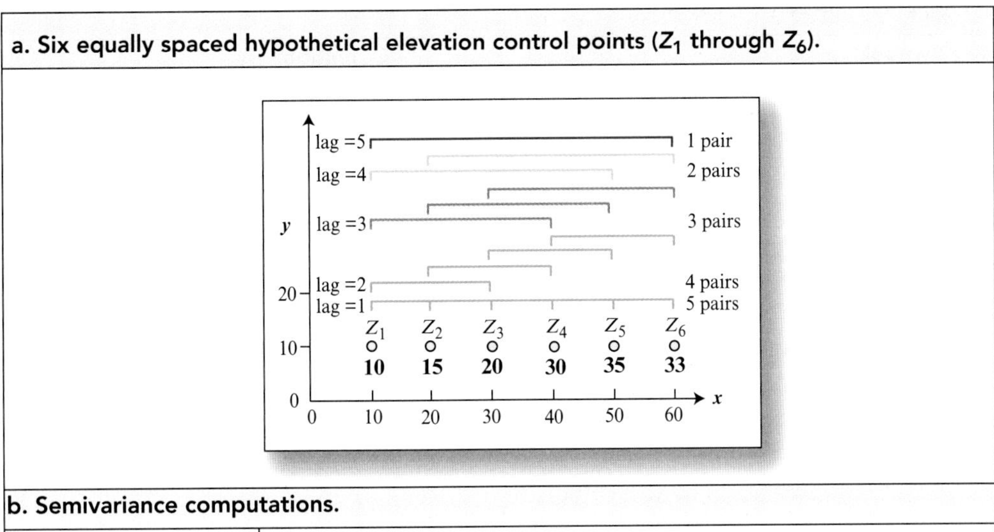

b. Semivariance computations.

	h				
	1	2	3	4	5
$(Z_1 - Z_{1+h})^2$	25	100	400	625	529
$(Z_2 - Z_{2+h})^2$	25	225	400	324	
$(Z_3 - Z_{3+h})^2$	100	225	169		
$(Z_4 - Z_{4+h})^2$	25	9			
$(Z_5 - Z_{5+h})^2$	4				
$\sum_{i=1}^{n-h} (Z_i - Z_{i+h})^2$	179	559	969	949	529
$2(n-h)$	10	8	6	4	2
γ_h	**17.9**	**69.88**	**161.5**	**237.25**	**264.5**

c. Empirical semivariogram model.

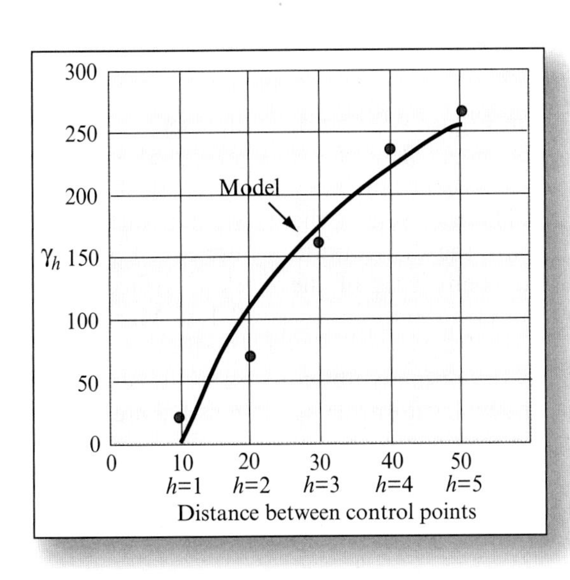

TABLE 9–3 Terminology and symbols in a typical empirical semivariogram (adapted from Curran, 1988; Johnston et al., 2001; Lo and Yeung, 2002; and Jensen, 2005).

Term	Symbol	Definition
Lag	h	The linear (horizontal) distance that separates any two locations (i.e., a sampling pair). A lag has length (distance) and direction (orientation).
Sill	s	The maximum level of the modeled semivariogram. The value that the variogram tends to when lag distances become very large. At large lag distances, variables become uncorrelated, so the sill of the semivariogram is equal to the variance of the random variable.
Range	a	Point on the h axis where the modeled semivariogram nears a maximum. The distance beyond which there is little or no autocorrelation among variables. Places closer than the range are autocorrelated, places farther apart are not.
Nugget variance	C_o	The location where the modeled semivariogram intercepts the $\gamma(h)$ axis. Represents the independent error, measurement error, or microscale variation at spatial scales that are too fine to detect. The nugget effect is a discontinuity at the origin of the semivariogram model.
Partial sill	C	The sill minus the nugget variance describes the spatially dependent structural variance.

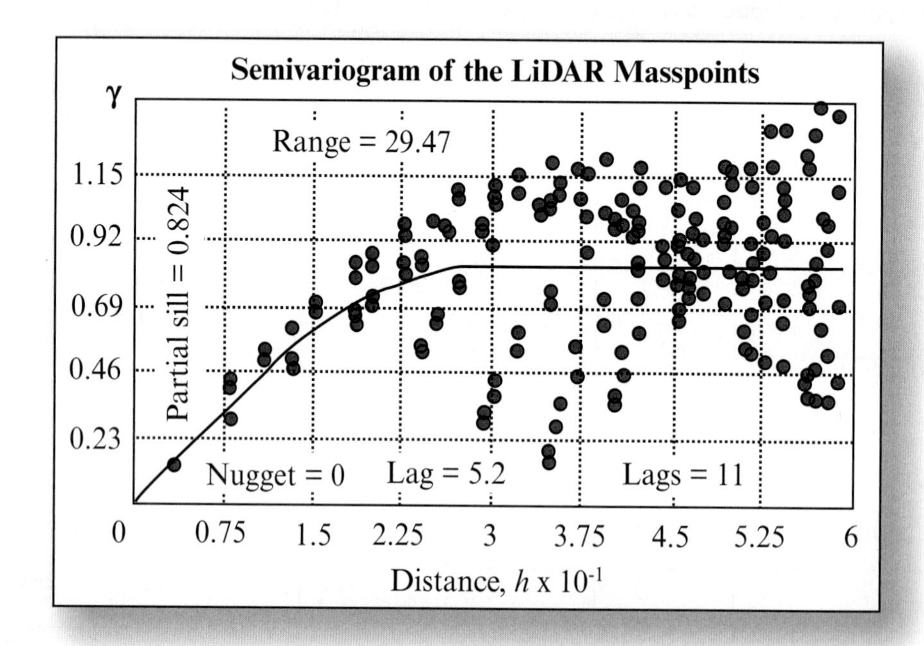

FIGURE 9–10 A semivariograph of the 37,150 LiDAR masspoints processed using spherical Kriging. This semivariogram contains autocorrelation information derived from all orientations (e.g., N, E, S, and W).

The line fitted to the data points in Figure 9-9 and in Table 9-2c is called a *semivariogram model*. The model is a line through the average semivariance versus average distance between point pairs. The user selects the functional form that best represents the distribution (e.g., spherical, circular, etc.). The coefficients of the function are empirically derived from the data.

It is possible to work with relatively few or many observations to predict the value at unknown locations using Kriging. For example, consider the relatively large LiDAR masspoint dataset. The semivariogram shown in Figure 9-10 contains detailed information about the range, partial sill, and nugget associated with the entire dataset. A spherical geostatistical Kriging algorithm was used to create the raster continuous surface from the 37,150 LiDAR masspoints. The analytically hill-shaded surface created using Kriging is found in Figure 9-11b. A color-coded version of the Kriged elevation surface with 19 class intervals is shown in Figure 9-11c. Many scientists use Kriging in a GIS to create continuous surfaces from individual control point observations. The procedure is not easy to understand, but the interpolated results are often quite useful.

Spline Interpolation

For millennia, humans have had the need to draw relatively complex curved lines. Before computers, this was

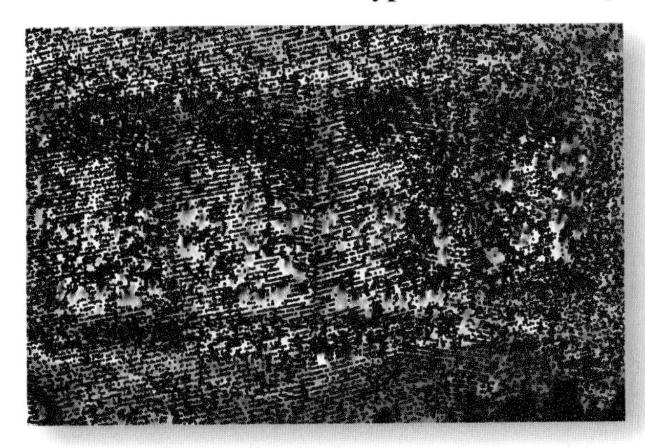

a. LiDAR masspoints.

b. Analytically hill-shaded surface created using Kriging.

c. Kriging matrix hypsometrically tinted using 19 class intervals and overlaid with 25 cm contours.

FIGURE 9–11 a) The 37,150 LiDAR masspoints overlaid on the 1 x 1 m color-infrared orthophotography. b) An analytically hill-shaded surface created using Kriging. The cell size is 0.25 x 0.25 m. c) The Kriged surface color-coded using 19 class intervals and overlaid with 25 cm contours.

performed manually using flexible pieces of wood or plastic called *splines* and lead weights called *ducks* to hold the spline in place (Figure 9-12). Very intricate curves can be constructed in this way. In fact, manual splines are still used to plan and build wooden boats and other objects (Waters, 2011).

In effect, the point where the duck touches the spline is a control point, much like the control points previously discussed. With the spline in place, properly anchored by control points, it is possible to predict the location at any point along the spline. This type of information can be used to interpolate between the LiDAR-derived elevation control points to create a new output dataset.

For example, consider a 2-dimensional view of just seven hypothetical elevation control points ranging from 99.0411 to 100.9093 feet above sea level (Figure 9-13a). You could think of this as a small mound of terrain adjacent to a stream. Connecting the ground control points with linear segments is useful but is "blocky" and probably does not really represent the true undu-

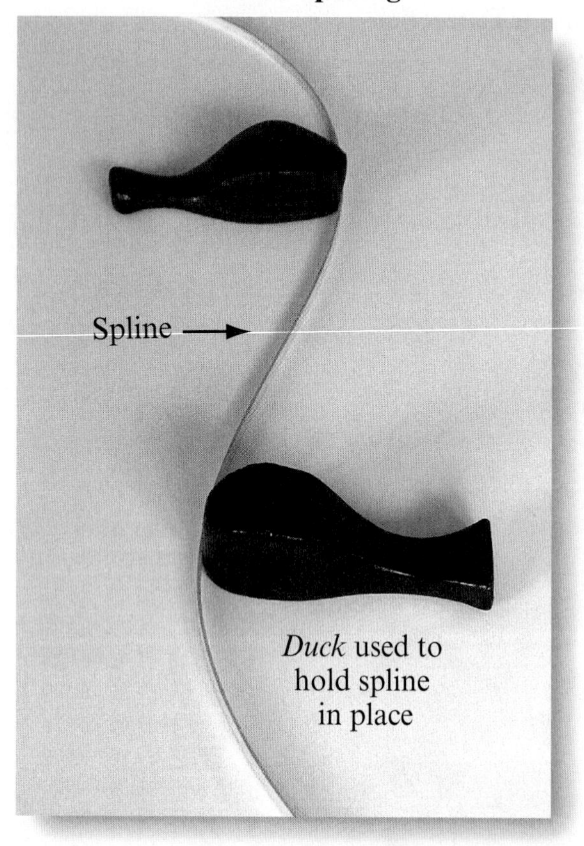

FIGURE 9–12 An example of lead ducks holding a flexible wooden spline in place.

lating nature of the terrain (Figure 9-13b). Therefore, we might want to densify the number of points using simple linear interpolation to more accurately represent the surface.

For example, if we wanted to determine the elevation at $x = 3.5$, we could linearly interpolate between point a and b in the dataset using the equation

$$f(x) = y_a + \frac{(x - x_a)(y_b - y_a)}{(x_b - x_a)} \tag{9.3}$$

where

$$f(3.5) = 100.1411 + \frac{(3.5 - 3)(99.2432 - 100.1411)}{(4 - 3)}$$

$$f(3.5) = 99.692 .$$

We could also decide to fit a polynomial equation to the seven points which is a generalization of linear interpolation. A sixth-order polynomial of the seven control points yields (Figure 9-13c)

$$f(x) = -0.0001521x^6 - 0.00313x^5 + 0.07321x^4 - 0.3577x^3 + 0.02255x^2 + 0.9038x + 100$$

$$f(3.5) = 99.652 .$$

Note that the polynomial interpolation using a single equation can be used to predict any new interpolated value.

Spline interpolation provides an accurate way to interpolate the values of new points. In the example, there are seven control points with six logical regions between them on the x-axis (Figure 9-13d). Splining uses lower-degree polynomials in each of the intervals, and selects the polynomial pieces such that they fit smoothly together. The resulting function is called a *spline*.

If we wanted to compute a new value at $x = 3.5$ in Figure 9-13d using spline interpolation, then we would use the equation associated with region [3,4], which yields the value $f(3.5) = 99.653$. Spline interpolation creates best-fit rubber sheet surfaces to the control points using polynomial equations. The mathematical surface passes through control points and minimizes sharp bends in the surface.

The LiDAR-derived elevation control points were subjected to spline interpolation to create a continuous raster of elevation values. A color-coded version of the splined elevation surface with 19 class intervals is shown in Figure 9-14c. Compare the results of the spline interpolation with the TIN, IDW, and Kriged surfaces.

Surface Processing of Raster 3-Dimensional Data

Elevation or other types of spatially continuous information stored in a matrix (raster) data structure can be visualized by displaying

- the distribution in black-and-white or color,
- the slope of the distribution, and
- the aspect of the distribution.

Black-and-White and Color Display

Elevation data interpolated to a grid using one of the aforementioned interpolation algorithms have the raster data structure shown in Figure 9-15a. Individual values are arranged in rows (i) and columns (j) with each cell having a unique value. For example, pixel (1,1) in the matrix has an elevation value of 4. If we want to display elevation in shades of gray then we can

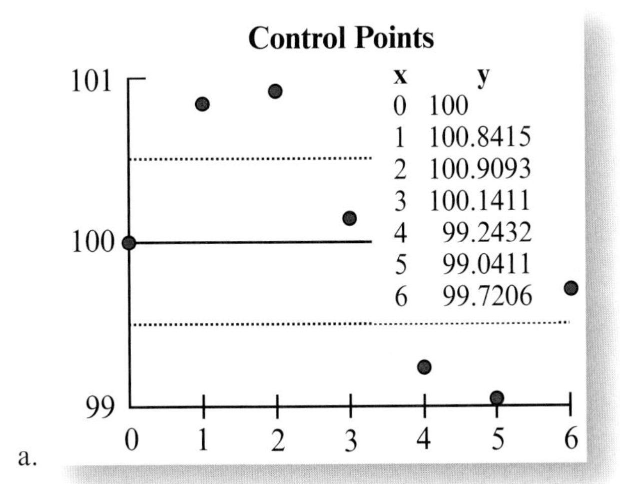

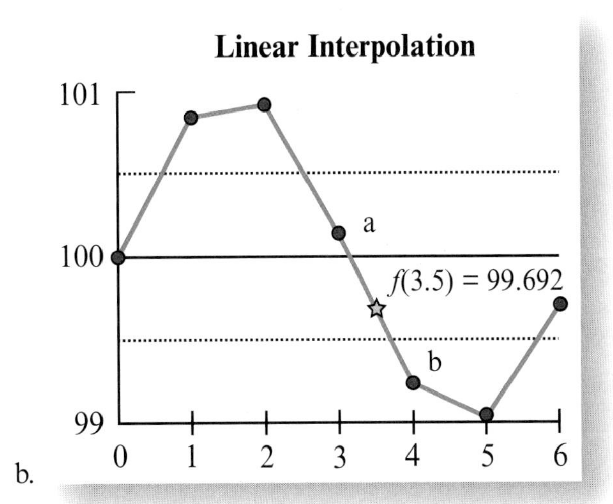

$$f(x) = y_a + [((x - x_a)\,(y_b - y_a))/(x_b - x_a)]$$
$$f(3.5) = 100.1411 + [((3.5 - 3)\,(99.2432 - 100.1411))/(4 - 3)]$$

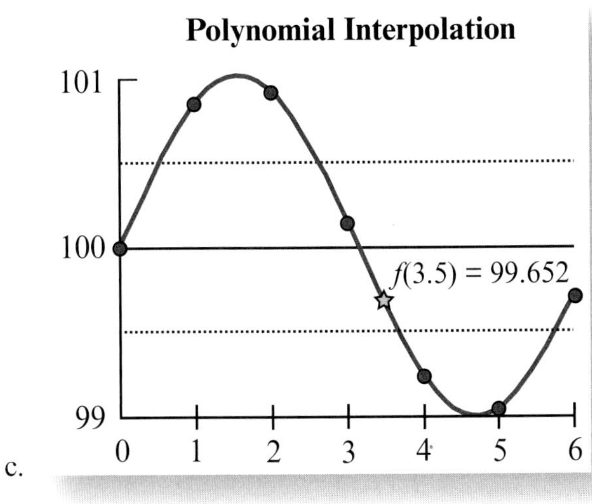

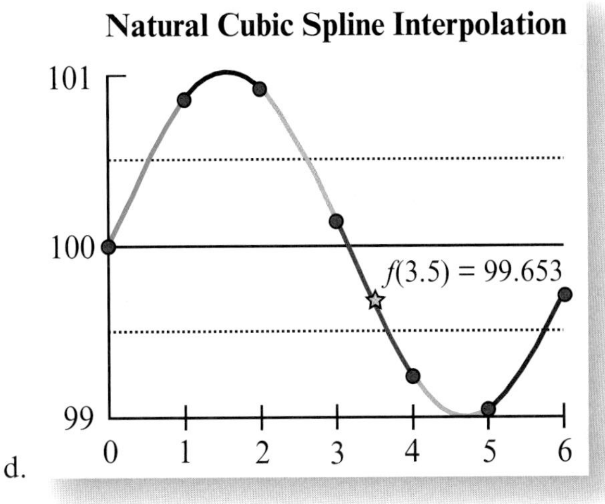

$$f(x) = -0.0001521x^6 - 0.00313x^5 + 0.07321x^4 - 0.3577x^3 + 0.2255x^2 + 0.9038x + 100$$

$$-0.1522x^3 + 0.9937x + 100 \quad \text{if } x \text{ e } [0,1]$$
$$-0.1258x^3 - 0.4189x^2 + 1.4126x + 99.8604 \quad \text{if } x \text{ e } [1,2]$$
$$0.1403x^3 - 1.3359x^2 + 3.2467x + 98.6377 \quad \text{if } x \text{ e } [2,3]$$
$$f(3.5) = 0.1579x^3 - 1.4945x^2 + 3.7225x + 98.1619 \quad \text{if } x \text{ e } [3,4]$$
$$0.05375x^3 - 0.2450x^2 - 1.2756x + 104.8259 \quad \text{if } x \text{ e } [4,5]$$
$$-0.1871x^3 + 3.3673x^2 - 19.3370x + 134.9282 \quad \text{if } x \text{ e } [5,6]$$

FIGURE 9–13 a) Seven hypothetical elevation control points. b) Linear interpolation of an elevation value at location $x = 3.5$. c) A sixth-order polynomial can be used to model the distribution of control points. d) Natural cubic spline interpolation used to interpolate between six separate regions along the x-axis. In this case, only the equation related to region [3,4] is used to compute a new value at location $x = 3.5$.

pass the elevation data through a black-and-white continuous tone look-up table. For example, if we wanted to display the value 4 as a dark gray then we could simply specify that any value of 4 encountered in the raster dataset would have a red, green, and blue (RGB) value of 4, 4, and 4 in the black-and-white look-up table (i.e., RGB = 4,4,4). The contents of the look-up table are constantly scanned by the computer and are used to create a pixel of the appropriate gray tone on the computer screen.

We can also display the pixels in the matrix in color. Pixel 4,4 in the dataset has a value of 11. Perhaps we want to display all elevation values in the dataset with a value of 11 as dark red. We simply enter the appropriate RGB values in the color look-up table associated

Spline Spatial Interpolation, Analytical Hill-shading, Hypsometric Tinting, and Contour Extraction

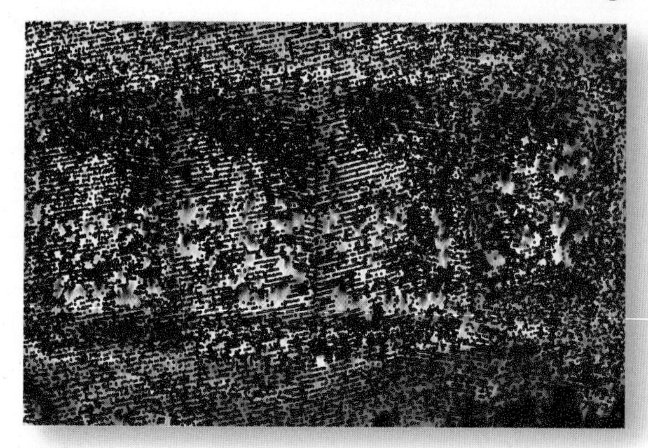

a. LiDAR masspoints.

b. Analytically hill-shaded surface created using Spline interpolation.

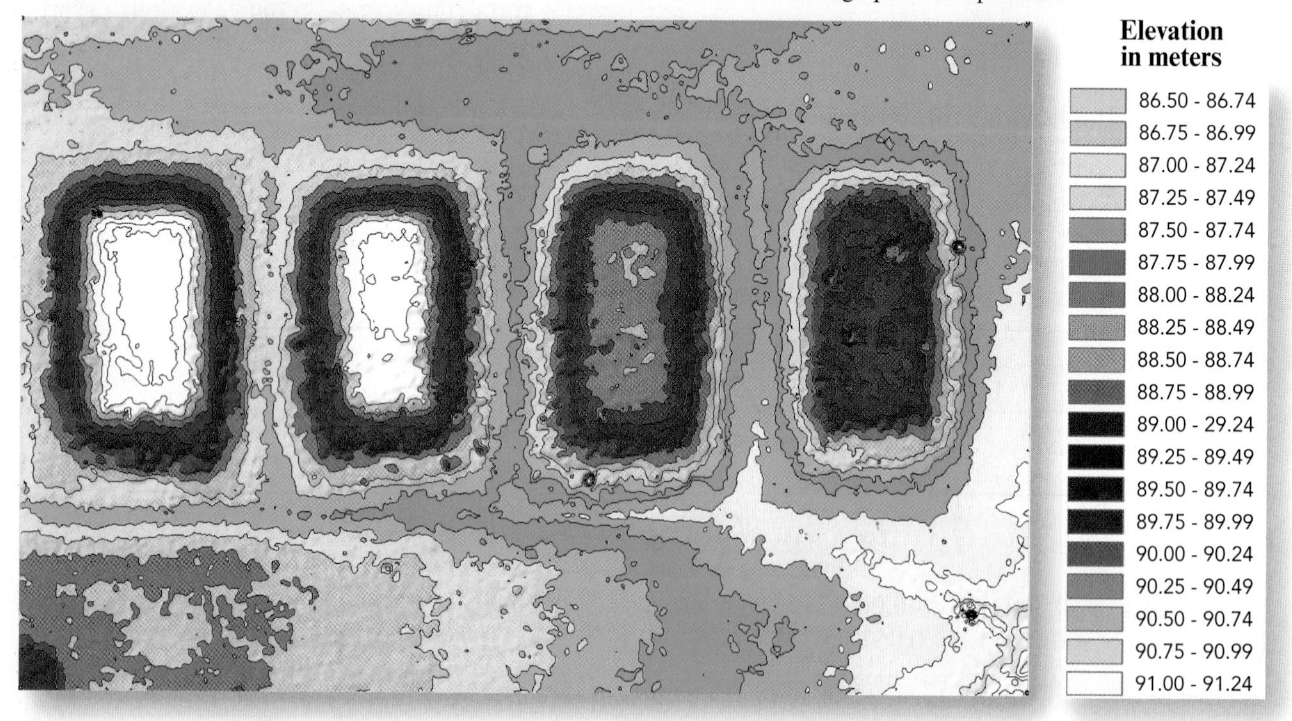

c. Splined matrix hypsometrically tinted using 19 class intervals and overlaid with 25 cm contours.

FIGURE 9–14 a) 37,150 LiDAR masspoints. b) An analytically hill-shaded surface created using spline interpolation. The cell size is 0.25 x 0.25 m. c) The Splined surface color-coded using 19 class intervals and overlaid with 25 cm contours.

with value 11 (i.e., RGB = 140, 11, 1). Every time a value of 11 is encountered, the computer consults the color look-up table and displays the pixel as dark red on the computer screen.

Slope Mapping Using Raster Data

Each cell in a matrix of elevation values can be modeled to compute the slope that exists at that cell (pixel). Slope derived from a matrix of elevation values is often computed using a nine-cell 3 x 3 spatial moving window such as the one shown in Figure 9-16a. The spatial moving window is applied systematically over the raster elevation dataset typically beginning at the upper left origin of the matrix (e.g., at location 1,1). As the window is passed over the original elevation values in the matrix, a slope value is computed for each cell (*e*) in the 3 x 3 matrix. This value is then placed at the appropriate location in the output slope matrix.

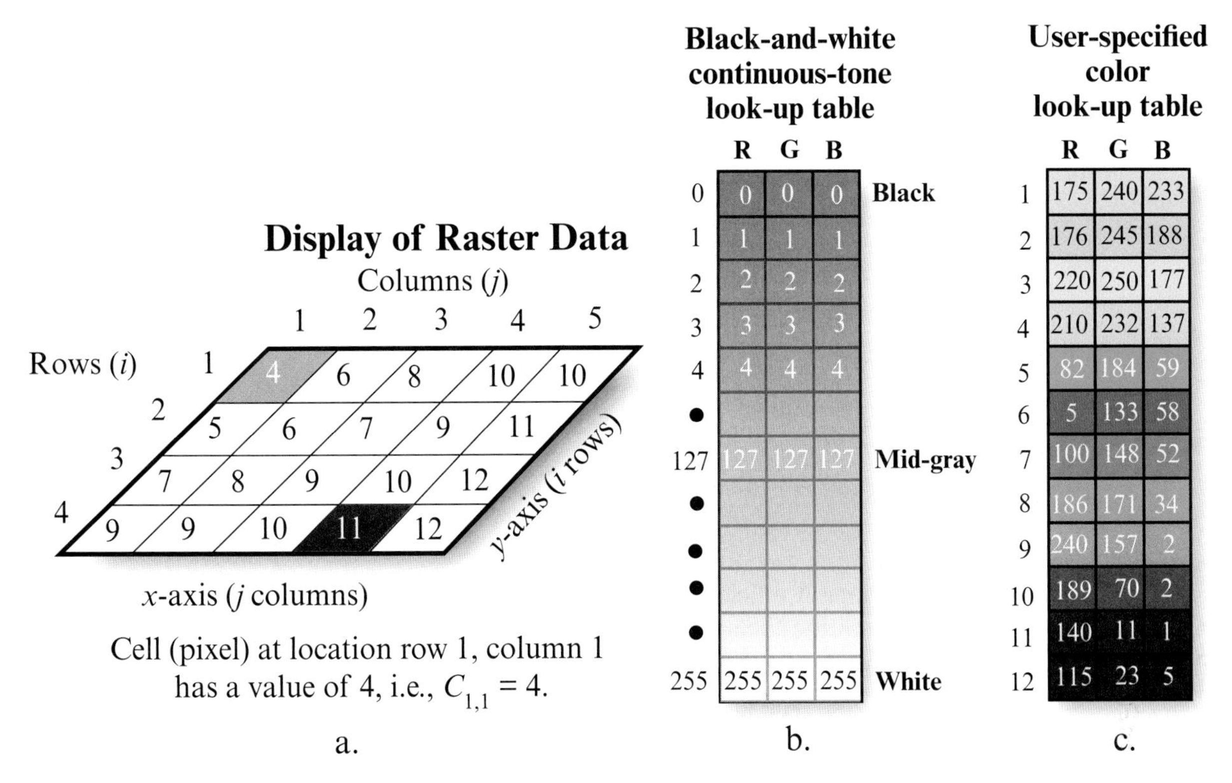

FIGURE 9–15 a) A raster (matrix) data structure. b) Display of a raster dataset using a continuous-tone 8-bit grayscale look-up table with values ranging from 0 to 255. c) User-specified color look-up table associated with the first 12 classes of the display of the elevation data in Figure 9-6c.

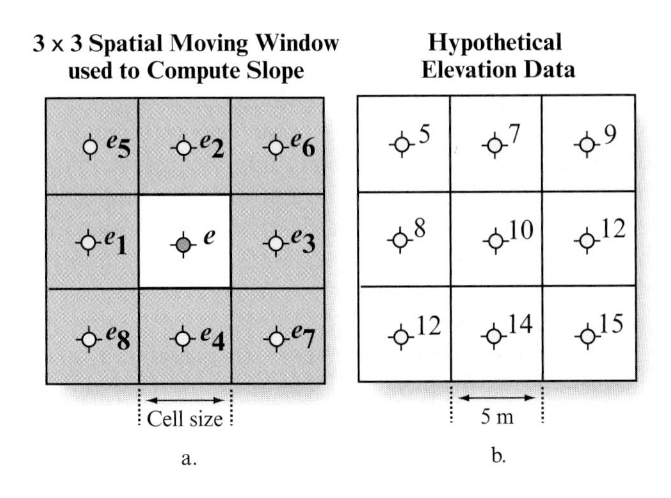

FIGURE 9–16 a) The structure of a 3 x 3 spatial moving window used to compute the slope of cell (e). The 3 x 3 window is applied systematically over the entire matrix of elevation values. Some slope algorithms use all eight of the surrounding cells while others use only the four nearest-neighbors (#e_1, e_2, e_3, and e_4) (adapted from Hodgson, 1998). b) Example elevation data used to demonstrate the computation of slope using Fleming and Hoffer (1979) and Horn (1981) methods.

Hodgson (1998) reviewed the characteristics of five of the most often used slope algorithms. Slope is normally computed by measuring the slope in two orthogonal gradients, typically west-to-east (*we*) and south-to-north (*sn*). Two of the most accurate methods of computing slope are summarized here.

Slope in degrees (e.g., 45°) can be computed from slope from two orthogonal directions using the equation (Hodgson, 1998):

$$Slope° = Tan^{-1}\left(\sqrt{Slope_{we}^2 + Slope_{sn}^2}\right) \quad (9.4)$$

where the $Slope_{we}$ and $Slope_{sn}$ variables in the equation are computed using selected cells in the 3 x 3 spatial moving window. Fleming and Hoffer (1979) and Ritter (1987) used just the four nearest-neighbors to the central point (e) under investigation in the spatial moving window (Hodgson, 1998):

$$Slope_{sn} = \frac{e_4 - e_2}{2 \times \text{cell size}} \text{ and}$$

$$Slope_{we} = \frac{e_1 - e_3}{2 \times \text{cell size}}.$$

Using these nearest-neighbor relationships, Equation 9.4, and the example elevation values found in Figure 9-16b, results in a slope of 38.8°:

$$Slope_{sn} = \frac{14-7}{10} = 0.7$$

$$Slope_{we} = \frac{8-12}{10} = -0.4$$

$$Slope° = Tan^{-1}\left(\sqrt{(-0.4)^2_{we} + (0.7)^2_{sn}}\right)$$

$$= Tan^{-1}\left(\sqrt{0.16_{we} + 0.49_{sn}}\right)$$

$$= Tan^{-1}(0.8062) = 38.9°$$

Hodgson (1998) through experimentation found this to be the most accurate and computationally efficient algorithm for computing slope representing the surface of a single cell.

The Horn (1981) algorithm uses Equation 9.4 and all eight cells in the 3 x 3 spatial moving average where the nearest cells are weighted more:

$$Slope_{sn} = \frac{(e_7 + 2e_4 + e_8) - (e_6 + 2e_2 + e_5)}{8 \times \text{cell size}} \text{ and}$$

$$Slope_{we} = \frac{(e_8 + 2e_1 + e_5) - (e_7 + 2e_3 + e_6)}{8 \times \text{cell size}}.$$

This is the slope algorithm used in ArcGIS.

A slope map derived from the IDW elevation matrix is shown in Figure 9-4b. Slope derived from the Kriged surface is shown in Figure 9-4c. Slope derived from the Splined surface is shown in Figure 9-4d. While there are similarities associated with the slope maps derived from the rasterized datasets (Figure 9-4b-d), there are also some significant differences, especially with regard to the location of the steepest slopes. The Splined dataset appears to have exaggerated the edges of objects in certain areas, increasing the steepness of slopes. The IDW and Kriged elevation matrices represent the surface slope more realistically.

Aspect Mapping Using Raster Data

The aspect (orientation) of each cell in an elevation matrix can be computed using some of the same information used to compute slope. Hodgson (1998) provided the algorithm in Table 9-4 to compute aspect, which incorporates the slope in the south-to-north ($Slope_{sn}$) and west-to-east ($Slope_{we}$) direction. Aspect maps associated with the IDW, Kriged, and Splined datasets are presented in Figure 9-5b–d.

TABLE 9–4 Algorithm used to compute the aspect of a surface element from the slopes in the west-to-east ($Slope_{we}$) and south-to-north ($Slope_{sn}$) directions (from Hodgson, 1998).

Aspect Algorithm

if $Slope_{sn}$ = 0 and $Slope_{we}$ = 0,
  Aspect = undefined
else
  if $Slope_{we}$ = 0,
    if $Slope_{sn}$ < 0,
      Aspect = 180
    else
      Aspect = 0
  else
    if $Slope_{we}$ > 0,
      Aspect = 90 – $\tan^{-1}$ ($Slope_{sn}$ / $Slope_{we}$)
    else
      Aspect = 270 – $\tan^{-1}$ ($Slope_{sn}$ / $Slope_{we}$)

Summary

This chapter introduced the characteristics of a triangulated-irregular-network (TIN) and how it can be used to visualize the information associated with control point measurements. The slope and aspect characteristics of the individual facets in the TIN are especially informative. The chapter then introduced several spatial interpolation methods used to populate a raster (grid) based on the characteristics of spatially distributed control points, including Nearest-neighbor interpolation, IDW interpolation, Kriging, and Spline interpolation. Various methods of visualizing the 3-dimensional data were demonstrated, including analytical hill-shading, hypsometric tinting, and the use of isolines (e.g., contour lines). Methods of computing the slope and aspect associated with pixels in a raster dataset were introduced. GIScientists and practictioners use a variety of these techniques on a daily basis to process and analyze 3-dimensional data. Additional information about isolines (e.g., contours) is found in Chapter 10.

Review Questions

1. Describe the characteristics of a facet in a TIN. How is a facet created? Are there constraints on the size and shape of the facet?

2. Describe how you would use analytical hill-shading, color hypsometric tinting, and lines of equal temperature (isotherms) to visualize the information content of

a TIN data structure containing land surface temperature values.

3. What algorithm would you choose to compute the slope associated with a pixel in a raster dataset?

4. Using the information presented in Figure 9-7, describe why the size of the output cell size is important when conducting spatial interpolation from control points to a raster.

5. You are required to interpolate 1,500 GPS-derived *x,y,z* spot height elevation values into a grid with 1 x 1 m spatial resolution pixels. Describe which of the raster interpolation methods (Nearest-neighbor, IDW, Kriging, Spline) you would use and why you think this method would provide the optimum results.

6. Why is the *range* important when analyzing a Kriging empirical semivariogram?

7. Based on the discussion in the text, when might you want to use a physical spline (i.e., a duck)?

8. You have decided to change the color look-up table in Figure 9-17c so that all the values in the raster dataset with a value of 10 are bright yellow. What would be the Red, Green, and Blue (RGB) values you would place in the color look-up table to make this change?

9. What do you believe is the most significant difference between IDW interpolation and Kriging geostatistical interpolation? Why is this important?

10. How would you locate a new *x,y,z* control point at the midpoint along one side of a TIN facet?

Glossary

Analytical Hill-shading: The synthetic illumination of a facet in a TIN dataset or a pixel in a raster dataset by light from a specific direction (e.g., NW at 345°) and at a specific elevation above the horizon (e.g., 45°).

Aspect: The cardinal direction that each facet is facing in a TIN data structure or that each pixel is facing in a raster data structure. It is measured as a cardinal direction in degrees (e.g., 0° [North], 180° [South]).

Control Point: An individual measurement obtained in the field or by a remote sensing instrument that has unique *x*, *y* coordinates and may also have a *z*-value (e.g., elevation above sea level).

Empirical Semivariogram: A graph that relates the semivariance to the amount of spatial separation (and autocorrelation) between control point samples in a geostatistical analysis.

Geostatistical Analysis: A special branch of spatial statistics that takes into account not only the distance between control point observations but also their spatial autocorrelation.

Inverse-Distance-Weighting (IDW) Interpolation: The determination of the *z*-value (e.g., elevation above sea level) at a new location using information from *n* nearby control points that are weighted in importance based on their distance to the new location.

Isoline: A line of equal magnitude above some arbitrary datum (e.g., a contour is an isoline of constant elevation above sea level).

Kriging: A generic name for a family of least-squares linear regression algorithms that are used to estimate the value of a continuous attribute (e.g., elevation) at any unsampled location using only attribute data available over the study area.

Nearest-neighbor Spatial Interpolation: Determination of the *z*-value (e.g., temperature) at a new location using information from *n* nearby control points. The value of the new location is assigned the value of the nearest-neighbor.

Pseudoscopic Illusion: This effect is created when a person views a 3-dimensional surface with the shadows falling away from the viewer. In this situation, the viewer can become confused and perceive low points as high and high points as being low. Having the shadows fall toward the viewer usually minimizes the pseudoscopic illusion effect.

Slope: The slope of a statistical surface (e.g., elevation) is the change in *z*-value (i.e., the rise) divided by the distance travelled (i.e., the run).

Spatial Interpolation: The process of identifying the *z*-value (e.g., elevation above sea level) at a new location based on the characteristics of *n* adjacent control points.

Triangular Irregular Network (TIN): A surface represented by a set of triangular facets with 3-dimensional coordinates at their vertices.

Variography: The geostatistical process whereby a spatially dependent model is fit to the ground control-point data and the spatial structure is quantified.

References

Brivio, P. A. and E. Zilioli, 2001, "Urban Pattern Characterization Through Geostatistical Analysis of Satellite Images," in J. P. Donnay, M. J. Barnsley and P. A. Longley (Eds.), *Remote Sensing and Urban Analysis*, London: Taylor & Francis, 39–53.

Curran, P. J., 1988, "The Semivariogram in Remote Sensing: An Introduction," *Remote Sensing of Environment*, 24:493–507.

Esri, 2010, *ArcGIS Geostatistical Analyst*, Redlands: Esri, Inc. (www.Esri.com/software/arcgis/extensions/geostatistical/index.html).

Fleming, M. D. and R. M. Hoffer, 1979, *Machine Processing of Landsat MSS Data and DMA Topographic Data for Forest Cover Type Mapping*, LARS Technical Report 062879. West Lafayette: Laboratory for Applications of Remote Sensing.

Hodgson, M. E., 1998, "Comparison of Angles from Surface Slope/Aspect Algorithms," *Cartography and Geographic Information Systems*, 25(3):173–185.

Horn, B. K. P., 1981, "Hill Shading and the Reflectance Map," *Proceedings of the IEEE*, 69(1):14-47.

Isaaks, E. H. and R. M. Srivastava, 1989, *An Introduction to Applied Geostatistics*, Oxford: Oxford University Press, 561 p.

Jensen, J. R., 2005, *Introductory Digital Image Processing: A Remote Sensing Perspective*, Upper Saddle River: Pearson Prentice-Hall, Inc., 526 p.

Johnston, K., Ver Hoef, J. M., Krivoruchko, K. and N. Lucas, 2001, *Using ArcGIS Geostatistical Analyst*, Redlands: Esri, Inc., 300 p.

Krige, D. G., 1951, *A Statistical Approach to Some Mine Valuations and Allied Problems at the Witwatersrand*, Master's Thesis, University of Witwatersrand, South Africa.

Lo, C. P. and A. K. W. Yeung, 2002, *Concepts and Techniques of Geographic Information Systems*, Upper Saddle River: Pearson Prentice-Hall, Inc., 492 p.

Maillard, P., 2003, "Comparing Texture Analysis Methods through Classification," *Photogrammetric Engineering & Remote Sensing*, 69(4):357–367.

Mark, D. M. and B. Smith, 2004, "A Science of Topography: Bridging the Qualitative-Quantitative Divide," in M. P. Bishop and J. Shroder (Eds.), *Geographic Information Science and Mountain Geomorphology*, Chichester: Springer-Praxis, 75–100.

Peucker, T. K. and N. Chrisman, 1975, "Cartographic Data Structures," *American Cartographer*, 2:55–69.

Peucker, T. K., R. J. Fowler, J. J. Little, and D. M. Mark, 1978, "The Triangulated Irregular Network," *Proceedings of the Digital Terrain Models Symposium,* St. Louis: American Society of Photogrammetry, May 9-11, 516–540.

Ritter, P, 1987, "A Vector-based Slope and Aspect Generation Algorithm," *Photogrammetric Engineering & Remote Sensing*, 53(8):1109–1111.

Slocum, T. A., McMaster, R. B., Kessler, F. C. and H. H. Howard, 2005, *Thematic Cartography and Geographic Visualization*, Upper Saddle River: Pearson Prentice-Hall, Inc., 518 p.

Waters, D., 2011, "Simple Spline Ducks," *Duckbuilding Magazine* (http://www.duckworksmagazine.com/03/r/articles/splineducks/splineDucks.htm).

Wolf, P. R. and B. A. Dewitt, 2000, *Elements of Photogrammetry with Applications in GIS*, Boston: McGraw Hill, Inc., 608 p.

Woodcock, C. E., Strahler, A. H. and D. L. B. Jupp, 1988a, "The Use of Variograms in Remote Sensing: I. Scene Models and Simulated Images," *Remote Sensing of Environment*, 25:323–348.

Woodcock, C. E., Strahler, A. H. and D. L. B. Jupp, 1988b, "The Use of Variograms in Remote Sensing: II. Real Images," *Remote Sensing of Environment*, 25:349–379.

10 CARTOGRAPHY USING A GIS

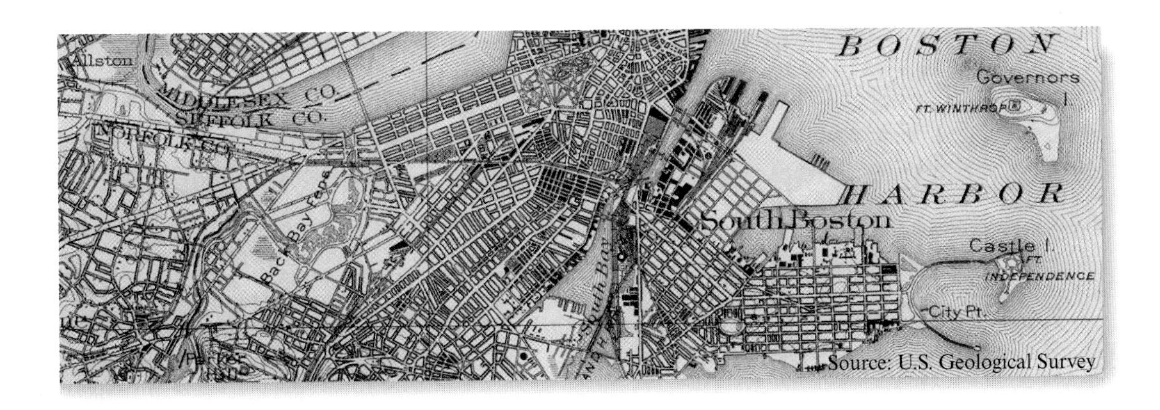

One of the most important uses of a geographic information system is the creation of general purpose and thematic maps that show the spatial distribution of phenomena such as geology, soils, vegetation, water, land use, population density, geographic place names, etc. Map-making using a GIS should be based on fundamental cartographic principles. Many of the cartographic principles have been with us for millennia.

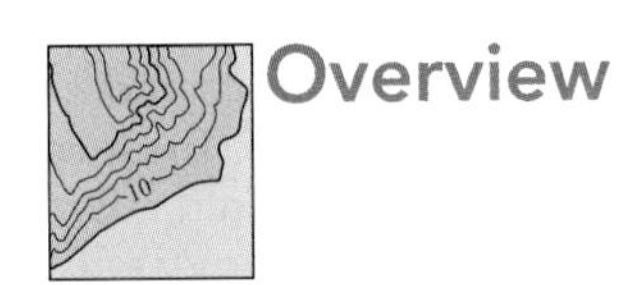

Overview

Many people who use a GIS to produce map products have no formal training in cartography. Consequently, the maps they create using a GIS may lack essential characteristics associated with good cartographic design principles. This reduces the probability that the information contained in the map is communicated to the map-reader successfully. The goal of this chapter is to present some fundamental cartographic design principles that will help you produce more accurate and aesthetically pleasing map products using a GIS.

The chapter begins with a brief history of some major cartographic milestones. Hopefully, the reader will realize that GIS analysis is closely aligned with cartographic science. The cartographic process is introduced to help the reader understand the practical and perceptual stages involved in map-making. Fundamental map design elements are described that can lead to high-quality cartographic products (e.g., layout, balance, use of color and symbols, the figure-ground relationship, north arrows and compass roses, scale bars, metadata). Detailed information about mapping point, line, and area features using a GIS are presented with examples. The reader should be better prepared to produce high-quality maps using a GIS after reading this chapter.

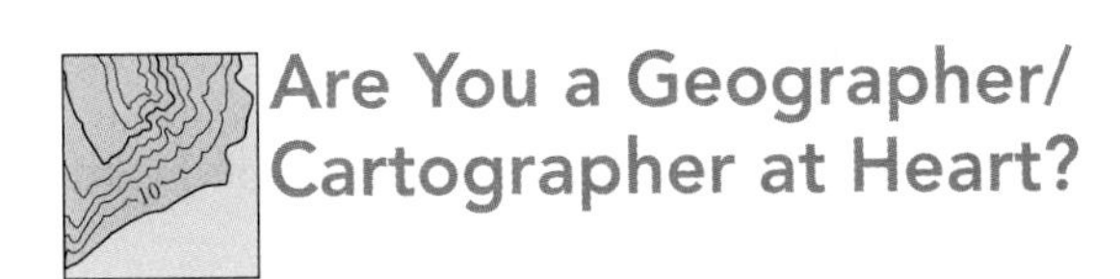

Are You a Geographer/ Cartographer at Heart?

Before delving into the history of cartography, let's see if perhaps you are really a geographer–cartogapher at heart, irrespective of your academic credentials or training. Carl Sauer, one of the great geographers of the twentieth century, described the characteristics of geographers, who are especially interested in maps and map-making (1956):

> ".... let me say [the] most primitive and persistent trait, is liking maps and thinking by means of them. We are empty handed without them in lecture room, in study, in the field. *Show me a geographer who does not need them constantly and want them about him, and I shall have my doubts as to whether he has made the right choice of life.* We squeeze our budgets to get more maps, of all kinds. We collect them from filling stations to antique shops. We draw them, however badly, to illustrate our lectures and our studies. However little a member of your institution may know what you are doing as a geographer, if he requires map information he will call on you. If geographers chance to meet where maps are displayed (it scarcely matters what maps) they comment, commend, criticize. *Maps break down our inhibitions, stimulate our glands, stir our imagination, loosen our tongues. The map speaks across*

the barriers of language; it is sometimes claimed as the language of geography. The conveying of ideas by means of maps is attributed to us as our common vocation and passion." [*italics added*]

Are cartographic products essential to your everyday activities? Do you like to study and analyze maps? Geographic information systems are used to design and produce many of the important, high-quality cartographic (map) products in use today.

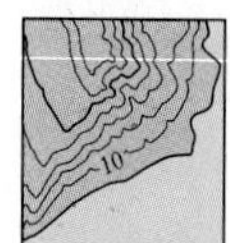

Historical Cartography

The word *cartography* (map-making) comes from the Greek *chartis* (map) and *graphein* (to write or draw). It is the science and practice of making representations of the Earth on a two-dimensional flat surface or three-dimensional globe. In order to appreciate the great strides that cartographic science has made through the centuries, it is instructive to introduce a select few of the major milestones and maps associated with the history of cartography. The reader is encouraged to read Norman J. W. Thrower's (1972; 1999) *Maps & Civilization: Cartography in Culture and Society* or consult the volumes of the *History of Cartography Project* for more detailed information (Harley and Woodward, 1987–2007).

Map of the World (*Imago Mundi*)
Centered on Babylon
Seventh or Sixth Century BC

FIGURE 10–1 One of the oldest world maps was carved into a clay tablet in the seventh or sixth century BC. The map depicts the world as a disc centered on Babylon on the Euphrates, surrounded by a circular landmass showing Assyria, Armenia, and several cities. These features are surrounded by the great bitter river or Salt Sea (used with permission from Zev Radovan, *Bible Land Pictures* / Alamy).

The Oldest Maps

Not surprisingly, the oldest surviving maps were not drawn on paper or parchment. Some of the oldest surviving maps were carved into mammoth bone, or scribed onto copper plates or clay tablets. For example, one of the oldest known world maps is the Babylonian Map of the World (*Imago Mundi*) inscribed on a clay tablet in the seventh or sixth century BC (Figure 10-1) (Gould, 1985). It was found at Sippar, in modern southern Iraq. With north at the top, the map depicts the world as a disc with Babylon on both sides of what appears to be the *Euphrates River,* surrounded by a circular landmass showing Assyria, Armenia, and several cities. These are surrounded by a "bitter river" (presumably the great ocean Salt Sea) and triangles which represent nearby districts (Smith, 1996). Only three of the triangles are visible in the clay tablet.

Many early maps contained very little geographic information because a) so little of the world had been explored, or b) political or religious leaders preferred to keep new geographic knowledge to themselves rather than sharing it with the general public. Geographic knowledge is a special type of power. Unknown areas were typically filled with drawings of real or mythical animals or imaginary landscapes to fill the void. Even when a location was well known, it was still difficult to place it in its proper geographic location on a map because the use of geographic coordinates (longitude and latitude) were unknown or the instruments necessary to measure longitude and latitude were not available (e.g., an accurate marine chronometer).

Medieval T-in-O Maps

A good example of medieval cartography is the tripartite (three-part) T-in-O map (derived from *orbis terrae* meaning orb, or circle of Earth). For example, Isidore, the Bishop of Seville (d. 636) created a T-in-O map in the seventh century for his encyclopedia, called the *Etymologiae.* Isidore's seventh-century map was printed in a book in 1472 by Gutherus Ziner (Figure 10-2a). This was the first map printed in a book in Europe

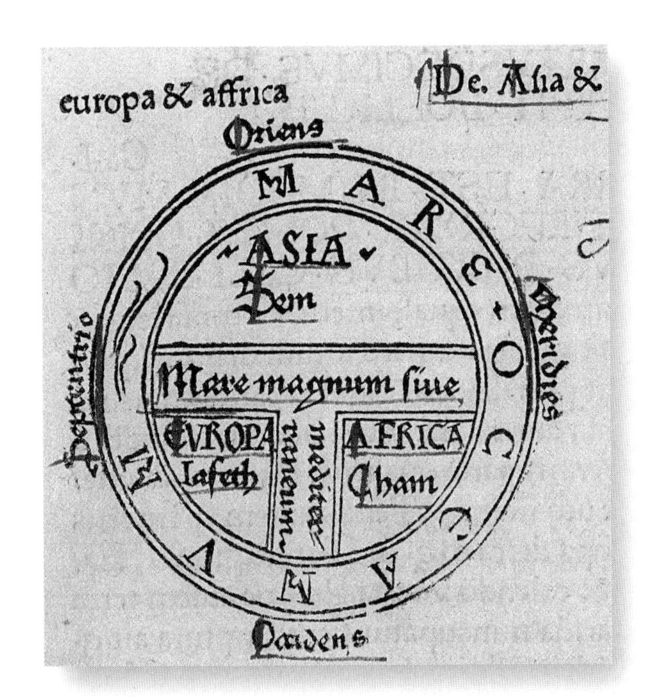

T-in-O Map

a. A T-in-O map created by Isidore of Seville in the seventh century. This T-in-O map was printed in a book in 1472 and shows the continents as domains of Noah's sons: Sem (Shem), Iafeth (Japheth), and Cham (Ham). Jerusaleum is at the center and east is at the top.

Ptolemy's World Map in 1482

b. Geographic information compiled by Ptolemy in his *Geographica* in 150 AD was finally made available to European cartographers in 1410. Ptolemy's maps contained much more accurate information than many of the fifteenth-century maps.

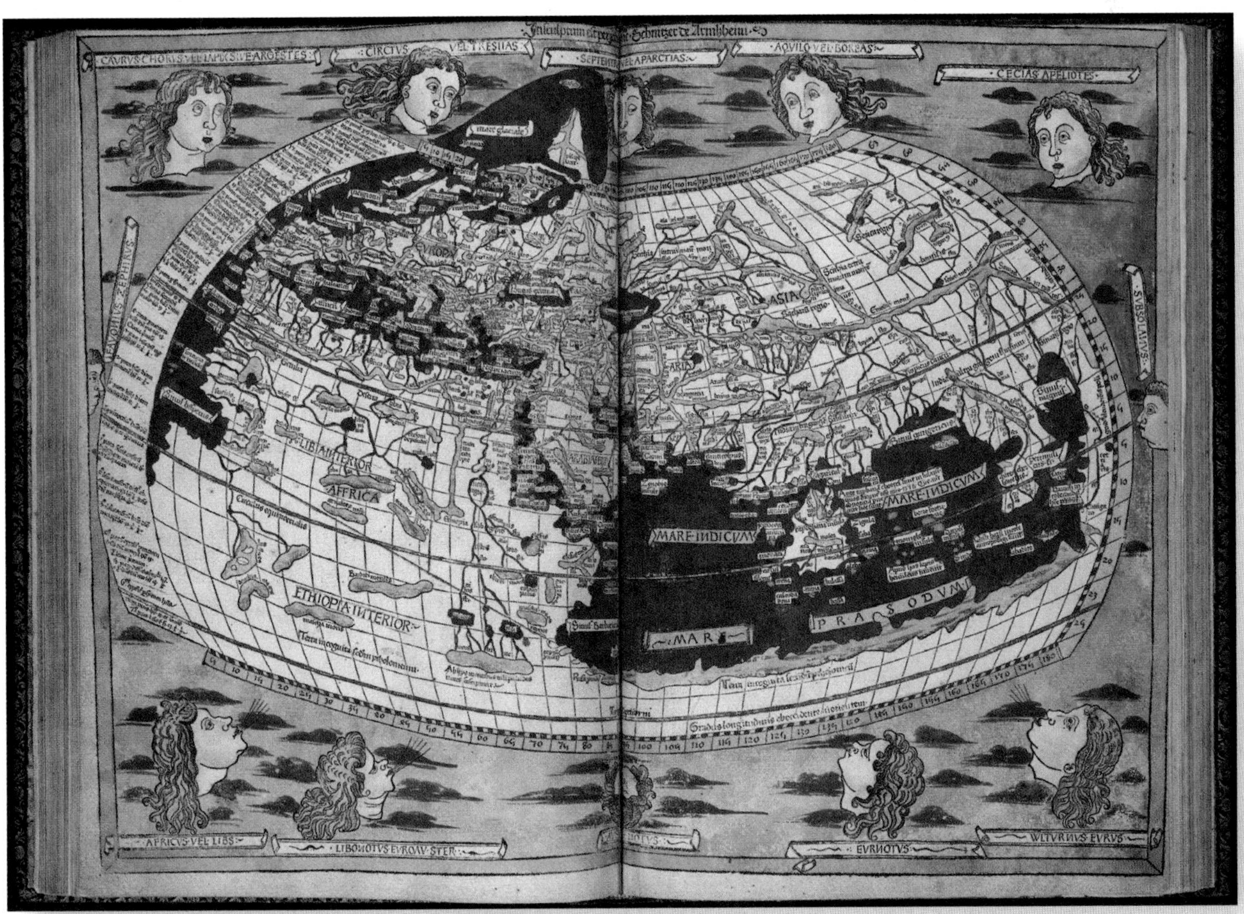

FIGURE 10–2 a) Seventh-century T-in-O map by Isidore of Seville printed in a book in 1472 by Guntherus Ziner (item #138.00.00 courtesy of the Library of Congress Rare Book and Special Collections Division). b) Ptolemy's World Map (ca 150 AD) printed in Ulm, Germany, by Lienhart Holle in 1482 complete with lines of latitude and longitude (item #140.02.00 courtesy of the Library of Congress Geography and Map Division).

(item #138.00.00; Library of Congress Rare Book and Special Collections Division, 2011).

The "T" in a T-in-O map represents a Christian cross with Jerusalem at the center of the world. It divided the world into the continents Asia, Europe, and Africa. Asia was as large as the other two continents combined. Because the sun rose in the east, Paradise (the Garden of Eden) was generally depicted as being in Asia (the Orient) and was situated at the top of the map. This is where we get the word "orienting" from. No southern regions are shown because a) the continents were not known at the time, or b) more southern climates were considered uninhabited or unattainable. The "O" in a T-in-O map is the encircling great world ocean or sea (*mare*). Early explorers assumed that it was possible to travel between the world's lands on the one world ocean which led to grand voyages of discovery. T-in-O map concepts persisted for many centuries. A more detailed T-in-O map called the Hereford *Mappa Mundi* (Map of the World) was published in 1300 AD (Hereford Cathedral, 2011).

Ptolemy's *Geographica* 150 AD

To demonstrate how long it took to obtain relatively accurate cartographic information, consider the work of Claudius Ptolemy (83–168 AD). Ptolemy was a Greek Roman citizen who became the librarian of the great Library of Alexandria in Egypt. He is best known by geographers for his book *Geographica* or *Cosmographia* (published ca 150 AD) which describes cartographic methods and incorporates the first use of longitude and latitude lines and locating features by celestial observations. Knowledge of these methods and the locational coordinates of numerous places were lost until Ptolemy's works were translated from Greek into Latin in Florence, Italy, about 1410. A reproduction of Ptolemy's World Map published in 1482 is shown in Figure 10-2b (item #140.02.00; Library of Congress Geography and Map Division, 2011).

Why were Ptolemy's maps so important in the middle ages when they were created more than 1,000 years earlier? The reason is that after 1,000 years, much of the geographic data in Ptolemy's maps (especially the use of geographic coordinates of places and new map projections) was superior to that found in maps produced during the middle ages. Ptolemy's book rocked the foundation of medieval map-making. As shown in the T-in-O maps, map-makers in the middle ages often based the size of countries, not on mathematical calculations, but on the importance of different places. The more important a place or country was for political or religious purposes, the bigger it appeared on the map. Ptolemy's *Geographica* changed cartography forever.

Age of Exploration, Printing, and Atlases

In 1440, German inventor Johannes Gutenberg invented the printing press process that, with refinements and increased mechanization, remained the principal means of printing until the late twentieth century. The inventor's method of printing from movable type, including the use of metal molds and alloys, a special press, and oil-based inks, allowed for the first time the mass production of printed books and maps. Maps were first printed using carved wooden blocks. Printing with engraved copper plates appeared in the sixteenth century and continued to be the standard until lithography was developed in the mid-1800s.

Major advances in cartography took place during the Age of Exploration in the fifteenth and sixteenth centuries. Cartographers responded with new world maps and navigation charts, with more accurate coastlines, islands, rivers, and harbors. Compass lines and other navigation aids were included, new map projections were devised, and new globes and atlases were constructed. Such maps, atlases, and globes were of great value for economic, military, and diplomatic purposes and were often treated as national or commercial secrets—classified or proprietary maps.

For example, consider the *Universalis Cosmographia* map drafted by the German cartographer Martin Waldseemuller (Figure 10-3). It is believed to be the first map to include the name *America* on it (see the enlargement in Figure 10-3) and the first to depict both North and South America as separate from Asia (Library of Congress American Memory Collection, 2011a). The name America was bestowed in honor of Amerigo Vespucci. There is only one surviving copy of the map, which was purchased by the U.S. Library of Congress in 2001 for $10 million. The wall map consists of 12 sheets, each 21 by 30 in., which produces a map of the world 4.5 x 8 ft. It was designated by its own inscription to be a marine chart and is dated 1507. It was one of the first maps to chart locations using latitude and longitude, following the example of Ptolemy.

The sixteenth through the eighteenth centuries were a time of great atlas production. An **atlas** is a collection of maps, traditionally bound into book form. As well as geographic features and political boundaries, many atlases also contain geopolitical, social, religious, and economic statistics and information. One of the most widely known atlases was the *Theatrum Orbis Terrarum* (Theatre of the World) created by Abraham Ortelius. The *Theatrum Orbis Terrarum* was first printed in 1570, in Antwerp, Belgium, and consisted of a collection of map sheets and text bound to form a book. It was not called an atlas. One of the maps in the *The-*

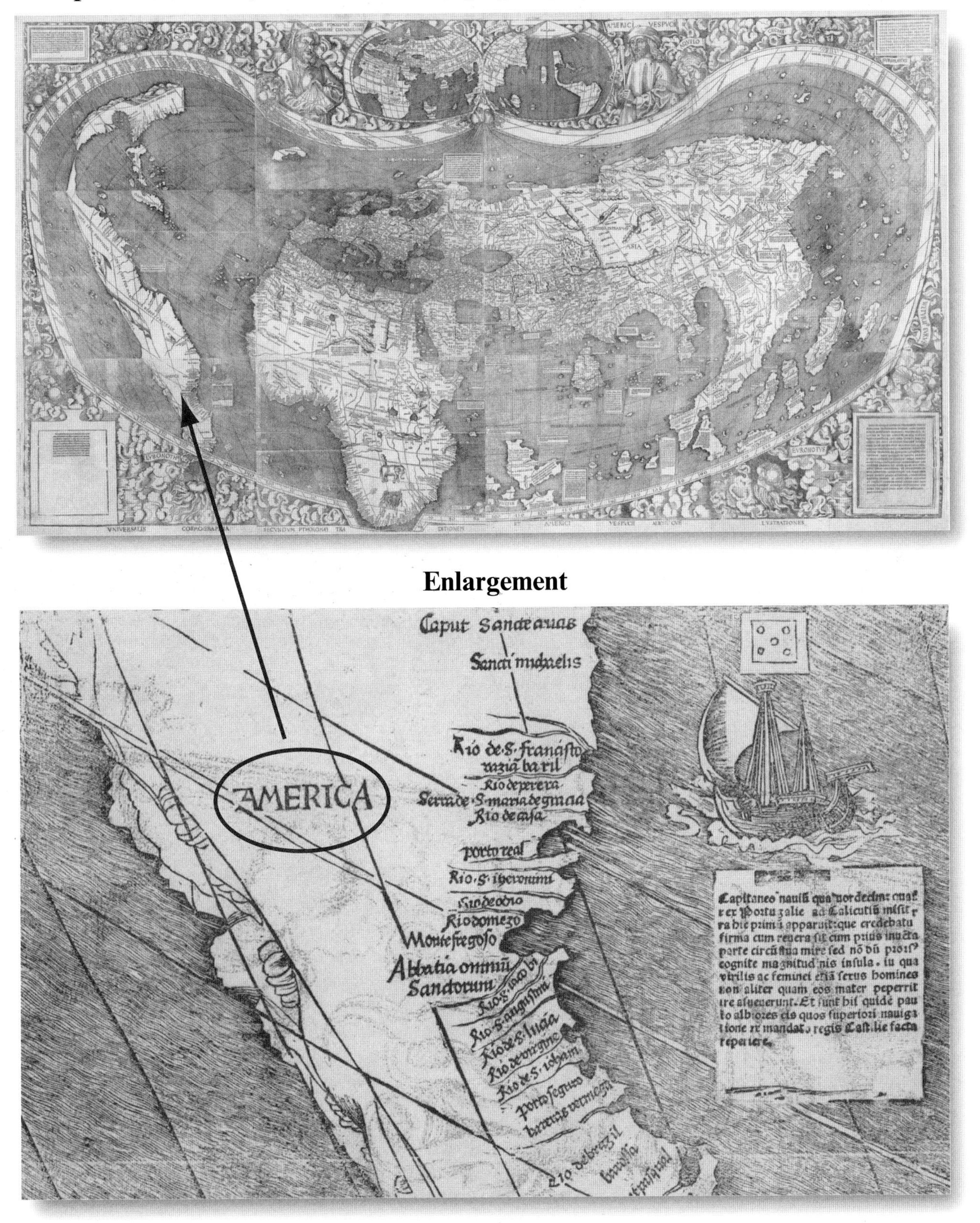

FIGURE 10–3 Martin Waldseemuller produced what was perhaps the first true world map based on relatively accurate longitude and latitude coordinate information. It was created in 1507 and consisted of 12 separate map sheets. Note the appearance of the word "AMERICA" in the enlargement (courtesy of Library of Congress Geography and Map Division).

The Map *Typus Orbis Terrarum* in the Atlas *Theatrum Orbis Terrarum* (Theatre of the World) Produced by Abraham Ortelius in 1570

FIGURE 10–4 A map from the *Theatrum Orbis Terrarum* atlas by Abraham Ortelius published in 1570 (courtesy of Library of Congress Geography and Map Division). Compare the information on the Americas in this map with the information found in the Martin Waldseemuller map of the world in Figure 10-3.

atrum is the *Typus Orbis Terrarum* shown in Figure 10-4 (originally published as a wall map in 1564). The Ortelius atlas is sometimes referred to as the climax of sixteenth-century cartography.

Ortelius regularly revised and incorporated new geographical information into the atlas, reissuing it in various formats until his death in 1598. Note the tremendous amount of new information found in the Ortelius atlas map *Typus Orbis Terrarum* 1570 (Figure 10-4) when compared with the information contained in the Martin Waldseemuller map of the world produced in 1507 (Figure 10-3). Studying maps through time teaches us about the historical development of geographical knowledge. Ortelius' atlas grew through 31 editions to encompass 167 maps by 1612. The Blaeu family continued to publish the atlas even after 1630.

Modern Map-making

Maps became increasingly accurate and factual during the seventeenth, eighteenth, and nineteenth centuries due in large part to more accurate surveying and time-keeping instruments. Many countries began to recognize the importance of accurate boundary and natural resource information which resulted in national mapping programs. For example, John Wesley Powell of the U.S. Geological Survey conducted two extensive surveys of the Colorado River region of the western U.S. beginning in 1871. Extensive terrestrial surveying took place. This spatial information was eventually incorporated into the map of the *Colorado River* by First Lieutenant George Wheeler (1873) (Figure 10-5) (Library of Congress American Memory Collection, 2011b). Maps such as this educated lawmakers and the public about the nature of the western lands and were used to make many decisions. Similar surveys were conducted in the latter part of the nineteenth century throughout

Parts of Northern and Northwestern Arizona and Southern Utah Atlas Sheet No. 67, 1873
by First Lieutenant George Wheeler, U.S. Army Corps of Engineers

FIGURE 10–5 A map of the *Colorado River* region of Arizona and Utah by First Lieutenant George Wheeler in 1873. The map incorporated the work of expeditions throughout the region from 1871–1873, most notably those of John Wesley Powell (map courtesy of the Library of Congress American Memory Collection, Geography and Map Division).

the world, especially by colonial powers (e.g., England, France, Spain) who controlled foreign lands in India, Africa, South America, Asia, etc.

Nevertheless, much of the world remained poorly mapped until the widespread use of aerial photography following World War I and World War II. Modern cartography is based on 1) a combination of accurate ground observations often involving total station surveying (which uses GPS), photogrammetry, and remote sensing, and 2) new thematic map products derived from GIS analysis.

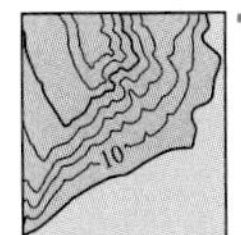

The Cartographic Process

The map is a truly remarkable invention of humankind. Maps are created to communicate the information present in spatial data to a map-reader. Sometimes the map is made just for the map-maker. At other times the map is created for a very particular or larger audience. In any case, it is hoped that the information that is portrayed in the map is useful and leads to an improved quality of living for humans, flora, and fauna.

The goal is to communicate the spatial information portrayed on the map as effectively and efficiently as possible. Ideally, reading a map is both a pleasing and enlightening experience for the map-reader. As demonstrated in the previous section, cartographers have been designing maps to communicate spatial information for millennia. Therefore, cartographers know a tremendous amount about how maps should be designed and how to communicate the information in a map effectively. This collective wisdom has been passed down from generation to generation of cartographers and is often implemented using the Cartographic Process (also referred to as the Map Communication Model) (Slocum et al., 2005).

The **Cartographic Process** generally consists of the five steps summarized in Figure 10-6. The first step is very important. The cartographer must first have some idea in his or her mind that a particular set of spatial data might reveal some interesting patterns (Buckley and

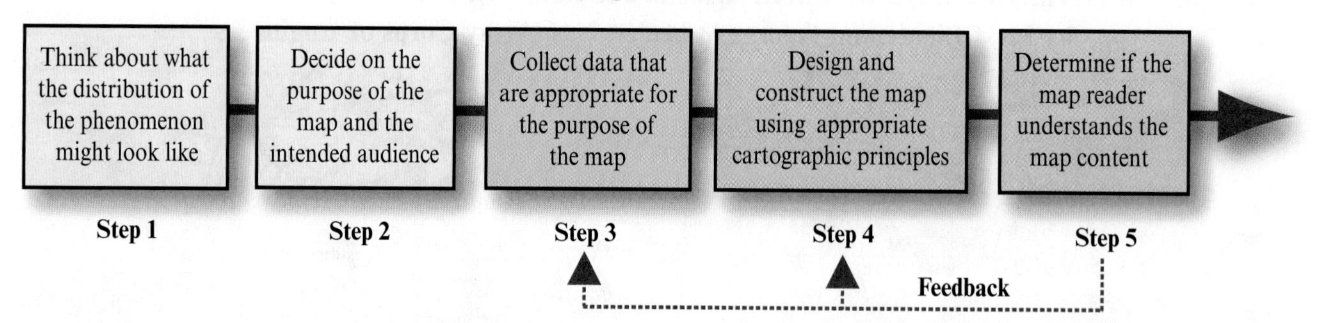

FIGURE 10–6 The Cartographic Process is used by cartographers to create high-quality cartographic products (maps) that communicate the desired spatial information to the map-reader (often referred to as the user). It is often necessary to iterate the data collection, cartographic design, and construction part of the process if the map-reader does not understand the desired spatial relationships portrayed in the map (adapted from Slocum et al., 2005).

Field, 2011). Otherwise, data will not be collected and no map will be made. He or she does not have to know exactly what the data will look like when mapped, but it is useful when the map-maker at least conceptualizes a preliminary version of the map in his or her mind. Therefore, cartographers must be capable of analytical thought, which translates real or anticipated spatial data into a 2- or 3-dimensional perceptual cartographic product.

Sometimes a map is created for the benefit of the map-maker to gain insight into the spatial relationships between one or several variables. At other times, the map is produced for a specific audience. Therefore, the cartographer must exercise good judgment during Step 2 when the purpose of the map and its intended audience is carefully considered. Unfortunately, map-makers, including many scientists, often fail to appreciate the background or the map-reading capabilities of the map-reader audiences. When this occurs, there is a general breakdown in the cartographic process resulting in the map not being as valuable as it might be. Significant time and resources can also be wasted by the cartographer if the characteristics of the intended audience are not taken into consideration.

Step 3 is concerned with data collection. Perhaps the cartographer only has a relatively small sample of spatial data at the beginning of the cartographic process that stimulates his or her interest in making a map. It is often necessary to collect a significant amount of additional unbiased spatial information in order to make the map as complete and as accurate as possible. This often involves using the in situ and/or remote sensing data collection procedures described in Chapter 3.

The map is actually constructed in Step 4. Ideally, the cartographer uses standard cartographic design principles which have been passed down through the years to symbolize the point, line, area, and volume information inherent in the map. Failure to use standard cartographic practices can result in a map that a) does not portray the cartographic information accurately, or b) causes the map-reader to misinterpret the map data. It is very important to point out that the cartographer should make sure that the design principles applied to the map are not used to lie or propagandize. Monmonier (1996) documents how unethical cartographers and lay persons have used certain types of cartographic principles to lie with maps. A map is a contract between the cartographer and the map-reader. The map-reader has every right to expect that the cartographer designs and constructs the map so that the spatial information in the map is as accurate in its portrayal as possible.

Ideally, the map communicates the spatial information clearly to the map-reader who then gains new insight about the thematic phenomena under consideration (Step 5). Unfortunately, sometimes the map-reader simply does not understand the spatial information being portrayed in the map, even when it is mapped as accurately as possible. When this occurs, the cartographer is hopefully told about this situation. He or she then re-evaluates the entire cartographic process and decides what must be done to improve the cartographic communication. Often this involves collecting additional spatial data, changing the map design, and re-creating the map once again. Some spatial data are more difficult to communicate than others, so there may be several iterations between Steps 3, 4, and 5. Once the cartographer is satisfied that he or she has successfully communicated the desired information to the user(s), then the final map is created and published or served to as many interested parties as possible. Unfortunately, some groups or governments suppress the geospatial information portrayed in maps to keep the general public uninformed. The greater the distribution of accurate spatial information, the higher the probability that good decisions will be made so that

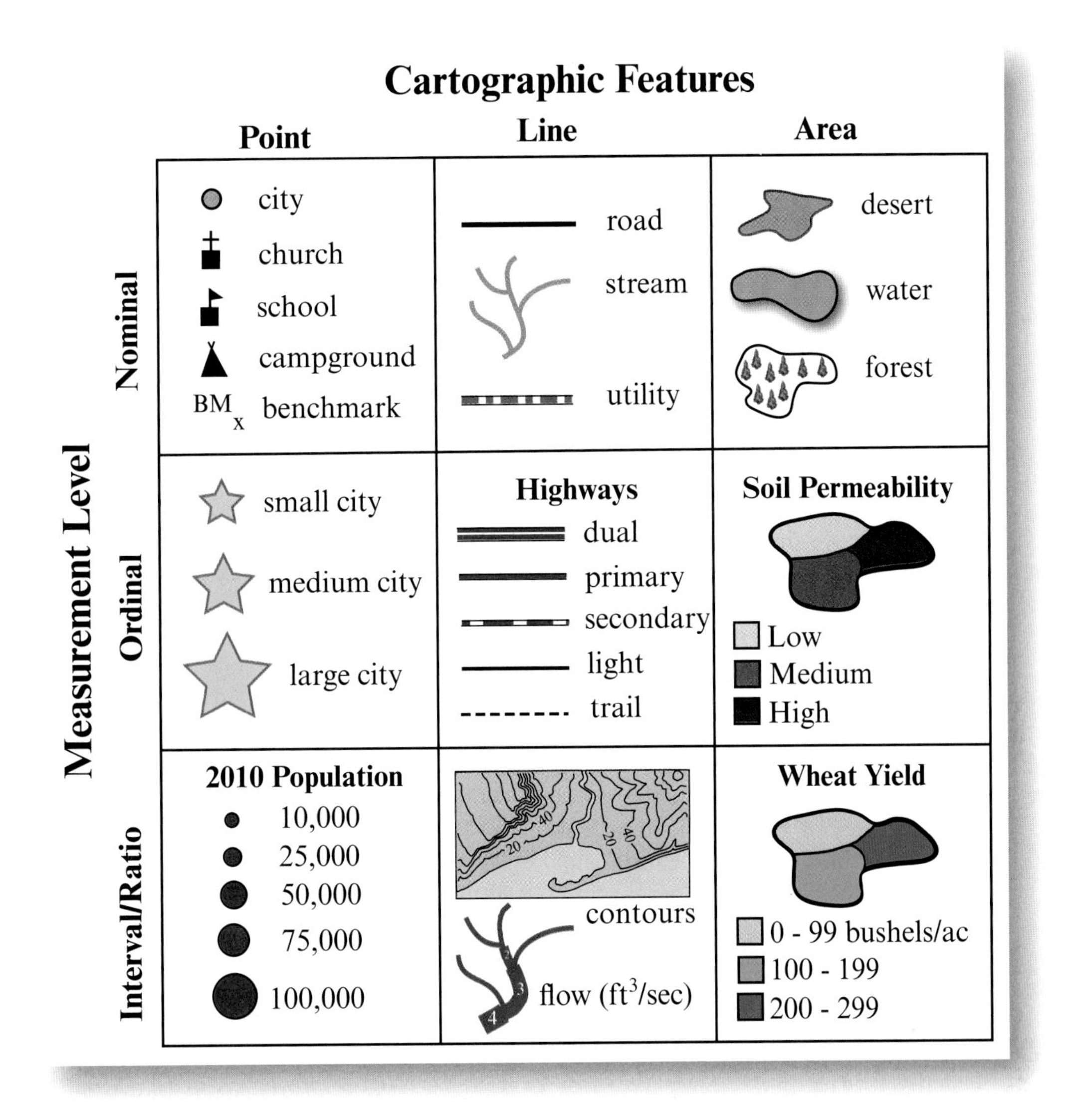

FIGURE 10–7 Examples of point, line, and area cartographic features and nominal, ordinal, and interval/ratio measurement levels.

humans, flora, and fauna can live in a sustainable world. Good cartography contributes to good governance and sustainable development.

Now that you understand the cartographic communication process, you can proceed to look more closely at the levels of measurement (nominal, ordinal, interval, and ratio) and types of data (point, linear, area, and volume) that will be mapped (Figure 10-7). The fundamental elements of map design can then be introduced.

Feature Type and Measurement Level

The data portrayed in maps may range in feature type (point, line, area, and surface/volume) and measurement level (nominal, ordinal, interval, and ratio). It is instructive to review these characteristics.

Feature Type

Real-world phenomena consist of point, line, area, and surface/volume features. *Point features,* such as a city, church, school, campground, or benchmark, exist at a single geographic location (Figure 10-7). The location of the point feature is represented by a single x,y-coordinate pair. It is important to note that when we are considering whether a feature is a point feature or not, that the scale of observation is very important. For example, everyone knows that we live in cities that occupy geographic space and that not all of us within a city reside at a single location. Therefore, if we were mapping the geographic extent (area) of a city at a very detailed scale, e.g., 1:5,000, then we would not be concerned with mapping the city as a point observation. Rather, we would be considering the city as an area feature (to be discussed shortly). However, if we are making a map depicting the spatial distribution of all the cities in Illinois, the United States, or the world, it would be necessary to map the cities at a much coarser scale, e.g., 1:10,000,000, wherein the cities would be considered to be point features that exist at discrete locations that do not occupy geographic area. Thus, the scale of our investigation often dictates whether something is considered a point or an area feature.

Linear features such as roads, streams, or utility lines occupy more than a single location and are associated with at least two geographic coordinates (Figure 10-7): one *x,y*-coordinate pair at the beginning and another *x,y*-coordinate pair at the endpoint. Many linear features have very intricate twists and turns associated with them and are characterized cartographically using many other *x,y* coordinate pairs between the beginning and ending coordinates.

Many of the features we map occupy a geographic area and are called *area features*. This means that the beginning and ending points of the polygon encompassing the feature will be the same. In other words, the polygon is closed. Good examples of geographic area features include deserts, water bodies, forest stands, etc. (Figure 10-7).

Sometimes we can obtain additional information about a geographic area such as its elevation above sea level, its barometric pressure, the amount of rainfall that fell during a recent storm, the population density of the area, etc. Usually this means that we have obtained discrete (single) biophysical measurements at many known locations throughout this geographic area. In addition, we can synthesize new measurements between the original measurements using spatial interpolation methods to create a more dense coverage of observations throughout the geographic area (interpolation methods were discussed in Chapter 9). After interpolation, each of the numerous observations contained within the geographic area has a unique *x,y*-coordinate pair plus a unique *z*-value (e.g., x = 1452000 E; y = 350000 N; and z = 100 ft. above sea level). We can make 3-dimensional views of these phenomena based on the *x,y,* and *z*-value information. For example, we can create a 3-dimensional view of the earth's topography using the *x,y,* and *z*-value (elevation) stored in a digital terrain model as shown in Figure 10-7 (several methods of displaying 3-dimensional information were discussed in Chapter 9).

We can also compute the volume associated with 3-dimensional surfaces. This is very important when we want to compare the volume of change from one time to the next. For example, we might want to determine the amount of rock material extracted from a rock quarry on the first of each month, the change in barometric pressure over a state every day, or the change in city population density every five years.

Geographic Measurement Level

Thus far we have introduced the point, line, area, and surface/volume characteristics of features that we can map using a GIS. Now it is important to talk about the attributes of these features. Sometimes we have very simple presence or absence (binary) information about a feature (e.g., a tree exists at coordinate *x,y*). At other times we might have very detailed quantitative information about the same feature (e.g., it exists at coordinate *x,y* and has a height of 30 ft.). The nature of these attribute observations dictate what kind of symbolization we typically use to communicate map information to the map-reader.

Fortunately, scientists have thought about these different levels of measurement as they relate to all types of measurement (not just geographic measurement). This has resulted in the development of the concept of **measurement levels,** which are used by geographers and GIScience practitioners to describe the nature of the data being mapped or evaluated. It progresses through nominal, ordinal, interval, and ratio scales of measurement, as listed in Table 10-1 and shown in Figure 10-7.

The *nominal* scale of measurement is easy to understand. If all we know about a point, line, or area feature is its location and name (e.g., the city of Memphis, TN; the *Mississippi River*, or the *Atlantic Ocean*), then we have nominal scale spatial information. Such nominal scale information in effect allows us to give place names to point, line, and area objects that exist in the real world but we cannot compare any quantitative characteristics associated with like objects. In effect, all objects or phenomena have equal value, i.e., A = B or B = A (Table 10-1). For example, we cannot say anything about the population of Memphis, TN, compared to the population of London, U.K. We can only say that the cities exist at specific *x,y*-coordinate locations. We cannot even say that one city is greater, lesser, or better than the other city in any dimension because the nominal scale spatial data will not support such comparisons.

Conversely, we can collect information about places using a simple *ordinal* level of measurement which would allow us to make some qualitative comparisons between phenomena. For example, we could look at all the cities in the world and classify them into three simple qualitative classes: small, medium, and large. Using such a system, Memphis, TN, would most likely be categorized as a small city while London, U.K., would

TABLE 10–1 Measurement levels with permissible operations (adapted from Burt et al., 2009).

Level	Permissible operations at each level include all operations valid at lower levels of measurement	Examples
1. Nominal	A = B or B= A, counting	Presence or absence of phenomena Land cover (e.g., forest), land use (e.g., recreation)
2. Ordinal	A<B or A>B or A=B	Residential area quality of living (good, better, best) Soil type A is more permeable than soil type B
3. Interval	Subtraction (A-B)	Temperature, ^{o}F (e.g., Area A is 10° cooler than Area B) Elevation above mean sea level
4. Ratio	Addition (A+B) Multiplication (AxB) Ratios (A/B) Square root Powers Logarithms Exponentiation	Precipitation on day 1 + precipitation on day 2 Density (e.g., persons /mile^2) Remote sensing vegetation indices (e.g., NIR/red) Stream discharge Shopping center square footage Wheat or rice yield

likely be classified as a large city. Therefore, we could logically say that Memphis (A) has a smaller population than London (B), i.e., A<B, even though we do not have the detailed quantitative information (Table 10-1). Similarly, consider the ordinal scale ranking of five road-carrying capacities utilized by the U.S. Geological Survey on their 7.5-minute topographic maps (Figure 10-7). Instead of just knowing that a road feature exists, we now have qualitative ordinal-scale information about whether the road is dual lane, primary, secondary, light, or trail. There are many other ordinal measurement scales such as good, better, and best; lowest, intermediate, and highest.

If we really want to compare the quantitative characteristics (e.g., population) of two features (e.g., two cities), it is necessary to have more precise *interval*- or *ratio*-scaled data. However, there is a very important distinction between interval- and ratio-scaled data. Having access to ratio-scaled data means that we can compute a meaningful *ratio* associated with the two numbers being compared. This is not possible using interval-scaled data. A simple example will clarify this observation.

Let us assume that 20 thermometers are placed on 20 asphalt driveways in the city and that 20 thermometers are placed on 20 lawns in the same city. Temperature measurements are made at all 40 locations at 2:00 pm in the afternoon. The average temperature of the 20 asphalt driveways is 100° F and the average temperature of the 20 lawns is 50° F. We can easily map this temperature information and provide the map-reader with information about the temperature of the land at 40 locations at 2:00 pm on this specific day. This is valuable information.

But can we say that the average asphalt driveway is twice as warm as the average lawn? This seems like a reasonable conclusion. Unfortunately, this statement is incorrect because the Fahrenheit measurement system is not based on a temperature at absolute 0°. For us to make a ratio of the two numbers and say that one is twice as warm as the other, the starting point in the measurements must be zero (0). Therefore, we would have to convert the Fahrenheit-scale measurements to temperatures in the Kelvin scale, where the starting point is zero (0). In fact, 50° F = 283 K and 100° F = 311 K). The ratio of 283/311 = 0.90. So, there is no way that the driveways exhibit twice the temperature as the lawns. In reality, the lawns exhibit approximately 90% of the temperature of the driveways.

Another good example of the use of ratio-scaled data is the computation of population density. Suppose you have population data for each county in your state. These data have a meaningful zero value. You also have information about the area of each county measured in miles^2. These data also have a meaningful zero value. Therefore, you can determine the population density of each county by computing the ratio between the county population and square miles in each county using the ratio

$$\text{Population density} = \frac{population}{miles^2} \tag{10.1}$$

Similarly, because base salary is zero ($0), observations made with a per capita income of $25,000 can be said to be one-half of the observations with a per capita income of $50,000.

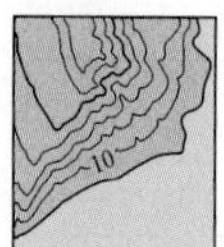

Map Design Fundamentals

A high-quality GIS can be used to design and produce beautiful maps that accurately and efficiently communicate important spatial information. Unfortunately, a GIS can also be used to make extremely bad maps that are visually unattractive and sometimes communicate the desired information very poorly. GIS-produced maps can also be used to lie, misinform, and introduce propaganda (Monmonier, 1996).

As previously noted, a major concern is that many people using a GIS to create a map have never taken a cartography course where map design fundamentals are introduced, including the ethics of map-making. Therefore, before discussing the cartographic options that can be used when mapping point, line, and area data, it is useful to first introduce some fundamental map design principles. Relatively brief instructions will be given concerning

- Map composition (i.e., layout in the map frame),
- Title,
- Typography (font, size, style, and color),
- Thematic content (and the *figure-ground* relationship),
- Geographic reference material (e.g., latitude–longitude graticule, grid),
- Scale (unit equivalent, representative fraction, scale bar),
- Legends,
- Orientation (e.g., North arrow),
- Metadata (carto-bibliography),
- Color, and
- Symbology.

Map Composition (Layout)

All the spatial and non-spatial information placed in a map (including 2-, 3-, and even 4-dimensional [time] maps) should be performed with the goal of producing a visually pleasing, accurate, and informative map or sequence of maps. The cartographer has great latitude when deciding where to place the various map components on the blank map frame which functions something like an artist's blank canvas. For example, suppose you were asked to make a map that depicts the population of South Carolina by county in 2000 using U.S. Bureau of the Census population data (Figure 10-8a). The shape of the area to be mapped has a major impact on the placement of features in the map frame. In this example, the shape of South Carolina lends itself well to the placement of the title centered at the top of the map and the legend, bar-scale, and north arrow placed in a pleasing format around the periphery of the state outline.

Good map design is learned, not inherited. The goal is to prepare an informative, yet uncluttered map that is easy to read. Fortunately, today's GIS allow GIScientists to rapidly select and move the various map features to different locations within the map frame and resize them to test different design ideas.

Title

The title of the map is extremely important. It represents a contract between the map-maker and the map-reader. The title should be very informative yet relatively short, if possible. It should accurately describe the thematic content of the map, e.g., the population of South Carolina; the enumeration unit, e.g., by county; and the most accurate date associated with the data, e.g., 2000. There are a variety of ways to order the title textual information. A subtitle can also be used if necessary.

The title should be created using an easily readable font that is usually the largest size type found on the map. It should be one of the first groups of type that the map-reader actually processes so that he or she understands the purpose of the map. Extremely unusual type fonts, extensive italics, and poor title placement should be avoided. In Figure 10-8a, the title was centered above the major thematic map content. Sometimes the title is placed at other locations depending upon the shape of the thematic content.

Typography

Typography is the art and science of creating alphanumeric type in various fonts, styles, and sizes. Typographers (experts in the creation and use of type) and cartographers have expended great effort creating *type* that is easy for lay persons to read and understand. Cartographers are primarily concerned with selecting the most appropriate type for a map based on its fundamental characteristics, including:

- font,
- size,

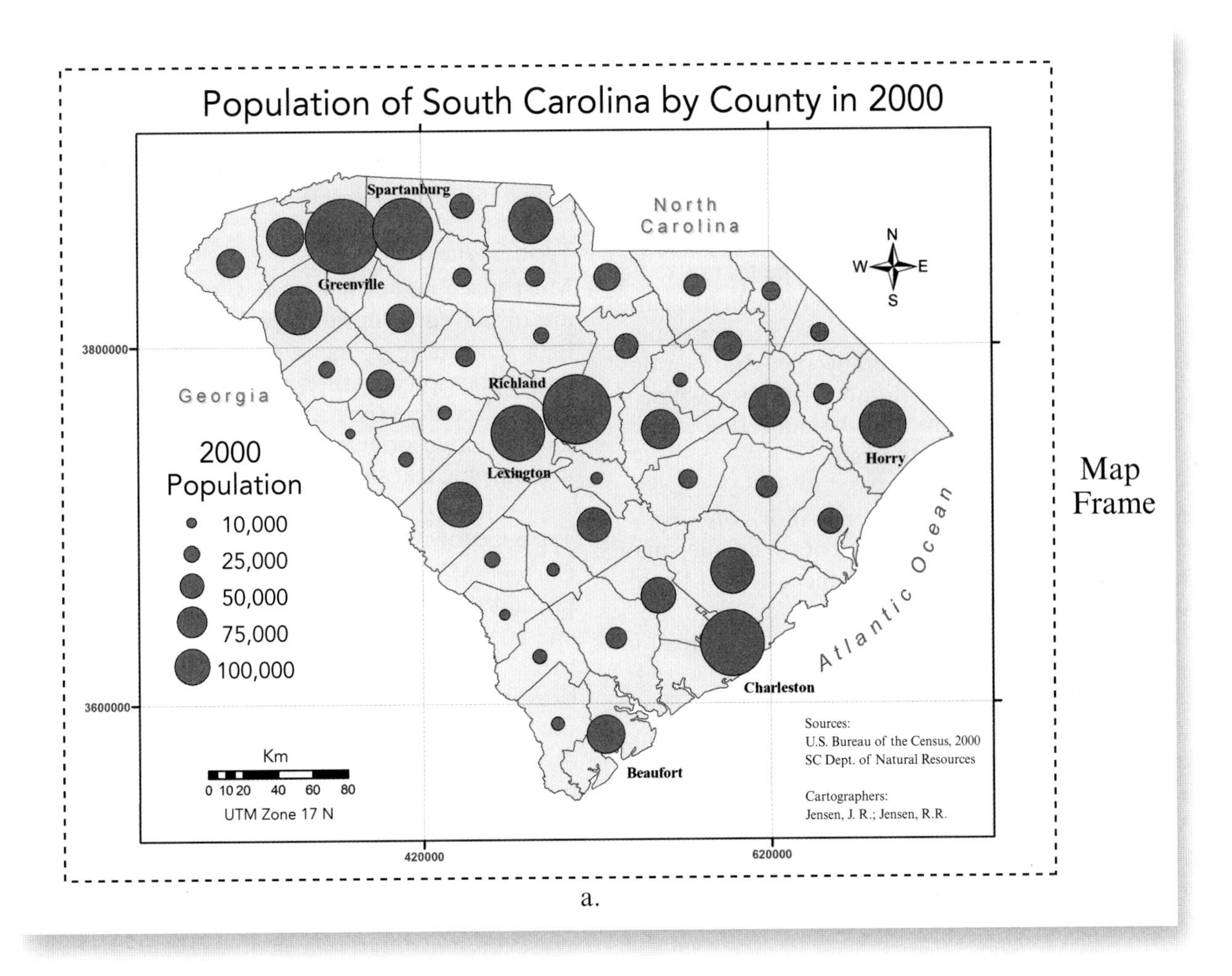

County	Population	County	Population	County	Population
Greenville	358012	**Darlington**	68346	**Dillon**	30506
Richland	315896	**Oconee**	65435	**Marlboro**	30279
Charleston	288372	**Greenwood**	63971	**Abbeville**	24611
Spartanburg	252842	**Laurens**	62822	**Barnwell**	22911
Lexington	215232	**Lancaster**	57912	**Fairfield**	22688
Horry	165741	**Georgetown**	54931	**Edgefield**	20529
Anderson	163654	**Kershaw**	49946	**Hampton**	20075
York	155044	**Cherokee**	49914	**Lee**	19009
Berkeley	152000	**Chesterfield**	40234	**Saluda**	17798
Aiken	146438	**Williamsburg**	38838	**Jasper**	17080
Florence	130492	**Colleton**	38698	**Bamberg**	16463
Sumter	113882	**Marion**	37001	**Calhoun**	14274
Beaufort	112537	**Newberry**	34597	**Allendale**	11661
Pickens	110394	**Chester**	34077	**McCormick**	9482
Dorchester	98611	**Union**	30979		
Orangeburg	92298	**Clarendon**	30711		

b.

FIGURE 10–8 a) A map of the population of South Carolina by county in 2000 used to demonstrate fundamental map design principles. b) The names and populations of the 46 counties (data courtesy of the U.S. Bureau of the Census and the South Carolina Department of Natural Resources).

- style, and
- color.

Font

Cartographers make maps that contain important thematic content. Therefore, the selection of the various type fonts used in a map should reflect the purpose of the map and the audience. If it is a serious cartographic project, then more serious or stately type fonts should be used. If the cartographic project is more light-hearted and illustrative, then more whimsical or popular type fonts may be used. Generally speaking, serious practictioners and scientists do not like to see whimsical or extremely ornate type fonts on maps that are addressing important, serious topics.

The font typeface selected is either *serif* or *sans serif*. A *sans serif* typeface is one that does not have the small ascending and descending parts of the letters of the alphabet called "serifs" at the end of strokes. Serif fonts are generally very pleasing to the eye, easier to read in a block of text, and impart elegance and character to the text. This paragraph is written using a serif Times New Roman MT Std font. The bold **Font** heading above is Avenir LT Std 55 Roman, a *sans serif* font. It is permissible when creating a map to use both *serif* and *sans serif* fonts in the same map composition, but one should be very careful and judicious in their use. The map of the Population of South Carolina by County in 2000 uses only two fonts: Avenir LT Std 55 Roman (*sans serif*) and Times New Roman MT Std (*serif*) (Figure 10-8a).

Type Size

The size of the type selected by a cartographer is usually measured in points (1 point = $\frac{1}{72}$ in.). Common text point sizes used in cartography include 8, 10, 12, 14, 16, 20, 24, 30, 36, 48, etc. Generally speaking, the size of the text should be commensurate with the importance of the information being portrayed and how it logically relates to other text in the map. Good cartographers carefully vary the size of the text to add interest to the map and make the map easier to comprehend. For example, the following fonts and type sizes were used to create the simple Population of South Carolina by County in 2000 map (Figure 10-8a):

- Title: Avenir LT Std 55 Roman, 20 pt.
- Legend: Avenir LT Std 55 Roman, 15 pt.
- *Atlantic Ocean*: Avenir LT Std 55 Roman, 14 pt., *italic*
- State names: Avenir LT Std 55 Roman, 12 pt., shadow
- County names: Times New Roman MT Std, 10 pt., **bold**
- Scale bar: Avenir LT Std 55 Roman, 9 pt.
- Source Metadata: Times New Roman MT Std, 9 pt.
- Grid coordinates: Avenir LT Std 55 Roman, 8 pt.

Type Style

Most place names (e.g., cities, roads, counties, states) are displayed in upright, plain (normal) text. Hydrologic features (e.g., the *Atlantic Ocean, Amazon River*) and topographic features (e.g., *Appalachian Mountains, Sierra Nevada, Alps*) are routinely displayed in italic and are often oriented along the general shape of the geomorphic feature.

Type Color

Cartographers often use colored text to highlight important phenomena in a map. Great care should be exercised when selecting the type color because garish, or overly intense, bright colors can overpower the reader, causing him or her to misunderstand or fail to extract the truly important thematic information in the map. A seasoned cartographer can use a GIS to select type colors that are commensurate with the phenomena being displayed (e.g., perhaps tropical tree species are annotated using pastel [light] green text and desert tree species are annotated using pastel brown text). In our example, only the *Atlantic Ocean* received color because it is a hydrographic feature (Figure 10-8a).

Thematic Content and the Figure-Ground Relationship

The **figure-ground relationship** is one of the most important concepts used in good cartographic design (Buckley and Field, 2011). Basically, the *figure* in a map is the most important thematic content. There may be several figures in the map of varying importance. The *ground* is the literal background information upon which the figure (important thematic content) resides. If the map is designed properly, the map-reader will first focus on the most important thematic content (the *figure*) and understand and appreciate its significance. The reader will then progress to the next most important thematic content. Finally, the reader will subconsciously progress toward the *ground* information, which may include all the ancillary data that supports the figure information, such as the scale bar, north arrow, grid reference system, and metadata.

For example, consider the Population of South Carolina by County in 2000 map (Figure 10-8a). While the title is certainly important, most readers will be drawn relatively quickly to the interesting red graduated

FIGURE 10–9 Examples of selected north arrows and compass roses (created using Esri ArcGIS®).

circles. The graduated circles are the most important figures (thematic content) on the map. They should appear to literally float on top of the ground which in this case is the outline of the State of South Carolina and its 46 counties. Note that the counties are displayed in pale green so as not to compete visually with the pastel red graduated circles associated with the population of each county. The legend also represents important figure information in the map. The graduated circles and quantitative information in the legend are intimately related to the graduated circles on top of each county. The legend represents the second most important figure on the map and is easily distinguished from the background.

The scale bar, north arrow, reference grid, and metadata are all important, but they are background information and not as important as the figure information. Therefore, it is imperative to decide early on in the map design process what are to be the most important *figures* (thematic content) and what will recede in importance and be the *background*. The cartographer then proceeds to design subtle, yet visually powerful hierarchical figure-ground map relationships. Dent (2002), Muehrcke (2005), and Slocum et al. (2005) provide detailed information about how to enhance the figure-ground relationship in map design.

North Arrows and Compass Roses

It is good practice to include north arrows and/or compass roses on maps whenever practical. North arrows and compass roses help the map-reader orient the map, i.e., understand where North, South, East, and West are on the map. Maps of the northern hemisphere usually contain a compass rose with a north-pointing arrow. A selected set of useful north arrows and compass roses is shown in Figure 10-9. Some of the north arrows depict only north while others show four or more cardinal compass directions. More scientific north arrows depict both true north and magnetic declination from true north for the geographic area being mapped (Figure 10-9).

North arrows and/or compass roses are usually placed on relatively homogeneous, uncluttered areas on the map such as in oceans, deserts, large forests, or blank areas of the map. They can be displayed in a variety of colors so they are easily discernible on top of whatever background they are superimposed upon. Novice cartographers tend to make the north arrows and/or compass roses too large. Note the relatively small and simple north arrow used in the map of the population of South Carolina (Figure 10-8a). It does not stand out, but is available if the map-reader needs to orient the map. North arrows and/or compass roses are usually placed around the periphery of the map frame.

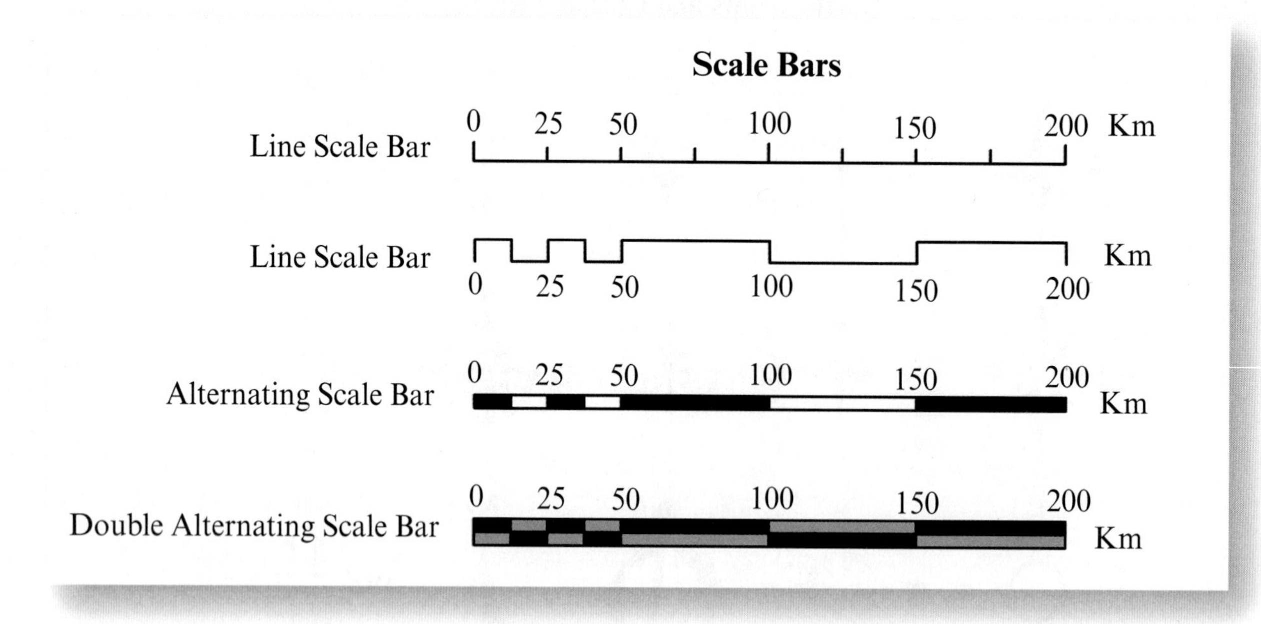

FIGURE 10–10 Examples of selected line, alternating, and double-alternating scale bars (created using Esri ArcGIS®).

Scale Bar

Few people create maps at a scale of 1 to 1 (i.e., 1:1). Therefore, almost all thematic maps are reductions of reality meaning that they are created at a scale smaller than 1 to 1. The map-reader is entitled to know about the scale of reduction. Therefore, all maps should contain detailed scale information. This information is typically communicated to the map-reader using several scale communication techniques:

- Representative Fraction,
- Dimensionless Ratio,
- Unit Equivalent, and
- Scale Bar.

For example, the U.S. Geological Survey's 7.5-minute topographic map series has a representative fraction scale of 1/24,000 and a dimensionless ratio scale of 1:24,000. This means that one unit on the map represents 24,000 units in the real world, i.e., one inch on the map represents 24,000 inches in the real world. Sometimes it is more convenient to describe the map scale in terms of unit equivalents. For example, the 1:24,000-scale map has a unit equivalent scale of 1 in. = 2,000 ft. Therefore, one inch on the map equals 2,000 ft. in the real world.

There is no problem placing representative fraction, dimensionless ratio, and unit equivalent information on the original map as long as the original map is never reduced or enlarged. However, if the original map is enlarged or reduced in any way, then the representative fraction, dimensionless ratio, and unit equivalent information are no longer accurate and map-users may extract inaccurate distance and area measurements.

Fortunately, there is a simple, graphic method for accurately communicating map scale information. A carefully crafted scale bar will convey accurate scale information irrespective of how the original map is reduced or enlarged. This is because a scale bar placed on the original map changes in size proportionally as the map is enlarged or reduced. Therefore, most high-quality thematic maps produced using a GIS or other cartographic software display scale bars around the periphery of the map. Linear, alternating, and double alternating scale bars are shown in Figure 10-10.

Cartographers are encouraged to keep scale bars relatively simple so that they don't detract from the important thematic content (*figure*) in the map. Alternating and double-alternating scale bars are often placed on GIS-produced maps because of the clarity of the subdivisions. The cartographer should use the most practical units in the scale bar (e.g., centimeters, meters, kilometers). Note that kilometers were used in the scale bars shown in Figure 10-10 instead of meters. The use of meters would have resulted in very large subdivision numbers (e.g., 25,000; 50,000; 100,000) which would make the scale bar much more complex and potentially confusing to the map-reader.

Legend

The map title and thematic content are probably the most important *figures* in a typical map. Next in importance is the legend, because it is used by the map-reader to accurately interpret the thematic content. Generally speaking, **legends** are used to show how the thematic information is organized and symbolized in the map. For example, the legend associated with the Population of South Carolina by County in 2000 map (Figure 10-8a) consists of just three components: a title, color proportional symbols, and text describing the quantitative value of the proportional symbols. Note that the legend is sufficiently large to catch the map-reader's attention, yet not so large as to compete with the map thematic content. Legends are usually placed around the periphery of the map and should add balance and good structure to the map design.

There is an infinite variety of legends that may be produced based on the nature of the point, line, area, and volume information being mapped. Subsequent sections will display examples of legends associated with point, line, area, and volumetric mapping.

Graticule or Reference Grid

Many high-quality thematic maps have a graticule of longitude/latitude lines or a reference grid displayed on them. The cartographer has to decide on a number of important parameters when designing the display of the graticule or reference grid. First, the system and units of measurement must be determined (e.g., latitude/longitude [degrees], Universal Transverse Mercator (UTM) map projection [meters], State Plane map projection [feet or meters]). In the Population of South Carolina by County in 2000 map, UTM coordinates are shown (Figure 10-8a). The cartographer then has to decide on the number of latitude/longitude or grid reference lines and whether the lines should lie on top of or below the thematic content. In this example, it was decided that only four grid lines would be used for the Population of South Carolina map, but the thin lines would be allowed to lie on top of the thematic content for orientation purposes. Finally, graticule or grid reference ticks and coordinates are placed systematically around the periphery of the map. In the South Carolina example, UTM Zone 17 N grid ticks in meters northing (e.g., 3,600,000 N) and easting (e.g., 420,000 E) help the reader to appreciate the geographic location and dimensions of the state of South Carolina.

Diagrams and maps not drawn to scale usually do not have graticules or reference grids. Conversely, thematic maps based on known map projections and coordinate systems should display the graticule or grid reference system whenever possible.

Geospatial Metadata

Geospatial **metadata** provide information about the data used to create the map or perform the GIS analysis. A metadata record is a file of information that captures the basic characteristics of a data or information resource. It represents the who, what, when, where, why and how of the resource as described in Chapter 4. Geospatial metadata is used to document geographic digital resources such as GIS files, geospatial databases, and Earth imagery. A geospatial metadata record includes core library catalog elements such as Title, Abstract, and Publication Data; geographic elements such as Geographic Extent and Projection Information; and database elements such as Attribute Label Definitions and Attribute Domain Values.

The U.S. Federal Geographic Data Committee (FGDC) provides detailed *Content Standards for Digital Geospatial Metadata* that must be used when creating geospatial information for federal map series [e.g., the USGS 7.5-minute topographic map series, the USGS digital orthophoto quarter quads (DOQQ)]. Geospatial metadata are critical to data discovery by the general public and are used extensively by the *Geospatial One-Stop* data portal and the *National Spatial Data Infrastructure (NSDI) Clearinghouse* (FGDC, 2011).

Metadata includes information about the sources of the information used to create the map. Unfortunately, unless they are providing maps for a nationally sponsored map series, most companies, organizations, and individuals rarely adhere to the rigorous federal metadata standards. At a minimum, an abbreviated amount of metadata should be displayed directly on the map describing the sources of map information and the cognizant cartographers who could be contacted to provide additional information (Figure 10-8a). More detailed metadata can be stored in a digital file associated with the map. These metadata would ideally include the Internet World Wide Web (www) address for every dataset used to produce the final map.

When a map is derived from an analysis of many geographic datasets, it is especially useful to have metadata about the history of the processing used to create the final map. Such information represents the genealogy or **geo-lineage,** of the map. Geo-lineage metadata is especially useful when the map products are used to present new scientific research findings, in very important public forums, or in litigation.

Map-users have the right to know about the origin and characteristics of the original geospatial data and about the data GIS analysis procedures used to create the final map. Ideally, every final map would contain sufficient geospatial metadata for the user to actually go to the original source documents and replicate the study. In reality, few maps provide sufficient geospatial metadata for this to be accomplished.

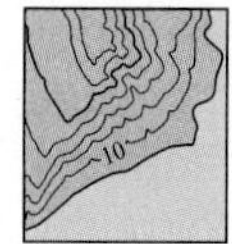

Mapping Point Data

Lay persons, scientists, surveyors, and government officials collect a tremendous amount of data at very specific point locations every day. They can be extremely large point measurements such as for an entire city or for very small features such as the geographic location of telephone poles, fire hydrants, well heads, surveyor pins, nesting sites, etc. In addition to knowing the geographic location of these point locations, they often collect quantitative (z-value) information about the point observation such as the population of the city, height of the telephone pole, the size of the fire hydrant nozzle, the volume of water coming out of the well head, the elevation at the surveyor pin, and the number of eggs in the nest.

Point phenomena can be mapped using a great variety of cartographic methods. Only a few of the most commonly used methods are presented here, including:

- Point mapping using simple symbols,
- Point mapping using graduated colors,
- Point mapping using proportional or graduated symbols,
- Point mapping using other symbols, and
- Point mapping using standard symbols.

Point Mapping Using Simple Symbols

Even simple maps of point data using simple symbolization can be very useful. For example, consider one of the most famous point maps ever created. There was a terrible cholera epidemic in the Soho district of London in 1854 (Figure 10-11). Dr. John Snow, an anesthesiologist, interviewed many of the surviving residents in the Soho community about those who died. Dr. Snow built upon the initial cartography of Edmund Cooper and plotted the geographic distribution of each cholera death as a rectangular black bar (Figure 10-11). This made houses with multiple deaths stand out on the map (Johnson, 2006). All of the evidence eventually helped Dr. Snow convince authorities that the source of the cholera was the public water pump on Broad Street (Figure 10-11). In Dr. Snow's words:

> With regard to the deaths occurring in the locality belonging to the pump, there were 61 instances in which I was informed that the deceased persons used to drink the pump water from Broad Street, either constantly or occasionally...
>
> The result of the inquiry, then, is, that there has been no particular outbreak or prevalence of cholera in this part of London except among the persons who were in the habit of drinking the water of the above-mentioned pump well.
>
> I had an interview with the Board of Guardians of St James's parish, on the evening of the 7th inst [September 7], and represented the above circumstances to them. In consequence of what I said, the handle of the pump was removed on the following day (John Snow, letter to the editor of the *Medical Times & Gazette*).

Thus, the geographic pattern of the point observations helped city officials prevent further loss of life and demonstrates how powerful simple point observations can be. His Soho map was perhaps the most comprehensive map study of a large-scale disease outbreak attempted to that date (Koch, 2004). Based on this work and other contributions, Dr. John Snow is now considered to be the father of modern epidemiology (UCLA Department of Epidemiology, 2011).

The geographic distribution of all the cities in South Carolina are mapped using simple point symbols in Figure 10-12a. The circular symbol is located at the x-, y-centroid of each city. Note that there is no quantitative information about the population of each city.

Point Mapping Using Graduated Colors

In addition to simply locating the geographic position of individual point observations, it is also possible to use graduated colors to provide more detailed quantitative information about each point location. For example, Figure 10-12b depicts the cities of South Carolina using eight colors and class intervals that range from 0 to 120,000 persons. The map-reader should be able to determine that Columbia, Greenville, Spartanburg, Rock Hill, Myrtle Beach, Hilton Head, and Aiken are the most heavily populated cities in South Carolina.

Point Mapping Using Proportional or Graduated Symbols

An even more visually compelling way of communicating the quantitative value of point symbols is to use **proportional symbols**. Basically, each map symbol (e.g., a circle) is made proportional in size (scaled) according to the point observation z-value. There are two funda-

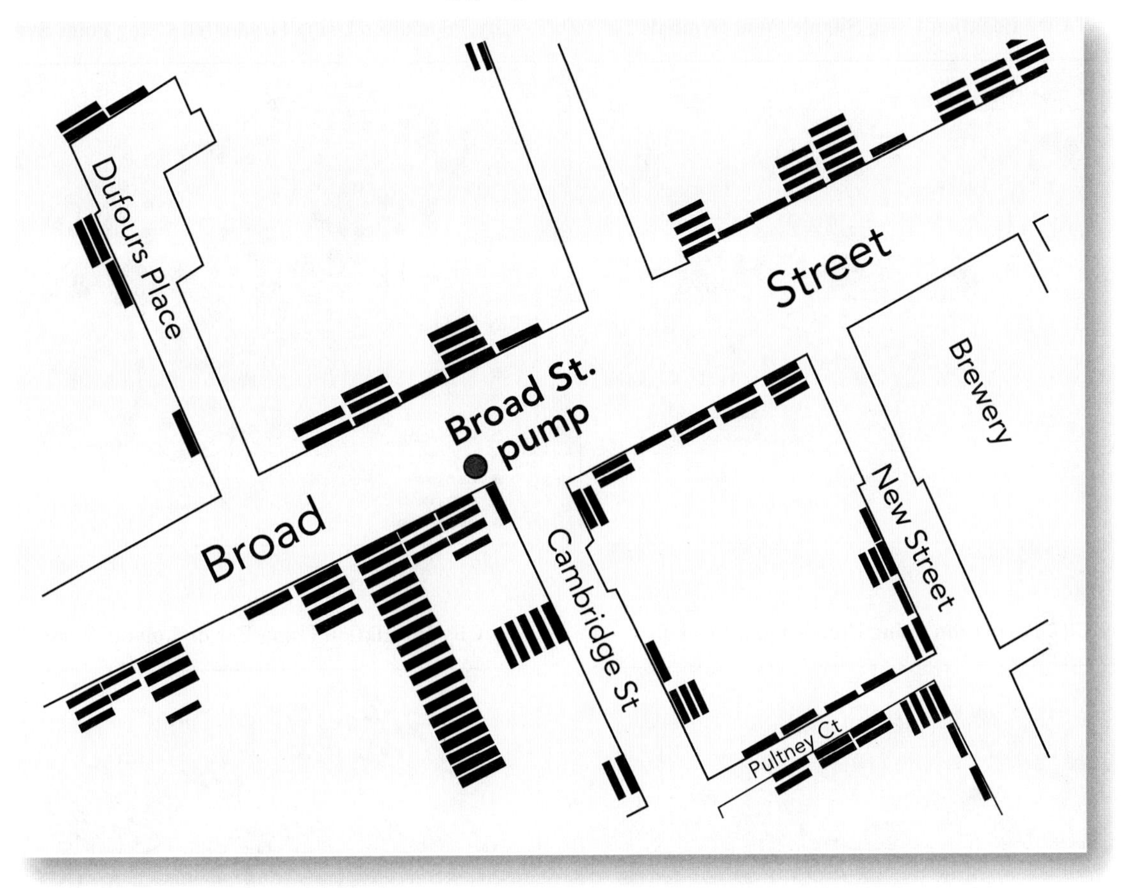

FIGURE 10–11 Dr. John Snow was an anesthesiologist who used interviews and cartographic principles to identify the potential source of a cholera epidemic in London in 1854. This is a redrafted enlargement showing the rectangular point symbols and the suspected Broad Street pump. For additional information about John Snow, read *The Ghost Map* (Johnson, 2006).

mental ways to proportionally scale point symbols: *apparent* (*perceptual*) and *absolute* scaling.

Apparent (perceptual) scaling was pioneered by psychologist James Flannery and scales the point observation z-value data to take into account the human tendency to underestimate the size of larger circles. Apparent scaling is applied to help the map-reader get the correct visual impression when viewing proportional symbols. For example, the perceptual scaling formula for proportional circles on a map is (Slocum et al., 2005):

$$r_i = \left(\frac{v_i}{v_L}\right)^{0.57} \times r_L \qquad (10.2)$$

where r_i is the radius of the circle to be drawn, r_L is the radius of the largest circle on the map, v_i is the data value for the circle to be drawn, and v_L is the data value associated with the largest circle. A map of the population of South Carolina cities based on perceptually scaled proportional circles is shown in Figure 10-12c. The proportional circles found in the legend are examples of what size a circle would be if a cities' population was exactly 10,000 or 100,000, etc. This is a very visually compelling map that communicates well the significant differences in South Carolina city populations.

Conversely, Edward Tufte (2001) opposes anything but *absolute scaling* of proportional symbols. He suggests that "The representation of numbers, as physically measured on the surface of the graphic itself, should be directly proportional to the numerical quantities represented." Tufte says cartographers should "tell the truth about data" and exclude compensation for human perceptual failings.

It is possible to map point observations using virtually any type of point symbol, e.g., diamonds, squares, triangles, spheres, bars, columns, etc. Any of these sym-

Point Mapping Symbolization

City Location Using Simple Point Symbols

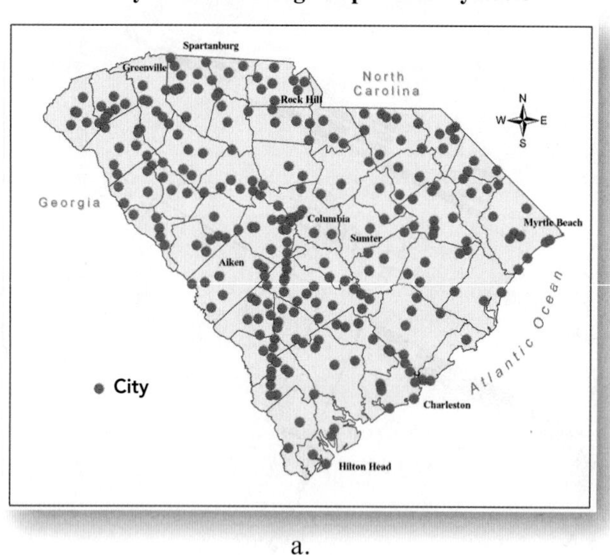

a.

City Population Using Graduated Color Point Symbols

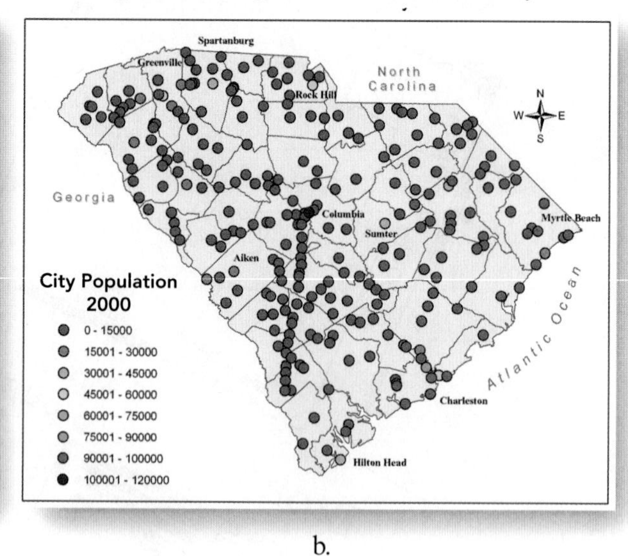

b.

City Population Using Proportional Symbols

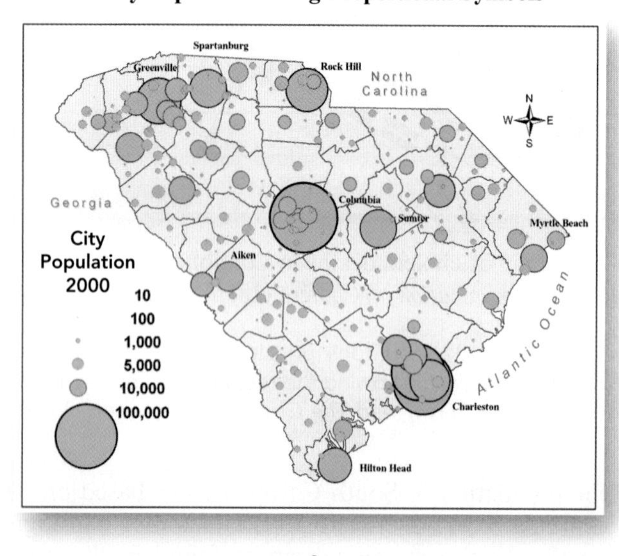

c.

City Population Using Bar or Column Symbols

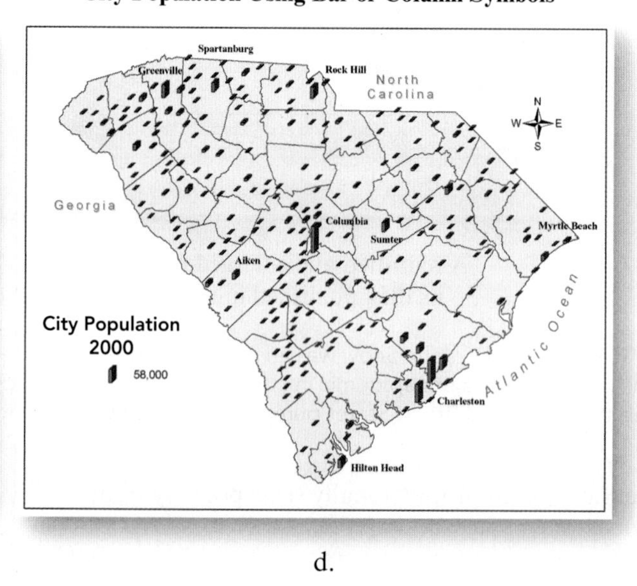

d.

FIGURE 10–12 Examples of selected point observation maps. a) Simple point symbolization. b) Graduated color symbolization. c) Proportional symbols. d) Bar (column) point symbolization (data courtesy of the U.S. Bureau of the Census and the South Carolina Department of Natural Resources).

bols can be scaled to be proportional to the *z*-value of the point observation. For example, graduated columns are used in Figure 10-12d to map South Carolina city populations. It is visually more informative than using simple point symbols or the graduated color symbolization shown in Figure 10-12a, b.

Standardized Point Symbols

GIS practitioners and/or cartographers have great latitude in the symbolization they use to map point data. However, because point symbolization problems have been with humankind for millennia, cartographers have designed many standardized point symbols that should be used whenever possible. The use of standardized point symbolization allows the same object to be easily interpreted by users throughout the world irrespective of language, religion, or background. For example, Figure 10-13 depicts the standardized point symbols for *control data* and *monuments* used by the U.S. Geological Survey topographic map series (USGS, 2009). Topographic map series throughout the world use similar standardized symbols to document

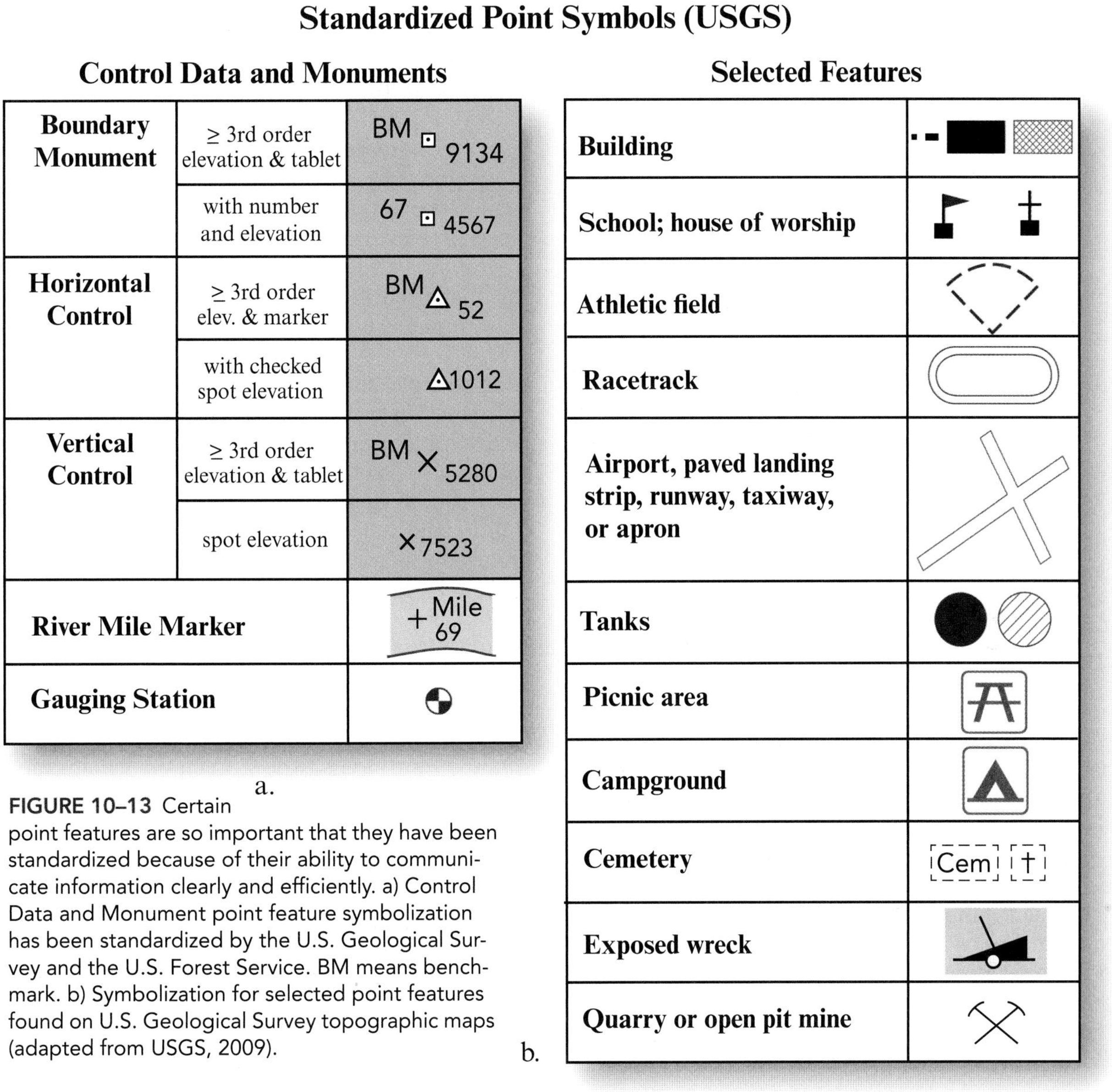

Standardized Point Symbols (USGS)

Control Data and Monuments

Boundary Monument	≥ 3rd order elevation & tablet	BM ⊡ 9134
	with number and elevation	67 ⊡ 4567
Horizontal Control	≥ 3rd order elev. & marker	BM △ 52
	with checked spot elevation	△1012
Vertical Control	≥ 3rd order elevation & tablet	BM × 5280
	spot elevation	×7523
River Mile Marker		+ Mile 69
Gauging Station		

a.

Selected Features

Building	
School; house of worship	
Athletic field	
Racetrack	
Airport, paved landing strip, runway, taxiway, or apron	
Tanks	
Picnic area	
Campground	
Cemetery	Cem
Exposed wreck	
Quarry or open pit mine	

b.

FIGURE 10–13 Certain point features are so important that they have been standardized because of their ability to communicate information clearly and efficiently. a) Control Data and Monument point feature symbolization has been standardized by the U.S. Geological Survey and the U.S. Forest Service. BM means benchmark. b) Symbolization for selected point features found on U.S. Geological Survey topographic maps (adapted from USGS, 2009).

boundary monuments and horizontal and vertical control points, and river mile markers on maps.

Other selected USGS standardized topographic map point symbols are shown in Figure 10-13b. Note that many are iconic, meaning that the symbol stands for itself and is easily identifiable such as a school, house of worship, picnic area, campground, cemetery, exposed wreck, and open pit mine or quarry (symbolized by crossed miner picks). Cartographers have spent many years designing high-quality, iconic point symbols. It is wise for novice map-makers using a GIS to carefully look for standardized, well-accepted point symbols before developing new symbols that may not communicate the point information as effectively.

Mapping Linear Data

The world is composed of a great variety of linear features. Some are natural phenomena such as rivers and shorelines. Others are perceptual linear features invented by humankind such as political boundaries and topographic contours. Some of the more important linear features portrayed on thematic maps include:

- boundaries
  - municipal
  - county
  - state

  - national/international
- hydrology
  - streams
  - rivers
  - shorelines
  - canals
  - levees
- transportation
  - roads
  - railroads
  - airport runways
  - tunnels
- transmission lines
  - cable
  - power
  - telephone
  - water
- lines of equal phenomena (i.e., isolines)
  - topographic
  - bathymetric
  - temperature
  - precipitation
  - atmospheric pressure
  - population density, etc.

These linear features may be symbolized and mapped using a variety of cartographic techniques, including line mapping using simple line symbolization and color, graduated line widths, and isarithmic mapping. Like standardized point symbols, the use of standardized linear symbolization allows the same linear feature to be easily interpreted by users throughout the world. For example, Figure 10-14 depicts selected standardized line symbols for transportation and hydrologic phenomena used by the USGS (2009). It is important to keep in mind that these standardized line symbols were developed for topographic mapping at relatively large scales (e.g., 1:24,000) and that adjustment of the symbolization is required when mapping at smaller scales.

Line Mapping Using Simple Line Symbolization and Color

Linear features may be mapped using relatively simple solid and dashed line patterns, line weight adjustments, and/or color. For example, note the logical progression in line weight and the use of color as the transportation features progress from trails to primary highways in the USGS standardized transportation symbolization shown in Figure 10-14. Also, note the use of superposition to identify highway or road under- or overpasses. There are thousands of secondary highway or light-duty roads in South Carolina. Mapping every one of these roads in South Carolina using simple 1-point black lines at this small scale would result in a thematic map that is almost completely black. Certain transportation features like railroads and railroad yards have been symbolized using the same line pattern for centuries (Figure 10-14).

Perennial streams and rivers are usually symbolized using standardized solid blue linework versus intermittent streams and rivers, which are symbolized using specially designed blue dashed lines. Of course, a cartographer is free to design new linear symbolization if he or she believes it will result in improved cartographic communication.

For example, consider the symbolization used to create a coarse scale map (1:2,400,000 before reduction) of the hydrology and transportation features for the State of South Carolina (Figure 10-15a-c). At this coarse scale, South Carolina perennial rivers were mapped using a solid blue line (1 point) (Figure 10-15a). Interstates (primary highways with a median strip) and primary highways were mapped using modified versions of the standardized symbolization shown in Figure 10-15b. Note how the increased line weight associated with the interstates (4 point) helps differentiate between interstates and highways (1 point). The hydrology and transportation information are superimposed in Figure 10-15c. Each of the cities in South Carolina is located beneath the road network to help the map-reader appreciate why certain highways are located where they are in the state. The hydrology occupies the lowest thematic level of the figure-ground relationship in this map.

Cartographers must be creative and make thoughtful thematic-mapping decisions based on the unique characteristics of the phenomena being mapped.

Flow Mapping Using Graduated (Proportional) Line Symbolization

Some phenomena increase or decrease in value as they progress through a linear network. For example, as tributary creeks and streams meet to form rivers, the amount of water typically increases as the network progresses downstream. Similarly, as rural secondary roads merge with primary roads and then interstates, the number of cars coming into the central business district in the morning may increase. It is possible to depict the nature of the flow in these networks by proportionally increasing the size of each downstream stream or road segment based on the added contribution of tributary streams or feeder roads. For example, Figure 10-7 displays the increase in water flow in a hydrologic stream network.

Standardized Linear Symbols (USGS)

Selected Transportation Features

Feature	Symbol
Primary highway	
Secondary highway	
Light duty road	
Unimproved road	
Trail	
Highway or road with median strip	
Highway or road under construction	
Highway or road underpass; overpass	
Highway or road bridge; drawbridge	
Highway or road tunnel	
Standard guage railroad	
Railroad yard	

a.

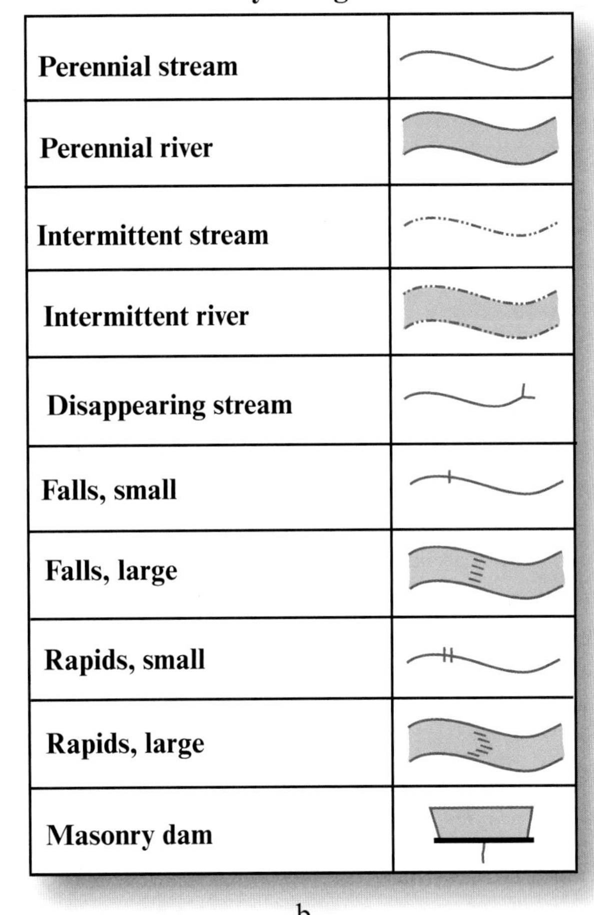

FIGURE 10–14 Certain linear features are so important that they have been standardized because of their ability to communicate information clearly and efficiently. a) Transportation feature symbolization has been standardized by the U.S. Geological Survey and the U.S. Forest Service. b) Hydrologic linear features found on U.S. Geological Survey topographic maps (adapted from USGS, 2009).

Isarithmic Mapping

Isarithmic mapping uses isolines (lines of equal value such as a contour that might be 10 ft. above sea level) to model smooth, continuous phenomena. There are two fundamental types of isarithmic maps:

- isometric maps and
- isopleth maps.

Isometric maps are created wherever the true data control points used to create the statistical surface actually exist at a particular geographic location. There is a tremendous variety of isometric maps. Only a select few are described in Table 10-2. The most common isometric map is the topographic contour map, which depicts lines of equal elevation above sea level.

It is also possible to create smooth statistical surfaces from *conceptual* data points and then create **isopleth maps** from these data. For example, it is possible to create a continuous surface of the population of South Carolina using conceptual data points associated with the centroid of each of the 46 counties. An isopleth map showing the population density per square mile of the state could then be derived from the conceptual point data. Isopleth maps require that the data be standardized to account for the geographic area over which

Examples of Line Mapping Symbolization

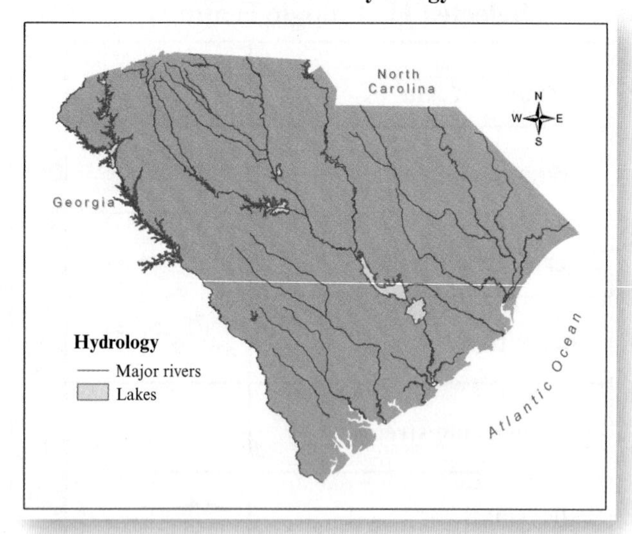

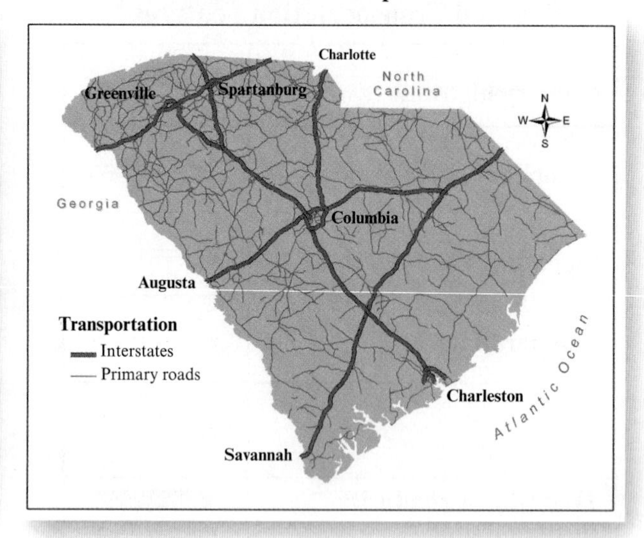

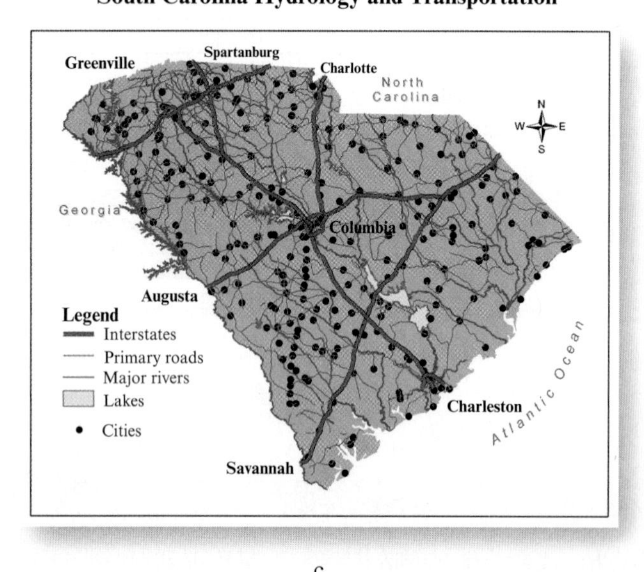

FIGURE 10–15 Examples of mapping selected South Carolina linear features, including a) hydrology, b) interstate (highways with a median strip) and primary highways, and c) hydrology, transportation, and cities (data courtesy of South Carolina Department of Natural Resources).

the conceptual data are collected. In the South Carolina example, this would require that the population of each county be divided by the total area of the county (e.g., mile^2) before creating the statistical surface and then selecting the isolines of interest (e.g., isolines with a population density interval of 100 persons per square mile).

Topographic and Bathymetric Contours

Lines of equal elevation (e.g., 10 ft.) above a datum (e.g., sea level) are referred to as topographic contours. The concept of contours has been around for a long time. Englishman Charles Hutton used contours to calculate the volume of a hill in 1777. Jean Louis Dupain-Triel used 20-m contour lines on a topographic map of France in 1791. It also included a topographic model cross-section to help map-readers understand the concept of contours (Konvitz, 1987).

Lines of equal depth (e.g., 20 ft.) below a datum (e.g., sea level) are called bathymetric contours or isobaths. In 1727, Dutch engineer Nicholas Cruquius drew the bathymetry of the *Merwede River* on a nautical chart using 1-fathom isobath intervals. The French geographer Philippe Buache used 10-fathom intervals on a nautical chart of the English Channel published in 1752. Government agencies and photogrammetric engineering firms all over the world spend a tremendous amount of money creating detailed contour (topographic) and isobath (bathymetric) maps.

TABLE 10–2 Selected types of isometric mapping based on the use of true data control points.

Name	Function
Contour - Topographic	Lines of equal elevation above a datum
Isobath - Bathymetric	Lines of equal depth below a datum
Isohyet	Lines of equal precipitation
Isotherm	Temperature
Isobar	Atmospheric pressure
Isostere	Atmospheric density
Isohume	Humidity
Isotach	Wind speed
Isopetic	Equal dates of ice formation
Isotach	Equal dates of ice thawing
Isogonic	Magnetic declination of the Earth's magnetic field
Isocline	Slope
Isohaline	Ocean salinity

Topographic and bathymetric maps consist of index, intermediate, and depression contours. As you might expect, the cartographic convention is to map topographic contours in brown and bathymetric contours in blue (Figure 10-16). Index contours are symbolized with a thicker line weight every *n*th contour (e.g., every fifth contour on most 1:24,000-scale USGS topographic maps in relatively rugged terrain). Intermediate contours are displayed using a smaller point-size line. Geographic areas above and below the datum with enclosed depressions are symbolized using intermediate contours with specially placed perpendicular hatch lines (Figure 10-16). Engineers often cut into the terrain or deposit material in diverse ways. These cuts and fills in the terrain often exhibit unique contour characteristics. For example, Figure 10-16 depicts the contours associated with a road that has been cut through a hill and fill material placed in a stream channel so that a road could pass over the stream channel.

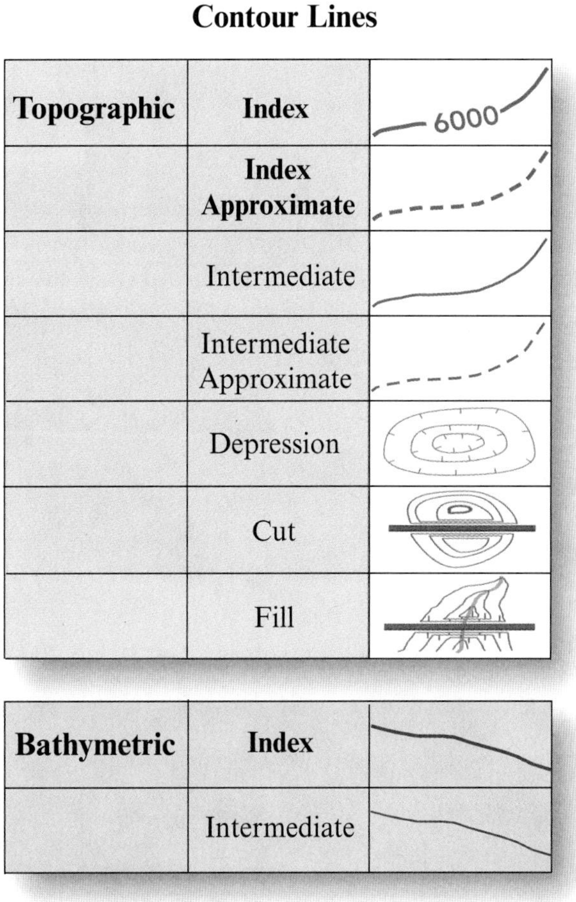

Contour Lines

Topographic	**Index**	6000
	Index Approximate	
	Intermediate	
	Intermediate Approximate	
	Depression	
	Cut	
	Fill	

Bathymetric	**Index**	
	Intermediate	

FIGURE 10–16 Isometric lines of equal elevation above a datum are called topographic contour lines. Isometric lines of equal elevation below a datum are referred to as bathymetric contour lines. It is customary to use index, intermediate, and depression contours to communicate important topographic and bathymetric elevation information. Approximate (dashed) topographic or bathymetric contours are used when the original input elevation data are less than ideal (symbols courtesy of U.S. Geological Survey).

It is useful to look at a real-world application of these topographic mapping principles. For example, consider the southern Menan Butte volcano in Madison County, ID. It is one of two cinder cone volcanoes in this area. The southern Menan Butte volcano is shown in a normal color 1 x 1 m high-spatial resolution aerial photograph collected by the U.S. Department of Agriculture National Agriculture Imagery Program (NAIP) in Figure 10-17a.

The USGS has created a digital elevation model (DEM) of this area (Figure 10-17b) with pixels spaced every 30 x 30 m (1 arc second) and elevation measured in feet above sea level (Maune, 2001). These data are part of the National Elevation Dataset (NED) and are available through the Internet via Geospatial One-Stop

Southern Menan Butte in Madison County, ID

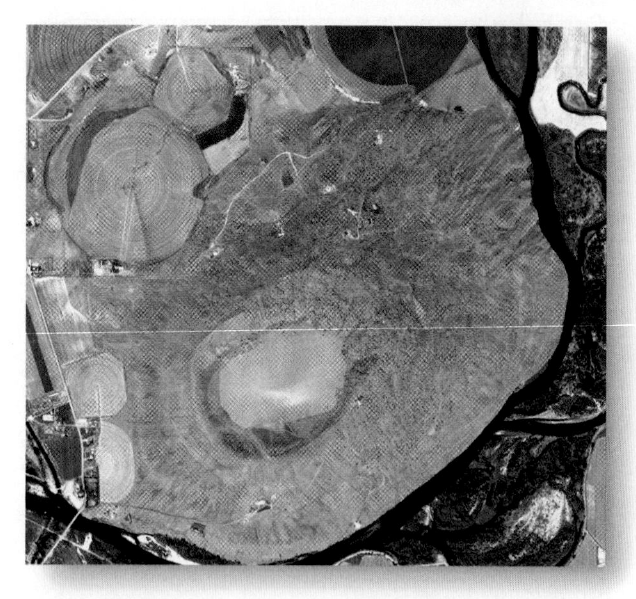

a. NAIP imagery (1 x 1 m) obtained on 31 July 2004.

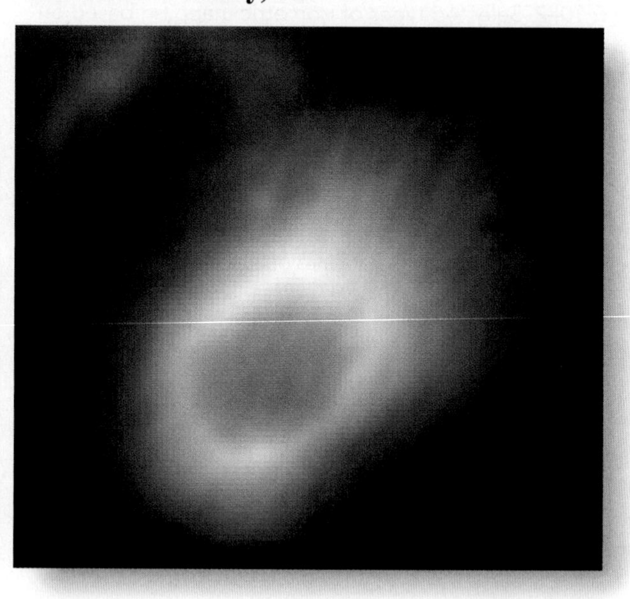

b. USGS Digital Elevation Model (30 x 30 m pixels).

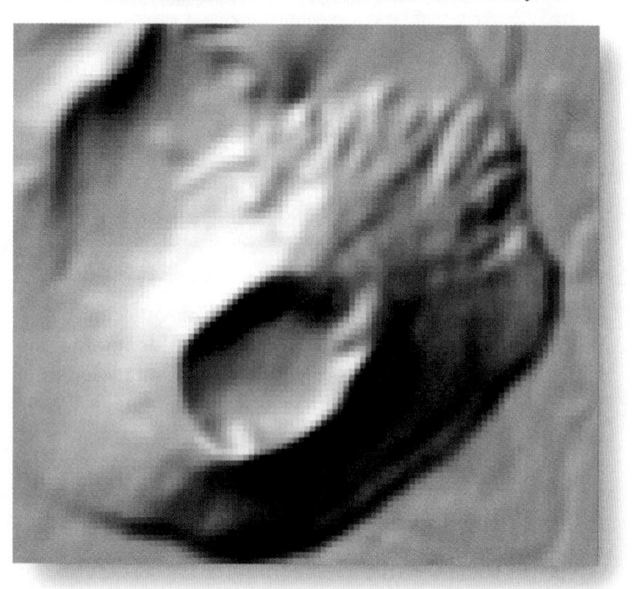

c. Hill-shaded version of USGS 30 x 30 m DEM.

FIGURE 10–17 a) USDA National Agriculture Imagery Program (NAIP) aerial photography rectified to 1 x 1 m spatial resolution. b) One arc-second (30 x 30 m) spatial resolution digital elevation model (DEM) extracted from the U.S. Geological Survey National Elevation Dataset (NED). c) A hill-shaded representation of the DEM with the light source from the northwest; 315° (data courtesy of the USDA National Agriculture Imagery Program and the USGS National Elevation Dataset).

(Maidment et al., 2007). A hill-shaded representation of the DEM is shown in Figure 10-17c. Methods for creating digital elevation models from individual point elevation measurements and analytically hill-shading them were described in Chapter 9.

Contour lines for the southern Menan Butte volcano were derived from the digital terrain model. The contours range from 4,800 ft. above sea level at the base of the volcano running along the river to 5,400 ft. above sea level. The highest point on the volcano is symbolized using a standard benchmark symbol. Topographic contour maps with contours every 10, 20, and 40 ft. are shown draped over the original digital elevation model in Figures 10-18a–c. Note that the steeper the slope, the more closely spaced the individual contour lines are. Also note that every fifth contour is an index contour. It is customary to label each of the index contour lines with its elevation value. Index contour elevation values were not labeled in these examples to avoid clutter and improve appreciation of the shape of the land. These three examples can be used to illustrate a useful cartographic design principle. Both the 20-ft and 40-ft contour-interval maps are useful and do an adequate job of representing the shape of the volcanic terrain. However, the 10-ft. contour interval map provides much more detailed topographic shape information for the map-reader. A 5-ft. contour interval map (not

Contours for Southern Menan Butte in Madison County, ID

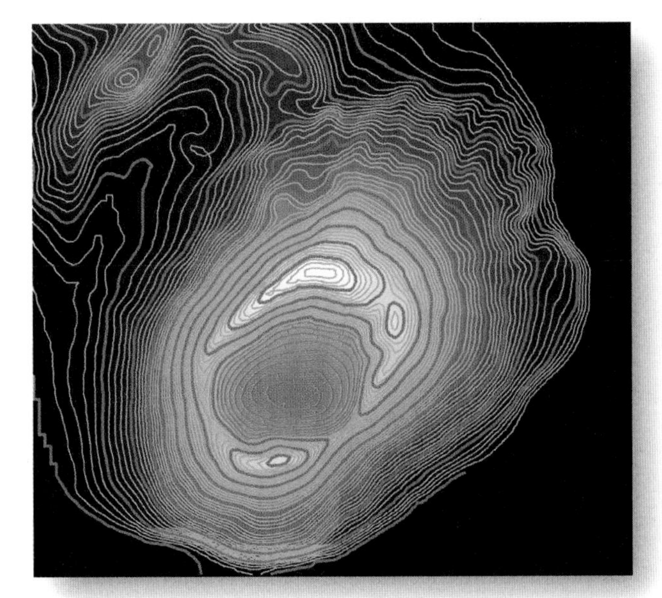

a. 10-ft. contours draped over 30 x 30 m DTM.

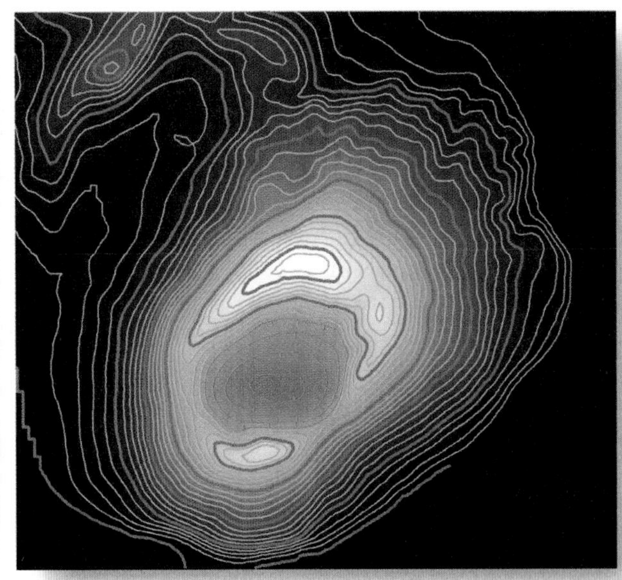

b. 20-ft. contour interval.

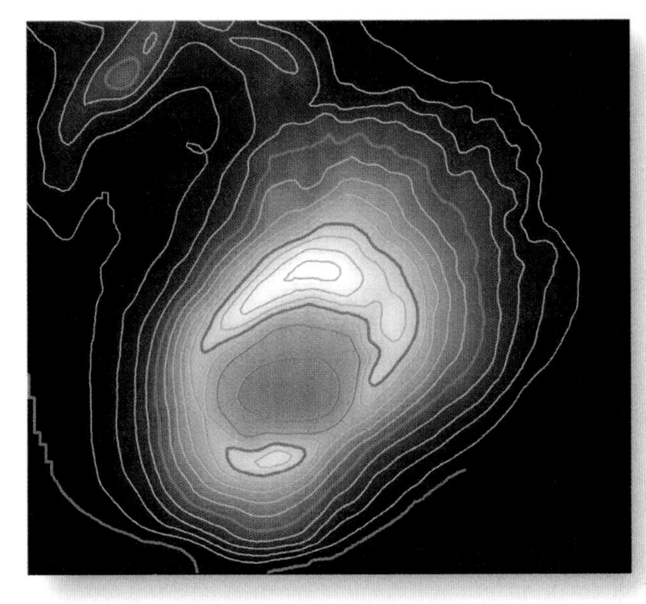

c. 40-ft. contour interval.

d. 20-ft. contours draped on NAIP imagery.

FIGURE 10–18 Contour maps of the Southern Menan Butte using three contour intervals. a) Use of a 10-ft. contour interval. b) Use of a 20-ft. contour interval. c) Use of a 40-ft. contour interval. Note the intermediate, index, and depression contour symbolization in a, b, and c. d) The 20-ft. contours are draped over the NAIP rectified aerial photography (data courtesy of the National Agriculture Aerial Photography Program and the U.S. Geological Survey).

shown) exhibited contours that were so dense at this scale of display that they were literally uninterpretable.

The top of the volcano has a depressed area with internal drainage. This was symbolized using depression contours. The 20-ft. contours are draped over the NAIP aerial photography in Figure 10-18d. Topographic contours are a wonderful invention that help map-readers understand the elevation of the terrain in quantitative terms and provides insight into topographic slope.

This section introduced just a few of the line mapping cartographic conventions. The reader is encouraged to consult a cartography text to obtain more detailed information when designing line maps using a GIS.

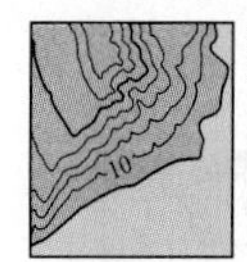

Mapping Area Data

GIS analysts often use a GIS as a cartographic mapping system to display geographic phenomena that occupy geographic *x,y* space in the landscape (e.g., land cover, soils, elevation, precipitation, temperature). The areal data may be in the form of individual pixels that occupy space or polygons that occupy space. The areal data may be nominal, ordinal, interval, or ratio-scaled as previously discussed. These areal geographic data may be mapped: 1) independent (unconstrained) by any administrative unit, or 2) according to whether they reside within a very specific administrative unit such as a city, county, state, country, watershed, watershed management district, school district, etc.

Thematic Mapping of Spatial Data Unconstrained by Administrative Unit Boundaries

Much of the spatial data mapped using a GIS is *unconstrained* by political or administrative units. Examples of spatially unconstrained data include elevation, slope, aspect, precipitation, temperature, wind speed, land cover, soil type, etc.

Interval and ratio-scaled unconstrained data such as elevation, temperature, precipitation, wind speed etc., may be mapped using the isarithmic techniques discussed in this chapter or methods specifically designed to analyze and display 3-dimensional data as described in Chapter 9.

Nominal and ordinal-scaled spatial information such as land cover and soil type may be mapped by simply displaying the raster (pixels) or vector (polygonal) data using carefully selected black-and-white or color symbolization. Qualitative color schemes are typically used that do not imply magnitude differences between legend classes. Rather, hues (colors) are used to highlight the primary visual differences between classes. Qualitative schemes are best suited to mapping nominal or categorical data (Brewer, 1994).

For example, consider the land cover map of Charleston, SC, shown in Figure 10-19. These land cover data are part of the South Carolina GAP Analysis database. There are 27 land cover categories in the classification scheme. The land cover map was derived from 30 x 30 m Landsat Thematic Mapper imagery obtained from 1991–1993. Each pixel in the nominal-scale thematic map was associated with only one of the 27 discrete land cover types described in the legend. The cartographer had to select 27 different color combinations that allowed the map-reader to distinguish among the 27 different land cover classes.

Also, consider the geology map of South Carolina shown in Figure 10-20. The geology data are in polygon format as opposed to the per-pixel format used in the previous illustration of the Charleston land cover (Figure 10-19). This map displays the spatial distribution of 22 different geologic classes of information. Once again, the cartographer had to select 22 unique color symbols. In this case, however, the cartographer also introduced texture into three of the color symbols to assist the map-reader to more easily comprehend the spatial information in the map. Stippling (the placement of random dots within a polygon) was introduced into the green, blue, and brown colors associated with the Chauga belt, Laurens thrust stack, and Pleistocene classes. Cartographers often mix texture with pastel colors (hues) to improve cartographic communication, especially when there are a large number of classes in the thematic map.

Thematic Mapping of Spatial Data Constrained by Administrative Units: Choropleth Mapping

Sometimes the nominal, ordinal, and interval/ratio-scaled spatial data are mapped according to specialized areal administrative units. This is referred to as **choropleth mapping**. Choropleth maps are the most commonly used and abused method of thematic mapping (Slocum et al., 2005). Therefore, it is useful to provide additional guidance on how to create useful and informative choropleth maps.

Choropleth Mapping

Choropleth mapping is performed by mapping spatial data that are constrained to lie within a *bona fide* administrative unit. The administrative unit may be based on political jurisdictions such as cities, counties, states, countries, school districts, emergency response districts, and tax zones, etc. The administrative units may also be associated with natural resource management districts or zones such as watersheds, water management districts, and forest districts.

There are a number of things to consider when creating a high-quality choropleth map, including the selection of the most appropriate:

- standardization,
- number of class intervals,
- class intervals, and
- symbolization.

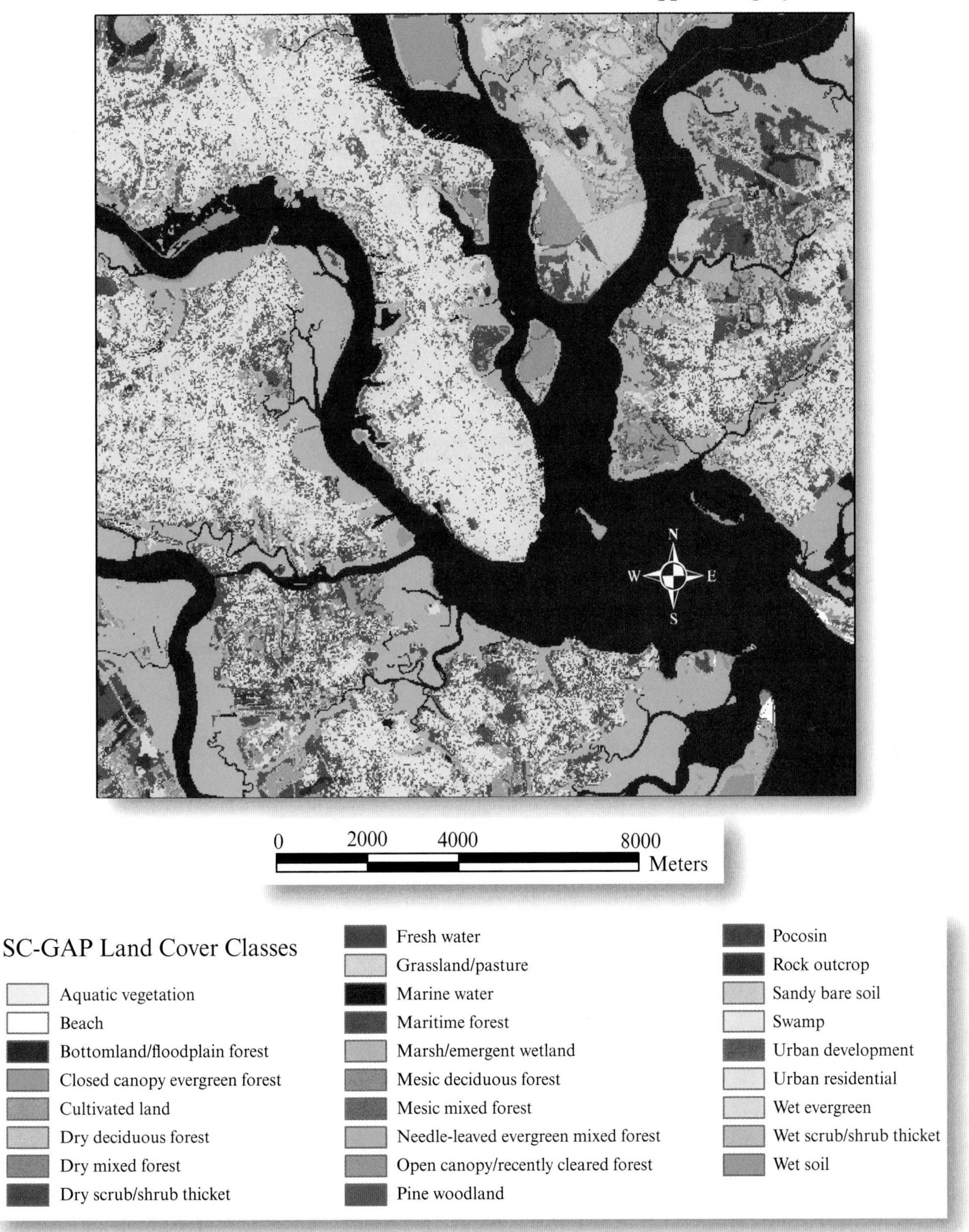

FIGURE 10–19 Nominal-scale land cover mapping using a simple qualitative color scheme applied to 27 classes. The per pixel land cover information was extracted from Landsat Thematic Mapper imagery obtained in the early 1990s. The data are part of the SC GAP Analysis program at a spatial resolution of 30 x 30 m pixels (data courtesy of South Carolina Department of Natural Resources).

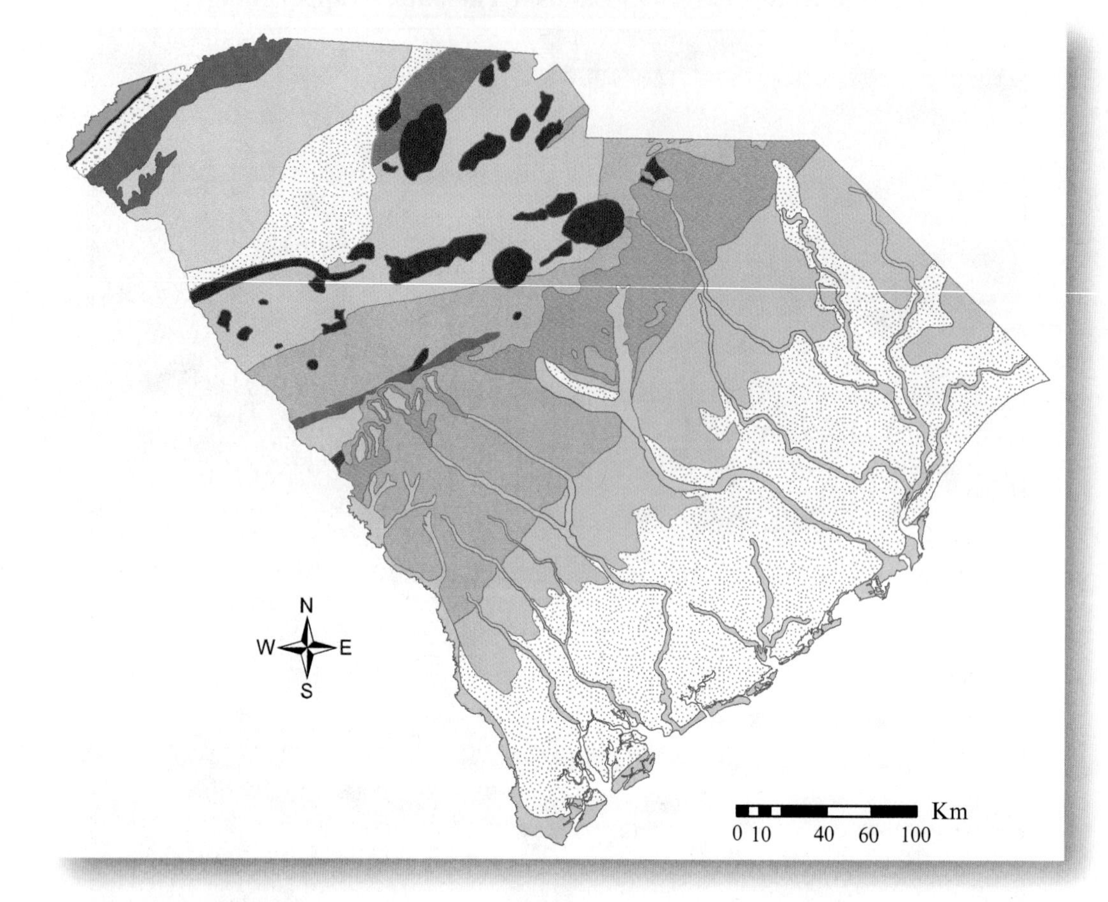

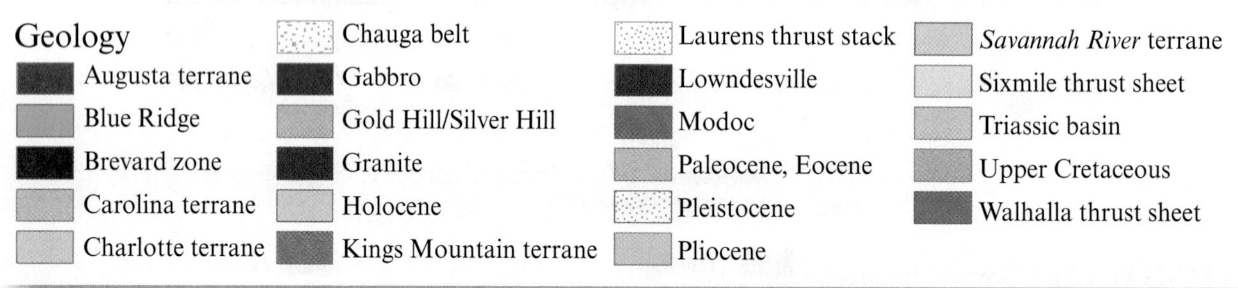

FIGURE 10–20 Nominal-scale land cover mapping of polygonal geology data using a simple qualitative color scheme applied to 22 classes (data courtesy of South Carolina Department of Natural Resources).

Standardization The size and shape of the administrative units can create special problems when performing choropleth mapping. Generally speaking, extremely large enumeration units tend to overshadow the contribution of relatively smaller, nearby enumeration units. The best choropleth maps contain enumeration units (e.g., counties) that are all approximately the same size.

In addition, one of the most important choropleth mapping considerations is whether or not to standardize the data by taking into account the geographic size of the enumeration unit. For example, assume that you know the number of persons that live in each county in your state. Unfortunately, some of your counties are two to three times larger in geographic area than others. In this circumstance, it would be appropriate for you to standardize these data before mapping by dividing each county's population by the size of the county measured in mile^2 or kilometer^2. This would yield county population density information that could be effectively mapped using choropleth mapping techniques.

Similarly, if you knew the amount of corn produced in every county in your state, you could divide this amount by the area (number of hectares) in each county to map corn per hectare production by county. You could also divide the amount of corn produced in each county by the total amount produced for your entire state. This would yield information on the proportion (%) of corn produced by county for the state. Standardization minimizes the impact of extremely large or small administrative units when applying choropleth mapping techniques.

Number of Class Intervals One of the most difficult decisions to make when conducting choropleth mapping is how many class intervals to use. If the cartographer uses too few classes, then a significant amount of generalization will take place and the map-reader may not get an accurate impression of the spatial relationships actually present in the spatial data. If too many classes are used, the map may be too noisy, obscuring once again the intrinsic spatial information present in the dataset. A general rule is to use between 5 and 15 classes depending upon the number of observations (Burt et al., 2009). Obviously, sometimes this rule of thumb is not applicable, especially when one is mapping a very complex dataset. Generally, as the number of observations increases, more classes can be used.

Scott (1979) provided the following algorithm for selecting the optimum number of classes or intervals (k):

$$k = 3.5sn^{-1/3} \qquad (10.3)$$

where n is the number of observations in the dataset, and s is the standard deviation of the dataset.

The cartographer should also take into account logical considerations when determining the number of classes. Grouping observations suggests to the map-reader that somehow the observations within a specific class interval are alike. Therefore, it is unwise to select a number of classes that force unlike observations into the same class. We break this rule if we place natural breakpoints within a class and not at a class boundary. For example, if we were working with temperature data it would be unwise to have a class interval that had class limits of –10° to +10° C suggesting that the temperatures below freezing can logically be grouped with those above freezing.

Choropleth Map Class Intervals There are a number of rules associated with class intervals. First, an observation should normally be associated with one and only one class interval. Therefore, the classes should be *mutually exclusive*. The upper bound of one class interval should not equal the lower bound of the next class interval. For example, consider the following three class intervals:

Class 1 = 3.0 to 4.0

Class 2 = 4.0 to 5.0

Class 3 = 5.0 to 6.0

Using this class interval scheme, observations with values of 4.0 and 5.0 could belong to two classes. A more appropriate mutually exclusive class interval scheme would be:

Class 1 = 3.0 to 3.99

Class 2 = 4.0 to 4.99

Class 3 = 5.0 to 5.99

There is no ambiguity as to which class the values of 4.0 and 5.0 belong. The class intervals selected must include all of the observations.

There are a number of ways to select the size of the class intervals. The most widely adopted methods include:

- *Natural Breaks* where a histogram of the original data is visually examined to determine logical breaks (often seen as gaps) in the data distribution. Whenever possible, it is important to respect natural breakpoints in the dataset. Examples of useful natural breaks that should be respected include 1) when mapping temperature in degrees Celsius, it is appropriate to use 0° C or 100° C as class limits; 2) for variables expressed as percentages, 50% represents a natural class limit because it is the breakpoint for a majority; 3) when mapping pH, 7.0 is the border between acidic and alkaline substances. It is unwise to disregard these and other natural, logical breakpoints when mapping certain very specialized phenomena.
- *Equal Interval* (or *equal steps*) wherein each class occupies an equal interval along the x-axis when the data are arranged in a histogram format. When it is not necessary to include specialized natural breakpoints as discussed above, it is good cartographic practice to create all of the class intervals so that they have the same width.
- *Quantile* method of classification wherein data are ranked-ordered and equal numbers of observations are placed in each class. Different names for this method are used depending on the number of classes, e.g., four- and five-class quantile maps are referred to as quartiles and quintiles. To compute

the number of observations in a class, the total number of observations is divided by the number of classes. To determine which observations should be placed in each class, one simply progresses through the rank-ordered data until the desired number of members in a class is obtained.

- *Mean ± Standard Deviation* where class boundaries are created by repeatedly adding or subtracting the standard deviation from the mean of the data. For example, consider the following four class intervals based on the use of 1 and 2 standard deviations (s) from the mean:

$$\text{Class 1} = \bar{x} - 2s \text{ to } \bar{x} - 1s$$

$$\text{Class 2} = \bar{x} - 1s \text{ to } \bar{x}$$

$$\text{Class 3} = \bar{x} \text{ to } \bar{x} + 1s$$

$$\text{Class 4} = \bar{x} + 1s \text{ to } \bar{x} + 2s$$

- *Maximum Breaks* wherein the original data are ordered from low to high, the differences between adjacent values are computed, and the largest of these differences serves as class breaks. Unfortunately, paying attention only to the largest breaks, the method often misses natural clusters of data along the histogram.
- *Optimal classification* methods using the Jenks-Caspall Algorithm or the Fisher-Jenks Algorithm (Slocum et al., 2009).

Most GIS allow the user to select among several types of class interval schemes. There is no single best method of classification. The cartographer must consider the purpose of the map and the knowledge of the intended audience when making class interval selections.

Choropleth Map Symbolization Map-makers must decide early in the map production process whether to use black-and-white or color symbolization when creating choropleth maps. When making this decision it is important to keep in mind that people can discriminate between about 15 grayscale classes. Conversely, it is possible for map-readers to discriminate between hundreds of different color classes. Introducing texture (e.g., random dots) or pattern (e.g., cross-hatching) to the black-and-white or color symbolization generally enhances the map-reader's ability to differentiate between classes. Another important consideration is that the production of hard-copy color maps is many times more expensive than the production of black-and-white maps. If all of the maps are to be displayed on a computer screen, then color choropleth mapping is generally preferable.

Great effort has gone into the development of symbolization for choropleth mapping. Here we will discuss several useful choropleth mapping color schemes, including 1) sequential color schemes, 2) diverging color schemes, and 3) spectral color schemes.

We will demonstrate the nature of several of these classification schemes using *ColorBrewer* designed by Cynthia Brewer and programmed by Mark Harrower and Andy Woodruff. ColorBrewer is a web tool for selecting color schemes for thematic maps, especially choropleth maps. It is a color diagnostic tool—not an online GIS. You cannot load your spatial data into ColorBrewer. Rather, you use the ColorBrewer interface to "test" a given color classification scheme to see if it suits your thematic mapping needs. ColorBrewer includes 35 basic color schemes with different numbers of classes for over 250 possible versions. Once you decide on an acceptable color scheme, the program lists the color specifications in a variety of color-space formats (e.g., CMYK, RGB, Hex, Lab, and AV3 [HSV]) that you can use in your GIS application software, e.g., ArcGIS®, IDRISI. ColorBrewer can be accessed at http://www.colorbrewer.org.

Sequential color schemes are ideal for mapping ordered data that progress from low to high (Figure 9-21a–c). Crucial lightness steps dominate the look of these sequential schemes, with light colors for low value data and dark colors for high value data. Sequential color schemes may also vary both the hue lightness and the single hue saturation (Brewer, 1994). Three selected sequential ColorBrewer color schemes are displayed in Figure 10-21a–c, including progressions in blue (Figure 10-21a), green (Figure 10-21b), and brown (Figure 10-21c). These sequential color schemes are pleasing to the eye because they are based on the use of soft pastel colors. It is good practice to avoid the use of intense, highly saturated colors.

The sequential red (brown) color classification scheme shown in Figure 9-21c was used to map the 2000 population density (persons per mile^2) of South Carolina counties (Figure 10-22a,b). The first choropleth map uses equal-area class intervals (Figure 10-22a). It highlights how a single coastal county (Charleston), two piedmont counties (Lexington and Richland), and two mountainous counties (Greenville and Spartanburg) have the highest population density in the state. The choropleth map created using the Jenks method of natural break selection places these same five (5) highest population density counties in the highest (darkest) class interval. Both maps are pleasing to the eye and convey approximately the same information. However, there are numerous subtle differences, which are a function of using two different class interval selection techniques.

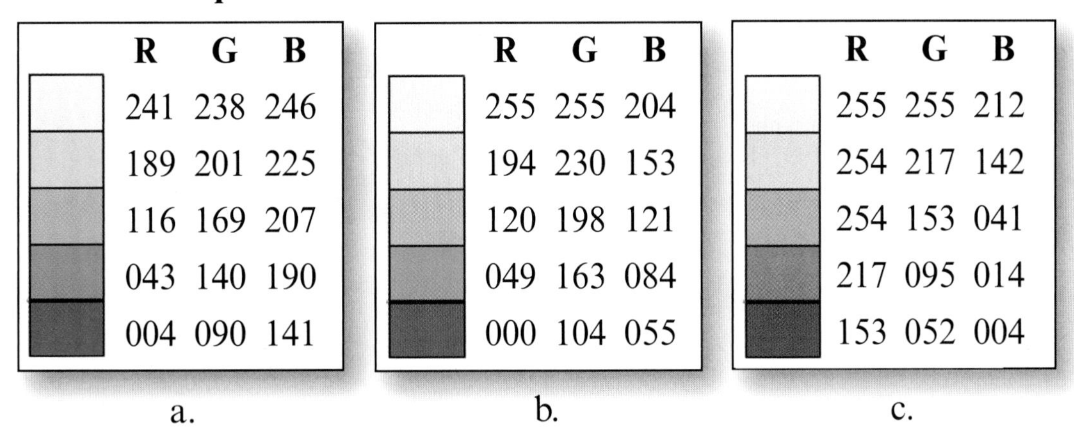

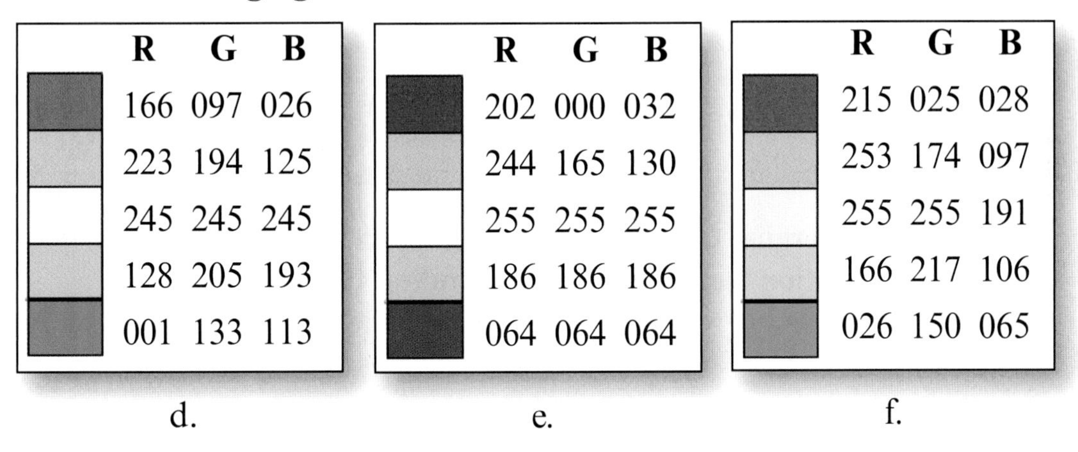

FIGURE 10–21 a-c) Three of the 18 sequential color schemes (blue, green, and brown) provided in the ColorBrewer system. Cartographers use ColorBrewer to experiment with various color classification schemes to determine the most appropriate color sequence. d-f) Three of the nine diverging color schemes provided in the ColorBrewer system. The RGB color values (or CMYK, Hex, Lab, or AV3 values) of the desired color sequence are input to the GIS when creating a choropleth map (©Cynthia Brewer and Mark Harrower and the Pennsylvania State University, *ColorBrewer:* Sequential and diverging color scheme specifications from ColorBrewer.org).

Diverging color schemes put equal emphasis on mid-range critical values and extremes at both ends of the data range (Brewer, 2009). The critical class or break in the middle of the scheme is typically emphasized with light colors, and very low and high data values are emphasized with dark colors that have contrasting hues (colors). Diverging color schemes are most effective when the class break in the middle of the sequence (the lightest middle color) is meaningfully related to the data being mapped. Use the break or class emphasized by a hue and lightness change to represent a critical value in the data such as the mean, median, or zero. Colors increase in darkness to represent differences in both directions from the meaningful mid-range value. Three selected diverging color schemes are displayed in Figure 10-21d–e, including progressions in green and brown (Figure 10-21d), black and red (Figure 10-21e), and green and red (Figure 10-21f). It is also possible for a mapmaker to use an unequal number of classes above and below the mid-range lightest point in the scheme (omitting some colors from a ColorBrewer scheme).

Two different diverging color classification schemes were used to map the 2000 population density (persons per mile^2) of South Carolina counties (Figure 10-22c,d). The five class intervals used in each map are based on standard deviation data characteristics. The choropleth map in Figure 10-22c uses diverging reds and grays with white as the central hue. Counties with population densities >2.5 standard deviations above the mean are shown in black. Counties with population densities < -0.49 standard deviation below the mean are shown in dark red. Note that most of the state is in this category. Figure 10-22d uses red and green diverging hues with beige as the central hue. This diverging color scheme is much more pleasing to the eye and makes it clear which of the 46 counties have

Sequential Color Scheme Choropleth Mapping of Population Density of South Carolina Counties in 2000 Persons per Square Mile

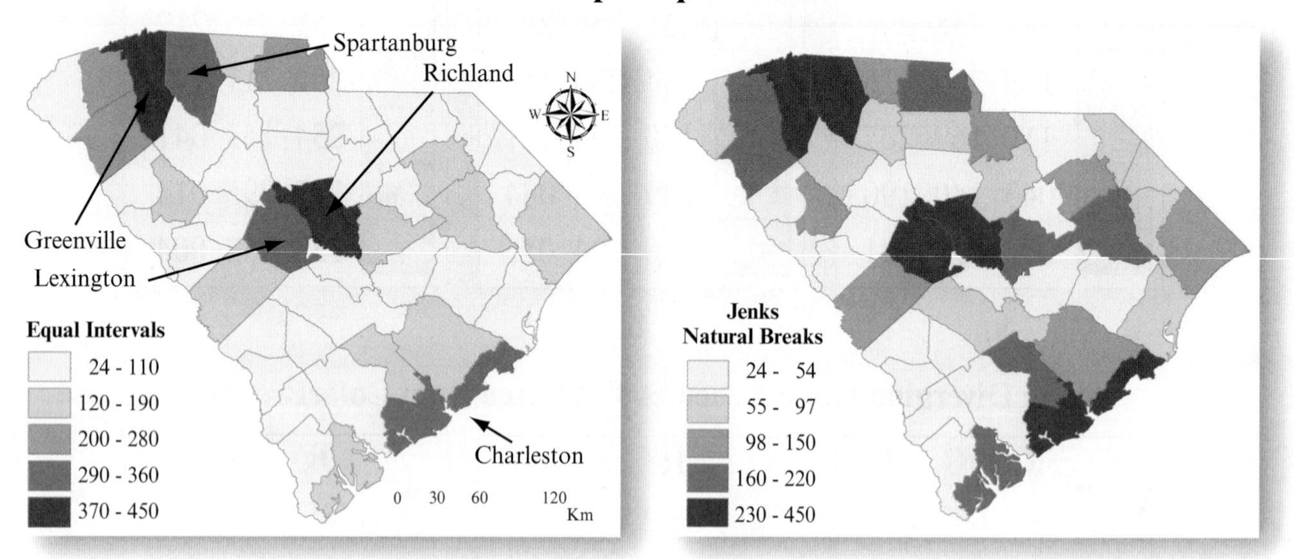

a,b. Equal area and Jenks natural breaks class intervals with the same sequential color classification scheme.

Diverging Color Scheme Choropleth Mapping of Population Density of South Carolina Counties in 2000 Persons per Square Mile

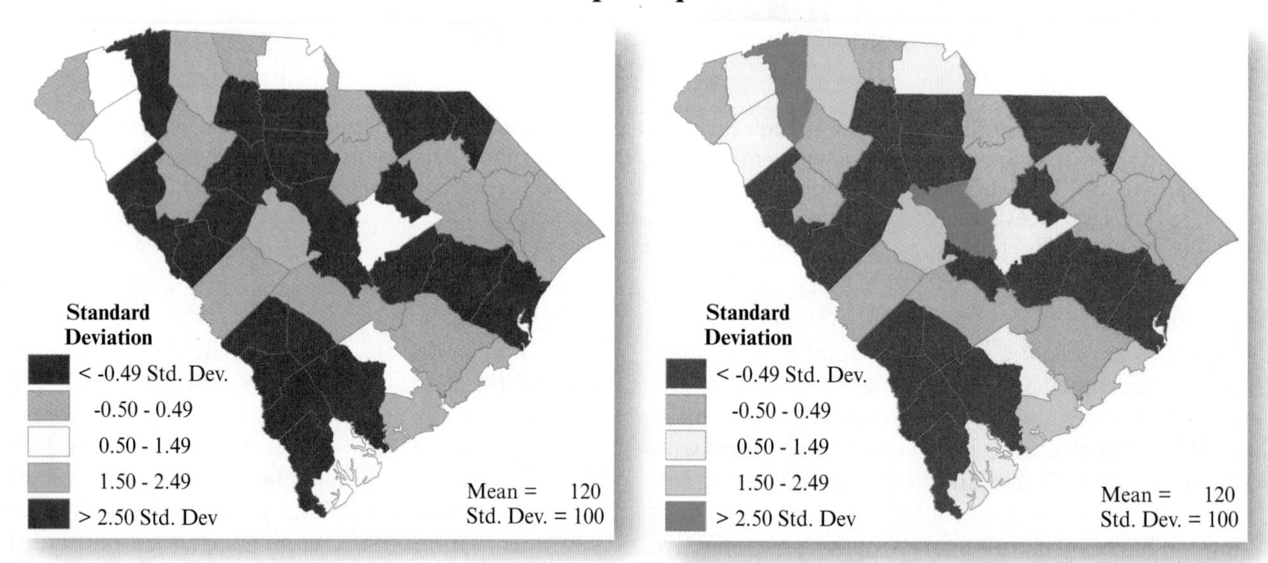

c,d. Standard deviation class intervals with two different diverging color classification schemes.

FIGURE 10–22 Examples of sequential and diverging color classification schemes used for choropleth mapping. The RGB characteristics of the color classification schemes are found in Figure 10-21 (data courtesy of U.S. Bureau of the Census and South Carolina Department of Natural Resources).

population densities >2.5 standard deviations from the mean (shown in bright green).

Spectral progression color schemes are composed of the sequence of colors associated with the electromagnetic spectrum. Typical colors include violet, indigo, blue, green, yellow, orange, and red often referred to as ROYGBIV (Figure 10-23).

Cartographers creating choropleth maps have to be careful as they select the method of standardization, the number of class intervals, and the symbolization

FIGURE 10–23 A spectral progression color scheme typically consists of an ordered sequence of colors associated with the electromagnetic spectrum such as violet, indigo, blue, green, yellow, orange, and red (ROYGBIV).

(e.g., qualitative, sequential, and diverging). Great care should be taken in the creation of the class interval legend so that it is easy to understand.

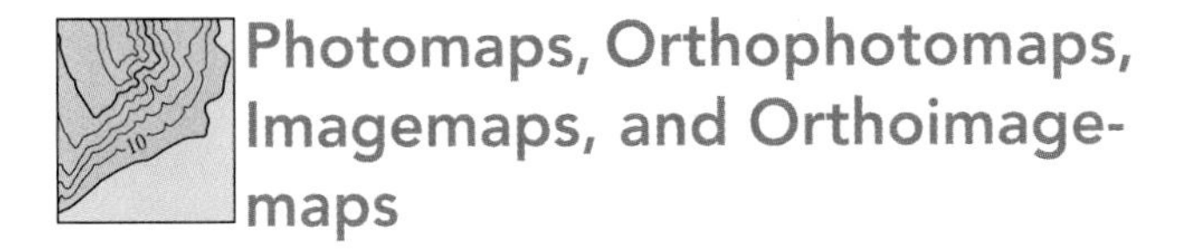

Photomaps, Orthophotomaps, Imagemaps, and Orthoimagemaps

It is common today to create maps that contain remotely sensed images (e.g., aerial photographs and other types of imagery) as the background information in the map. In fact, the public views a tremendous number of photomaps, imagemaps, and/or orthophotomaps everyday as they download spatial information from:

- Google Earth (www.earth.google.com),
- Google Maps (www.maps.google.com),
- Bing Maps (www.bing.com/maps), and
- other data providers.

Photomaps, imagemaps, and orthophotomaps have important geometric properties that should be considered when using them in a GIS. It is instructive to briefly introduce some of the basic characteristics so that these image-based products can be used wisely when performing GIS analysis or mapping.

Uncontrolled Photomaps (Photomosaics) and Imagemaps

It is possible to overlay several analog or digital vertical aerial photographs from a block of aerial photography to create an **uncontrolled photomap** (technically an **uncontrolled photomosaic**). While a photomosaic is visually informative, it should not be used to measure distances, areas, or directions because it has not been registered to a map projection (e.g., Universal Transverse Mercator) and the effects of relief displacement are still present in the photomosaic.

Similarly, it is possible to superimpose a number of unrectified remotely sensed images (e.g., Landsat Thematic Mapper or ASTER data) that overlap one another and create an **uncontrolled imagemap**. Once again, it is not wise to measure distances, areas, or directions using uncontrolled imagemaps because the data have not been registered to a map projection and may also contain significant error due to relief displacement.

Controlled Photomaps and Imagemaps

Individual aerial photographs in a block of aerial photography that have been geometrically rectified to a map projection (e.g., UTM) using ground control points (GCPs) and digital image rectification techniques are called *controlled photomaps* or *controlled photomosaics*. Similarly, individual remotely sensed images that have been geometrically rectified to a map projection using GCPs and digital image processing geometric rectification techniques are called *controlled imagemaps*.

For example, consider the five controlled imagemaps documenting the urbanization of Dubai from 2000 through 2008. To expand the possibilities for beachfront tourist development, Dubai, part of the United Arab Emirates, conducted massive engineering projects to create hundreds of artificial islands along its Persian Gulf coastline. Built from sand dredged from the sea floor and protected from erosion by rock breakwaters, the islands were shaped into recognizable forms, including two large palm trees. The first Palm Island constructed was Palm Jumeirah. The Advanced Spaceborne Thermal Emission and Reflection Radiometer (ASTER) on NASA's Terra satellite observed its progress from 2000 to 2008 (NASA Earth Observatory, 2009).

The false-color composite imagemaps shown in Figure 10-24 were created using ASTER bands 1, 2, and 3 (green, red, and near-infrared, respectively) each with a nominal spatial resolution of 15 x 15 m. The original imagery was geometrically corrected to a UTM map projection using GCPs and nearest-neighbor resampling techniques. The terrain is essentially flat in Dubai, so there is little need for ortho-rectification. In these false-color images, bare ground appears light brown, vegetation appears red, water appears dark blue, and buildings and paved surfaces appear light blue or gray.

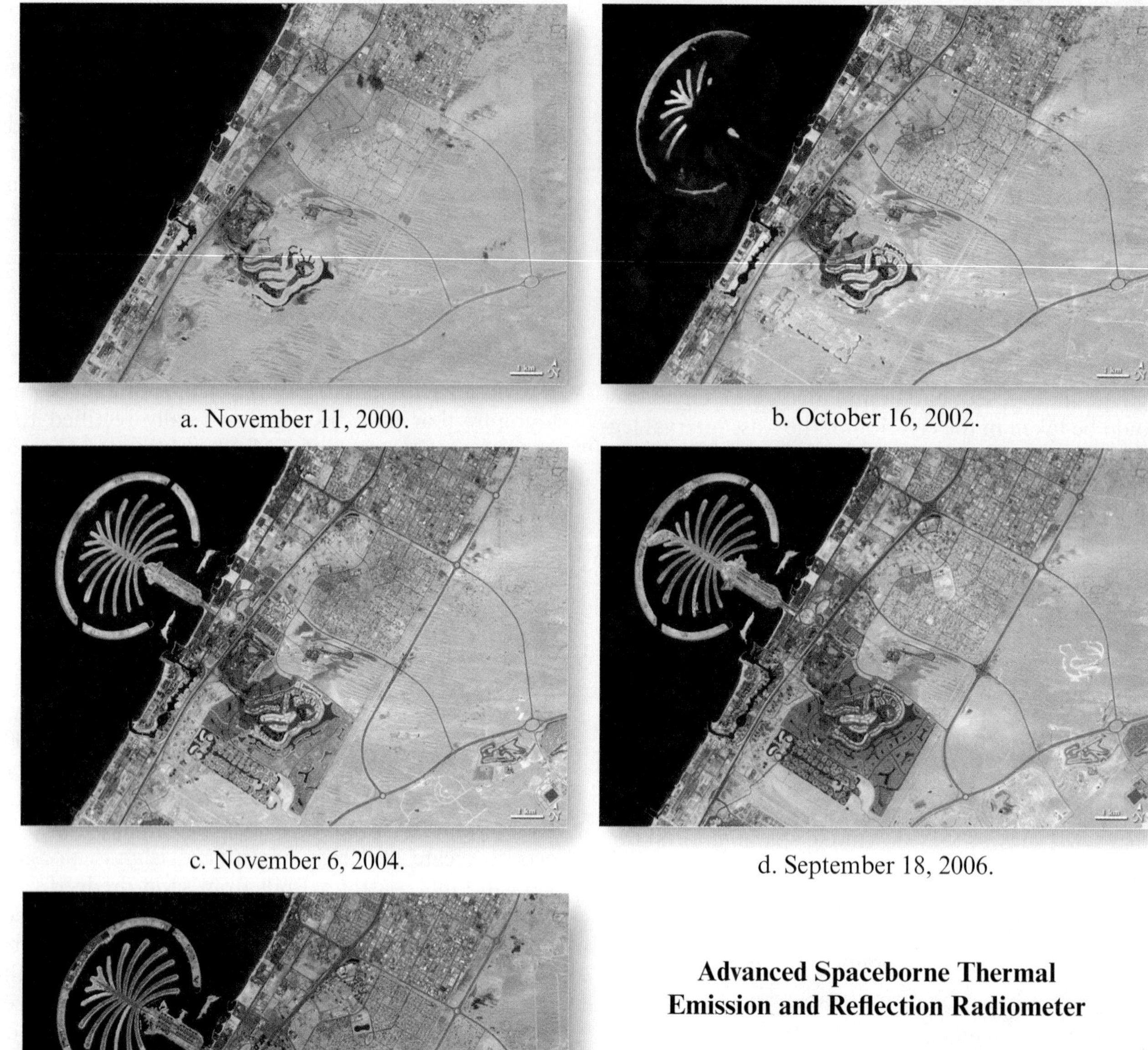

FIGURE 10–24 Five controlled imagemaps of Dubai, United Arab Emirates, produced by geometrically rectifying ASTER optical remote sensor data to a Universal Transverse Mercator (UTM) map projection using ground control points and digital image processing rectification techniques. The imagemaps overlay one another to within one pixel (e.g., RMSE = ±15 m) in a GIS and document the urbanization of Dubai from 2000 through 2008. Because the terrain is almost perfectly flat, relief displacement is virtually nonexistent in these imagemaps except for tall buildings. Therefore, accurate distance, area, and bearing calculations can be extracted from the rectified imagemaps (images courtesy of NASA's Earth Observatory).

The first image, acquired in November, 2000, shows the area prior to the island's construction. By October 2002, substantial progress had been made on Palm Jumeirah, with many sandy "palm fronds" inside a circular breakwater. Palm Jumeirah was almost finished in 2004. Inland, changes are just as dramatic between November 2000 and November 2008. In the earliest image, empty desert fills the lower right quadrant of the imagemap, because the urbanized area hugs the coastline. As the years pass, urbanization spreads inland, and the final image documents that the area is almost entirely developed with roads, buildings, and irrigated land (NASA Earth Observatory, 2009).

Controlled photomaps and controlled imagemaps are typically much more geometrically accurate than uncontrolled photomaps and imagemaps. Each pixel in these datasets has a unique map coordinate (as opposed to uncontrolled products, which only have image row and column coordinates). Therefore, controlled photomaps and controlled imagemaps are easily placed in a GIS and can be analyzed in conjunction with other spatial data. Some of the imagery displayed in Google Earth and Bing Maps are controlled photomaps or controlled imagemaps. Fairly accurate distance, area, and bearing information may be extracted from the controlled photomaps and controlled imagemaps. However, it is important to remember that controlled photomaps and imagemaps are not as geometrically accurate as orthophotomaps or orthoimage maps because they may still have errors associated with relief displacement.

Uncorrected Vertical Aerial Photograph

a.

Orthophotograph

b.

FIGURE 10–25 a) An uncorrected vertical aerial photograph of a power transmission line in rugged terrain. b) Planimetrically accurate orthophotograph after correction to remove roll, pitch, and yaw errors introduced by the aircraft at the instant of exposure and the effects of topographic relief displacement. Note that the transmission line is straight in the orthophoto (images courtesy of the U.S. Geological Survey).

Orthophotos, Orthophotomaps, Orthoimages, and Orthoimagemaps

Earth exhibits significant local relief (i.e., changes in elevation over relatively small distances). These changes in local elevation cause some objects within the instantaneous-field-of-view (IFOV) of the remote sensing system to be closer to the sensor while other objects within the IFOV are farther away from the sensor at the instant of exposure. These variations in local relief give rise to relief displacement in the imagery, where objects or features in the terrain are displaced from their true planimetric x,y location. For example, consider the uncorrected vertical aerial photograph of a power transmission line in the rugged terrain shown in Figure 10-25a. Relief displacement in the original aerial photography caused the linear power transmission line to appear distorted (crooked). If the Earth were completely flat (i.e., we lived on a very boring planet), we would not have to worry about the negative effects of relief displacement when creating photomaps or imagemaps.

Fortunately, it is possible to remove the effects of relief displacement in aerial photography or remotely sensed imagery. Individual aerial photographs in a block of aerial photography or other types of remote sensor data may be processed using ground control points (GCPs), digital terrain models (DTM), and fundamental photogrammetric techniques to remove the effects of terrain (and building) relief displacement. Aerial photography processed in this manner yields **orthophotos**. For example, the effects of relief displacement have been removed in the orthophotograph shown in Figure 10-25b. The power transmission line is now straight as an arrow, as it should be. Very accurate distance, area, and direction measurements can be made from the orthophoto. When the orthophotos or **orthoimages** are overlaid with point, line, and/or area thematic information they are called **orthophotomaps** or **orthoimagemaps**. Jensen (2007) describes how relief displacement is removed to create orthophotos and orthoimages.

A large-scale orthophotomap of a portion of downtown Beaufort, SC, is shown in Figure 10-26. The 1 x 1 ft. spatial resolution color-infrared digital aerial photography was processed using photogrammetric techniques and a digital terrain model to create the color-infrared orthophoto. The street centerlines, street names, and parcel boundary data are overlaid on the orthophoto creating an orthophotomap. There is con-

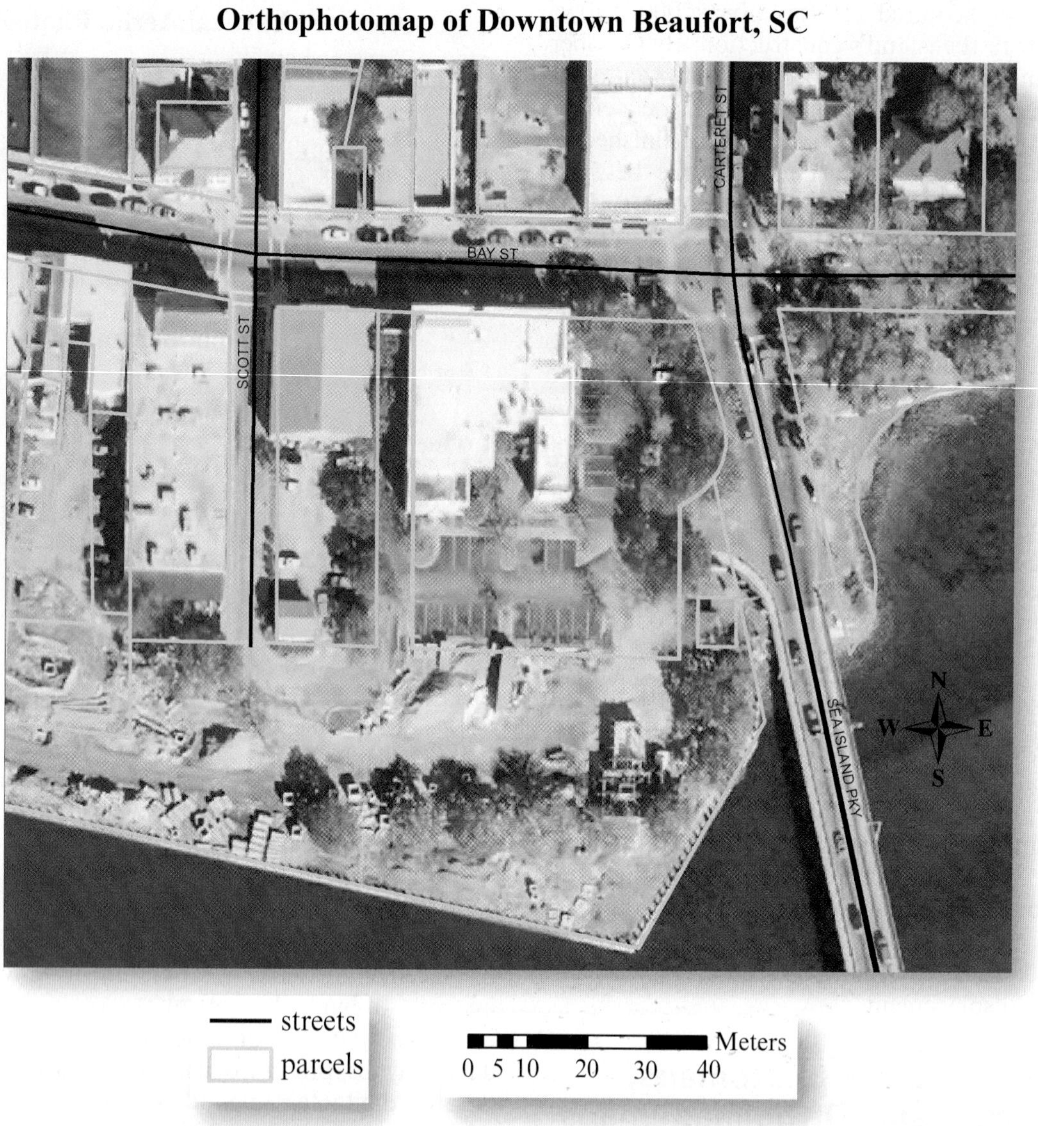

Orthophotomap of Downtown Beaufort, SC

FIGURE 10–26 An orthophotomap consisting of a color-infrared orthophoto of Beaufort, SC, overlaid with street centerlines, street names, and parcel information (data courtesy of Beaufort County GIS Department).

siderable local relief in this part of the city. The street centerlines and parcel boundaries (Cowen et al., 2008) would not overlay the imagery correctly if the effects of relief displacement were still present in the color-infrared imagery. The ortho-rectification process removed the effects of relief displacement and caused every pixel in the orthophoto to be in its correct *x,y* location making it well-suited for use with other geospatial data in the county GIS.

Some of the imagery available from Google Earth, Bing Maps, and other data providers are orthophotos or orthoimagery. Very accurate distance, area, and direction information can be extracted from these data. The map-user should always consult the metadata associated with each type of imagery to determine if the imagery are uncontrolled, controlled, or ortho-rectified. This is a very important consideration when making cartographic products using a GIS. The more geometrically accurate the remote sensor data, the better it will register with other spatial data in the GIS.

National Digital Orthophoto Programs

Two of the most important agencies providing orthoimagery used in the creation of orthophotomaps are the U.S. Geological Survey and the U.S. Department of Agriculture.

USGS Digital Orthophotos The USGS has been creating orthophotos of the United States for many years. You can use the USGS *EarthExplorer* program at http://edcsns17.cr.usgs.gov/EarthExplorer/ to identify available orthophoto coverage. Each of the digital orthophotos has detailed metadata to facilitate its use in GIS. Below is some additional information about USGS digital orthophotos.

A USGS Digital Orthophoto Quadrangle (often referred to as a DOQ) is a computer-generated image of a National Aerial Photography Program (NAPP) aerial photograph in which the image displacement caused by terrain relief and camera tilt has been removed. The DOQ combines the image characteristics of the original photograph with the georeferenced qualities of a map. DOQs may be based on black-and-white (B/W), natural color, and/or color-infrared (CIR) aerial photography, all with 1 x 1 m nominal spatial resolution. Most of the USGS orthophotos were acquired in the early spring of the year during "leaf-off" conditions.

The USGS produces three types of DOQs (EROS, 2009):

- *3.75-minute (Quarter-quad) DOQs* cover an area measuring 3.75-minutes longitude by 3.75-minutes latitude. Quarter-quad DOQs are often referred to as **DOQQs** and are available for much of the U.S.
- *7.5-minute (Full-quad) DOQs* cover an area measuring 7.5-minutes longitude by 7.5-minutes latitude. Full-quad DOQs are primarily available for Oregon, Washington, and Alaska. Limited coverage is available for other states.
- *Seamless DOQs* are available for free download from the Seamless site (www.seamles.usgs.gov).

USDA National Agriculture Imagery Program (NAIP) This program acquires imagery during the agricultural growing seasons in the continental United States. A primary goal of NAIP is to make true color digital orthophotos available to governmental agencies and the public within a year of data acquisition. NAIP is administered by the USDA's Farm Service Agency (FSA) through the Aerial Photography Field Office (APFO) in Salt Lake City. The "leaf-on" imagery is used as a base layer for GIS programs in the FSA's County Service Centers, and is used to maintain the USDA Common Land Unit (CLU) boundaries.

The NAIP normally acquires imagery on a three- to five-year cycle; however, some states acquire NAIP imagery annually. NAIP imagery products are available as digital ortho quarter quad tiles (DOQQs):

- *NAIP Digital Ortho Quarter Quad Tiles (DOQQs)* have a nominal spatial resolution of 1 x 1 m. Most of the aerial photography is natural color (blue, green, and red) with much of the new digital photography collected in the blue, green, red, and near-infrared portions of the spectrum. Each individual image tile within the mosaic covers a 3.75 x 3.75-minute quarter quadrangle. The DOQQs correspond to the USGS topographic quadrangles previously discussed. All individual tile images and the resulting mosaic are rectified to a UTM map projection and NAD 83.
- *NAIP Compressed County Mosaics (CCM)* are generated by compressing DOQQ image tiles into a single mosaic that is clipped by county boundaries.

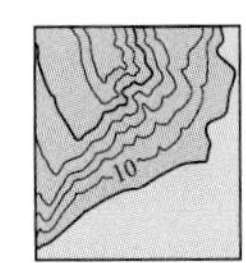

Summary

This chapter provided a brief history of some major cartographic milestones. It then introduced how a GIS can be used to create high-quality cartographic products that contain point, line, and area data at various levels of measurement (e.g., nominal, ordinal, interval, and ratio). The cartographic process was discussed to obtain an appreciation of the iterative map-making process. Numerous map design principles were discussed and demonstrated using cartographic examples. Various types of controlled and uncontrolled photomaps and imagemaps as well as orthophotos and orthophotomaps were discussed to document when they are appropriate for use in a GIS for map-making purposes.

GIS users would be wise to learn even more about fundamental cartographic design principles so that the maps they make using a GIS communicate the geospatial information accurately to the map-user. This will hopefully lead to more useful decision making to improve the quality of life and have sustainable development.

Review Questions

1. Why is so much attention given to Claudius Ptolemy's maps, originally compiled in approximately 150 AD?

2. Why did it take so long for cartographers to compile an accurate map of the world? What were some of the major obstacles that had to be overcome to obtain geographic data and map it accurately?

3. What geographic measurement level (e.g., nominal, ordinal, interval, ratio) is information on land cover, soil type, temperature ^{o}F, population density, atmospheric pressure?

4. You are required to make a map depicting the topography of the area surrounding your home. You will be using a hill-shaded digital terrain model, 1-ft. con-

tours overlaid on the digital terrain model, roads, building footprints, and place names. Describe the figure-ground relationship of these features and how you would use the figure-ground information to create a thematic map.

5. You are creating a thematic map that shows the spatial distribution of 10 different soil types. Describe how you will select the colors you will use for each of the 10 classes. What are some general cartographic guidelines that you will use as you select the symbolization?

6. You have used a GIS to analyze data and are now ready to produce a map of your results. The map will first be produced in hard-copy format at a scale of 1:24,000. However, the map will also be provided as a portable document file (PDF) that can be displayed on computer screens throughout the world. What type of scale information will you include in the body of your map to ensure that the scale information is always accurate when viewed?

7. You are making a proportional symbol map of the population density of the 100 most densely populated cities in the world. Would you use apparent (perceptual) scaling or absolute scaling of the proportional symbols? Why?

8. Why is it important to consider using standardized symbolization for point, line, and area features when creating a map?

9. You are making a contour map at a scale of 1:5,000 with 1-ft. contours. Describe the symbolization you would use for a) the line width for regular, index, and depression contours; and b) contour line color.

10. What is the difference between an uncontrolled photomosaic in a hilly area and an orthophoto of the same area at the same scale? Which will yield the most accurate horizontal measurements? Why?

Glossary

Atlas: A collection of maps, traditionally bound into book form.

Cartographic Process: A sequence of processes used by cartographers to create high-quality maps that accurately communicate the desired spatial information to the map-reader.

Choropleth mapping: Mapping nominal, ordinal, and interval/ratio-scaled data according to specialized areal administrative units such as watersheds, counties, states, or countries.

DOQQ: The USGS produces digital-orthophoto-quarter-quadrangles at a spatial resolution of 1 x 1 m encompassing an area 3.75-minutes of longitude and 3.75-minutes of latitude.

Figure-Ground Relationship: The *figure* in a map is the important thematic content. There may be several figures in the map of varying importance. The *ground* is the literal background information upon which the figure (important thematic content) resides and may include administrative units such as states or counties, graticule, scale bar, legend, north arrow, and metadata.

Geo-lineage: Metadata about the history of the processing used to create the final map.

Isarithmic Mapping: Uses isolines to model two types of continuous phenomena: isometric surfaces that actually exist in reality (e.g., elevation, temperature) and isopleth surfaces that are conceptual in nature (e.g., population density).

Isometric Mapping: A special type of isarithmic mapping used when the data control points used to create the statistical surface actually exist at a particular geographic location (e.g., elevation, temperature).

Isopleth mapping: A special type of isarithmic mapping used when the data control points used to create the statistical surface are conceptual and may not exist at all locations on the surface (e.g., population density, per capita income).

Legend: A cartographic device used to show how the thematic information in a map is organized and symbolized. It usually consists of a title, classes, class intervals, and/or symbolization.

Measurement Levels: Data may be described as having nominal, ordinal, interval or ratio measurement levels.

Metadata: Information about the data used to perform the GIS analysis and/or create a map.

Orthoimage: A remotely sensed image that has been geometrically rectified to a standard map projection and the effects of relief displacement removed.

Orthophoto: A specially prepared aerial photograph that has the metric characteristics of a planimetric map with the photographic detail provided by the aerial photograph. Distortion caused by terrain relief displacement has been removed.

Orthophotomap or Orthoimagemap: Orthophotos or orthoimages overlaid with point, line, and/or area thematic information.

Proportional Symbol: A special type of point symbol (e.g., a circle) that is made proportional in size (scaled) according to the point observation *z*-value.

Typography: The art and science of creating alphanumeric type in various fonts (e.g., Times New Roman, Avenir), styles (e.g., *serif* or *sans-serif,* bold, italic), and sizes.

References

Brewer, C. A., 1994, "Color Use Guidelines for Mapping and Visualization," Chapter 7 in *Visualization in Modern Cartography*, edited by A. M. MacEachren and D. R. F. Taylor, New York: Elsevier Science, 123–147.

Buckley, A. and K. Field, 2011, "Making a Meaningful Map: A Checklist for Compiling More Effective Maps," *ArcUser*, 14(4):40–43.

Burt, J. E., Barber, G. M. and D. L. Rigby, 2009, *Elementary Statistics for Geographers*, 3rd Ed., New York: Guilford, 653 p.

Cowen, D., Coleman, J., Craig, W., Domenico, C., Elhami, S., Johnson, S., Marlow, S., Roberts, F., Swartz, M. and N. Von Meyer, 2008, *National Land Parcel Data: A Vision for the Future*, Washington, D.C.: National Academy Press, 158 p.

Dent, B., 2002, *Cartography: Thematic Map Design*, 5th Ed., New York: McGraw-Hill, 448 p.

EROS, 2009, *Digital Orthophoto Quadrangles*, Sioux Falls, SD: EROS Data Center, http://eros.usgs.gov/products/aerial/doq.php.

FGDC, 2011 *Geospatial Metadata*, Washington only for D.C.: Federal Geographic Data Committee, www.fgdc.gov/metadata.

Gould, P., 1985, *The Geographer at Work*, London: Toutledge, pages 9–10.

Harley, J. B. and D. Woodward, 1987-2007, Volumes in the *History of Cartography Project*, Wisconsin: History of Cartography Project, www.geography.wisc.edu/histcart/#Project.

Hereford Cathedral, 2011, Hereford *Mappa Mundi* (Map of the World), London: Hereford Cathedral.

Jensen, J. R., 2007, *Remote Sensing of the Environment: An Earth Resource Perspective*, Upper Saddle River: Pearson Prentice-Hall, 592 p.

Johnson, S., 2006, *The Ghost Map*, New York: Riverhead Books, 358 p.

Koch, J., 2004, "The Map as Intent: Variations on the Theme of John Snow," *Cartographica*, 39(4):1–14.

Konvitz, J., 1987, *Cartography in France 1660–1848: Science, Engineering & Statecraft*, 214 p.

Library of Congress, 2011, *An Illustrated Guide: Geography and Maps*, http://www.loc.gov/rr/geogmap/guide/gmillint.html.

Library of Congress American Memory Collection, 2011a, Martin Waldeesmuller's *Universalis Cosmographia*, Washington: Library of Congress, http://memory.loc.gov/cgi-bin/query/h?ammem/gmd:@field%28NUMBER+@band%28g3200+ct000725C%29%29.

Library of Congress American Memory Collection, 2011b, George Wheeler's *Map of the Colorado River*, Washington: Library of Congress, http://memory.loc.gov/cgi-bin/query/h?ammem/gmd:@field%28NUMBER+@band%28g4330+np000069%29%29.

Library of Congress Geography and Map Division, 2011, Claudius Ptolemy, *Geographia*, Ulm: Lienhart Holle, 1482, Washington: Library of Congress (140.02.00).

Library of Congress Rare Book and Special Collection Division, 2011, *T-O Map of the World*, Washington: Library of Congress, http://myloc.gov/Exhibitions/EarlyAmericas/AftermathoftheEncounter/DocumentingNewKnowledge/MappingtheWorld/ExhibitObjects/TOMapoftheWorld.aspx.

Maidment, D. R., Edelman, Heiberg, E. R., Jensen, J. R., Maune, D. F., Schuckman, K. and R. Shrestha, 2007, *Elevation Data for Floodplain Mapping*, Washington, D.C.: National Academy Press, 151 p.

Maune, D. F., (Ed.), 2001, *Digital Elevation Model Technologies and Applications*, Bethesda: American Society for Photogrammetry & Remote Sensing, 538 p.

Monmonier, M., 1996, *How to Lie with Maps*, 2nd Ed. Chicago: University of Chicago Press, 222 p.

Muehrcke, P. C., 2005, *Map Use: Reading, Analysis and Interpretation*, 5th Ed., Madison: J. P. Publications, 544 p.

NASA Earth Observatory, 2009, *The Urbanization of Dubai*, http://earthobservatory.nasa.gov/Features/WorldOfChange/dubai.php.

Sauer, C. O., 1956, "The Education of a Geographer," *Annals* of the AAG, 46:287–299. Presidential address given by the President of the Association of American Geographers at its 52nd annual meeting, Montreal, Canada, April 4, 1956.

Scott, D. W., 1979, "On Optimal and Data-Based Histograms," *Biometrika*, 66:605–610.

Slocum, T. A., McMaster, R. B., Kessler, F. C. and H. H. Howard, 2005, *Thematic Cartography and Geographic Visualization,* 2nd Ed., Upper Saddle River: Pearson Prentice-Hall, 518 p.

Smith, C. D., 1996, "Imago Mundi's Logo: The Babylonian Map of the World," *Imago Mundi*, 48:209–211.

Snow, J., 1855, *On the Mode of Communication of Cholera*, London: John Churchill, 139 p.

Thrower, N. J. W., 1972, *Maps & Man: An Examination of Cartography Based on Culture and Civilization*, Upper Saddle River: Pearson Prentice-Hall, Inc.

Thrower, N. J. W., 1999, *Maps & Civilization: Cartography in Culture and Society*, Chicago: University of Chicago Press, 326 p.

Tufte, E., 2001, *The Visual Display of Quantitative Information*, 2nd Ed., Cheshire, Conn: Graphics Press, 220 p.

UCLA Department of Epidemiology, 2011, *John Snow*, http://www.ph.ucla.edu/epi/snow.html.

USGS, 2009, *Topographic Map Symbols*, Washington, D.C.: U.S. Geological Survey, 4 p.

11 GIS Hardware/Software and Programming

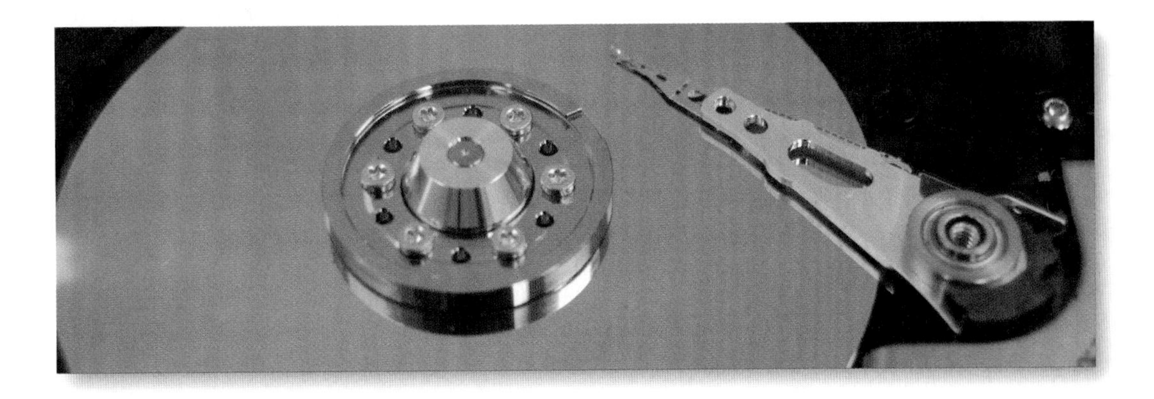

The computer hardware and GIS software that are used to perform GIS analysis can make the difference between success and failure for a given project. This chapter describes some of the basic alternatives that should be considered when selecting the most appropriate hardware and software for GIS analysis.

Overview

This chapter begins with an overview of computer hardware characteristics that are of value when conducting GIS research, including type of computer, central processing unit (CPU), system memory, mass storage, display, input and output devices, etc. The hardware associated with typical GIS laboratories is discussed. GIS data storage and archiving considerations are reviewed.

GIS software should be easy to use and functional. Important GIS software characteristics are introduced, including commonly used GIS software, operating systems, data capture and data formats, databases, cartographic output capabilities, and cost. GIS software customer support is also important and can be satisfied through online manuals and help, person-to-person dialog, user groups, and online training and workshops.

High-quality GIS software has significant capabilities. However, there is often a need to perform some type of geospatial analysis that is not available in the standard GIS software. When this situation occurs, a well-trained GIS professional may be able to program new geospatial code that can function within the standard GIS software. The fundamental characteristics of performing GIS-related computer programming are reviewed. An example of object-oriented programming using the Python language is provided.

GIS Hardware Considerations

As briefly introduced in Chapter 1, GIS analysis requires specially configured hardware and software. The following sections describe the fundamental characteristics of some of the most important computer hardware and software considerations for GIS applications.

Type of Computer

All GIS software vendors list the minimum system requirements necessary to run their GIS software. Keep in mind that these are the minimum requirements. Computers with components that exceed the minimum requirements will be more useful for GIS analysis. If the computer has only the minimum hardware required to run the GIS software, the software will probably run slowly and will most likely dominate the operating system's resources. This is especially a problem if you are a "multitasker" who frequently has other programs running at the same time as the GIS software (e.g., word processor, graphics program, Internet browser).

Computers used for GIS analysis can be organized into three main categories: personal computers, computer workstations, and mainframe computers.

Personal Computers

Personal computers are the workhorses of the GIS industry (Figure 11-1). These include relatively inexpensive computers such as desktops, laptops, and tablets. They have much greater clock speeds and can process instructions faster than their predecessors because they have 32- to 64-bit registers (word size) compared to the 8-bit registers used historically. Many GIS-related companies provide their employees with high-quality personal computers because of their low initial cost and inexpensive maintenance requirements. Interestingly, it seems that one can always purchase a "good" personal computer for GIS analysis for under $3,000. Ideally, the computer should have >6 GB of RAM, a large hard disk (>500 GB), a rewritable disk drive (e.g., DVD-RW), a cursor, and a good graphics display system (monitor and video card). Common operating systems suitable for personal computers include Microsoft Windows products (e.g., Windows 7) and the Macintosh OS X Lion operating system. These operating systems allow computers to be networked and have access to the Internet.

Computer Workstations

Computer workstations usually contain more powerful processors, more RAM, larger hard disk drives, and very high-quality graphics display capability. These improved components allow workstations to perform GIS analysis more rapidly than a personal computer. However, the cost of a workstation is usually two to three times more than the cost of a personal computer. The most common workstation operating systems are UNIX, Linux, and various Microsoft Windows products.

Mainframe Computers

Mainframe computers perform calculations more rapidly than personal computers and workstations, and they are able to support hundreds of users simultaneously. Mainframes are ideal for intensive CPU-dependent tasks such as overlay analysis, large database operations, and raster rendering. If desired, the output from mainframe processing can be passed to a personal computer or workstation for less intensive processing. Mainframe computers are usually expensive to purchase and maintain. Also, GIS software for mainframe computers is more expensive.

Central Processing Unit (CPU)

One of the most important things to consider when obtaining a computer for GIS analysis is the speed of the **central processing unit (CPU)**. The CPU is the processing part of a computer and consists of a control unit and arithmetic logic unit. The CPU performs the following functions:

- numerical integer and/or floating point calculations, and
- directs input and output from and to mass storage devices, color monitors, printers, plotters, digitizers, etc.

CPU efficiency is measured in terms of how many millions of instructions per second (MIPS) it can process. Current CPUs process >4 million instructions per second. This number will continue to increase. In 1985, Gordon Moore (co-founder of Intel, Inc.) made an observation that each new computer chip contained roughly twice as much capacity as its predecessor with chips being released roughly every 18–24 months. He reasoned that if this trend continued, computing power would increase exponentially. This observation has come to be known as Moore's Law and still appears to be accurate today. Since 1971, the number of transistors on Intel chips has increased from 2,300 on the 4004 microprocessor to >2 billion transistors. Following this trend, CPU efficiency measured in MIPS has increased exponentially.

Many personal computers, workstations, and especially mainframe computers have multiple CPUs. A single CPU functions in a serial manner. The presence of multiple CPUs allows parallel processing to take place. The operating system and/or GIS software is able to parse (distribute) different tasks to the several CPUs, dramatically improving processing speed.

Memory (Read-Only and Random Access)

Computers used for GIS analysis have many other characteristics that must be considered, such as **Read-Only Memory (ROM)** and **Random Access Memory (RAM)**. ROM retains information even after the computer is turned off because power is supplied by a battery that occasionally must be replaced. When a computer is turned on, the computer examines the information stored in the various ROM registers and uses this information to proceed. Most computers have sufficient ROM for GIS analysis.

RAM is the computer's primary temporary workspace. Unlike ROM, all the data stored in RAM are lost when the computer is turned off. Computers should have sufficient RAM for the operating system, GIS software, and any spatial data that must be held in temporary memory while calculations are performed. Because of this, the amount of RAM is one of the most important considerations when purchasing a computer for GIS analysis. As mentioned in Chapter 1, it is good

Personal Computers Are Ideal for GIS Analysis

FIGURE 11–1 Properly configured personal computers and computer workstations are ideal for GIS analysis. In this example, the personal computer is being used to perform on-screen digitizing. A tracing device, such as keyboard direction keys or the mouse cursor and specialized GIS software, are being used to extract the coordinates of point, line, or area objects of interest. The outline (and area) of several large buildings (shown in red) have been extracted from the natural color orthophoto (data courtesy State of Utah).

practice to have more than 6 GB of RAM for GIS analysis.

Operating System

The **operating system** is the first program loaded into memory (RAM) when the computer is turned on. The operating system controls all of the computer's higher order functions and resides in RAM at all times. The operating system provides the user interface, controls multitasking, handles input and output to the hard disk and all peripheral devices such as DVDs, scanners, printers, plotters, and color displays. All GIS software must communicate with the operating system.

As noted, some of the most common operating systems are Microsoft Windows 7 and Macintosh OS X Lion. These operating systems are single-user operating systems that are designed for a single person working independently at a desktop or laptop computer. Other operating systems are designed to manage multiple user requests at the same time. These operating systems include Microsoft Windows OS, UNIX, and Linux.

Display

The display of raster and vector GIS data on a computer screen is an important part of all GIS projects. Careful selection of the display properties of a personal computer or workstation will provide an optimum environment for visually examining spatial data. A standard computer displays approximately 1024 x 768 pixels on the computer screen. A high-quality personal computer or workstation for GIS analysis should be able to display substantially more pixels on the screen, e.g., 1900 x 1200 (Figure 11-1). This allows the GIS user to view many more pixels at one time when displaying maps and images.

It is often important during GIS analysis to be able to display a tremendous range of colors on the computer screen. The number of rows and columns of pixels that can be displayed on the screen and the number of colors that can be displayed are controlled by the characteristics of the computer graphics memory located inside the computer attached to the system bus. It is ideal to have 512 MB to 1 GB of video memory for GIS applications. This allows each individual pixel on the video screen to be able to display one of 16.7 million colors (commonly referred to as 24-bit color resolution). Having the ability to display up to 16.7 million colors is ideal for all GIS cartographic mapping and especially useful when displaying color-composite remotely sensed images.

Input Devices

Two of the most widely-used methods used to extract new geographic information from analog (hardcopy) maps and historical aerial photographs are: a) digitization using a digitizing table, or b) on-screen digitization from scanned hard-copy materials.

Digitizing Using a Digitizing Table

Digitizing tables are used to transfer points, lines, and areas from hard-copy (analog) paper maps or aerial photographs into digital points, lines, and areas that can be analyzed using the GIS software (refer to Figure 3-1b). This is done by securing the hard-copy map or photograph to the table. The analyst then identifies individual points on the map or photograph that can also be identified on a reference digital map or image displayed on the computer screen. The hard-copy map and the digital map displayed on the computer screen will most likely have completely different geometries. The relationship between the hard-copy *x,y* coordinates of selected features and the digital *x,y* coordinates of the same features is used to develop a geometric transformation that allows all the points, lines, or areas digitized on the map or aerial photograph to be registered with other spatial information in the GIS. This process is commonly called **table digitizing**.

On-screen Digitizing

On-screen digitizing requires that the map or image already be in a digital format having been scanned using one of the scanning instruments discussed in Chapter 3. The scanned map or image data are then rectified to a standard map projection. The digital map or image can then be displayed on the screen and the analyst uses the cursor to identify point, line, and/or area features of interest. The geometric characteristics of the objects of interest are saved for further analysis. Building perimeters are being extracted from the natural color orthophoto in Figure 11-1.

When digitizing from paper maps or digital maps and images, great care must be taken to assure that accurate information is obtained. As noted in Chapter 4, all spatial data contain error. The geometric accuracy of the source material after it has been geometrically rectified should be known (e.g., the root-mean-square-error—RMSE). Geometric error present in the rectified digital dataset will find its way into all derivative products.

Output Devices

A GIS should be able to output high-quality maps, images, charts, and diagrams in both small (e.g., A size plots 8.5 x 11 in.) or large formats (e.g., E size plots 36 x 48 in). To accomplish this, both small and large format printers are required. Inexpensive ink-jet or color laser printers can be used for small format printing, and E-sized plotters can be used for large formats. Other kinds of output devices include dye-sublimation printers and traditional pen plotters.

GIS Laboratories

A GIS laboratory consists of many networked personal computers or workstations that have GIS software installed on each computer or served from a central location. A hypothetical GIS laboratory is shown in Figure 1-9. A real GIS computer laboratory is shown in Figure 11-2. In this laboratory, the computers are connected via a local area network (LAN) that allows multiple users to access spatial data from a common source (e.g., a file server). All of the laboratory computers are connected to the Internet, which allows users to quickly and efficiently download existing spatial data and communicate with one another. All the computers have access to high-quality input (e.g., coordinate digitizing table, scanner) and output devices (E-size plotters and a color laser printer). Each computer has access to >5 TB of mass storage and the ability to backup important files locally or at a common repository. Whiteboards are present to list tasks and promote discussion among the GIS analysts. The digital overhead projector allows the instructor to demonstrate concepts and interactively perform GIS analysis.

GIS Data Storage and Archiving Considerations

Much money, time, and effort goes into the acquisition, analysis, and display of GIS data. Therefore, archiving the geospatial data is an important consideration. This section describes some of the different options available for temporary storage and long-term archiving of GIS data.

Rapid Access Mass Storage and Backup

To quickly access GIS data, users usually store the data on devices such as hard disks, CD-ROMs, DVDs, flash drives, and/or in the "cloud." This allows users to effectively store the data while still being able to quickly

FIGURE 11–2 This typical GIS computer laboratory consists of multiple high-end personal computers with single, very fast CPUs, access to >5 TB of mass storage, high resolution computer screens (up to 1920 x 1080) with 512 MB to 1 GB of video memory, cursors, connection to a local area network (LAN), and access to the Internet. All of the computers have access to the color laser printer and scanner and to several devices not shown including a digitizing table and E-size inkjet plotter. The digital overhead projector allows the instructor to display items of interest and perform real-time GIS analysis.

access it. It is common for GIS laboratories to have several terabytes of hard disk storage capacity. These large hard disks may be associated with personal computers or workstations or they may be network drives that are accessible by numerous workstations at one time. Flash drives are another useful way to store and back up data. In fact, many GIS analysts use flash drives to back up their GIS-related data every day. Commercial backup services are also available through numerous providers on the Internet. For a fee, they will back up hard drives and store data in real-time. These commercial backup services form the basis of "cloud computing," which is described in Chapter 12.

Ideally, each computer is backed up at least once every week. Useful and efficient backup and archiving programs are available for common operating systems. Writable CDs and DVDs are also used for quick backups and archiving.

Long-term Data Storage and Archiving

After a GIS project is completed, you will probably want to archive the data used in the project. The best media to archive GIS-related data appear to be DVDs with a projected longevity of >100 years under low humidity storage conditions. However, one must be certain to store the hardware necessary to extract data from the DVD in the future. It is wise to always store a complete computer system (e.g., the computer, monitor, keyboard, DVD player, etc.) that can read and write to the DVD media as part of the archiving process. This ensures that you can always access the data archived on a DVD in the future. Unfortunately, there are numerous stories about GIS users who carefully archived the data (e.g., on magnetic disks or tapes) but now do not have access to hardware and software that can read the archived data.

GIS Software Considerations

The GIS software selected is critical to the successful completion of the GIS project or research. A good rule of thumb is to always use GIS software that has a very good reputation. You may be making decisions based on the output from the GIS analysis that can impact people, flora, and fauna. Your reputation will be dependent upon how carefully you structure the research question or application and the proper use of algorithms and procedures within the GIS software.

GIS Software

Some commonly-used GIS software programs are listed in Table 11-1. The information provided in the table does not endorse any particular GIS software program. Before purchasing GIS software, analysts should carefully evaluate its functions and capabilities to see if they match current and potential GIS analysis requirements. In most cases, representatives from the GIS software companies will be pleased to visit and demonstrate the capability of their software. Analysts should ask the software representative to demonstrate specific types of geospatial analysis that are of special interest.

GIS software, much like computer operating systems and other software, has evolved from simple applications using "command line" instructions to user-friendly programs with sophisticated Graphical User Interfaces (GUI). This has enabled people to more comfortably use a GIS. Many GIS software programs are designed for specific purposes (e.g., hydrologic modeling using a GIS), while others contain a more comprehensive suite of GIS functions. There is no "one-size-fits-all" GIS software package that everyone should use. Below is a brief discussion of three commonly used GIS software programs: ArcGIS® for Desktop, GRASS, and IDRISI.

ArcGIS® for Desktop

The Environmental Systems Research Institute (Esri) markets the popular Arc series of GIS software. Esri is a market leader in GIS, and its GIS products include ArcGIS® for Desktop and ArcGIS® for Desktop Advanced. Almost all of the functionality necessary for vector and raster GIS operations are contained within this software. In addition, the software allows users to import many different kinds of vector and raster data. These data can be edited, analyzed, queried, and displayed in a number of ways. For additional functionality, Arc products typically provide extension modules that can be purchased for specific project applications. A spatial database engine that is very comprehensive and allows for advanced database modeling is also a part of Arc software.

Arc products run on both Windows and UNIX operating systems. Esri continues to release timely versions of Arc products that improve on existing releases. User comments and suggestions play a key role in the update and release of the software. Esri has a devoted following of users that are a significant resource when GIS problems or questions arise. The user-community maintains active blogs and usually responds quickly to GIS software questions. In addition, Esri provides access to a substantial amount of base geographic data that are provided with the software. These data can be downloaded from their website (www.Esri.com/data/free-data/index.html). As part of their GIS software, Esri provides web mapping services.

Esri has devoted substantial resources to developing ArcGIS® Online, a cloud-based GIS that uses Esri's cloud infrastructure. Currently, users may manage data, create and share maps, and access Esri's spatial dataset. Esri is expected to add more features and abilities to ArcGIS® Online in the future.

Arc products allow for easy user modification and enhancement. Esri provides an online site where Arc users are able to share computer code that can be integrated into the GIS. This is described in more detail in the Programming section of this chapter. More information about Esri software can be found at their website (www.Esri.com). The annual Esri User Conference in San Diego, CA, attracts thousands of users. It is the largest gathering of GIS-related professionals each year.

GRASS

The Geographic Resources Analysis Support System (GRASS) was developed by the U.S. Army Construction Engineering Research Laboratory from 1982 to 1995 as public-domain GIS software. Since that time, GRASS has evolved into a robust GIS with a wide range of users in many scientific areas. This raster-based software is **open-source** meaning that it can be downloaded, installed, and used without any cost or license fee to the user. GRASS is used in academic and commercial settings throughout the world.

GRASS has grown more complete as additional versions have been released. GRASS runs on most UNIX operating systems, including Linux, Solaris, and on the Mac OS. It can also run in Windows (natively or with optional Cygwin tools), although work is underway on an improved Windows version. GRASS provides raster, vector, image processing, remote sensing, 3-dimensional visualization, and cartographic functions. More information about GRASS, including how to download the software, can be found at its website (www.grass.fbk.eu/index.php).

IDRISI

IDRISI GIS and image processing software is developed and supported by the Clark Labs at Clark University. IDRISI is supported by the not-for-profit IDRISI Project. Users in 175 countries have adopted IDRISI GIS software products for diverse geospatial applications. These applications include natural re-

TABLE 11–1 Commonly-used GIS software programs and selected characteristics. The greater the capability, the greater the number of ***.

GIS Software	Operating System	Data Input	Vector/Raster Processing	Vector/Raster Data Handling	Carto-graphic Output	Integration of Remote Sensing
AccuGlobe	Windows	***	**	**	*	
AGIS	Windows		*	*		
ArcGIS® for Desktop	Windows	****	****	****	****	****
AUTOCAD	Windows/UNIX	***	***	***	****	***
AUTOCAD Raster Design	Windows/UNIX	*	***	****	**	***
Cadcorp SIS Map Modeller	Windows	**	***	***	**	*
Caliper Maptitude	Windows	****	***	***	****	
CARIS Carta	Windows	***	***	***	***	*
ERDAS ER Mapper	Window/UNIX	****	***	***	***	****
ERDAS IMAGINE (Intergraph)	Windows/UNIX	****	****	****	****	****
GRASS	Windows/Mac/ Linux/UNIX	***	****	****	****	**
IDRISI Taiga	Windows	****	****	****	****	****
ILWIS	Windows	**	***	***	*	***
Intergraph	Windows/UNIX	****	****	****	****	****
Kosmo Desktop	Windows/Linux	***	**	**	**	*
LandSerf	Windows/Mac/ Linux/UNIX	***	***	****	**	*
Manifold	Windows	****	****	**	*	
MapInfo	Windows/UNIX	***	***	***	****	**
OpenJump	Windows/Mac/ Linux/UNIX	**	**	**		
PCI Geomatica	Windows/UNIX	***	***	***	*	****
Quantum GIS	Windows/Mac/ Linux/UNIX	*	*	**	*	
SPRING	Windows/UNIX	***	***	***	**	***
SuperMap DeskPro	Windows/UNIX	***	***	***	*	

source management, land use planning, land cover mapping, environmental change analysis, and many others. The current version, IDRISI Taiga, runs on Windows computers.

IDRISI is primarily a raster-based GIS, but it also provides several stand-alone vector applications that enhance geographic analysis and output. One of these, CartaLinx, provides topology building and editing, feature extraction, and many other functions. This has helped IDRISI to expand its vector capabilities. IDRISI also developed a Land Change Modeler extension for both IDRISI and ArcGIS® software. The modeler analyzes and predicts land cover change and assesses the implications of change for biodiversity. More information about IDRISI can be found at their website (www.clarklabs.org).

Cost

Companies, public agencies, and academic institutions have limited financial resources that must be used carefully. Therefore, the cost of a commercial GIS software program is a serious consideration. Although the cost of GIS software has decreased in the past several years, it is still expensive. This may be the result of the still closed-source nature of most GIS software. The price for a single GIS software license is highest for commercial users, somewhat lower for public agencies, and much lower for academic institutions.

Open-source GIS

If software cost is a concern, open-source GIS, such as GRASS, may be the best solution. Other open-source GIS software is also available (e.g., Quantum GIS, PostGIS, and OpenGIS). Similar to commercial software, each open-source GIS software program will have strengths and weaknesses. It is suggested that users fully investigate the capabilities and reputation of open-source software before committing to it.

Operating System

Different types of GIS software are able to run on all of the major operating systems (Windows, Mac OS, etc.; Table 11-1). Users should select GIS software that runs using an operating system that they are comfortable with. This will help reduce the learning curve as you begin working with the GIS software. If you are going to run the GIS software on your personal computer, be aware that you may have to upgrade to a new or different operating system in order to run the GIS software. If you are installing the GIS on an existing computer you must also be sure that the computer has a sufficiently fast CPU, enough memory (RAM), and adequate hard disk space for the GIS software to run efficiently.

Data Capture and Data Formats

One of the most important considerations when choosing GIS software is determining what kinds of digital data it will accept, process, and output. A GIS should be able to input data in several ways. A digitizing table (Figure 3-11b) and/or on-screen digitizing (Figure 11-1) are commonly used to extract geometric information from hard-copy maps or aerial photographs. Of course, digitizing a paper map into a GIS goes beyond just tracing lines on a digitizing table. For example, when using high-quality GIS software, there are many tolerances and parameters that you can define so that the amount of error introduced when digitizing is minimized. After the digitized data have been input into a GIS, the software must allow the user to edit, analyze, query, and output the data as accurately and efficiently as possible. Some GIS software packages have both complete digitizing and editing functionality while others do not. Selecting GIS software that has a comprehensive digitizing capability can be very important, especially if a substantial amount of the data to be analyzed will come from hard-copy maps or aerial photographs.

You may be required to analyze spatial data that others have already digitized, scanned, or otherwise converted into a digital format. Therefore, support for importing spatial data provided in many different formats is an important consideration. For example, a GIS that is able to import a Joint Photographic Experts Group (*.jpeg or *.jpg) image will save time and frustration as this a very common raster data format. At a minimum, a GIS should be able to read and import the public-domain data commonly found on the Internet for both vector and raster data files. An example of this is the TIGER/MAF/Line files provided by the U.S. Bureau of the Census (www.census.gov). These data are topologically correct and can usually be used almost immediately for address-matching (geo-coding) and routing applications (Chapter 7). Another example is the shapefiles provided by the United States National Wetlands Inventory (www.nwi.gov). A good GIS should be able to import these data directly with minimal input from the user.

GIS analysts often receive data in uncommon formats. Ideally a GIS is able to quickly import these data. For example, many spatial datasets often come in the form of an ASCII text file. These files usually contain spatial (x, y, and z) data and attribute information. A GIS should be able to quickly read and import these ASCII data into a spatial data layer with an accompanying database that contains the attribute information.

Additional file formats you may need to import include Tagged Image File Format (*.tif), Windows Bitmap (*.bmp), ERDAS Imagine (*.img), and others. In addition, the GIS should be able to output to formats that support vector features, such as Adobe Illustrator (*.ai) or Encapsulated Postscript (*.eps). Maps produced using a GIS are often "freshened up" in graphic arts programs such as Adobe Illustrator.

Exporting data files or GIS databases in different GIS data formats is another consideration. The program must be able to output spatial data in formats that other GIS software packages can read. For example, the IDRISI GIS software can read spatial data output by ArcMap™ and vice-versa.

Incorporation of Vector, Raster, and GPS Data

Many GIS programs are either vector or raster-centric. The ability of a GIS to effectively integrate raster and vector data—even if the GIS favors one form of data over the other—is another consideration. Also, the ability to convert raster data to vector data and vector data to raster data is important. Data acquired from a Global Positioning System unit are critical to many GIS investigations. A GIS should be able to directly import data from GPS units.

Database Management

Database management is a critical capability found in high-quality GIS. As discussed in Chapter 5, the database forms much of the basis of GIS analysis and decision making. Purchasing a GIS with common and advanced database capabilities will ultimately make some tasks easier. Database management, maintenance, and multiple-user access are important considerations. Finally, the ability of the GIS to interface with external database management systems such as Oracle may make a difference when considering which GIS software to use. If you have a GIS without these capabilities, you may end up spending considerable time and resources trying to integrate these capabilities into your existing GIS.

Cartographic Output

Cartographic output, including maps, tables, charts, etc., is critical to most GIS projects. Chapter 10 provides fundamental information about how to prepare cartographic products using a GIS. Some GIS software have little or no capability to create high-quality cartographic products while others have great capability. When a GIS does not allow high-quality graphics to be exported as maps, charts, and figures, then an external graphic arts program must often be used, such as Adobe Illustrator. Having to purchase an additional graphic arts program increases the cost of GIS analysis and should be considered when determining what GIS software to purchase.

GIS Software Support

There is often a relatively steep learning curve associated with the use of GIS software. Therefore, the quality of the online manuals, help, and customer support are very important considerations.

Online Manuals and Help

Most GIS analysts rely heavily on the GIS software's online support. For example, the online user-friendly help interface for ArcGIS® for Desktop is shown in Figure 11-3. In this example, the user requested information about the attribute "Table Window" via the Table of Contents icon in the help menu. Information about selected topics can also be obtained using the "Favorites" tab or by providing keywords to the software's internal search engine.

Customer Support

GIS analysts occasionally need to speak with representatives from the GIS software company to help solve specific problems or issues with the software. These issues may range from software installation to software bugs encountered. The ability to call, send an email, or talk with a person who can help you quickly solve your problem is very valuable. GIS software vendors typically provide some level of customer service or support.

GIS Software User Groups

When a GIS software program has a large and relatively loyal following it is generally easier for the GIS analyst to find solutions to GIS-related problems. This is especially true when the software has formal or informal user groups that are active online. Usually, you can post a technical issue or problem at one of the user sites and multiple users will quickly respond. As you become more proficient in GIS, you should also participate and respond when you are able to provide meaningful feedback about a GIS-related question. This kind of participation helps everyone as the GIS user-community grows.

Software Maintenance Contracts

Some GIS software companies offer packages where users can purchase yearly maintenance contracts that provide annual updates of the software. This is critical if the need to maintain current software versions is important because of collaboration with other companies or individuals. The cost of software maintenance can be expensive, and it is usually billed in addition to the initial cost of the software. Also, be aware that many GIS software vendors now offer the fundamental GIS capabilities as a base product, but require you to purchase additional add-on or special purpose modules that may be essential to what you want to accomplish. This can be costly, especially when you thought the base product had all the capabilities you would need to perform the GIS analysis.

You may have little to say about the software you initially use. However, as time goes on and you gain experience, you will probably have the opportunity and responsibility to make decisions about GIS software. GIS software must be within budget, maintainable, user-friendly, and be able to perform all of the spatial analysis functions required. You will likely use the GIS

A User-friendly “Help” Interface

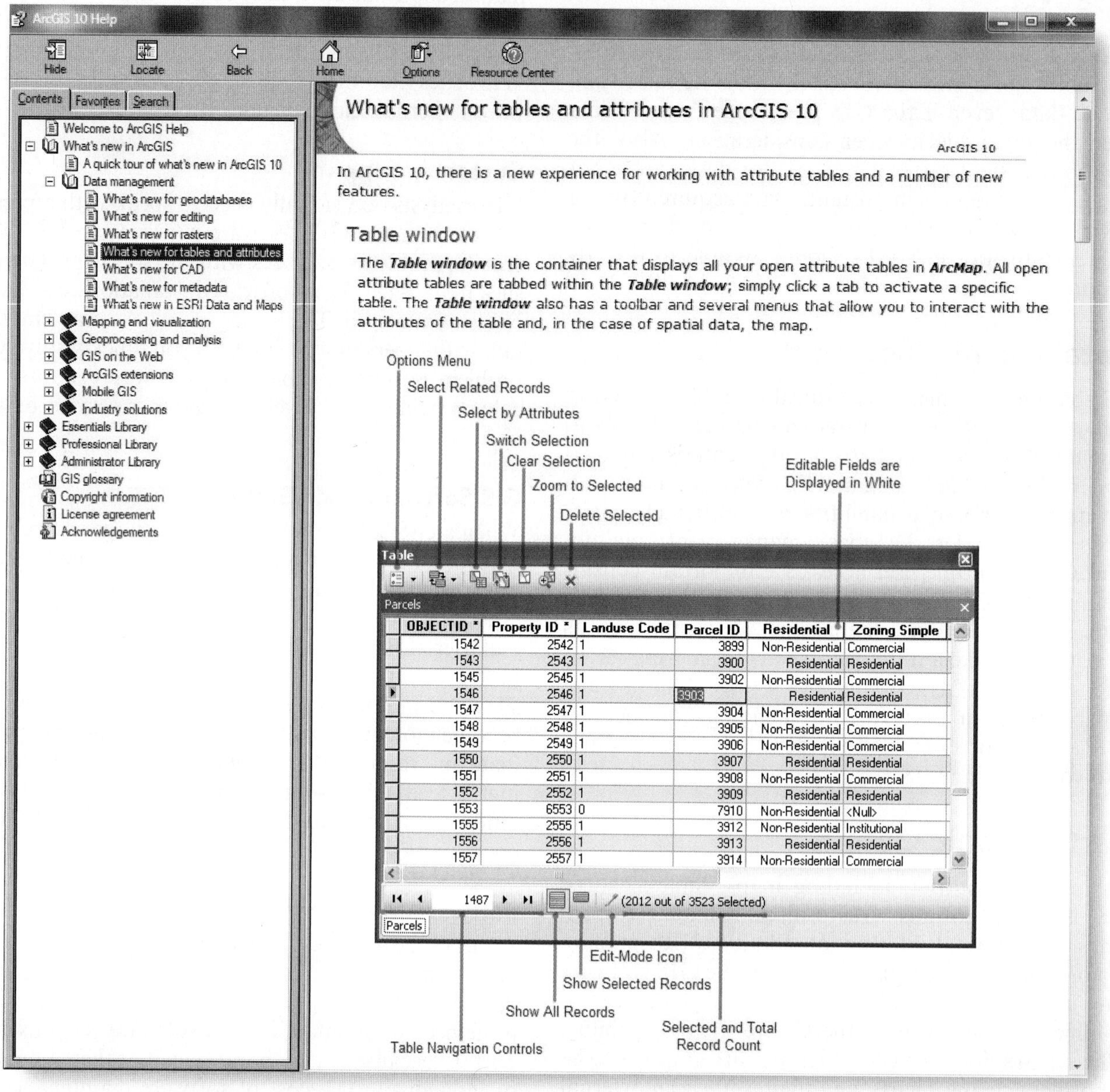

FIGURE 11–3 High-quality GIS software provides detailed online "Help" about a great variety of general and software specific topics. The GIS analyst can request help on a topic selected from a Table of Contents, from a list of favorite topics, or by providing key words to an internal search engine. This example provides detailed information about the "Table Window" in ArcGIS® and its various components (user interface courtesy of Esri, Inc.)

software for very diverse geospatial applications. Therefore, it is wise to select a GIS that has broad capabilities.

Online Training and/or Software Workshops

An efficient way to train new GIS users is through online training and/or software workshops. While these kinds of courses and materials do not always provide all of the GIS theory, they can help new GIS users become quickly acquainted with the operational characteristics of specific software programs. This may help to alleviate the pressure on other employees to train new GIS users to perform simple tasks. For example, Esri maintains a "Virtual Campus" suite of online classes that users can take at any time (www.training.Esri.com). These courses cover most of the basic GIS procedures and many of the more advanced modeling and geospatial analysis tasks.

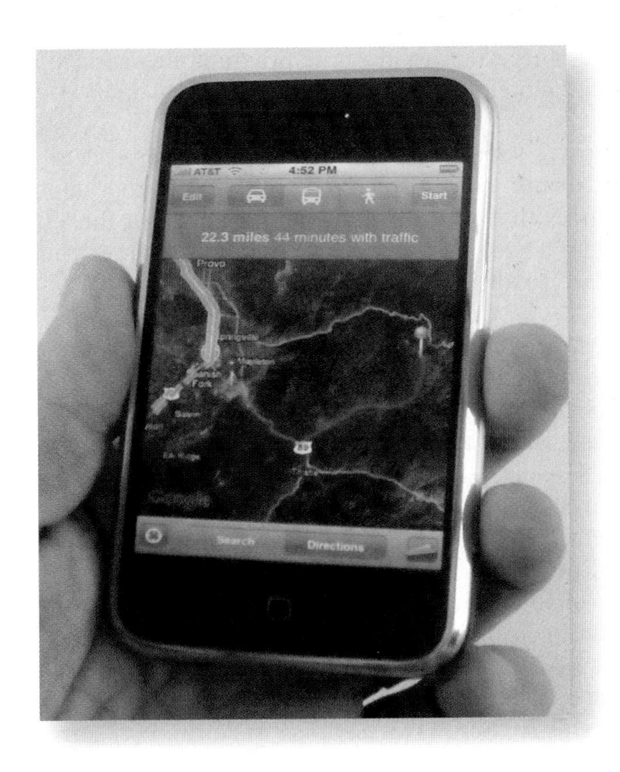

FIGURE 11–4 A cellular phone with navigation capability. The navigation capability is based on principles of GIS network analysis coupled with near real-time GPS positioning.

Integration of External Code and Software Modification

As discussed later in this chapter, you will probably encounter a time when the "out-of-the-box" GIS software does not perform a specific spatial analysis function you need. When this occurs, the ability to modify functions and/or add functionality to the software via programming is very important.

Hand-held GIS

As computer hardware has become more powerful (e.g., more and faster RAM, more and faster CPUs) it has also become miniaturized. In fact, cell phones and other hand-held devices now have incredible computing power. Because of this, GIS software has been developed for use on hand-held devices such as cell phones or personal digital assistants (PDAs).

Hand-held GIS software ranges from stand-alone programs such as Esri's *ArcPad* to more network-based mapping programs such as *Google Maps* and *MapQuest*. These mapping capabilities are available on hand-held devices such as the *iPhone* (Figure 11-4) and many *Android*-based smart phones. Stand-alone GIS software, such as that found on *ArcPad,* provides much of the functionality of larger GIS software programs, and also allows users in the field to add, modify, and/or query data in real time. For example, assume you are given the task of locating and documenting the attributes of all the trees in your hometown. This would probably require many days of field work where you identify each tree's location, species, height, diameter-at-breast-height (DBH), and leaf-area-index (LAI). A PDA that allows you to input all of this information along with GPS-measured location coordinates would be very helpful.

Programming and GIS

A review of current GIS job openings reveals that GIS computer programming is a very valuable skill. This is because GIS software does not always provide all the spatial data analysis functions, database manipulation, or cartographic output alternatives that might be needed. This does not mean that all GIS software is inadequate or poorly designed. Rather, it is simply a result of the dynamic nature of geographic and spatial analyses where questions, functions, and methods are continuously evolving. When a GIS software company is made aware of functions or procedures that are lacking, they often make an effort to develop new functions or procedures and release them in a future edition of the software. Unfortunately, GIS analysts cannot always wait until the function or procedure becomes available. Therefore, most high-quality GIS software provides ways for users to modify existing functions and/or add new functionality to the GIS software.

Below are some examples of special-purpose programs written to function within existing GIS software:

- the creation of a new map projection (Ipbuker and Bildirici, 2005),
- development of an algorithm to remove geometric distortion in hyperspectral imagery (Jensen et al., 2011),
- aggregation of spatial data obtained at multiple spatial scales (Strager and Rosenberger, 2007),
- advanced visualization techniques (Sorokine, 2007),
- the creation of a stand-alone GIS package with full vector and raster integration designed specifically for Amazon Basin research (Jensen et al., 2004).

When Should You Program?

GIS analysts who can program are never limited by the functionality of an existing GIS software program. If they can conceptualize a spatial analysis procedure, they should be able to program it. Computer code may be written that automatically 1) performs many spatial analysis tasks while you are away from the computer, 2) creates customized GIS interfaces, 3) performs repetitive tasks, and/or 4) automates complex GIS modeling.

An important question to ask when determining whether or not to create a program is: "Will it take more time to write, compile, and debug the new program than it will to complete the task manually?" Generally speaking, if doing the task manually is quicker, then you probably should not create a new program. However, if you will save time in the long run by writing a program for a fairly common task that you will use over and over again, then it is usually worth the effort to create the program—even if the initial programming will take longer than doing it manually.

The following section describes the basics of geographic programming and one of the programming languages commonly used for scripting in GIS applications and for stand-alone programs—Python. The section also describes a stand-alone application for geometrically correcting hyperspectral raster remote sensor data.

Computer Programming Basics

A computer program is a set of instructions used by the computer to complete a task or set of tasks. Computers understand only one language—machine language—and most early programs were written in this language. Fortunately, today very little programming is done in machine language. Modern computer programming allows users to write code in a user-friendly language that is compiled (or interpreted) into machine language—usually as an executable file or a library. In addition, computer programming has matured over the past 30 years, from procedural or in-line programming to object-oriented programming.

How Can You Learn to Program?

Learning a computer programming language can be difficult—especially given the complexity of computer language syntax and structure. However, beginning programmers should not be overwhelmed by the magnitude and capabilities of modern computer programming languages. Rather, they should focus on the small parts of the language that they will use and concentrate on how to use the language to create a useful GIS function. In addition, there are numerous tutorials and "cookbooks" that provide valuable programming basics. College students seeking to learn more about computer languages are encouraged to take an introductory programming class. However, an introductory programming class in a computer science department will probably not introduce you to many of the techniques necessary to integrate programming code into a GIS. Therefore, some college geography departments offer geographic programming courses that focus primarily on spatial analysis functions. Other college departments may also provide specific programming courses that present unique applications in their own fields. Those not in college can find online courses geared to all skill levels.

Most beginning programmers start by writing a simple GIS-related program. They then compile it, debug it, and add it to the functionality of the GIS software. This process takes time and effort. Seasoned programmers realize that if they have encountered a spatial analysis problem, chances are that other researchers or scientists have encountered exactly the same problem and may have already solved it. Therefore it is often useful to check web emporiums or other locations to see if the problem has already been solved.

One of the best Internet sites for GIS code and add-ins is Esri's ArcScripts (arcscripts.esri.com/). Esri software users post computer code at this location that expands the functionality of Esri software. The code can be searched by type of software (e.g., ArcMap™, ArcINFO, etc.), type of programming language (e.g, Visual Basic, C++, Python, etc.), and type of problem that the code addresses (e.g., advanced topology construction). Even if you cannot find code that directly addresses a specific need, you may still find code that addresses a similar problem to use as a starting point. Other Internet forums and textbooks can also provide solutions to many geographic computing problems and issues. People searching for specific geospatial functions can also type in the nature of the problem in any of the common search engines (e.g., *Google*, *Yahoo!*, etc.). Always make sure that proper credit is given when using another person's code to solve a problem or as a starting point in the creation of your own program to solve a problem.

Object-Oriented Programming

Object-Oriented Programming (OOP) relies on objects that contain discrete sections of code. These objects are called into programs on an as-needed basis and objects can be used in more than one program. One of the benefits of OOP is that objects or functions can be created that contain many of the same properties of existing objects (called "inheritance") and objects can contain other objects (Ralston, 2002). Object-oriented programming is a collection of cooperating objects, as opposed to the traditional view in which a program was seen as a collection of functions, or simply as a list of instructions to the computer. In OOP, each object is capable of receiving and processing data, and sending and receiving messages to or from other objects. Each

Visual Basic Window in ArcGIS®

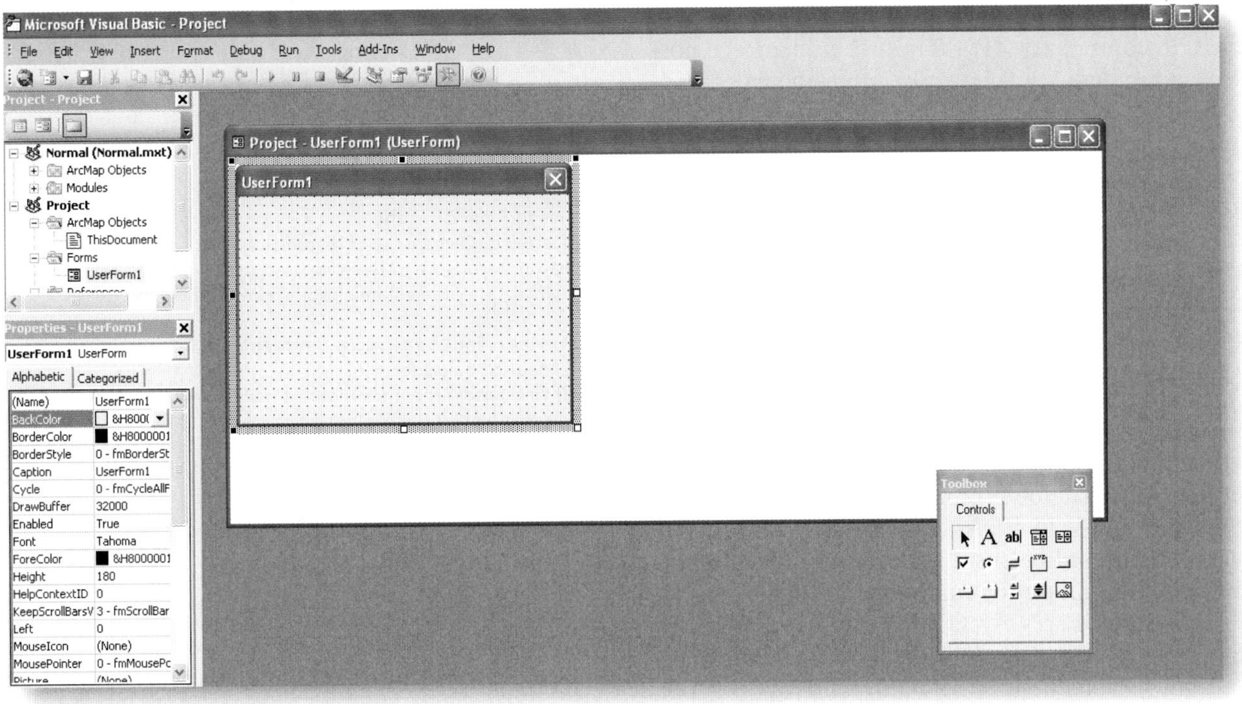

FIGURE 11–5 The Visual Basic Editor window available in ArcGIS® is used to integrate and/or modify functions (user-interface courtesy of Esri, Inc).

object is an independent set of instructions with distinct roles and responsibilities. This form of programming allows for relatively quick software development. Another OOP advantage is that it is easier to locate and fix errors within the code because you can compile and debug each object independently. Contrast this with trying to find an error when you have 10,000 lines of code. When called upon, objects within a program communicate with each other by sending messages between each other.

Objects are important because they are reusable in multiple programs and can be used incrementally to create large software systems. In the GIS community, this functionality allows users to expand existing software in small steps while error-checking throughout the process. Once an object is created, it can be enhanced for greater functionality and added to multiple programs. Therefore, many GIS users find that creating a geographic "toolbox" that contains many objects that can be quickly added to existing software is useful. In fact, the goal of a geographic programming course may be for each student in the class to create their own toolbox of programming objects that are most pertinent to their areas of interest. For example, a forester's toolbox might include functions that calculate the amount of biomass in a forest stand given basal area and/or leaf-area-index from a set of points.

ArcObjects It is relatively simple to add functionality in Esri's GIS sofware. A screen shot of the Visual Basic Editor window that can be accessed from ArcGIS® is shown in Figure 11-5. Within this Editor, there are a large number of objects defined for use in GIS analysis called **ArcObjects**. To use these objects, you are only required to know what the objects are and how they work. However, there are some challenges to using ArcObjects, such as you must have a basic understanding of computer programming languages, and the large number of objects can make it difficult to find the objects that you need. However, ArcObjects allows you to do everything that you can do in ArcGIS® for Desktop and more, thus giving users great flexibility. Esri provides charts that describe some of the basic properties of each object. In addition, Esri maintains an Esri Developer Network website (edn.Esri.com/) dedicated to integrating geography and mapping capabilities into applications.

Python—A Commonly Used Programming Language When GIS software was first developed, programmers and vendors quickly realized that there was a need for users to be able to modify the software to add functionality. Initially, vendors provided proprietary languages to accomplish this because there were no standard customizing systems available. However, today there are many computer languages that can be easily integrated into a GIS (e.g., C++, Visual Basic,

Delphi, Python, etc.). This chapter does not endorse or suggest a particular language. Rather, one programming language will be described that is commonly used in the GIS community—Python. It should also be noted that computer language syntax often changes rapidly. This should not keep you from learning a particular language because once you are able to program in a particular language, it is usually not very difficult to migrate to another language.

Python is a generic, interpreted scripting language that supports object-oriented computer programming (Karssenberg et al., 2007). Python's intellectual property rights are held and protected by the Python Software Foundation. Because Python is open-source, it is free to use—even for commercial products—and it can be distributed without cost or permission. Python is able to run on Windows, Linux/Unix, Mac OS X, OS/2, Amiga, hand-held PDAs, and mobile phones. Python has been used extensively in the GIS community and is the foundation for many of the functions that are currently in Esri's ArcGIS® suite. In fact, in the "Arc Toolbox" that is available in several ArcGIS® applications, users can right-click on many of the tools and select "Edit." A text window with Python code is opened where users can modify the existing function to meet their needs. The example in Figure 11-6 provides information about the Average Nearest Neighbor Python tool.

Also, the code in these functions can be copied and pasted into another window that can be used for an additional function. This is another example of using existing code and not starting from scratch when implementing code for additional functionality in a GIS. Python can be downloaded from www.python.org.

When you install ArcGIS® on your computer, you are usually required to install Python. This enables you to modify functions, create new functions, or to build stand-alone GIS programs that can be used any number of times. Researchers have used Python for data analysis, processing, statistical analysis, and many other applications since Esri released ArcGIS® version 9.0.1 (Shi, 2007).

In addition to the functionality that Python has within ArcGIS®, there is an environmental modeling language called PCRaster where Python also plays a large role. In PCRaster, you can install a Python extension that enables you to write functions in Python. Finally, Python can easily be used to "steer" code written in other languages (Oliphant, 2007). Thus, Python can be used to unify code written in a variety of different languages.

Example of the Python User-interface

```
File  Edit  Format  Run  Help  Windows  Help
"""
Tool Name: Average Nearest Neighbor
Source Name: NearestNeighbor.py
Version: ArcGIS 10
Author: ESRI

This tool performs the nearest neighbor measure of spatial
clustering. Given a set of features, it evaluates whether these
features are more or less clustered than we might expect by
chance.  The nearest neighbor approach involves:

(1) Measuring the distance between each feature and its
    nearest neighbor
(2) Calculating the mean nearest neighbor distance
    (observed)
(3) Calculating the mean nearest neighbor distance for
    theoretical random disribution (expected)
(4) Comparing the observed and expected by calculating a
    Z score for their difference.
(5) Displaying the results of whether or not the Z Score
    is significant
"""
################### Imports ###################

import os as OS
import sys as SYS
import subprocess as SUBPROCESS
import locale as LOCALE
from numpy import *
import Utilities as UTILS .....etc....
```

FIGURE 11–6 An example of the Python user-interface that is available to users by selecting the "Edit" option after right-clicking on many of the commands in Arc Toolbox. This particular tool is associated with computing the Average Nearest Neighbor (user-interface courtesy of Esri, Inc).

GIS Programming Integration

Often, the best way to perform specialized GIS analysis that is not provided in the software is to use the existing software interface (and objects) to create the functions. Python is often chosen for GIS programming integration because of its open source properties and the ease in using Python to integrate code into ArcGIS®.

Consider the following hypothetical situation. You need to determine the statistics of land cover classes in 500 m, 1000 m, and 1500 m buffers around deer vehicle collision points. How can you use scripting to assist in your task? What is the advantage of using scripting instead of the traditional method of accomplishing the same task?

One advantage is that once the method is scripted it becomes much faster than the traditional method. Another advantage is the ease of changing certain parameters of the model. For example, what if you wanted results using 800 m, 1600 m, and 2400 m buffers? It is easier to run the scripted version than the traditional method, which can take considerable time.

There are also disadvantages associated with scripted alternatives. Scripts can take longer to create, debug, and deploy. Also, if a script is not designed so that it is flexible for future applications or different users, then changing one thing can possibly break the whole script or cause it to behave in an unpredictable manner.

Stand-alone GIS Programming Applications

Occasionally it may be useful to create a stand-alone program that can be distributed to others without requiring any GIS software. An example of this may be if you would like to distribute a small program to your clients, but you don't think it is necessary for them to purchase a GIS software program. You could simply create an application that allows them to perform the special function — and perhaps not much else. For example, assume you are working with farmers to integrate precision agriculture techniques in the orange groves of south Florida. When the oranges are harvested, they are placed in a large plastic container called a "goat." A combine picks up each goat and deposits the oranges in the back of a truck. To determine general yield trends a farmer could collect a GPS point where each goat is collected. You could quickly develop a program that allows the farmer to plot the distribution of the collection points. The farmer could do this and predict general crop yields from certain parts of his or her farm without needing to purchase a full GIS/GPS software suite.

Python is a complete and complex program language that allows users to also create stand-alone programs to perform spatial analysis or other functions. The following example presents a case where raster hyperspectral imagery needed to be corrected using digitized lines (vectors) and carefully selected ground control points (Jensen et al., 2011).

Airborne hyperspectral data are acquired differently than aerial frame photography. Each line of an airborne push-broom image is collected perpendicular to the flight path and is independent from the preceding line. Each line has varying perspective geometric properties, and the ground location of pixels along each line can change dramatically from line to line because of the pitch, roll, and yaw of the aircraft. Unfortunately, these kinds of errors cannot be corrected using ground control points alone, and it is not possible to correct these errors with standard raster and vector GIS and remote-sensing software packages. Therefore, a Python program was written that incorporated traditional ground control points plus reference lines along roads or other linear features. The ground control points and the reference line data were identified in the reference image and in the uncorrected hyperspectal data (Figure 11-7a, b). The rectified hyperspectral data are overlaid on the orthophoto in Figure 11-7c (Jensen et al., 2011).

Summary

This chapter described some of the characteristics of the computers used to perform GIS analysis and information about GIS software. The chapter also described the importance of computer programming in a GIS environment. It is recommended that students who are planning to be GIS professionals learn the fundamental characteristics of a GIS-compatible computer programming language (e.g., Python). This will allow them to program new functions within existing GIS software or create new stand-alone programs. This will make the GIScientist more marketable as he or she is not limited by the capability of the standard GIS software.

Review Questions

1. Describe the differences between a personal computer and a computer workstation. Is one type of computer preferred over the other for GIS analysis?

2. What are the general characteristics of a GIS computer laboratory used for instructional purposes?

3. What are the best media to use to back up or archive GIS data in the near- and long-term?

4. Describe some of the main considerations when choosing a GIS software package.

5. Why is it necessary for GIS users to have access to graphic displays that have high spatial and spectral resolution?

6. Give an example of when you might use programming during a GIS project.

7. What is object-oriented programming and what is its significance to GIS software?

8. Describe the different types of computer memory and why they are important in GIS analysis.

9. Why are online user-groups associated with any type of GIS software important? How might they save you valuable time or resources?

Geometric Rectification of Hyperspectral Imagery Using a Python Script

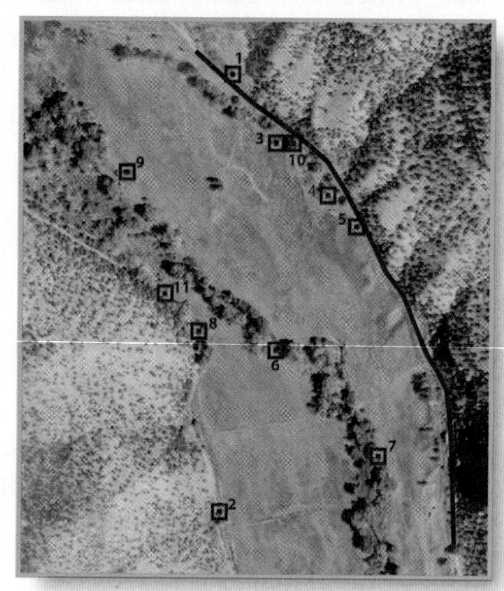

a. Geometrically correct reference orthophoto with control points and reference line.

b. Distorted hyperspectral image with control points and reference line (in red).

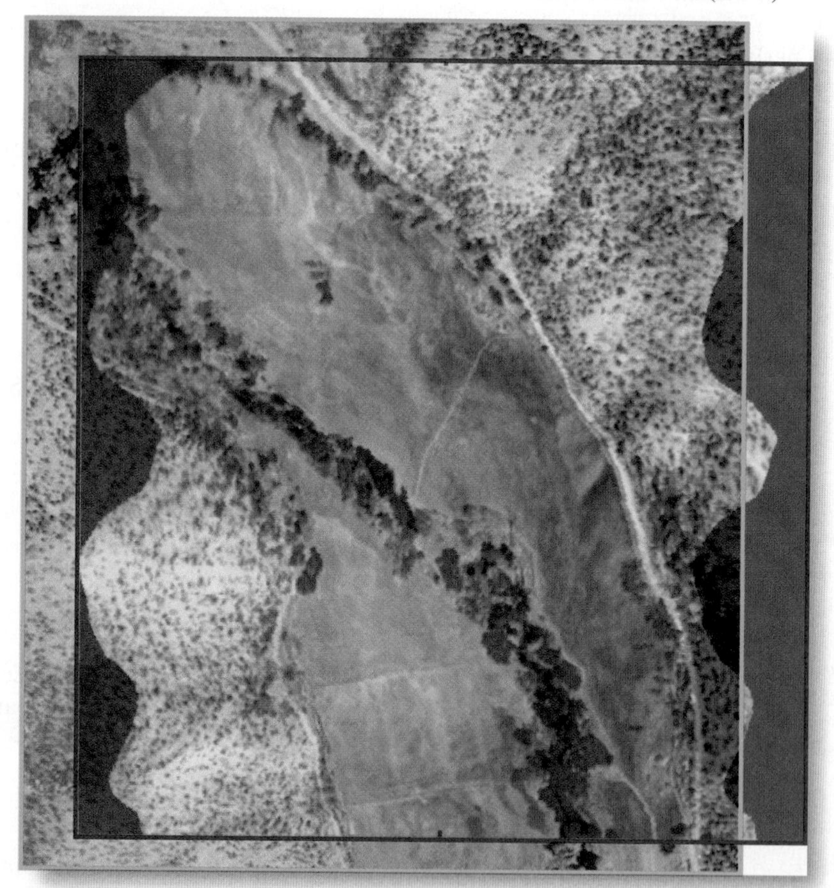

c. Geometrically corrected hyperspectral image overlaid on the reference image.

FIGURE 11–7 A Python program was used to geometrically correct distorted hyperspectral data. a) A 1 x 1 m spatial resolution NAIP orthophoto with ground control points and a control line in black. b) Distorted 2 x 2 m hyperspectral image (three of 248 bands displayed) with ground control points and control line in red. c) Geometrically corrected hyperspectral image overlaid on the NAIP orthophoto (background image courtesy of USDA; adapted from Jensen et al. [2011], courtesy of Bellwether Publishing, Ltd., used with permission).

10. When would it be necessary to create a stand-alone program rather than adding functionality to existing GIS software?

Glossary

ArcObjects: A set of spatial objects that can be easily integrated into Esri ArcGIS® software.

Central Processing Unit (CPU): The processing part of the computer that consists of a control unit and arithmetic logic unit.

Object-Oriented Programming: A computer programming method that uses objects to create applications and computer programs.

On-Screen Digitizing: The process of digitally tracing points, lines, and/or areas on digital maps or images displayed on the computer screen using a pointing device such as a mouse.

Open-Source Software: Software that can be downloaded, installed, and used without any cost or license fee to the user.

Operating System: Controls all of the computer's higher-order functions and resides in RAM at all times. It provides the user interface, controls multitasking, and handles input and output to the hard disk and all peripheral devices.

Python: A generic interpreted scripting language that supports object-oriented programming.

Random Access Memory (RAM): Memory that is lost when the power is turned off. A computer must have enough RAM for the operating system, software, and any spatial data that must be held in temporary memory.

Read Only Memory (ROM): Memory that retains information even after power is turned off.

Table Digitizing: The process of digitizing points, lines, and areas on a hard-copy map or image that is placed on a tablet digitizer.

References

Ipbuker, C. and I. O. Bildirici, 2005, "Computer Program for the Inverse Transformation of the Winkel Projection," *Journal of Surveying Engineering,* 131(4):125–129.

Jensen, J.R., 2005. *Introductory Digital Image Processing A Remote Sensing Perspective*, Upper Saddle River, NJ: Pearson Prentice Hall.

Jensen, R. R., Hardin, A. J., Hardin, P. J. and J. R. Jensen, 2011, "A New Method to Correct Push-broom Hyperspectral data Using Linear Features and Ground Control Points," *GIScience & Remote Sensing*, 48(4):416–431.

Jensen, R. R., Yu, G., Mausel, P., Lulla, V., Moran, E. and E. Brondizio, 2004, "An Integrated Approach to Amazon Research — the Amazon Information System," *Geocarto International,* 19(3):55–59.

Karssenberg, D. A., de Jong, K. and J. van de Kwast, 2007, "Modelling Landscape Dynamics with Python," *International Journal of Geographical Information Science*, 21(5):483–495.

Oliphant, T. E., 2007, "Python for Scientific Programming," *Computing in Science & Engineering*, 9(3):10–20.

Ralston, B. A., 2002, *Developing GIS Solutions with MapObjects and Visual Basic*, Albany, NY: Onword Press.

Shi, X., 2007, "Python for Internet GIS applications," *Computing in Science & Engineering*, 9(3):56–59.

Sorokine, A, 2007, "Implementation of a Parallel High-performance Visualization Technique in GRASS GIS," *Computers & Geosciences*, 33(5):685–695.

Strager, M.P. and R.S. Rosenberger, 2007, "Aggregating High-priority Landscape Areas to the Parcel Level: An Easement Implementation Tool," *Journal of Environmental Management*, 82(2):290–298.

12 Future Considerations

Courtesy of Dave Cowen and Mike Morgan, Univ. of South Carolina

The future of GIScience in general, and GIS in particular, is bright. The United States Department of Labor and other organizations have recognized GIS and its allied geotechnologies as a key emerging industry with numerous career opportunities (Gewin, 2004; Mondello et al., 2008; USDOL/ETA, 2011). GIS analysis procedures are robust, with technical improvements being made daily.

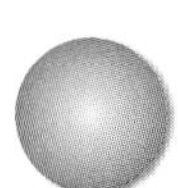

Overview

This chapter begins by discussing GIS career and education considerations. Wage and employment trends in GIS-related occupations are presented in addition to comments about public and private sector employment, certification, and continuing education. Various GIS technical considerations are discussed, including cloud computing and GIS; web-based GIS; mobile GIS; the collection of Volunteered Geographic Information; improvement in data formats and standards; and 3-dimensional visualization. Public access to geospatial data and legal/privacy issues are introduced. The chapter concludes with observations about the increased integration of remote-sensing science and GIS.

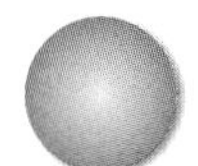

GIS Career and Education Considerations

People trained in GIScience, and GIS in particular, have the potential to be well-employed in the public or private sectors. If possible, they should also align themselves with the most appropriate professional organization that will help not only themselves but also the profession. GIS professionals should not be too narrow in expertise. They should know as much as possible about advances in GIS and in the other mapping science technologies (e.g., geodesy, surveying, GPS, cartography, and remote sensing). If possible, it would be beneficial to a) obtain initial and advanced degrees in GIScience, and/or b) become certified as a GIS professional and then participate in continuing education to stay current in the field. The following sections provide additional information on these important topics that may impact your future as a GIS professional.

GIS Careers in the Public and Private Sectors

Currently, there are many GIScience employment opportunities in the public or private sectors. The O*NET program is the nation's primary source of occupational information (USDOL/ETA, 2011). The O*NET database contains information on 974 standardized occupation-specific descriptors. The database, available to the public at no cost, is continually updated by surveying a broad range of workers from each occupation. A search of the O*Net database using the keyword "GIS" identified many GIS-related occupations and their wage and employment trends through 2018. Just a few of the GIS-related occupations are listed in Table 12-1.

It is clear from Table 12-1 that a) there are a great number of GIS-related jobs already in existence, b) there is significant demand for more people in the field from 2008 to 2018 (>100,000), with a projected growth in many occupations from 7% to ≥20%, and c) most of the GIS-related occupations pay well at the entry level. The top industries associated with the future occupa-

TABLE 12–1 Selected GIS-related occupations and wage and employment trends defined by the U.S. Department of Labor Employment and Training Administration (USDOL/ETA, 2011; O*Net Online, http://online.onetcenter.org/find/quick?s=gis).

Code	Occupation	Wages & Employment Trends
15-1199.04 15-1199.05	**Geographic Information Scientists and Technologists** **Geographic Information Systems Technicians**	Median wages (2010): $38.10 hour; $79,240 annual (for both codes) Employment (2008): 209,000 employees Projected job openings (2008–2018): 72,600 Projected growth rate: Average (7 to 13%) Top industries (2008): 1. Government 2. Professional, Scientific, and Technical Services
17-3031.02	**Mapping Technicians**	Median wages (2010): $18.22 hour; $37,900 annual Employment (2008): 77,000 employees Projected job openings (2008–2018): 29,400 Projected growth rate: Much faster than average (≥20%) Top industries (2008): 1. Professional, Scientific, and Technical Services 2. Government
17-1021.00	**Cartographers and Photogrammetrists**	Median wages (2010): $26.21 hour; $54,510 annual Employment (2008): 12,000 employees Projected job openings (2008–2018): 6,400 Projected growth rate: Much faster than average (≥20%) Top industries (2008): 1. Professional, Scientific, and Technical Services 2. Government
17-1022.01	**Geodetic Surveyors**	Median wages (2010): $26.39 hour; $54,880 annual Employment (2008): 58,000 employees Projected job openings (2008–2018): 23,300 Projected growth rate: Faster than average (14 to 19%) Top industries (2008): 1. Professional, Scientific, and Technical Services 2. Government
17-2099.01	**Remote Sensing Scientists and Technologists**	Median wages (2010): $45.57 hour; $94,780 annual Employment (2008): 27,000 employees Projected job openings (2008–2018): 10,100 Projected growth rate: Average (7 to 13%) Top industries (2008): 1. Government 2. Professional, Scientific, and Technical Services
19-3092.00	**Geographers**	Median wages (2010): $35.00 hour; $72,800 annual Employment (2008): 1,000 employees Projected growth (2008–2018): 1,000 Projected growth rate: Much faster than average (≥20%) Top industries (2008): 1. Government 2. Professional, Scientific, and Technical Services

Notes:
Projected Growth is the estimated change in total employment over the projection period (2008–2018).
Projected Job Openings represent openings due to growth and replacement.
Industries are broad groups of businesses or organizations with similar activities, products, or services. Occupations are considered part of an industry based on their employment. There are hundreds of specific occupations within the "Government" and within the "Professional, Scientific, and Technical Services" industries. Detailed occupation lists can be viewed at http://www.onetonline.org/find/industry?j=17-1022.01&i=93.

tions are "Government" or "Professional, Scientific, or Technical Services."

GIS Careers in the Public Sector

Public GIS employment will provide you with many opportunities to use GIS for the public good and to interact with citizens on a regular basis. Public employees trained in GIS help monitor and protect natural resources, plan our cities, and monitor and maintain our infrastructure (roads, waterways, etc.). National Homeland Security and defense-related agencies such as the National Geospatial-Intelligence Agency (NGA) will also be hiring a great number of GIS professionals in coming years.

Many people trained in GIS are drawn to public sector employment because of the perceived stability of employment. Although specific duties will vary by job, important aspects of GIS jobs will continue to be a) maintaining large spatial databases, b) integrating these databases with other databases, and c) conducting GIS analysis and modeling.

Working for a public agency will require you to provide regular reports/presentations to governmental organizations, such as city/county councils, planning agencies, public interest groups, etc. Therefore, verbal, written, and graphic communication skills are indispensable, particularly when describing the results and significance of GIS-related studies.

Unless formally "classified" as secret by the government, most of the data and projects that you work on in the public sector are available to the general public via Freedom of Information Act laws (discussed later). Public employees (except those in sensitive defense or homeland security-related occupations) are generally allowed to publish the results of their GIS-related studies in popular or peer-reviewed literature. GIScience professionals working in pubic colleges and universities are expected to publish their research in peer-reviewed journals.

GIS Careers in the Private Sector

Working for a private GIS-related firm will most likely require you to a) prepare proposals, often in response to a government or commercially sponsored Request for Proposal (RFP), and b) work on very specific projects with relatively tight schedules. Many private sector employees are able to propose very specific GIS-related projects that are of great interest to them. To some this is an important private sector consideration. Once again, verbal, written, and graphic communication skills are very important.

GIS-related data and results created while working in the private sector may be proprietary to the company or firm. You may or may not be allowed to publish your results in popular or refereed-journal literature. Proprietary methods, procedures, and patents are the life-blood of many commercial firms that must maintain a competitive intellectual and economic advantage to survive.

To help prepare you to perform well in both the public and private sectors, you should have a sound knowledge of GIS fundamental principles and be proficient using the most widely adopted GIS software.

Association with Professional Organizations

Professional organizations are usually nonprofit entities that seek to further a particular profession, the interests of people engaged in the profession, and the public interest in the profession. There are many professional organizations that help promote GIS in the United States and throughout the world. There are real benefits to belonging to some of the GIS-oriented professional organizations. Some of the major geospatial-related organizations and their unique characteristics are listed in Table 12-2. Additional geospatial organizations are identified in the Appendix.

As a GIS professional, it is important for you to contribute to the GIS community as a whole by joining and participating in professional organizations. Many of these professional organizations hold annual meetings, where GIS users come to present GIS research results. These conferences are excellent places to network with other GIS professionals and create professional relationships that may be mutually beneficial. Other benefits to participating in a professional organization include

- *Professional development*—Scholarly refereed journal publications, manuals, newsletters, websites, online resources, conferences, and many other venues provide members with support and development opportunities. Most GIS professionals have the desire to share their knowledge with others as they mature in their careers. Professional organizations provide an excellent medium to do so.
- *Employment opportunities*—Members have access to proprietary job opportunity announcements and lists that are constantly updated.
- *Current affairs*—The organization keeps its membership informed about major advancements in the field and political activities that may impact the profession or individuals in the profession.
- *Membership information*—Upon request, professional organizations may provide a list of members including member skills. This allows people to determine who to contact when they encounter specific problems or when they need advice on various topics. The membership list informs others about you, your skill set, and your organization or company.
- *Local and regional involvement*—Many national/international organizations have regional or local chapters where you can interact with professionals in your geographic region. These chapters help foster local professional relationships.
- *Resumé building*—Being a member of a professional organization is an important addition to your resumé. It suggests you have a serious commitment to the field.
- *Leadership opportunities*—Most professional organizations provide leadership development and service opportunities for its members through committee service and administrative positions. For example, members often serve on committees or

TABLE 12–2 GIS-related professional organizations.

Organization	Characteristics
American Congress on Surveying and Mapping (ACSM)	Founded in 1941, ACSM's goal is to advance the sciences of surveying and mapping and related fields. It consists of three independent member organizations with more than 5,000 surveyors, cartographers, and other geospatial professionals. On July 13, 2011, the ACSM Congress voted to turn over administrative and financial control of ACSM to the National Society of Professional Surveyors (NSPS), one of the member organizations (http://www.acsm.net/).
American Society for Photogrammetry & Remote Sensing (ASPRS)	ASPRS: The Imaging and Geospatial Information Society is a scientific association serving more than 7,000 professionals worldwide (http://www.asprs.org/). Its mission is to "promote the ethical application of active and passive sensors; the disciplines of photogrammetry, remote sensing, geographic information systems, and other supporting geospatial technologies; and to advance the understanding of geospatial and related sciences." It publishes *Photogrammetric Engineering & Remote Sensing.*
Association of American Geographers (AAG)	The AAG is a scientific and educational society founded in 1904. It has more than 10,000 members and 60 specialty groups, including: cartography, GIS, and remote sensing. It publishes the *Annals of the AAG* and the *Professional Geographer* (www.aag.org).
Canadian Association of Geographers (CAG)	Founded in 1951, the CAG is the national organization representing practicing geographers from public and private sectors and from universities (www.cag-acg.ca/en).
Cartography and Geographic Information Society (CaGIS)	CaGIS became an independent corporation in 2004. It is composed of educators, researchers, and practitioners involved in the design, creation, use, and dissemination of geographic information. It provides an effective network that connects professionals who work in the broad field of cartography and geographic information science both nationally and internationally. It publishes *Cartography and Geographic Information Science.*
European Umbrella Organization for Geographic Information (EUROGI)	Founded in 1993, EUROGI's mission is to maximize the availability, use, and exploitation of geographic information throughout Europe to ensure good governance, economic and social development, environmental protection and sustainability, and informed public participation (http://www.eurogi.org/).
Geospatial Information & Technology Association (GITA)	GITA is an educational association serving the global geospatial community. It is an advocate for anyone using geospatial technology to operate, maintain, and protect the infrastructure, which includes organizations such as utilities, telecommunications, and the public sector (http://www.gita.org/).
GIS Certification Institute	The institute offers certification as a Geographic Information Systems Professional (GISP). A GISP must meet the minimum standards for educational achievement, professional experience, and manner in which he or she contributes back to the profession. A GISP has their background scrutinized and reviewed by independent third party non-profit organizations (e.g., AAG, NSGIC, UCGIS, GITA, and URISA) (http://www.gisci.org/).
Management Association for Private Photogrammetric Surveyors (MAPPS)	Founded in 1982, MAPPS is the national association of commercial firms in the surveying, spatial data, and GIS fields in the United States. MAPPS member firms are engaged in surveying, photogrammetry, satellite and airborne remote sensing, aerial photography, hydrography, aerial and satellite image processing, GPS and GIS data collection and conversion services (http://www.mapps.org/).
University Consortium for Geographic Information Science (UCGIS)	Founded in 1991, the UCGIS emphasizes the multidisciplinary nature of GIS and the need for balance and cooperation among the numerous geospatial disciplines. Its goal is to serve as an effective, unified voice for the geographic information science research community (http://www.ucgis.org/).
North American Cartographic Information Society (NACIS)	Founded in 1981, NACIS promotes communication and cooperation among the producers, disseminators, curators, and users of cartographic information. It promotes and coordinates activities with all other professional organizations and institutions involved in cartographic information to improve graphicacy and understanding of cartographic materials through education (http://www.nacis.org/).
Urban and Regional Science Association (URISA)	Founded in 1963, URISA —*The Association for GIS Professionals*— is a provider of learning and knowledge for the GIS community. Its goal is to provide educational experiences and create a connected community. It is a multidisciplinary association where professionals from all parts of the spatial data community come together to share concerns and ideas (http://www.urisa.org/).

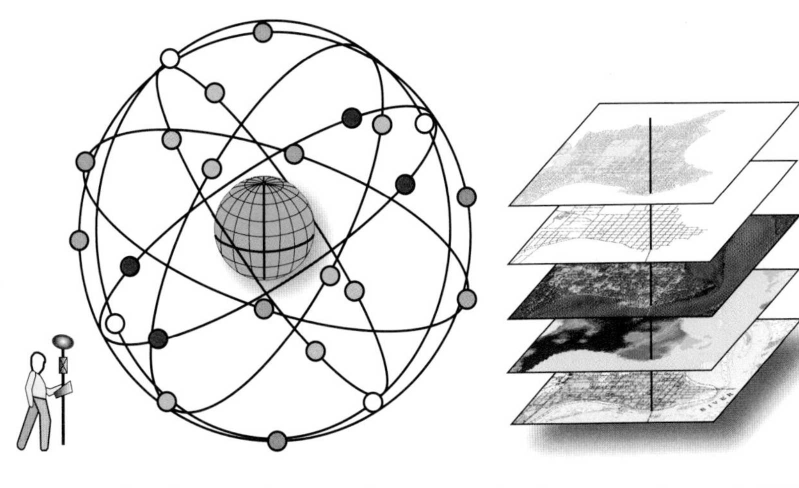

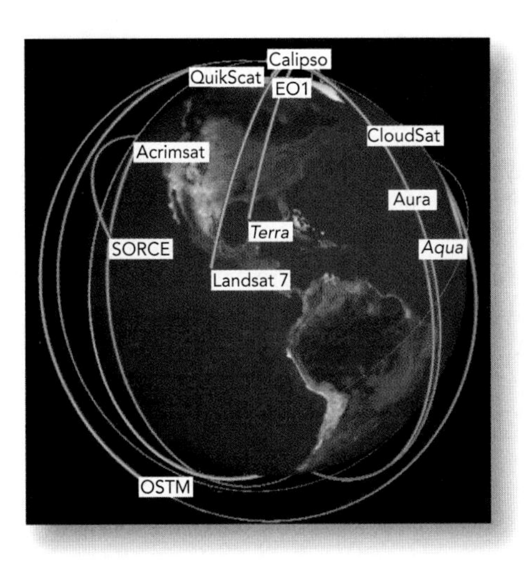

FIGURE 12–1 The mapping sciences include a) geodesy (including the use of global navigation satellite systems [GNSS] such as the U.S. GPS) and surveying; b) cartography and GIS (data courtesy of Beaufort County GIS Department); and c) remote sensing of the environment. The orbital tracks of 11 selected earth resource satellites on August 11, 2011, are shown [courtesy of NASA JPL (2011)]. These allied geotechnologies will continue to become even more integrated.

boards and can be elected to regional or national positions of leadership.

- *Political action*—Professional organizations often speak for the collective organization at various levels of government. In certain instances, they may retain lobbyists or organize political action committees to further the professional organization's goals or to protect its membership from unfair trade practices.
- *Continuing education*—Special workshops and continuing education courses are provided for continuing education credit. This is very important for maintaining specializations, registration, and/or certification.
- *Certification, registration programs*—Many societies or organizations provide rigorous certification or registration programs.

Unfortunately, many GIS professionals choose not to join professional organizations for a variety of reasons (e.g., not enough time; membership fees are considered too expensive; no desire to be part of an organization). Membership in professional societies or organizations helps keep you up to date technically and politically, engages you with other people with similar professional interests, and assists you with certification/recertification. It also demonstrates to potential future employers that you are serious about GIS as a profession.

Knowledge about Other Mapping Sciences (Geotechnologies)

Geodesy (including the use of global navigation satellite systems [GNSS] such as the U.S. Global Positioning System), surveying, cartography, GIS, and remote sensing constitute the **mapping sciences** or geotechnologies (Bossler et al., 2002) (Figure 12-1). Significant advances will continue to be made in all of these technologies. In addition, the technologies will become more integrated with one another. For example, GIS network analysis applications have benefited tremendously from more accurate road network centerline data obtained using GPS units mounted on specially prepared cars. Entire industries are now dependent on high spatial resolution satellite and airborne remote sensor data as geographic background imagery for their search engines (e.g., *Google Earth*, *Google Maps*, *Yahoo Maps*, *Bing Maps*). Remote-sensing data collection has benefited from advancements in GPS measurements that are used to improve the geometric accuracy of images and image-derived products that are used so heavily in GIS applications. Terrestrial surveying has been revolutionized by improvements in GPS technology, where measurements as accurate as ± 5 to 10 cm in x, y, and z are now possible.

It is important to constantly read and study about advances in the mapping sciences. The more knowledge you have about the characteristics of all of the geotechnologies, the higher the probability that you will make wise decisions when designing and conducting a GIS analysis or modeling project.

GIS Certificates, Certification, and Licensure

Many people believe that GIS-related professionals should be held to high ethical and data analysis standards so that the products they derive are as accurate as possible. There are several methods that can be used to document a GIS professional's ethical and technical GIS expertise, including

- GIS certificates,
- GIS certification, and/or
- licensure (registration).

It is useful to review the characteristics of these alternatives.

GIS Certificates

A **GIS certificate** is a formal award or acknowledgement given to a student after completing a sequence of academic courses or training programs. Many universities in the U.S. offer GIS certificates after students complete a sequence of GIS-related courses. For example, they may receive a bachelor's degree in geography or geoscience with a certificate in GIS. The certificate requirements are determined by the sponsoring institution. Unfortunately, at the present time there is no course content or certification standardization among institutions. Therefore, the value of a GIS certificate varies as a function of the certificate requirements, quality of the faculty or people providing the instruction, and where the certificate was awarded.

Some standardization of course content may be on the horizon as more institutions develop curriculum associated with the *Geographic Information Science & Technology Body of Knowledge* (Dibiase et al., 2006). In addition, the U.S. Geospatial Intelligence Foundation (USGIF) Accreditation Certification Program now enables colleges and universities to accredit their geospatial intelligence programs that accompany their college degrees. The USGIF Academy's Geospatial Intelligence Certification Program is the first of its kind and should help develop a well-qualified workforce for the geospatial intelligence community (http://usgif.org/education/accreditation).

GIS Certification

GIS certification is the process by which GIS professionals are recognized by an unbiased third party to have expertise in GIS. Certification requirements also vary by the organization that provides the certification. The certification process may require a) official documentation of formal academic education, degrees, and continuing education; b) years of service in the profession with *bona fide* GIS-related companies, universities, laboratories, etc.; c) passing a written or verbal examination; and/or d) letters of recommendation from respected professionals in the field who vouch for the applicant's knowledge and character.

Three major GIS certification programs include Geographic Information System Professionals, ASPRS Certification, and Esri Technical Certification.

The GIS Certification Institute The *GIS Certification Institute* (GISCI; http://www.gisci.org/) has certified more than 5,000 Geographic Information System Professionals (GISPs). To be certified, GIS professionals must document their experience in three areas: education, professional experience, and contributions to the profession. Points are awarded in each category, and minimum-point thresholds must be reached in each category and in total points to become a GISP. Of the three areas, more emphasis is placed on professional experience than education and professional contributions. Only those professionals who have at least four years of experience in GIS may be considered for certification. Each application is evaluated by an independent third-party organization and certification lasts for five years. After five years, certified professionals may apply for renewal, at which time the professional must document his or her continuing education, professional experience, and contributions to the profession again. This ensures that GIS professionals continue to educate themselves, develop professionally, and contribute to the profession. Also, all GISPs must agree to adhere to an ethical code of conduct.

The GISCI is considering implementing a test of basic GIS proficiency that would be required of all GISPs (Luccio, 2007). The addition of a written test would make the GISP certification more rigorous.

ASPRS Certification The American Society for Photogrammetry & Remote Sensing (ASPRS; http://www.asprs.org/) offers professional certification in several GIS-related areas:

- Certified Photogrammetrist,
- Certified Mapping Scientist—Remote Sensing, and
- Certified Mapping Scientist—GIS/LIS.

The minimum years in the profession varies with each certification area. A peer-review committee examines the applicant's experience, training, service to the profession, and four letters of recommendation from professionals in the field. The applicant must also pass a written examination in the area of specialization.

ASPRS also offers certification for *technologists* in each of the above categories for those with less professional experience. For those still in school, provisional certifications are available to senior and graduate-level students who have studied GIS and its allied technologies. In this case, students take the exam within 6-months of graduation and, if successful, the certification is provisional until the experience requirements are met.

ASPRS encourages certified persons to continue their professional development. ASPRS certified professionals must apply for recertification every five years, at which time they must document their continuing education in the field, their professional contributions to the field, and once again be recommended by four peers. It is not necessary at this time to sit for another exam.

Esri Technical Certification Esri provides software-specific certification for its GIS product line (http://training. Esri.com/certification/index.cfm). Esri's certification is available at both "Associate" and "Professional" levels in seven substantive areas in three GIS software environments, including Desktop, Developer, and Enterprise.

Esri's certification is based on tests (one test per level in each substantive area) that are administered throughout the world. The tests contain software specific questions that verify best practices. As such, Esri's certification options provide a way for employees (and potential employees) to demonstrate to their employers that they are proficient with Esri software and practices. Esri evaluates all test questions after a new software release to ensure that the questions are relevant and up to date with the software. Although software versions change regularly, those already certified maintain their certification for life. Unlike the other certification programs discussed, Esri's certification does not evaluate nor require any other information, such as education or professional service, for certification. To receive Esri Technical Certification, one simply needs to pass the test(s).

Potential GIS Licensure

GIS Licensure (sometimes referred to as registration) is the granting of a license to practice in a profession. Licensure is usually regulated by states or other governing bodies. Licensure requirements are often put forth in formal legislation (GISCI, 2011). For example, laws require you to have a license to practice medicine, to drive, to hunt, and to fish. The surveying profession has "model laws" in each state that require land surveyors to be registered. A photogrammetrist can also become a registered land surveyor. At the present time there are no "model laws" that require a GIS professional to become licensed or registered. This may change in the future. Perhaps all GIS professionals will eventually be required to be registered before they can perform GIS data analysis. This would have a tremendous impact on the GIS educational system and profession.

Continuing Education

GIS has changed remarkably since its inception and this trajectory is expected to continue as hardware and algorithms are continually improved (Baumann, 2009). Because of this, it will be necessary to continually educate yourself about advances in GIS hardware, software, data, and analysis techniques. Doing so will increase your marketability in the GIS industry. While at first this may seem difficult, continuing education is a hallmark of many fast-evolving professions like GIS. In fact, continuing education is an important part of the GISP and ASPRS certification process.

Many nonprofit organizations (e.g., ACSM, ASPRS), two-year community colleges, colleges, and universities offer continuing-education GIS-related courses. Most provide formal continuing-education credit for the courses. Some GIS software companies provide short courses and other education opportunities. For example, Esri's Virtual Campus (http://training.Esri.com/gateway/index.cfm) offers courses associated with much of its software.

You must be able to adapt to changes in your job description and to changes in the marketplace. The U.S. Department of Labor Statistics estimated in a 2010 News Release that an individual between the ages of 18 and 44 will change jobs 11 times in his or her lifetime (BLS, 2010). This kind of job/career movement makes it necessary for workers to be very flexible. Hopefully, you can stay within the GIS-related profession of your choice by constantly updating your knowledge and skills.

GIS Technical Considerations

With more and more people entering the field, geographic information science will continue to develop rapidly. More academics and private company scientists are working on GIS problems than ever before. The number of GIS users increases daily. The users provide feedback to GIScientists about what needs to be improved. This leads to constant improvement in GIS software and user-friendliness. The following subsections identify several important GIS technical considerations.

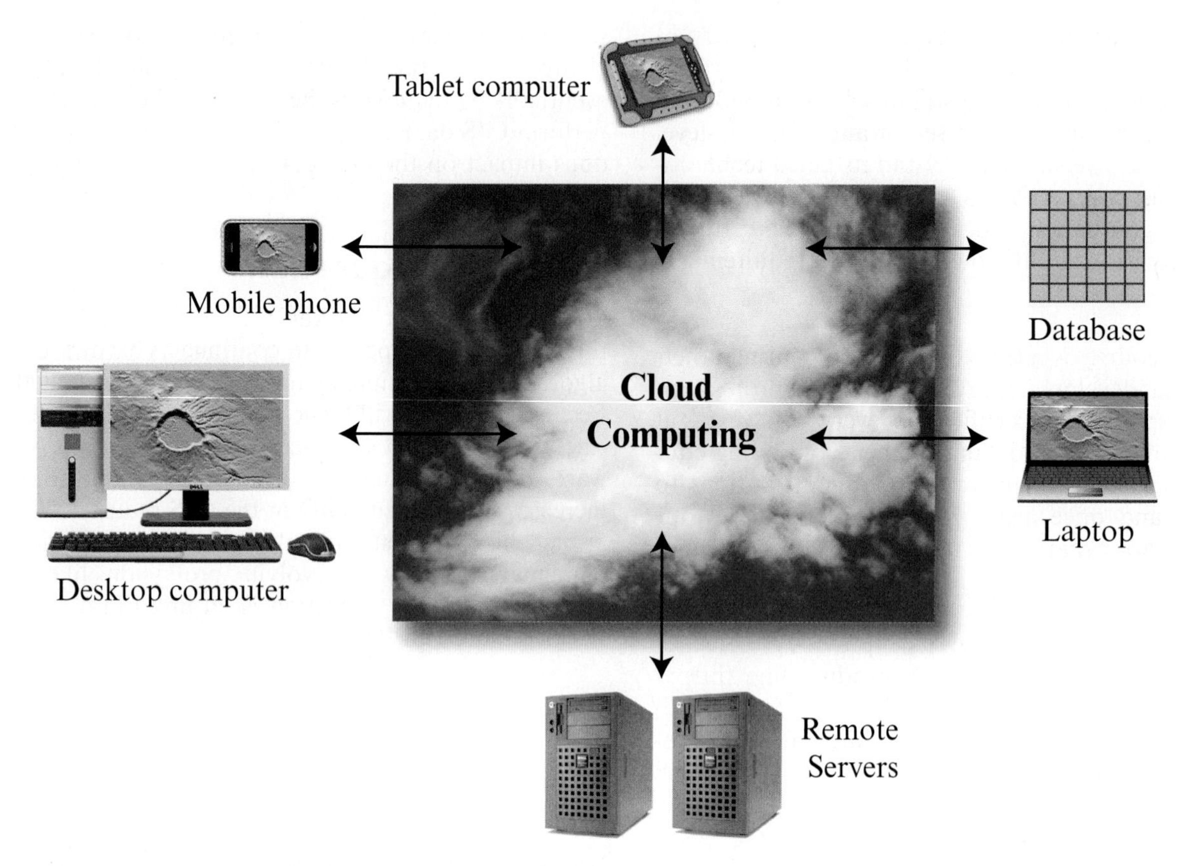

FIGURE 12–2 In a cloud-computing environment, remote servers typically serve GIS-related data and applications software to a variety of devices such as mobile phones, tablet computers, laptops, and desktop PCs. Cloud computing will become more important as cloud providers become more prevalent and the access speed to and from the cloud improves.

Cloud Computing and GIS

Cloud computing generally refers to the practice of storing data in a remote location that can be accessed via the Internet. However, this definition only scratches the surface of what cloud computing will become. Cloud computing is rapidly becoming a technological trend that almost every industry that provides or uses hardware, software, and data storage will utilize (Kouyoumjia, 2010). In addition to simple data storage, cloud computing also includes the serving of software from remote locations, minimizing the need to install software locally on single computers. The shift from locally installed software to true cloud computing and remote serving of software is just beginning (Hayes, 2008). Cloud computing is the next step in the evolution of on-demand information technology services and products. Cloud computing may eventually lead to a future where we do not compute on local computers. Rather, computing will occur on centralized facilities operated by third-party computer and data storage utilities. In a cloud-computing environment, the data or software stored on remote servers is provided via the Internet to all types of computers, as shown in Figure 12-2.

At the present, there are two main types of cloud computing: public and private. In the public cloud, the infrastructure and services are owned and sold by a separate organization. Data space on the public cloud is available to all computer users. Private cloud computing is available for companies or organizations that are not comfortable placing their data files in a public cloud. A private cloud provides data storage in a remote location that is maintained behind a restrictive firewall.

There are several advantages to cloud computing. The cloud is always on and always available as long as there is connection to the Internet. This results in increased availability of data, software and services at virtually any location. For example, data, software and services stored in the cloud can be accessed with any of the devices shown in Figure 12-2. This provides users access to both data and software anywhere at anytime using any technology. Most cloud-computing providers offer multiple storage and service models that fit customers' needs. In addition, most providers offer pay-as-you-go and try-before-you-buy for most of their services. This allows users to adjust their cloud resource usage through time and test out different cloud scenarios.

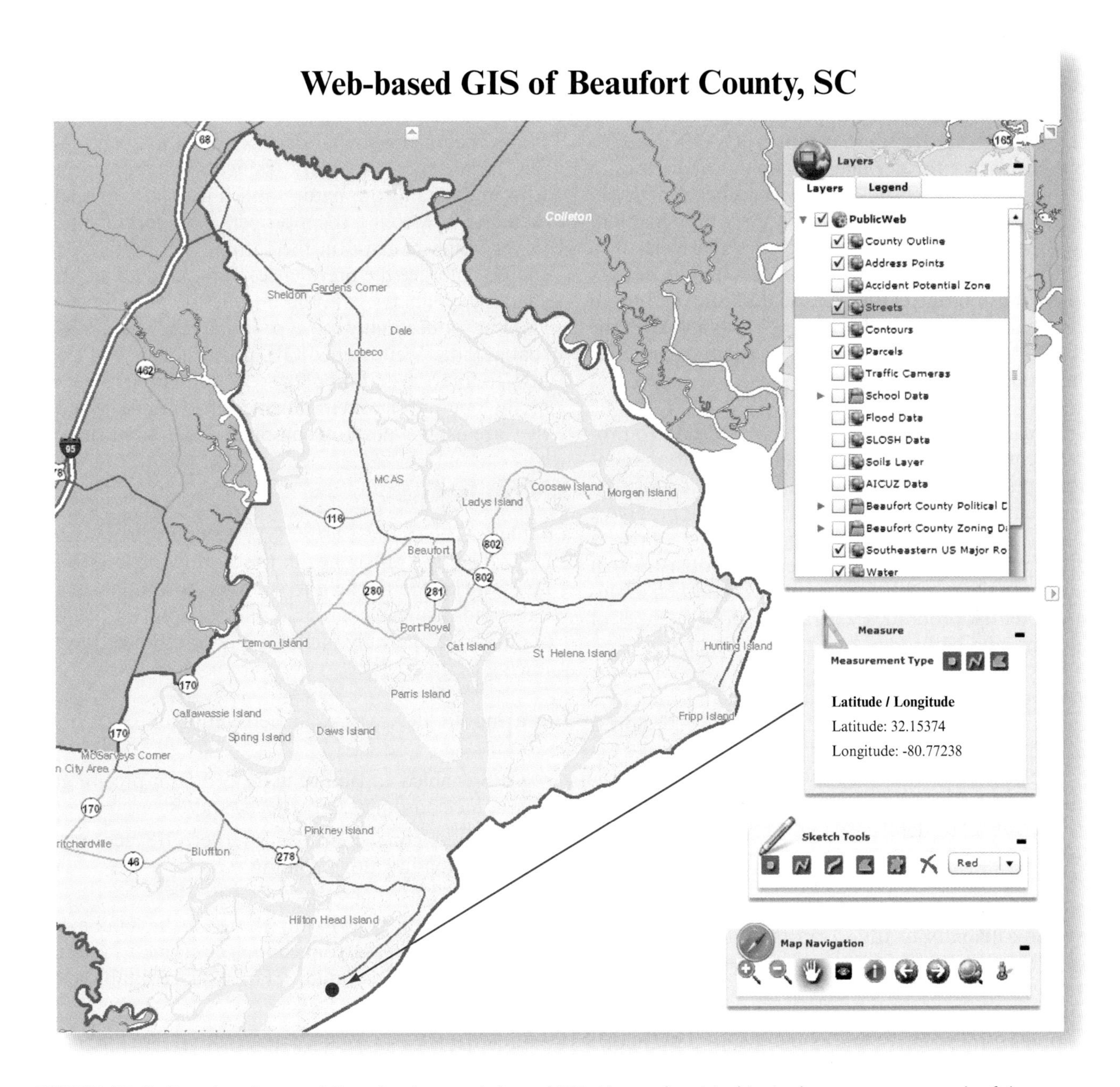

FIGURE 12–3 Beaufort County, SC, maintains a web-based GIS. Users who visit this site have access to much of the geospatial information the county maintains and also to selective GIS tools. Users may select multiple thematic layers to display on the map using the "Layers" window. Users may also navigate, measure, and sketch on the map. For example, the latitude/longitude coordinates of a user-selected location on Hilton Head Island (the red dot) are shown. A limited amount of data query may also be performed using online tools (courtesy of Beaufort County GIS Department).

While cloud storage and computing will continue to grow and evolve, there are some limitations. The data transfer rate between an individual computer and the cloud can be very slow. This is a serious problem when massive geospatial datasets must be accessed via the cloud. Privacy and security are two other concerns with cloud computing. In some cases, customer or government data security issues may preclude storing sensitive data on the cloud (Kouyoumjia, 2010).

Web-based GIS

Web-based GIS is the distribution of GIS data, data analysis, and other GIS-related services over the Internet (Figure 12-3). Web-based GIS usually does not require any GIS application software on an individual's computer. Rather, only an Internet connection and browser interface are required to access and use the web-based GIS software. While many web-based GIS software applications already exist, web-based GIS will continue to become more prevalent. In addition to the common mapping tools found online (e.g., *Google Maps, Yahoo! Maps, MapQuest, Bing Maps*), more and more private companies and public agencies will provide online GIS-mapping utilities for users to access. For example, the Beaufort County, SC, GIS Department currently provides many mapping capabilities to the public on its website (http://webgis.bcgov.net/publicsite/publicviewer.html#). Online users have many of the same tools and query capabilities that exist in a desktop GIS environment (Figure 12-3). The county administrators control the type, quality, and amount of geospatial and attribute data that are available over the web. Privacy issues are discussed in a subsequent section in this chapter.

Many real estate firms also use web-based GIS to provide agents and prospective buyers with up-to-date information about the location and features of property, apartments, and homes. These firms usually provide a web-based geographic search capability (e.g., within a certain part of the city or in a specific school district) in addition to the normal search criteria used when evaluating potential properties (e.g., asking price, number of bedrooms and bathrooms, square footage, etc.).

Many organizations provide spatial data and databases online, and websites are being continually developed that can directly process spatial data. For example, Esri's ArcXML provides ArcWeb services and Microsoft's web mapping service provides spatial functionality (Wadembere and Ssewanyana, 2010). Powerful web-mapping services such as *Google Earth, Yahoo!Maps, Bing Maps*, etc. will continue to improve their mapping capabilities and features. These vendors have the capability to transform the GIS software industry by making significant improvements to the existing geospatial software so that it becomes a web-based GIS system. Users will then be able to conduct all of their processing online using one of the vendor's special web-based GIS interfaces. In the beginning, it may not be possible to perform all of the GIS functions found within the major GIS software packages. But as time goes on, it is very likely that the free or inexpensive web-based GIS user interfaces will include more and more sophisticated tools for geospatial analysis and modeling.

Desktop versus Web-based GIS

With the increased mapping and analysis abilities of web-based mapping applications and programs, a few GIS professionals fear that too much web-based GIS functionality will make the importance of GIS professionals—and desktop GIS software—wane. However, as noted in multiple chapters in this book, the intelligent use of spatial data and spatial-data analysis requires a high level of knowledge about geospatial data and how to analyze or model it accurately. Many people who currently use web-mapping applications do not fully understand the limitations and issues associated with spatial data and spatial-data analysis, and therefore may make incorrect assumptions and decisions when using spatial data provided in a web-mapping application. Properly trained GIS professionals who understand the nature and limitations of spatial data and how to use them properly will continue to be in very high demand in the future. GIS professionals should embrace the prevalence of spatial data and GIS spatial data analysis via the Internet because these services introduce many more people to the usefulness of spatial data. Well-trained GIS professionals will know how to analyze and model geospatial data irrespective of the computing environment, for example, whether they are using a desktop computer or a mobile device.

Mobile GIS

Mobile GIS is the use of GIS technology and data away from the office, i.e., in the field. Mobile GIS enables workers in the field to capture, store, analyze, update, and display geographic information (Esri, 2007). Mobile GIS typically includes one or more of the following technologies:

- a mobile device (e.g., tablet computer, cell phone, etc.),
- GPS-enabled capability used to obtain precise geographic coordinates of objects, and/or
- a wireless connection for Internet GIS access and data uploading/downloading.

Mobile GIS will grow in importance as tablet computers and wireless data connections continue to improve and function more rapidly. For example, tablet GIS programs such as

- *TerraGIS* (http://www.fasterre.com/en/products/terrapad/terrapad.html),
- *GISRoam* (http://gisroam.com/),
- *PocketGIS* (http://www.pocket.co.uk/index.php), and
- *Star Pal* (http://www.starpal.com/)

are able to utilize the tablet's GPS and cellular data connections.

Mobile GIS software allows users to modify forms and input geographic and attribute information to the custom form(s). For example, assume you are given the task of cataloging all municipal-owned trees along streets in part of a city. A tablet computer with mobile GIS software, GPS capability, and a cellular data connection can be used to identify the spatial location of each tree. A custom-made form viewed on the mobile device can be populated with information about each

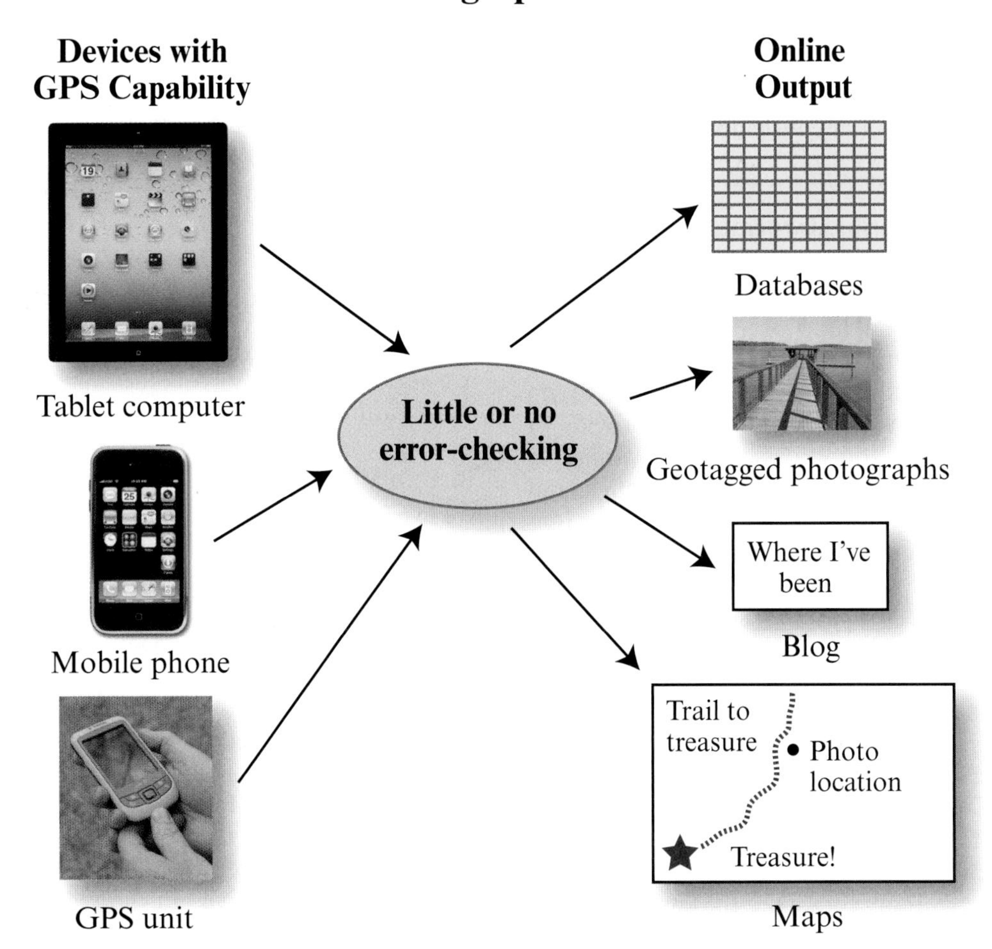

FIGURE 12–4 Volunteered geographic information is another important component of the future of GIS. More and more individuals will be able to contribute to the body of geographic knowledge. Unfortunately, the reliability (and therefore the usefulness) of the data must be carefully monitored as it is used in databases, blogs, and geospatial games and recreation (iPad 2 photograph courtesy of Alliance images / Alamy; iPhone photograph courtesy of D. Hurst / Alamy).

tree, including species name, common name, diameter-at-breast-height (DBH), and general condition of the tree. The geographic coordinates of the tree are input automatically via the tablet's GPS. A photograph of the tree can be obtained directly by the tablet and geotagged to the form. After inputting all of the information, the complete record can be uploaded to a central dataset via the cellular data connection and archived.

Mobile smart phones usually come equipped with some kind of mobile mapping software, such as *Google Maps*. Mobile mapping applications will become more powerful as cell phones and other mobile devices come equipped with improved GIS software, faster CPUs, larger screens, improved GPS capabilities, and faster Internet connections.

Volunteered Geographic Information

The Internet and the people that use and contribute to it are continuously changing. In fact, according to Flanagin and Metzger (2008), 35% of Internet users have created and posted content online, 26–34% have shared something that they created themselves online (e.g., photographs), about a third (32%) have rated a product, person, or service using an online rating system, 20% have created a personal profile that others can see, and approximately 8% have a blog. When coupled with the fact that more than 70% of adults in the U.S. are online, it is obvious that a large proportion of people in the U.S. are participating in the creation and use of information.

Volunteered Geographic Information (VGI) is created when Internet users voluntarily share geospatial information. Increased demand in recent years for free spatial data has spurred the growth of VGI (Zielstra and Hochmair, 2011) (Figure 12-4). The amount of spatial data is growing rapidly, the methods for obtaining spatial data are increasing, and the ways that people use spatial data are expanding. Web services that support user-generated or user-modified maps and spatial data continue to grow at a rapid pace. This has been spurred on by the increase in the number of devices that can easily collect and disseminate data with geographic attributes (Elwood, 2008). Cell phones and tablet computers geotag photographs with geographic coordinates that can be instantaneously uploaded to the Internet.

Volunteered Geographic Information Quality

The quality of VGI is a serious concern (Figure 12-4). For example, users are given an opportunity to tag photographs at geographic locations when using *Google Earth*. The locations of these photographs are generally considered to be "correct" with little or no oversight—although most programs do provide a "misplaced" reporting option or something similar to help identify misplaced features. Those who collect and ultimately post this information usually do so voluntarily and with little or no training. The results may or may not be accurate or reliable (Goodchild, 2007). Other places where users may post spatial data include *Wikimapia*, *OpenStreetMap*, and *GoogleMyMaps*.

Other spatial data, such as street networks, can also be uploaded for use on the Internet. Like geotagged photographs posted in a blog, these data have very little error-checking. Zielstra and Hochmair (2011) compared some of the differences between digital street data provided free to the public versus proprietary data available for sale. The authors compared the datasets on the basis of data quality and data completeness. They found that the open-source (free) data were generally more complete in rural areas while the purchased data tended to be more complete in urban areas.

The creation and use of VGI will expand tremendously. GIS professionals should carefully follow the literature on this topic to ensure that they use volunteered geographic information wisely.

Improvements in Data Formats and Standards

One of the most important issues in GIS continues to be the development of consistent data standards throughout the industry. According to the U.S. Federal Geographic Data Committee (FGDC, 2011), **data standards** facilitate the use, sharing, creation, and distribution of spatial data. Data standards define the format and use of spatial and tabular data. Despite these benefits, there is not one unifying data standard for GIS data. In the future, with the collective efforts of government, private industry, and GIS users, unifying GIS data standards will probably be developed.

There is also a great need to unify the standards for vector data, raster data, and geodatabases. There continues to be disagreement on specific data formats and other issues. Unified GIS data standards will facilitate having an "Open" GIS standard. An "Open" GIS standard will allow practitioners to use almost any type of computer or GIS software knowing that their data output will be compatible with all other GIS software systems. The Open Geospatial Consortium (OGC: http://www.opengeospatial.org/) has worked on data standards for many years.

Three-dimensional Visualization

Three-dimensional visualization of the terrain and urban infrastructure will become increasingly important in the future.

Terrain Visualization

We live in a 3-dimensional world. People have great experience navigating in and understanding the terrain portrayed in three dimensions. This is one of the reasons that the "Terrain" option is one of the major viewing alternatives on *Google Earth*. For example, consider the 3-dimensional visualization of the flat terrain in Utah Valley in Utah County, UT, which transitions into the rugged *Wasatch Mountains* shown in Figure 12-5. The first illustration presents the digital elevation model (DEM) using a simple grayscale scheme where darker shades represent lower elevations and brighter shades represent higher elevations (Figure 12-5a). It is informative but difficult to interpret. The original DEM subjected to analytical hillshading is shown in Figure 12-5b. It is even more informative because it displays the terrain with synthetic shadows falling toward the viewer, which increases the viewer's ability to identify important 3-dimensional terrain characteristics. Contours can easily be extracted from the DEM (Figure 12-5c). One-hundred-meter contours draped over the hill-shaded DEM provide a very informative terrain visualization experience (Figure 12-5d).

Improvements will continue to be made in the collection of accurate 3-dimensional terrain information using a) soft-copy photogrammetric software applied to stereoscopic aerial photography, b) LiDAR, and c) interferometric RADAR (discussed in Chapters 3 and 9).

Urban Infrastructure Visualization

Three-dimensional GIS analysis in urban/suburban environments will become very important. Improvements in terrestrial surveying using Total Stations (Chapter 3) and terrestrial LiDAR sensors will provide extremely accurate three-dimensional exterior and interior coordinate information to be used in 3D GIS building information models (BIM). For example, Figure 12-6 displays detailed building infrastructure information in three dimensions for a part of the University of South Carolina campus in Columbia, SC (Morgan,

3-Dimensional Terrain Visualization

Utah Valley and the *Wasatch Mountains*

a. 30 x 30 m Digital Elevation Model.

b. Hill-shaded DEM.

c. 100 m contours overlaid on DEM.

d. 100 m contours overlaid on hill-shaded DEM.

FIGURE 12–5 Visualization of the terrain in a part of Utah Valley in Utah County, UT. a) The original DEM. b) Analytically hill-shaded DEM. c) 100 m contours extracted from the original DEM. d) 100 m contours overlaid on the hillshaded DEM (data courtesy of the U.S. Geological Survey).

3-Dimensional Urban Infrastructure Visualization

a. Aerial photograph of a part of the University of South Carolina campus.

b. 3-dimensional extruded buildings.

c. Interior rooms in the 3-dimensional buildings.

FIGURE 12–6 Building interior 3-dimensional information will become increasingly important. a) An oblique aerial photograph of a part of the University of South Carolina. b) Three-dimensional buildings extruded. c) Individual rooms in the individual buildings (courtesy of Dave Cowen and M. Morgan, Dept. of Geography, University of South Carolina).

2010). An aerial oblique view of the terrain is shown in Figure 12-6a. Individual buildings are extruded to their true height in Figure 12-6b. Individual rooms within the extruded buildings are shown in Figure 12-6c. Planners and scientists will have increasing access to previously unavailable exterior and interior building infrastructure information for a variety of 3D GIS applications.

New spatial-data standards are being developed to more accurately and efficiently process the expected increase in 3-dimensional GIS analysis. For example, the Open Geospatial Consortium (OGC) is developing the *City Geography Markup Language* (*CityGML*). It is an open information model for the representation, storage, and exchange of virtual 3D city models. It provides a way to describe objects with respect to their geometry, topology, semantics, and appearance and it defines five different levels of detail. *CityGML* allows users to employ virtual 3D city models for sophisticated analysis and display tasks in different application domains such as pedestrian navigation, environmental simulations, urban data mining, facilities management, real estate appraisal, and location-based marketing (Open Geospatial Consortium, 2011).

Geospatial Public Access and Legal Considerations

Several legal issues will likely have an impact on the future of GIS, including public data access, GIS data liability, and invasion of privacy.

Public Data Access

The access to public data—including spatial data—is an important issue that GIS users will encounter in the future. Access to these data is usually legislated through the Freedom of Information Act or similar legislation.

Freedom of Information Act

Most government agencies must conform to freedom of information or open records laws that allow data collected at taxpayer expense to be made available to anyone who requests the data at the cost of data reproduction (e.g., the cost of the person's time to burn a CD and the cost of the CD itself). The **Freedom of Information Act (FOIA)** is a U.S. federal law that governs the disclosure of information and documents by the U.S. government. It was signed into law in 1966 and has been amended several times. FOIA gives any person the right to acquire federal agency records unless the records (or parts of the records) are protected. In 1996, the Electronic Freedom of Information Act Amendment was signed into law. This revised law makes it possible for people to have access to electronic information without making a formal FOIA request. This amendment is especially relevant to GIS and its users because many government agencies make spatial data available on a website that anyone can download and use. If spatial data that have been collected by the federal government are not available for download, a formal FOIA request may be made to the agency that collected the data. After making the formal request, the agency will usually provide the data at the cost of reproducing the data. Digital data provided by governmental agencies usually adhere to an accuracy standard.

Most states in the U.S. have some version of the FOIA—usually they are called *Open Records Acts* or *Sunshine Laws*. Specific regulations—including who may request the information and what they may do with it—vary by state. Local governments and municipalities may have different laws (or interpretations of laws) than other government entities. It is wise to investigate a government agency's policies before assuming that all public data will be made available. Before collecting any new data, it is best to determine if the data have already been collected by the government.

Creating, storing, and serving public GIS data is a costly endeavor for many government agencies. Furthermore, the expense of maintaining a publicly accessible GIS is considerable. Some public agencies have decided to recoup some of the cost of these operations by selling GIS-related data and data services to the public. Others argue that this activity contradicts the purpose of both *FOIA* and *Open Records Laws* because citizens have a right to free access to data acquired by public agencies. Any excessive fees for the data could limit that right.

Conversely, some data held by public agencies can be extremely valuable to private individuals or companies who use the data for economic gain. These people or companies could probably afford to pay for the data. Their demand for "free" data can place a large burden on the public agencies responsible for providing the data. Therefore, public agencies often make decisions about the distribution of geospatial data on a case-by-case basis.

GIS Data Liability

Access to data collected by public government agencies has also raised various liability concerns. Spatial data are usually acquired for a very specific purpose. Sometimes the data are subsequently used for completely different or even inappropriate purposes. For example, if a dataset was designed to be used in a regional study

GIS Liability Statement

Data Access and Usage Agreement

GIS Services

Division of Information and Operations

Sedgwick County Government

Sedgwick County, Kansas

Please Read Carefully

It is understood that, while Sedgwick County Geographic Information Services (SCGIS), City of Wichita GIS, (data suppliers of the aerial photography and the road centerline within Wichita), participating agencies, and information suppliers, have no indication and reason to believe that there are inaccuracies in information provided, SCGIS, its suppliers make no representations of any kind, including, but not limited to, warranties of mechantability or fitness for a particular use, nor are any such warranties to be implied with respect to the information, data or service furnished herein. In no event shall the Data Providers become liable to users of these data, or any other party, for any loss or damages, consequential or otherwise, including but not limited to time, money, or goodwill, arising from the use, operation or modification of the data. In using these data, users further agree to indemnify, defend, and hold harmless the Data Providers for any and all liability of any nature arising out of or resulting from the lack of accuracy or correctness of the data, or the use of the data. No person shall sell, give or receive for the purpose of selling or offering for sale, any portion of the information provided herein.

I Agree

FIGURE 12–7 Sedgwick County Geographic Information Services (SCGIS) requests potential users to agree to a data access and usage agreement. The goal is to protect the county from inappropriate use of publicly available geographic information (courtesy Sedgwick County Geographic Information Services, http://gis.sedgwick.gov/; © Copyright, 2011, Sedgwick County, Kansas).

that crosses multiple state lines or perhaps multiple ecosystems, it might be inappropriate to use the dataset for a local-scale study. When this occurs, it is possible that inaccurate conclusions could be drawn from the data or poor decisions made.

Therefore, just as maps often have a liability statement that describes their intended use and limitations, many government agencies describe the liability of their GIS data and data products. This is done to ensure that the public agency is not liable for poor decisions made using the spatial data or for possibly illegal actions. Often, potential users of the geospatial data are required to acknowledge that they have read and understand the liability statement before they are permitted to download the data. For example, consider the Sedgwick County Kansas Geographic Information Services data access and usage agreement shown in Figure 12-7. Statements such as these will become more prevalent as public agencies protect themselves from inappropriate use of publicly available geographic information.

Fourth Amendment Privacy Considerations

Onsrud et al. (1994) raised concerns about combining geographic datasets with other databases and making these combined data available to the public. They stated that some GIS datasets—although legal—may be highly controversial and considered intrusive to most citizens. Many of their original concerns are relevant today. In his book *Spying with Maps*, Monmonier

Inground Pools in a Residential Neighborhood

FIGURE 12–8 It is a straightforward task to identify the location of all the inground swimming pools using high spatial resolution aerial photography. The intersection of the location (address) of the swimming pools with a list of current swimming pool permits is an easy way to identify unpermitted pools (photography courtesy of Lexington County Property, Mapping and Data Services).

(2002) warned readers to beware of the unintended consequences of otherwise benign uses of GIS and spatial data.

In the United States, the Fourth Amendment guarantees freedom from unreasonable search. Unreasonable search is an important legal consideration that will likely play a significant role in the use or misuse of geospatial information in the future. For example, high-spatial-resolution remote-sensor data have been available for many decades. However, the placement of such data in a GIS and the analysis of the data by local governments to monitor compliance is considered by some to be unreasonable search. Below are some examples of what many would consider unreasonable search.

- The town of Riverhead, NY, used *Google Earth* image data to locate all the swimming pools in the city. This information was intersected with a list of current swimming pool permits. The city discovered about 250 unpermitted pools. The city subsequently required pool owners to obtain the required permits or be fined (Elgan, 2010). The process is straightforward to implement, as demonstrated in Figure 12-8 using an entirely different southeastern U.S. residential neighborhood.
- Many municipalities mandate a minimum amount of insulation in homes to reduce energy consumption. To help ensure that all homes meet this minimum amount, does a government official driving down the street or flying overhead in a helicopter on a cold winter day with a scanning thermal infrared thermometer have the right to examine your home to determine if it has adequate insulation?
- Does your cellular phone company have the right to distribute locational information gathered by your mobile phone to law enforcement if you are suspected of a crime?
- Does a rental car company have the right to monitor the speed of the cars? If so, can the rental company charge a premium if the renter regularly exceeds the speed limit? A rental car company in Connecticut tracked its customers by GPS and fined them for exceeding 79 miles per hour (Monmonier, 2002).
- Does a government agency or company have the right to create and/or share spatial data and information about your home or land (appraised value, square footage, number of bedrooms and bathrooms, building footprint, etc.) that can then be queried by anyone? In the United Kingdom, thieves used *Google Earth* imagery to identify backyard ponds where rare fish were located. The thieves

broke into the backyards and stole the fish that they intended to sell later (Elgan, 2010).

- Some data providers routinely provide terrestrial profile views of all the properties on both sides of the road. Sometimes these photographs capture images of people on the street at the time of data acquisition and even people inside their homes or offices. Is this an invasion of privacy?
- Does the government have the right to collect geospatial information about your property to determine if there are illegal activities taking place? For example, it is a simple matter to obtain high-spatial-resolution aerial photography to identify small marijuana plots being grown outside. High spatial resolution thermal infrared imagery can in certain instances be used to identify extremely high-temperature buildings where methamphetamine is being manufactured or marijuana plants are being grown inside.

What constitutes illegal search and/or invasion of privacy will become very important topics that will impact the type of data that can be collected, shared, and analyzed using a GIS. It is important that GIS practitioners stay up to date on such legal matters. A GIS with appropriate data can be used to improve the quality of life or it can be used for illegal purposes. GIS practitioners must be law-abiding citizens with ethical values.

People often unknowningly give up personal information. For example, the photographs obtained using personal cellular phones or digital cameras are often automatically geotagged with precise geographic information (latitude and longitude) about the location where the photograph was taken. While this is a wonderful source of information to identify where and when a photograph was acquired, many people do not realize this information was collected. They often post the photograph online (e.g., in a blog), and the privacy of the individual is unwittingly compromised. For example, Figure 12-9 contains geographic and other information about a geotagged photograph.

Information in a Typical Geotagged Photograph

File	
	Name: Image.121.jpg
	Size: 939 KB
	Modified: 08.11.11 12.33.17 pm
	Imported: 08.11.11 12.35.08 pm
Exposure	
	Shutter: 1/211
	Aperture: *f* / 2.8
	Exposure: Normal program
	Focal Length: 3.85 mm
	Sensing: One-chip color area
	Flash: Off
	Metering: Average
	ISO Speed: 64
	GPS Latitude: 40° 14′ 42.60″ N
	GPS Longitude: 111° 38′ 21.60″ W

FIGURE 12–9 An image taken by a personal cell phone or digital camera may contain information about shutter speed, focal length, and geographic location. In this example, the latitude and longitude values were also saved with the photograph. Many users do not realize their photographs are geotagged and unwittingly allow others to know where the photograph was taken.

Integration of Remote Sensing and GIS

Improvement in remote-sensing science will have a significant impact on GIS. Advances in the number of data-collection platforms and platform stability will improve the timeliness and spatial accuracy of remote-sensing–derived products. Advances in the sensor systems placed on the platforms will provide new types of biophysical and urban/surburban information for use in GIS investigations. Improvement in remote-sensing digital image processing will extract more useful and accurate geospatial information.

Advances in Data Collection Platforms

Satellite, suborbital aircraft, and mobile (e.g., car or van) platforms are becoming more reliable. Improvement in inertial guidance systems and GPS allow for more accurate information about the platform position and orientation at the time the remote sensor data are collected. This improves the ability to more accurately geometrically rectify the remote-sensing–derived products. The more geometrically accurate the remote sensor data, the easier it is to place the data in a GIS where it can be modeled with other geospatial information.

There will also be an increased use of unmanned aerial vehicles (UAV). Numerous vendors now provide relatively inexpensive stand-alone systems that can be programmed to obtain different types of remote sensor data over areas at user-specified altitudes. The use of UAVs will continue to be strictly controlled by federal aeronautics agencies to protect the public from objects falling out of the sky.

Advances in Remote Sensing Systems

Engineers are constantly developing improved remote-sensing systems that collect entirely new or improved remote sensor data. For example, NASA's proposed Hyperspectral Infrared Imager (HyspIRI) to be launched 2013–2016, will have increased spectral sensitivity in hundreds of spectral bands from 380 to 2500 nm with 60 x 60 m spatial resolution (NASA, 2011). Numerous agencies around the world are developing improved synthetic aperture RADAR (SAR) systems that obtain data in multiple frequencies and polarizations (PolSAR), providing data both day and night and during inclement weather. Ground-penetrating RADAR (the sensor is placed on the ground) is revolutionizing the detection of objects below the ground surface. Anthropologists and civil engineers use the sub-surface geospatial information to determine where to excavate.

Significant advancements in airborne and terrestrial LiDAR data collection are taking place that will improve the quality of natural and urban digital elevation models and provide detailed biophysical information about vegetation (especially forest characteristics) (e.g., Maidment et al., 2007; Raber, 2007). Airborne bathymetric LiDAR provides detailed sub-surface bathymetric information in relatively shallow waterbodies. Terrestrial LiDAR (the sensor is placed on the ground) is being used to densify 3-dimensional information about buildings, overpasses, topography, trees, etc. This type of information is also heavily used by the motion picture industry to create synthetic 3-dimensional views of cities for manipulation using digital image processing.

Organizations and government agencies are mining historical remote sensor data to prepare national or worldwide image mosaics and/or change detection products. Typical datasets include Landsat imagery of the world (Esri, 2011a), land cover, biomass, impervious surface, elevation, tree canopy (USGS, 2011), and urban extent (Schneider et al., 2009). See the Appendix for additional types of remote-sensing–related geospatial products.

Until recently it was not possible for remote-sensing instruments to see inside most structures. New terrestrial Z-backscattering X-ray technology (the sensor is stationary on the ground or can be placed in a van) can penetrate relatively thick metal containers, tractor trailers, and homes. The photo-like X-ray image is especially good at locating soft, fleshy material like bananas, vegetation, and human bodies (American Science and Engineering, 2011). This remote-sensing technology is being used operationally to locate explosives, persons hiding in cars or trucks, and illicit drugs. This technology can also be used to save lives such as when people are trapped inside an attic during rising flood water. As with all remote-sensing technology, it has the potential of being used appropriately and inappropriately.

Advances in Digital Image Processing

Great strides are being made in the processing of the aforementioned types of remote sensor data to extract land use/land cover, biophysical, and topographic information. Much of this geospatial information finds its way into a GIS, where it is analyzed in conjunction with other geospatial information to solve problems.

Improvements in soft-copy photogrammetry are revolutionizing the ability of GIS practictioners to extract detailed building infrastructure information (e.g., building footprints) and detailed topographic information from high-spatial-resolution digital (and analog) aerial photography.

At one time, hyperspectral data were relatively difficult to analyze. More user-friendly hyperspectral analysis software is making it more straightforward for individuals to extract information from hyperspectral data (Im and Jensen, 2009; ITT, 2011).

Analyzing RADAR imagery has always been relatively difficult. Improved RADAR digital-image processing techniques are making it much easier to process the multi-frequency and multi-polarization RADAR data to extract land use/land cover and biophysical information. Interferometric SAR data yield relatively accurate digital-elevation information when there is little vegetation canopy present.

Object-oriented image-segmentation will be used much more frequently to extract homogeneous polygons of information in imagery as opposed to per pixel information (e.g., Jensen et al., 2009; Wang et al., 2010). These algorithms take into account both the spatial and spectral characteristics of the remote sensor data, not just the spectral characteristics. They are especially useful for analyzing high-spatial-resolution multispectral imagery. Geographic object-based image analysis (GEOBIA) is developing as a field for contextual analysis of imagery, LiDAR/DEM, RADAR and information from GIS geodatabases to identify and classify objects for direct input to GIS (Blaschke et al., 2008).

Significant improvements in LiDAR and terrestrial LiDAR data processing is making it much easier to extract extremely dense digital terrain and vegetation structure characteristics from the masspoint cloud (refer to Chapters 3 and 9).

Remote-sensing change detection has always been a relatively complex process. Advances in digital-image-processing change-detection algorithms will make it relatively straightforward to obtain change information from multiple-date images (e.g., Jensen and Im, 2007; Esri, 2011b).

GIS software companies are ramping up their ability to a) ingest diverse types of remote sensor data; b) analyze the data within the GIS software; and c) output the remote-sensing–derived information so that it can be used in conjunction with other spatial information during GIS analysis. GIS and remote-sensing science will become very integrated in the future.

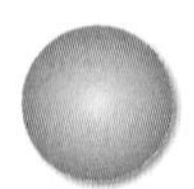

Summary

People trained in GIScience and GIS in particular should have bright futures. In this chapter, several future considerations were discussed. Barring unforeseen events, GIS-related work in the public and private sectors should increase, as documented by the U.S. Department of Labor (USDOL/ETA, 2011). Membership in professional organizations is a very effective way to strengthen your GIScience credentials and make significant contributions to the body of knowledge. You also need to stay informed about advances in the other mapping sciences (geotechnologies). Obtaining certificates, certification, and perhaps eventually a license are important future considerations.

Significant advances in GIS technology, techniques, and software will take place. Important areas to follow include cloud computing; web-based GIS; mobile-GIS; data formats and standards improvement; the creation and appropriate use of volunteered geographic information; and 3-dimensional visualization. It is important to stay abreast of new developments in the public access to GIS data. GIS and remote-sensing science will become increasingly integrated.

Roger Tomlinson, one of the major contributors to the development of GIScience, recently said:

> "I'm very positive about the future of GIS. It's the right technology at the right time. When I think of all the major problems that we face throughout the world today—overpopulation, food shortages, reduced agricultural production, adverse climate change, poverty—these are all quintessentially geographic problems. These problems are all concerned with the human relationship to the land, and this is where GIS can make its biggest contribution. GIS is the technology of our times and is uniquely suited to assist in solving the problems that we face" (Baumann, 2009).

Review Questions

1. What are some of the advantages and disadvantages of being employed as a GIS expert in the public or private sector?

2. Why are local and state government agencies concerned about the liability associated with the geospatial data they provide to the public via their websites?

3. What are two of the main privacy concerns associated with GIS data?

4. How do you think mobile GIS will evolve? Describe two applications in which mobile GIS technology would be very important.

5. What are some of the benefits and limitations associated with volunteered geographic information?

6. What are the differences between GIS certificates, GIS certifications, and licensure?

7. What is the Freedom of Information Act? Why is it important to GIS practitioners?

8. Why is it important to continue to educate yourself in the principles and practice of GIS? What does it mean to be "flexible" within the GIS profession?

9. What are geotagged photographs? What are the privacy concerns associated with geo-tagged photos?

10. Why are professional organizations useful to the GIS professional? How might membership in a professional organization benefit you?

11. What do you think about the future of GIS? What are some of the most important changes or challenges that will take place?

Glossary

Cloud Computing: The practice of storing files and software in a remote location that can be accessed via the Internet.

Data Standards: Specifications that facilitate the use, sharing, creation, and distribution of spatial data.

Freedom of Information Act (FOIA): A U.S. federal law that governs the disclosure of information and documents by the U.S. government.

GIS Certificate: A formal award or acknowledgement given to a student after completing a sequence of GIS academic courses or training programs.

GIS Certification: The process whereby individuals are certified by a third party to have expertise in GIS. The requirements for certification vary by the granting third party.

GIS Licensure: The granting of a license to practice a profession. Licensure is usually regulated by state legislation.

Mapping Sciences: The mapping sciences consist of geodesy (including the use of global navigation satellite systems [GNSS] such as the U.S. GPS), surveying, cartography, GIS, and remote sensing.

Mobile GIS: The use of GIS technology and data away from the office, i.e., in the field.

Nonprofit Professional Organizations: Organizations that seek to further a particular profession, the interests of people engaged in that profession, and the public interest.

Volunteered Geographic Information (VGI): Web users create information with geographic coordinates that is voluntarily incorporated into various Internet applications.

Web-based GIS: The distribution of GIS data, data analysis, and other GIS-related services over the Internet.

References

American Science and Engineering, 2011, *Z Backscatter*, Billerica, MA: American Science and Engineering (http://www.as-e.com/products_solutions/z_backscatter.asp).

Baumann, J., 2009, "Roger Tomlinson on GIS History and Future," *GEOconnexion International Magazine*, 8(2):46–48.

Blaschke, T., Lang, S. and G. Hay, 2008, *Object-Based Image Analysis: Spatial Concepts for Knowledge-Driven Remote Sensing Applications*, New York: Springer, 836 p.

BLS, 2010, "Number of Jobs Held, Labor Market Activity, and Earnings Growth among the Youngest Baby Boomers: Results from a Longitudinal Survey," Washington, DC: Bureau of Labor Statistics (http://www.bls.gov/news.release/pdf/nlsoy.pdf).

Bossler, J. D., Jensen, J. R., McMaster, R. B. and C. Rizos, 2002, *Manual of Geospatial Science and Technology*, London: Taylor & Francis, 623 p.

DiBiase, D., DeMers, M., Johnson, A., Kemp, K., Luck, A.T., Plewe, B. and E. Wentz, 2006, *Geographic Information Science & Technology Body of Knowledge*, Washington: Association of American Geographers.

Elgan, M., 2010. "Big Brother is Searching You: Is it OK to Violate the Fourth Amendment, as Long as You Use New Technology To Do It?" *Computerworld*, August (http://www.computerworld.com/s/article/9181298/Big_Brother_is_searching_ you_?).

Elwood, S., 2008, "Volunteered Geographic Information: Key Questions, Concepts and Methods to Guide Emerging Research and Practice," *GeoJournal*, 72:133–135.

Esri, 2007, *GIS Best Practices Mobile GIS*, Redlands: Esri, Inc. (http://www.Esri.com/library/bestpractices/mobile-gis . pdf).

Esri, 2011a, *Esri Introduces Landsat Data of the World*, Redlands: Esri, Inc. (http://www.Esri.com/news/arcnews/spring11articles/Esri-introduces-landsat-data-for-the-world.html).

Esri, 2011b, *Landsat Change Matters Viewer*, Redlands: Esri, Inc. (http://www.Esri.com/landsat-imagery/viewer.html).

FGDC, 2011, *Standards—Federal Geographic Data Committee*, Washington: Federal Geographic Data Committee (http://www.fgdc.gov/standards).

Flanagin, A. J. and M. J. Metzger, 2008, "The Credibility of Volunteered Geographic Information," *GeoJournal*, 72:137-148.

Gewin, V., 2004, "Careers and Recruitment Mapping Opportunities," *Nature*, 427:376–377.

GISCI, 2011, *Geographic Information System Certification Institute Program* (http://www.gisci.org/certification_ program _description.aspx).

Goodchild, M. F., 2007. "Citizens as Sensors: The World of Volunteered Geography," *GeoJournal*, 69:211–221.

Hayes, B., 2008, "Cloud Computing: As Software Migrates from Local PCs to Distant Internet Servers, Users and Developers alike go along for the Ride," *Communications of the ACM*, 51:9–11.

Im, J. and J. R. Jensen, 2009, "Hyperspectral Remote Sensing of Vegetation," *Geography Compass*, Vol. 3 (November), DOI: 10.1111/j.1749-8198.2008.00182.x.

ITT, 2011, *ENVI–Environment for Visualizing Images*, Boulder: ITT (http://www.ittvis.com/ProductsServices/ENVI .aspx).

Jensen, J. R. and J. Im., 2007, "Remote Sensing Change Detection in Urban Environments," in R. R. Jensen, J. D. Gatrell. and D. D. McLean (Eds.), *Geo-Spatial Technologies in*

Urban Environments Policy, Practice, and Pixels, 2nd Ed., Berlin: Springer-Verlag, 7–32.

Jensen, J. R., Im, J., Jensen, R. and P. Hardin, 2009, "Chapter 19: Image Classification," in *Handbook of Remote Sensing*, D. Nellis and T. Warner, Eds., Boca Raton: CRC Press, 82–102.

Kouyoumjian, V., 2010, "The New Age of Cloud Computing and GIS," *ArcWatch*, January, 2010 (http://www.Esri.com/news/arcwatch/0110/feature.html).

Luccio, M. 2007, "GIS—the Greater Extent: GIS Professional Certification," *Professional Surveyor Magazine*, July 2007 (http://www.profsurv.com/magazine/article.aspx?i=1911).

Maidment, D. R., Edelman, S., Heiberg, E. R., Jensen, J. R., Maune, D. F., Schuckman, K. and R. Shrestha, 2007, *Elevation Data for Floodplain Mapping*, Washington: National Academy Press, 151 p.

Mondello, C., G. Hepner and R. Medina, 2008, "ASP&RS Ten-year Remote Sensing Industry Forecast Phase V," *Photogrammetric Engineering & Remote Sensing*, 74(11):1297–1305.

Monmonier, M., 2002, *Spying with Maps*, Chicago: University of Chicago Press, 339 p.

Morgan, M. F., 2009, *CAD-GIS Interoperability Issues for Facilities Management: Enabling Inter-disciplinary Workflows*, unpublished Masters Thesis, Columbia: Department of Geography, University of South Carolina.

NASA, 2011, NASA Earth Science Decadal Survey Studies: *HyspIRI*, Washington: NASA Goddard Space Flight Center (http://decadal.gsfc.nasa.gov/hyspiri.html).

NASA JPL, 2011, *Eyes on the Earth 3D*, Pasadena: California Institute of Technology (http://climate.nasa.gov/Eyes/eyes.html).

Onsrud, H. J., Johnson, J. P. and X. Lopez, 1994, "Protecting Personal Privacy in Using Geographic Information Systems," *Photogrammetric Engineering & Remote Sensing*, 60:1083–1095.

Open Geospatial Consortium, 2011, *The OGC Seeks Comment on City Geography Markup Language (CityGML) V1.1*, Wayland, MA: Open Geospatial Consortium (http://www.opengeospatial.org/ogc).

Raber, G., Hodgson, M. E. and J. R. Jensen, 2007, "Impact of LiDAR Nominal Posting Density on DEM Accuracy, Hydraulic Modeling, and Flood Zone Delineation," *Photogrammetric Engineering & Remote Sensing*, 73(7):793–804.

Schneider, A., Friedl, M. A. and D. Potere, 2009, "A New Map of Global Extent of Urban Area from MODIS Satellite Data," *Environmental Research Letters*, 4(4): doi:10.1088/1748-9326/4/4/044003.

USDOL/ETA, 2011, *O*Net Online*, Washington: U.S. Department of Labor/Employment and Training Administration (www.onetonline.org/find/quick?s= GIS).

USGS, 2011, *National Land Cover Database 2006: Land Cover, Impervious Surfaces, Tree Canopy, Orthophoto, and Elevation,* Washington: U.S. Geological Survey (http://seamless.usgs.gov/index.php).

Wadember, I. and J. K. Ssewanyana, 2010, "Future IT Trends for GIS/Spatial Information Management," *Scientific Research and Essay,* 5:1025–1032.

Wang, Z., Jensen, J. R. and J. Im, 2010, "An Automatic Region-Based Image Segmentation Algorithm for Remote Sensing Applications," *Environmental Modelling & Software*, 25(10):1149–1165.

Zielstra, D. and H. H. Hochmair, 2011, "Free versus Proprietary Digital Street Data," *GIM International*, 25:29–33.

APPENDIX: SOURCES OF GEOSPATIAL INFORMATION

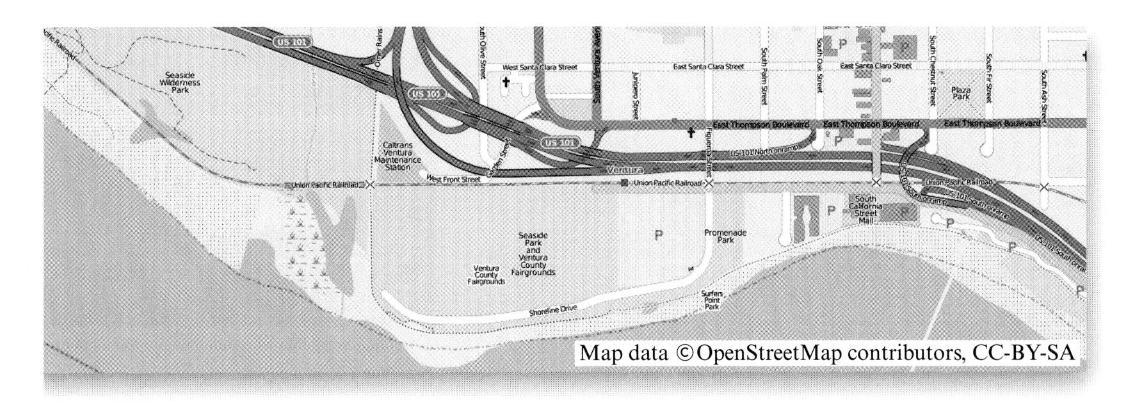

Obtaining timely, accurate, geospatial information is one of the most important and challenging activities of a GIS investigation. Chapter 3 introduced numerous types of geospatial data that are often analyzed in a GIS. This Appendix provides additional information about how to access selected types of geospatial data using the Internet. The thematic datasets listed are not exhaustive, but will hopefully point you in the appropriate direction to obtain some of the most commonly used types of geospatial data.

This Appendix begins by introducing four federal geospatial data repositories, including 1) *EarthExplorer*, 2) *The National Map*, 3) *Geo.Data.gov.*, and 4) the *Bureau of the Census*. An open-source geospatial data repository—*OpenStreetMap*—created using volunteered geographic information (VGI) is discussed. A single commercial geospatial data repository—*Esri ArcGIS Online*—is introduced for demonstration purposes. The remainder of the Appendix is devoted to a discussion of selected thematic datasets (e.g., elevation, hydrology, land use/land cover). Selected sources of public remote sensor data are provided (several commercial sources of remote sensor data were presented in Chapter 3). The Appendix concludes with a list of the Internet addresses of the GIS-data clearinghouses in each of the 50 states.

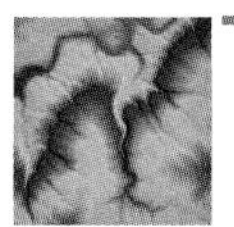

Table of Contents

USGS *EarthExplorer* User Interface

Geographic Search Area

a.

Results of a Search for NLCD2006

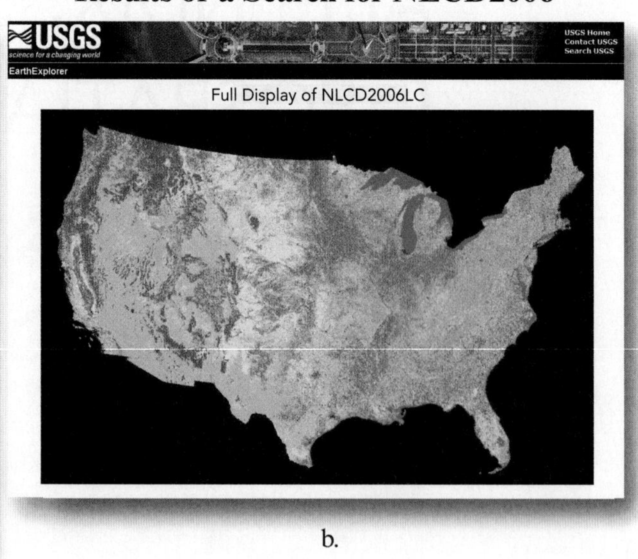

b.

FIGURE A–1 a) The USGS *EarthExplorer* user interface. The geographic search area is available online. A search for the USGS 2006 National Land Cover Dataset (NLCD) of the conterminous U.S. has been selected. b) The results of the search for the 2006 NLCD is shown (http://edcsns17.cr.usgs.gov/NewEarthExplorer/).

Land Use/Land Cover and Biodiversity/Habitat Data

- NLCD—National Land Cover Dataset (USGS)
- C-CAP—Coastal Change Analysis Program (NOAA)
- GAP Analysis Program (USGS)
- NWI—National Wetlands Inventory (USFWS)
- NPN—U.S. National Phenology Network

Network (Road) and Population Demographic Data

- MAF/TIGER—Master Address File/Topologically Integrated Geographic Encoding and Reference System (Bureau of the Census)
- 2010 Census Demographic Data Census (Bureau of the Census)
- LandScan (Oak Ridge National Laboratory)

Remote Sensor Data—Public

- ASTER—Advanced Spaceborne Thermal Emission and Reflection Radiometer (NASA)
- AVHRR—Advanced Very High Resolution Radiometer (NOAA)
- AVIRIS—Advanced Visible Infrared Imaging Spectrometer (NASA)
- Declassified Satellite Imagery (USGS)
- DOQ—Digital Orthophoto Quadrangles (USGS)
- Landsat Multispectral Scanning System (MSS), Thematic Mapper (TM), and Enhanced Thematic Mapper Plus (ETM^+) (NASA/USGS)
- LiDAR—Light Detection and Ranging (USGS)
- MODIS—Moderate Resolution Imaging Spectrometer (NASA)
- NAIP—National Agriculture Imagery Program (USDA)

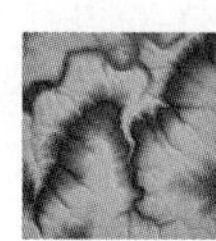

Federal Geospatial Data Repositories

The wonderful thing about federal geospatial data repositories is that the data are in the public domain and available at no expense. Only a select few of the many federal geospatial repositories are introduced here.

USGS *EarthExplorer*

One of the best places to look for both vector and raster geospatial data is at the U.S. Geological Survey's *EarthExplorer* website (http://earthexplorer.usgs.gov/). At this site, users are able to select a place or region by typing in the name of a location, entering geographic coordinates, or drawing on a map (Figure A-1a). Once the geographic area has been identified, the user can identify specific types of data from the menu. For example, the user interface in Figure A-1a was used to locate the 2006 National

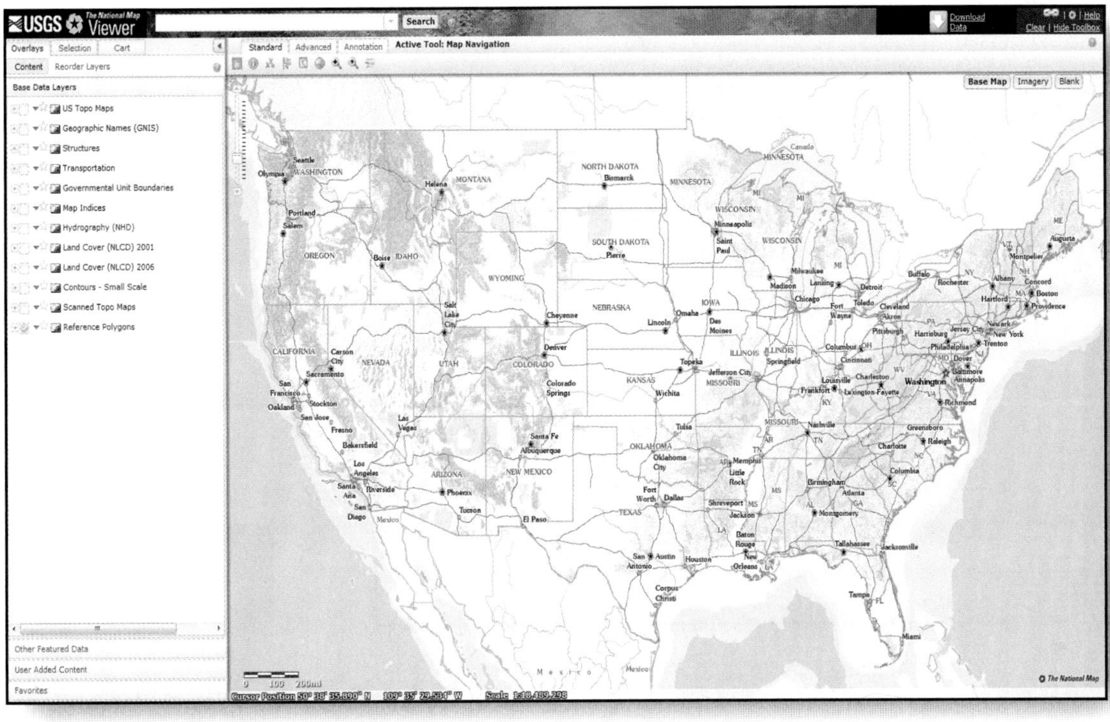

FIGURE A–2 *The National Map* user interface is especially useful for locating information about geographic boundaries, terrain elevation, geographic names, hydrography, land cover, orthoimagery, structures, and transportation (http://nationalmap.gov/viewers.html).

Land Cover Dataset (NLCD). The results of the search are provided in a separate window shown in Figure A-1b. The user then has the option of discarding the search or ordering a digital copy of the 2006 NLCD. Much of the data from a variety of agencies and organizations can be queried and downloaded from this website.

Users must register with *EarthExplorer* to save searches and order data. It is easy to locate and download vector and raster files—especially remote-sensing data files. Some datasets can be downloaded immediately. Other datasets take a few hours or a couple of days for the data to be extracted and then made available via FTP. Normally, users are not sent to additional sites to order data. This is an advanced search engine that is most useful for those who know the type and characteristics of the geospatial data they are looking for.

USGS *The National Map*

Managed by the National Geospatial Program (NGP), *The National Map* viewer provides data visualization and download of all eight *National Map* datasets and US Topo products (Carswell, 2011). *The National Map* includes geographic boundaries, elevation, geographic names, hydrography, land cover, orthoimagery, structures, and transportation. The majority of *The National Map* effort is devoted to acquiring and integrating medium-scale (nominally 1:24,000-scale) geospatial data for the eight base layers from a variety of sources and providing access to the resulting seamless coverages of geospatial data (Figure A-2).

One of the most useful data layers of *The National Map* is the US Topo data. US Topo is the new generation of digital topographic maps arranged in the traditional 7.5-minute quadrangle format. Digital US Topo maps look like the traditional paper topographic maps but provide modern technical advantages that support wider and faster public distribution and enable basic, on-screen geographic analysis (http://nationalmap.gov/ustopo/index.html).

The *National Atlas* within *The National Map* is very interactive and contains many different data layers that users can select. *The National Map* also provides mapmaking tools for users to create on-demand maps using a variety of spatial data layers.

Geo.Data.gov

On October 1, 2011, *Geodata.gov* became *Geo.Data.gov*, within the Data.gov infrastructure. With this move, the U.S. national geospatial assets were brought together to make it easier to browse and access over 400,000 maps,

***Geo.Data.gov* User Interface**

GEO.DATA.GOV
Login Register Data.gov Help Feedb
Home Gallery Browse Search
Search for geodata
Search

Browse
This page shows a sample implementation of a browse tree that you can customize. The browse capability allows users to browse a subset of classified resources in the catalog.

Map Files
Offline Data
Static Map Images
ISO Topic Category
Administrative and Political Boundaries
Agriculture and Farming
Atmosphere and Climatic
Biology and Ecology
Business and Economic
Cadastral
Cultural, Society and Demography
Elevation and Derived Products
Environment and Conservation
Facilities and Structures
Geological and Geophysical
Human Health and Disease
Imagery and Base Maps
Inland Water Resources
Locations and Geodetic Networks
Military
Oceans and Estuaries
Transportation Networks
Utilities and Communication

88161 filtered results TIGER Richland County Filter Clear
Showing 1-10 1 2 3 4 5 > Last
TIGER/Line Shapefile, 2008, county, Richland County, SC, Address Ranges
TIGER/Line Shapefile, 2008, county, Richland County, SC, All Lines
TIGER/Line Shapefile, 2008, county, Richland County, SC, Feature Names
TIGER/Line Shapefile, 2010, county, Richland County, SC, Current Other Identifiers Relationship File
TIGER/Line Shapefile, 2009, county, Richland County, SC, Current Other Identifiers Relationship File
TIGER/Line Shapefile, 2009, county, Richland County, SC, Current Address Ranges Relationship File
TIGER/Line Shapefile, 2008, county, Richland County, SC, Address Range-Feature Name
TIGER/Line Shapefile, 2009, county, Richland County, SC, Current Address Range-Feature Name Relationship File
TIGER/Line Shapefile, 2010, county, Richland County, SC, All Roads County-based Shapefile
TIGER/Line Shapefile, 2010, county, Richland County, SC, Current Address Ranges Relationship File

a.

Map Viewer

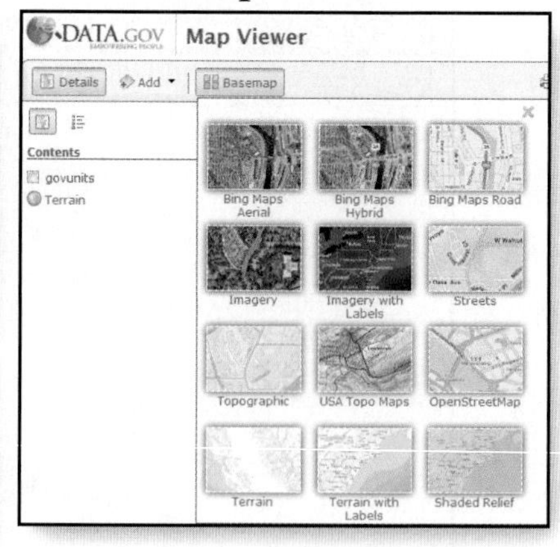

b.

FIGURE A–3 a) This is the browser interface of the *Geo.Data.gov* website. The browse catalog on the left contains information about Content Type (not visible) and ISO Topic Categories. In this example, the user selected the Transportation Networks topic category and specified "TIGER Richland County South Carolina" in the filter. The results of the search identified all of the TIGER data for Richland County from 2008 to 2010. The user can evaluate the metadata associated with each file or download the data by clicking on the desired dataset and following a few simple instructions. b) A map viewer at the site provides twelve basemaps that can serve as a backdrop to be overlaid with information the user locates using the "Add" icon (http://geo.data.gov/viewer/webmap/viewer.html).

datasets, and services (Figure A-3a). In addition, the services, mapping and visualization capabilities, and data standards behind these sites also became accessible. This work was done in coordination with a refresh of the Geospatial Platform, which remains the online home for the Federal Geographic Data Committee's guidance, policies, and standards.

Geo.Data.gov allows the user to search for geospatial information by specifying Content Type and ISO Topic Categories (Figure A-3a). The user can then refine the search using the text filter provided. In this example, the Transportation Network category was identified and then filtered using the request for information about "TIGER Richland County South Carolina." The result is a list of U.S. Census Bureau TIGER data for Richland County from 2008 through 2010. The website also provides a map viewer where users can select from one of twelve backdrop datasets to be overlaid with information using the "Add" icon (Figure A-3b). It is an especially good search engine if you are interested in demographic data and basic spatial data. This website is ideal for the less experienced user that is not absolutely sure what geospatial data they are looking for.

U.S. Census Bureau

If users do not want to use the *Geo.Data.gov* search engine to locate public domain data, they can often go directly to the source of the data. For example, the U.S. Census Bureau website provides a wealth of geospatial data, as shown in Figure A-4. It offers several file types for mapping census geographic data based on data found in their MAF/TIGER database. The most important parts of the site for many GIS studies are the TIGER/Line Shapefiles and the Cartography Boundary Files.

TIGER/Line® Shapefiles: TIGER/Line files can be downloaded for individual counties or entire states. The files contain features such as roads, railroads, rivers, as well as legal and statistical geographic areas. This is the U.S. Census Bureau's most comprehensive dataset and is designed for use with a GIS.

Cartography Boundary Files: The cartographic boundary files are simplified representations of selected geographic areas from the U.S. Census Bureau's MAF/TIGER geographic database. These boundary files are specifically designed for small-scale thematic mapping. Generalized boundary files are clipped to a simplified version of the

U.S. Census Bureau

FIGURE A–4 The U.S. Census Bureau user interface provides access to U.S. demographic data as well as the extensively used MAF/TIGER/Line database. The Geography area of the interface is highlighted (www.census.gov).

U.S. outline. The data are ideal for small-scale (limited detail) mapping projects clipped to the shoreline.

Open-source Volunteered Geographic Information (VGI) Repositories

There are numerous open-source geospatial data repositories. One of the most respected is OpenStreetMap.

OpenStreetMap

OpenStreetMap (OSM) is like *Wikipedia*, except that it provides free, open source geographic information such as street maps to the world (http://www.openstreetmap.org/) (Figure A-5). The project was started because much of the spatial data people think they can freely use for mapping and GIS applications actually have legal restrictions. Data from copyrighted maps or any other proprietary data are strictly prohibited in OpenStreetMap. The goal of OSM is to provide free access to geospatial data to stimulate creativity. Volunteers like you collect geographic data about an area of interest or community from a variety of sources. Some committed volunteers systematically map whole cities over a period of time, or organize mapping parties to intensively map a particular area over an evening or a weekend. In 2011, OSM had more than 400,000 registered users.

Ground-based surveys are usually performed by a person with a GPS unit who is walking, riding a bicycle, or riding in a car or boat. Geographic data can also be extracted using simple image-based, onscreen tracing procedures using rectified aerial photography or satellite imagery. Some government agencies have released data for use in OSM. Much of these data have come from the U.S. public domain sources (e.g., Landsat imagery, TIGER data). In 2010, Microsoft allowed the OSM community to use *Bing* vertical aerial imagery as a backdrop in the OSM editor. Once the geographic data have been collected, they are uploaded into the OSM website. A simple editing interface (Figure A-5) is then used to "attribute" the geographic data, e.g., label a line segment as a road, stream, or power line and symbolize it. This is usually done by the same person who uploaded the geographic data, or by other interested registered OSM users. OSM provides detailed geographic data in some locations including building footprints and feature names (Figure A-5), and minimal information in other areas. Of course, the geometric and attribute accuracy of OSM data is dependent

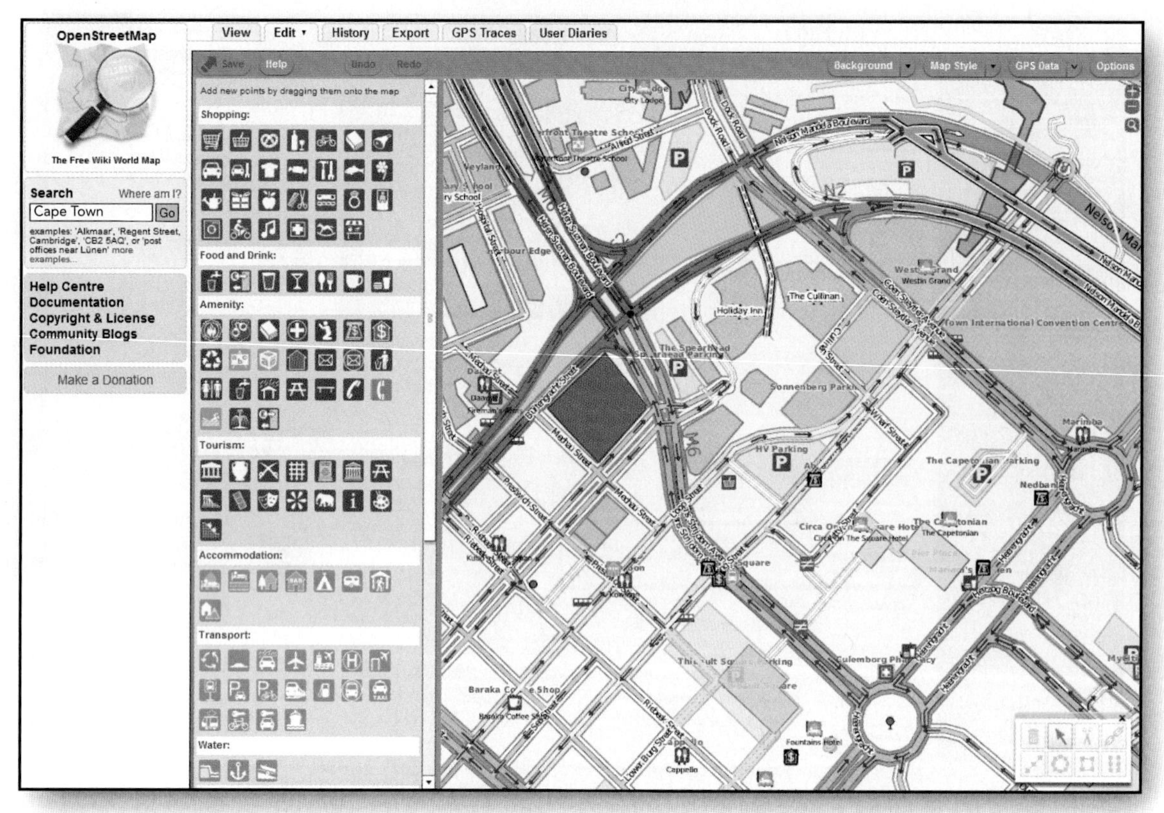

FIGURE A–5 The open-source OpenStreetMap repository mainly contains data input by volunteers with some public domain data from federal agencies. This illustration depicts the geographic data associated with downtown Cape Town, South Africa. The interface is in editing mode where volunteers can add points, lines, and polygons to the database and provide symbolization and attribute information using the icons shown (Map data © OpenStreetMap contributors, CC-BY-SA).

upon the quality of the geographic data provided by the volunteers.

Mobile hand-held receivers (e.g., Garmin) and cell phones (e.g., iPhone) can be used to view OSM data. It is also possible to use an open source geographic information system (e.g., Quantum GIS at http://qgis.org/) to extract OSM data and save it is as an ArcGIS shapefile. During the 2010 Haiti earthquake, OSM and volunteers used high spatial resolution satellite imagery to map the roads, buildings, and refugee camps of Port-au-Prince in just two days. They created the most complete digital map of Haiti's road network. The resulting data and maps were used by numerous international relief organizations.

Commercial Geospatial Data Repositories

There are numerous commercial geodata search engines such as *Google Earth*, *Bing*, *Esri ArcGIS Online*, and others. The *Esri ArcGIS Online* database is introduced for demonstration purposes.

Esri ArcGIS Online

The *Esri ArcGIS Online* website offers information associated with basemaps, demographic maps, reference maps, and specialty maps (Figure A-6).

Basemaps: World Imagery, World Street Map, World Topographic Map, World Shaded Relief, World Physical Map, World Terrain Base, USA Topographic Maps, and Ocean Basemap.

Demographic Maps: Details about the U.S. population, including average household size, median age, population density, retail spending potential, etc.

Reference Maps: World Boundaries and Places, World Boundaries and Places Alternate, World Reference Overlay, and World Transportation.

Specialty Maps: DeLorme World Basemap, World Navigation Charts, and Soil Survey Maps.

Esri ArcGIS Online links to several of the government data repositories previously discussed. It also provides

Esri ArcGIS Online

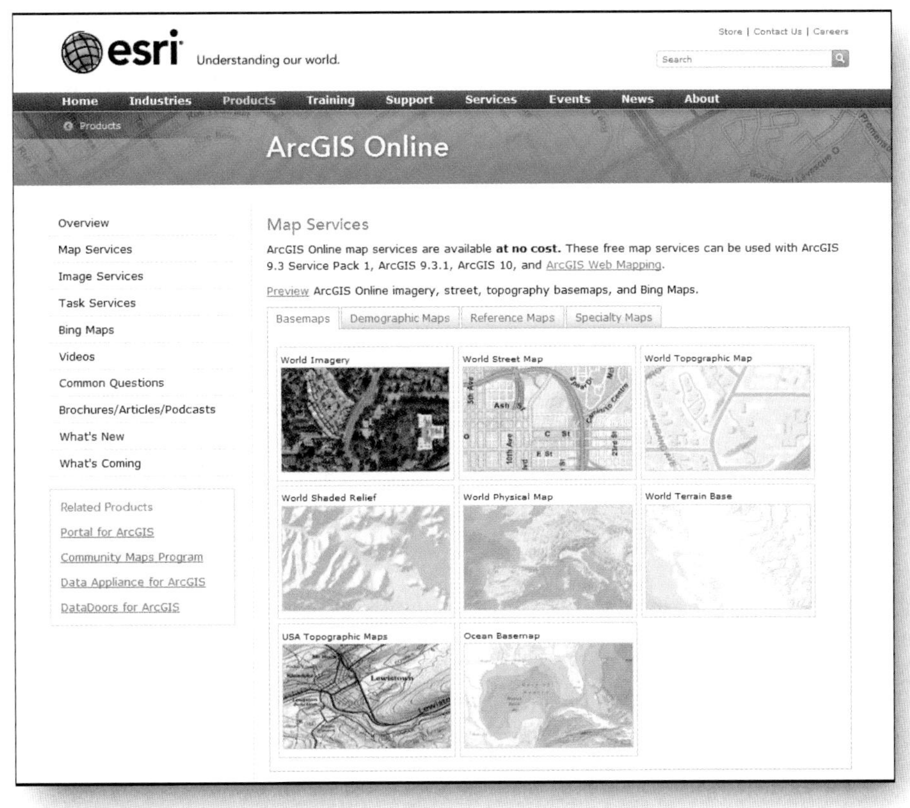

FIGURE A–6 The Esri ArcGIS Online interface provides access to basemaps, demographic maps, reference maps, and specialty maps (user interface courtesy of Esri, Inc.).

access to ArcGIS Online map and image services. It is an especially good location for obtaining U.S. Bureau of the Census data. Data provided at this free site are relatively easy to import and use in Esri's ArcGIS software.

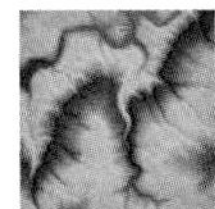

Digital Elevation Data

Accurate digital elevation information is very important for many applications. Numerous commercial photogrammetric engineering and mapping companies provide access to high-quality, digital-elevation information for a fee.This section focuses on public domain sources of digital elevation information.

- DRG—Digital Raster Graphics (USGS, www.libremap.org)

Sometimes it is useful to analyze historical topographic information. Fortunately, the original hard-copy USGS topographic maps were scanned to create digital raster graphics (DRGs) from the 1:24,000-, 1:25,000-, 1:63,360- (Alaska), 1:100,000-, and 1:250,000-scale topographic map series. Coverage includes the standard series quadrangle maps of the U.S. and its trusts and territories. The image inside the map neatline is georeferenced to the surface of the earth and fit to the Universal Transverse Mercator projection. The horizontal positional accuracy and datum of the DRG matches the accuracy and datum of the source map. The maps were scanned at a minimum resolution of 250 dpi. Historical DRGs may be downloaded free from http://libremap.org/.

Several other important sources of digital elevation information are presented in Table A-1, including:

- GTOPO30—Digital elevation model of the world (USGS)
- NED—National Elevation Dataset (USGS)
- Topographic and Bathymetric Information (USGS, NOAA)
- Topographic Change Information (USGS)
- SRTM—Shuttle RADAR Topography Mission (NASA JPL)

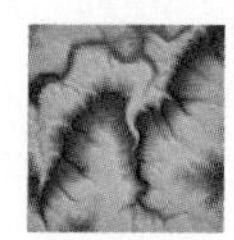

Hydrography Data

Hydrologic information is critical to the successful modeling of many natural (e.g., streams) and human-made (e.g., canals) geospatial relationships. Table A-2 summarizes the availability of detailed hydrologic information from:

- NHD—National Hydrologic Database (USGS)
- EDNA—Elevation Derivatives for National Applications (USGS)

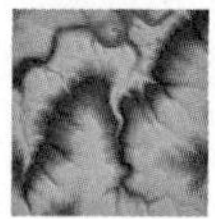

Land Use/Land Cover and Biodiversity/Habitat Data

Land use is the human use of the terrain. Land cover is the biophysical material present on the surface of the Earth such as vegetation, soil, water, rocks, etc. The land cover is the habitat for animals, birds, and aquatic species. Several of the more important land use/land cover and biodiversity/habitat resources are presented in Table A-3, including:

- NLCD—National Land Cover Dataset (USGS)
- C-CAP—Coastal Change Analysis Program (NOAA)
- GAP Analysis Program (USGS)
- NWI—National Wetlands Inventory (USFWS)

In addition, there is *The National Phenology Network.* Phenology is the study of nature's calendar. For example, it looks at when peach trees blossom, when alligators build their nests, when salmon swim upstream to spawn, or when corn is fully ripe. The National Coordinating Office of the Network is a resource center that facilitates and encourages widespread collection, integration, and sharing of phenology data and related information. Source: *USA National Phenology Network, 1955 East 6th Street, Tucson, AZ 85721.*

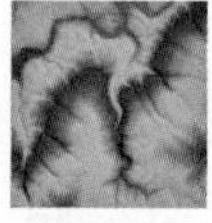

Network (Road) and Population Demographic Data

Topologically correct road-network information is indispensable for navigation and business decision making. The U.S. Census Bureau provides the MAF/TIGER—Master Address File/Topologically Integrated Geographic Encoding and Reference System free of charge to the public. Details are provided in Table A-4. The U.S. Census Bureau also provides information aggregated to various spatial enumeration districts.

LandScan created by the Oak Ridge National Laboratory predicts the spatial distribution of people at different times of day anywhere in the world at a spatial resolution of 1 x 1 km (Table A-4).

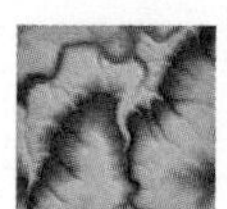

Remote Sensor Data—Public

Remote-sensing data are available from orbital and aerial platforms and sensors. Table A-5 provides information about some of the remote-sensing systems commonly used to collect data analyzed using a GIS.

- ASTER—Advanced Spaceborne Thermal Emission and Reflection Radiometer (NASA)
- AVHRR—Advanced Very High Resolution Radiometer (NOAA)
- AVIRIS—Advanced Visible Infrared Imaging Spectrometer (NASA)
- Declassified Satellite Imagery (USGS)
- DOQ—Digital Orthophoto Quadrangles (USGS)
- Landsat Multispectral Scanning System (MSS), Thematic Mapper (TM), and Enhanced Thematic Mapper Plus (ETM^+) (NASA/USGS)
- LiDAR—Light Detection and Ranging (USGS)
- MODIS—Moderate Resolution Imaging Spectrometer (NASA)
- NAIP—National Agriculture Imagery Program (USDA)

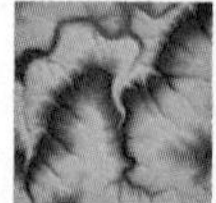

State GIS Data Clearinghouses

States maintain a substantial amount of publicly available geospatial data in GIS data clearinghouses (Table A-6). These websites generally list GIS data by category (e.g., elevation, hydrology, transportation).

References

Carswell, W. J., 2011, *National Geospatial Program*, Washington, DC: U.S. Geological Survey, 2 p.

Gesch, D. B., 2007, Chapter 4: "The National Elevation Dataset," in Maune, D. F., Ed., *Digital Elevation Model Technologies and Applications—The DEM Users Manual* (2nd ed.), Bethesda, MD: American Society for Photogrammetry & Remote Sensing, 99–118.

TABLE A-1 Digital Elevation Data.

Data	Description	Example
GTOPO30	GTOPO30 is a global digital elevation model with a horizontal grid spacing of 30 arc-seconds (approximately 1 x 1 km). It was derived from numerous sources of topographic information. It has been used extensively for regional, continental, and global studies and for numerous global change applications. Compare this GTOPO30 DEM of Mt. Kilimanjaro with the SRTM DEM to appreciate the coarse resolution of the GTOPO30 data. Source: *http://eros.usgs.gov /#/Find_Data/ Products_and_ Data_Available/gtopo30_info.*	 Mt. Kilimanjaro
NED—National Elevation Dataset	The National Elevation Dataset is the 30 x 30 m resolution elevation layer of *The National Map*. NED has evolved into a multi-resolution dataset that provides the best available elevation data, including 3 x 3 m or better LiDAR-derived elevation data. Source: *http://ned.usgs.gov.* See Gesch (2007) for a detailed description of the National Elevation Dataset characteristics.	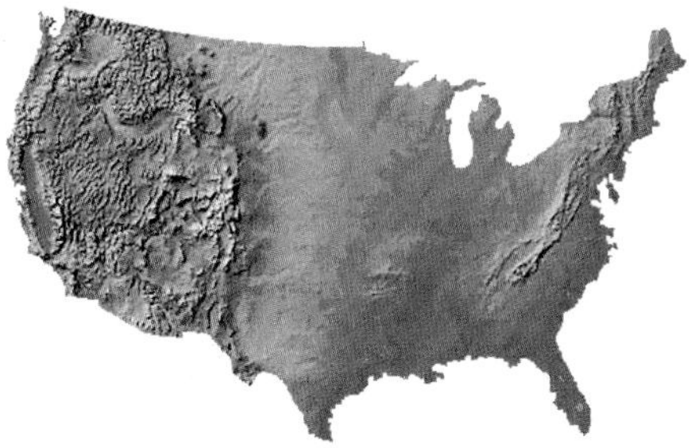
Topographic-Bathymetric Information	Topographic-bathymetric (topobathy) data are merged topography (land elevation) and bathymetry (water depth) data in a single product useful for inundation mapping and other applications. Topography data come from the National Elevation Dataset (NED). Bathymetry data are provided by the NOAA GEOphysical DAta System (GEODAS). The example depicts topobathy data of a part of the Puget Sound, WA. Source: *http:// topotools.cr.usgs.gov/topobathy.viewer/.*	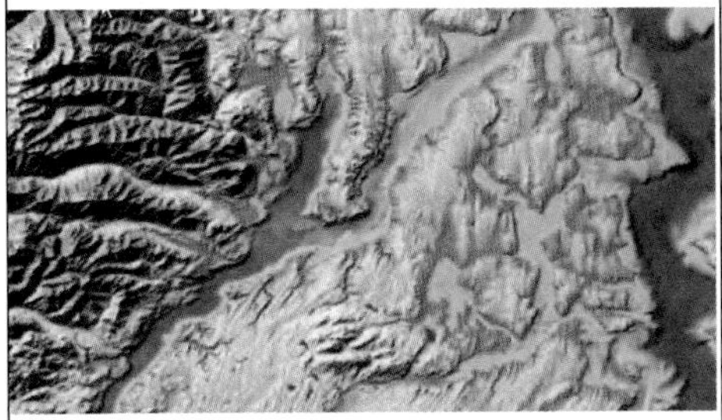
Topographic Change Information	The need for information on the extent of human geomorphic activity resulted in the creation of the first-ever accounting of topographic change across the U.S. The primary types of topographic changes resulting from human geomorphic activity include surface mining, road construction, urban development, dam construction, and landfills. The example shows: (left) NED DEM of a gold mine in Carlin, NV; (right) cut (blue) and fill (red) areas identified using SRTM-derived DEM. Source: *http://topochange.cr.usgs.gov/.*	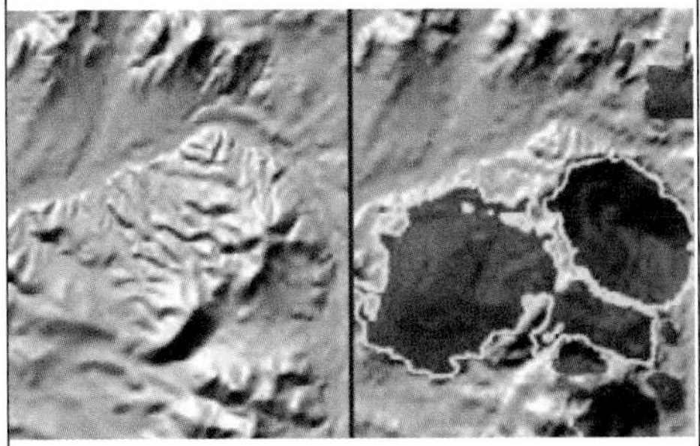
SRTM—Shuttle RADAR Topography Mission	SRTM data were obtained by the Space Shuttle *Endeavour* in 2000. SRTM acquired data for over 80 percent of the Earth's land surface between 60 degrees N and 56 degrees S latitude. SRTM images are available at no charge as FTP downloads. Compare the GTOPO30 DEM of Mt. Kilimanjaro with the SRTM DEM to appreciate the fine spatial resolution of the SRTM-derived DEM. Source: *http://eros.usgs.gov/#/Find_Data/Products_and_ Data_ Available/SRTM.*	

TABLE A-2 Hydrologic Information.

Data	Description	Example
NHD—National Hydrography Dataset	The NHD is the surface water component of *The National Map*. The NHD is a digital vector dataset easily used in GIS hydrologic analysis. It contains features such as lakes, ponds, streams, rivers, canals, dams, and stream gages. These data are designed to be used in general mapping and in the analysis of surface-water systems.The NHD contains vector-surface-water-hydrography information obtained from topographic maps and additional sources. It is available nationwide as medium resolution at 1:100,000-scale and as high resolution at 1:24,000-scale or better. In Alaska, the NHD is available at 1:63,360-scale. A few "local resolution" areas are available at varying scales. The hydrography of the United States is organized by drainage areas. The sub-basin 8-digit Hydrologic Unit Code (HUC) drainage area is the most practical area for high resolution NHD. Subregions (4-digit HUCs) are composed of varying numbers of sub basins. The NHD is available in an Esri personal geodatabase format known as NHDinGEO, a file-based geodatabase format, and in Esri shapefile format known as NHDGEOinShape. The NHD is organized by hydrologic units, but can be downloaded in various geographic extents. This map displays NHD data of Hobble Creek, UT. Source: *http://nhd.usgs.gov/*.	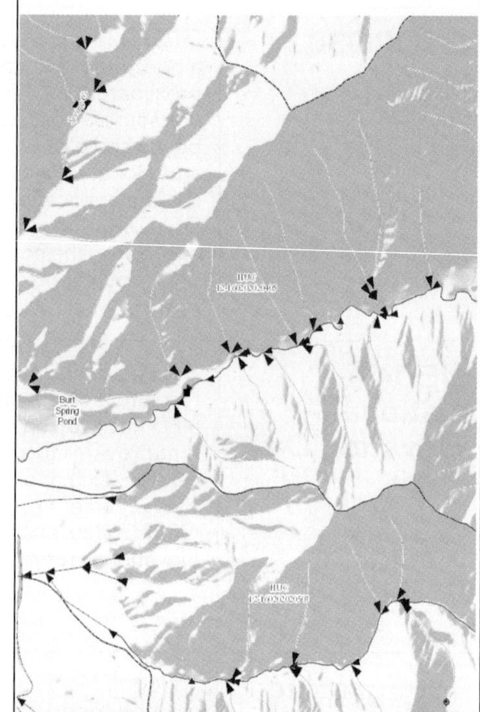
EDNA—Elevation Derivatives for National Applications	EDNA is a multilayered database derived from the NED, which has been hydrologically conditioned for improved hydrologic flow modeling. The seamless EDNA database provides 30 x 30 m raster and vector data layers including: Aspect Contours Filled DEM Flow Accumulation Flow Direction Reach Catchment Seedpoints Reach Catchments Shaded Relief Sinks Slope Synthetic Streamlines Hydrologically conditioned elevation data, processed to create hydrologic derivatives, can be useful in many topologically based hydrologic visualization and investigative applications. Drainage areas upstream or downstream from any location can be accurately traced, facilitating flood analysis investigations, pollution studies, and hydroelectric power generation projects. This is a map of reach catchment seedpoints. Source: *http://edna.usgs.gov/*.	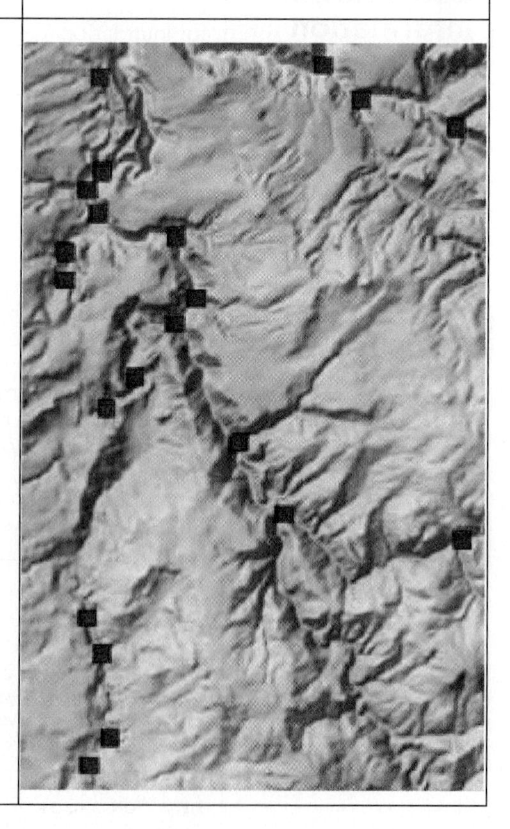

TABLE A-3 Land Use/Land Cover and Biodiversity/Habitat Information.

Data	Description	Example
NLCD—National Land Cover Dataset 1992, 2001, 2006	The Multi-Resolution Land Characteristics (MRLC) Consortium developed the NLCD, which is a 16- to 21-class land cover dataset of the United States derived from 30 x 30 m Landsat TM data. The NLCD state datasets are extracted from larger regional datasets that are mosaics of Landsat TM scenes. NLCD 1992 is a land cover dataset. NLCD 2001 is a land cover database composed of three elements: land cover, impervious surface, and canopy density. NLCD 2006 also quantified land cover change between 2001 to 2006. The land cover in Washington, DC, in 1992 is shown. Source: *http://www.mrlc. gov/index.php.*	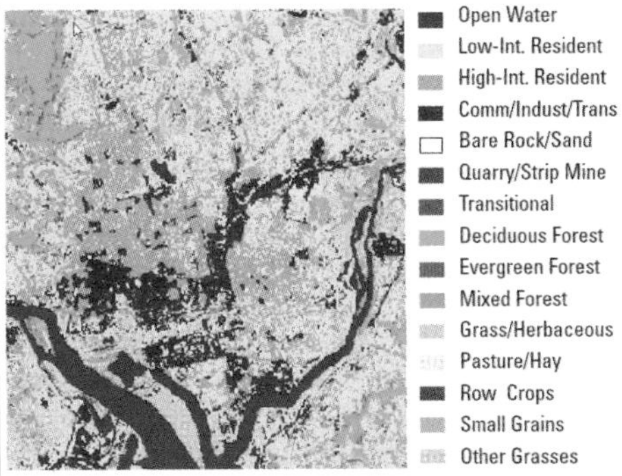
C-CAP—Coastal Change Analysis Program	C-CAP is a database of land cover and land cover change for the coastal regions of the U.S. produced every 5 years. C-CAP provides inventories of coastal intertidal areas, wetlands, and adjacent uplands. C-CAP products consist of land cover maps for each date of analysis, as well as a file that highlights what changes have occurred between these dates. NOAA also produces high resolution C-CAP land cover products, for select geographies. C-CAP provides the "coastal expression" of the NLCD, and contributes to the Earth Cover layer of the National Spatial Data Infrastructure. The example shows C-CAP data of Pearl Harbor, HI. Source: *http://www.csc.noaa. gov/digitalcoast/data/ccapregional/.*	
GAP Analysis Program	The GAP Analysis Program is part of the National Biological Information Infrastructure (NBII). The goal is to keep common species common by protecting them *before* they become threatened. GAP activities focus on the creation of state and regional databases and maps that depict patterns of land management, land cover, and biodiversity. These data can be used to identify "gaps" in conservation where an animal or plant community is not adequately represented on the existing network of conservation lands. The example depicts the U.S. GAP land cover map which contains 551 Ecological Systems and modified Ecological Systems. Source: *http://gapanalysis.usgs.gov/.*	
NWI—National Wetlands Inventory	The U.S. Fish & Wildlife Service's National Wetlands Inventory provides current geospatial data on the status, extent, characteristics, and functions of wetland, riparian, deepwater, and related aquatic habitats in priority areas to promote the understanding and conservation of these resources. The NWI serves online map information for 82% of the conterminous United States, 31% of Alaska, and 100% of Hawaii. The goal is to complete and maintain a seamless digital wetlands dataset for the nation that will become the Wetlands Data Layer of the NSDI. The NWI example is of Crayvik, FL. Source: *http://www.fws.gov/ wetlands/index. html.*	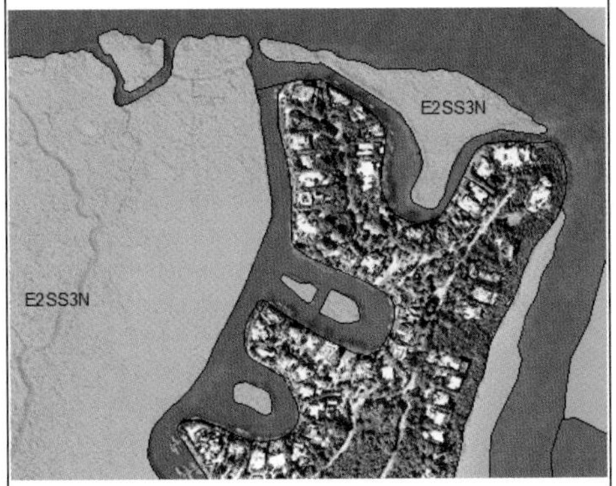

TABLE A-4 Network (Road) and Population Demographic Information.

Data	Description	Example
MAF/TIGER/ Line	TIGER/Line® Shapefiles are spatial data extracts from the U.S. Bureau of the Census MAF/TIGER database (Master Address File/Topologically Integrated Geographic Encoding and Reference System), containing features such as topologically correct roads, railroads, and rivers, as well as legal and statistical geographic areas. They are made available to the public at no charge and are typically used to provide the digital base map for GIS or mapping software.The TIGER/Line® Shapefiles do not include demographic data, but they contain geographic entity codes that can be linked to the Bureau's demographic data, available on American FactFinder described below. The TIGER /Line® Shapefiles are provided in four types of coverages: County-based State-based Nation-based American Indian Area-based Source: *http://www.census.gov/geo/www/tiger/shp.html.*	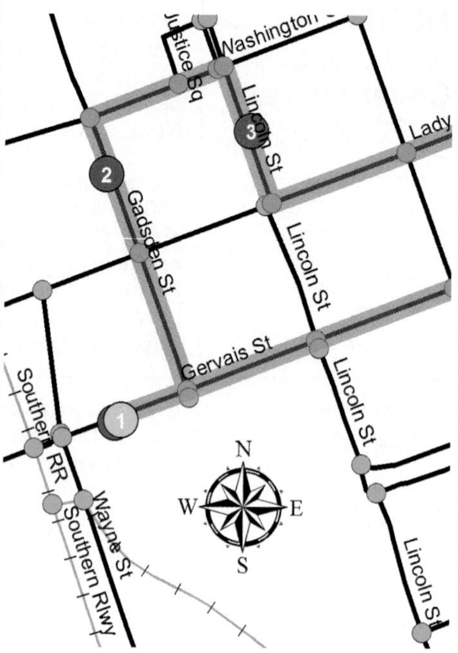
2010 Census Population Demographics	The 2010 Census reported that 308.7 million people live in the United States, a 9.7 percent increase from the 2000 Census population of 281.4 million. Below are some of the most important 2010 U.S. Census products (tabular and feature-based) and a brief description of each. Other developed countries usually have sites available to download and analyze census demographic information. *American FactFinder (AFF)* The AFF is a data access system that will find and retrieve geographic information and plot the information on an interactive map. Source: *http://factfinder2.census.gov/faces/nav/jsf/pages/index.xhtml.* *Cartographic Boundary Files* Generalized, digital files suitable for use with GIS in small-scale thematic mapping. Source: *http://www.census.gov/geo/www/cob/.* *Census 2010 County Block Maps* Color maps, showing census blocks, voting districts, and other feature details. Source: *http://www.census.gov/geo/www/maps/pl10_map_suite/cou_block.html.* *Voting District/State Legislative District Reference Maps* Color maps, showing voting districts and/or state legislative districts. Source: *http://www.census.gov/geo/www/maps/pl10_map_suite/vtd_sld.html.*	
LandScan Population Distribution Modeling	LandScan was developed by Oak Ridge National Laboratory (ORNL) through funding by the DOD and the DOE. At approximately 1 x 1 km, LandScan is the highest resolution global population distribution data available and represents an ambient population (average over 24 hours). The LandScan algorithm uses spatial data and image analysis technologies and a multivariable dasymetric modeling approach to disaggregate census counts within an administrative boundary. LandScan population distribution models are tailored to match the data conditions and geographical nature of individual countries and regions. The LandScan dataset is available free to U.S. government agencies. Others, such as educational institutions or research scientists, must register with LandScan to determine license fees (if any) for obtaining LandScan resources. Source: *http://www.ornl.gov/sci/landscan/index.shtml.*	

TABLE A-5 Remote Sensor Data—Public.

Data	Description	Example
ASTER — Advanced Spaceborne Thermal Emission and Reflection Radiometer	ASTER is carried onboard NASA's *Terra* satellite. ASTER began data collection in 2000 and consists of three sensors that obtain images in multiple spatial resolutions (15 x 15, 30 x 30, and 90 x 90 m). ASTER is the only high-resolution imaging sensor on *Terra*. The primary goal of the ASTER mission is to obtain high-resolution image data in 14 channels (including thermal infrared) over the entire land surface, as well as black-and-white stereo images. With a revisit time of between 4 and 16 days, ASTER provides repeat coverage of changing areas on Earth's surface. This is an ASTER image of the Patagonia Glacier in Chile obtained on May 2, 2000. Source: *http://visibleearth.nasa.gov/view_rec.php?id=2044.*	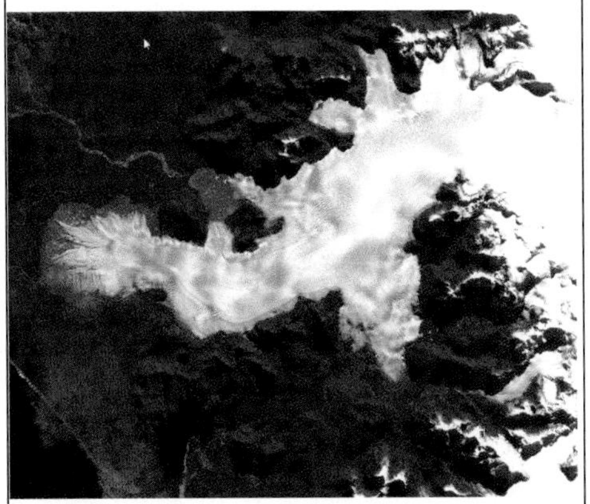
AVHRR— Advanced Very High Resolution Radiometer	The Advanced Very High Resolution Radiometer (AVHRR) is an optical multispectral scanner flown aboard NOAA orbiting satellites. The instrument measures reflected sunlight and emitted radiation (heat) from Earth in the visible (Channel 1), near-infrared (Channel 2), and thermal infrared (Channels 3, 4, and 5) regions of the electromagnetic spectrum. There is fairly continuous global coverage since June 1979, with morning and afternoon acquisitions available. The resolution is 1.1 x 1.1 km at nadir. This is an image of the Gulf Stream off North and South Carolina. Source: *http://eros.usgs.gov /#/Find_Data/Products_and_Data_Available/AVHRR.*	
AVIRIS— Airborne/ Visible Imaging Spectrometer	AVIRIS is a unique optical sensor that delivers calibrated images of the upwelling spectral radiance in 224 contiguous spectral channels (bands) with wavelengths from 400 to 2500 nanometers. The main objective of the AVIRIS remote-sensing system is to identify, measure, and monitor constituents of the Earth's surface and atmosphere based on molecular absorption and particle scattering signatures. Research with AVIRIS data is predominantly focused on understanding processes related to the global environment and climate change. This is an AVIRIS image of the lower portion of San Francisco Bay, California. Source: *http://aviris.jpl.nasa.gov/.*	
Declassified Satellite Imagery	Almost 90,000 declassified satellite images are maintained in the USGS EROS declassified satellite image archive. The images were captured by a variety of intelligence satellites, including CORONA, ARGON, LANYARD, KH-7, and KH-9 between 1960 and 1980. Coverage is global, but the geographic distribution is uneven. Some images are high resolution (although not georeferenced). This is an image of the western edge of Dakar, Senegal, Africa, acquired by the KH-7 satellite in 1966. Source: *http://eros.usgs.gov/#/Find_Data/Products_and_ Data_Available/Declassified_Satellite_Imagery_-_2.*	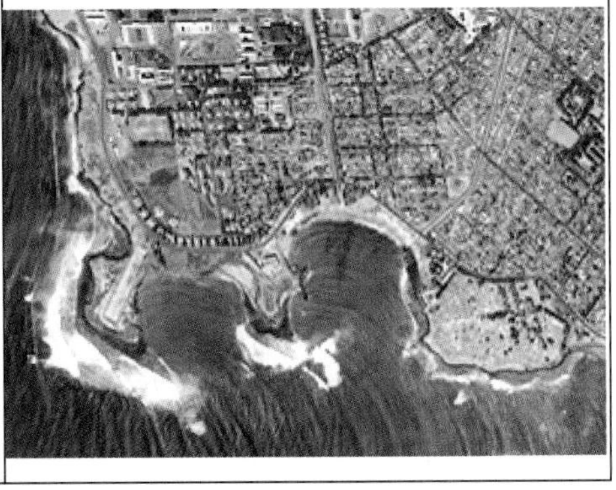

TABLE A-5 (continued) Remote Sensor Data—Public.

Data	Description	Example
DOQ—Digital Orthophoto Quadrangles	A Digital Orthophoto Quadrangle (DOQ) is a computer-generated image of an aerial photograph in which the image displacement caused by terrain relief and camera tilt has been removed. The DOQ combines the image characteristics of the original photograph with the georeferenced qualities of a map. DOQs can be black-and-white (B/W), natural color, or color-infrared (CIR) images with 1 x 1 m ground resolution. They cover an area measuring 3.75-minutes longitude by 3.75-minutes latitude or 7.5-minutes longitude by 7.5-minutes latitude. A CIR DOQ of downtown Washington, DC, is shown. Source: *http://egsc.usgs.gov/isb/pubs/factsheets/fs05701.html.*	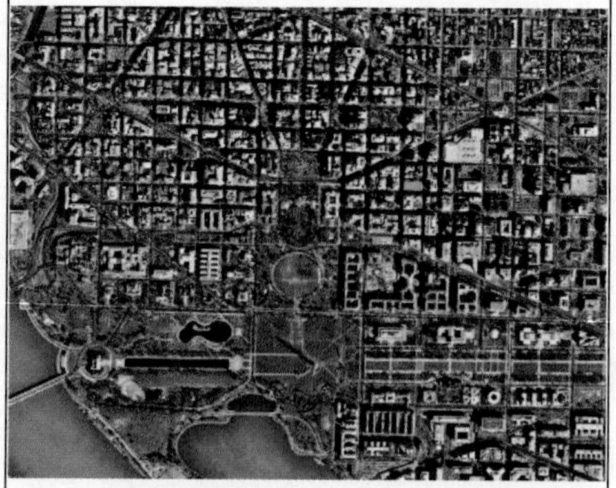
Landsat—MSS, TM ETM$^+$	The first two Earth Resources Technology Satellites (ERTS) were launched in 1972 and 1975. They were subsequently renamed Landsat satellites. Additional Landsat satellites were launched in 1978, 1982, 1984, 1993 (did not achieve orbit), and 1999. The Landsat satellites have carried a variety of sensors, including the Multispectral Scanning System (MSS; 80 x 80 m), Thematic Mapper (TM; 30 and 60 m), and Enhanced Thematic Mapper (ETM+; 15, 30 and 60 m). All USGS Landsat data acquired from 1972 to the present are available at no charge and with no user restrictions. The Landsat 7 imaged draped over an SRTM digital elevation model is in southern Malawi, Africa, near the Mozambique border. Source: *http://landsat.gsfc.nasa.gov/images/archive/f0005.html.*	
LiDAR— Light Detection and Ranging	LiDAR data collection is one of the most important sources of digital surface models that provide detailed information about the *x,y*, and *z* location of masspoints for all features on the surface of the earth. With accurate processing, the masspoints can be edited to produce bare-earth digital terrain models. Additional processing can yield biophysical information about the vegetation. LiDAR can also be used to obtain bathymetric information in shallow clear water. *Click* is the USGS Center for LiDAR Information Coordination and Knowledge at *http://lidar.cr.usgs.gov/.*	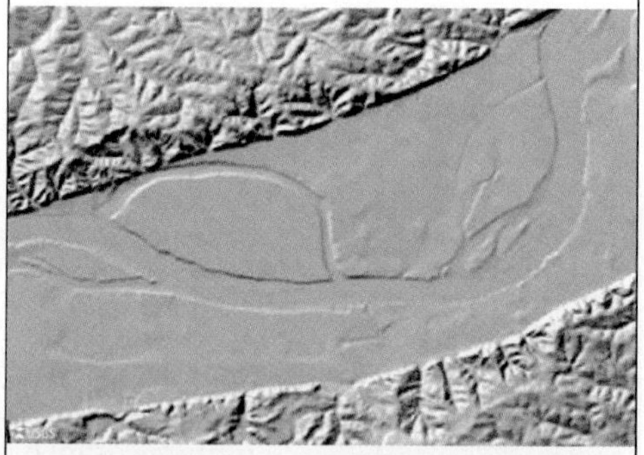
MODIS—Moderate Resolution Imaging Spectrometer	The Moderate Resolution Imaging Spectrometer (MODIS) is flown on both the NASA *Aqua* and *Terra* satellites. It collects data in 36 spectral bands at three spatial resolutions: 250 x 250, 500 x 500, and 1000 x 1000 m. MODIS collects imagery of the entire Earth every 1 to 2 days. The data are excellent for regional, continental, and global analyses of relatively small-scale problems such as dynamic land, ocean, ice, and atmospheric processes and global environmental change. Source: *http://modis.gsfc.nasa.gov/gallery/#.*	

TABLE A-5 (continued) Remote Sensor Data—Public.

Data	Description	Example
NAIP—National Agriculture Imagery Program	The NAIP acquires imagery during the agricultural peak growing seasons for the conterminous United States. The "leaf-on" orthophoto images are at 1 x 1 m or 2 x 2 m spatial resolutions. The 1 x 1 m imagery provides updated digital orthophoto imagery. The 2 x 2 m imagery supports the USDA Farm Services programs that require current imagery acquired during the agricultural growing season but do not require a higher resolution. Included in this imagery category is 1 x 1 m data acquired through certain state programs as "leaf-off." Source: *http://www.fsa.usda.gov/FSA/apfoapp?area=home&subject=prog&topic=nai.*	

TABLE A–6 State GIS Data Clearinghouses.

State	GIS Clearinghouse Website
Alabama	http://portal.gsa.state.al.us/Portal/index.jsp
Alaska	http://www.asgdc.state.ak.us/
Arizona	http://agic.az.gov/
Arkansas	http://www.geostor.arkansas.gov/G6/Home.html
California	http://atlas.ca.gov/
Colorado	http://coloradogis.nsm.du.edu/Portal/
Connecticut	http://magic.lib.uconn.edu/
Delaware	http://datamil.delaware.gov/geonetwork/srv/en/main.home
Florida	http://www.fgdl.org/
Georgia	http://gis.state.ga.us/
Hawaii	http://hawaii.gov/dbedt/gis/download.htm
Idaho	http://www.insideidaho.org/
Illinois	http://www.isgs.uiuc.edu/nsdihome/ISGSindex.html
Indiana	http://www.igic.org/
Iowa	http://www.igsb.uiowa.edu/nrgislibx/
Kansas	http://www.kansasgis.org/
Kentucky	http://technology.ky.gov/gis/Pages/default.aspx

TABLE A–6 (continued) State GIS Data Clearinghouses.

State	GIS Clearinghouse Website
Louisiana	http://lagic.lsu.edu/
Maine	http://www.maine.gov/megis/
Maryland	http://www.marylandgis.net/index.jsp
Massachusetts	http://www.mass.gov/mgis/
Michigan	http://www.michigan.gov/cgi
Minnesota	http://www.mngeo.state.mn.us/chouse/index.html
Mississippi	http://www.gis.ms.gov/portal/home.aspx
Missouri	http://www.msdis.missouri.edu/
Montana	http://nris.mt.gov/gis/
Nebraska	http://www.dnr.state.ne.us/databank/geospatial.html
Nevada	http://www.nbmg.unr.edu/DataDownloads/VirtualClearinghouse.html
New Hampshire	http://www.granit.unh.edu/
New Jersey	https://njgin.state.nj.us/NJ_NJGINExplorer/index.jsp
New Mexico	http://rgis.unm.edu/
New York	http://www.nysgis.state.ny.us/http://rgis.unm.edu/
North Carolina	http://www.nconemap.com/
North Dakota	http://www.nd.gov/gis/
Ohio	http://ogrip.oit.ohio.gov/Home.aspx
Oklahoma	http://www.seic.okstate.edu/
Oregon	http://gis.oregon.gov/
Pennsylvania	http://www.pasda.psu.edu/
Rhode Island	http://www.edc.uri.edu/RIGIS/
South Carolina	http://www.gis.sc.gov/data.html
South Dakota	http://www.sdgs.usd.edu/
Tennessee	http://www.tngis.org/
Texas	http://www.tnris.org/
Utah	http://gis.utah.gov/

TABLE A–6 (continued) State GIS Data Clearinghouses.

State	GIS Clearinghouse Website
Vermont	http://www.vcgi.org/dataware/
Virginia	http://gisdata.virginia.gov/Portal/
Washington	http://metadata.gis.washington.edu/geoportal/catalog/main/home.page
West Virginia	http://wvgis.wvu.edu/
Wisconsin	http://www.sco.wisc.edu/wisclinc/
Wyoming	http://www.wyoming.gov/loc/04222011_1/statewideIT/gis/Pages/default.aspx

GLOSSARY

Accuracy The extent to which the attribute and positional (*x,y,z*-location) data correspond to their real-world counterparts.

Address Matching The most common type of geocoding, which plots street addresses as points on a map.

Adjacency Information about the neighborhoods of different objects.

Analog-to-Digital Conversion The transformation of analog (hard-copy) data such as a historical map or aerial photograph into digital information.

Analytical Hill-shading The synthetic illumination of a facet in a TIN dataset or a pixel in a raster dataset by light from a specific direction (e.g., NW at 345°) and at a specific elevation above the horizon (e.g., 45°).

ArcObjects A set of spatial objects that can be easily integrated into Esri ArcGIS software.

Area Measurement of the geographic region enclosed by a polygon.

Aspect The cardinal direction that each facet is facing in a TIN data structure or that each pixel is facing in a raster data structure. It is measured as a cardinal direction in degrees (e.g., 0° [North], 180° [South]).

Atlas A collection of maps bound as a book.

Azimuthal Projection to a plane placed tangent to (just touching) the globe at a point.

Bathymetry The study of the underwater depth of lake, sea, or ocean floors.

Buffering The creation of a polygon that is a specified distance (e.g., 100 m) around a point, line, or area (polygon) feature.

Cartographic Process A sequence of processes used by cartographers to create high-quality maps that accurately communicate the desired spatial information to the map reader.

Census The systematic collection of information about the members of a population. Each of the persons, places, or things of interest in the study area are investigated.

Central Processing Unit (CPU) The processing part of the computer that consists of a control unit and arithmetic logic unit.

Choropleth Mapping Mapping nominal, ordinal, and interval/ratio-scaled data according to specialized areal administrative units such as watersheds, counties, states, or countries.

Class A collection of objects with the same attributes. Especially useful in geodatabases.

Clipping An operation that extracts a geographic area of the input layer using the outside boundary of a polygon in the clip base layer.

Cloud Computing A model of computer use in which data and/or services stored on the Internet are provided to users on a temporary basis.

Common Key A term used when the primary key and the foreign key have the same field name in two related databases.

Completeness The extent to which the data exhaust the universe of all possible items.

Conformal A map projection is conformal when at any point the scale is the same in every direction. Unfortunately, the size of most areas is distorted. No flat map can be both equal-area and conformal at the same time.

Connectivity Information about the links between spatial objects.

Continuous Geographic Features The type of geospatial data that exists continuously in the landscape. Examples include elevation, temperature, atmospheric pressure, and slope.

Control Point An individual measurement obtained in the field or by a remote sensing instrument that has unique *x*, *y* coordinates and may also have a *z*-value (e.g., elevation above sea level).

Coverage A georelational vector storage framework developed by Esri with built-in topology for geographic information.

Crowd Sourcing The outsourcing of tasks traditionally performed by an employee or contractor to an undefined, large group of people or community (i.e., a crowd), through an open call usually via the Internet.

Data Models Define how real world spatial features are represented in a GIS.

Data Standards Specifications that facilitate the use, sharing, creation, and distribution of spatial data.

Database Management System (DBMS) Computer software used to add, edit, query, analyze, and report on the attributes contained in the database.

Datum A reference surface against which position measurements are made.

Developable Surface A developable surface is a simple geometric form capable of being flattened without stretching. Many map projections can be organized according to the developable surface used such as a cylinder, cone, or plane.

Digital Image Processing The analysis of digital remote sensor data using special-purpose software for preprocessing (radiometric and geometric), enhancement, classification, and change detection.

Digital Tracing A computer process that identifies (traces) features in a utility or natural network that are connected such as streams in a hydrologic network. A network element such as an edge or junction can only be included in a digital trace if it is in some logical way connected to other elements (e.g., edges, junctions) in the network.

Digitization The process of converting information found in hard-copy (analog) maps, images, and diagrams into digital information. Hopefully, the digitized information can then be rectified and analyzed with other geospatial information using a GIS.

Discrete Geographic Features Discrete geospatial data generally consist of points (e.g., the centroid of a building), lines (e.g., a road network), or polygons (e.g., building footprints).

DOQQ The USGS produces digital-orthophoto quarter-quadrangles at a spatial resolution of 1 × 1 m encompassing an area 3.75-minutes of longitude and 3.75-minutes of latitude.

Ecological Fallacy The belief that all observations within an area will exhibit the same or similar values for a particular characteristic.

Edge Enhancement The process of enhancing edges in an image or map to make them more identifiable.

Edge Impedance The cost of traversing network edge segments (e.g., roads) or passing through junctions.

Elevation A specific type of height (orthometric), which is what most people think of as height above mean sea level.

Empirical Rule In a normal distribution, about 68% of the observations will fall within one standard deviation of the mean, about 95% will fall within two standard deviations of the mean, and almost 100% (99.7%) will fall within three standard deviations of the mean.

Empirical Semivariogram A graph that relates the semivariance to the amount of spatial separation (and autocorrelation) between control point samples in a geostatistical analysis.

Enclosure Information about spatial features that enclose other spatial features.

Equal-area (also referred to as Equivalent) A map projection is equal-area if every part on the map, as well as the whole, has the same area as the corresponding part on the Earth, at the same reduced scale. No flat map can be both equal-area and conformal at the same time.

Equidistant Maps that show true distances only from the center of the projection or along a special set of lines.

Erasing Deletes a part of the input layer using the erase base layer as a template for the geographic area to be deleted. The output layer contains only those input layer features that are outside the erase region.

Error Matrix A table used to calculate producer's and user's accuracies, overall accuracy, and Kappa Coefficient of Agreement.

Euclidean Distance The simple, straight-line distance between two projected points.

Features Summarized by Geographic Area Geographic data summarized by an enumeration district such as a watershed, school district, county, state, or country.

Federal Geographic Data Committee (FGDC) Interagency U.S. committee that promotes the coordinated development, use, sharing, and dissemination of geospatial data on a national basis.

Figure-Ground Relationship The figure in a map is the important thematic content. There may be several figures in the map of varying importance. The ground is the literal background information upon which the figure (important thematic content) resides and may include administrative units such as states or counties, graticule, scale bar, legend, north arrow, and metadata.

Foreign key The primary field in a second database that links with the primary key to combine two or more databases.

Freedom of Information Act (FOIA) A U.S. federal law that governs the disclosure of information and documents by the U.S. government.

Fuzzy Tolerance The distance within which individual discrete points are snapped to form a single point during geographic editing.

Geocoding The process of finding a geographic location from an address.

Geodatabase An object-based vector model that maintains topologically integrated spatial datasets.

Geodesy The scientific discipline concerned with determining the size and shape of the Earth and the location of points upon its surface.

Geographic Information System (GIS) A spatial information system used to import, edit, visualize, analyze, and output spatial and non-spatial information stored in a computer database.

Geoid The equipotential surface of the Earth's gravity field that best fits global mean sea level.

Geo-lineage Metadata about the history of the processing used to create the final map.

Geometric Utility (Directed) Networks A special type of network where travel along the edges (e.g., pipes, streams) is usually only allowed in one direction.

Georeferencing The ability to locate objects and/or areas accurately in geographic space.

Georelational Data Model A vector data model that stores spatial and attribute information in separate files.

Geostatistical Analysis A special branch of spatial statistics that takes into account not only the distance between control point observations but also their spatial autocorrelation.

Geotagging The process of adding geographical identification metadata to various media such as terrestrial photographs, videos, etc.

GIS Certificate A formal award or acknowledgement given to a student after completing a sequence of GIS academic courses or training programs.

GIS Certification The process whereby individuals are certified by a third party to have expertise in GIS. The requirements for certification vary by the granting third party.

GIS Licensure The granting of a license to practice a profession. Licensure is usually regulated by state legislation.

GIScience The body of theory and knowledge that seeks to improve our understanding about the nature of geographic data and how it may be collected, analyzed, and viewed using the logic found within the mapping sciences (i.e., cartography, geodesy, GIS, surveying, and remote sensing of the environment).

Global Navigation Satellite System (GNSS) The generic term for various constellations of satellites used to determine the geographic location of features on the surface of the Earth. Important GNSS include the United States' GPS, the European Galileo system, the Russian GLONASS, and the Chinese COMPASS.

Global Positioning System (GPS) The NAVigation System using Timing And Ranging (NAVSTAR) Global Positioning System is a U.S.-owned utility that provides users with position, navigation, and timing services. It consists of a constellation of 24 to 32 satellites that operate in six different orbits.

Graticule A graticule is often superimposed on a globe and consists of the spherical coordinate system based on lines of latitude (parallels) and longitude (meridians).

Great Circle A circle is formed on the surface of a sphere by a plane that passes through the center of the sphere. The Equator, each meridian, and each other full circumference of the Earth forms a great circle.

High-frequency Filter A raster image–enhancement that emphasizes the high-spatial-frequency detail in a map or image.

Horizontal Datum A collection of points on the Earth that have been identified according to their precise northerly or southerly location (latitude) and easterly or westerly location (longitude).

Humanware The characteristics and capabilities of the people responsible for designing, implementing, and using a GIS (sometimes referred to as liveware).

Hyperspectral Remote Sensing The collection of spectral data in tens or hundreds of bands in the electromagnetic spectrum. NASA's AVIRIS and MODIS are hyperspectral remote sensing systems.

Identity An operation that computes the geometric intersection of the input layer features and identity layer features. The input features or portions thereof that overlap the identity layer features receive the attributes of the identity layer features.

Indicatrix A geometric deformation indicator that is an infinitely small circle on the surface of the Earth projected as a small ellipse on a map projection plane. It is used to measure and graphically illustrate the geometric distortion associated with various map projections.

Information System Computerized tools that assist people to transform data into information.

Intersection The intersection of two map layers is based on the use of the AND connector, which computes the geometric intersection of the input layer and the base feature layer. Only those features or portions of features that overlap in both the input layer and the base layer are written to the output layer.

Inverse-Distance-Weighting (IDW) Inter-polation The determination of the z-value (e.g., elevation above sea level) at a new location using information from n nearby control points that are weighted in importance based on their distance to the new location.

Isarithmic Mapping Uses isolines to model two types of continuous phenomena: isometric surfaces that actually exist in reality (e.g., elevation, temperature) and isopleth surfaces that are conceptual in nature (e.g., population density).

Isoline A line of equal magnitude above some arbitrary datum (e.g., a contour is an isoline of constant elevation above sea level).

Isometric Mapping A special type of isarithmic mapping used when the data control points used to create the statistical surface actually exist at a particular geographic location (e.g., elevation, temperature).

Isopleth mapping A special type of isarithmic mapping used when the data control points used to create the statistical surface are conceptual and may not exist at all locations on the surface (e.g., population density, per capita income).

Kriging A generic name for a family of least-squares linear regression algorithms that are used to estimate the value of a continuous attribute (e.g., elevation) at any unsampled location using only attribute data available over the study area.

Kurtosis A measure of the peakedness of the distribution of data values.

Laplacian Edge Enhancement A second derivative filter (as opposed to the gradient, which is a first derivative) that is invariant to rotation, meaning that it is insensitive to the direction in which the edges run.

Legend A cartographic device used to show how the thematic information in a map is organized and symbolized. It usually consists of a title, classes, class intervals, and/or symbolization.

LiDAR Remote sensing using Light Detection and Ranging technology where near-infrared laser energy is transmitted toward the terrain or blue-green laser energy is transmitted into a water body and the characteristics of the back-scattered energy are recorded and processed.

Linear Spatial Filter A filter for which the value ($V_{i,j}$) at location *i,j* in the output image or map is a function of some weighted average (linear combination) of values located in a particular spatial pattern around the *i,j* location in the input image or map.

Line-in-polygon Overlay The overlay of a line layer on a polygon layer.

Local Raster Operation Each pixel (cell) at location *i,j* in a raster dataset may be considered to be a local object. The value of this pixel can be operated upon independent of neighboring pixels (cells).

Location-Allocation Modeling The process of finding the best location(s) for one or more new facilities (e.g., a fast-food restaurant) that will service a given set of points (e.g., homes) and then assigning those points to the new facilities. The process takes into account factors such as the number of facilities available, their cost, and the maximum impedance (e.g., distance or time) from a facility to a point.

Logical Consistency Careful application of the same rules and logic throughout a dataset.

Low-frequency Filter A raster image-enhancement that de-emphasizes or blocks the high-spatial frequency detail in the map or image.

MAF/TIGER/Line File The U.S. Bureau of the Census Master Address File/Topologically Integrated Geographic Encoding and Referencing network geodatabase. The files contain information about each street segment, including: street name, beginning and ending address for each side of the street, and the postal code on each side of the road.

Manhattan Distance The "around-the-block" measurement of distance.

Many-to-many A database relationship where many records in one database can be related to many records in another database.

Many-to-one A database relationship where many records in a database may correspond to one record in another database.

Map Algebra Arithmetic and algebraic local operations applied to multiple registered raster datasets.

Map Projection A systematic transformation of the 3-dimensional Earth (or other body) onto a flat plane surface.

Mapping Sciences The mapping sciences consist of geodesy (including the use of global navigation satellite systems [GNSS] such as the U.S. GPS), surveying, cartography, GIS, and remote sensing.

Masspoints LiDAR-derived elevation datapoints located systematically across flightlines.

Maximize Attendance Location-Allocation Modeling Used to solve neighborhood store location problems where the proportion of demand allocated to the candidate facility or facilities falls within a specified time or distance to the demand points (e.g., 5 minutes or 7 miles).

Maximize Market Share Location-Allocation Modeling Used to locate facilities that maximize market share.

Mean The arithmetic average of a dataset.

Mean Center A measure of central tendency that can be used to determine the center of a spatial distribution plotted in geographic or Cartesian coordinates.

Measurement Levels Data may be described as having nominal, ordinal, interval, or ratio measurement levels.

Median The middle value of an ordered dataset.

Median Filter Ranks the pixel values found within the $n \times n$ neighborhood from lowest to highest and selects the median value, which is then placed in the central value of the neighborhood.

Metadata Information about the data used to perform the GIS analysis and/or create a map.

Minimum/Maximum Filter Examines the values of adjacent pixels in a user-specified region (e.g., $n \times n$ pixels) and then replaces the value of the central pixel with the minimum or maximum value.

Mobile GIS The use of GIS technology and data away from the office, i.e., in the field.

Mode The most commonly occurring value in a dataset.

Modifiable Areal Unit Problem Occurs when spatial areas are analyzed using enumeration units that are poorly suited for what is being studied.

Moran's I A measure of the spatial autocorrelation in a dataset.

Multispectral Remote Sensing Sensors that collect data in several bands in the electromagnetic spectrum. The Landsat Enhanced Thematic Mapper Plus, Quick-Bird, and GeoEye-1 are multispectral sensor systems.

National Hydrography Dataset (NHD) A topologically correct geodatabase of surface water hydrography created from digitized topographic maps and other sources. It is available nationwide at medium resolution 1:100,000–scale and at high resolution 1:24,000–scale. In Alaska, the NHD is available at 1:63,360–scale. In a few geographic areas, the NHD is available at various "local resolutions."

National Spatial Data Infrastructure (NSDI) The NSDI includes geospatial framework foundation data (e.g., geodetic control, digital orthophotos), framework thematic data (e.g., cadastral, transportation), and other types of thematic spatial data (e.g., soils, land cover) used by the United States and other governments throughout the world to manage natural and cultural resources.

National Spatial Reference System (NSRS) Consists of the horizontal and vertical datums used by the U.S. National Geodetic Survey.

NAVigation System using Timing And Ranging (NAVSTAR) Global Positioning System (GPS) The primary navigation system for the U.S. government. NAVSTAR GPS consists of a constellation of 24 to 32 satellites.

Nearest-Neighbor Ratio An analysis that determines whether the spatial distribution of points is dispersed, random, or clustered. It is the observed nearest-neighbor distance divided by the expected distance for a random distribution.

Nearest-neighbor Spatial Interpolation Determination of the z-value (e.g., temperature) at a new location using information from n nearby control points. The value of the new location is assigned the value of the nearest-neighbor.

Neighborhood Raster Operation Modifies the value of each focal pixel in the context of the values of the pixels surrounding it.

Network A system of interconnected lines (edges) and intersections (junctions) that represent possible routes from one location to another.

Network Cost (Impedance) The cost of traversing a network. Whenever something such as a car or bus travels over a network element (e.g., a road) and/or passes through an intersection (junction), it accumulates network costs based on the impedance characteristics of the edge or intersection.

Network Service Area The geographic region that encompasses all parts of the network that can be reached within a certain impedance (cost) value.

Node The beginning and ending points of an arc.

Nonprofit Professional Organizations Organizations that seek to further a particular profession, the interests of people engaged in that profession, and the public interest.

Normal Distribution A bell-shaped distribution where the mode, median, and mean are approximately equal.

Object-Based Vector Model A vector data model that uses objects to store both spatial and attribute data in a single system.

Object-Oriented Programming A computer programming method that uses objects to create applications and computer programs.

Oblate Ellipsoid or Oblate Spheroid A sphere where the polar axis is shorter than the equatorial axis.

Olympic Filter Using all the values in an $n \times n$ region, the highest and lowest values are dropped and the remaining values are averaged.

One-to-many A database relationship where one record in a database may correspond to many records in another database.

One-to-one A database relationship where one record in each database corresponds to one record in another database.

On-Screen Digitizing The process of digitally tracing points, lines, and/or areas on digital maps or images displayed on the computer screen using a pointing device such as a mouse.

Open Geospatial Consortium (OGC) A group of more than 100 universities, corporations, and government agencies whose mission is to make GIS interoperable by building links that allow the accurate and efficient transfer of information derived using many of the most popular commercial and public geographic information systems.

Open-Source Software Software that can be downloaded, installed, and used without any cost or license fee to the user.

Operating System Controls all of the computer's higher-order functions and resides in RAM at all times. It provides the user interface, controls multitasking, and handles input and output to the hard disk and all peripheral devices.

Origin–Destination Matrix A matrix that contains information about the cost (usually measured in distance or time) from each of n origins to each of m destinations.

Orthoimage A remotely sensed image that has been geometrically rectified to a standard map projection and the effects of relief displacement removed.

Orthophoto A specially prepared aerial photograph that has the metric characteristics of a planimetric map with the photographic detail provided by the aerial photograph. Distortion caused by terrain relief displacement has been removed.

Orthophotomap or Orthoimagemap Orthophotos or orthoimages overlaid with point, line, and/or area thematic information.

Perimeter The outside edge of a polygon. It is measured by determining the length of each of the n line segments associated with a polygon and then summing them.

Pixel A 2-dimensional picture element that is the smallest nondivisible element of a digital image.

Point-in-Polygon Overlay The overlay of a point layer on a polygon layer.

Polygon-on-Polygon Overlay The overlay of a polygon layer on a polygon layer.

Positional Accuracy A measure of how close the geographic coordinates of features in a spatial dataset are to their real-world geographic coordinates (both horizontal and vertical).

Precision A measure of the "exactness" of a measurement.

Primary Key (Key Field) A unique identifier used to relate databases.

Proportional Symbol A special type of point symbol (e.g., a circle) that is made proportional in size (scaled) according to the point observation z-value.

Pseudoscopic Illusion This effect is created when a person views a 3-dimensional surface with the shadows falling away from the viewer. In this situation, the viewer can become confused and perceive low points as high and high points as being low. Having the shadows fall toward the viewer usually minimizes the pseudoscopic illusion effect.

Python A generic interpreted scripting language that supports object-oriented programming.

Quadrat A user-defined geographic area that is usually square or rectangular and is used in quadrat analysis.

Quadrat Analysis A technique used to determine the uniformity of points distributed in a number of quadrats.

RADAR Remote sensing using Radio Detection and Ranging technology in which microwave energy is transmitted toward the terrain and the characteristics of the back-scattered energy are recorded and processed.

RADAR Interferometry The process whereby radar images of the same location on the ground are recorded by a) two radar antennas on the same platform, or by b) a single antenna on a platform on two different occasions.

Radiometric Resolution The sensitivity of a remote sensing detector to differences in signal strength as it records the radiant flux reflected, emitted, or backscattered from the terrain.

Random Access Memory (RAM) Memory that is lost when the power is turned off. A computer must have enough RAM for the operating system, software, and any spatial data that must be held in temporary memory.

Random Sample A sample where every observation has an equal chance of being selected.

Raster Data Structure A data structure that uses a grid consisting of rows, columns, and cells to represent spatial data.

Raster Map Overlay Occurs when local operations are applied to multiple raster layers.

Raster-to-Vector Conversion The act of converting raster data to points, lines, or polygons.

Read Only Memory (ROM) Memory that retains information even after power is turned off.

Relational Database A database where unique identifiers are used to link two or more databases or tables together.

Remote Sensing The measurement or acquisition of information of some property of an object or phenomenon by a recording device that is not in physical or intimate contact with the object or phenomenon under study.

Remote Sensing Process The process of extracting useful information from remotely sensed data by: 1) identifying the in situ and remote sensing data to be collected, 2) collecting the data, 3) extracting information from the data, and 4) presenting the information.

Rhumb Line A line on the surface of the Earth crossing all meridians at the same angle. A rhumb line shows true direction.

Route The path (edge) from one location to another.

Sampling A procedure concerned with the selection of a subset of individuals from within a population to yield some knowledge about the whole population and especially to make predictions based on statistical inference.

Shapefile A georelational vector dataset developed by Esri that contains non-topological attribute and spatial data.

Skewness A measure of the asymmetry of a distribution of data values.

Slope The slope of a statistical surface (e.g., elevation) is the change in z-value (i.e., the rise) divided by the distance traveled (i.e., the run).

Spatial Autocorrelation Measures the spatial ordering and spatial dependency of geographic data to indicate whether neighboring or adjacent values vary together.

Spatial Data Any data or information that have spatial attributes (e.g., latitude/longitude).

Spatial Decision Support System (SDSS) A spatial information system that supports business or organizational decision-making activities.

Spatial Frequency The number of changes in value per unit distance for any particular part of a raster map or image.

Spatial Interpolation The process of identifying the z-value (e.g., elevation above sea level) at a new location based on the characteristics of n adjacent control points.

Spatial Resolution A measure of the smallest angular or linear separation between two objects that can be resolved by a remote sensing system.

Spatial Statistics Statistics used to quantitatively describe and assess certain spatial characteristics of landscapes.

Spectral Resolution The number and size of specific wavelength intervals (referred to as bands or channels) in the electromagnetic spectrum to which a remote sensing instrument is sensitive.

Splitting Divides the input layer into a number of smaller layers based on the characteristics of the base layer. Each new output coverage contains only those portions of the input layer features overlapped by the split coverage polygons.

Standard Deviation Average deviation about the mean.

Standard Distance A measure of how dispersed a spatial distribution is about the mean center.

Stratified Random Sample A sample where the observations are stratified to account for the known variation in the population.

Structured Query Language (SQL) A unique database computer language commonly used for data query.

Symmetrical Difference An operation that computes the geometric intersection of the input-layer features and the base layer features. Features or portions of features in the input and update features that do not overlap are written to the output layer.

Table Digitizing The process of digitizing points, lines, and areas on a hard-copy map or image that is placed on a tablet digitizer.

Target Market Share Location-Allocation Modeling Used to solve targeted market share competitive facility location problems.

Temporal Accuracy Refers to how up to date a dataset is.

Temporal Resolution How often in situ or remotely sensed data are collected for a particular area.

Thermal-infrared Remote Sensing Remote sensing technology that measures energy emitted from the terrain in two primary regions of the electromagnetic spectrum: 3–5 μm for hot targets and 8–14 μm for general terrain and water bodies.

Topology The mathematical study of the properties of objects that are not distorted under continuous deformations. The geometric characteristics of features in a GIS that have topology cannot be changed regardless of how the data may be altered through projection or data transformation.

Transportation (Undirected) Network A network where travel along the edges (e.g., road, railroad, subway, pedestrian walkway) may be in any direction that is allowed.

Triangular Irregular Network (TIN) A surface represented by a set of triangular facets with 3-dimensional coordinates at their vertices.

Turn Impedance The cost of making a turn in the network.

Typography The art and science of creating alphanumeric type in various fonts (e.g., Times New Roman, Avenir), styles (e.g., serif or sans-serif, bold, italic), and sizes.

Ultraspectral Remote Sensing Data collection in many hundreds or even thousands of bands in the electromagnetic spectrum.

Union The intersection of two map layers, which preserves all of the features in both the input-polygon layer and the base-polygon layer.

Value Attribute Table A table associated with a raster dataset that describes the number of times that a cell value occurs in a dataset.

Variance The average squared variation about the mean.

Variography The geostatistical process whereby a spatially dependent model is fit to the ground control-point data and the spatial structure is quantified.

Vector Data Structure A data structure that uses points, lines, and polygons to represent spatial features.

Vector-to-Raster Conversion The act of converting points, lines, or polygons into a raster data format.

Vertical Datums A collection of spatially distributed points on the Earth with known heights either above or below mean sea level.

Vertices Points along a line (between the beginning and ending node) that define a line.

Volunteered Geographic Information (VGI) Web users create information with geographic coordinates that is voluntarily incorporated into various Internet applications.

Web-based GIS The distribution of GIS data, data analysis, and other GIS-related services over the Internet.

SUPPLEMENTAL CREDITS

Figures 1-2(c-d), 1-9(a-d), 3-4(a-c), 3-8, 3-11(a-b), 3-14(a-c), 3-18(b-d), 3-31, 3-33, 3-34, 7-22(a-c), 9-12, 10-11, Chapter 11 Opener, 11-2, 12-2, 12-4(c,e): Photographs by John R. Jensen.

Figures 3-7(a-b), 11-1, 11-4: Photographs by Ryan R. Jensen.

Figures 2-10(a), 2-11(b), 2-12(a), 2-15(a), 2-16(a), 2-18, 2-19, 2-20, 2-21, 2-22, 4-1, 5-16, 5-17(b), 5-18, 10-9, 10-10, 11-3, 11-5, 11-6, A-6: The ArcGIS® ArcMap™ and ArcCatalog™ graphical user interfaces are the intellectual property of Esri and are used herein by permission.

SUPPLEMENTAL CREDITS

[illegible]

[illegible]

[illegible]

INDEX

D

E

F

G

M

O

P

Notes

NOTES

Notes

NOTES